D1238601

Unionism,
Economic Stabilization,
and Incomes Policies

STUDIES IN WAGE-PRICE POLICY

Unionism, Economic Stabilization, and Incomes Policies

European Experience

ROBERT J. FLANAGAN
DAVID W. SOSKICE
LLOYD ULMAN

THE BROOKINGS INSTITUTION
Washington, D.C.

331.88
F58u

Library of Congress Cataloging in Publication data:

Flanagan, Robert J.
  Unionism, economic stabilization, and incomes
policies.

  (Studies in wage-price policy)
  Includes index.
  1. Wage-price policy—Case studies. 2. Collective
bargaining—Case studies. 3. Trade unions—Case
studies. I. Soskice, David, 1942– . II. Ulman,
Lloyd. III. Title. IV. Series.
HC79.W24F52 1983   331.88   83-71459
ISBN 0-8157-2856-5
ISBN 0-8157-2855-7 (pbk.)

1 2 3 4 5 6 7 8 9

THE BROOKINGS INSTITUTION is an independent organization devoted to nonpartisan research, education, and publication in economics, government, foreign policy, and the social sciences generally. Its principal purposes are to aid in the development of sound public policies and to promote public understanding of issues of national importance.

The Institution was founded on December 8, 1927, to merge the activities of the Institute for Government Research, founded in 1916, the Institute of Economics, founded in 1922, and the Robert Brookings Graduate School of Economics and Government, founded in 1924.

The Board of Trustees is responsible for the general administration of the Institution, while the immediate direction of the policies, program, and staff is vested in the President, assisted by an advisory committee of the officers and staff. The by-laws of the Institution state: "It is the function of the Trustees to make possible the conduct of scientific research, and publication, under the most favorable conditions, and to safeguard the independence of the research staff in the pursuit of their studies and in the publication of the results of such studies. It is not a part of their function to determine, control, or influence the conduct of particular investigations or the conclusions reached."

The President bears final responsibility for the decision to publish a manuscript as a Brookings book. In reaching his judgment on the competence, accuracy, and objectivity of each study, the President is advised by the director of the appropriate research program and weighs the views of a panel of expert outside readers who report to him in confidence on the quality of the work. Publication of a work signifies that it is deemed a competent treatment worthy of public consideration but does not imply endorsement of conclusions or recommendations.

The Institution maintains its position of neutrality on issues of public policy in order to safeguard the intellectual freedom of the staff. Hence interpretations or conclusions in Brookings publications should be understood to be solely those of the authors and should not be attributed to the Institution, to its trustees, officers, or other staff members, or to the organizations that support its research.

Foreword

Is it not possible for a country to contain inflation and maintain or improve the international competitiveness or profitability of its industry without paying a steep price in unemployment, lost output, and lost income? Could the dilemma be resolved—or at least diminished—if wage determination under collective bargaining were brought under restraint? Or are such policies doomed to failure because they are the product of economic misdiagnosis? Does the adoption of an incomes policy invite the adoption of lax monetary and fiscal policies—or is demand management more likely to be "accommodative" when wage costs are unrestrained? If wage restraint is desirable as a component of macroeconomic policy, is it obtainable? Could union leaders ever bargain with discretion—without provoking disaffection at the grass roots and without weakening the centralized union and bargaining structures on which the success of incomes policies typically depends? Could union members be adequately compensated for wage restraint by tax cuts, by more generous social welfare programs, or by measures designed to give workers a share in the management or even the ownership of enterprises? If not, could the authority of union officers and the integrity of bargaining structures be shored up by the adoption of labor relations policies intended for that purpose? If so, would such policy bargaining—or "democratic corporatism"—be politically feasible?

These and other questions motivated the authors of this volume. So as to do justice to institutional and political variety and a diversity of policy approaches, the authors analyze experience since the Second World War, particularly in the 1970s, for each of nine countries of Western Europe. The opening chapter discusses developments that significantly influenced the systems of labor relations and the wage-determining processes in all or most of the countries. A brief theoretical section introduces two analytic models that guided the authors in their evaluation of developments in the various countries and in their assessment of the potential role of incomes policy in moderating movements in real as well as money wages. The concluding chapter draws on experience in the individual countries in order to assess union behavior, especially during the stagflationary period of the 1970s, and to evaluate the prospects for incomes policy in the years ahead.

Robert J. Flanagan is professor of labor economics in the Graduate School of Business at Stanford University. David W. Soskice is a fellow of University College, Oxford. Lloyd Ulman is professor of economics at the University of California, Berkeley. All three wrote this book as members of the Brookings associated staff.

This is the sixth in the Brookings series of Studies in Wage-Price Policy. The research upon which it is based was supported in part by a grant from the Sloan Foundation and a supplementary grant from the German Marshall Fund. The views expressed here are those of the authors and should not be ascribed to the Sloan Foundation or the German Marshall Fund, or to the officers, trustees, or other staff members of the Brookings Institution.

BRUCE K. MACLAURY
President

May 1983
Washington, D.C.

Acknowledgments

Any study such as this is subject to the limitations as well as the advantages inherent in an examination by a small team of authors of institutional behavior and policymaking in a variety of historical and cultural settings. Certainly it could not have been undertaken without help from many talented and well-informed persons in trade union movements, management, and public and academic life who were kind enough to offer insight and information. The authors acknowledge particularly their indebtedness to Lars Aarvig, Odd Aukrust, Claire Beauville, Per Bransten, Clair Brown, E. H. Phelps Brown, Wim Driehuis, Sabine Erbès, Karl-Olof Faxén, John Goldthorpe, Bent Hansen, H. ter Heide, Alfred Klose, Carsten Kowalczyk, Georges de Menil, Thierry de Montbrial, Andrew Oswald, Alessandro Pizzorno, Wolfgang Pollan, Mario Regini, Jean-Daniel Reynaud, Derek Robinson, Michele Salvati, Spiros Simitis, Hannes Suppanz, Aage Tarp, Sigurd Tveitereid, Erwin Wekssel, and Pieter de Wolff.

The authors also benefited greatly from the critical comments and suggestions of Anne Romanis Braun, Daniel J. B. Mitchell, Joseph A. Pechman, George L. Perry, and Charles L. Schultze. Paul Farnham, Sanford M. Jacoby, Peter Rappoport, Anthony P. Rodrigues, and Elaine Sorensen rendered excellent research assistance. Joan J. Lewis of the Berkeley Institute of Industrial Relations and El Vera Fisher of Stanford University provided expert administrative and clerical support.

Research, clerical, and library assistance were also generously provided by the Institute of Industrial Relations, the University of California, Berkeley, the Oxford Institute of Economics and Statistics, and the Graduate School of Business at Stanford University.

The manuscript was edited by David Howell Jones; its factual content was verified by Judith Cameron and Penelope Harpold. The index was prepared by Florence Robinson.

R.J.F.

D.W.S.

L.U.

ix

Contents

Tables

xvi CONTENTS

Figures

I

Wage Problems since the Mid-Sixties

This book is about trade-union power and efforts to restrain its use in the general economic interest. We are concerned with such efforts in nine countries in Western Europe, where experimentation with policies of wage restraint—whether official or tacit—has been more determined and more varied than it has been in North America. We concentrate on the period beginning in the latter part of the 1960s, but we draw on earlier experience when necessary to provide appropriate perspective on the objectives and achievements of incomes policies. The perspective is of particular interest because the period on which this study is focused began with a widespread acknowledgment of the failure of what might be referred to as the first generation of postwar incomes policies.

The first phase of incomes policy occurred in the decade following the end of World War II. There was widespread agreement in most European countries that policies of reconstruction—which were designed to foster investment and the growth of output capacity and to improve international competitiveness and the balance of trade—required that real wages be directly restrained, notwithstanding the initially high levels of unemployment associated with postwar shortages of capital stocks.[1] The popularity of formal incomes policies was impaired by the worldwide price inflation associated with the Korean War, but in some countries, such as the United Kingdom and the Netherlands, they registered rather dramatic success in reducing real wages and assisting the transition to long-term growth policies under conditions of excess supply in labor markets. By the mid 1950s domestic labor was no longer in significant excess supply in Europe, and recourse to incomes policies diminished.[2] Very low levels of unemployment were reached and sustained in most of the countries in our sample, but increased international trade and competition and continuing improvement in the terms of trade

1. Anne Romanis Braun, "The Role of Incomes Policy in Industrial Countries since World War II," *IMF Staff Papers*, vol. 23, no. 1 (March 1975), pp. 4–5.
2. William Fellner and others, *The Problem of Rising Prices* (Paris: Organisation for European Economic Co-operation, 1961), pp. 35–38, wherein overall excess demand is judged to have prevailed during the investment boom of 1955–57.

1

combined with—and contributed to—high rates of growth in output and productivity to help keep price inflation moderate.[3] In this conjuncture of events, it might appear that incomes policies on the pattern of those of the 1950s were neither necessary nor appropriate.

Nevertheless, policies of wage restraint were again resorted to in the 1960s. Instead of reduction of excess supply (and unemployment) by holding down real wages, however, the reason for them became prevention or retardation of the development of inflationary pressures as full-employment growth policies were pursued. In those days it was still a prime object of macroeconomic policy to minimize the level of unemployment, which, in the absence of constraints on the balance of trade, was generally believed by policymakers to be dependent on the level of aggregate demand for money. But the rate of inflation was seen to be dependent, at least in the short run, on the level of unemployment, and empirical Phillips curve relations indicated that this was particularly true at low rates of unemployment. In pursuing expansionist demand policies to reduce unemployment to the low levels to which they were generally committed in the 1960s, therefore, authorities ran the risk of accelerating inflation—and, in the process, generating a crisis in the balance of trade. But contractionary policies were believed to be inefficient in the sense that they would extract a heavy price in the form of increased unemployment for a relatively small reduction in the rate of inflation. So the objective of incomes policy in the 1960s was to improve the Phillips tradeoff between unemployment and inflation and to enable the fiscal and monetary authorities to pursue expansionist policies that could minimize the former without unduly increasing the latter.

The first generation of incomes policies was generally centered on specific guidelines for wage and price growth. Although the guidelines ranged from statements urging "noninflationary behavior" to outright wage and price freezes—that is, a zero rate of growth for all incomes—the most common wage norm was based upon the growth of economy-wide productivity and implied stable unit labor costs. This general guideline was frequently supplemented by certain exceptions to the general rule in order to permit flexibility of allocations, encourage advances in productivity, or achieve certain distributional objectives,

3. Organisation for Economic Co-operation and Development, *Economic Growth 1960–1970: A Mid-Decade Review of Prospects* (Paris: OECD, 1966), table 4, p. 26, and pp. 96–100; Paul McCracken and others, *Towards Full Employment and Price Stability* (Paris: OECD, 1977), pp. 37, 45.

such as increases in the relative wage of the least well paid workers.[4] By design, however, guidelines were a type of "nominal" incomes policy— that is, a policy designed to reduce inflation through symmetric reductions in money wages and prices. "Real" incomes policies, which by design are intended to reduce real wages, will be discussed later.

Failures of the First Generation of Incomes Policies

By the end of the 1960s, most of the first-generation experiments in the United States and most European countries had been abandoned or greatly de-emphasized. Although there were some instances of short-term restraint of increases in money wages, these periods of apparent effectiveness were often terminated by waves of wildcat strikes, wage explosions, and severe disruptions in national systems of industrial relations. There was even less evidence of short-term price restraint, so in several countries, the net effect of incomes policies was a reduction in real wages. Restraint on real wages was compatible with improved profitability and international competitiveness, but in the case of nominal incomes policies, where no effect on real wages was intended, this outcome stemmed from more effective enforcement of the wage side of the policy than of the price side, with subsequent costs in macroeconomic stability that will be detailed later. The policies failed, moreover, to prevent lower unemployment rates in the second half of the decade from being accompanied by sharply higher rates of inflation. Furthermore, the failure of first-generation policies to achieve their long-term objective of shifting the perceived tradeoff between unemployment and inflation was independent of both the structure of the collective-bargaining institutions and the design and enforcement of the policy itself. In particular, the results of a policy were insensitive to the degree of centralization of bargaining institutions, the degree of political support by the trade-union movement, or the degree of compulsion used in the enforcement of the policy. Nevertheless, the factors behind the failures of the first-generation incomes policies are instructive in the effort to understand developments during the 1970s.[5]

---

4. For a clear statement of the principle, some exceptions, and their application to the United States, see *Economic Report of the President, January 1962*, pp. 185–90.

5. This section draws on findings reported in Lloyd Ulman and Robert J. Flanagan,

Many first-generation incomes policies failed because they were applied to problems for which other policies would have been more appropriate but were perceived as being politically infeasible or at least costly. In many instances, the policies were initiated in periods of substantial excess-demand inflation, during which the discretionary exercise of market power was either not present or not obvious. In these situations, which cover many applications of incomes policy in Europe during the 1960s, deflation or devaluation might have been the more appropriate policy, given the underlying economic conditions, but the political and economic costs of these alternatives were regarded as too high.

In an important sense, then, the case for the first-generation incomes policies was the case against the alternatives. This case seemed stronger than it really was, however, because the costs of an incomes policy itself were underestimated. These costs were underestimated in part because there was insufficient appreciation of the nature of the incentives required for sustained cooperation by labor unions and business with an incomes policy, especially when the effect of the policy was to restrain real wages. Even unions with close ties to the incumbent political party—a situation that is more frequent in many European countries than in the United States—need rewards for accepting restraint on money wages, and by design or implementation, first-generation policies failed to provide significant rewards for cooperation. In particular, the distributional implications of most of the policies were not advantageous to labor, and efforts by national union officials to cooperate with the incomes policy objectives of their governments eroded the institutional authority of the officials over the rank-and-file membership. In fact, cooperation by national union officials with government incomes policy objectives in several countries brought about reductions in real wage growth that were followed by grass-roots revolt, wildcat strikes, and the wage explosions of the late 1960s. In some countries a significant reaction against the centralized bargaining structures that had exercised wage restraint and explicit demands for decentralized negotiations in the future resulted.

The experience with first-generation policies suggested that at best they were short-run policies suited to conditions of excess supply in

Wage Restraint: A Study of Incomes Policies in Western Europe (Berkeley: University of California Press, 1971).

labor markets. Under such conditions incomes policy might succeed in breaking through an inflation sustained by unrealistic expectations. But even this more limited function for incomes policy seemed dubious if rewards for cooperation between unions and management were not embedded in the policy itself.

Changed Economic Circumstances

Nevertheless incomes policies were not fatally discredited by their misadventures during the 1960s. To begin with, circumstances surrounding their apparent failure did little to bolster general confidence in monetary-fiscal deflation as either an efficient or even a feasible anti-inflationary alternative. Its efficiency was called into question because the grass-roots strikes and wage explosions, which originated in France in 1968 and spread subsequently through most of Western Europe, occurred during a recovery from the recessions of 1966–67, a recovery characterized by relatively modest demand pressures and in some countries by relatively slack labor markets. The question of feasibility was joined to the question of anti-inflationary efficiency as a result of the recession of 1970–71, which occurred in the aftermath of the waves of worker unrest. Increased unemployment failed to exert a concomitant slackening in price inflation. While this in itself was a disappointment, it was also believed that the authorities were inhibited in their recourse to demand deflation by fear that worker militancy, having recently been provoked by lagging real wages and tightened production standards in the second half of the 1960s,[6] would be rekindled by increasing unemployment to levels that might prove high enough to overcome what was later to become known as the momentum or inertia of wage inflation.[7]

But if governments initially associated significant economic and

6. David Soskice, "Strike Waves and Wage Explosions, 1968–1970: An Economic Interpretation," in Colin Crouch and Alessandro Pizzorno, eds., *The Resurgence of Class Conflict in Western Europe Since 1968*, vol. 2: *Comparative Analyses* (New York: Holmes and Meier, 1978).

7. A group of experts reported to the OECD: "Perhaps, in retrospect, policy-making in the period from 1969 to 1971 was too much affected in some countries by the sense of unease to which the discord in labour markets—and in the streets—had given rise. But it is important not to under-estimate the influence that this sense of unease may have had on those who held the responsibility for economic policy as unemployment began to rise." McCracken and others, *Towards Full Employment*, p. 52.

political costs with exclusive reliance on demand-management policies during the early 1970s, earlier incomes policy approaches seemed poorly designed to address the economic constraints placed on collective bargaining institutions by the macroeconomic shocks of the late 1960s and early 1970s. Domestic and international developments, including sharp increases in the prices of food and raw materials and the quadrupling of the price of oil in the fall of 1973, limited the prospects for real wage gains through standard bilateral collective bargaining arrangements. While national governments sought to restrain money wages, simple wage guidelines were less likely than ever to meet the institutional needs of unions. As the 1970s progressed, a new generation of incomes policies emerged in response to the changed economic circumstances. As a background, we review these circumstances and the nature of the constraints that they imposed on collective bargaining institutions.

Wage Explosions

The decline of the first generation of incomes policies coincided roughly with a series of strikes and national wage explosions in the late 1960s and early 1970s that ultimately spread through most of the countries in this study. These explosions elevated money wage inflation from the predominantly single-digit rates of the 1960s to the double-digit plateau of the 1970s (see table 1-1)—significantly higher than the predictions of most models in which wage inflation was in large measure determined by unemployment and prices. More important for purposes of macroeconomic stability, the acceleration in nominal compensation produced a sharp increase in real wages (table 1-1), as money wages ran significantly ahead of prices, particularly in the manufacturing sector, where world prices imposed a ceiling on the extent to which increased labor costs could be passed through into export prices.[8] A second wage acceleration in several countries occurred around 1974–75, following the sharp increases in world prices of oil, raw materials, and food in 1973–74. Since there was no comparable explosion in the rate of growth of labor productivity during the 1970s, the sharp increase in money wage inflation caused an upward shift in the rate of growth of unit labor costs.

8. For a more extensive development of this point, see Jeffrey D. Sachs, "Wages, Profits, and Macroeconomic Adjustment: A Comparative Study," *Brookings Papers on Economic Activity, 2:1979*, pp. 269–312. (Hereafter *BPEA*.)

Table 1-1. *Rates of Growth of Nominal and Real Hourly Compensation in Manufacturing in Selected Countries of the OECD, Selected Periods, 1962–79*
Average annual percentage change

Country	1962–69	1969–73	1973–75	1975–79
Austria				
Nominal	8.4[a]	13.3	16.2	9.0[b]
Real	4.8[a]	7.2	6.7	3.4[b]
Denmark				
Nominal	10.3	14.5	19.2	10.6[b]
Real	4.2	6.9	6.1	0.5[b]
France				
Nominal	8.5	12.8	19.9	15.1
Real	4.4	6.2	6.4	4.9
Germany				
Nominal	7.9	12.8	12.5	7.9
Real	5.3	7.1	5.6	4.1
Italy				
Nominal	9.6	19.4	27.7	19.3
Real	5.4	12.1	8.1	n.a.
Netherlands				
Nominal	11.7	15.0	17.6	8.2
Real	6.3	7.7	6.9	2.2
Norway				
Nominal	9.0	13.0	18.9	11.7[b]
Real	5.0	4.8	7.6	2.7[b]
Sweden				
Nominal	9.2	12.6	17.7	13.2
Real	5.2	5.4	7.2	3.2
United Kingdom				
Nominal	7.5	14.9	26.2	15.0
Real	3.5	6.4	5.1	1.3
United States				
Nominal	4.7	7.5	10.2	9.3
Real	1.9	2.4	0.1	1.5

Sources: Earnings and compensation data for Austria, Denmark, and Norway: Swedish Employers Confederation (SAF), *Wages and Total Labour Costs for Workers: International Survey, 1960–1970* and *1968–1978* (Stockholm: SAF, May 1972, October 1980); for all other countries: U.S. Bureau of Labor Statistics, "Estimated Hourly Compensation of Production Workers in Manufacturing, Ten Countries," February 1980, and unpublished data provided by the U.S. Bureau of Labor Statistics. Consumer price data on all countries: International Monetary Fund, *International Financial Statistics*, various issues.
n.a. Not available.
a. 1963–69.
b. 1975–78.

It is by no means clear that there is a common explanation for these developments in each country in which they have been observed. In cross-country comparisons of the wage-determination process, no single statistical model has been found to provide a satisfactory explanation of the wage behavior observed in various countries.[9] Furthermore, while the variability in the structure of empirical wage-determination models across countries is not generally predictable from existing theoretical models, it is understandable when the different conventions regarding appropriate wage standards that become established reference points in setting wages in various countries are understood. Although the conventions may vary from country to country, within a country a convention may survive and take on a life of its own because unions and firms generally have incentives to set their compensation practices with reference to the practices of other unions and firms in the market.[10] In exploring the wage problem in the 1970s we shall devote particular attention to institutional peculiarities and the changing function of collective bargaining in establishing these conventions in European labor markets and to the efforts of public policy institutions to alter the wage-determination process in order to achieve reductions in nominal and real wages.

Strikes and Worker Militancy

The importance of collective bargaining to the European wage problem is signaled by the apparent significance of increasing militancy on the part of workers in the wage acceleration of the late 1960s and early 1970s. In general, there is no clear-cut relation among worker militancy, the level of strike activity, and wage changes. With worker militancy unchanged, for example, an increase in militancy on the part of employers or the government is likely to increase strike activity and induce more modest wage changes. On the other hand, increased worker militancy will not be associated with an increase in work stoppages if employers find it less costly to concede a wage increase without a strike. But a combination of increased strike activity and a wage acceleration well in excess of the predictions of standard economic models of wage behavior suggests a combination of rising worker militancy and (somewhat weaker) employer resistance.[11]

9. See, for example, William D. Nordhaus, "The Worldwide Wage Explosion," *BPEA, 2:1972,* pp. 431–64; George L. Perry, "Determinants of Wage Inflation around the World," *BPEA, 2:1975,* pp. 403–35.

10. For a discussion of this point, see Arthur M. Okun, *Prices and Quantities: A Macroeconomic Analysis* (Washington, D.C.: Brookings Institution, 1981), pp. 104–05.

11. For a discussion of these points, see Soskice, "Strike Waves and Wage Explosions," particularly p. 231.

Table 1-2. *Number of Industrial Disputes in Selected Countries of the OECD, Selected Periods, 1965–79*[a]

Annual averages

Country	1965–68	1969–70	1971–73	1974–76	1977–79
Denmark	24	62	90	162	253
France	1,687[b]	2,574	3,838	3,872	3,254[c]
Italy	2,903	3,975	4,711	3,827	2,596
Netherlands	25	64	18	10	20
Norway	7	10	10	23	13
Sweden	12	88	51	81	114
United Kingdom	2,196	3,511	2,533	2,407	2,440
United States	4,502	5,708	5,167	5,584	4,839

Source: International Labour Office, *Yearbook of Labour Statistics, 1970,* table 30, pp. 790–91; *1978,* table 24, pp. 626–28; *1980,* table 25, pp. 636, 638–39.
a. Data for Austria and Germany are not available.
b. 1965–67; data for France were not tabulated for 1968.
c. 1977–78.

It is this combination that characterized European labor markets during the late 1960s and early 1970s. After two decades of on the whole placid industrial relations that gave rise to conjectures of "the withering away of the strike," work stoppages increased significantly in most of the countries of this study (see table 1-2) and were associated with the wage explosions noted earlier. Increased worker militancy therefore appears to have contributed significantly to the initial wage accelerations, and strike activity, including unofficial or wildcat strikes, remained at higher levels until the late 1970s.[12]

The acceleration of money wages did not bring about a parallel increase in prices. Constrained in export markets by relatively modest world price increases, many producers of tradable goods were unable to pass along the full labor cost increase into prices. Real wage increases exceeded the growth of labor productivity, and the distribution of income

12. Note that the notion of worker militancy used here is different from the traditional concept of union power—the degree of monopoly in labor markets—which is often measured by the fraction of the labor force that is unionized. For union power in the traditional sense to have been a source of the wage explosions, the degree of union monopoly power in labor markets would have to have increased during the late 1960s and early 1970s. From the evidence of the statistics on union membership, however, a significant shift in this direction did not occur in most countries. This, in combination with the apparent influence of worker militancy on wage increases during the period, suggests the possibility of a divergence between the maximum bargaining power of a union—that is, the degree of monopoly power—and the bargaining power that is actually exercised. This theme will be explored more extensively later.

Table 1-3. *Net Profit Shares and Rates of Return in Manufacturing in Selected Countries of the OECD, Selected Periods, 1965–76*[a]

Country	1965–69	1970–73	1974–76
Denmark[b]			
Profit share	42.0	39.8	34.3[c]
France			
Rate of return	10.0	11.6	8.0
Germany			
Profit share	27.8	21.4	16.6
Rate of return	19.5	15.0	11.4
Italy			
Profit share	24.8	20.7[d]	n.a.
Rate of return	11.4	10.3[d]	n.a.
Netherlands			
Profit share	29.2	28.7	30.8
Sweden			
Profit share	21.9	23.9	24.2
Rate of return	11.2	12.0	12.3
United Kingdom			
Profit share	22.9	18.1	8.5
Rate of return	10.6	8.3	3.7
United States			
Profit share	22.9	18.9	20.2
Rate of return	12.2	8.6	7.1

Sources: T. P. Hill, *Profits and Rates of Return* (Paris: Organisation for Economic Co-operation and Development, 1979), tables 6.2 and 6.4, pp. 123, 125; Mervyn King and Jacques Mairesse, "Profitability in Britain and France: A Comparative Study, 1965–75" (Paris: National Institute of Statistics and Economic Research, 1978), table 2.1.

n.a. Not available.

a. Profit share is net operating surplus divided by net value added. Rate of return is net operating surplus divided by net capital stock.

b. Gross profit share.

c. Data are for 1974–75.

d. Data are for 1970–72.

shifted toward labor. At the same time there was a significant decline in profitability, particularly in the export sector of European economies (see table 1-3). As falling rates of return reduced incentives to investment, European policy authorities came to regard low profitability as a significant barrier to expansion during the recessions of the 1970s and began to think of incomes policy as an instrument to achieve the real wage reductions that were considered necessary for full employment. This interest in real incomes policies that would achieve asymmetrical restraint in wages and prices presents a significant contrast to North American experience, in which the required adjustments in real wages were more modest and, in design at least, incomes policies continued to be nominal throughout the 1970s.

The wage explosions and industrial unrest of the late 1960s had a profound effect on the climate for incomes policy during the 1970s. In the first instance, these developments reduced the willingness of policymakers to risk a repetition of such disruptions by responding to inflationary pressures with sharply deflationary policies. At the same time, unions were even less disposed to go along with incomes policies than they had been in the 1960s. Following the surge of often unofficial strike activity during the late 1960s, union leaders in centralized bargaining systems had reason to be wary of restraining wage demands during the 1970s for fear of a more fundamental rank-and-file rejection of existing institutional arrangements. Union leaders also came under pressure because international developments and the extensive growth of the public sector in most European countries reduced the potential growth of disposable real income, even in the absence of cooperation in incomes policy arrangements.

World Price Increases and International Recession

A second major change in the economic circumstances confronting incomes policy in the 1970s was the change in the international terms of trade associated with the substantial increases in the world prices of oil and raw materials during 1972–74. These increases began with a general expansion in the economies of developed countries in 1972 that led to shortages in many raw materials markets and a sharp increase in the prices of industrial commodities. At the same time a decline in the world grain harvest contributed to an increase in food prices. In 1973 the Arab oil embargo and a subsequent series of price increases by the Organization of Petroleum Exporting Countries (OPEC) quadrupled the price of oil and further shifted the terms of trade against the developed countries.

The magnitude of the world price increases and their influence on inflation in the United States and the countries in this study are summarized in table 1-4. Columns 1–4, which show the rate of increase of import and export prices for each country during 1972–74 and the subsequent deceleration in 1974–75, indicate the magnitude of changes in the terms of trade for the countries in this study. The influence of these changes on domestic prices varies with the importance of international trade in the economies of the various countries. In columns 5–10 the price increases recorded in columns 1–4 are weighted by the shares of exports and imports in 1972 gross domestic product (GDP) and total domestic demand respectively to provide an estimate of the

Table 1-4. *Export and Import Prices in Selected Countries of the OECD, 1972–74 and 1974–75*ᵃ

Average annual rate of change

| Country | Export prices | | Import prices | | At world pricesᵇ / Indicator of external price influencesᶜ | | | | | | Change in effective exchange rates | | Indicator of external price influencesᵈ (total) | |
| | | | | | Exports | | Imports | | Total | | | | | |
	1972–74 (1)	1974–75 (2)	1972–74 (3)	1974–75 (4)	1972–74 (5)	1974–75 (6)	1972–74 (7)	1974–75 (8)	1972–74 (9)	1974–75 (10)	1972–74 (11)	1974–75 (12)	1972–74 (13)	1974–75 (14)
Austria	17.0	8.4	16.8	7.7	5.6	2.8	5.6	2.5	11.2	5.3	5.7	2.6	7.0	3.5
Denmark	17.6	10.5	24.6	8.6	5.4	3.2	7.3	2.5	12.7	5.7	2.7	2.9	10.7	3.8
France	11.8	14.9	20.1	6.9	2.0	2.6	3.3	1.1	5.3	3.7	-2.8	8.4	6.5	0.8
Germany	16.5	8.2	20.9	3.4	3.6	1.8	4.2	0.7	7.8	2.5	6.8	0.5	4.6	2.2
Italy	11.4	6.3	25.5	1.4	2.3	1.3	5.0	0.3	7.3	1.6	-10.5	-5.0	13.0	3.8
Netherlandsᵉ	17.0	6.3	20.4	6.0	7.8	3.0	9.3	2.8	17.1	5.8	3.5	1.7	13.4	4.1
Norway	23.4	4.4	22.5	8.6	9.5	1.8	9.1	3.5	18.6	5.3	5.3	3.0	13.6	2.8
Sweden	14.6	15.0	19.1	8.8	3.6	3.7	4.5	2.0	8.1	5.7	-1.1	3.5	8.6	3.9
United Kingdom	10.1	11.0	22.6	4.3	2.2	2.4	4.9	0.9	7.1	3.4	-7.6	-7.8	11.3	7.3
United States	15.7	10.5	26.9	9.1	0.9	0.6	1.7	0.6	2.6	1.2	-3.4	-0.7	3.1	1.2

Source: OECD, "Prices and Incomes Policies in an Overall Setting," CPE/WP4(77)2 (Paris: OECD, April 25, 1977), p. 4.

a. National accounts deflators for goods and services.

b. Assuming unchanged effective exchange rates.

c. Export and import price increases of columns 1, 2, 3, and 4 multiplied respectively by the share of exports in the GDP in 1972 and by the share of imports in total domestic demand in 1972.

d. Columns 9 and 10 adjusted for changes in effective exchange rates.

e. 1974 figures adjusted for reexported oil.

contribution of world price increases to domestic price inflation. It is clear after adjusting for the volume of international trade that the effects of the shift in the terms of trade on domestic price levels were far more severe for European countries than for the United States and that the macroeconomic adjustment problems were correspondingly larger. Even the data in columns 5–10, however, do not fully reflect the domestic price implications of changing terms of trade, since they include the effect of changes in the exchange rates during the period (see columns 11 and 12). In columns 13 and 14 the total external price influence is adjusted for the changes in effective exchange rates. The data in table 1-4 indicate that world price influences alone tended to generate double-digit inflation for several of the countries in this study during the period 1972–74, as real wages failed to adjust to the changing terms of trade.

The surge of world prices, which was without precedent in the postwar period, significantly constrained the potential achievements of collective bargaining. Most dramatically, after a long period in which collective bargaining had been conducted in an environment of significant growth in real income, the shift in the terms of trade sharply reduced the prospects for gains in real earnings, particularly in the traditionally unionized manufacturing and service sectors.[13] With a substantial redistribution of real resources from developed countries to the oil-producing and raw-materials-producing countries, efforts by unions in industrial countries to maintain and advance the real incomes of workers could only succeed if profitability were further reduced and international competitiveness lessened. Otherwise, any attempt to protect real incomes by means of increases in money wages stimulated instead a second round of wage and price increases that added to the cost pressures initiated by external events. Collective bargaining organizations and other private institutions that had developed social mechanisms for distributing the gains from economic growth were poorly suited to the new environment, in which the fundamental problem was to allocate the inevitable losses in real income among various social groups. One case for incomes policy during this period was therefore to develop mechanisms to mediate the distributional issues raised by the adjustment to

13. The prospects for gains in real earnings were also reduced by a slowdown in the rate of growth of potential output, which was associated with decelerating growth of the labor force and labor productivity in most of the countries during the 1970s. See Jacques R. Artus, "Measures of Potential Output in Manufacturing for Eight Industrial Countries, 1955–78," *IMF Staff Papers*, vol. 24, no. 1 (March 1977), pp. 1–25.

Table 1-5. *Current-Account Balance as a Percentage of Gross Domestic Product in Selected Countries of the OECD, 1973–76*

Country	1973	1974	1975	1976
Austria	−1.5	−1.5	−0.8	−3.8
Denmark	−1.8	−3.0	−1.4	−5.0
France	−0.3	−2.3	0.0	−1.7
Germany	1.2	2.5	0.9	0.7
Italy	−2.0	−5.2	0.3	−1.7
Netherlands	2.9	2.9	1.8	2.7
Norway	−1.6	−5.2	−8.8	−12.2
Sweden	2.2	−1.6	−2.3	−3.3
United Kingdom	−1.1	−4.2	−1.6	−1.2
United States	0.0	0.0	0.8	0.0

Sources: OECD, "Prices and Incomes Policies in an Overall Setting," p. 7.

reduced growth of real incomes and to minimize the development of secondary wage and price pressures.

From the perspective of macroeconomic policy, the extraordinary increase in international prices represented the principal incident of cost-push inflation during the postwar period. Since the increased cost pressures were not fully accommodated by monetary and fiscal policies in the larger countries, the world price increase was followed by a major recession, in which unemployment rates in most countries reached their highest postwar levels and important sectors of structural unemployment, particularly for youth, emerged. The oil price increase contributed to a deterioration in international competitiveness and current-account deficits (historically a precursor of first-generation incomes policies) that were only partially reduced by the subsequent recession and exchange-rate adjustment. Data on the current-account balance as a percentage of gross domestic product during the mid 1970s for the United States and the countries covered in this study are presented in table 1-5. With the exception of the Netherlands, which has substantial natural gas deposits, and Germany, the countries in the study experienced current-account deficits throughout the period. (Specific details concerning the sources of and policy responses to the deficits will be discussed in the chapters on individual countries.) In several countries, however, deficits persisted after the main effects of the oil price shock had passed and served to focus policy interest on the determination of labor costs. Thus, while the impetus to the inflation of the mid 1970s was attributable to factors beyond the reach of domestic policies, the repercussion of the world

Table 1-6. *Public Expenditure as a Percentage of Gross Domestic Product in Selected Countries of the OECD, Selected Periods, 1955–76*[a]

Country	1955–57	1967–69	1974–76
Austria	29.0	36.4	39.9
Denmark	25.5	35.5	46.4
France	33.5[b]	39.4	41.6
Germany	30.2[b]	33.1	44.0
Italy	28.1[b]	35.5	43.1
Netherlands	31.1	42.6	53.9
Norway	27.0	37.9	46.6
Sweden	n.a.	41.3	51.7
United Kingdom	32.3	38.5	44.5
United States	25.9	31.7	35.1

Source: OECD, *Public Expenditure Trends* (Paris: OECD, June 1978), table 2, pp. 14–15.
n.a. Not available.
a. All percentages computed at current prices.
b. Not fully comparable with other years.

price increases and domestic macroeconomic adjustment, including wage determination, renewed interest in incomes policy as an instrument of facilitating domestic adjustment to severe external shocks.

Public Expenditures and Taxation

Both internal and external factors constrained the abilities of labor unions to advance the welfare of their members through traditional collective bargaining techniques during the 1970s. Prominent among the domestic influences was the growth of taxation, which was tied to the growing claim on resources by the public sector in each of the countries in the study. Table 1-6 shows the percentage of gross domestic product represented by public expenditures in the periods 1955–57, 1967–69, and 1974–76. These data document not only the relative growth of the public sector, as measured by expenditures, but also the acceleration in that growth in most of the economies between the late 1960s and the mid 1970s. The acceleration was particularly rapid in Denmark, Germany, the Netherlands, and Sweden and was tied in many instances to expansion of transfer payments and social-service programs supported politically by labor unions and labor parties.

The general expansion of government activity along with the relatively slow growth of labor productivity in the public sector brought about a

Table 1-7. *Employment in the Public Sector as a Percentage of Total Employment in Selected Countries of the OECD, 1965 and 1975*[a]

Country	1965	1975
Austria	n.a.	n.a.
Denmark	20.9[b]	24.3
France	12.4	14.2
Germany	9.8	13.9
Italy	9.6	12.2
Netherlands	11.5	13.5
Norway	13.6	19.3
Sweden	15.3	25.4
United Kingdom	15.7	21.7
United States	18.0	19.9

Source: OECD, *Public Expenditure Trends*, table 4, p. 19.
n.a. Not available.
a. Comparisons in time are more significant than comparisons across countries, because there remain some large conceptual differences among various countries' definitions of the public sector.
b. 1970.

general increase of the public sector's share of employment (see table 1-7). In a general sense, this development increased the proportion of the employed labor force that was more or less sheltered from the effects of demand-management policies and may have reduced the responsiveness of wages to variations in unemployment.

The rapid expansion of the public sector required an increase in taxation in order to reduce claims on private goods and services and to finance public sector activities. While the structure of the tax systems differs considerably among the countries in this study, all make considerable use of personal income taxes as a source of revenue.[14] The need to finance the expansion of the public sector, along with the effect of inflation on marginal tax rates in unindexed tax systems, tended to push workers in many countries into increasingly progressive ranges of the tax rate schedules. In addition, many social benefits provided by the public sector were financed by social security contributions that were generally assessed on earnings, although nominally split between workers and employers. The contributions of employees directly reduced

14. Among the countries in this study taxes on income and profits constituted from 19–20 percent of total tax revenues in Italy and France to about 57 percent in Denmark. Social security taxes ranged between 6 percent of tax revenues in Denmark and 42 percent in France and Italy. OECD, *Revenue Statistics of OECD Member Countries, 1965–1974* (Paris: OECD, 1976), p. 76.

Table 1-8. *Marginal and Average Income Tax and Contributions to Social Security Paid by the Average Production Worker in Selected Countries of the OECD, 1974*

| Country | Marginal rate[a] (percent of increase in earnings) | | | Average rate[a] (percent of earnings) | | | |
	Income tax	Employee contribution to social security	Total (t_m)	Income tax	Employee contribution to social security	Total (t_a)	Progressivity[b]
Austria	26	8	34	13	12	25	1.36
Denmark	56	4	60	39	4	43	1.40
France	17	8	25	8	8	16	1.56
Germany	33	11	44	19	14	33	1.33
Italy	12	7	19	5	7	12	1.58
Netherlands[c]	26	16	42	15	20	35	1.20
Norway	39	9	48	25	8	33	1.45
Sweden	62	1	63	36	2	38	1.66
United Kingdom	33	5	38	25	6	31	1.23
United States	26	6	32	20	6	26	1.23

Source: OECD, *The Tax/Benefit Position of Selected Income Groups in OECD Member Countries, 1974–78* (Paris: OECD, 1980), table 23, p. 117; table 29, p. 120; table 37, p. 124.

a. Tax rates are for a single person and reflect the combined effects of state, local, and federal taxation.

b. Defined as t_m/t_a, where t_m is the marginal total tax rate and t_a is the average total tax rate.

c. Data are for 1976.

disposable income received from gross earnings, and there may have been a further indirect reduction to the extent that contributions of employers were shifted back onto workers.

The data in table 1-8 describe the marginal and average income tax rates and the employee social security tax rates applicable to the average earnings of a production worker in the United States and the countries included in this study. The final column also provides a measure of the progressivity of the total taxation on incomes—that is, including contributions of employees to social security—for an average production worker. The measure is the elasticity of tax payments with respect to an increase in pretax nominal income, or t_m/t_a, where t_m and t_a, respectively, are the marginal and average tax rates. If the elasticity equals unity, the tax system is proportional; if t_m/t_a exceeds unity, the system is progressive.

In the mid 1970s there were clearly wide variations among countries in the extent to which the money wages of an individual at the mean of the wage distribution for production workers translated into nominal changes in disposable income. Only Austria, France, and Italy tax incomes at a lower rate than does the United States, which is tied with

Italy for the least progressive system of income taxation among the countries covered in table 1-8. The progressivity of the tax systems derives from the income tax; rates of employee contributions to social security either are strictly proportional or are regressive, except in Norway. The degree of progressivity is greatest in the Scandinavian countries, where a 10 percent increase in money wages may yield as little as a 6 percent increase in disposable nominal income for the average production worker.

Nevertheless, the data in table 1-8 do not fully reveal the effect of some national tax systems on the environment of collective bargaining in the 1970s. In the first instance, the data in the table are for workers in the middle of the production-worker wage distribution. Workers receiving higher gross incomes are taxed at significantly higher marginal rates, and the unions that represent them might be less likely to acquiesce in wage increases that unions representing workers who are closer to the average would accept. At a minimum, sharply progressive tax systems can be a source of conflicting wage objectives between unions representing blue-collar workers and unions representing white-collar and professional workers and so introduce instability into national collective bargaining systems. To the extent that unions form their notions of equitable relative wages on the basis of gross rather than disposable wage differentials, the conflicting objectives introduced by the tax system have the potential for becoming an independent source of wage push. Yet efforts to compensate for the effects of the tax system with higher nominal wage increases can be self-defeating. In economies with high rates of inflation and steeply progressive unindexed income tax rates, it may be impossible for unions to advance real disposable earnings at *any* rate of increase in money wages. In addition to circumscribing the abilities of unions to advance the welfare of their members by pursuing traditional collective bargaining objectives, the increasing progressivity of effective tax rates further undermined the likely efficacy of simple first-generation incomes policies based on a single wage guideline and applicable to all workers, irrespective of tax status.

Nonwage Labor Costs

Both the environment of collective bargaining and the degree of inertia in wage and price changes have also been influenced by the growing importance of nonwage labor costs in the compensation package. The growth of nonwage labor costs reflects choices by an array of political and collective bargaining institutions. As governments—often in response to pressure from labor unions—pursue policies that increase the redistribution of income from the active population to the inactive, by way of the development of more extensive health and welfare policies, greater social welfare charges have been imposed on employers by government at various levels. At the same time there have been significant increases in private fringe benefits as unions have responded to the demands of their members during a period when growth of real wages combined with the effects of high rates of inflation on marginal tax rates may have increased the attractiveness of nonpecuniary compensation. (See tables 1-9 and 1-10 for data on the growing importance of nonwage labor costs.) The existence of statutory contributions by employers to social security drives a wedge between the total labor costs incurred by employers and those labor costs that are determined by collective bargaining and wage drift. With the growth of statutory charges, the resistance of employers—particularly those competing in world markets—to increases bargained for collectively grew and raised demands for explicit trades between statutory elements of labor cost and those obtained through collective bargaining. As a consequence, the potential for bargaining impasses and strikes increased during the period.

Two aspects of the growth of nonwage labor costs have tended to render fluctuations in unit labor costs more countercyclical with the passage of time. First, the percentage of total labor costs related to hours of employment has declined. Second, the growth in the fixed component of labor costs—nonwage payments that are not computed as fractions of the base wage—has reduced the incentive for employers to respond to increases in product demand by hiring more workers. (It should not have reduced their incentive to lay off or dismiss workers in response to declining demand; those options have traditionally been less available to European employers than to American employers, however, and they were reduced further by union-backed legislation as well as by bargaining and strikes in the 1970s.)

The Collective Bargaining Environment

Each of the developments reviewed above imposed constraints that implied a diminished function for traditional collective bargaining institutions in advancing the welfare of union members. These constraints,

Table 1-9. *Nonwage Labor Costs as a Percentage of Total Labor Costs, Total Economy, in Selected Countries of the OECD, 1965 and 1974–76*[a]

Country	1965	1974	1975	1976[b]
Austria	17.5	17.9	18.5	n.a.
France	24.1	24.9	25.7	25.6
Germany	14.0	17.7	18.3	18.8
Italy	27.5	28.8	28.5	28.4
Netherlands	15.2	22.3	22.3	22.7
Norway	6.8	15.1	15.0	n.a.
Sweden	10.4	19.7	21.8	24.4
United Kingdom	8.9	10.5	11.3	12.2
United States	8.7	12.6	13.0	13.3

Source: OECD, "Fixed Employment Costs," CPE/WP4(78)1 (Paris: OECD, May 31, 1978), p. 33.
n.a. Not available.
a. Employers' contributions to social security programs, private pensions, insurance programs, and employer payroll taxes that are not compensation to employees. Data for Denmark are not available.
b. Estimate.

Table 1-10. *Nonwage Labor Costs as a Percentage of Total Labor Costs in Manufacturing in Selected Countries of the OECD, 1965, 1975, and 1978*

Country	1965	1975	1978
Austria	41.0	45.1	46.2
Denmark	14.1	17.1	17.6
France	40.2	40.3	43.7
Germany	29.7	34.1	40.8
Italy	45.0	47.9	51.4[a]
Netherlands	31.6	40.8	43.0
Norway	22.2	29.9	30.1
Sweden	19.0	32.2	38.1
United Kingdom	13.8	17.4	19.7
United States	17.1	24.0	26.0

Source: SAF, *Wages and Total Labour Costs for Workers: International Surveys, 1965–75* (Stockholm: SAF, May 1977); see also ibid., *1968–78*.
a. 1977.

moreover, occurred during a period in which both inflation and unemployment were of growing significance. While the resistance of employers was in most instances insufficient to restrict negotiated settlements to the reduced "room" for pay increases, unions, which could not by themselves alter the nature of the constraints, were in an unpleasant dilemma. To ignore the implications for collective bargaining and use the conventional methods of unions for advancing the welfare of their members would simply have exacerbated the stagflation problem and retarded the speed with which domestic economies adjusted to external shocks, but acceptance of the implications would have threatened the institutional role of labor unions.

It is clear that the first generation of incomes policies, which typically consisted of announcement of a rule for income growth to the parties to collective bargaining, was poorly suited to resolution of this dilemma. If unions had restrained money wage demands and had otherwise altered traditional objectives in ways that facilitated macroeconomic adjustments, they would have had to require compensating gains for their members and institutional protection for themselves. But neither of the parties to traditional collective bargaining was directly responsible for the factors that threatened the institutional viability of unions, so the dilemma was unlikely to be resolved within the traditional framework of collective bargaining. On the other hand, the more important domestic constraints were tied to taxation of various forms. Since the governments that wished to encourage restrained increases in money wages were a source of the threat to the traditional role of unions, there was room for a deal, but with a very different approach to incomes policy. The circumstances that led to a second generation of incomes policies encouraged the development of multilateral bargaining arrangements—with national governments as explicit parties to the negotiations—in order to work out the forms that compensation and institutional protection would take. The development and effectiveness of these institutions is analyzed in the country chapters.

Theoretical Bases

It is interesting that the policymakers of Europe should have returned so persistently to an instrument whose record has been as spotty and unreliable as the record of incomes policy has been. That record raises the question whether incomes policies are inherently ineffective, even self-defeating, given the nature of the underlying inflationary process, or whether the design and administration of past policies have been inadequate to cope with the institutional forces that they were designed to resist. In this section we shall consider circumstances in which institutional restraint is possible and incomes policy is therefore in principle feasible.

Nominal and Real Policies

In order to discuss the potential role of incomes policies, we return to the distinction between real and nominal policies. A "nominal" policy is an incomes policy designed to alter nominal magnitudes, such as absolute prices, money wages, and the money supply, while leaving unchanged real magnitudes, such as relative prices, real wages, unemployment, output, and profitability. A nominal policy therefore changes all nominal magnitudes in the same proportion. Historically, nominal incomes policies have been the dominant variety of incomes policy experiments in the United States and, during the 1960s, in Western Europe. In contrast, a "real" policy is designed to alter at least some real magnitudes. Policies designed to reduce the rate of inflation without restraining real wages or changing unemployment—by attempting to alter expectations directly, for instance—are nominal policies in principle, even if some real variables are affected in the process. On the other hand, policies with the aim of restraining real wages, bolstering profitability, improving international competitiveness, or enabling unemployment to be reduced are examples of real policies, although they may also help to bring down the rate of inflation.[15] In the remainder of this section we shall consider circumstances in which nominal and real incomes policies seem feasible in principle. Economic developments reviewed in the preceding section, particularly the acceleration of real wages and subsequent squeeze on profits, have led to a considerable emphasis on real incomes policies in European countries during the 1970s.

The International Monetarist Model

A natural starting point in consideration of economies with substantial foreign sectors is with the labor market behavior and possibilities for

15. A similar distinction between real and nominal incomes policies is drawn by M. J. Artis, "Incomes Policies: Some Rationales," in J. L. Fallick and R. F. Elliott, eds., *Incomes Policies, Inflation, and Relative Pay* (London: Allen & Unwin, 1981), pp. 6–22; related distinctions appear in Palle Schelde Andersen and Philip Turner, "Incomes Policy in Theory and Practice," *OECD Economic Outlook, Occasional Studies,* July 1980, p. 33, and Karl-Olof Faxén, "Incomes Policy and Centralized Wage Formation" (Stockholm: SAF, February 1982), p. 3. The use of real incomes policies during the 1970s in some European countries can be seen as a variant of James Meade's suggestion that demand-management policies be used "to maintain a steady rate of growth of money expenditure . . . [and] to use wage-fixing institutions and policies to maintain full employment." James E. Meade, *Wage-Fixing* (London: Allen & Unwin, 1982), p. 8.

incomes policy implied by the international monetarist model (IMM).[16] In this, as in other models that we shall consider, most of the salient points can be made by postulating an economy artificially restricted to a single-product market in which profit-maximizing businesses produce manufactured goods with the aid of labor and imported raw materials. Each unit of manufactured goods, which may be sold or bought on the world market, requires in production one unit of raw materials.

The labor-market behavior implied by the IMM rests on three propositions. First, world markets function under conditions of perfect competition, so domestic producers face an infinitely elastic demand curve at the world price of manufactures. Second, the supply of labor increases with the real wage. Together these first two propositions determine the supply of output, since the marginal production costs consist of payments for labor and imported raw materials. Equilibrium in labor markets occurs when the real wage rate (W/P) equals the marginal product of labor [$MPL(1 - t)$] adjusted for the ratio of the world price of materials to the world price of manufactures (t).[17] Labor market equilibrium, in which $W/P = MPL(1 - t)$ to determine the full employment level, E_0, that corresponds to the natural rate of unemployment, is illustrated by the intersection of the demand [$MPL(1 - t)$] and supply (E_s) schedules in figure 1-1.

The third proposition is that money wages will rise more or less rapidly than expected prices depending on whether there is excess demand for or excess supply of labor. Therefore, the disequilibrium behavior of the economy depends on the determinants of the expected rate of inflation. With fixed rates of exchange it would be expected that the increase in domestic prices would be equal to the increase in world prices. In the case of floating rates, the rational expectation of price inflation would be equal to the expected rate of growth of the money supply.

The introduction of unions and collective bargaining into the international monetarist world alters the equilibrium but leaves the basic mechanisms of the model unchanged. Instead of the original labor supply condition, the presence of unions may introduce an expected negotiable

16. The concepts presented in this section are simple, and the analysis, which has been compressed to the greatest extent possible, helps to build the intellectual case for the value of an incomes policy. Readers who find the material too technical, however, may be able to pass over it and still read the chapters on individual countries profitably.

17. Since a unit of materials has to be used in each unit of output, its cost, $P_w t$, must be subtracted from the marginal revenue product as conventionally defined.

Figure 1-1. *Real Wages and Employment in the International Monetarist Model*

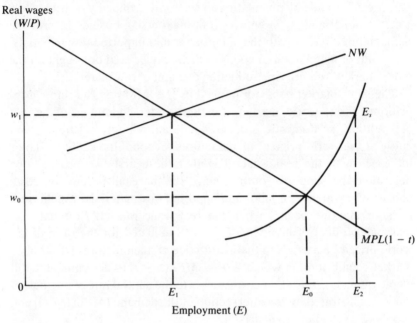

Employment (E)

real wage (the NW schedule in figure 1-1) that varies positively with the level of employment (a determinant of the relative bargaining strength of union and employers) but exceeds the reservation wage. In this conventional representation of union bargaining behavior, variations in the rate of negotiated wage change can be produced solely by variations in the resistance of employers, which reflect changes in product market conditions. In disequilibrium, money wages will rise more or less rapidly than expected prices according to whether at the existing level of employment, the expected negotiable real wage is higher or lower than the actual real wage. It can be seen that the main effect of introducing collective bargaining has been to alter the equilibrium to employment level E_1, where both the real wage and the natural rate of unemployment are higher than under competition.[18] The new equilibrium implies involuntary unemployment of $E_2 - E_1$. Under the assumption that unions

18. The conclusion that the natural-rate result is preserved under collective bargaining is in line with the observation in the survey article on inflation by two leading international monetarists that a wide range of bargaining models, including those based on the Nash cooperative solution, imply the natural-rate result; see David Laidler and Michael

always exploit their market power fully—that is, they operate on the *NW* schedule—collective bargaining influences the natural rate of unemployment in this model but can be responsible for initiating episodes of inflation only when the unions' degree of monopoly—or bargaining—power increases.

The international monetarist model with fixed exchange rates clearly precludes either real or nominal incomes policies. Nominal policies are precluded since world prices are exogenous, and altering domestic wages would therefore alter relative prices. Real policies are ruled out by the existence of a unique natural rate of unemployment equilibrium: any reduction in the growth of money wages in relation to world price inflation would expand employment, but this would produce a subsequent increase in money wages greater than inflation, since the rise in employment would have pushed the expected negotiable wage above the actual.

If exchange rates are flexible, however, a nominal incomes policy is possible. An exogenous reduction in money wages, even if confined to one sector, will generate rational expectations of such a cut in all nominal magnitudes including the money supply and the exchange rate. But this assumes the absence of built-in wage and price lags, which impart inertia to the inflationary process in the face of deflationary monetary policy and would call for real or relative sacrifice by laggards who comply with an incomes policy. And, as before, a real policy is not possible on account of the unique real equilibrium of the economy.

Variable Bargaining Intensity

If collective bargaining can make a contribution of its own to the inflationary process, however, there is a case for incomes policy even within the framework of the international monetarist model. Our approach to union behavior relies on a notion accepted as commonplace by practitioners and observers of industrial relations: that unions may bargain with varying degrees of intensity, or militancy, even when economic and structural conditions—including the degree of organization and the coverage of collective bargaining—are held constant.

The difference between variable bargaining intensity and the conventional bargaining models can be illustrated by dropping the previous

---

Parkin, "Inflation: A Survey," *Economic Journal,* vol. 85 (December 1975), pp. 757–58. For the first explicit model of this, see George de Menil, *Bargaining: Monopoly Power versus Union Power* (Cambridge: MIT Press, 1971).

Figure 1-2. *The Maximum Negotiable Wage and the Minimum Acceptable Wage under Collective Bargaining*

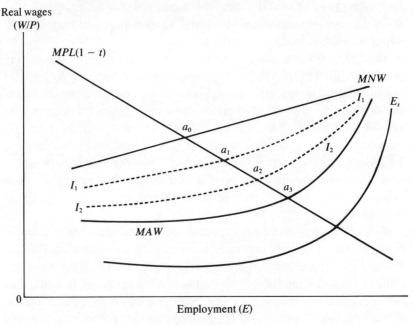

assumption that the real wage actually negotiated by the union is the maximum obtainable (now represented as schedule *MNW* in figure 1-2). This maximum, which represents a union's potential bargaining power, depends in part on the employer's ability to pay and his ability and willingness to resist union demands. Profit-maximizing bargaining behavior by employers will lead to an attempt to obtain a least-cost combination of settlement costs and strike losses. Employer resistance thus depends on conditions of supply and demand in labor markets, which affect both strike costs and settlement costs. Employer resistance also depends on the effective coverage or extent of collective bargaining and on the structure of collective bargaining, including the degree to which it is centralized and the resources and authority at the disposal of associations of employers. Finally, the maximum negotiable wage depends on the prevailing attitudes, or bargaining militancy, of the workers themselves, since the employer's propensity to resist depends on his estimate of his employees' willingness to go out and remain on strike and hence of the estimated cost of resistance to the union's demands.

Worker attitudes and bargaining structures can also determine the level of the minimum acceptable wage (*MAW* in figure 1-2). At any given level of employment, the minimum acceptable wage is the highest wage that workers will insist on and cannot be prevented from striking for. More generally, workers behave as if they had certain minimally acceptable levels of real or relative wages or of profits in relation to wages. Workers behave, moreover, as if they also had maximum acceptable levels of effort, discomfort, and hazard and quite frequently minimum acceptable levels of job security and income security. Above such levels, these various attributes of employment can be regarded as mutual substitutes, and tradeoffs among them will be revealed by collective bargaining or competitive forces. But the levels themselves constitute a set of minimum constraints.

Collective bargaining targets also depend in part on the degree to which authority is centralized within the union structure and on the level at which collective bargaining is carried out. In competitive product markets the conditions that govern the elasticity of the derived demand for labor indicate that bargaining power will tend to increase with the centralization of collective bargaining. With greater centralization—industry bargaining rather than plant bargaining, for example—the scope for consumer substitution in response to wage-induced price increases is reduced, and the employment losses associated with a wage increase are smaller than they would be with decentralized bargaining. Under imperfect product-market competition, however, the broader the level—plant, company, industry, economy—at which organizational bargaining policy is made, the more restrained it tends to be. There are a number of reasons for the comparative restraint exercised by more centralized unions in this situation, the most important of which is the pervasive presence in different forms of the prisoner's dilemma, or public goods problem. Local unions, bargaining independently, are likely to feel—as long as profits remain positive—that the wages they negotiate have a trivial effect on the industry price level and hence on the level of their employment. It will thus be in their interest to bargain with maximum intensity, whether or not other local unions are doing so. Each local will therefore bargain with maximum intensity. Wage restraint on their part, if unmatched by other unions bargaining independently, will cause losses in both real and relative earnings to the extent that other unions fail to exercise similar restraint.[19] On the other hand, the relation between wage

19. The level of employment within a decentralized bargaining unit, however, may depend on the relative level of profitability and costs prevailing therein when the

increases and price increases is more obvious to centralized bargaining institutions. Similarly, bargaining is likely to be less restrained if an industry is represented by a number of craft unions, each of which exerts a relatively small degree of leverage on total costs and product price, than if it is represented by a single industrial union.

Individual national unions, unless very large, are also unlikely to believe that their own independent negotiations will affect government policy with respect to aggregate demand. If the elasticity of demand for labor in the industry is low, such a union will attempt to bargain for a relatively high real wage, independent of the policies of other unions. The result could be a higher overall level of real wages than the government is prepared to accept, so it will reduce aggregate demand, thus increasing unemployment. A centralized federation, on the other hand, would be able to negotiate a lower overall real wage and thus avert this consequence. The broader economic perspective of a more widely based union has constituted an important reason for granting such organizations authority over narrower bodies, contributing to an ability to hold down both the minimum acceptable demands of union members and the degree of bargaining intensity within the zone of discretion.

If minimum acceptable wages are below levels obtainable through maximum exploitation of bargaining power, union negotiators bargain within a zone of discretion, indicated in figure 1-2 by the gap between the minimum acceptable wage (*MAW*) and maximum negotiable wage (*MNW*) schedules. Within the zone of discretion, the union can make its choice of bargaining intensity. For example, the lines I_1I_1 and I_2I_2 in figure 1-2 represent two possible schedules of constant bargaining intensity within the zone of discretion. The actual real wage is determined by the intersection of the chosen intensity schedule and the demand curve for labor—the equilibrium is at point a_1, for example, if the union

---

employing unit is part of a multiplant and multinational firm. In such an instance, the plant might lose employment if its unit operating costs were to exceed operating costs plus whatever capital expenses would have to be incurred in expanding capacity in some other location. Two developments have tended to increase the importance of this type of restraint on decentralized bargaining systems. The first is the growth of multinational firms. The second is rising unemployment, which, by creating excess capacity, has tended to reduce the critical wage differential at which reductions in force might be expected to occur in high-cost units. Not until the end of the 1970s, however, did these two developments reach a scale large enough to challenge the historic generalization that the wage behavior of decentralized union institutions is less restrained than the wage behavior of centralized structures.

bargains with the intensity of I_1I_1. A general increase in the militancy of the organized work force could therefore cause increased wage and price inflation.

The effect would be indistinguishable from the effect of an increase in the degree of union organization or collective bargaining coverage in a situation in which it was assumed that unions always bargain at full potential. Increases in the militancy of labor, as reflected in part by the increase in strike activity in the late 1960s and 1970s discussed earlier in this chapter, raise both the equilibrium real wage and the natural rate of unemployment. With variable bargaining intensity there is a clear case for a real incomes policy, for if the government can persuade the unions to reduce their bargaining intensity, its incomes policy allows the government a tradeoff between higher employment and lower real wages. (In figure 1-2, incomes policy gives the government the choice of locating the economy on the strip between a_0 and a_3.)

Profitability, International Competitiveness, and Incomes Policy

Under perfectly competitive conditions and flexible exchange rates, only nominal incomes policies are possible. With allowance for variable bargaining intensity, the international monetarist model can contemplate a category of real incomes policy in which the growth of real wages is moderated in order to permit business firms to increase output and employment. During the 1960s, however, and especially during the 1970s, moderation of real wages was urged on the grounds that it was necessary to increase or restore international competitiveness and profitability, following periods of excessive growth in real wages, in order to stimulate investment. Concern for reaching higher actual levels of employment tended to be secondary; indeed, these incomes policies were apt to be accompanied by deflationary measures.[20] Incomes policies designed to increase profitability or competitiveness would be redundant under conditions of perfect competition; the widespread and in some cases prolonged decline in profitability noted earlier cannot easily be reconciled with competitive theory.

For four reasons, the assumption of perfect competition also makes it more difficult to account for certain types of macroeconomic behavior. First, positive cyclical correlations of real wages and employment are

20. Ulman and Flanagan, *Wage Restraint*, pp. 245–46.

difficult to reconcile with the assumption of diminishing marginal productivity that is incorporated in the international monetarist model. Second, the existence of external constraints on the level of domestic activity is difficult to reconcile with the notion that unemployment is always at the natural rate and the natural rate is consistent with external balance. But for governments concerned with preserving external balance, unemployment has had to reflect world economic conditions. (The international monetarist model must explain the rise in unemployment in the late 1970s as a consequence of increasing natural rates of unemployment in individual countries.) Third, a combination of declining terms of trade between manufacturers and suppliers of raw materials (notably including energy), real wages increasing in relation to trend productivity, and falling unemployment does not fit well with the competitive model. This combination characterized the behavior of some economies—Italy and the United Kingdom, for example—in the aftermath of 1973, but it is ruled out in the previously discussed models, where real wages and the marginal productivity of labor schedules are normalized for trend productivity growth. Finally, on the microeconomic side, there is considerable agreement that in most Western European economies prices are set with reference both to average costs of production and to world prices, and there is considerable evidence that output is generally limited by demand rather than by lack of profitability.[21]

The foregoing observations do not make a conclusive case against the assumption of perfect competition. Most of the situations discussed can be reconciled with a perfectly competitive framework with the aid of appropriately tailored assumptions about lags, disaggregation, uncertainty, market disequilibrium, or changes in taxes, preferences, or technology. Nevertheless, a model of oligopolistic competition, based on the importance of retention of customers and the retardation or

21. McCracken and others, *Towards Full Employment*, pp. 304–08; Wynne A. H. Godley and William D. Nordhaus, "Pricing in the Trade Cycle," *Economic Journal*, vol. 82 (September 1972), pp. 853–82; Paolo Sylos Labini, "Prices and Income Distribution in Manufacturing Industry," *Journal of Post-Keynesian Economics*, vol. 2 (Fall 1979), pp. 3–25; OECD Economic Surveys, *France*, February 1972; Michael K. Evans, *An Econometric Model of the French Economy: A Short-Term Forecasting Model* (Paris: OECD, 1969); Gerhard Fels, "Inflation in Germany," p. 599; Lars Calmfors, "Inflation in Sweden," pp. 504–09; and Odd Aukrust, "Inflation in the Open Economy: A Norwegian Model," pp. 135–38, all in Lawrence B. Krause and Walter S. Salant, eds., *Worldwide Inflation: Theory and Recent Experience* (Washington, D.C.: Brookings Institution, 1977).

prevention of entry by new firms is also consistent with the phenomena described above without the need for ad hoc elaborations. The relevance of oligopolistic competition extends beyond highly concentrated national markets. Many international markets with many suppliers can be fragmented into a web of national, regional, or local markets, in each of which suppliers are conscious of their interdependence and aware that their individual actions can attract new or cross entries. Oligopolistic competition can therefore apply to domestic markets where prices are based entirely on costs as well as to markets exposed to international trade in which prices are set as weighted averages of costs and world prices, including instances in which prices are based solely on the world price. In each case, suppliers produce what is demanded at the price set, rather than the amount that equates marginal cost to price.[22]

A central feature of the oligopolistic competition model is its reliance on the notion of a kinked product demand curve. This feature reflects the fact that the supplier who wants the lowest "common" price is able to impose that price by refusing to follow price increases by any other company; other suppliers must then price roughly in line in order to protect their shares of the market. Price cutting is usually ruled out by fear of retaliation. So long as the price does not attract entry, including increased import competition, this desired price will be (roughly) the monopoly price. More generally, the desired price—and hence the market price—is chosen to retard or prevent entry into the market.

Contrary to the usual kinked-demand-curve argument, however, a rise in costs will cause a rise in the sustainable, entry-preventive market price. Therefore, in a closed economy the entry-preventive—or entry-retarding—price will be a markup on the long-run average costs of production, the markup reflecting both the fixed costs of entry and any difference between the operating costs of potential entrants and of existing firms. With import competition, on the other hand, the entry-preventive price is the price at which the good in question is sold in other

22. This approach also has a number of points in common with the customer theory of pricing developed by Arthur Okun. In perfectly competitive markets buyers can switch between suppliers at no cost. But, as Okun points out in characterizing the seller-buyer relationship as an implicit contract, this is rarely the case in practice. Instead, the supplier establishes a reputation of reliability with customers. At the same time, the buyer in industrial markets is generally well aware of competitors' prices and, in an effort to minimize costs, will not tolerate any significant long-run price differential. The supplier can thus safeguard his share of the market by charging prices broadly in line with those charged by his competitors. See Okun, *Prices and Quantities*, pp. 134–78.

national markets—that is, the world price. In fact, immediate retaliation against penetration by imports—by reducing domestic prices to world levels—has not been profitable as long as the share of imports in the domestic market has remained small, and, of course, extensive import penetration has occurred.

Hence we take the domestic price level (P) to be a weighted average of the world price of manufactures and a markup on the average cost of production at standard capacity operation. Consider the two extreme cases. In pure markup pricing the domestic price is completely unrestrained by the world price. If the world price is assumed to be constant, a given increase in money wages will raise the domestic price in relation to the world price, as a result of which competitiveness is reduced. At the same time the real price of imports, $P_M/P = t(P_W/P)$, is also reduced, so that the rise in the domestic price level is less than proportionate to the rise in the money wage level, as determined by the ratios of the cost of labor and the cost of imported materials, respectively. The increase in real wages will have been "paid for" by a decline in the real price of imports. At the other extreme, where domestic prices are set equal to world prices, the rise in the real wage has no effect on competitiveness; its entire effect is to reduce profitability. In the mixed case, in which the domestic price is a weighted average of the world price and a markup, both competitiveness and profitability are reduced. This case is depicted in figure 1-3.

The relation between real wages, aggregate employment, and incomes policy under conditions of oligopolistic competition can now be seen with the assistance of figure 1-3. The $MPL(1 - t)$ schedule has been drawn with an upward-sloping segment in order to examine an equilibrium that is consistent with increasing productivity of labor. Given a kink in the oligopolistic product demand curve at an output level corresponding to the employment level E_0, the real marginal revenue product schedule, AAA, coincides with the MPL schedule for employment levels up to E_0, at which point it jumps vertically downward. If we assume for the moment that the I_1I_1 schedule represents the constant level of union bargaining intensity, the intersection of AAA with I_1I_1 (point a at employment level E_0) corresponds to the intersection between marginal revenue and marginal cost above the profit-maximizing level of output. Therefore, E_0 is an equilibrium level of employment, and it is determined by monetary or fiscal policy which sets the aggregate demand for output. At E_0, unions will bargain the real wage w_0.

Figure 1-3. *Real Wages and Aggregate Employment*
under Conditions of Oligopolistic Competition

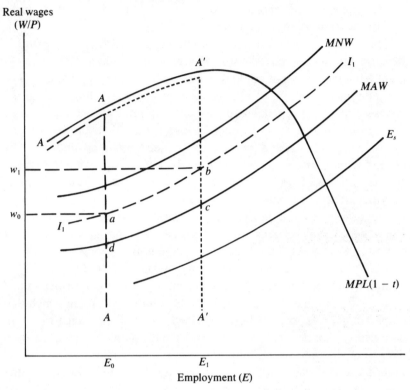

An increase in aggregate demand will shift the kinked real marginal
revenue product curve to the right—to $A'A'$, for example, the extension
of AAA in figure 1-3. The expansion of output will therefore establish a
new equilibrium, b, at a higher level of employment, E_1, and, if the
bargaining intensity remains at I_1I_1, a higher real wage, w_1. The higher
real wage implies a reduction of profitability. Profit-maximizing businesses, however, will produce the new level of output, since marginal
profitability—the gap between $MPL(1 - t)$ and W/P—is still positive.
Thus, in contrast to the unique natural rate of unemployment equilibrium
of the international monetarist model, there will be a range of potential
equilibria under oligopolistic competition, even at constant bargaining
intensity (so long as $MPL [1 - t] \geq I_1I_1$). Although real wages rise as
demand increases, it will still pay businesses to produce the output

demanded, since the higher wages do not eliminate profits. But it will not pay them to produce more than the increase in aggregate demand, since, at any given level of aggregate demand, the kinked demand curve imposes a prohibitive cost on expansion.

There are, however, two conditions under which an expansion in demand and the associated rise in the real wage could prevent employment from increasing or could require a reduction in employment. The first condition would prevail if positive profits were eliminated in the course of an upswing in demand, so that a lower rate of real wages would be required to sustain employment at a level to the right of the intersection between $MPL(1 - t)$ and the curve of chosen bargaining intensity. The second would arise as a result of the effect of an expansion in demand on the balance of trade. An expansion in demand directly increases imports, while a rise in domestic prices in relation to world prices caused by the associated rise in the negotiated rate of real wages decreases exports and further increases imports. An increase in employment would therefore have to be balanced by a reduction in real wages to increase competitiveness if equilibrium in the balance of trade were to be maintained. Whether the higher level of employment could be maintained depends upon the exchange rate regime. A limiting case, in which that employment level cannot be maintained, is when exchange rates are completely flexible and there are no capital flows. In that case an imbalance of trade would be precluded by depreciation, which would reduce the real wage rate at the higher level of employment, but the latter would be unsustainable, given the ability of the unions to increase the real wage. The outcome, as under the first condition, would be either an acceleration of inflation at the higher level of employment or a reduction in demand and employment to their original levels. And in the former case, the authorities would come under pressure to protect the international value of their currency and "manage" their exchange rates. There will, in fact, be a unique level of employment consistent with constant inflation, at any given level of world aggregate demand, if there are immobility of capital and complete flexibility of exchange rates. This is because the balance of trade deteriorates as employment—or output—increases, for the reasons cited above; hence, a unique level of employment will be required for a zero trade deficit, at least if world demand is constant. A decrease (increase) in world demand will of course decrease (increase) the zero-deficit level of employment.

The other limiting case—that of fixed exchange rates—imposes no external constraint on the level of employment, but only so long as the government is able to finance an accumulating deficit. In this analysis exchange rates are assumed not to be completely flexible. This assumption is not unrealistic. In the quarter-century preceding the decade of the 1970s exchange rates were fixed, although adjustable; during the 1970s floating was imperfect—"dirty," or "managed"—and official policy remained constrained to preserve external equilibrium.

The function of a real incomes policy in an environment of reduced competitiveness and profitability now becomes apparent. Note that competitiveness and profitability (at standard capacity) can be reduced in two ways. First, with an expansion of aggregate demand, an increase in employment from E_0 to E_1 under conditions of constant bargaining intensity—along I_1I_1, for example—would be associated with an increase in real wages and a reduction in competitiveness, as noted earlier. Second, an increase in bargaining intensity—from I_1I_1 to MNW, for example—at a given level of employment E_1 would also bring about the combination of constant unemployment, higher real wages, and lower competitiveness and profitability, as determined by the relative weights assigned to the markup over costs and to world prices. Only if the increase in bargaining intensity were sufficient to raise the real wage rate above the $MPL(1 - t)$ schedule would employment be reduced.

Conversely, competitiveness and profitability may also be increased in one or both of two ways: first, by what one might regard as a classical contraction of aggregate demand, under constant bargaining intensity, a decrease in employment from E_1 to E_0 would be accompanied by a reduction in the real wage rate and by an increase in competitiveness and the rate of profits; second, by a reduction in bargaining intensity at a given level of employment, as when there is a move down from I_1I_1 toward the MAW schedule. Securing such a moderation of real wages through a reduction in bargaining intensity instead of through deflation and unemployment has constituted an important rationale for incomes policies in many Western European countries during the 1970s. Incomes policy has also been used in tandem with both expansionist and contractionist demand management. In the former case, by reducing the level of bargaining intensity during an upswing, the policy could in principle prevent real wages from rising with an increase in employment from E_0 to E_1 and thus prevent profitability and competitiveness from declining— a policy combination that would move the equilibrium from a to c, for example, instead of from a to b. In the latter case, incomes policy has been used to increase the effectiveness of deflation in increasing profit-ability or competitiveness and hence in minimizing recourse to unem-ployment, as when necessary to maintain balance-of-trade equilibrium following an adverse movement in the terms of trade—a downward shift in $MPL(1 - t)$, a policy combination, for example, that would move the equilibrium from b to d instead of from b to a. Finally, in cases in which it was necessary to secure the assent of the unions to contractionist monetary or fiscal policy, deflation itself might be regarded as a target of incomes policy.

The Scandinavian Model

The issues of profitability and competitiveness have also arisen in those countries—principally in Scandinavia—in which the inflation process under fixed exchange rates is believed to be described by a two-sector model originally developed by the Norwegian economist Odd Aukrust.[23] The Aukrust model makes a now-familiar distinction between the open sector of the economy, consisting of export and import-competing industries, and a sheltered sector consisting of industries that compete in domestic markets. The rate of growth of labor productivity is normally greater in the open sector. Since prices in the open sector must equal world prices if firms are to remain competitive, profit margins in the open sector will remain stable if money-wage inflation in the sector equals the rate of world price inflation plus the rate of growth of labor productivity in the sector. A combination of labor market competition and the egalitarian spirit of collective bargaining will tend to transmit the money-wage increases obtained in the open sector to the sheltered sector. Price inflation in the sheltered sector is equal to money-wage inflation *minus* the rate of growth of labor productivity in that sector. Since the latter is relatively low, domestic price inflation will exceed the rate of growth of world prices.

There is nothing that guarantees that under collective bargaining wages in the open sector will be mechanically determined by the

---

23. The basic references on the short-run and long-run versions of the model are Odd Aukrust, "PRIM I: A Model of the Price and Income Distribution Mechanism of an Open Economy," *Review of Income and Wealth,* series 16, no. 1 (March 1970), pp. 51–78, and idem, "Inflation in the Open Economy: A Norwegian Model." For a discussion of the applicability of the model to Sweden, see Gösta Edgren, Karl-Olof Faxén, and Clas-Erik Odhner, *Wage Formation and the Economy,* tr. by Margareta Eklof (London: Allen & Unwin, 1973).

"room" provided by increases in labor productivity and world prices, particularly since the principal elements of compensation—negotiated rates, wage drift, and social charges—are largely determined independent of each other. As increases in compensation exceed the room, profits in the export sector will be squeezed, as noted earlier in the chapter, and the rate of domestic price inflation will increase. As in the previous model, there is a role for incomes policy to contain compensation increases to the room consistent with maintaining competitiveness.

Plan of the Book

Thus, under the circumstances outlined above, there is a case for incomes policy to thwart or reverse episodes of worker militancy and, in so doing, to reduce real wages, lower the equilibrium rate of unemployment, and restore competitiveness and profitability. Yet this case for incomes policy runs counter to the traditional trade union objective of advancing the real incomes of members and is unlikely to receive significant support unless unions can secure a quid pro quo in other forms of economic compensation for union members or in measures of institutional protection designed to compensate unions for the loss of support of their members with increased organizational authority and security. The actual incomes policy mechanisms adopted in the pursuit of this good in the 1970s have varied widely, reflecting international differences in underlying economic circumstances and in the behavior of trade unions and political institutions. The center of this book consists of an analysis of the nature and effectiveness of the incomes policy mechanisms adopted in nine Western European countries. These chapters provide the raw material from which we draw our comparative conclusions on the achievements of European incomes policies in the final chapter. In the country chapters we analyze the underlying macroeconomic conditions, the principal factors that appear to have motivated the bargaining behavior of trade unions, and the principal incomes policy choices, with particular attention to the endogeneity of policy choices with respect to particular political and economic factors.

We also attempt to evaluate the effects of particular policy episodes on wage and price behavior. In various instances we have used econometric methods of policy analysis to assist in the evaluation. At times, however, the assumptions underlying econometric evaluation techniques were not satisfied by the underlying economic and institutional behavior. In some countries, there was extensive structural change in the wage-determination process associated with shifts of worker militancy or employer resistance. Because these and other factors that influence the intensity of bargaining are not easily specified in a regression analysis, standard evaluation techniques may confound such unspecified institutional influences with the effects of incomes policy.[24] In others, incomes policies operated more or less continuously throughout the period under study, although the form of the policy changed from time to time. Here the overall effects of the policies could not be estimated, given the lack of a base "policy-off" period, although the marginal effect of policy changes could at times be assessed. Where these difficulties have not been insuperable, we have used econometric evaluation techniques to obtain summary measures of the likely effects of policies on wage and price behavior. Many of the effects of incomes policies, however—particularly on the behavior of trade unions and political institutions—cannot be neatly revealed by statistical procedures, and in these instances, we have used other methods.[25]

The country chapters could be organized around any of several themes that arise in the study of incomes policy. Nevertheless, in analyzing these countries we were struck by one outstanding fact of their incomes policy experience: countries with a similar initial approach toward incomes policies at the beginning of the decade sometimes ended up in quite different circumstances as the decade proceeded. We have chosen to order the individual country chapters around this perspective.

The first three chapters, covering the experience in Austria, the Netherlands, and Norway, analyze countries that began the decade with a relatively formal policy apparatus for achieving wage and price

---

24. Both Lipsey and Parkin and Oi have produced forceful critiques of incomes policy evaluation procedures that failed to allow for the effects of a policy on the entire structure of the wage-determination process. R. G. Lipsey and J. M. Parkin, "Incomes Policy: A Re-appraisal," *Economica*, vol. 37 (May 1970), pp. 115–38; Walter Y. Oi, "On Measuring the Impact of Wage-Price Controls: A Critical Appraisal," in Karl Brunner and Allan H. Meltzer, eds., *The Economics of Price and Wage Controls*, Carnegie-Rochester Conference Series on Public Policy, vol. 2 (Amsterdam: North-Holland Publishing Company, 1976). Procedures that do provide such flexibility require significant periods of stability in the wage-determination process to provide a base against which policy-induced changes can be measured. Such periods of stability appear to have been elusive in some countries in recent times.

25. These and related issues are also discussed in Andersen and Turner, "Incomes Policy in Theory and Practice."

restraint. By the end of the decade, however, the experience of the countries in achieving wage and price restraint had differed sharply.

The second trio of countries, West Germany, Sweden, and the United Kingdom, began the decade with systems of tacit restraint in lieu of formal systems of incomes policy. Yet the experience of these countries throughout the decade was as diverse as that of the first group.

Denmark, Italy, and France began the decade with wage and price determination unrestrained by either formal or tacit incomes policies. Italy and France also began the decade without particularly effective collective bargaining systems; in each case labor markets had fairly weak institutional structures that were dominated by employers.

In the final chapter we shall discuss the reasons that groups of countries with such different initial policy conditions experienced a somewhat similar mixture of policy effectiveness.

II

Austria

As the emphasis in incomes policy during the 1970s shifted from the guideline formulations that characterized most experiments of the 1960s to a search for approaches based on consensus or social contract, the Austrian social partnership of labor, management, and government attracted considerable attention as an approach to incomes policy. On the face of it, the Austrian policy is in sharp contrast to the experience of other countries, particularly because of its durability and lack of direct government involvement or sanctions. The policy was initiated by the principal labor and management organizations and has survived for more than twenty-five years of variable economic conditions. Participation is voluntary and decisions must be unanimous. Many attribute Austria's favorable experience with growth, inflation, and strikes to the existence of the institutional framework for review of Austrian wage and price decisions, but these claims are difficult to evaluate by standard methods because there have been few periods when there was no institutional effort to exercise restraint. Whether the Austrian experience with growth, inflation, and strikes is a result of the consensus for restraint or a precondition of its durability is therefore explored in this chapter.

Close study of the policy reveals much about the necessary institutional conditions for a durable social contract, but it also indicates why these may not be sufficient conditions for the success of the policy and why, as even Austrian officials acknowledge, the Austrian policy probably shares the poor export prospects of most unique institutional arrangements.

Economic Developments

By the evidence of most aggregative indexes of economic activity, the performance of the Austrian economy compares favorably with developments in other European countries during the fifteen years

We are greatly indebted to Fidelis Bauer, Charles Gulick, Alfred Klose, Wolfgang Pollan, and Erwin Weissel for their detailed critiques of a draft of this chapter.

Table 2-1. *The Growth of Real Output, Austria, Germany, Italy, the United Kingdom, and the EEC Five, Selected Periods, 1955–73*

Annual average rate of change, 1963 prices

Country or group of countries	1955–60	1960–64	1964–69	1969–73
Austria	5.51	4.62	4.23	6.27
Germany	6.41	5.07	4.62	4.52
Italy	5.40	5.45	5.61	4.06
United Kingdom	2.49	3.14	2.50	2.95
European Economic Community Five[a]	5.33	5.44	5.26	4.98

Source: D. T. Jones, "Output, Employment, and Labour Productivity in Europe since 1955," *National Institute Economic Review*, no. 77 (August 1976), pp. 72–85.

a. Belgium, France, West Germany, Italy, and the Netherlands.

preceding 1974. The period was characterized by only mild fluctuations in real factors around a substantial economic growth trend (see table 2-1). The behavior of the unemployment rate, moreover (see figure 2-1), indicates that, until 1974, the labor market was virtually insulated from the consequences of the modest real fluctuations around the Austrian growth trend.[1]

Although the data in table 2-1 indicate that the overall Austrian growth rate compares favorably with those of other European economies, there are important deviations in two periods. First, during the early 1960s, economic growth in Austria was slower than in the late 1950s and also slower than the growth rates of its principal trading partners. Although the slower growth of output and subsequent industrial investment had its roots in developments in the export sector, it was not traced to unusual wage-cost pressures. Instead, Austrian exports were placed at a growing competitive disadvantage by a combination of external polit-

1. The relatively high rates of growth and modest fluctuations in unemployment are attributable in part to a highly elastic labor supply made possible by the extensive importation of foreign workers. Indeed, the ebb and flow of foreign workers signals the tightness of the labor market and also the fact that in Austria, as elsewhere in Europe, some policies succeed much more in stabilizing unemployment statistics than in stabilizing unemployment. Following a period of rapid increase in the proportion of foreign workers in the Austrian labor force during the early 1970s, when the pace of the boom greatly strained labor markets, more than 33,000 workers were "exported" between 1974 and 1975 as the recession deepened in Austria. See Felix Butschek, "Continuous Reporting System on Migration" (Paris: Organisation for Economic Co-operation and Development, July 1976).

Figure 2-1. *Economic Indicators, Austria, 1960–79*

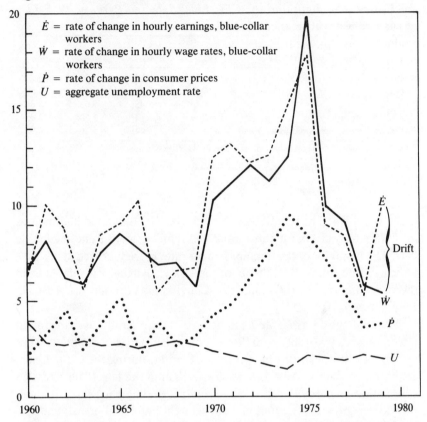

Sources: Organisation for Economic Co-operation and Development, *Main Economic Indicators: Historical Statistics, 1955–1971,* and *1960–1979* (Paris: OECD, 1973, 1980); data provided by Oesterreichisches Institut für Wirtschaftsforschung, Vienna.

ical developments and internal structural rigidities. With the progressive integration of the European Economic Community (EEC), tariffs on intra-EEC trade were reduced, placing the exports from Austria and other nonmembers at a competitive disadvantage. This was only partially offset by expanded trade possibilities through Austria's membership in the European Free Trade Association (EFTA). The second factor was the adverse composition of Austrian exports during the early 1960s. Because basic metals constituted a relatively large share of exports, the declining world trade in and prices of these commodities had a disproportionately large effect. Finally, membership in the EFTA exposed Austria to increased competition from imports. Here domestic factors in labor markets were apparently important, since an increase in Austrian unit labor costs in relation to those of its trading partners in the EFTA was associated with an increase in the share of imports in gross national product (GNP). Aside from this development (in 1965–67), there is little indication that domestic market developments were a significant factor in the slowdown in economic growth.[2]

Beginning in 1968, Austria moved into a strong, export-led upswing that continued into mid 1974, when pressures from the oil price increases drove the country into recession along with the rest of Europe. During this period, Austrian growth exceeded that of Europe and its major trading partners (see table 2-1). Until the recession beginning in late 1974, moreover, Austria escaped two economic calamities experienced by most of the other countries in this study. The first was the wage explosion of the late 1960s; the second was the recession of the early 1970s. Austria was apparently subject to neither the market pressures nor the distributional pressures on wage determination that occurred in other countries. The Austrian economy had been operating further below capacity than those of most other European countries in the years immediately before 1968. There were no real wage losses during the period, moreover. Changes in real wages and gross industrial profit shares (prices minus unit labor costs) are graphed in figure 2-2. The rate of change of real wages reached a postwar peak, narrowing profit margins, in the near-recession of 1966–67. Real wage growth in the remainder of the 1960s was lower as profit shares recovered, but more in line with the secular increase in labor productivity.

The pattern of behavior of real wages during the late 1960s is consistent with the countercyclical wage policy, which will be discussed further below, of the Austrian trade unions at the time. More important, the comparative stability of Austrian money wages during the late 1960s may be attributable to lack of earlier deterioration of real wages under the Austrian incomes policy. In contrast, incomes policies that effectively reduced gains in real wages in several other Western European countries during the mid 1960s appear to have contributed to the explosions in money wages at the end of the decade.[3]

---

2. For a more extensive analysis of the slowdown in Austrian growth during the early 1960s, see OECD Economic Surveys, *Austria*, May 1967, pp. 8–11.

3. For a discussion of the possible influence of European incomes policies on wage explosions in the late sixties, see chapter 1; see also Lloyd Ulman and Robert J. Flanagan, *Wage Restraint: A Study of Incomes Policies in Western Europe* (Berkeley: University of California Press, 1971), pp. 216–57.

Figure 2-2. *Rates of Change in Real Wages and Prices minus Unit Labor Costs in Industry, Austria, 1961–78*

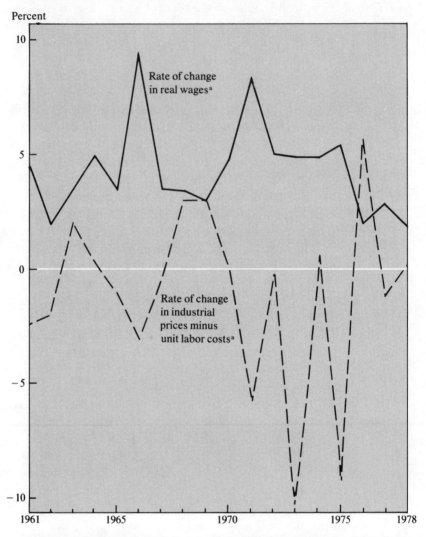

Sources: GDP deflator for industrial activity, United Nations Statistical Office, *Yearbook of National Accounts Statistics, 1979*, vol. 2: *International Tables* (New York: UN, 1980), p. 429; monthly earnings in industry and CPI, OECD, *Main Economic Indicators, 1960–1979*, pp. 192, 194; unit labor costs in industry, OECD Economic Surveys, *Austria*, various issues.
   a. Real wages are monthly earnings in industry divided by the consumer price index and industrial prices are the gross domestic product deflator for industrial activity.

It is perhaps more surprising that the export-based economy of Austria was insulated from the general European recession of the early 1970s. In fact, a decline in the growth rate of industrial exports was offset by a rise in tourism attributable in part to the fact that Austria avoided the European wage explosion. Since German tourist expenditures account for three quarters of Austrian tourist earnings, the economy also benefited from the appreciation of the deutsche mark.[4] The result was a substantial growth of demand pressure followed by an acceleration in wage drift (see table 2-5 and related discussion below) and prices. Austria's ability to avoid this recession is one reason for the country's increased inflation and the subsequent deterioration of the balance of payments during the early 1970s. The relative cost problem is illustrated in figure 2-3. Since the early 1970s, wages and unit labor costs in Austrian industry have continued to rise in relation to those of its principal trading partners. Most notably, the wage pressure continued through the 1974–75 recession, fueled by large negotiated increases in 1975, despite a tax reform early in the year that added 2.5 percent to personal disposable income. Although Austria came through the 1974–75 recession better than most countries of the Organisation for Economic Co-operation and Development (OECD), the wage-cost pressures documented in figure 2-3 continued to contribute to an unusually large external deficit in 1976–77. These same cost pressures also squeezed the profits of Austrian manufacturers. Unit labor costs generally increased more rapidly than producer prices during the first half of the 1970s, unlike the trend during the 1960s (see figure 2-2). As were other countries in this study, Austria was under pressure to produce the adjustments in real wages that would maintain or restore international competitiveness. To the extent that incomes policy was to be a part of the policy mix, the economic problems required a real rather than a nominal incomes policy.

Hard-Currency Option

With the deterioration of the balance of payments in the 1970s, the central element of the macroeconomic policy setting in which Austrian incomes policy was embedded was the hard-currency option. At the

4. In general, tourism is an unusually strong factor in the Austrian economy and balance of payments. Tourist receipts amount to 7 percent of Austrian gross national product (the highest of any Western economy) and 23 percent of exports (second highest after Spain). OECD Economic Surveys, *Austria*, July 1972, p. 32.

Figure 2-3. *Unit Labor Costs and Wages in Austria in Relation to Those of Its Principal Trading Partners, 1964–75*[a]

Source: OECD Economic Surveys, *Austria,* July 1976, p. 44.

a. West Germany, Switzerland, Italy, the United Kingdom, the United States, Sweden, and France, weighted according to their importance as markets for Austrian exports in 1974.

b. Unit labor costs in Austria in relation to trade-weighted unit labor costs of its principal trading partners, industry only; 1974 = 100.

c. Total hourly labor costs in Austrian industry as a fraction of total hourly labor costs in industry in Austria's principal trading partners, in common currency units. Data for 1975 are provisional.

suggestion of the trade unions (and with the concurrence of employers) Austria tied the schilling, first to movements in a basket of currencies, later, in 1976, to the deutsche mark—a decision that essentially required reducing the Austrian rate of inflation to approximately the German rate. Although there has recently been some broadening of the range in which the schilling is permitted to vary, the essential connection remains. Since the German inflation rate has been less than the U.S. rate, the Austrian schilling has appreciated in relation to currencies that are pegged to the dollar and currencies that have depreciated in relation to the dollar.

Maintaining the hard-currency option in the face of the appreciation of the schilling with respect to the currencies of most trading partners has imposed significant requirements on domestic economic policy. In addition to increasing the demand for imports, the policy places the export sector under considerable pressure. With major changes in exchange rates ruled out, export industries must accept world prices and control costs as best they can. Uncertainty concerning either the future development of domestic labor costs or movements in world prices will reduce incentives to invest in the export sector and encourage a shift of resources toward the domestic production sector. This is where the institutional prerequisites for a hard-currency option become most obvious. If normal profit margins are to be maintained, trade unions must accept a growth of real compensation that is parallel to the growth of labor productivity. More rapid increases in labor costs will compress profits and lead to either a flow of resources out of the export sector or abandonment of the hard-currency option via devaluation. The trade union support of the hard-currency option is highly unusual, since it implies the acceptance of considerable self-restraint; union cooperation in an incomes policy has been a precondition to the maintenance of the option. (For a case in which policymakers were unable to implement a hard-currency option because of lack of cooperation by unions, see the chapter on Denmark.)

Labor-Market Institutions

On the surface, there are two striking characteristics that differentiate the Austrian approach to prices and incomes policy from experiments in other countries: the virtual absence of government in the initiation and implementation of the policy and the absence of compulsion. The durability of a policy under these conditions implies a unique set of underlying labor-market institutions or a policy that has no important effect on economic behavior.[5]

From an institutional perspective, the Austrian approach to prices and incomes policy grew out of the severe economic disruption in the immediate postwar years and a desire to avoid the internal conflicts that had generated a particularly harsh interwar history. One result was a reduction in political competition and the establishment of a coalition government that ruled until 1966. In the labor market, paradoxically, the durability of the policy reflects the postwar revival of one institution with deep roots in Austrian history—the professional chambers—and an important structural change in the trade unions. Although none of these changes was initiated with a view to developing a viable framework for the regulation of wage and price inflation, the resultant structural features constitute a list of the necessary conditions for sustaining a policy based on a consensus of economic interest groups.

The case for a coalition government in postwar Austria went beyond the desire for political stability during a period of economic hardship and reconstruction. There was also a desire to avoid a repetition of the tragic experience of the First Austrian Republic (1918–38), when political and class differences culminated in a brief civil war in February 1934, the establishment of the Dollfuss regime, and a suspension of many civil liberties, including the right to form trade unions.[6] This was succeeded by the German occupation, a period during which leaders of varying political persuasions shared the same concentration camps. The view that postwar political arrangements should seek to avoid the self-destructive conflicts of the First Republic was reinforced by the need to present a united front to the four-power occupation forces and to restore self-government as soon as possible. The result was a coalition government of the Austrian People's party (Christian Democrats) and the

5. For additional detail on these issues, see Hannes Suppanz, "The Institutional Framework," in Hannes Suppanz and Derek Robinson, *Prices and Incomes Policy: The Austrian Experience* (Paris: OECD, 1972), pt. 1; Erich Spitaller, "Incomes Policy in Austria," *IMF Staff Papers*, vol. 20 (March 1973), pp. 170–202; Fritz Klenner, *The Austrian Trade Union Movement* (Brussels: International Confederation of Free Trade Unions, 1956).

6. For a definitive social history of the First Republic, with extensive discussion of trade union behavior, see Charles A. Gulick, *Austria from Habsburg to Hitler* (Berkeley: University of California Press, 1948); see also Heinrich Benedikt, ed., *Geschichte der Republik Österreich* [History of the Republic of Austria] (Vienna: Verlag für Geschichte und Politik, 1954).

Austrian Socialist party (Social Democrats), which together attract close to 90 percent of electoral support. The political consensus has undoubtedly been an important precondition for establishing economic cooperation, since there have traditionally been ties between the major economic interest groups and the major political parties. Most of the support of the Socialist party is from workers, and nearly all the leaders at all levels of the workers' organizations are in the Socialist party. Members of the employer, professional, and agricultural organizations are almost exclusively in the People's party.[7]

In economic affairs, Austria had developed an unusually extensive system of economic interest group representation long before World War II. The highest and broadest levels of representation are through the chambers—institutions rooted in nineteenth-century Austria that have no parallel in the other countries of this study. Each of the chambers was established by an act of Parliament to serve the economic interests of a particular group, and membership in an appropriate chamber is required by law. Although the enabling legislation specifies the rights and obligations of the chambers, they are autonomous bodies, and the government cannot legally give directives to them.

From the perspective of Austrian wage and price policies, the chambers of Commerce and Labor are the most prominent of these organizations.[8] Both are organized at the provincial (regional) level but also have a central or federal chamber to deal with problems that are national in scope. At the federal level the chambers have much to do with the formulation of economic and social legislation of interest to their members. The government is required to obtain the appraisal of the chambers on draft legislation before it is submitted to Parliament, and more generally, the chambers represent their members' interests in Parliament and at the ministries. Beyond this there are important differences.[9]

The Chamber of Commerce, originally established by regulations and legislation passed in 1848 and 1850, provides legal representation for the

7. Overall, about two thirds of union members vote for Socialist candidates, another 3 percent for Communists, and the remainder for candidates of the People's party. The voting allegiance of some 90 percent of the members of the organizations of employers and agriculture is to the People's party.

8. The Chambers of Agriculture are represented but are of minor importance. Separate chambers also exist for lawyers, physicians, dentists, and other professions.

9. The government can circumvent the chambers if it has a mind to, however, by having draft legislation submitted by an individual member of Parliament. There is no sanction, moreover, if the government submits a bill without consulting the chambers.

interests of owners of businesses and managers in the private sector.[10] Although this chamber represents the economic interests of its members in the legislative process, it differs from the Chamber of Labor in representing its employer constituency in collective bargaining.[11] It is the only institution, moreover, through which employers obtain representation in the Austrian incomes policy. Therefore, the decisionmaking process by which differences among employers are resolved *within* the chamber is of interest in a study of the factors contributing to the durability of the Austrian wage and price policy. The chamber sees its task as a problem of simultaneously balancing the special interests of the six professional branches and taking actions that do not disrupt the general economic climate.[12] Since an internal decisionmaking approach based on majority rule may persistently override the interests of some sections of the chamber and lead to disaffection and ultimately to demands for some alternative channel of representation, the enabling legislation specifies that the chamber must attempt to reach unanimous decisions. Unanimous decisionmaking at the chamber level has become the rule, and conflicts so difficult as to require recourse to majority rule are rare.

Austrian workers have access to three varieties of institutional representation: chamber, trade union, and works council. Originally established by legislation in 1920, the Chamber of Labor is the most nearly universal in its membership. Membership is compulsory, assuring representation of the economic interests of both union and nonunion workers, and the activities of the chamber are financed by payroll deductions. In contrast to the employer side of the market and despite the fact that it is legally a party to labor agreements, the Chamber of Labor takes no direct part in collective bargaining. This is left to the

10. Organizationally, the chamber is further subdivided at the national and regional levels into six professional sections representing industry, commerce, transport, tourism, small-scale production (including some construction and services), and finance, credit, and insurance.

11. Contrary to the convention elsewhere, the main voluntary association of manufacturing employers, the Association of Austrian Industrialists, acts as a lobby for industrial interests but takes no direct part in collective bargaining or incomes policy deliberations. There is indirect representation, however, since many officials of the association also hold positions in the Chamber of Commerce.

12. For an interesting review of adversary interests within the various labor market and political organizations, see Murray Edelman, *National Economic Planning by Collective Bargaining: The Formation of Austrian Wage, Price, and Tax Policy after World War II* (Urbana: University of Illinois Press, 1954), pp. 14–15.

Austrian Trade Union Federation, in which membership is voluntary. By lobbying at the legislative level for changes in the legal and social framework, the Chamber of Labor seeks instead to alter the general conditions under which unions operate. Furthermore, the chamber acts as the intellectual brain trust and research arm of the trade-union movement. One result of this bifurcation of responsibilities is that labor has dual representation—through the chamber and the federation—in the incomes policy institutions, a feature that will be discussed at greater length below.

The present institutional structure of Austrian unions dates from the end of World War II (1945), when Austrian trade unionists formed a new Austrian Trade Union Federation, the Oesterreichischer Gewerkschaftsbund (OeGB), whose members have represented 60 to 65 percent of the employed workers in the country throughout the postwar period. Simultaneously, there was a structural reorganization that greatly centralized bargaining, finances, and authority within the labor movement and increased its potential power in economic affairs. In contrast to the uncoordinated multiunion structure fragmented along craft and political lines that had dominated the Austrian labor movement before the end of the First Republic, the new federation consists of sixteen unions organized generally along industrial lines, although the largest organization is now the union of salaried workers in the private sector. Public employees are concentrated in four unions, which include both salaried and wage employees. Thus, there is none of the fragmentation of the labor movement along political, confessional, or occupational lines observed in most other European countries. Instead, workers of different political persuasions are represented by separate party caucuses within the national unions. Disputes based on political differences tend to be resolved in the internal deliberations of the unions and the OeGB, much as the economic chambers internalize most factional disputes. In general, it appears that the postwar organizational structure of the Austrian labor movement leaves less room for interunion competition than is typical in most other countries.

Other features of the union structure appear to reduce institutional barriers to responsive wage adjustments and to centralize authority in the union movement in a manner conducive to an incomes policy. For example, contracts are usually renegotiated every twelve to eighteen months by all unions. This feature, in combination with the relatively small number of unions, reduces the prospects of persistent inertia in wage inflation that can result from long-term contracts and interunion wage imitation in collective bargaining systems with contracts of unequal duration and staggered expiration dates. While the sixteen unions appear to have considerable autonomy in formulating their wage policy and conducting collective bargaining, moreover, the centralization of authority in the OeGB probably exceeds that of any other democratic trade union movement and vests the federation with considerable influence over the activities of the affiliated unions. In particular, the OeGB controls the finances of the sixteen unions and appoints and employs the secretary of each. This centralization of authority within the federation is further maintained by an indirect system of electing union officials. The rank and file vote directly only for representatives to works councils in the firms that employ them. (In nonunion establishments, works council representatives are simply elected by the employees.) In unionized firms, these are usually the same as the local union representatives or shop stewards. These representatives elect the higher union representatives, who in turn elect the officials of the Trade Union Federation. The position of most senior union officials therefore seems on the whole insulated from the pressures of the rank and file, an arrangement that may contribute to their freedom to participate and cooperate through long periods in the incomes policy arrangements.

Works councils, which are established by federal law and are legally distinct from trade unions, provide plant-level representation to union and nonunion employees. Both the election of works council members and the interrelation between collective negotiations and works council activities provide greater institutional protection to the OeGB and its affiliates than exists elsewhere. In other countries, works council representatives in union plants may not be union members, and shop stewards and the representatives may be in competition with each other. From our point of view, however, the most interesting feature of the works councils is that they have the authority to negotiate plant-level supplements to the trade union agreements and hence are a source of wage drift. The difficulties that this authority creates for unions and union wage policy will be discussed in the following section.

Union Wage Policy

The centralization of authority within the Austrian trade union movement, along with the structural reforms instituted at the close of World War II, has permitted a better-coordinated wage policy than would have been possible in the First Republic. As in the Netherlands, the exigencies of the postwar economic reconstruction task, along with the necessity of accommodating the occupation forces, had a substantial influence on postwar union wage policy. Following an initial surge of nationalization—of banks, electric utilities, and much heavy industry—unions seemed to agree that the rate of capital accumulation required for rapid recovery could be best achieved by having wealth in private hands and by pursuing a wage policy consistent with growth objectives. Since then, union wage goals have been directed toward considerations of productivity, solidarity, and cyclical stabilization.

Austrian unions do not dispute that wage growth can contribute to price inflation, and they have generally agreed that gains in real wages should parallel the secular rate of growth of labor productivity (as required by the hard-currency option). Although the national productivity trend of about 3 percent a year is normally mentioned in official discussions, thus making this aspect of union wage policy consistent with the guidelines developed under incomes policy experiments in many Western nations during the 1960s, it appears that sectoral trends in productivity also receive some attention in the formulation of wage demands. In addition, the unions seek wage compensation for price increases in order to maintain their real gains. Except in public-sector agreements, however, they have not generally adopted automatic indexation schemes, which would conflict with the countercyclical goal discussed below.

During the 1960s these guides for general wage growth were purported to have been mitigated by the unusual countercyclical orientation of official negotiated wage policy in Austria. As a matter of policy, unions generally attempted to exercise restraint in their wage claims during an expansion but to press for somewhat more than the productivity-price orientation would imply during a recession. As a matter of practice, the effectiveness of the countercyclical wage policy may have been limited. In our econometric analysis of Austrian wage behavior (reported in table 2-5, below) we find that negotiated changes are quite sensitive to unemployment. Although a successful countercyclical wage policy would have a stabilizing influence on wage incomes throughout the cycle, it should also have a destabilizing influence on output and employment. In particular, by thwarting the operation of the classical macroeconomic adjustment to a balance-of-payments deficit, a successful countercyclical wage policy would be inconsistent with the goal of external stability. As noted earlier, it was exactly this difficulty that led the unions to abandon the countercyclical wage policy in the 1970s for the hard-currency option, with which the earlier wage policy would be inconsistent.

The orientation of the trade union movement toward redistribution of income marks the sharpest departure from trade union wage objectives in other countries and may have contributed significantly to relatively favorable wage and price behavior before the 1970s. Although Austrian trade unions share with other labor movements the egalitarian ethic that income should be distributed according to personal need, they do not regard the collective bargaining system as the primary mechanism of redistribution. In fact, Austrian unions do not challenge the employer view that wage differentials should reflect the contributions of various groups of workers to output, and they do not make redistribution of the national income a primary objective of wage negotiations. More specifically, the solidaristic objective does not (as in Scandinavia) imply a commitment to a narrowing of the wage structure by negotiating relatively high wage gains for poorly paid workers, but refers instead to the notion that stronger and weaker unions should share equally from the gains of economic growth. As a result, the broader redistributional objective—distribution according to need—is channeled into the legislative process, and as a consequence the strains upon collective bargaining have been reduced. This is surely a mitigating factor in the postwar Austrian inflation and hence a feature of basic importance to the durability of the Austrian policy, since the efforts of other countries in this study to secure redistribution of income through changes in the structure of negotiated wages have themselves become engines of inflation.[13] Unlike the situation in these countries, the wage policy of the Austrian unions is largely geared toward creation of employment rather than redistribution.

Nevertheless, the strains on collective bargaining have not been entirely eliminated, since one consequence of the successful pursuit of redistribution in Parliament has been an increase in various social charges.[14] In fact, the most striking fact about the remuneration of labor in Austria is the magnitude of the gap between earnings received directly by workers and the labor costs paid by employers. While the gap between wages and total labor costs is generally larger in Europe than in North

13. See, in particular, the chapters on Norway, Sweden, Denmark, and the United Kingdom.

14. Social charges include pay for nonworking days, social security contributions, taxes on wages, recruiting and training costs, and other social welfare benefits paid by employers.

America, the difference between the two concepts of labor costs is larger in Austria than in any other European country. The average hourly earnings of Austrian manufacturing workers are among the lowest in Europe. In 1964, moreover, the total hourly labor cost of Austrian manufacturing workers was the lowest in Europe, despite the fact that the proportion of social charges—70 percent of the earnings in 1964— was virtually the largest in Europe. Throughout the subsequent decade, both hourly earnings and social charges increased in relation to those in other European countries.[15] Despite agreement on the structure of wages, the high rate of social charges provides a basis for conflict between employers and labor over wage increases that may present more serious problems to the economy at large. Workers may find their wages low in relation to earnings received for comparable work in neighboring countries, while employers find themselves under competitive pressure, given the wedge driven between costs and direct incomes by social charges. As Austrian labor costs have increased in relation to those of Austria's trading partners during the 1970s (see figure 2-2), employers have made increasing efforts during collective bargaining to reach an understanding with the OeGB over the future development of legislated social charges.

In practice these general union wage goals are not followed rigidly, and wage drift—the difference between the rate of change of actual and scheduled, or negotiated, wages—is an important element in the general development of earnings. In a broad sense, the drift is the result of two features of negotiations. As in other countries, unions in Austria tend to negotiate increases in money wages that the marginal employer can live with, recognizing that wage drift is likely in firms with relatively strong market positions. In part, wage drift is a by-product of a wage policy that seeks to minimize the probability that wage increases will force inefficient firms out of business. The magnitude and behavior of wage drift, however, also reflect the relation between the industry-level and regional-level official negotiations involving unions and the Chambers of Commerce on the one hand and the plant-level works councils on the other. In all industrial relations systems with centralized authority and bargaining, unions face a delicate organizational conflict between the purported gains in power and influence from centralization and the maintenance of some control over all levels of the union structure. The

15. Comparisons in the preceding paragraphs are based on data in G. F. Ray, "Labour Costs in OECD Countries, 1964–1975," *National Institute Economic Review*, no. 78 (November 1976), pp. 58–62.

inability to match the economic terms of a centralized agreement exactly with the diversity of economic circumstances facing the plants to which the agreement must be applied has contributed to the presence of wage drift in advanced economies with centralized bargaining institutions. The existence of drift itself challenges the ability of unions to control through bargaining the earnings that workers receive, and ultimately, if the drift component of earnings becomes sufficiently large, it may lead workers to question the value of union membership. The allegiance of the rank and file in a centralized bargaining system may be further weakened by the general lack of participation in bargaining and other affairs.

For these reasons, Austrian unions have been uncomfortable with the gap between actual earnings and negotiated minimum wage rates. As the gap increased during the late 1950s and early 1960s, some unions began to negotiate explicitly over the rate of increase of *actual* earnings in an effort to close the gap. Since the existence of drift establishes a different base for rates and earnings, the negotiated percentage increase in earnings is usually smaller than the negotiated percentage increase in rates, and the immediate effect of the contract is a reduction in wage drift. Subsequently, the works councils attempt to bring the rate of increase of earnings up to the rate of increase of negotiated rates specified in the official collective bargaining agreements, and this process may generate positive wage drift, contrary to the objectives of the unions.

Despite the close interaction between the union and the works councils at the plant level, there appears to be considerable competition between the two bodies on wage issues. Although the rate of increase of negotiated rates provides a loose limitation on works council wage claims, there are no real sanctions on works councils that exceed this figure, and the unions are concerned with the discrepancy between wage rates and earnings sufficiently to press employers during discussions within the Austrian incomes policy institutions to resist more strongly the works council pressure for wage increases.

Incomes Policy Institutions

The collaboration that forms the basis of the current Austrian incomes policy institutions dates from 1947 and is deeply rooted in special historical circumstances. It was noted earlier that the traumatic events associated with the end of the First Austrian Republic and the subsequent Nazi occupation strongly influenced the development of attitudes congenial to consensus among virtually all economic interest groups. These events, along with the views of the postwar occupation forces, effectively precluded the emergence of a rightist coalition in political affairs. The resultant stability of the postwar political coalition of the Socialist and People's parties facilitated the subsequent economic collaboration of the various economic interest groups.

The impetus to a private social contract in the immediate postwar years was related to a shortcoming in the government bureaucratic structure. With GNP at about a third of the prewar level, the Austrian government was faced with a sizable reconstruction effort. In the efforts at economic planning and regulation that followed, regulatory tasks were assigned to various ministries with little appreciation of the complex interdependencies in economic life.[16] The ministries, for their part, were inclined to take uncoordinated actions that coincided with the immediate desires of their constituents but contributed to a substantial postwar inflation. This structural characteristic of attempts to regulate economic behavior is not unique to Austria, but the potentially disruptive effect on postwar reconstruction efforts led the four main interest organizations—the OeGB and the chambers of Agriculture, Commerce, and Labor—to negotiate privately a series of five agreements between 1947 and 1951 that explicitly considered the interests and interdependencies between various sectors.[17] During this period labor negotiated relatively large wage increases for women and unskilled workers and attempted to protect real earnings in the face of price increases negotiated to permit higher incomes for other economic interest groups, such as agriculture. Although the government was not a direct participant in negotiations, the agreements usually assumed that subsequent changes would be made in tax and social insurance legislation to prevent losses in real income of wage earners and the beneficiaries of various social security programs. At the conclusion of the first agreement the four interest groups joined in an Economic Commission, which practiced surveillance without sanctions over the agreements.

16. Edelman notes that the postwar "readjustment was treated as if it involved separable price, wage, subsidy, and fiscal problems, for these questions were assigned to different governmental organizations for disposition." See Edelman, *National Economic Planning*, p. 19. More generally, this book provides an excellent reference on developments in Austrian wage, price, and income distribution policies for 1947–51.

17. For details, see ibid., pp. 23–56.

The Parity Commission

The current incomes policy institutions grew out of an inflation in the mid 1950s that coincided with wage settlements in some of the industrial branches, which apparently challenged the authority of the OeGB to set the standards of wage policy but nevertheless yielded small gains in real income. In contrast with the situation in other countries, the policy institutions that emerged in Austria were not the result of direct government initiation. This unusual abstinence, as well as the inherently voluntary nature of the resultant approach, is apparently a result of an idiosyncrasy of the Austrian constitution, by which the authority of a cabinet minister cannot be superseded by the collective decisions taken by a commission. Thus the muted official role of government in the current arrangement appears to be as much a matter of legal necessity as official preference.[18]

A Parity Commission for Wages and Prices—sometimes referred to as "Joint Price and Wage Commission" or "Joint Commission"—was first proposed on a one-year trial basis in 1956 by the president of the Trade Union Federation and was agreed to by the president of the Federal Chamber of Commerce. Although approved by a cabinet resolution, the commission was established voluntarily and has no legal authority behind it. As will soon become clear, the creation of the Parity Commission has tended to protect the institutional authority of the OeGB over the wage policy of its constituent unions and to prevent a fragmentation of the collective bargaining process such as existed during the First Republic.

Although not the initiating force, the government has a definite

18. In 1952 the Supreme Court of Austria ruled that the Economic Directorate, a commission established in 1951 to coordinate decisions on price controls, rationing, and other economic policies, was unconstitutional. The directorate had been presided over by the Austrian chancellor, and the members were the vice-chancellor and eight cabinet ministers. Although the OeGB had no role in the directorate and the three chambers and the Austrian National Bank had only advisory roles, all decisions had to be unanimous. More generally, "the Austrian Constitution limits the powers of the Cabinet as a whole, those of its committees, as well as those of any single minister with respect to exercising control over the fiscal activities of individual ministries. . . . Coordination at this level, then, even when exercised by such bodies as the Joint Commission, largely takes the form of voluntary agreements and understandings." OECD Economic Surveys, *Austria,* June 1970, p. 44.

presence: the federal chancellor presides over the commission, and its members include representatives of the ministries of Finance, Social Affairs, Trade, Manufacturing, Industry, and Agriculture and Forestry. This presence may be more form than substance, however, since the government typically abstains on wage and price decisions. The remainder of the commission consists of two representatives each from the chambers of Commerce, Labor, and Agriculture and the OeGB. In the absence of a legal basis for the institution, participation is voluntary and, as in the chambers, decisions must be unanimous, a feature that may have been important in reducing the incentives of any one party to drop out of the institution. The formation of the Parity Commission in the face of constitutional limitations on an official government role provides an interesting contrast with countries, such as the Netherlands, that initiated incomes policies backed by strong official sanctions at about the same time. At the level of the Parity Commission, the Austrian approach may illustrate the importance of consensus over authority and coercion in the establishment of durable incomes policy institutions. Alternatively, the consensus at that level may exist because of the authority and coercion that can be exerted within the constituent interest groups.

The Subcommittee on Wages consists of two representatives each from the Chambers of Commerce and OeGB and one representative each from the Chambers of Labor and Agriculture. The chair rotates between the Chambers of Commerce and the OeGB. Although the subcommittee is a review body, its powers seem modest in comparison to those of incomes policy institutions in other countries. There is no wage guideline or rule that it enforces, and it has no ultimate authority to influence the size of the wage increase or any other benefits provided by the contract. Instead, "The principal role of the Subcommittee for Wages in this system is in *deciding when to approve new wage negotiations,* thus *influencing the period of validity of collective agreements* and *helping to ensure a balanced wage policy"* (emphasis in original).[19] While this statement accurately describes the authority of the Subcommittee on Wages, it is probably misleading as to the potential effects of the policy. Under the ground rules, the individual unions must apply to the Subcommittee on Wages for permission to commence negotiations over a new contract. These requests, however, must be forwarded to the subcommittee by way of the OeGB, which conducts its own review

19. Austrian Federal Press Service, *The Rational Approach to Labour and Industry,* tr. by John Wilde (Vienna: AFPS, 1973), p. 13.

of the bargaining demands. In this capacity the Trade Union Federation
acts as a screen and can recommend delays and even adjustments of
negotiating demands to unions before the request reaches the subcommittee. This no doubt shields the subcommittee from some proposals
that would be substantially at variance with current economic objectives.
It also greatly increases the institutional authority of the OeGB, which
in its screening capacity may be better able to coordinate the wage
demands of individual unions and prevent invidious differentials from
developing. Although there is no legal requirement to obtain prior
approval of the Parity Commission (via the Wage Subcommittee) before
beginning negotiations, the procedure has been accepted without challenge by the unions.

The Subcommittee on Prices is presided over by the representative
of the Chamber of Commerce and includes representatives of the
Ministry of Finance, the Ministry of Trade, Manufacturing, and Industry, and the other interest-group organizations represented on the
Parity Commission. In contrast to the wage procedure, firms seek
subcommittee approval for the actual magnitude of price increases. The
subcommittee does not work with a rigid formula, but rather attempts to
limit price increases to unavoidable increases in costs. Negotiated wage
increases in central collective bargaining agreements provide a justification for price increases, but increases negotiated by works councils at
the plant level generally do not. In principle this distinction should stiffen
the bargaining resistance of employers faced with demands for wage
increases in excess of gains in productivity and may explain why wage
drift in Austria does not follow the regularities observed in other
countries. Firms are not entirely happy with the subcommittee process,
because their arguments for cost-based increases are frequently countered by an interesting coalition of the OeGB, Chamber of Labor, and
government representatives, who argue that the proposed price increases
are excessive and will trigger demands for wage increases by the unions.
Ultimately, some compromise is usually reached, since the subcommittee also requires unanimity for decisions. Failing this, a price request is
passed along to the full Parity Commission for a decision.

Nevertheless, there are certain features of the price policy that limit
its probable effect on price developments.

First, the price-review function of the Parity Commission and its
Subcommittee on Prices covers the pricing of about 20 percent of
Austrian output—industrial commodities, for the most part—and the

prices of services, public-sector commodities (including the output of nationalized industries), exports, and imports are unregulated.

Second, even within the industrial sector, participation in the price-review procedure is voluntary. In practice, the employers' associations have agreed that their members will not increase prices without the approval of the Parity Commission or Subcommittee on Prices, but it is doubtful that this agreement would guarantee participation if regulation were perceived as truly stringent.

There is, however, an indirect incentive for firms to participate in the review procedures of the Subcommittee on Prices. Since 1973, the minister of trade, manufacturing, and industry has had the authority to regulate a price for six months if the four interest organizations jointly report a price increase and if the minister finds that the increase is not justified. If the price increase is submitted to the Subcommittee on Prices, it is "justified," and the minister cannot intervene. Nevertheless, the ministerial procedure has never been used. Although the labor representatives have attempted to initiate the procedure on several occasions, their efforts have been blocked by the Chamber of Commerce. At the same time, the existence of the procedure may be sufficiently threatening to encourage firms to participate in the Parity Commission procedures. Government contractors may also feel obliged to submit proposed price increases for review.

Third, in determining whether proposed price increases are justified by unavoidable cost increases, the Subcommittee on Prices must rely on information provided by the company, and although this information is at times inadequate, the subcommittee has no authority to subpoena the company's accounts or examine them in greater detail.

Fourth, producers cannot be forced to cut prices when costs decline—for example, as a result of reduced tariffs or declining prices of raw materials on world markets. Finally, both the subcommittee and the Parity Commission work on the principle of unanimity in decisions on proposed price increases. Given the fact that participation in the policy is voluntary, this decision rule may be essential to keep the institution together. It is also possible, however, that the only set of conditions that is consistent with durable participation is inconsistent with real policy impact.[20]

20. In addition to the voluntary review procedures of the Subcommittee on Prices, statutory authority exists for the minister of trade, manufacturing, and industry to impose maximum prices for certain basic commodities and services directly after

With these limitations, the actual effectiveness of the price side of the Austrian incomes policy is doubtful. It is more likely that the appearance of symmetrical treatment of wages and prices was needed by the unions to make wage restraint more palatable to the rank and file. In practice, literal symmetry in the effect of policies on wages and prices is a characteristic of nominal, but not of real, incomes policies. A truly symmetrical treatment of prices under the Austrian policy would therefore have interfered with the real wage adjustments that were required during the 1970s.

Tax-Wage Bargains

Dissatisfied with the degree of wage and price stability attained by the Parity Commission's voluntary procedures, the government on one occasion attempted to obtain wage restraint in exchange for tax relief. In late 1966, the government approached the labor market partners and the monetary authorities separately and proposed an earlier implementation of income tax cuts along with a relaxation of monetary policy in exchange for wage and price restraint in 1967 and 1968. The subsequent understanding produced a one-quarter postponement of wage negotiations, smaller wage claims than had been made earlier, and increased contract duration in exchange for tax cuts in October 1967.[21] Industrial wage rates "rose by 6.6 percent between 1967 and 1968, more than one percentage point below the rise recorded in 1967, and less than in any year since the recession in 1958–59. Wage drift did not become positive until the end of the year in spite of some increase in overtime working."[22]

Subsequent tax reforms occurred on a four-year statutory schedule (with an additional interim adjustment in 1973). Although there was a second attempt to achieve a combined wage-tax bargain in 1974–75, the OeGB refused in this instance to connect problems of taxation with wage increases. The tax revision for 1975 was completed in the spring of 1974, prior to the wage negotiations in the fall and winter of 1974–75; union representatives subsequently rejected suggestions of employers that the reduction in personal income tax rates should be taken into account in

securing the agreement of other ministries and in consultation with the Parity Commission, which includes representation of the chambers and government ministries. Direct price regulation is applicable to items that account at most for 20 percent of the consumer price index, but in recent years the authority has for the most part been exercised over the pricing of certain agricultural commodities.

21. OECD Economic Surveys, *Austria*, May 1967, p. 23; May 1968, pp. 21–22.
22. Ibid., July 1969, p. 12.

the negotiations; and the wage round yielded unusually large increases in negotiated rates. (See econometric evidence on wage behavior below.) The 1977–78 bargaining offered a similar phenomenon with a reversed sign: the OeGB succeeded in simultaneously restraining negotiated wage increases and turning aside suggestions for a tax reduction, despite the fact that inflation continued to increase the effective tax rates faced by many workers. The wage stance was consistent with the countercyclical wage policy of the unions, but the tax stance reflected the view of the OeGB leadership that it was necessary to pay the bill for the successful fiscal policy of the recession in 1975–76. Again, distributional issues were secondary to general policy considerations in the interactions between Austrian wage policy and fiscal policy.

Changing Objectives

From the end of World War II until the early 1970s, the main objective of the various efforts at social partnership was the creation of a favorable climate for growth by preventing an outbreak of inflation from uncoordinated and mutually inconsistent income claims by the various economic interest groups. After 1973, however, the attention of the Parity Commission shifted to the problem of maintaining full employment, growth, and external balance. With respect to the employment objective, discussions within the Parity Commission succeeded in the avoidance of layoffs during the recession, particularly in nationalized industries, by means of labor hoarding and short-time work. With the export of foreign workers and an increase in government expenditures for selected programs, the modest employment effects of the recession in private industry were more than offset by the increase in employment in public and private services. At the same time, the Trade Union Federation, concerned with employment objectives, had abandoned its countercyclical wage policy for the hard-currency option.

Policy Analysis and Evaluation

At several points in the preceding description of the structure and operations of the main labor market and incomes policy institutions, we raised the question of their actual effects. We now turn to the problem of evaluating the effect of the policy on the development of prices, wages, and aspects of income distribution. Given the continuity of the

Austrian approach to prices and incomes policy during the postwar period, the basic method of econometric evaluation of incomes policy by means of comparisons between "policy-on" and "policy-off" periods is not feasible. Given the durability of the Parity Commission, there simply is no policy-off period during the years for which data are available.

Despite this constraint, we can examine two evaluative issues in our review of econometric evidence on wage and price movements in Austria. First, we shall simply ask whether the models that best explain Austrian wage and price behavior are consistent with the decision rules that are purported to be applied by the OeGB and the incomes policy institutions in the formulation and approval of requests for wage and price increases. The decision rules applied by the Price Subcommittee of the Parity Commission correspond to a strict cost-markup view of the pricing process. This implies that demand pressure in the product market will influence product prices only indirectly, through its effects on the costs of materials and labor. The absence of an independent role for demand should be reinforced if officially controlled price changes are kept nearly constant throughout the cycle. Similarly, the countercyclical wage policy of the trade unions should, if successful, tend to insulate wage movements from labor market pressures.

Next, we shall ask how well the Austrian consensus-building institutions coped with the pressure put on wage and price formation in a period when macroeconomic shocks of largely external origin would most challenge their effectiveness in modifying economic behavior. The 1970s brought a number of shocks to the Austrian economy that ended the relatively tranquil economic environment of the Parity Commission deliberations. First, the expansion continued well into the 1970s and raised the classical problem of whether *any* form of incomes policy can effectively restrain transactions prices in a strong excess-demand inflation. This raises the question of the interaction between negotiated wages and wage drift during the period. Second, Austria instituted a value-added tax (VAT), effective at the beginning of 1973, which added to price pressures and exacerbated the existing demand-based impetus. Third, the oil price increases of 1974 added further direct and indirect pressure on prices from the supply side, given the importance of international prices in Austrian inflation, and ultimately forced the country into a recession.

In pursuing the latter question, we shall examine the stability of the price- and wage-determination process in recent years, when external events should have subjected the policy to strains. Price and wage equations estimated from data through 1971 or 1972 will be used to predict subsequent price and wage changes, which are then compared with actual changes. This is a limited "test" of policy effectiveness, since it asks only whether the existence of the incomes policy institutions was sufficient to ensure that prices and wages were generated by the same process that prevailed before the macroeconomic shocks. But while it is possible to predict what price and wage changes would have been *if* that process had prevailed, we do not know what changes actually would have occurred during 1973–76 in the absence of the Parity Commission. Within these confines we shall examine Austrian price and wage behavior.

Price Behavior

In this section we shall estimate models of adjustments in producer prices (measured by changes in the gross domestic product [GDP] deflator), compare the results to the price-adjustment process implied by the decision rules of the Price Subcommittee, and compare actual and predicted changes in producer prices for the period 1972–75. As noted above, the Price Subcommittee takes a cost-markup approach to pricing decisions, permitting price adjustments to cover cost increases.[23] Prices reviewed in the subcommittee's voluntary procedures receive only a 20 percent weight in the consumer price index (CPI), but represent a larger component of the GDP deflator, which excludes the prices of some items that also are not subject to the review procedure. The government has indicated, moreover, that it attempts to insulate the prices of commodities that are subject to direct government controls from market pressures (just as the trade unions claim to pursue a countercyclical wage policy).

Thus, an empirical issue of importance in Austria, as elsewhere, is the sensitivity of prices to the rate of excess demand in the product market. From a policy perspective, the absence of a relation between demand and prices implies that standard monetary and fiscal policies will exert only an indirect influence on prices through their effects on

23. We are indebted to Wolfgang Pollan of the Oesterreichisches Institut für Wirtschaftsforschung (WIFO), the Austrian Institute for Economic Research, for assistance in the price analysis.

wages and other elements of cost. We have therefore examined the data
for the respective influence on prices of elements of cost and demand,
first in isolation and subsequently in a combined regression. Demand
pressures on the product market are represented by a GDP gap variable
(*GDPGAP*),[24] and cost pressures are represented by changes in unit
labor costs (*ULC*) and changes in import prices ($\dot{P}_m$).

The results, which are reported for 1957–71 and 1957–75 in table 2-2,
indicate that Austrian pricing is well described by a cost-markup model
and that demand pressures on the product market have not played a
strong direct role in domestic price formation. The very simple model in
which prices simply adjust to the rate of excess demand in product
markets is clearly dominated by the cost-markup formulation, even for
the period preceding the external shocks of the 1970s. When included
alone (regressions 1 and 6), the *GDPGAP* variable does not attain normal
standards of statistical significance, although it is correctly signed; when
included with the cost variables—rates of change of unit labor costs and
import prices—in regressions 3 and 8, the *GDPGAP* remains statistically
insignificant and has a negligible effect on the coefficients of the cost
variables. The cost-markup specification, however (regressions 2 and
7), describes price movements reasonably well for the period.[25] (Compare, for example, the standard error of the regression for the product-
market demand and cost-markup specifications.) Export prices, however, attain statistical significance only when data for 1972–75 are added,
suggesting that the Aukrust mechanism was not in general descriptive
of the Austrian inflationary process. The statistical qualities of the
regressions with export price changes are inferior to the cost-markup
specifications.

The regression estimates for 1957–71 describe the structure of the
price-determination process during the first fifteen years of the Parity
Commission, a period generally free of severe macroeconomic shocks.
Embedded in the coefficients are whatever influence this institution

24. The variable *GDPGAP* is the residual from the following regression: ln *GDP* =
$a_0 + a_1 TIME + e$, in which *GDP* is an index of gross domestic product at constant
prices and *TIME* is a linear time trend.

25. We obtained equivalent results from unreported regressions in which a measure
of capacity utilization was substituted for *GDPGAP* in the regressions analysis. Our
results also coincide with an OECD regression analysis in which it was found that a
similar cost-markup model tracked changes in the GNP deflator well for the period
1958–71. A test for independent influence of demand, moreover, failed, although a
measure of *labor*-market demand was inexplicably used in the analysis. See OECD
Economic Surveys, *Austria,* August 1973, pp. 40–41.

Table 2-2. *Price Change Regressions, Austria, 1957–71 and 1957–75*

Regression number and period	Constant	Independent variable[a] GDPGAP	ULC	$\dot{P}_m$	$\dot{P}_x$	Summary statistic R^2	Durbin-Watson	Standard error
1957–71								
1	3.671	23.03	. . .	. . .	. . .	0.15	2.14	1.17
	(11.91)	(1.52)						
2	2.126	. . .	0.308	0.175	. . .	0.77	2.12	0.63
	(6.61)		(4.33)	(3.21)				
3	2.215	9.862	0.300	0.158	. . .	0.80	2.55	0.62
	(6.80)	(1.17)	(4.28)	(2.85)				
4	−1.460	. . .	0.362	. . .	0.036	0.59	2.09	0.84
	(0.29)		(3.91)		(0.70)			
5	5.177	20.515	0.356	. . .	−0.030	0.65	2.19	0.81
	(0.76)	(1.39)	(3.99)		(0.44)			
1957–75								
6	4.593	38.535	. . .	. . .	. . .	0.15	0.59	2.26
	(8.86)	(1.75)						
7	1.864	. . .	0.415	0.192	. . .	0.88	1.99	0.86
	(5.27)		(6.88)	(4.18)				
8	1.911	15.350	0.419	0.162	. . .	0.90	2.43	0.81
	(5.75)	(1.81)	(7.42)	(3.54)				
9	−5.66	. . .	0.351	. . .	0.081	0.82	2.06	1.09
	(1.72)		(3.28)		(2.24)			
10	−4.05	21.60	0.369	. . .	0.064	0.86	2.12	0.98
	(1.33)	(2.19)	(3.82)		(1.92)			

Sources: *GDPGAP, ULC, $\dot{P}_m$,* Oesterreichisches Institut für Wirtschaftsforschung (WIFO), the Austrian Institute for Economic Research; $\dot{P}_x$, International Monetary Fund, *International Financial Statistics,* 1977 supplement, vol. 30 (May 1977), pp. 84–85.

a. Definitions:

GDPGAP = actual minus trend real gross domestic product (see text for computational details)

ULC = rate of change of unit labor costs (wages and salaries, including employer social security contributions, divided by GNP at constant prices)

$\dot{P}_m$ = rate of change of import prices

$\dot{P}_x$ = rate of change of export prices

Numbers in parentheses are *t*-statistics.

may have had on price determination. We examined the stability of this structure in the face of strong external shocks by comparing subsequent price changes with the changes predicted on the basis of models estimated on the 1957–71 data. The results appear in table 2-3. Clearly, the models that tracked the data well for 1957–71 consistently underpredicted price changes by large margins (in relation to the standard errors of the regressions) during the subsequent period of shocks in the economy, even when the effects of rapidly rising import and export prices are accounted for. These findings are at least suggestive that whatever success the Parity Commission may have had before 1971, its activity may have had on price determination. We examined the stability of this was not sufficient to maintain the same process of price formation in 1972–75. As noted, however, we have no way of predicting price changes

Table 2-3. *Actual Changes minus Predicted Changes in the GDP Deflator, Austria, 1972–75*

	Regression number	
Year	2	3
1972	2.7	2.4
1973	1.3	1.0
1974	1.6	1.6
1975	1.4	1.8

Source: See table 2-2 and text.

during this period in the absence of Parity Commission procedures. A comparison of the regression results for 1957–71 in table 2-2 with the results for 1957–75, moreover, indicates that the main source of instability was in the coefficient of the unit labor cost (regressions 2 and 7) and *GDPGAP* (regressions 3 and 8) variables. These increased in magnitude and significance with the addition of the 1972–75 data. Finally, the constant term, representing the combined influence of all factors omitted from the analysis, does not shift significantly in the later period, as might be expected with a breakthrough of "discretionary" pricing.

To examine the effects of direct price controls, which apply to only about 20 percent of the CPI, changes in regulated and nonregulated consumer prices are reported in table 2-4. In administering its price-control authority, the government purports to pursue a policy of contra-cyclical increases in regulated prices, and for modest economic fluctuations the data are consistent with this strategy. Price increases of directly regulated items are relatively large in the relatively weak markets of 1967 and 1968 and the mid 1970s. But regulated price increases were kept lower than those of unregulated items as market pressures grew in the late 1960s and early 1970s. As the expansion lengthened, it became increasingly difficult to maintain the official restraint, and in 1972, regulated price changes exceeded unregulated changes.[26]

Wage Behavior

In reviewing money-wage behavior in Austria during the period of Parity Commission operations, we are, as in the preceding section,

26. The relaxation of regulated price restraint no doubt contributed to the underprediction of 1972 price increases reported in table 2-3. The introduction of a value-added tax on January 1, 1973, a factor not included in the estimating equations, is an important source of the 1973 underprediction.

Table 2-4. *Changes in Regulated and Unregulated Consumer Prices, Austria, 1967–76*

Average percentage change from preceding year

Year	Prices	
	Regulated	Unregulated
1967	8.8	2.5
1968	3.4	2.2
1969	2.0	3.1
1970	2.4	4.5
1971	3.2	4.5
1972	6.4	5.9
1973	5.4	7.7
1974	11.6	9.6
1975	10.6	7.6
1976	6.7	6.1

Source: WIFO.

interested in whether the influences on wage movements are consistent with the stated objectives of the policy and whether the existence of the Parity Commission was sufficient to keep money wages on track during the 1974–77 period of macroeconomic shocks. As in most countries, the incomes policy institutions in Austria deal most directly with official or negotiated wages. Yet a classical problem faced by all incomes policies is the resourcefulness of market forces in influencing actual earnings when contractual wages are restrained. In our analysis of wage behavior, therefore, we examined the behavior of and interactions between both negotiated rates and wage drift. We incorporated both our own analyses and the work of Austrian economists.[27]

The earlier discussion of the collective bargaining and incomes policy institutions suggested that negotiated money wages were expected to develop on the basis of changes in prices and labor productivity (with some ambiguity as to whether economywide or sectoral productivity was the dominant influence), labor-market pressures were muted through a contracyclical objective in union wage policy, and there was some effort to limit wage drift in the negotiating process. The concern of

27. One interesting and possibly suggestive feature of analyses of wage and price inflation by Austrian economists is the inattention accorded the possible effects of the institutions for wage and price review. In general, the work cited below does not include explicit discussion of potential effects of the wage-price review activities on the structural models, or whether the review procedures are sufficiently forceful to have any effect at all.

employers with the effect of increased social payments, moreover, led to efforts to seek union agreement to a tradeoff between wages and social programs. We shall examine the performance of models suggested by these considerations.

We first estimated the parameters of a standard Phillips curve model of negotiated wage determination for 1959–73.[28] This is basically a model of domestic inflation in which the main propagating factor is the rate of excess demand in labor markets, although the approach is sufficiently flexible to include effects from trade-union pressure. The result of our analysis is reported as regression 1 in table 2-5. Although the Austrian wage-setting institutions claim to pursue a wage policy that reduces the cyclical amplitude of wages, the regression results indicate that whatever the actual effect of the policy, changes in blue-collar wage rates are significantly related to labor-market pressure. This result is consistent with the findings in studies by Austrian economists covering about the same period.[29] On the other hand, the relation between negotiated rates and price changes for this period, during which prices were on the whole stable, is negative and statistically insignificant. Although very few Austrian collective agreements contain formal indexation arrangements and the result confirms findings by Suppanz and Nowotny, Rothschild,

28. We also considered the power of the Aukrust or Scandinavian model of wage determination for Austria. An analysis of Austrian data for the period 1960–74 indicates that price formation in both the exposed and sheltered sectors coincides closely with the propositions of the model. Prices in the export sector move in line with world prices, and price changes in the sheltered sector are consistent with a fixed markup over unit labor costs. On the other hand, the characteristics of the wage equations vary systematically from the Scandinavian model. In the exposed sector, wage changes are significantly related to labor-market demand pressures as well as the "room" provided by the growth of productivity and world prices, and there is only a partial spillover to the sheltered sector. See Helmut Frisch, "Eine Verallgemeinerung des skandinavischen Modells der Inflation mit einer empirischen Analyse für Oesterreich" [A generalization of Scandinavian models of inflation with an empirical analysis of Austria], *Empirica Zeitschrift des Oesterreichischen Instituts für Wirtschaftsforschung,* vol. 2 (1976), pp. 197–218.

29. Worgotter, for example, finds that negotiated wages seem to have been more sensitive than earnings to labor market pressure during 1959–73 and that the period 1968–73 was marked by increasing negotiated wage flexibility. See Andreas Worgotter, "Lohn- und Preisgleichungen für Oesterreich" [Wage and price equations for Austria], *Empirica Zeitschrift des Oesterreichischen Instituts für Wirtschaftsforschung,* vol. 1 (1975), pp. 57–77. Suppanz also notes the strong influence of job vacancies on negotiated rates in a very thorough study of Austrian wage determination in the 1960s. See Hannes Suppanz, "Die Lohndrift in Oesterreich" [Wage drift in Austria], *Monatsberichte,* vol. 45, no. 7 (1972), pp. 290–319.

Table 2-5. *Negotiated Wage Rate and Drift Regressions, Blue-Collar Workers, Austria, 1959–73 and 1959–76*

Period and dependent variable	Constant	Independent variable[a]				Summary statistic		
		U_t^{-1}	$\dot{P}_{t-1}$	$(\dot{W} - \hat{\dot{W}})_{t-1}$	DIFF	R^2	Durbin-Watson	Standard error
1959–73								
1. Rate	3.047	12.650	−0.262	...	...	0.80	2.08	1.03
	(3.56)	(5.49)	(0.90)					
2. Drift	−0.188	0.510	0.238	...	...	0.09	2.14	1.28
	(0.18)	(0.18)	(0.66)					
3. Earnings	2.808	13.353	−0.033	...	...	0.65	1.97	1.76
	(1.93)	(3.41)	(0.07)					
4. Drift	−0.188	0.510	0.238	0.175	...	0.11	2.19	1.33
	(0.17)	(0.17)	(0.64)	(0.47)				
5. Drift	−1.337	2.061	0.288	...	−0.176	0.20	2.12	1.26
	(0.95)	(0.67)	(0.80)		(1.21)			
1959–76								
6. Rate	2.422	4.794	0.986	...	...	0.62	2.42	2.29
	(1.40)	(1.25)	(3.52)					
7. Drift	−0.238	4.419	−0.272	...	...	0.22	2.43	1.37
	(0.23)	(1.93)	(1.63)					
8. Earnings	2.138	9.356	0.710	...	...	0.62	2.06	2.30
	(1.23)	(2.43)	(2.53)					
9. Drift	−0.238	4.419	−0.272	−0.175	...	0.29	2.23	1.35
	(0.23)	(1.95)	(1.65)	(1.15)				
10. Drift	−1.794	6.324	−0.135	...	−0.210	0.38	2.35	1.26
	(1.55)	(2.38)	(0.59)		(1.70)			

Sources: Hourly rates of wages, earnings, drift, unpublished data provided by Hannes Suppanz and WIFO; unemployment rate, unpublished data provided by Wolfgang Pollan, WIFO; $\dot{P}$ computed from Organisation for Economic Co-operation and Development, *Main Economic Indicators*, various years.

a. Definitions: Dependent variables are hourly rates of wages, earnings, and wage drift of blue-collar workers in manufacturing. Data on wage rates include increases associated with reductions in weekly hours of work. The unemployment rate is adjusted for changes in the definition of unemployment. $\dot{P}$ is the rate of change of the consumer price index. The proportionate difference between an index of blue-collar and white-collar earnings rates, *DIFF*, is defined as 100 [log (blue-collar earnings) − log (white-collar earnings)]. Numbers in parentheses are absolute values of *t*-statistics.

and Schwödiauer, the statistical result first appears to be at variance with purported criteria for union wage objectives.[30] The latter authors attribute the result to certain lags in the responsiveness of wages imposed by the duration of labor agreements. Price increases triggered by large wage increases in a negotiating year may be followed by smaller deferred wage increases during the second year of the contract. The result can be a negative correlation between changes in negotiated wages and in prices, and the coefficient is unlikely to attain statistical significance, since the sequence does not occur every year.[31] Finally, the Phillips

30. Suppanz, "Die Lohndrift in Oesterreich," p. 309; Ewald Nowotny, Kurt W. Rothschild, and Gerhardt Schwödiauer, *Bestimmungsgründe der Lohnbewegung* [Reasons for the wage movement] (Vienna and New York: Springer-Verlag, 1972).

31. Nowotny and others, *Bestimmungsgründe der Lohnbewegung*, pp. 129–30.

curve model of wage adjustments tracks the data through 1973 better than a model that relates negotiated rates to the rates of change of labor productivity and prices—that is, the general approach of the Wage Subcommittee.[32] In general, the main stated objectives of wage policy by the Trade Union Federation and the incomes policy institutions are not reflected strongly in the data. The countercyclical wage policy of the unions has frequently been mentioned as an important element of stabilization in Austria during the 1960s, despite the fact that, as noted, such a policy could increase fluctuations in output and employment and interfere with classical mechanisms of adjustment to balance-of-payments disequilibria. The regression results, however, raise doubts concerning the extent to which the official wage policy was achieved. Instead, the findings indicate that negotiated wage drift did not exhibit significant cyclical variation during the 1960s.

For the wage-drift component of total earnings, we examined the behavior of drift in a standard Phillips curve model (regression 2) and tested for two aspects of compensatory influences in the behavior of wage drift. One version holds that drift will tend to fill the gap between the equilibrium wage and contractual wages, thus undermining attempts to restrain negotiated wages through incomes policy. The second aspect concerns the tendency of wage drift in some countries to nullify collective bargaining efforts to narrow the wage structure. (See in particular the chapters on Scandinavian countries.)

For 1959–73, we find no significant relation between wage drift for blue-collar workers, unemployment, and price changes. Although the raw data indicate cyclical movements in drift in the late 1960s and early 1970s (see table 2-6), the relations for the early 1960s were sufficiently loose (in part because of a large structural component of unemployment) to dominate the overall findings.

Tests for compensatory behavior yielded similar results. The first or general compensatory hypothesis predicts that drift will be unusually large (small) when actual negotiated wage changes are unusually low (high) in relation to the values predicted on the basis of normal structural relations and the current values of key determinants of adjustments to money wages. The hypothesis implies a negative relation between drift and the gap between actual and predicted negotiated wages, where the

---

32. The evidence on this point is from Worgotter, "Lohn- und Preisgleichungen," in which the performance of both models is compared.

Table 2-6. *Sources of Growth in Industrial Earnings, Austria, 1967–75*

Year	Standard rates in industry Percentage change	Percentage distri-bution	Drift Percentage change	Percentage distri-bution	Earnings in industry Percentage change	Percentage distri-bution
1967	6.8	165	−2.7	−65	4.1	100
1968	6.7	140	−1.9	−40	4.8	100
1969	5.8	60	3.8	40	9.6	100
1970	5.2	39	8.0	61	13.2	100
1971	11.4	67	5.5	33	16.9	100
1972	9.2	63	5.4	37	14.6	100
1973	11.0	71	4.5	29	15.5	100
1974	12.8	83	2.6	17	15.4	100
1975	13.8	102	−0.3	−2	13.5	100

Source: OECD Economic Surveys, *Austria,* August 1971, p. 18; July 1976, p. 16.

predicted wage is based on structural relations during a nonpolicy period. Formally, if negotiated rate changes can be predicted by the model

$$\hat{W} = a_0 + a_1 U_t^{-1} + a_2 \dot{P}_{t-1},$$

then the amended drift regression is

$$DRIFT_t = b_0 + b_1 U_t^{-1} + b_2 \dot{P}_{t-1} + b_3(\dot{W} - \hat{W})_{t-1} + \epsilon_t,$$

and the compensatory hypothesis predicts $b_3 < 0$. In regression 4 of table 2-5, b_3 is positive and far from statistically significant. On the average, drift has not tended to compensate for unusually low or unusually high negotiated changes in wage rates, so in the short run, restraint in collective bargaining could produce a slower rate of increase in earnings.

We examined the distributional version of compensatory drift behavior by including a variable for the proportionate difference in white-collar and blue-collar earnings (*DIFF*). For 1959–73 we observe the expected negative sign (in regression 5), but it is well below normal standards of statistical significance. This of course is consistent with the purported absence of strong redistributional goals in Austrian wage determination. This independence of general wage movements from broad changes in the wage structure is in sharp contrast to our findings for other countries in the study and is an important feature of the Austrian

Table 2-7. *Actual Changes minus Predicted Changes in Wages,
Austria, 1974–76*

Percent

Year	Wage rates (regression 1)	Wage drift (regression 2)	Earnings (regression 3)
1974	1.92	0.6	2.50
1975	13.34	−4.42	8.97
1976	2.58	−2.88	−0.27

Source: Computed on the basis of the regression results in table 2-5.

wage-determination process. When wage policy is used to achieve employment objectives rather than major redistributional objectives, efforts to restrain the rate of growth of money wages are not undermined by wage pressures that arise from market response to union efforts to alter the wage structure or from disagreements among different parts of the labor force concerning what the appropriate distribution of wages should be.

To examine the stability of Austrian wage determination under the Parity Commission during the period of macroeconomic shocks, we used regressions 1 through 3 to predict changes for 1974–76 and then compared actual and predicted changes for each wage concept in table 2-7. It is clear that the dramatic departure occurred in the wage negotiations in 1975. Wage drift appears to have moved in a compensatory manner in both 1975 and 1976, virtually offsetting the underprediction of negotiated wages in the latter year.

Although the 1975 explosion in negotiated wages was preceded by tax reforms that were designed to increase real incomes, it appears to be largely attributable to factors beyond the control of the social-partnership institutions. The first factor, a familiar problem in consensus policy efforts, was a major error in the economic forecast that provides a background for union wage demands and collective bargaining. In September 1974 the Oesterreichisches Institut für Wirtschaftsforschung (WIFO) forecast a growth rate of 4 percent in real GNP and an inflation rate of 9.5 percent for 1975. The OECD forecasts were similar. Collective bargaining was conducted with this strong forecast as a frame of reference, but the actual real GNP *declined* at a rate of 2.5 percent, while the inflation rate was 8.4 percent. Once the forecast error and the developing recession became apparent, wage increases responded rapidly, dropping from 22.8 percent in the first quarter to 12.3 percent in the fourth. Nevertheless, many agreements providing for large wage increases had been completed and approved before the forecasting error became apparent. There was also a 5 percent reduction in working hours in 1975 (under the terms of an agreement reached by the social partners in the late sixties), accompanied by compensatory movements in hourly wages. Thus, some part of the prediction error for 1975 reflects this factor.

The prediction errors shown in table 2-7 signal extensive structural change in the underlying wage relations, and the nature of these changes can be inferred by comparing the regression results for the two periods in table 2-5. Although the variables are the same, the addition of data for only three years yields substantial changes. For negotiated rates the direct labor-market effect is no longer significant, but lagged consumer price changes are now statistically significant, with a coefficient that indicates no money illusion. (Both changes may be strongly influenced by the 1975 observation.) Drift now shows a labor-market influence and a suggestion of a distributional compensatory influence in regression 10.

It is easier to describe these findings than to infer their implications for Parity Commission operations. For while the data in table 2-7 indicate significant deviations of negotiated wages in 1975 and 1976 from earlier structural relationships, it is hardly surprising that a period of extensive price increases would sensitize institutional responses to inflation. (Note that given the estimates in the top half of table 2-5, accelerating price inflation *lowered* the predicted negotiated wage increases for 1974–76.) The huge forecasting error and the hours-of-work reduction, moreover, were influences beyond the immediate control of the Parity Commission. From this perspective, there is not a clear pattern that signals a breakdown in the effectiveness of the Parity Commission.

During the period since 1975, moreover, the OeGB has generally adopted positions favoring wage restraint. As output and employment prospects declined in the export industries, the president of the OeGB suggested in late 1976 that wage increases in the 1976–77 wage round should be based on the room for wage increases in the export sector, in order to protect the hard-currency option. This seemed to imply wage increases of no more than 7 percent and led to some conflict between unions representing workers in export industries and unions in profitable sheltered industries, such as banking and insurance. By late 1977 and early 1978, the threat of massive layoffs and short-time work (under the guise of widespread retraining) in some nationalized industries even led

to a discussion of possible reductions in money wages. Although negotiated increases in money wages in late 1977 generally fell in the range of
6 to 7 percent, they implied a real increase of 1 to 1.5 percent (before
taxes). In early 1978, union publications suggested the necessity of
accepting a decline in real wages, and union spokesmen urged employers'
organizations to resist more strongly the wage demands of works
councils.[33]

Distribution

The procedures and standards of the Parity Commission do not appear
to have unusual implications for distribution. The general approach to
both wage decisions and price decisions implies stable functional shares
but nothing in particular about the wage structure. The procedures would
therefore be a major source of conflict only if the principal labor-market
organizations had distinctly different distributional objectives. Distributional considerations do not seem to be an important element of the
ideology of Austrian collective bargaining, however—see the discussion
of union wage policy—or in the actual determination of wages—see the
discussion of the regression analysis of wages—although they are an
important objective of domestic political and legislative activity. The
existing wage structure is generally accepted by unions, and to the extent
that changes in the functional distribution of income are desired, the
legislative process is regarded as the appropriate forum.[34] Indeed,
Austria is the only country in this study in which union wage policy has
been primarily directed at the securing of employment rather than at
egalitarian or other objectives.

The question might be asked whether there were major shifts in the
functional distribution despite the apparent intentions of the unions and
the Parity Commission and also whether the wage structure was acceptable so long as it did not change sufficiently to perform an allocative
function. A somewhat misleading picture of the secular behavior of
functional shares is given by national-account statistics, which describe

33. See Anton Benya, "Auch in rauheren Zeiten festen Kurs!" [Even in hard times
a straight course], *Arbeit und Wirtschaft*, vol. 32 (January 1978), pp. 2–4.

34. On the other hand, little research has been done and hence there is very little
organized knowledge of questions of income distribution in Austria. In particular, there
is little knowledge of the effects of the extensive Austrian social programs on the
distribution of incomes.

a general decline in the share of nonlabor income—income from entrepreneurship, property, and self-employment—in national income, with
a particularly sharp drop during the 1970s.[35] In Austria, as elsewhere in
Europe, the principal secular element behind the data is the decline of
self-employment, which is a corollary of the changes in the structure of
employment that accompany growth and industrialization. When the
share of wages is adjusted for changes in the employment structure, the
wage share is virtually unchanged between 1955 and 1975. Further
adjustment for cyclical influences on relative shares using multiple
regression techniques indicated a small but statistically significant negative trend in the wage share of national income.[36]

Although there has been little change in properly measured functional
shares in Austria, there have been significant changes in the wage
structure. In contrast to the wage-determination process observed in
Scandinavian countries, however, both negotiated wages and drift
appear to favor the less-skilled workers in Austria. Blue-collar rates
increased in relation to white-collar wages during the period under study,
with some weak tendency for compensatory movements in wage drift.
In a more extensive analysis of blue-collar wages for 1962–71, disaggregated by skill and industry, Suppanz found that wage drift generally
reinforced negotiated wage changes across skill levels (although, as
noted above, he found evidence of compensatory behavior) and that
both were largest for unskilled workers. On the average the cumulative
drift during the period was 5.75 percent for unskilled labor, 5 percent for
semiskilled, and 5.5 percent for skilled. Parallel findings emerged for the
skill structure of wages within the white-collar group.[37]

Suppanz does not assign union wage policy a large role in the

35. See, for example, OECD Economic Surveys, *Austria,* July 1976, p. 18.

36. Data in this paragraph were provided by the Austrian Institute for Economic
Research. The regression equation referred to is

$$WAGE\ SHARE = 61.83 - 47.77\ GDPGAP - 0.15\ TIME.$$
$$(127.35)\quad (2.70)\qquad\qquad (2.81)$$
$$R^2 = 0.44;\ \text{Durbin-Watson} = 1.11;\ \text{standard error} = 1.02$$

The *GDPGAP* is defined as in the analysis of price behavior, *TIME* is a linear time
trend, and the regression is estimated from annual data for 1955 through 1971.
Comparisons of actual and predicted values for 1972–75 were generally within one
standard error of the regression. The largest prediction error (+2.0) occurred in 1975
and is apparently attributable to the outcome in negotiations for that year as discussed
above.

37. Suppanz, "Die Lohndrift in Oesterreich," pp. 303–04.

equalization of the wage structure, and in fact there are well-known
competitive mechanisms that would tend to narrow the skill structure of
wages during periods of strong labor-market pressure—such as the latter
part of the period covered by the Suppanz study.[38] A recent investigation
of the industrial wage structure examines the effect of labor-market
pressure on interindustry wage dispersion in Austria.[39] A seemingly
paradoxical feature in the data is the *increased* dispersion in both time
and piece rates since the late 1960s, despite the tightening labor markets
that would normally pull poorly paid workers into higher-wage jobs for
which there was a shortage of workers. Pollan notes, however, that the
Austrian expansion was accompanied by a rapid influx of foreign workers
who increased the relative supply of workers with limited skills. His
econometric estimates indicate that both factors had the predicted effect
on the industrial wage dispersion, but the magnitude of the foreign-
worker effect overwhelmed the labor-market effect. (The growth in
industrial wage dispersion was particularly marked after 1973, when the
recession reinforced the foreign-worker influence.) From our perspective, these studies indicate that the wage differentials are reasonably
fluid and that if Austrian unions do not seek to achieve major changes in
the wage structure, neither do they seek to maintain the existing structure
rigidly. Indeed, these studies provide evidence of the sensitivity of the
wage structure to market forces and indicate that the trade unions and
the incomes policy institutions have not suppressed the allocative role
of the wage structure.

Achievements and Tensions

The Austrian approach to prices and incomes policy provides an
important case study of the institutional and economic prerequisites to
a durable consensus or social contract. Many of the prerequisites and
lessons seem particularly clear because of the extensive contrasts now
possible with the less durable policies of other countries. Yet so many
of the prerequisites are rooted in rather special historical antecedents

38. See Melvin W. Reder, "The Theory of Occupational Wage Differentials,"
American Economic Review, vol. 45 (December 1955), pp. 833–52.
39. Wolfgang Pollan, "Der Einfluss des Konjunkturverlaufes und der Fremdarbei-
terbeschäftigung auf die Industrielle Lohnstruktur" [Cyclical behavior of the interindustry wage structure in Austria], *Monatsberichte*, vol. 50, no. 2 (1977), pp. 63–70.

and accidents that we doubt that the Austrian blueprint is exportable. We have some questions, moreover, concerning its future viability. Nevertheless, we begin by reviewing what we take to be the elements behind the postwar consensus to date.

First, there are likely to be large diseconomies of scale in developing a consensus policy as the number of parties that must be heard increases. In Austria, the number of participants has been kept small—for practical purposes, the government and the four principal interest groups—by internalizing disputes within the main interest organizations and by adopting the principle of unanimity in decisions at virtually all levels of the interest groups and the Parity Commission. By internalizing the settlement of disputes, the system may also tend to discourage the adoption of extreme positions as part of a public bargaining posture. So far, those that do not participate directly, such as the various professional chambers, have apparently remained satisfied with their salary-deter-mination procedures and have not requested representation. Most Austrian observers doubt that the Parity Commission procedures could successfully accommodate additional participants.[40]

Second, largely for historical reasons, postwar Austria has experi-enced considerable political consensus. In 1966, the coalition govern-ment that had been in power since the end of World War II dissolved and was succeeded by a government of the People's party. Subsequently, the Socialist party came to power in 1970. The strains on operations of the Parity Commission created by these political changes were appar-ently minor and brief, thanks to both the determination of the social partners and the postwar changes in the labor union structure that effectively internalized the political competition that had divided some unions during the First Republic. (For a polar example of the effects of political fragmentation on the implementation of anti-inflation policy, see the chapter on Denmark.)

Third, the ability to resolve conflicts internally rests on the strong centralization of powers within the interest organizations. The use of

40. The number of participants is also small because many individuals fulfill several roles simultaneously. The most notable example is the president of the Trade Union Federation, who is also the speaker of the Nationalrat, the chamber of Parliament at whose pleasure the chancellor and cabinet serve, and the president of the metalworkers' union, which often takes an important part in wage negotiations. Similar examples are fairly common (irrespective of the party in power), almost never lead to conflict-of-interest allegations, and appear to reduce conflict between the objectives of political and economic institutions.

indirect voting systems by each of the organizations tends to shield the highest-level officials who deal with national economic and social objectives from direct accountability to the lower levels of the organizations.[41] The OeGB probably has more control over the financial and personnel affairs of its constituent unions, moreover, than does any other Western labor federation.

To judge from the experience of other countries, however, the fundamental question raised by an apparently durable system of wage restraint built on centralized collective bargaining institutions is how a rank-and-file revolt is avoided. During the period under review, Austria alone has been spared both substantial wildcat strike activity and a wage explosion; wage drift, while present, does not appear to be as serious as in other countries. Despite the centralization of authority within Austrian labor market institutions, a structure of negotiations that is by European standards decentralized and integration of shop stewards into higher levels of the Socialist party and labor organizations have apparently minimized the gap between the leaders and the rank and file, although some tensions remain. While there are sixteen national unions, there is considerable bargaining at the regional level, so the results of official negotiations are not so remote from the work place as in Scandinavia, for example.[42] The negotiated limitations on wage drift, moreover, may carry some force in subsequent wage council negotiations. Organizationally, however, there appears to be a more determined effort to integrate even shop stewards into the social-economic partnership. In contrast to those in other countries, Austrian shop stewards in many respects appear to be trainees for union and political leadership, moving successively into positions of local or regional union leadership, the regional parliament, and later a national union or party position. The organizations have attempted to avoid the isolation of the shop steward that has occurred in other centralized bargaining systems.[43]

41. This is somewhat less true for the Chambers of Commerce, whose voting system combines elements of direct and indirect voting.

42. For example, a recent survey by the Austrian Central Statistical Office reported 1,487 collective agreements in effect at the end of 1976. Of these, 312 were "comprehensive" agreements (145 at the national level); 969 were "supplementary" agreements (424 at the national level); and 206 were supplementary plant-level agreements. The last figure is a minimum estimate, since many plant agreements go unreported. See *Statistische Nachrichten,* no. 9 (1977).

43. It can be noted, however, that rank-and-file revolt is usually observed where centralized policies achieve, however briefly, some wage restraint. Perhaps the real reason for Austria's cooperative rank and file is that no real restraint was achieved in the first place.

Fourth, although Austria has a major commitment to redistribution, distributional conflict has been channeled into the legislative process, thereby reducing the pressure on the collective bargaining and incomes policy institutions. Unions and employers largely agree that wages should be distributed according to the worker's contribution to production, while income distribution according to the criterion of need occurs through legislation. There appears to be general agreement, moreover, that the existing wage structure and the existing functional distribution of income are appropriate by the first criterion. This was confirmed in the empirical analysis of wage determination, in which no systematic tendency of wage drift was found to compensate for changes in the earnings distribution. In fact, the skill structure of wage drift appears to reinforce the structure of negotiated wages. In summary, we found no evidence in Austria that changes in the wage or earnings distribution presented a significant impetus to inflation.

More generally, the durability of the Austrian "social partnership" may rest in part on its lack of emphasis on redistributional objectives, which have undermined policy experiments in other countries. Throughout the existence of the Parity Commission, the emphasis has been on receiving gains in income through economic growth, and as a result there has been little policy attention to and very little research on questions of distribution. The neutral stance toward distributional issues by both the main economic interest groups and the incomes policy institutions may be an element of the relatively favorable experience with inflation in Austria. (Compare, for example, the Austrian experience with the effects of distributional conflicts on the inflationary process in Scandinavian countries.)

Fifth, the extent to which the policy itself has had a significant independent effect on prices and wages is not entirely clear. Earlier we noted the barriers to conducting the normal statistical test for policy impact. Nevertheless, within the limitations noted, it appears that Parity Commission apparatus has had some difficulty in coping with the main period of economic strain since its formulation. Price changes since 1972 have deviated substantially from predictions based on past cost-markup relationships. Only the deviations for 1972 and 1973 can be explained by cost-related factors—that is, the introduction of the value-added tax. Wages were more on track than prices during the mid 1970s, with the notable exception of 1975. This exception appears to be largely the result of factors outside the control of this social partnership, however. Perhaps the main contribution to macroeconomic stability has been the willingness of the labor unions to subscribe to the hard-currency option for the purpose of restoring international competitiveness and, in principle, to accept the self-discipline in wage negotiations that this implies. In practice, the policy has fallen short of its goal, for there was a shift in resources toward the sheltered sector, particularly private services, in the mid to late 1970s.

In our view, however, the more important economic challenge to the future viability of the Austrian social partnership—and a limitation on the success of the hard-currency option—is a consequence of efforts to contain distributional disputes within the legislative process. This consequence has been the substantial and increasing importance of legislatively determined social charges in total labor costs. The trade unions have not generally practiced compensatory wage restraint as social charges have increased, and the resultant cost pressures (see figure 2-2) threaten the export performance of Austrian industry. Since 1973, economic growth has apparently been too weak to accommodate increased labor costs associated with increased social security charges. As noted above, the pressure on prices has been particularly severe in the export sector, where the balance-of-payments deficit increased to 7 percent of GNP in 1976.

In conclusion, there are many signs that the social partnership has worked well as a device for exchanging information between the government and the main labor-market interest organizations, reducing uncertainty in economic policy and thereby reducing fluctuations that might result from misinformation. It may also have been a factor that spared Austria the wage explosion of the late 1960s. The institution, however, appears to have functioned more effectively during the long period of growth with mild fluctuations than during the sharp economic shocks that began in 1974. Indeed, we cannot at this stage rule out the possibility that the formal social partnership structures have obscured real events.[44]

44. Or, as one Austrian economist remarked, "The cat has vanished and only the grin remains."

III

The Netherlands

For nearly two decades after the end of the war the Netherlands produced an international paragon of incomes policy; but in the early 1960s Humpty Dumpty had a great fall. He has yet to recover his early form, and new strains to which Dutch collective bargaining was subjected during the 1970s—by the exploitation of natural gas and the consequent appreciation of the currency, by exceptional increases in government spending, especially transfer payments, and in taxation, and by a distinctly egalitarian development of union policy with respect to wages and also salaries—have embittered industrial relations. Nevertheless, the task of reconstruction has never been abandoned, and indeed a patchwork system of incomes policy—consisting in part of central social-contract bargaining and in part of official wage and price guidelines—has evolved.

The Dutch experience invites comparison with the Swedish, for the economies of both countries have been subjected to the same types of external and internal pressures. Both economies are small, highly industrialized—about a third of their respective labor forces are engaged in industry—and highly exposed to international trade; however, in 1976, the Netherlands, with a gross domestic product (GDP) only about 20 percent greater than the Swedish, devoted 44 percent of GDP to exports, while Sweden devoted only 25 percent to exports.[1] Thus people in both countries had reason to pay great attention to the postwar liberalization and expansion of international trade and to its possible effect on industrial structure and industrial relations. Yet both countries assigned top priority to the establishment of high rates of employment; and in the Netherlands, as in Sweden, unemployment generally remained below 2 percent from the mid 1950s until the end of the 1960s. In both countries,

1. See OECD Economic Surveys, *Netherlands,* February 1977, p. 10, for a diagram which shows that, among fourteen countries of the Organisation for Economic Co-operation and Development (OECD) in 1971–73, only Norway, Ireland, and Luxembourg had a higher ratio of exports to gross national product than the Netherlands and Belgium. In relation to their GNP, the ratio of exports to total demand of the latter two countries was clearly exceptional. See also OECD Economic Surveys, *Netherlands,* March 1978, Statistical Annex, International Comparisons.

moreover, economic egalitarianism has been strongly supported as a policy objective—and in both countries there were destabilizing economic and institutional reactions to the narrowing of income differentials. As a result, the objective of domestic price stability in both countries was generally subordinated to the requirements of a high rate of employment, egalitarianism, and external equilibrium. Although the Central Bank of the Netherlands sought to prevent the growth of the money supply from exceeding the extra liquidity requirements associated with the prospective growth of real income, the former president of the bank acknowledged that the objective of price stability had to be sacrificed.[2]

The Dutch Slant on Inflation: Emphasis on Domestic Causes and Incomes Policy

Despite their similarity in circumstances and objectives, observers and advocates in the two countries have tended to emphasize different aspects of the problems of inflation and unemployment or to derive different policy implications from their respective approaches. The Dutch seem to have been somewhat more conventional than the Swedes in their analysis of inflation, somewhat less so in their view of unemployment. Although these differences in approach or emphasis may reflect environmental and institutional differences, they also yield somewhat different policy implications and so are of more than academic interest.

The Swedes adopted and indeed anticipated in practice the Aukrust model, which stresses the dominance of external developments in causing domestic inflation. This type of analysis in principle leaves little scope for incomes policy. Wage inflation which is associated with—that is, is either "permitted" or required by—an increase in world prices and world demand should not be blamed for domestic price inflation, which is in any event consistent with the maintenance of equilibrium in the balance of payments. Where wage increases have not exceeded their "room," there is no room for incomes policy. If wage increases do exceed the room offered by increases in world prices and sectoral productivity, there may indeed be occasion for incomes policy. On the other hand, since the penalty for excessive wage increases may take the

2. M.V. Holtrop, "On the Effectiveness of Monetary Policy: The Experience of the Netherlands in the Years 1954–69," *Journal of Money, Credit and Banking*, vol. 4 (May 1972), pp. 283–311.

form of nearly automatic reduction in employment in the same sectors in which these increases are assumed to originate—the exposed sectors— the probable magnitude of such transgressions is not regarded as great. This argument holds when the exchange rate is fixed; to some it is a variant of the most important argument in favor of fixed exchange rates. Thus the Aukrust focus on inflation minimizes the potential importance of incomes policy to which, it so happens, the Swedes had been opposed long before the model appeared.

On the other hand, the approach taken by Aukrust and Edgren-Faxén-Odhner (EFO) allowed scope for demand management in determining the levels of output and employment in the economy: as long as increases in the cost of labor are contained within their room, any slack in the open sector might be taken up by increasing domestic demand—through such policies as releasing investment reserve funds and temporary subsidies, for example—although expansion of demand should preferably be associated with "active labor-market policies" to eliminate inflationary bottlenecks.

The Dutch approaches to analysis of both inflation and unemployment make a potentially more important case for incomes policy. In approaching inflation, they have tended to give equal emphasis to the influence of domestic labor and that of product markets. In a recent study, de Wolff and Driehuis found that annual percentage changes in contract wages in manufacturing during the period 1953–72 could best be estimated as an increasing function of unlagged changes in consumer prices (PC), lagged changes in labor productivity (HM) and profit rates (ZM), and the sum of changes in direct taxes and social security payments by employees ($SF + TD$).[3] Such contractual changes were not sensitive to changes in the rate of capacity use (QM, measured as the ratio of actual to potential output in the manufacturing sector) or to lagged price changes. These variables, however, together with changes in labor productivity and in the degree of unionization (UM), did help to account for changes in wage drift in the manufacturing sector, although the coefficient on the price variable was low and, like the other two coefficients, did not exceed its

3. Pieter de Wolff and Wim Driehuis, "Postwar Economic Developments in the Netherlands, with Special Reference to Inflation" (University of Amsterdam, April 1977), pp. 103 ff. This paper was delivered at the Brookings Conference on Stabilization Policy held in Rome, May 30–June 4, 1977. A revised and abbreviated version of it can be found in Richard T. Griffiths, ed., *The Economy and Politics of the Netherlands since 1945* (The Hague: Martinus Nijhoff, 1981).

standard error. Combining the drift and contractual equations, de Wolff and Driehuis obtained the following combined wage-sum equation in the manufacturing sector:

$$WM = 0.95\,PC_{-\frac{1}{4}} + 0.34HM_{-\frac{1}{4}} + 0.52GM_{-\frac{1}{4}} + 0.07ZM_{-1} + 0.15UM$$
$$+ 0.41(SF + TD) + 0.02\,DM + 1.00SEM - 0.45,$$

where *SEM* represents social security payments by employers and *DM* is a dummy variable for the year 1969 to allow for certain corrections in the official data.

Just as the Aukrust model (in its pure form) makes no allowance for domestic influence on wage determination in the exposed sector, so this Dutch model makes no explicit allowance for foreign influences in this sector. De Wolff and Driehuis did find, however, that contractual wage changes in manufacturing were the most consistently important determinants of wage changes in the services, building, and agricultural sectors. They had hypothesized that manufacturing was the key sector for wage determination in the Netherlands, since negotiations in the others follow those in the metal trades and other manufacturing industries. This statistical finding is also consistent with the Aukrust model, which hypothesizes that economywide wage increases originate in and are determined by wage increases in the exposed sector, whether for institutional or competitive reasons.

Our own estimating equations also point to a pronounced influence of domestic price changes—as well as unemployment levels—on changes in money wages, especially contractual rates. The coefficient on the consumer price index (*CPI*) variable in the wage drift (*WD*) equations, 3 and 3a in table 3-1, is notably reduced in magnitude and loses significance after correction for simultaneous-equation bias, but the coefficient in the negotiated wage-change equations, 1 and 1a, remains at approximately unity and strongly significant. This suggests that Dutch collective bargaining has contained a strong cost-of-living component and, further, that increases in the cost of living have been translated into wage increases primarily through the mechanism of collective bargaining. We have also estimated a set of equations (2, 4, 6, and 2a, 4a, 6a) which include a variable measuring changes in world prices (*PW_{-1}*) in place of domestic consumer price changes, and the former in conjunction with productivity changes (*QN*) can be taken as an indicator of demand cum ability to pay, along the lines of the Scandinavian model. This influence seems to be confined entirely to the domain of collective bargaining, as a comparison between the *PW* coefficients (and their associated *t*-statistics) in the *WN* and the *WD* equations suggests.

Evidence that movements in compensation were responsive to the room created by variations in world prices and domestic productivity, however, does not imply that wage increases were contained within the confines of that room. The sums of the *PW* and *QN* coefficients in *WN* equations 2 and 2a and *WT* equation 6 are substantially in excess of unity, which suggests that negotiated wage increases tended to emerge as increases in unit labor costs over world prices. Table 3-2, adapted from de Wolff and Driehuis, shows that wage increases exceeded increases in producer prices plus sectoral labor productivity in the manufacturing sector as well as in the sheltered construction and services sectors. The Aukrust influence appears during 1963–70, when the excess was smallest in the manufacturing sector, but during the first half of the 1970s, this pattern was sharply reversed. In this connection it might be noted that the relatively large and positive coefficients on the dummy variable *D2* in the *WN* and *WT* equations suggest the existence in 1971–75 of strong domestic influences on wage increases, in addition to those imparted by increases in prices and productivity.

Thus, although wage movements have been directly affected by forces that are primarily external, Dutch concern with influences on wage inflation that are primarily internal seems not to have been misplaced. Some of the results presented in table 3-1, moreover, are an aid to understanding the strong and persistent interest in incomes policy evinced by the Dutch. An obvious limitation of such policies is that direct restraint on collective bargaining can merely cause more wage drift. Our *WD* equations include negotiated wage increases (*WN*) among their explanatory variables, and, correspondingly, the *WN* equations include drift (*WD*) among *their* explanatory variables. Equation 3 suggests that drift may be negatively related to negotiated increases. In the corrected equation 3a, however, the *WN* coefficient is greatly diminished in magnitude and loses significance. Even in equation 3, the *WN* coefficient is only −0.4, suggesting that if incomes policy is assumed to be effective in reducing a negotiated increase by a certain amount, less than half of such a reduction would pop up in increased drift. The negatively signed *WD* coefficients in the *WN* equations, moreover, suggest that part of the increase in wage drift induced by prior restraint on *WN* would itself tend to restrain a subsequent rise in *WN*, although this *WD–WN* relation loses significance after correction for bias.

Table 3-1. Wage-Change Regressions, the Netherlands, 1957–76

Dependent variable[a]	Explanatory variable[b]												Summary statistic		
	CPI	PW_{-1}	WN	WD	QN	U	SS	DIF_{-1}	S_{-1}	D1	D2	Constant	R^2	Standard error	Durbin-Watson
	Ordinary least squares regressions														
1. WN	1.08 (4.75)	…	…	-0.61 (-2.45)	0.25 (1.73)	-1.37 (-3.48)	-0.54 (-1.17)	…	…	-1.39 (-1.24)	2.23 (1.95)	5.13 (3.91)	0.92	1.34	2.96
2. WN	…	0.58 (3.60)	…	-0.39 (-1.36)	0.76 (4.46)	-2.30 (-3.56)	-0.17 (-0.31)	…	…	-3.43 (-3.08)	2.97 (2.31)	7.53 (5.37)	0.89	1.58	3.06
3. WD	0.62 (2.16)	…	-0.40 (-2.22)	…	…	-1.05 (-2.84)	-0.08 (-0.22)	0.23 (1.06)	0.10 (1.16)	…	…	4.28 (5.75)	0.52	1.17	2.10
4. WD	…	-0.02 (-0.17)	-0.04 (-0.34)	…	…	-0.42 (-0.72)	-0.05 (0.12)	0.41 (1.69)	0.11 (1.06)	…	…	3.70 (3.30)	0.35	1.36	1.89
5. WT	0.77 (2.86)	…	…	…	0.35 (2.15)	-1.59 (-3.54)	-0.39 (-0.71)	0.19 (0.66)	0.27 (2.11)	-3.87 (-2.64)	3.14 (2.25)	8.96 (4.96)	0.91	1.46	2.20
6. WT	…	0.46 (2.79)	…	…	0.73 (4.40)	-2.45 (-4.05)	-0.06 (-0.11)	0.24 (0.85)	0.26 (1.98)	-5.30 (-4.36)	3.34 (2.44)	11.11 (7.60)	0.91	1.48	2.75

Instrumental variables regressions

1a. WN	1.03 (4.11)	...	...	-0.31 (-0.62)	0.27 (1.72)	-1.25 (-2.83)	-0.57 (-1.17)	...	...	-1.40 (-1.18)	2.67 (1.97)	...	4.42 (2.59)	0.91	1.42	2.85
2a. WN	...	0.58 (3.55)	...	-0.21 (-0.43)	0.76 (4.39)	-2.25 (-3.40)	-0.19 (-0.32)	...	...	-3.34 (-2.92)	3.15 (2.32)	...	7.00 (3.87)	0.88	1.61	3.07
3a. WD	0.26 (0.45)	...	-0.14 (-0.37)	...	...	-0.79 (-1.54)	-0.04 (-0.10)	0.35 (1.25)	0.12 (1.22)	...	...	...	3.78 (3.69)	0.44	1.26	1.97
4a. WD	...	-0.08 (-0.56)	0.05 (0.32)	...	...	-0.27 (-0.44)	-0.06 (-0.14)	0.45 (1.82)	0.12 (1.16)	...	...	...	3.13 (2.52)	0.32	1.39	2.10

a. *Dependent variables*
WN: Annual percentage change in negotiated or contractual wages, adjusted for timing factors. Source: Central Bureau of Statistics.
WD: Annual percentage change in wage drift. Source: Same as for WN.
WT: Annual percentage change in total wage bill. Source: Same as for WN.
b. *Explanatory variables*
CPI: Annual percentage increase in the consumer price index. Source: OECD, *Main Economic Indicators*, various issues.
PW: Annual percentage increase in export prices for manufactured goods from market economies, used as a proxy for world prices. Source: United Nations, *Yearbook of International Trade Statistics*, various issues.
QN: Annual percentage increase in real GDP/civilian employment, used as a proxy for productivity. Sources: OECD, *National Accounts Statistics, 1952–76*, and OECD, *Labour Force Statistics*, various issues.
U: Registered civilian unemployment rate. Sources: 1957–73, U.S. Bureau of Labor Statistics, Division of Foreign Labor Statistics; 1974–1976, OECD Economic Surveys, *Netherlands*, March 1978.
D1: Dummy variable taking the value 1 for 1959–62.
D2: Dummy variable taking the value 1 for 1971–75.
SS: Annual percentage increase in social security contributions paid by employers. Source: Same as for WN.
DIF: Annual percentage increase in hourly wage rates of adult male office personnel minus annual increase in hourly wage rates of adult male manual workers, used as a proxy for white collar–blue-collar differences. Source: *Statistical Yearbook of the Netherlands*, various issues. (N.B. For 1974–76, these figures refer to *weekly* earnings.)
S: Annual percentage change in the ratio of operating surplus plus entrepreneurial income from the rest of the world to national income, used as a proxy for profitability. Source: OECD, *National Accounts Statistics, 1952–76*.
Numbers in parentheses are *t*-statistics.

Table 3-2. *Average Annual Increases in Wage Rates minus the Sum of the Average Annual Increases in Producer Prices and Labor Productivity, the Netherlands, Selected Periods, 1953–75*
Percentage points

Sector	1953–62	1963–70	1971–75
Manufacturing	2.0	1.4	3.8
Construction	0.8	3.0	0.7
Services	0.8	3.4	2.7
Total economy	1.0	2.1	1.7

Source: Pieter de Wolff and Wim Driehuis, "A Description of Post War Economic Policy in the Netherlands," in Richard T. Griffiths, ed., *The Economy and Politics of the Netherlands since 1945* (The Hague: Martinus Nijhoff, 1981), p. 25.

The Dutch have experimented with incomes policies during virtually the entire postwar period, so it is not possible to assess the effectiveness of any of these experiments by using some policy-off period as a control. We did insert a dummy variable ($D1$) for the period 1959–62, however, when the policy took a distinctive form. (Wage norms were supposed to be based on sectoral increases in productivity.) The $D1$ coefficients are negative, which could signify policy effectiveness in restraining increases in negotiated and total wages (although currency revaluation could well have helped to exert a restraining influence during this period). We shall therefore discuss institutional behavior directly and in conjunction with specific incomes policy experience, following some observations on the Dutch interpretation of some of the variation in their unemployment.

The Dutch Slant on Unemployment: Structural Causes and Incomes Policy

The approach of the Dutch to unemployment, which is somewhat less orthodox than the Swedish approach, has tended to stress certain alleged structural aspects of unemployment and has reinforced their interest in incomes policy. This is not to imply that the Dutch have neglected conventionally recognized causes of unemployment, including changes in the balance of payments. And it can hardly be maintained that the Swedes have slighted structural factors: although the Aukrust-EFO model explains inflation in the absence of structural imbalances in the economy, the longer-standing Rehn model, which served as the basis for Swedish labor-market policy, emphasized the importance of imbalances in causing both inflation and unemployment. The latter model, however, was concerned primarily with structural problems arising on the supply side of the labor market—with occupational and geographic immobilities of labor and associated rigidities in wage *structures*. The Dutch, on the other hand, stressed demand-supply relationships, notably alleged excess supply of labor in relation to capital and excessively high wage *levels* in relation to the cost of capital. As Haveman has pointed out, however, the great growth of their income transfer programs should also have operated, on the supply side, to increase recorded unemployment in relation to excess labor supply.[4]

Nevertheless, the Dutch took their tack early in the postwar period. One reason they did so is that during the war, the country's stock of physical capital suffered extensive damage—something that did not happen, of course, in Sweden. A second reason consisted of the postwar continuation of a historically high rate of increase in the Dutch population and labor force, which included repatriations from Indonesia (in 1948) and migration from Surinam. The prevalence of a relatively high rate of unemployment—in excess of 2.5 percent—through the mid 1950s has therefore been attributed to a shortage of capital; de Wolff and Driehuis have shown that during this period, the unemployment rate tended to exceed the percentage of idle capacity.[5] By the second half of the 1960s, this was no longer the case, and from the late 1950s to 1971, unemployment rates were low. During the first six years of the 1960s, unemployment was less than 1.5 percent, and it fell below rates of unused capacity. Thereafter, however, the relation between unemployment and idle capacity was again reversed; after declining from a recession high in 1967, unemployment rose sharply during the 1970s and it had reached the earlier peak of 5 percent by 1976–77.[6]

Thus there has been a tendency to regard the relatively high—although declining—levels of unemployment of the late 1960s and the still higher and rising unemployment of the 1970s as including a growing structural component. Although the sharp increase in unemployment after 1973 has been associated with a severe international recession in demand and hence with a sharp increase in idle capacity, the fact that the rate of

4. Robert H. Haveman, "Unemployment in Western Europe and the United States: A Problem of Demand, Structure, or Measurement?" *American Economic Review*, vol. 68 (May 1978, *Papers and Proceedings, 1977*), pp. 44–50.

5. De Wolff and Driehuis, "Postwar Economic Developments," pp. 3, 3a, 32.

6. OECD Economic Surveys, *Netherlands*, March 1979, p. 6, table 1.

unemployment has exceeded the rate of unused capacity has revived discussion of capital shortage. The more recent capital-shortage unemployment is distinguished from the earlier variety because, it is claimed, it has been associated with higher capital–labor ratios and more capital-intensive investment. This phenomenon was adduced to account for the sluggish recovery in employment, together with sharp increases in productivity, that followed the recession of 1967.[7] It has been regarded as a fallout from a much-remarked tendency toward increased industrial concentration in the Netherlands, as elsewhere in Western Europe, with an attendant liquidation of small-scale, relatively labor-intensive firms, plant closures, and an increase in collective dismissals.[8] And behind increased concentration, it was argued, lay the expansion of international trade and competition and an acceleration of the rate of wage inflation during the early 1960s, furnishing an incentive to increase productivity by substitution of capital for labor, within and among enterprises.

To those who recall the great American automation scare of the early 1960s, this argument has a familiar ring. And while explanations that point toward structural unemployment tend to appeal to the general public as self-evident, they tend to strike conventional economists as a priori ambiguous and difficult to validate convincingly. Two objections at least are invariably raised. The first is that a rise in the general level of wages will tend to elicit an equal proportionate increase in prices, including the prices of capital goods; in that event, the rise in wages would not create an incentive for management to substitute capital for labor. Second, labor displaced by technological change could be absorbed elsewhere, and if not, most of the increase in unemployment might properly be ascribed to a deficiency in aggregate demand.

In the case of a small and open economy, however, the first objection loses much of its force, for firms in export and import-substitute industries may be unable to raise prices more rapidly than their foreign competitors. If this means that prices cannot rise in equal proportion to money wages and other labor costs, real wages will rise and profit margins will be squeezed; and if prices of capital goods do not rise as

7. Ibid., May 1969, pp. 10–11.
8. Ibid., May 1973, pp. 16–17; Economist Intelligence Unit, *Quarterly Economic Review, Netherlands,* 2d quarter (June 1970), pp. 12–13; Bram Peper, "The Netherlands: From an Ordered Harmonic to a Bargaining Relationship," in Solomon Barkin, ed., *Worker Militancy and Its Consequences, 1965–75: New Directions in Western Industrial Relations* (New York: Praeger, 1975), p. 125.

rapidly as labor costs, firms will have an inducement to make labor-saving investments "in order to remain competitive." In this respect, the Netherlands can be contrasted with the United Kingdom. In the United Kingdom export prices have often tended to outpace world prices as domestic labor costs have risen. This has tended to squeeze profits and also to produce chronic balance-of-payments problems; but it has tended per se to blunt the incentive to substitute capital for labor, which would increase productivity. In the Netherlands, on the other hand, de Wolff and Driehuis found that export prices have tended to rise less rapidly than the export prices of competitors, at least until the 1970s, and even then Dutch export prices in general appear not to have risen more rapidly than those abroad.[9] But restraint in relative export prices did not appear to inhibit increases in Dutch labor costs. In 1970, for example, total hourly compensation in the Netherlands was three times as great as it had been in 1960, whereas in Germany total compensation was only 2.4 times the 1960 level. Between 1970 and 1975, hourly compensation doubled in the Netherlands, whereas it rose 1.6 times in Germany. During the long period 1960–78, compensation in the Netherlands increased 8.3 times; in Germany, 5.3 times. OECD comparisons showed that both hourly labor costs and earnings (measured in U.S. dollars) in the Netherlands rose more rapidly than trade-weighted averages of costs in a combination of its principal trading partners between 1964 and 1978.[10]

With Dutch export prices constrained by world export prices and Dutch labor costs rising more rapidly than labor costs abroad and more rapidly than the room allowed them by increases in world prices and sectoral productivity, Dutch employers are alleged to have been under an incentive to offset the rise in hourly costs with more rapidly rising productivity by greater concentration on labor-saving activities and investment. Two types of fragmentary evidence might be regarded as consistent with the operation of such a mechanism. The first consists of the very high rate of increase in productivity that occurred in the Netherlands in the 1960s and early 1970s. Thus data appearing in a report to the OECD by a group of independent experts indicate that the average yearly increases in industrial productivity in the Netherlands in 1960–69 (6 percent) and in 1969–73 (8 percent) were higher than in any of

9. OECD Economic Surveys, *Netherlands,* March 1978, pp. 11–12.
10. Ibid., February 1977, diagram 10, p. 24; March 1979, diagram 1, p. 11.

the other eight major industrial countries surveyed except Japan.[11] Rapid increases in productivity were matched by rapid increases in real wages and, after the 1960s, by a steady decline in employment in manufacturing and mining.[12] In the latter years, as we shall see, these increases in costs and productivity reflected a complex interplay between industrial policy (involving natural gas development), social welfare policy, and collective bargaining. Nevertheless, this constellation of developments is not inconsistent with the outcome of a process of structural displacement.

The existence of such a process is suggested more strongly when developments in productivity and employment are considered in conjunction with evidence of a different sort. This suggests that in fact the cost of labor rose in relation to the "user cost of capital"—or that the latter fell in relation to the former. The user cost of capital is a measure developed by Driehuis for the Netherlands and is determined by the price of investment goods, the interest rate, and certain corporate tax allowances.[13] De Wolff and Driehuis find that the wage–user-cost ratio was higher in the 1960s than in the 1950s and higher in the first half of the 1970s than in the 1960s.[14] In this connection it might be noted that Dutch manufacturers import most of their machinery;[15] hence the appreciation of the guilder in the 1970s—which was caused by increased output and export of natural gas—tended to hold down the rate of increase in capital costs.

The skeptic's second objection to this structural interpretation of unemployment—that displacement in one sector can be matched by absorption in another—is more difficult to turn aside. Yet some developments have been interpreted as evidence of increased structural unemployment. The Central Planning Bureau has compiled official estimates of man-years of total unemployment, has divided these into cyclical and structural components and, in turn, has divided the latter into four subcategories, including "structural, narrowly defined" as "unemployment resulting from qualitative discrepancies between de-

11. Paul McCracken and others, *Towards Full Employment and Price Stability* (Paris: OECD, 1977), table 6, p. 147.

12. Employment in these sectors declined from 1.273 million in 1965 to 1.134 million in 1973 (and thence to 1.090 million in 1975). OECD Economic Surveys, *Netherlands*, February 1977, table 5, p. 20.

13. Wim Driehuis, *Fluctuations and Growth in a Near Full Employment Economy* (Rotterdam: Rotterdam University Press, 1972), pp. 39–40.

14. "Postwar Economic Developments," table 4, p. 7.

15. OECD Economic Surveys, *Netherlands*, March 1978, p. 11; March 1979, p. 25.

mand and supply of labour and quantitative lack of job outlets to the extent this is not cyclical." Such narrowly defined structural unemployment rose steadily from 8,000 man-years in 1970 to 90,000–95,000 man-years in 1976, an elevenfold increase. Total structural unemployment, in contrast, increased only twofold, from 81,000 to 170,000 man-years, while total, including cyclical, unemployment increased four times, from 56,000 to 240,000.[16] Upward displacement of an inverse cyclical relationship between unemployment and job vacancies during the 1960s and especially after 1973 is suggested in figure 3-1. There has also been a steady rise in the ratio of the "labor reserve"—unemployment plus employment in special government work programs—to the dependent labor force: between 1964 and 1973, this measure rose from 0.8 percent to 2.9 percent.[17] Disincentive effects of the expanded transfer payment programs could make for developments of this nature, as could industrial concentration and induced technological change; increased unemployment in relation to vacancies, however, has been associated with an apparent decline in the marginal employment–output ratio of the economy.[18] Figure 3-2 suggests only a loose positive relation between associated changes in employment and real GDP, rather than a strong relation in the earlier years that was subsequently broken. It can be seen, however, that all but two of the absolute decreases and smallest increases in employment for corresponding changes in output—those in 1957 and 1967—occurred during the years 1972–76.

Another note of caution might be sounded by considering the fact that the sheltered commerce and service sectors together accounted for an increase in employment of 356,000. Employment in the total private sector increased by only 200,000, and employment in mining and manufacturing actually declined by more than 90,000 during the decade preceding the oil crisis of 1973. These labor-intensive and income-elastic sectors could thus be regarded as having absorbed employment from the sectors in which much greater growth in productivity occurred. At the same time, their absorptive potential might have been restrained by a decline in profitability in those sectors—which indeed was mainly responsible for the decline in the overall fall in the share of nonlabor income in value added in the total private sector, despite relatively rapid

---

16. Ibid., February 1977, pp. 14–16; March 1978, pp. 15–16.
17. Ibid., March 1976, p. 14, n. 5.
18. Ibid., p. 14.

Figure 3-1. *Associated Rates of Unemployment and Job Vacancies,
the Netherlands, 1957–76*

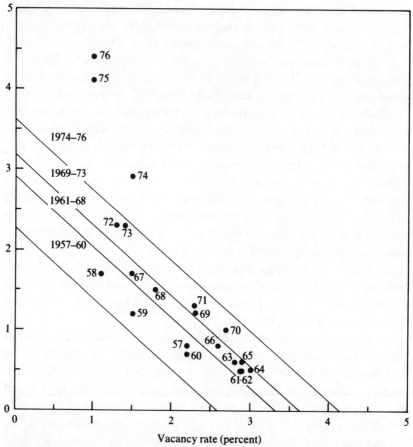

Unemployment rate
(percent)

Vacancy rate (percent)

Sources: OECD, *Main Economic Indicators,* various issues; OECD, *Labor Force Statistics,* various issues.

rates of sectoral inflation.[19] It might be argued that an Aukrust mechanism
operated imperfectly in this case: that the wage increases transmitted to
the sheltered sectors could not be wholly covered by the price increases
that they generated (see table 3-2).

But if this has been the case, should the unemployment phenomena
mentioned above be regarded as structural rather than as manifestations

19. Ibid., February 1977, pp. 19–23.

Figure 3-2. *Associated Changes in Employment and Real Gross Domestic Product, the Netherlands, 1956–76*

Percentage change
in employment

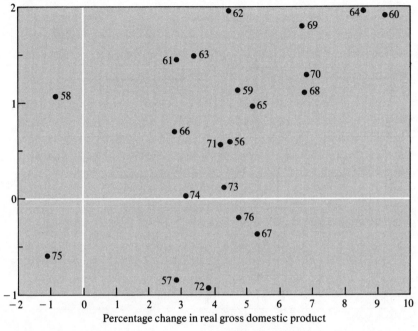

Percentage change in real gross domestic product

Sources: Percentage change in civilian employment, OECD, *Labor Force Statistics,* various issues; OECD Economic Surveys, *Netherlands,* March 1978; *GDP/P,* percentage change in gross domestic product in purchasers' values, at 1970 prices, OECD, *National Accounts Statistics,* various issues.

of deficient demand? If prices in the sheltered sectors were allowed to rise sufficiently to cover wage increases less the relatively small increases in productivity in those sectors, the necessary expansion of domestic liquidity would create circumstances favorable for higher rates of wage and price inflation in the open sectors—and consequently unfavorable for equilibrium in the balance of payments and for maintaining increased levels of employment. The existing distribution of income between wages and profits in the sheltered sectors, as in the open sectors, can indeed be maintained if wage increases are all determined externally and also if productivity movements in the open sectors are independent of these wage increases. But if these Aukrust conditions are departed from, increases in money wages may produce excessively large increases in real wages, in the price of labor in relation to the price of capital, and in

Figure 3-3. *Diagrammatic Representation of Structural Unemployment*

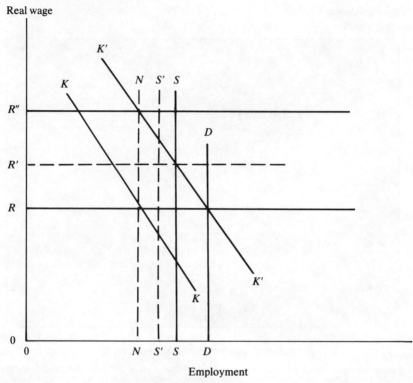

Real wage

Employment

unemployment. To the extent that this unemployment cannot be significantly reduced by demand management alone—and to the extent that it could be reduced by the provision of additional capital (through increases in the proportion of income devoted to investment)—it might be regarded as structural in nature and claim kinship with the type of unemployment prevailing in the first postwar decade. This comparison can perhaps be visualized with the aid of figure 3-3.

Since figure 3-3 purports only to illustrate one possible interpretation of the relation between real wages and unemployment, it is a heroic abstraction—if not a heroic artificiality. It is drawn in highly stylized fashion in order to underscore the element of unreality: thus the aggregate labor demand functions KK and $K'K'$ are straight lines and the supply function SS depicts a potential labor force that remains constant and is completely unresponsive to changes in real wages. The postwar capital shortage until the mid 1950s is then depicted by a level of demand at KK and of unemployment measured by $0S$-$0N$ at real wage $0R$. Higher levels of labor demand following the growth in capital stock are represented by $K'K'$. At real wages short of $0R'$, $K'K'$ generates very high levels of employment, $0S$, and excess demand for labor—$0D$-$0S$ at the original wage $0R$, for example—such as prevailed during most of the 1960s. But when real wages are raised higher than $0R'$, demand falls short of supply once again; this is alleged to have begun to occur after the mid 1960s. This third situation is represented by the intersection of $0R''$ and $K'K'$, which is drawn artificially to yield the same levels of employment and unemployment as the intersection of $0R$ and KK—to show that the capital–labor ratio is higher in the former case—the result of the substitution process induced by the rise in the real wage.

The structural version of unemployment that has been emphasized in the Netherlands dovetails with the eclectic view of wage inflation. The former assigns a causal or a contributory role to cost inflation; the latter looks to domestic as well as external origins of increases in wages and other labor costs and includes institutional influences among the domestic origins. The policy inferences are that demand management alone cannot be expected to reduce inflation or unemployment, but that wage-restraint policies, in conjunction with demand management, are potentially helpful in directly reducing both unemployment and inflation. Thus the Dutch have sought to assign maximum responsibility to the "social partners" for restraining wage increases, and they have been more willing than most others to encourage explicit participation by both government and private organizations in formal and continuing incomes policies.

Vertical Pluralism

Government participation was in part necessitated, in part motivated, by the pluralistic structure of Dutch unionism and employer organizations. The Netherlands and Belgium are the only countries in Western Europe that have more than one central union federation of blue-collar workers, none of which is Communist-led. In contrast to other northern European countries, the Socialist-affiliated union movements in these two countries have been unable to achieve exclusive status but have been obliged to coexist both with Catholic confederations and with a

Protestant movement in the Netherlands or a federation allied with a Liberal party in Belgium. The Netherlands emerged from World War II with three large union federations: the Nederlands Verbond van Vakverenigingen (NVV), the Netherlands Federation of Trade Unions, a Socialist group; the Nederlands Katholiek Vakbond (NKV), the Netherlands Catholic Trade Union Federation; and the Christelijk Nationaal Vakverbond (CNV), the Protestant National Trade Union Federation. In 1947, the affiliates of the NVV had about 300,300 members, or 12 percent of the country's wage and salary earners; the NKV had 224,900, or 9 percent; and the CNV had 119,100, or 6 percent. Another 146,900, or 6 percent, were organized in independent, largely white-collar unions.[20] By 1975, membership in the NVV had grown to 638,800, in the NKV to 360,400, in the CNV to 228,100, and in the independents to 437,600.[21] In 1976, the NVV and the NKV merged into the FNV, or Dutch Federation of Trade Unions, but this unification is not complete and has been a long time coming.

Diversity appeared early and survived the two wars and the intervening depression. It reflects a historical division of Dutch social and political life among the three religious and ideological pillars—Protestant, Catholic, and Socialist. Thus Windmuller, in his perceptive and scholarly study of labor relations in the Netherlands, observes that by the beginning of the century, even Marxist unionists were beginning to learn the lesson, administered in the form of a disastrous strike in which they were not joined by Protestant and Catholic organizations, that "the fundamental ideological and religious cleavages in Dutch society extended vertically down to the level of the working class and that these cleavages were at least as important in determining worker loyalties and attitudes as horizontal class stratification."[22] The Socialist NVV was the historic champion of unity, but not even the dissolution of its formal ties with the Socialist party during World War II could convert clandestine cooperation within the Dutch resistance movement and the establishment of a Council of Trade Union Federations into institutional unity.[23] The immediate postwar period witnessed a move by the Socialists to transform their party into a nonideological group with broader ap-

20. J. P. Windmuller, *Labor Relations in the Netherlands* (Ithaca, N.Y.: Cornell University Press, 1969), table 2, p. 183.

21. Wil Albeda, "Changing Industrial Relations in the Netherlands," *Industrial Relations,* vol. 16 (May 1977), p. 141.

22. Windmuller, *Labor Relations in the Netherlands,* pp. 26–30; quotation from p. 30.

23. Ibid., pp. 92–106.

peal, along the lines of the British Labour party, but it also witnessed the launching of a unity movement, which, with the participation of the Communists, staged a number of politically motivated strikes at a time when the NVV, at some cost in members lost, and the other two federations were cooperating in the national effort to rebuild the economy. The response of the Catholic church was to reaffirm its prohibition against joining non-Catholic, especially Socialist, organizations. Not until the Catholic bishops finally, in 1965, withdrew their interdiction and also acquiesced in the elimination of a dual structure that had formerly given the church direct authority within the Catholic union-movement was it feasible to move to unification of the two federations.[24] Even then, the Protestant federation, CNV, remained aloof. The ethic of Dutch Protestantism has tolerated a transition from nineteenth-century paternalism in labor relations to a doctrine of "mutual responsibility," but not to worker control, or "power," as envisaged by the NVV, and it remains strong enough to sustain the Dutch Protestant unionist's traditional reluctance to sanction strikes.

"Vertical pluralism" has been reflected in parallel national and local unions in the same industrial jurisdictions and enterprises, and it has meant parallel local as well as central federations. It also brought into being three central federations of employers for industry and large-scale enterprises—the nondenominational Centraal Sociaal Werkgevers-Verbond (CSWV), the Central Social Federation of Employers; the Nederlands Katholiek Werkgevers Verbond (NKWV), the Netherlands Catholic Employers' Federation; and the Verbond van Protestants-Christelijke Werkgevers in Nederland (VPCW), the Federation of Protestant Employers. Many of the associations for individual industries have been affiliated with both nonconfessional and confessional federations, however, and the two confessional federations merged their staffs in 1967 and formed the Federatie van de Katholieke en Protestants-Cristelijki Werkgeversverbonden (FCWV), a common Federation of Catholic and Protestant Employers.[25] The tendency seems to have been toward a looser relationship among the different pillars on the employer side than on the union side; if so it is probably related to a lack of discipline and formal authority either possessed or exercised by the federations of employers over member firms.[26] In this respect, these federations stand in contrast not only to the Swedish and German associations of employers

24. Ibid., pp. 21, 121–28.
25. Ibid., pp. 247–51.
26. Ibid., p. 257.

but even to the Dutch union federations, which acquired considerable authority over their respective constituent unions. Also, the looser relationship among the employer associations may reflect the fact that ideological and confessional divisions did not imply differences in economic outlook or industrial relations behavior for firms, while in some respects, such as their attitudes toward strikes and toward management, they did for the union movements.

But if ideological divisions made it difficult for the union side to achieve structural unification, they did not prevent harmonious coexistence or close cooperation much of the time. Although the NVV's own brand of religion calls for unity of all workers in one union movement, the leaders of the NVV have pursued that objective by attempting to persuade their opposite numbers in the other federations rather than through pursuing jurisdictional warfare. There has been no Dutch equivalent of the old American Federation of Labor doctrine of exclusive jurisdiction or of the derivative concept of exclusive representation implemented in the American National Labor Relations Act. Since 1943 (except for a hiatus between 1954 and 1957), formal coordinating machinery has been in existence not only at the level of the central federations but also at city federation, local union, and plant levels. Parallel national and industrial unions were established, membership dues were equalized, and organizing drives were coordinated.[27] The intermovement relationships could be portrayed by an institutional version of the kinked oligopolistic demand curve: the traditional ideological forces have been so strong that competitive dues setting or organizing—the equivalents of competitive price cutting—would not appreciably benefit the aggressor while it could trigger retaliatory activity that would weaken all three groups.

The union activity most obviously analogous to competitive price cutting is competitive wage cutting or, alternatively, competitive wage raising. The former is a way to "organize the employer"; the latter is an appeal to the wage earner. During the interwar period, including the Great Depression, the three union movements demonstrated their ability to work together for the establishment of industrywide bargaining in order to resist downward pressures on wage levels that would have been conducive to competitive wage cutting—at the same time that cartels were being formed in product markets to resist competitive price cutting.

27. Ibid., pp. 139–42, 147.

Immediately after World War II, the three union movements cooperated in a program of wage restraint in an environment that might otherwise have been conducive to competitive wage raising. Thus wage-restraint policies could provide a modest institutional safety net for the three confederations, although they would also strain the ties existing between the confederations and their respective bargaining affiliates.

At the same time, the Dutch have developed a tradition of active involvement by the government in union activities and collective bargaining, which Windmuller traces back at least to World War I, when the government began to subsidize the unions' unemployment funds as part of the wartime relief program.[28] And in 1937 the minister of labor, after long opposition from the employers, acquired legislative authority both to extend collective agreements to nonsignatory firms and to declare agreements void in whole or in part.[29] Governmental power to extend agreements is of course found in other European countries, but in the Netherlands it tends to underwrite the oligopolistic understanding among the three principal federations as well as to protect union standards in general. (Subsidization of union funds also minimized the competitive incentive.) Finally, while the operation of Dutch incomes policy after World War II depended critically on the efforts of the Stichting van den Arbeid (SvdA), the Foundation of Labor, a group representing the private interests—the unions, business, and agriculture—which had been formed during the wartime occupation, the government was also involved. Involvement by the government could furnish, if only as a by-product, protection to the federations against competitive leapfrogging, although Dutch unions and firms, like their Swedish counterparts, were opposed to government intervention. Wage restraint was underpinned by the Buitengewoon Besluit Arbeidsverhoudingen (BBA), the Extraordinary Decree on Labor Relations, of 1945, which, in addition to prohibiting contested quits and discharges without official permission, established a minimum work week of forty-eight hours and prohibited employers from paying wages higher than those approved by the College van Rijksbemiddelaars (CvR), the Board of Government Mediators.

This board, which had been established in 1940 to help set wages in wartime, was given the authority to approve, reject, or extend the terms of collective agreements. Although it acted only after consultation with

28. Ibid., p. 43.
29. This authority paralleled the grant of similar governmental powers with respect to cartel agreements. See ibid., pp. 73–76.

the foundation, with which it originally enjoyed close relations, and although it functioned as an independent nongovernmental agency, it possessed considerable authority. The members of the board have been prominent and practicing members of academic and other professions rather than full-time government specialists. Thus the board's authority in the domain of collective bargaining is balanced by its independence of the government. As a result it has been able, in effect, to mediate between the foundation—that is, the private parties—and the government in matters of wage policy, and, in so doing, it has served as a convenient, and prestigious, scapegoat for each side. The board's independence of the government meant, according to J. Pen, that the minister of social affairs could "shrug his shoulders at too detailed questions concerning wages in Parliament." And while the board has invariably consulted the foundation on proposed settlements in individual sectors, the latter has consulted the board before making the recommendations that the latter invariably adopted. "The interplay between the two," as Pen put it, "was such that the chairman of the Mediators could maintain that he was the Foundation's messenger-boy, while the latter institution could depict itself as a powerless and innocent advisory body. The opposite, too, could be maintained, as circumstances might require."[30]

After 1950, the foundation was further but similarly circumscribed by the creation of another official body, the Sociaal-Economische Read (SER), the Social and Economic Council, which government ministers are obliged by law to consult on important social and economic measures, naturally including wage and price policy. Like the Board of Mediators, the SER is an independent agency rather than a government agency. A third of its approximately forty-five members are representatives of labor organizations; another third represent industry and agriculture; the remainder are independent experts, most of them university professors, who enjoy an enviable status in this progressive society. Thus the federations were represented on the council, which is designed to be independent of the government, although it has naturally acted in consultation with government agencies and has relied heavily on information and forecasts supplied by the Central Planning Bureau, which itself has maintained considerable autonomy. As a result, the Dutch

30. J. Pen, "The Strange Adventures of Dutch Wage Policy," *British Journal of Industrial Relations,* vol. 1, no. 3 (October 1963), p. 320.

bargaining parties have not operated as independently as their Swedish counterparts in determining wage policy. The more explicit and formal roles assigned to the government and to the community at large have been associated with more explicit acceptance of the need for formal policies of wage restraint. But parallel unions—as well as parallel employer associations—would in any event require some governmental pressure as insurance against defection from the oligopolistic front. If the NVV had been able to enjoy an institutional monopoly position comparable to that possessed by the Swedish Confederation of Trade Unions (LO), this element of insurance might not have been required, although Dutch society might still have believed it essential to assert official jurisdiction over a sphere of activity that it regarded as vested with a critical public interest.

But if Dutch incomes policy continued a prewar tradition of government intervention in collective bargaining, it also continued a parallel tradition of union involvement in public affairs. The latter tradition also dated back to the period of World War I, when unions officially participated in the national relief effort and when, in 1919, a High Council of Labor, composed of representatives of the federations of unions and employers, together with senior civil servants and private experts, was set up to advise the minister of social affairs.[31] Like the tradition of government intervention, this corporatist tradition was reinforced by the "pillarization"—but not polarization—of political life as well as of industrial relations, and it thus limited whatever influence the NVV was able to achieve through its alliance with the Socialists. The Dutch parliamentary system had to be organized by fragile coalitions, and when this system proved incapable of responding to crisis conditions during the 1930s, the union movements demanded direct participation in policymaking. The High Council of Labor acquired greater importance in the area of social legislation, so, "In retrospect, the Council ought to be viewed as a predecessor of the decisionmaking machinery in labor relations and social-economic affairs which was developed after World War II."[32] And the habits and spirit of accommodation and cooperation, which the High Council fostered and required and which were powerfully reinforced by a common enemy in wartime, formed an invaluable legacy that enabled the designers of postwar incomes policy to rely exclusively

31. Windmuller, *Labor Relations in the Netherlands*, pp. 63–65.
32. Ibid., p. 65.

on the Foundation of Labor in the early years. The establishment of the tripartite Social and Economic Council in 1950 was attributed by Windmuller in part to the fear that "the Foundation's existence was linked too precariously to shared wartime sufferings,"[33] but the influence and participation of the private interests survived and indeed remained dominant for another decade.

The First Postwar Decade: The System Seems to Work

The task for which the Dutch devised their postwar instruments of intervention and cooperation was restraint of real wages and consumption in order to increase investment and employment and to secure equilibrium in the balance of payments. As the result of the introduction of a "social minimum budget" in 1945, real wages were set at levels too high to be consistent with these policy objectives. (In figure 3-3, the real wage level $0R$ is associated with an excess supply of labor, or $0_S - 0_N$ unemployment.) Since real wages were supposedly set at "social minimum" levels, the task of wage policy was not to seek increased employment, competitiveness, and growth by reducing real wages, which would be indicated in figure 3-3 by the intersection of the demand function KK and the fixed supply SS below $0R$, but rather by holding real wages constant, thereby allowing investment and, with it, productivity to advance. As Pen wrote, "With the social minimum an advance had been given on later increases in productivity."[34] Hence money wage increases were not to exceed increases in the cost of living, while prices could be raised only to cover increases in nonlabor costs, mainly import prices, after notification to the Ministry of Economic Affairs. The Foundation of Labor collated and reconciled the claims that originated in the various sectors, then negotiated general wage increases with the Board of Mediators, which in turn reflected the macroeconomic thinking of the government and the Central Planning Bureau. Thus the foundation, together with the mediators, sought to make a decentralized system of wage determination function like a centralized, synchronized system.

The new system was not supposed to generate uniform percentage wage increases across industries and occupations, however. Under a

33. Ibid., p. 289.
34. Pen, "Dutch Wage Policy," p. 322.

guiding criterion of equal pay for equal work, the union movements sought both to eliminate—or prevent the emergence of—interindustrial wage differences and to permit the development of occupational differentials that could help to overcome the shortages of skilled labor that were associated with the prevailing high levels of overall unemployment. The Dutch, like the Swedes, sought to avoid inefficient wage emulation, but they approached the problems of shortages and inappropriate wage structures through a projected nationwide system of job evaluation and classification rather than through primary reliance on curve shifting through "active labor market policy." The Board of Mediators, the three union federations, and the employer federations all subscribed to the notion that disputes over relative wages could be resolved by the application of "scientific" and "objective" criteria that would lead to the assignment of the correct number of points for each job.[35] And their faith was reinforced, under the authority of the Extraordinary Decrees of 1945, by the imposition of fines and even jail sentences on those rogue employers who paid unscientifically and unethically high "black wages."[36]

In any event, the outcome of the general policy was satisfactory when judged with reference to the policy targets. The direct real-wage target was hit in the center. Between 1947 and 1954, consumer prices rose 32 percent, as did gross weekly earnings of adult male industrial workers in general and weekly and hourly earnings of skilled workers in particular; hourly and weekly earnings of the semiskilled and unskilled rose 33 percent.[37] Unemployment jumped sharply between 1950 and 1952, from less than 3.5 percent to 5 percent, but it declined for the entire decade. Driehuis's wage-estimating equation for the subperiod 1951–54 assigns no explanatory function to either the level of unemployment or the rate of change, a result that, following Lipsey and Parkin, he attributes to the operation of the wage policy.[38] The ultimate objectives of economic policies were also achieved. Investment increased and so did productivity, which rose 44 percent between 1950 and 1954.[39] Finally, the balance

35. Martin P. Oettinger, "Nation-wide Job Evaluation in the Netherlands," *Industrial Relations,* vol. 4 (October 1964), p. 46.

36. Pen, "Dutch Wage Policy," p. 319.

37. Data presented in Windmuller, *Labor Relations in the Netherlands,* pp. 340–41.

38. Driehuis, *Fluctuations and Growth,* p. 118. The variable in question is defined as one minus the unemployment rate, which is referred to as the "utilization rate of labor."

39. Angus Maddison, *Economic Growth in the West: Comparative Experience in Europe and North America* (New York: Twentieth Century Fund, 1964), table I-2, p. 240; table H-1, p. 231.

of payments moved into strong surplus after the Korean crisis, to which
the government and the parties had responded in 1951 by agreeing to a
temporary reduction in real wages. This ad hoc intervention was generally regarded as highly effective at the time and can be seen in retrospect
as the precursor of wage policy in the 1970s. Attention, however,
continued to be focused on the search for criteria and cooperative
institutional arrangements that could place incomes policy on an effective, continuing basis.

1954–59: The System Comes under Strain

Meanwhile, the rise in profitability that ensued as real wages lagged
behind productivity made the unions increasingly restive; and the
Catholic (NKV) and Protestant (CNV) federations began to reassert
their traditional preference for decentralized bargaining and settlements
that could reflect differences in profitability. Their dissatisfaction was
exacerbated as the employers in growing firms and industries, themselves frustrated by their inability to grant increases in relative wages
under the central policy, resorted increasingly to the payment of illegal
"black" wages and to "rank inflation"—that is, upgrading.[40] (Wage
drift, which had averaged about 0.7 percent annually between 1948 and
1954, rose to 2.5 percent in 1955 and 3.3 percent in 1956.[41]) So in 1954 the
wage policy was relaxed to permit so-called welfare wage rounds, which
permitted real wages to advance at an equal rate with national income.
The new policy also allowed for some differentiation. It provided for
extra increases for skilled workers (still in short supply), for some
narrowing of differentials among the five geographic wage zones that the
Board of Mediators had established in 1945, and for special adjustments
indicated by job-evaluation systems; moreover, the new policy did not
prescribe "compulsory" wage rounds. Driehuis found that for the period
1954–59, when this policy was in effect, it appears to have been effective
in restraining the rate of wage inflation. As in the period 1951–54,
unemployment had no significant part in effecting wage changes, but the
coefficients on his productivity-change and price-change variables were
now greater.[42]

40. De Wolff and Driehuis, "Postwar Economic Developments," p. 39.
41. Windmuller, *Labor Relations in the Netherlands,* table 17, p. 390.
42. Driehuis, *Fluctuations and Growth,* pp. 120–21.

Policy influence during the second half of the 1950s, however, reflected two episodes in which the welfare formula was abandoned in favor of more stringent restraint. In 1955, wages were restrained below the increase in productivity, apparently as a corrective to a 16 percent increase the year before. In 1957, wages were held below the rate of price inflation when a sharp swing into deficit on current account induced fiscal-monetary contraction and a jump in unemployment to more than 3 percent. Neither intervention permitted differentiation in wage increases; the 1957 increase covered only compensation for a new contributory pension system and for a nationwide rent increase. This episode resembled the 1951 episode, which was also associated with a balance-of-payments emergency, but in 1957 the cooperative leaders of the union federations came under strong criticism from the grass roots, and some of the unions suffered losses in membership.[43] At the same time, many firms chafed under a price policy that generally denied price increases in response to wage increases in excess of 3 percent.

1959–62: A Strange Adventure of Dutch Wage Policy

In principle a policy that prescribed uniform treatment of wages and uniform treatment of prices (except in response to changes in the prices of imported inputs) was bound to run into trouble in a high-employment economy, since it made no allowance for divergences in sectoral movements in productivity. In principle overall price stability could be achieved either under a policy that prescribes uniform wage increases and differentiated sectoral price changes or under a policy that prescribes differentiated wage increases and rules out price increases in response to wage increases. The former approach, however, which in its American and British versions in the early 1960s allowed money wages to rise uniformly with increases in overall productivity, could not realistically hope to secure price reductions in the high-growth sectors—especially when the latter were exposed to international competition—and thus to avoid both a redistribution of income in favor of profits and domestic price inflation. (A policy based on the Aukrust model, which allows uniform wage increases in accordance with the above-average increases in productivity—and world prices—in the open sector avoids the distri-

43. Windmuller, *Labor Relations in the Netherlands*, p. 353.

butional problem but explicitly renounces the objective of domestic price stability.) The second approach reconciles the distributional and price-stability objectives, but it contemplates the creation and preservation of wage inequalities within the same occupational markets, which can simultaneously violate canons of equity and efficiency.

The Dutch adopted a hybrid policy in 1959. Whereas their old policies had called for uniform treatment of both wages and prices across sectors, the new one called for some differentiated treatment of both. Money wages were generally to rise in accordance with productivity in each sector, but more than proportionately in sectors, such as services, in which productivity increased slowly and less than proportionately in sectors in which productivity notably exceeded the economywide average. Prices generally were to remain steady except that they were to be reduced where wage increases were held below gains in productivity, to balance increases in unit labor costs in the slow-growth sectors. The new policy reflected a change in government that, for the first time since the end of the war, consigned the Labor party to the opposition and correspondingly reduced the influence of the NVV. As a result the egalitarian objectives of the NVV, which would have been better served by a uniform wage policy along Swedish lines, were compromised in order to accommodate the preferences of the employers, and also of the two confessional federations, by allowing greater differentiation and decentralization. But these objectives were thwarted, first by the lack of objective data on sectoral productivity, and second by a pronounced tightening of labor markets and renewed concern over the external balance.

As a result of the absence of detailed productivity data, "bargaining about wages became bargaining about output and input figures. These discussions sometimes assumed surrealistic proportions,"[44] according to Pen, as the negotiators clamored in vain for enlightenment from the Central Bureau of Statistics. But lack of data failed to prevent the policy guidelines from becoming increasingly complex and inoperable. The limit was reached when the Central Planning Bureau, the government, and the Foundation of Labor jointly negotiated a formula for 1962 under which each sector's indicated pay increase reflected the projected economywide increase in productivity as well as its own sectoral increase in productivity, with the latter assigned three times the weight of the

44. Pen, "Dutch Wage Policy," p. 324.

former. It was a formula, according to Pen, "which raised a good many laughs."[45]

Furthermore, the policy came into effect under highly unpropitious circumstances, as labor markets tightened severely. Unemployment fell below 1 percent in 1961 and 1962 for the first time, and Driehuis's estimations suggest that money wages were responsive to employment rates between 1959:3 and 1962:4, whereas they had not been earlier.[46] And money wage inflation increased sharply, from 2.4 percent in 1959 to 8.1 percent the following year, and totaled 24 percent between 1959 and 1962.[47] Nevertheless, the negative coefficients on the dummy variables for 1959–62 (D1) in the WN and WT equations in table 3-1 suggest that the rate of wage inflation might have been even greater in the absence of both this policy and a revaluation of the guilder, which occurred in 1961 following a revaluation of the deutsche mark. These two policy changes were regarded as complementary by the authorities at the time. Previous incomes policies had not been accompanied by revaluations; on the other hand, they were associated with more slack in the labor markets. Indeed, in some respects this 1959–62 episode continued a Fabian strategy that could be regarded as an attempt to prolong an originally favorable cost position in international trade and to stimulate investment and growth in productivity.[48] The rise in money wages between 1959 and 1962 was almost matched by a contemporaneous increase of 20 percent in productivity, whereas retail prices rose only 9 percent. Thus, while money wages and real wages rose sharply, unit labor costs increased hardly at all (in domestic currency). In figure 3-3, the increase in capital stock in relation to labor, the result of past investment and the cause of the increased productivity, is depicted by the rise in demand from KK to $K'K'$, while the increase in real wages and increased labor shortage associated with the low rate of unemployment can be represented by a rise from $0R$ to a new level short of $0R'$.

But policy in 1959–62 followed tradition in another respect. The intended increase in wage dispersion did not occur. Wage drift increased greatly,[49] and in 1959 a reduction in the workweek from six eight-hour

45. Ibid., p. 326.

46. Driehuis, *Fluctuations and Growth,* pp. 123–24.

47. Ibid., pp. 196–98.

48. William Fellner and others, *The Problem of Rising Prices* (Paris: Organisation for European Economic Co-operation, 1961), p. 175.

49. Windmuller, *Labor Relations in the Netherlands,* table 17, p. 380.

days—which exceeded the general European level—to five days swept across the economy instead of proceeding gradually from industry to industry, as the government had wished. The government, therefore, anxious about domestic cost inflation and the effect of revaluation—especially since it had underestimated prospective increases in productivity—once again intervened directly in collective bargaining and in associated pricing decisions. It prohibited the negotiation of further wage increases until existing multiyear contracts had expired, and it also prohibited employers in the construction industry from raising prices after granting a wage increase, thereby precipitating a strike. In these and other situations, the government all but bypassed the quasi-independent Board of Government Mediators.

Thus if incomes policy did achieve some restraint during this period, it also incurred two considerable social costs. In the first place, the fiasco surrounding the attempts to secure productivity data "deprived the wage policy of its objective basis," as Pen wrote.[50] This marked the failure of the second Dutch endeavor to resolve distributional issues with reference to what had been advanced as objectively neutral, or "scientific," formulas, the first having been job evaluation. This failure might have marked the beginning of wisdom, but it also contributed to the end of optimism and togetherness. The other social cost consisted of a blow to the belief that effective restraint could be achieved under less centralized bargaining and with less government intervention. We again quote Pen: "The main reason for this disenchantment undoubtedly lay in the paradox, that since 1959 more freedom had been promised, but what had actually come about was more interference."[51] All parties in the Foundation of Labor were now very unhappy—the employers, who still had to contend with shortages and prohibitions against black wages; the confessional unions, whose objective it was to secure free and decentralized bargaining; and the leaders of the NVV, who continued to favor centralization with restraint as a way to secure a planned and egalitarian economy, but who were unwilling to continue paying the cost, in disaffection of its members, when government intervention was divorced from that political objective.

50. "Dutch Wage Policy," p. 325.
51. Ibid., p. 326.

1963–70: The Crumbling of Consensus

Notwithstanding the disappointing experience of 1959–62, the Dutch continued their attempts to operate incomes policy under conditions of excess demand in the labor markets. Despite the opposition of the large-scale firms, which increasingly resorted to the payment of black wages, incomes policy continued to be supported by the nonconfessional employers' associations, many of whose smaller and less efficient member firms feared the elimination of wage restraints during a period of labor shortage. It was also supported vigorously by Governor Holtrop of the Central Bank, who, contrary to the view that excess demand was responsible for the failure of incomes policy, later argued that it was the failure of that policy which led to the creation of excessive liquidity after 1963.[52] Indeed, it was Holtrop who, according to Windmuller's account, was the main architect of the successor to the policies of 1959 and 1961.[53] The new policy, which was adopted in 1963, differed from its immediate predecessors by dropping growth in sectoral productivity as a criterion for wage changes in favor of a universal norm based on growth in economywide productivity, but it retained emphasis on a consensual approach. The general norm was to be negotiated by the Foundation of Labor, representing only labor and management, and the government, but their negotiations were to be guided by recommendations issued by the tripartite Social and Economic Council, whose semiannual reports were in turn based on economic forecasts by the independent Central Planning Bureau. Following their discussions with the government, the central union and employer federations would meet with their constituent organizations in the various industries to ensure that the individual settlements would not exceed the overall target. Thus the foundation was to replace the Board of Mediators in guiding and reviewing the industry negotiations. The board retained the power to set aside any proposed settlement, however, if the parties in the foundation failed to reach agreement on its appropriateness, or if the board itself believed that the settlement exceeded the target. If the foundation and the

52. Holtrop, "Effectiveness of Monetary Policy," p. 308.
53. Windmuller, *Labor Relations in the Netherlands*, p. 300.

government failed to agree on a central norm, moreover, the latter had standby authority to impose a temporary emergency wage freeze. Thus this system required, first, that consensus had to be reached within the Social and Economic Council; second, that the consensus had to survive negotiations with the government; and third, that the consensus had to influence the actual negotiators at the industry level.

The Fallibility of Control Norms

But neither of the two assumptions on which this elaborate edifice was to rest—the ability to produce distributionally neutral productivity norms and the ability to regenerate an effective social consensus— proved to be tenable. As a necessary condition for the maintenance of labor's share in the national income, the wage norm once again had to be based on forecasts of short-term movements in average productivity— rather than on past trends, as contemporary British and American policies specified. But forecasting productivity in a highly dynamic economy placed too heavy a burden on the Central Planning Bureau, which, as noted earlier, had underestimated short-term growth in 1961. It did so again in 1963 and 1964, when productivity increased 9 percent instead of a predicted 4 percent. Thus when negotiated wages jumped more than 14 percent, the sky did not fall in. On the contrary, as Albeda wrote, "Instead of the prophesied unemployment, unexpected high real earnings were the result of this aggressive wage policy."[54] The current account did swing into deficit, but the principal victims were the incomes policy and its supporting institutions; the foundation was obliged to raise its target in order to narrow the differential between actual and permissible wage increases. Albeda concluded:

It is understandable that confidence in the Government's and the Foundation's ability to assess possible wage increases was still further weakened when the wage explosion was such a success. Had the unions been too cautious throughout the postwar years? Was the relatively low standard of living in the Netherlands a result perhaps of the meekness of the trade unions? Would a more aggressive wage policy not have led to greater efficiency and increased mechanisation and investment?[55]

54. Wil Albeda, "Recent Trends in Collective Bargaining in the Netherlands," in International Labour Office, *Collective Bargaining in Industrialized Market Economies* (Geneva: ILO, 1973), p. 324.
55. Ibid.

The episode also aroused suspicion that official forecasts were conservatively biased out of concern with balance-of-payments equilibrium—and indeed the current account did swing sharply into deficit.[56] After failing to reach agreement within the foundation in 1966 and again in 1967, the unions insisted on the elimination of the overall norms.

Big Firms versus Small Firms—and Incomes Policy

Difficulty in forecasting was the lesser of the two evils that plagued Dutch incomes policy during the second half of the 1960s. A greater problem was presented by the erosion of a predisposition to consensus that had survived its wartime origins but became weakened by the economic recovery that it had helped to promote. Economic growth was attended by structural change and increased diversity of interests, both political and economic. One source of structural change consisted of the liberalization and growth of world trade. This contributed to increased industrial concentration and the expansion of large-scale enterprises, which reacted to international competitive pressures by seeking to bring their labor costs under better control. Controlling labor costs involved linking wages more directly with output at the plant level and in general emphasizing company-level industrial relations at the expense of industrywide and central bargaining. This development was by no means confined to Holland, but it assumed particular importance in a country where, as in Germany, labor costs had remained below international levels and where, unlike in Germany, great emphasis had been placed on centralized incomes policies. Some of these firms, like Philips and Hoogovens, bargained outside the employer associations and, as we have seen, resorted to the payment of black wages, partly in order to obtain and motivate labor. In so doing, their interests sometimes diverged from those of the associations and their smaller and less profitable affiliates. Hence in 1970, when a wildcat strike on the Rotterdam docks was settled by a lump-sum wage payment that was subsequently duplicated throughout the country, it was reported that

56. Windmuller, *Labor Relations in the Netherlands,* p. 303, refers to an analysis by Pieter de Wolff, the former director of the Central Planning Bureau, and C. A. van den Beld, which did reveal a tendency for the bureau's forecasts to underestimate economic activity.

there is a notable lack of solidarity among employers; it seems that some large and profitable firms would not mind raising wages to such an extent as to bankrupt some of their weaker brethren and so to alleviate competition and solve their own labour problem.[57]

This is an interesting example of "competitive bargaining," whereby a "dominant" firm can increase its share of a product market at the expense of less profitable competitors by adopting a more relaxed bargaining stance toward the union in the common jurisdiction.[58]

At the same time the wage practices of some of the larger firms threatened to undermine wage policy. In 1965 the Philips Company negotiated a three-year agreement with specified annual increases and a cost-of-living escalator clause. The purpose was to project the firm's labor costs with greater certainty—an objective that became increasingly urgent after the wage explosions of 1963–64. The employer paid the insurance premium in this case, contrary to some implicit contract theories, with wage increases that exceeded the current norm. Both the long-term nature of the agreement and the indexation provisions, moreover, ran directly counter to the policy of annually determined wage changes. In short, the forces making for increased concentration combined with the success of the wage policy in holding down levels of labor costs to impair the continuing effectiveness of incomes policy and to weaken the centralized wage-setting institutions on which it depended.

Discord and Decentralization on the Union Side

A similar negative feedback occurred on the union side. The process began in the mid 1950s, when discontent with the unions over their support of policies of wage restraint was first manifested. Continued union restraint was reflected in the facts that between 1956 and 1966 there were fewer strikes per year in the Netherlands than there were during the depression period of 1933–39 and that, with only twenty-seven working days lost per thousand wage earners, it remained in a select group of nearly strike-free countries that included West Germany (twenty-eight), Sweden (six), Switzerland (four), and Austria (fifty-six).[59] But rank-and-file unrest was manifested in a number of wildcat

57. Economist Intelligence Unit, *Quarterly Economic Review: Netherlands*, no. 4 (1970), p. 3.
58. Lloyd Ulman, "Connective Bargaining and Competitive Bargaining," *Scottish Journal of Political Economy*, vol. 21, no. 2 (June 1974), pp. 103–07.
59. See Windmuller, *Labor Relations in the Netherlands*, table 19, p. 394; table 20, p. 396.

strikes, despite the fact that Dutch law, like German law, confined the strikes to organizations involved in central negotiations and to disputes arising out of them and despite the opposition of the unions themselves.[60] In 1963, wildcat strikes preceded the scrapping of the norm and the wage explosion of the following year;[61] in 1966, a wildcat strike led by an unofficial "action committee" of construction workers touched off riots in Amsterdam;[62] in 1969–70, Holland's participation in the continental wildcat movement, which was precipitated by a sudden doubling of the rise in the consumer price index following the introduction of the value-added tax (VAT), was not supported by the official unions until the Foundation of Labor decided to extend throughout the country a lump-sum payment of 400 florins, which had been won in a strike led by Soviet-leaning Communists and Albanian-trained Maoists in a Rotterdam shipyard.[63] (A partial exception consisted of an official one-hour strike against a wage control decree in December 1970, but this was essentially a political demonstration.)

While the law on strikes tended to underwrite the authority of the unions and their federations, legal encouragement of employee works councils strengthened the possibility that those elective institutions, which had proliferated and grown in popularity among union members in the 1950s, could change their consultative and company-oriented nature and fill a vacuum created by union bargaining restraint. When the Foundation of Labor decided that it had better extend throughout the country the lump-sum settlement won by the Rotterdam shipyard workers in 1970, the unions in most cases left it to the works councils to secure the extra payments, which were in excess of the centrally negotiated settlement.[64] And union apprehensions were raised when a new Works Council Act, which was passed in 1971, extended employee rights of consultation to include virtually the entire range of employee concerns outside wage determination.[65]

Although union membership in the three federations generally increased during the 1950s and 1960s, and remained constant as a pro-

60. Ibid., pp. 318–25, 164.

61. Peper, "The Netherlands," pp. 130–31.

62. Windmuller, *Labor Relations in the Netherlands*, pp. 174–75.

63. Peper, "The Netherlands," pp. 133–34; Albeda, "Recent Trends," pp. 325–26; Economist Intelligence Unit, *Quarterly Economic Review: Netherlands*, no. 4 (1970), p. 3.

64. Albeda, "Recent Trends," p. 329.

65. Peper, "The Netherlands," pp. 146–48.

portion of the dependent work force,[66] union leaders recalled their loss of members in 1957 and feared that rank-and-file dissatisfaction with wage restraint would cause defection. The first reaction of some unions was to secure institutional protection by negotiating certain gains that would either be restricted to their members, who in the aggregate constituted about a third of the work force in the mid 1960s, or would strengthen the unions organizationally. They included educational programs and other union activities financed by employers, vacation funds for union members financed by deducting part of the pay of nonmembers, employer rebates of union dues, and even compulsory membership as a condition of employment (in the printing industry).[67] But these attempts encountered strong opposition. They ran afoul of the prevailing union ethic which holds that union membership should involve an active relationship, marked by voluntary sacrifice. They were not exactly popular with nonmembers: worker unrest in 1966 was touched off by what proved to be successful wildcat resistance to a proposed members-only vacation fund in the Amsterdam construction industry.[68] The central federations of employers were also opposed, because some of these members-only schemes were virtually the equivalent of black wages and thus threatened control by the associations over employer bargaining, although the federations were not unsympathetic to the problems posed to their "social partners" by wage restraint.[69]

Union reaction to rank-and-file unrest also took another form, which was designed to strengthen the institutional ties of the unions with the rank and file. In 1964, the NVV Metal Workers Union began to develop a system of "plant work" by union-designated shop-floor representatives that would parallel the works councils.[70] But of more ominous portent to Dutch incomes policy was the insistence by the larger unions, including the organizations of construction, metal, and factory workers, on re-

66. Windmuller, *Labor Relations in the Netherlands,* pp. 183–85.

67. Tinie Akkermans and Peter Grootings, "From Corporatism to Polarisation: Elements of the Development of Dutch Industrial Relations," in Colin Crouch and Alessandro Pizzorno, eds., *The Resurgence of Class Conflict in Western Europe since 1968,* vol. 1 (New York: Holmes and Meier, 1978), pp. 162–63; Windmuller, *Labor Relations in the Netherlands,* pp. 194–200; Albeda, "Recent Trends," p. 330; Peper, "The Netherlands," p. 131.

68. Windmuller, *Labor Relations in the Netherlands,* p. 175.

69. Ibid., p. 198.

70. Ibid., pp. 427–30; Albeda, "Recent Trends," pp. 329–30; Albeda, "Changing Industrial Relations," p. 138; Akkermans and Grootings, "From Corporatism to Polarisation," pp. 167–68.

turning to the traditional Dutch system of decentralized, industry-level bargaining. In 1965, following the Philips agreement, the three federations proposed to eliminate the review procedures established under the 1963 policy, and subsequently, following the inability of the foundation and the Social and Economic Council to agree on a norm in 1966 and 1967, review by the labor and employer federations came to an end. In 1968 the foundation rejected a request by the government to restrict negotiated reductions in the workweek as inconsistent with the principle of free collective bargaining.

Dutch experience in the 1960s, on both the employer and the union sides, taught an important lesson, in two parts, about the relation between incomes policy and bargaining structures. First, to be effective an incomes policy must contribute to a strengthening of the authority and influence of the centralized institutions. But second, if an incomes policy is ineffective, it may contribute to a weakening of these centralized institutions on which a voluntary policy depends.

The Limits of Government

With the crumbling of consensus, the government sought to establish a mandatory policy. The government was to be empowered to promulgate norms, as it had done in the past, and a governmental or independent agency was to be empowered to enforce the norm, whether by requiring advance approval of individual collective agreements or by "unbinding" offending contracts after the fact. Acting under the standby authority provided in the 1963 agreement, and also under legal authority provided by the Extraordinary Decree of 1945, the government, in 1967, announced a wage norm; after that norm had been generally ignored in collective bargaining, the Board of Mediation proceeded to reject agreements covering more than half a million employees. The following year the minister of social affairs unbound three agreements that provided for a half-hour reduction in the workweek, after the unions had declined to negotiate smaller reductions voluntarily. And the government sought a new legislative mandate by introducing a bill that would enable it to extend wage agreements or freeze wages, including drift, temporarily—although only after consultation with the Social and Economic Council, the Foundation of Labor, and a new Wage Advisory Committee—to invalidate collective agreements, and, as a last resort, to require their advance approval by the Board of Government Mediators.

The government set the new law aside by approving a new engineering contract that ran for two years and that also contained a cost-of-living escalator clause. This prompted the resignation of the minister of economic affairs, but the government hoped to work out a central wage norm with the parties for 1971. The gesture failed, however; whereas the union federations had found the prospective passage of the wage law a sufficient stimulus for agreement with employers on a norm in 1969, they evidently did not find in the government's abstention from invoking that law a sufficient stimulus for tripartite agreement in 1970. The government then issued a wage modification decree, calling for a modified freeze of six months' duration; this could be regarded as an exercise of authority under the new law. But parliamentary approval of this measure had been preceded by a one-hour protest strike called by the NVV and the NKV, which Peper referred to as "the most widespread exhibition of industrial and political action witnessed in postwar Netherlands."[71] As a result, after a new government was elected in the summer of 1971, it nullified the decree and agreed not to use the powers to invalidate bargaining agreements that were provided in the Law on Wage Formation. Thus the sequence of union opposition, government enactment, intensified union opposition, and government withdrawal was followed twice between 1969 and 1971, before and after passage of the legislation.

The Ineffectiveness of Policy

With incomes policy unable to command support from the unions and the big firms beyond what was necessary to cope with an economic emergency, it left little apparent imprint on an economy in which inflation and international competitiveness occasioned continuing concern but where expectations of emergency had a way of being falsified by events. In the 1960s, the Netherlands had a high-growth, high-inflation economy. Manufacturing productivity increased at an average rate of 7 percent a year, a rate that was about a full percentage point higher than growth in Germany, France, Italy, and the United States.

But the relative increase in hourly compensation, 11.4 percent, was even greater; and unit labor costs rose more rapidly in the Netherlands than in any other European country in our study, including Sweden and

71. Peper, "The Netherlands," p. 133.

Denmark, where increases in productivity matched those in the Netherlands. It could no longer be claimed that the Dutch were nursing their early postwar cost advantage, an outcome for which incomes policy used to receive a generous share of credit.

The economy itself had become more subject to cost pressures in the 1960s. Both productivity and real wages rose more rapidly in 1963–70 than in 1953–62, but the share of profits in national income declined, and average profit rates were lower in 1963–70 than they had been in 1953–62.[72] The decline in profitability, however, was smaller in the exposed sectors of the economy than elsewhere: whereas the rise in unit labor costs in relation to producer prices was greater after 1962 than before in the construction and services sectors, the converse was true in the manufacturing sector (see table 3-2). This may help to explain why support for incomes policy was stronger in the small-scale sectors of the economy than in the large-scale sector—and also why incomes policy lacked the impetus provided by a crunch on international competitiveness.

Finally, it might be noted that wages in relation to the cost of capital were higher between 1963 and 1970 than they had been between 1953 and 1962.[73] Since much of the Dutch capital equipment is imported, a rise in Dutch labor costs in relation to the price of capital equipment was consistent with a rise in Dutch labor costs in relation to labor costs in countries in which that equipment was manufactured. If the rise in wages in relation to capital costs induced substitution of capital for labor in the aggregate, it may thereby have contributed both to the relatively large increase in Dutch productivity and to any "structural" increases in unemployment[74] and in unemployment in relation to vacancies that occurred in the 1960s, as suggested in figure 3-1. According to Driehuis's equations, money wages were much less responsive to unemployment rates in 1963–68 than they had been in 1959–63.[75] (The rates of wage and price inflation were as high in 1967–68, when unemployment was 2 percent, as they had been in 1960, when unemployment was less than 1

72. De Wolff and Driehuis, "Postwar Economic Developments," table 4, p. 7; table 9, p. 15.

73. Ibid., table 4, line 8, p. 7. The ratio "wage rate to user cost of capital" rose from 69.3 to 93.6.

74. OECD Economic Surveys, Netherlands, May 1969, pp. 10–11.

75. Driehuis, Fluctuations and Growth, pp. 123, 125. The coefficient of the "labor utilization" variable is lower and not significant in the later period.

percent.) This is consistent with a conjecture that an adverse change in the inflation-unemployment relation might have been partly generated by increased labor costs. It is likewise consistent with Driehuis's general conclusion that "this sub-period equation does not show specific characteristics of wage policy."[76] Our equations in table 3-1 also lend support to this view if the negative coefficient on the dummy variable for 1959–62 can be interpreted as indicative of less restraint in subsequent years than there had been during a period when wage policy was already weakening.

The Troubled Seventies

The 1970s might have increased the supply of a vital ingredient in the formula for building social consensus in a small country, as concern over the international competitiveness of Dutch industry increased and was added to anxiety over rising inflation and unemployment and declining profitability. Growth in manufacturing productivity declined after 1973 from an annual average rate of 8 percent in 1970–73 to 4.7 percent, and it was no longer greater than elsewhere. But it did remain close to the growth rates in Germany and France, the two leading countries. Hourly and unit labor costs in domestic currency continued to rise more rapidly than in Germany. Unit labor costs measured in common currency, moreover, rose more rapidly in the Netherlands than in all the larger industrial countries during the 1970s except the United Kingdom and the United States after 1972, which indicated a loss of competitiveness.[77] The Netherlands' share of the total international market for manufactures did not decline as a result of the rise in its relative costs, but, since Dutch relative export prices fell, loss of its share of the market was minimized at the expense of profitability and hence future competitiveness. Private operating surplus fell steadily and steeply in relation to net domestic product—from 25 percent in 1970 to 20 percent in 1978 (see table 3-3, below). In this connection it is also pertinent to recall that, whereas the

76. Ibid., p. 126.

77. OECD Economic Surveys, *Netherlands,* March 1979, pp. 10, 12–13; Barbara Boner and Arthur Neef, "Productivity and Unit Labor Costs in Twelve Industrial Countries," *Monthly Labor Review,* vol. 100, no. 7 (July 1977); Arthur Neef, *Unit Labor Costs in the United States and Ten Other Nations* (Washington, D.C.: Bureau of Labor Statistics, July 1972).

average negative wage gap (increases in wage rates less increases in producer prices plus productivity) had been greater in the sheltered construction and services sector than in the exposed manufacturing sector between 1963 and 1970, it was greater in manufacturing in the first half of the 1970s (see table 3-2). And in a strong investment recovery in 1976–78, the bulk of the activity occurred in the sheltered sectors of the economy, such as services, agriculture, and nonresidential construction.[78]

Why did Dutch labor costs continue to rise in relation to costs elsewhere, especially in Germany, and in relation to export prices? And why did they do so in the face of an unemployment rate that nearly quadrupled from 1.2 percent of the labor force in 1970 to 4.5 percent in 1978? (In the latter connection, we might note the positive and significant coefficients on the dummy variables for the years 1971–75 [D2] in the WN and WT equations in table 3-1.) In attempting to find answers to these questions, especially the first, one turns naturally to certain distinguishing characteristics of the Dutch economy and its system of industrial relations in this period. We shall consider the rise of natural gas production and of the price of natural gas, the scale of social welfare programs, indexation of wages, decentralizing tendencies on both sides that have helped to frustrate attempts at centrally negotiated social contracts, egalitarian union policies and white-collar reaction, and some "nonmaterial" demands put forward by the unions as a quid pro quo for wage restraint.

Natural Gas, the "Curse in Disguise"

When relative unit labor costs were declining in local currency while they continued to rise in common currency, the disparity was attributed in part to the effect of natural gas production. The production of gas had increased from 1.7 billion cubic meters in 1965 to 31.7 billion cubic meters in 1970 and rose to 97.3 billion in 1976;[79] and, as a result of a policy decision following the jump in oil prices in 1973–74, its price gradually rose to equality with the price of petroleum substitutes. The effect, of course, was to provide the Dutch economy with an increase in an extremely important export and import substitute, but in so doing it

78. OECD Economic Surveys, *Netherlands*, March 1979, pp. 16–18.
79. Ibid., March 1978, table 9, p. 31.

contributed to an appreciation of the guilder. Between 1971 and 1977, the guilder appreciated 17.5 percent with respect to the currencies of Holland's principal suppliers and as much as 28.5 percent in relation to those of its customers.[80] A heavier currency should have restrained the rise in labor costs of manufactured exports—on the demand side by stiffening employer resistance to wage increases and on the supply side by moderating the rise in living costs. In the latter connection, it should be noted that, since Dutch wages have been formally indexed to consumer prices, an automatic channel for such deceleration has existed. A relative decline in Dutch unit labor costs in local currency during the mid 1970s was consistent with the operation of this type of international market restraint, but it was insufficient to prevent the increase in relative costs in common currency.

Increased unemployment is also consistent with this unresponsiveness, or insufficient responsiveness, of labor costs—although of course it mainly reflected the downward shift in foreign demand after the oil price increase of 1973–74. Employment lost in a relative contraction in manufacturing export volume and a relative increase in import substitutes could not begin to be replaced by increased output in the highly capital-intensive natural gas industry.[81] The Dutch sought to hold down the rate of appreciation by encouraging capital outflows through relatively low interest rates,[82] but this tended to encourage capital-intensive investments. Thus, the effect of an appreciating currency would be a reduction in the price of imported capital goods in relation to nonresponsive wages, while the effect of monetary measures to retard appreciation would be a reduction in the financial cost of capital and a relaxation of downward pressures on wages. In any event, the association between the rise in Dutch labor costs in relation to foreign labor costs on the one hand, and to domestic capital costs on the other, has been regarded as having been highly conducive to labor-saving investment during the 1970s;[83] and the fact that investment in machinery, including replacement investment in the export sector, trended upward (in 1975 prices) between 1970 and 1978, while investment in nonresidential construction remained stagnant has been taken as confirmation of this hypothesis.[84] Also roughly

80. Ibid., p. 12.
81. Ibid., p. 31.
82. Ibid., pp. 12–13, 36.
83. De Wolff and Driehuis, "Postwar Economic Developments," table 4, p. 7.
84. Ibid., p. 7; diagram 5, p. 17; and p. 19. OECD Economic Surveys, *Netherlands,* February 1977, p. 9.

consistent with this hypothesis is the fact that productivity increased more rapidly than output in manufacturing throughout the 1970s so that employment declined.[85]

As a result, policies to promote employment by increasing exports and domestic demand were joined by policies to combat structural unemployment. In 1977 reflationary policies were adopted; but because of the belief that the higher unemployment levels of the 1970s included an increased structural component, these policies were designed "to pay special attention to job-creating aspects."[86] Wage-cost subsidies were introduced to offset the tendency of rising wage costs to accelerate the obsolescence of existing capital. A system of investment premiums was designed to favor small business, and larger projects had to qualify for extra premiums on the basis of new jobs created.[87]

Thus the argument that the development of natural gas production proved to be a "curse in disguise," or the carrier of "Dutch disease," because it caused a relative increase in Dutch unit costs was true only insofar as the currency appreciation that it tended to induce was not balanced by sufficiently strong demand pressure on domestic labor costs. (The opposite argument has also been made: tying a country's currency to the "heavy" currency of a strong competitor, as the Dutch did in effect when they joined the currency Snake in 1972, should have a "bracing" or "disciplinary" effect on domestic costs.) But it has also been alleged that the expansion of the natural gas industry has actually tended to increase rates of inflation in both the wage and nonwage components of domestic labor costs.

In the first place, increased natural gas production enabled the current external account to move from deficit to surplus and thus tended to remove the type of immediate constraint which has been conducive per se to the development of a consensual policy of wage restraint. The loss of cost competitiveness that ensued should itself have provided an alternative stimulus to moderation, as suggested earlier, but it lacked the quality of urgency inherent in an overall current deficit.

In the second place, since the level of labor productivity in gas production is very high, the relative expansion of this sector raised the economywide growth rate of productivity. The latter, according to an

85. OECD Economic Surveys, *Netherlands*, March 1980, table 6, p. 28; table D, p. 71; and table E, p. 72.

86. Ibid., October 1977, p. 34.

87. Ibid., March 1978, p. 30; March 1979, pp. 45–46.

OECD report, "was an important consideration in centralized pay negotiations."[88] This could have contributed to increasing unit labor costs in the sectors employing the great bulk of the work force and to the rise in labor costs in relation to international levels in the open sector. (It could have produced the same effects even if the wage guidelines had been taken from the Scandinavian model, since increases in productivity in the entire open sector would reflect the influence of the expansion of the natural gas industry.)

Transfers and Taxes

The Dutch tax and transfer system was another growth industry that placed a burden of accommodation on the system of collective bargaining. As background, total public expenditures rose dramatically in the 1970s—from 50.7 percent of GDP in 1972 to 60.5 percent in 1977. (In Sweden, growth was even faster, from 50 percent to 67 percent, but Germany, France, and the United Kingdom still devoted less than 50 percent of national income to public expenditures in 1977.[89]) Transfers and subsidies, which had doubled as a proportion of current GDP between 1955–57 and 1967–69, rose by half again in 1974–76, when they reached more than 27 percent, the highest in the OECD.[90] Social security benefits alone rose in relation to wages and salaries, from 19 percent in 1961 to 32 percent in 1970 to 46 percent in 1978.[91]

Increased expenditures were accompanied by increased taxes and contributions to social security, which also rose in relation to material income and GDP. Total tax receipts rose from 36.5 percent of net national income in 1961–65 to 42.1 percent in 1966–70 and to more than half the national income—51.9 percent—in 1975–77. Social security taxes alone increased from 10.6 percent to 20.2 percent throughout the entire period.[92]

In 1976 policies were announced that were designed both to limit the growth of public spending and taxing and also to halt the increase in

88. Ibid., March 1979, p. 9.
89. Ibid., p. 7, n. 2.
90. Rudolf Klein, "Public Expenditure in an Inflationary World," prepared for the Brookings Project on the Politics and Sociology of Global Inflation (November 1978), table 1.
91. OECD, *National Accounts Statistics, 1980.*
92. OECD Economic Surveys, *Netherlands,* March 1979, p. 8, n. 3.

export volumes of natural gas, which were to begin declining in 1980.[93] In the 1970s (1970–78), however, the "burden" of taxes and social security contributions kept pace with expenditures[94] because a large proportion of the incremental revenue from higher natural gas prices and production accrued to the public sector, which enabled increased social security benefits to be financed by transfers from the central government to the social security funds. (The latter increased from 5.2 percent of expenditures in 1974 to 10.9 percent in 1977.) Tax revenues from natural gas were expended in order to compensate for the deflationary effects of the gas price increases, and in part these expenditures took the form of subsidizing employer contributions to social security in order to moderate the rate of increase in total labor costs. It has been suggested, with the aid of hindsight, that if the authorities had instead reduced taxes on wage earners, wage inflation might have been minimized, and it should be noted that the amounts transferred to the social security funds have been linked to negotiated wage increases.[95] The negative coefficients of the *SS* variables in our *WN* equations, while lacking in significance, suggest that increases in contributions to social security may have induced somewhat greater employer resistance to union demands. If so, the subsidies should have made for lower employer resistance and greater negotiated wage increases, so that lesser increases (than otherwise) in nonwage labor costs would have been offset to a considerable extent by larger increases in wage costs.

On the other hand, de Wolff and Driehuis interpreted a positive coefficient on an explanatory variable that combines changes in social security premiums and direct taxes on employees in their wage-change estimating equation for 1953–72 to mean that "workers do not seem to be fully prepared to pay for the inactive part of the population, as well as for collective goods."[96] Thus, if these employee taxes, rather than employer taxes, had been held down by subsidy, a more moderating effect might have been exerted on negotiated wage increases and on total labor costs.

It has also been claimed that the great increase in the magnitude and variety of transfer payments must have created serious disincentives to work, thereby simultaneously increasing reported unemployment and

93. Ibid., March 1978, pp. 36, 53; March 1979, p. 8.
94. Ibid., March 1979, p. 8.
95. Ibid., March 1978, pp. 33–34.
96. De Wolff and Driehuis, "Postwar Economic Developments," p. 86.

wage inflation. Halberstadt cited as presumptive evidence of a disincentive effect, first, the fact that in 1976–77 more than a quarter of the working population fifteen to sixty-five years of age—1.3 million out of 4.7 million—received some form of transfer payment, mainly unemployment, sickness, and disability compensation and social assistance, and, second, that the number of recipients of disability benefit payments alone increased from 164,000 in 1968 to 530,000 in 1976–77, when they accounted for more than 10 percent of the working population. Halberstadt interpreted this increase in disability recipients as

to a large extent . . . nothing more than an expensive way of providing unemployment benefits and of retiring people at an early age—over half of all male workers, for instance, become beneficiaries of disability or similar programs after the age of fifty-seven.[97]

It might be noted that sick leave rose steadily as a percentage of total work hours, from 7.2 percent in 1968 to 10 percent in 1978.[98] It is also relevant to add that unemployment benefits rose, in relation to the modal wage, between 1973 and 1979. In 1979 unemployment benefits equaled 85 percent of the average wage (net of taxes) for the first 130 days and 82 percent thereafter up to two years.[99]

Evidence of actual effects of transfer programs on labor supply and hence on reported unemployment and inflation (Haveman's thesis, referred to earlier) is still rather indirect and ambiguous. An OECD study derived an upward shift in the unemployment-vacancy relationship (see our figure 3-1) in the 1970s from a regression equation that included a dummy variable taking the value of unity after 1968, the year in which the disability insurance program was introduced.[100] The positive dummy coefficient in this unemployment-estimating equation might be juxtaposed with the positive coefficients on the $D2$ variables in our wage-estimating equations, suggesting that the expansion of transfer payments had something to do with the adverse displacement of the wage change–unemployment relation by making unemployment more "voluntary" in nature.

But disaggregation suggests that the rise in the ratio of unemployment

97. Victor Halberstadt, Comments on Robert H. Haveman, "The Dutch Social Employment Program," in John L. Palmer, ed., *Creating Jobs: Public Service Employment and Wage Subsidies* (Washington, D.C.: Brookings Institution, 1978), pp. 273–74.

98. OECD Economic Surveys, *Netherlands,* March 1980, table E, p. 73.

99. Ibid., pp. 30–31.

100. Ibid., p. 26.

to vacancies may have reflected the operation of other forces, although not necessarily to the exclusion of the growth in transfer payments. The rise in unemployment in relation to vacancies was concentrated among women in the last half of the 1970s, and their high and rapidly rising unemployment rates in relation to male rates have been regarded as a sectoral problem characterized by relatively high rates of increase in female participation in the labor force and the tendency for female employment to be concentrated in the service sectors. Female unemployment appears to have been caused primarily by a shortage of employment opportunities rather than by increased transfer payments.

On the other hand, male unemployment has been suspected of reflecting the increased availability of social welfare payments because, while unfilled vacancy rates for men rose steadily after 1974, when female vacancy rates were falling sharply, and regained their 1969–73 levels in 1979, male unemployment rates, although declining slightly after 1977, remained at twice their 1969–73 levels.[101] Shortages of male industrial workers, measured by the excess of unfilled vacancies over the number of unemployed, especially of skilled labor in the metal trades and construction, were a source of concern in the late 1970s. During the upswing of 1977–79, these shortages rose from 40 percent of vacancies in industry to 49 percent; in metalworking (in the export sector) they rose from 33 to 67 percent.[102] Meanwhile, industrial and manufacturing employment continued to decline—in 1979 employment in manufacturing stood at 80 percent of its 1970 level.[103] But manufacturing productivity continued to rise more rapidly than output, as it had throughout the decade (in contrast to the latter half of the 1960s), so it was uncertain whether production was effectively constrained by the reported shortages of labor.

Nor is any of the evidence referred to above inconsistent with the view that increased benefits and other transfer payments have been the effect as well as the cause of unemployment and inflation. Dutch welfare policies were motivated by broad egalitarian trends and other social concerns, and their growth began before the pronounced upswings in unemployment in the mid 1960s and in the 1970s. But these welfare transfers were also intended as compensation for the unemployed. The

101. Ibid., pp. 21–29.
102. Ibid., p. 30.
103. Ibid., table D, p. 72, and table E, p. 73.

disability insurance program, which, according to Halberstadt, acquired the characteristics of unemployment compensation, began in 1968 after the sharp rise in unemployment in 1966–67. And an accelerated rise in the benefit–wage ratio in 1975–78—1.9 percentage points a year from 1.2 in 1969–74—followed the steep increase in unemployment during the first half of the 1970s. The cause-and-effect hypothesis also passed a crude statistical test in the form of a pair of estimating equations. In the first the unemployment rate was estimated by including a lagged benefit–wage ratio as an explanatory variable, the coefficient of which is positively signed, which is consistent with the results of the OECD equation that used a dummy variable. In the second the benefit ratio itself was estimated with the aid of a lagged unemployment rate variable, and that too has a positive coefficient.[104]

Diversion of proceeds from exploitation of natural gas to provide compensation for the unemployment to which it contributed—through currency appreciation—was done partly at the strong insistence of the union federations. The latter included social transfer programs as an important element of compensation for wage restraint in a series of intended social contracts that we shall discuss in a later section. Since sufficient wage restraint could offset the adverse effects of currency appreciation on costs, increased transfer payments required to elicit such restraint might have operated indirectly to reduce, rather than increase, inflation and unemployment. But if sufficient wage restraint was not forthcoming, unrequited increases in benefits could have strengthened the bargaining position of the unions by reducing the cost and hence the fear of joblessness among employed wage earners and also by making the jobless less disposed to remain actively in the labor market. (The effect of increased transfer payments in strengthening the

104. These estimating equations for 1960–78 are

$$\text{unemployment rate} = 0.56 + 0.10 \text{ benefit ratio}_{-1} - 0.70 \text{ vacancy rate}_{-1},$$
$$\qquad\qquad (0.81) \quad (5.67) \qquad\qquad\qquad (-3.64)$$
$$R^2 = 0.77; \text{Durbin-Watson} = 1.08; \text{standard error} = 0.77$$

$$\text{benefit ratio} = 21.36 + 5.21 \text{ unemployment rate}_{-1},$$
$$\qquad\qquad (13.62) \quad (7.75)$$
$$R^2 = 0.78; \text{Durbin-Watson} = 0.53; \text{standard error} = 4.07$$

where benefit ratio = social security benefits as a percentage of wage and salary income (t-statistics in parentheses). Unemployment rates from OECD, *Main Economic Indicators,* July 1981 and earlier issues; social security benefits and wage and salary income from OECD, *National Accounts, 1961–1978,* vol. 2: detailed tables and certain issues; vacancies from OECD, *Main Economic Indicators: Historical Statistics, 1960–79;* labor force from OECD, *Labour Force Statistics, 1968–1979,* and earlier issues.

ability of the unions to maintain at least the level of real wages in the face of declining demand for labor can be depicted in figure 3-3 by a leftward shift in supply from SS to $S'S'$. At wage $0R''$, $0S$-$0S'$ could be regarded as "voluntary" unemployment and $0S'$-$0N$ as "involuntary"— that is, composed of individuals who would prefer work to compensated leisure at wage $0R''$ after employment had declined to $0N$.)

Such strengthening of the unions' collective bargaining position could have two additional consequences. First, it could increase the need for wage restraint and make the government still more disposed to offer increased transfer payments of one variety or another as a quid pro quo; if so, these could ensure an upward spiraling of the unions' collective bargaining power and of their federations' political bargaining power. Second, strengthening of the unions' collective bargaining position could be reflected in their ability to shift the burden of payment that the authority had sought to levy on the wage earners through increased taxes and premiums. Table 3-3 shows that a 50 percent increase in benefit payments in relation to net domestic product (column 1) from 1970 to 1978 was accompanied by a 25 percent reduction in after-tax wages and salaries (column 2), which indicates that those employed did indeed make some payment. But the fact that the share of wages and salaries before taxes (column 3) remained constant, while the share of nongas profits before taxes fell by a fifth (column 4) is indicative of the limited responsiveness of the bargaining system to pressures emanating from both an appreciating currency and an expansive welfare policy.

Wage Indexation

Wage indexation has received a substantial share of the blame for the behavior of wage costs in the 1970s, for it became fully developed just in time to confront the pressures generated by the natural gas and social welfare explosions. Union interest in automatic escalation had been awakened by the breakdown of central negotiations in 1964 and the Philips agreements of 1965 and 1968, which, like many important American arrangements, provided for wage escalation in a multiyear contract. In 1970 the contracts in engineering and trade, which were negotiated after rank-and-file unrest, also provided for indexation, and they set a general pattern.[105] At the end of the 1960s, only about 10

105. Economist Intelligence Unit, *Quarterly Economic Review: Netherlands*, no. 1 (1970), pp. 2–3; no. 2 (1970), p. 3.

Table 3-3. *Benefit Payments, Wages, and Operating Surplus: Shares in Net Domestic Product, the Netherlands, 1970–78*

Year	Benefits/ NDP (1)	After-tax wages and salaries/ NDP (2)	Wages and salaries/ NDP (3)	Private operating surplus/ NDP (4)	Public operating surplus/ NDP (5)
1970	20.39	23.97	50.14	24.54	2.35
1971	21.78	22.77	50.55	23.18	2.12
1972	22.99	21.45	49.90	23.52	2.26
1973	23.71	19.49	49.42	23.77	2.27
1974	25.22	18.93	50.53	22.05	2.79
1975	28.12	19.53	52.00	18.68	3.89
1976	28.46	18.34	50.06	20.40	4.62
1977	29.15	18.45	50.11	19.63	4.87
1978	30.24	17.70	50.04	19.51	4.75

Source: OECD, *Main Economic Indicators*, main aggregates, detailed tables, 1960–78.
Definitions:
1. Benefits include social security benefits, social-assistance grants, casualty-insurance claims, unfunded employee-welfare benefits.
2. After-tax wages and salaries = wages and salaries − (wages and salaries/wages and salaries + entrepreneurial income of unincorporated enterprises) × direct taxes on income − social security contributions.
3. Private operating surplus = total operating surplus − central government operating surplus.
4. Public operating surplus = central government operating surplus.
5. NDP (net domestic product) = GDP − consumption of fixed capital.

percent of the work force had been covered by escalator clauses in collective agreements; two years later, coverage was virtually complete.[106]

During the 1970s, the "price compensation" component of the average wage bill increase of the "modal employee"—married, with two children—rose in relation to the total wage increase (see table 3-4). During the first half of the decade both the total increase and the price-compensation part increased more rapidly than in the preceding five-year period, and in the second half of the 1970s, the rates of increase in both were lower than in 1971–75. In 1975–78, the average annual rate of increase was about the same as it had been in 1961–65, but the rate of price compensation was nearly twice as great as it had been in the earlier period.

The policymakers had entertained reservations about wage indexation since the mid 1960s. They were opposed to the Philips agreement because they believed that long-term collective agreements were inconsistent with the operation of a central incomes policy and its system of annual review and determination, and indexation was an integral part of

106. OECD Economic Surveys, *Netherlands*, May 1973, p. 39.

Table 3-4. *Wage Increases and Component Parts, the Netherlands, Selected Periods, 1961–78*

Component	1961–65	1965–70	1971–75	1975–78
Total wage bill increase	9.6	11.1	14.1	9.9
Price compensation	4.1	5.1	8.6	7.6
Real income	5.5	6.0	5.5	2.3

Source: OECD Economic Surveys, *Netherlands*, March 1979, table 2, p. 8.

such long-term agreements. Employers joined the opposition during the 1970s. In 1975, the failure of negotiated wage increases to reflect the sharp recession that had begun the previous year was ascribed to the operation of the contractual escalator clauses. While wage drift was responsive to increased unemployment, declining to negative levels for the first time since 1962, contractual increases responded to increased inflation and declined only slightly, so real wages continued to rise.[107] In 1977, a series of strikes was the result of an attempt by the employers to eliminate the escalator clauses. The employers lost the strikes and the clauses were retained, although the employers did obtain an agreement to study possible modifications of the indexing provisions.[108]

Official concern over indexation rests on the assumption that the elimination, suspension, or reduction of indexation would reduce to some extent the total negotiated package and hence the level or the rate of increase in real wages. The unions lent plausibility to this assumption when they began to formulate their demands in real terms—"1 or 2 percent on top of inflation," for example. But of course indexation has never constituted a necessary condition for real-wage bargaining. That it was not necessary is indicated first by the coefficients of unity on the CPI variables in the negotiated wage change equations 1 and 1a, for these equations cover a period that began in 1957, long before formal indexation came into vogue. It is interesting that a similar wage-estimating equation for Italy also has a unit coefficient, enabling us to place the famous *scala mobile* in similar historical perspective—more as effect than as cause of bargaining sensitivity to changes in the cost of living. It is arguable that indexation was instrumental in propping up real wages in the face of rising unemployment during the 1970s. But the fact is that real wages were not merely maintained but rose strongly—and it

107. Ibid., February 1977, p. 14, n. 11.
108. Albeda, "Changing Industrial Relations," p. 143.

is also arguable, as we have seen, that the unemployment was the result of bargaining power augmented by transfer payments rather than a constraint upon it. Thus, table 3-4 shows that real wages rose as rapidly in 1971–75, when unemployment averaged 2.7 percent, as in 1961–65, when unemployment averaged 0.8 percent.

In the bargaining process escalator clauses can be substituted for shorter contract duration and vice versa. Automatic escalation per se could produce bigger cost increases within the span of a fixed-term agreement if price increases occurred that could not have been foreseen at the beginning of the contract period. That of course is why unions have usually sought to insist on escalation—or on interim "reopenings" for wages—as a condition of their acceptance of long-term agreements. The 1965 agreement between Philips and the three metalworkers' unions was of three years' duration, and it was followed by a number of four- and five-year agreements elsewhere, all with escalator clauses that permitted wage adjustments to take place at six-month intervals. Thus it was possible that wages could be revised more frequently under the long-term contracts than under the more common one-year agreements. By 1970, escalation had spread to the latter as well.[109] The spread of escalation during an inflationary period, moreover, suggests that the alternative would have been a tendency to negotiate agreements of shorter duration. Before the mid 1960s the government had occasionally acquiesced in semiannual wage reviews during periods of rapid price inflation.[110] And in 1974, government wage regulations provided for price compensation to be paid within three months after the expiration of current agreements instead of after the normal interval of four months.[111]

On the other hand, formal indexation has not prevented the exercise of real-wage restraint. Even under formal indexation arrangements, ways could be found whereby increases in productivity or in the entire cost of living would not be fully compensated for by increases in contractual wages. In a growing economy, real wages could be re-strained, as they were in 1973 when the unions subscribed to an agreement that provided for full cost-of-living compensation but also for a money wage increase, 3.5 percent, which was less than the forecast increase in productivity of 4–4.5 percent. It also provided for a reopening, however, if the increase in productivity turned out to exceed the forecast, doubtless

109. De Wolff and Driehuis, "Postwar Economic Developments," pp. 45, 46.
110. Windmuller, *Labor Relations in the Netherlands*, p. 374.
111. OECD Economic Surveys, *Netherlands*, June 1974, p. 47.

with the bad 1964 forecast in mind.[112] The government memorandum "Blueprint 1981" was aimed at a repetition of this form of restraint: the total contractual wage increase, 2–3 percent, should at most equal the projected rise in productivity, which in turn would equal the projected inflation rate, leaving no room at all for a rise in real contractual wages.[113]

Indexation itself has not always been complete, moreover, and it has been negotiable. Its approval by the Social and Economic Council in 1976 was made subject to the condition that the consumer price index to which wages are indexed be purged of such "impure" elements as changes in indirect taxes and adverse changes in the terms of trade. These conditions were in fact met, although ad hoc wage adjustments have sometimes been made in response to indirect tax increases.[114] In 1978 the minister of social affairs offered to relax some of the restrictive policy measures proposed in Blueprint 1981 if the unions agreed to an explicit ceiling on price compensation.[115] In 1979, the agreement set a flat rate ceiling on the price compensation of wage earners in the private sector.[116]

Finally, it might be noted that, in 1973, "price compensation" was placed on a progressive, or tiered, basis—with full compensation for the lowest paid, three-fourths compensation for an intermediate income range, and only half for the higher income levels. In general, the object has been to protect real wages up to and including the income level of the "modal employee."[117] This, like other egalitarian measures that will be discussed later, may have had inflationary repercussions; but the latter should not of course be ascribed to indexation proper. In general, then, escalation has not operated as an inflationary deus ex machina; it can be seen rather as a reflection of the extent to which the unions have been able to advance and protect real wage levels under adverse market conditions.

The Elusive Social Contract

The unions' interest in explicitly formulating their bargaining objectives in real terms set the stage for attempts at a new generation of incomes policies in the 1970s, of the compensated, or social-contract,

112. Ibid., May 1973, p. 56.
113. Ibid., March 1979, p. 30.
114. Ibid., March 1976, p. 20, n. 14.
115. Ibid., March 1979, p. 50.
116. Ibid., March 1980, p. 65.
117. Ibid., p. 45.

variety. The inefficiency of conventional collective bargaining, apparently manifested in inflation and fiscal drag, plus concern over rising unemployment disposed the unions to seek their real objectives through political bargaining with the government as a partial substitute for collective bargaining with employers. Governments were equally disposed to enter political negotiations with the unions in the hope of concluding a social contract that would minimize increases in unit costs and prices. Political bargaining entailed costs to both sides—to the unions in restraints on collective bargaining, to the government in loss of parliamentary sovereignty. But a prewar tradition of pillarization and democratic corporatism had established the principle of union involvement in official policymaking. And the postwar tradition of incomes policy was strong; even after its collapse during the 1960s, the unions accepted the need for official wage policy, at least in "emergencies." The shock of novelty would be less severe in the Netherlands than in most of the other countries. The question remained whether, in the American patois, bargaining in good faith could produce a settlement.

The unions took the initiative in 1969, when they requested that budgetary policies be thrown into the same pot with pay demands in central bargaining. The Social and Economic Council unanimously recommended that, in exchange for a limitation of increases in real wages below anticipated and actual increases in productivity, the government agree to maintain the current freeze on prices, to reduce planned cuts in income and investment taxes, and to postpone planned increases in the value-added tax and in rents. The SER's recommendations were, for the most part, accepted by the government; moreover, they helped to abate the controversy surrounding the Wage Control Act (which the government insisted on passing but then agreed not to implement).[118] But the private agents could not bind their principals: wage drift more than doubled in 1969 and 1970; the wildcats broke out; the unions increased their contractual demands; central negotiations broke down; and the government unilaterally imposed a six-month pay pause at the beginning of 1971.[119]

118. Ibid., June 1974, p. 29; April 1970, pp. 32–33; Economist Intelligence Unit, *Quarterly Economic Review: Netherlands,* no. 3 (1969), pp. 2–3.

119. The pause, however, incorporated both the union demands and the flat increment won by the Rotterdam labor strikes. OECD Economic Surveys, *Netherlands,* November 1971, pp. 27–28; Akkermans and Grootings, "From Corporatism to Polarisation," p. 170.

Another social contract, dubbed as such for the first time, was concluded in 1972 (for 1973), with the Labor party back in the government. It provided again for a lag of real wages behind productivity in exchange for a continued freeze on profits, abandonment of planned restrictions on sickness insurance and family allowances, abandonment of a planned increase in the VAT, and government intentions to reduce the workweek to forty hours by 1975 and otherwise to reduce unemployment.[120] But once again the central parties failed to carry the precincts. Attempts to implement the wage agreements in sectoral bargaining ended in strikes in 1972 and 1973, and central bargaining broke down every year thereafter.[121] In 1974 and 1976, the government again imposed wage freezes, under the authorization of a Special Powers Act.[122]

Thus the wage freeze continued to serve the function of substituting the authority of government for the authority of the union federations—and of the employer associations as well. By tacit agreement it almost became part of policy bargaining, as a backstop and a quid pro quo to the government for policy concessions made at the central level.

But wage freezes were effective at most for very short periods, and price controls were really no more effective in restraining labor costs; large and medium-sized companies were required to justify intended price increases mainly on the basis of increased nonlabor costs, including taxes, but during the latter half of the 1970s, internal price increases were primarily restrained by appreciation.[123] Profit margins, which were fixed in absolute terms in the trade sector in lieu of price controls, were being squeezed. But since the profit squeeze was seen as a result of the lack of prior wage restraint, it was regarded more as a source of unemployment than of restraint on costs. In 1977, therefore, when the increase in productivity proved less than anticipated, the general rule against raising prices in response to rising labor costs was suspended.[124] The 1969 and 1972 social contracts, which had permitted extra wage increases in the event of unpredicted increases in productivity, provided no symmetrical treatment on the down side. To keep prices down in the

120. OECD Economic Surveys, *Netherlands,* May 1973, pp. 47, 56–57.

121. Akkermans and Grootings, "From Corporatism to Polarisation," p. 171; Albeda, "Changing Industrial Relations," p. 133; OECD Economic Surveys, *Netherlands,* February 1977, p. 13.

122. OECD Economic Surveys, *Netherlands,* March 1976, p. 17.

123. Ibid., March 1980, p. 46.

124. Ibid., February 1978, pp. 131–33, and March 1977, p. 27.

138   THE NETHERLANDS

face of rising labor costs, the government was obliged to resort to
subsidies. In 1976, it reduced corporate income taxes following a rise in
minimum and other wages.[125] But the subsidies, as we know, frequently
took the form of reducing the employers' contributions to social security
and did more to offset increases than to moderate them. They did not
offset them sufficiently to protect profitability, and they could not be
increased indefinitely without further loss of control by the authorities
over economic performance.

Since it appeared that neither the unions nor the authorities would or
could shoulder more of the "collective burden"—that is, taxes, social
security premiums, and nontax public revenues—on the national income,
it seemed necessary, in 1976, to reduce the relative size of that burden,
in the interest of increasing profits, investment, and employment in the
private sector. It had been rising by an average of 1.5 percentage points
a year throughout the previous decade; it was henceforth to be restrained
under a new "one percent" policy.[126] Subsidies were maintained, with
a wage-cost subsidy paralleling an investment subsidy to discourage
labor-saving investment, as noted earlier. The unions were not satisfied;
they wanted a profit-sharing measure (VAD) like the Swedish Meidner
Plan, whereby a portion of "excess" profits would be paid out through
the issuance of special share certificates that would be held in a union-
administered fund and ultimately disbursed to the old-age pension
fund.[127] They tacitly accepted a report of independent experts in the
Social and Economic Council, however, which held that profits were
too low, as a result of excessive increases in labor costs;[128] and they
agreed that real wages should stop rising—although not that they should
start falling.[129] Nevertheless, no central deal was concluded, and another
six-month freeze was imposed in the first half of 1976.

These attempts to forge social contracts were not fruitless, but they
did show how difficult it is to substitute political bargaining for collective
bargaining. During the second half of the 1970s the rate of increase in
money wages and real wages declined significantly (see table 3-4), while

125. Ibid., February 1977, p. 32.
126. Ibid., pp. 33–34.
127. Economist Intelligence Unit, *Quarterly Economic Review: Netherlands*, no. 2
(1976), p. 4; no. 3 (1976), p. 5; OECD Economic Surveys, *Netherlands*, March 1978,
pp. 28–29.
128. OECD Economic Surveys, *Netherlands*, March 1976, p. 48.
129. Economist Intelligence Unit, *Quarterly Economic Review: Netherlands*, no. 4
(1976), p. 2; no. 4 (1975), pp. 3–4.

the decline in the share of private operating surplus in net domestic product (NDP) was arrested (see table 3-3). And judging from the angry reaction of unionists in the early 1970s and the reported labor shortages later on, the makeshift policy of central social-contract bargaining followed by mandated freezes may not have been ineffective in restraining contractual wage increases to some extent. The intent has been to compensate the union federations for their acceptance of contractual wage guidelines, which formed the basis of the government's budget proposals, and also for their acceptance of the frequent wage freezes, by means of policy concessions in such areas as taxation, social security benefits, minimum wage increases, and rent controls. And the idea has also been to compensate management for these concessions with subsidies. But on each side, the organizations that received concessions were frequently not the organizations that were called on to exercise restraint. Neither the firms, with unsatisfactory income statements still before them, nor the national unions, with restive members behind them, were satisfied. The targets of their dissatisfaction were their respective central federations.

There was a disposition on the part of sectional employer associations and individual firms to feel that resistance to union demands and increases in labor costs at the central level was not as strong or effective as it could be. If the central negotiators accepted a standard of growth in productivity that was based on the expansion of the capital-intensive natural gas industry as a yardstick for wage increases, the dissatisfaction of employers is understandable. In any event, it was reflected in an increased disposition to take strikes—a reversal of the attitude prevailing in the 1960s, when labor markets had been tighter and when more aggressive employers were trying to expand market shares. Employer militancy apparently paid off in 1973, when the Industriebond, a newly formed and militant grouping of large national unions within the NVV, was obliged to call off a number of strikes in the metal industry. On the other hand, a series of shutdowns the preceding year ended with the employers agreeing to pay for benefits that a court injunction had earlier forbidden the unions to pay to their striking members.[130] And, in 1977, as noted earlier, the employers lost a number of short strikes in their unsuccessful

130. Akkermans and Grootings, "From Corporatism to Polarisation," p. 171; Peper, "The Netherlands," pp. 135–36; Economist Intelligence Unit, *Quarterly Economic Review: Netherlands,* no. 2 (1973), p. 2; no. 3 (1973), p. 14.

attempt to remove indexation provisions from collective agreements. The unions were able to neutralize the financial resources of the employer associations by striking selectively, while the latter, lacking the authority enjoyed by their German and Swedish counterparts to order sympathetic lockouts, could not capitalize on either their financial resources or the growing general softness of the labor markets.

Thus this testing of the waters would seem to have disproved a belief that the unions' political bargaining power grossly exceeded their economic bargaining power; indeed, employers tended to the belief that, as one of them put it, "We are trying to play chess, while they are playing football." Yet the lesson might not have been lost on the central negotiators. A report of the independent experts that called for wage restraint in the interest of higher profits was issued despite some apprehension of mediation-minded neutrals in the Social and Economic Council, who were made somewhat unhappy by what struck them as a German-style "concertation," or concerted action, procedure. The employer representatives were discreetly urged to refrain from loud applause in order to minimize the public embarrassment of the representatives from the union federations.

Indeed, the embarrassment of the union federations had been of long standing. During the 1970s, it reflected the increased militancy and radicalization of the NVV Metal Workers Union, which had traditionally set the pattern for settlements during decentralized bargaining and which (as in Sweden) was most likely to grow restive under central bargaining conducted by the federations.[131] In 1971 the metalworkers lost their pattern-setting role when an unexpired two-year contract prevented them from joining the scramble to negotiate new settlements at the end of the wage freeze in midyear. Although their contract, with its generous indexation clause,[132] had remained in effect, the metalworkers considered themselves to have fallen behind, and their dissatisfaction contributed to the breakdown of central negotiations and an outbreak of strikes in 1972. They were not disposed to follow the lead of the NVV and the

131. De Wolff and Driehuis, "Postwar Economic Developments," pp. 106–12, estimated "wage sums" in the construction, services, and agricultural sectors by including contractual wage increases in manufacturing among the explanatory variables. The coefficients are large, positive, and significant and are to this extent consistent with a pattern-setting hypothesis.

132. Increases in indirect taxes and in import prices were not eliminated in calculating indirect wage increases under this agreement. OECD Economic Surveys, *Netherlands*, April 1970, p. 33.

other two federations in negotiating the social-contract agreement at the end of 1972, moreover, and they struck again in 1973.

Meanwhile, the NVV metalworkers were acquiring allies. In 1971, they joined with unions in textiles, chemicals, and other manufacturing jurisdictions to form a new organization, the Industriebond, whose combined membership, 185,000, constituted nearly a third of the total membership of the NVV.[133] At first the metalworkers' unions in the NKV and the CNV withheld their support and concluded separate agreements during the 1972 strikes, but in 1973 a solid front was maintained. Thus a subfederation of decentralizers was being formed, the president of the NVV metalworkers calling for unrestrained bargaining, "American style," and younger elements of the radical left calling for increased militancy. This did not signify either an organizational break with the NVV or a radicalization of collective bargaining; the metalworkers were reported to be seeking help from the new president of the NVV in calling off their strike in 1973. But the Industriebond's leaders were certainly not interested in moderating their economic demands, either in the interest of the NVV-supported Labor party of the old left, which was attempting to forge a new governing coalition in 1972, or in furtherance of a merger of central federations, which occurred in 1976. These considerations were very much taken into account by the president of the NVV when he put together the social-contract agreement in 1972. That agreement was designed to forestall another wage freeze and, in the process, to avoid friction between the NKV and the CNV and their respective political allies, who were still in office. But this was compensation for the federations—not for the unions in the Industriebond.

Egalitarianism and White-Collar Organization

One reason that the NVV, like the LO in Sweden, originally supported centralized negotiations was that they apparently offered a superior opportunity to reduce differentials in labor income. The LO's efforts have been persistent, they have gone well beyond equal pay for equal work, and they provoked almost systematic reaction from more highly paid workers and employers in the form of wage drift. In Holland, however, this situation has been almost reversed. The Socialist federa-

133. Economist Intelligence Unit, *Quarterly Economic Review: Netherlands,* no. 4 (1972), p. 4 n.

tion has had to work in harness with the traditionally less egalitarian-minded confessional federations, especially the Protestant CNV; central negotiations and incomes policies, moreover, have reflected the influence of bourgeois parties—notably the sectoral productivity experiments in 1959–62. And the pressure for greater egalitarianism has frequently come from below. But the egalitarian influence has tended to prevail in both countries: in Sweden, because the centralized system managed to trump the grass roots with "drift compensation" and other neutralizing devices; in Holland, because a weaker central system has sought to maintain itself by accommodating to pressures from important bargaining affiliates.

Thus Albeda described the introduction of a minimum wage for unskilled workers after the wage explosion of 1964 as the most important outcome of that episode.[134] The extra pay increase, 2.5 percent, won in the wildcat strikes of 1970 took the form of flat lump-sum bonuses. The most important bargaining issue raised during the Industriebond's strikes in 1972 and 1973 was the demand that occupational wage and salary differentials be reduced by restricting cost-of-living increases to flat absolute amounts for higher-paid groups and that salaried employees, including junior management, be covered by the same agreement as wage earners. These objectives were endorsed by the NVV and the NKV. The settlement provided for indexation that varied inversely with income class, and part of the general increase took the form of a flat sum.[135] In 1974 a Special Powers Act, designed to cope with the oil crisis, was supposed "to ensure that much of the burden of the terms of trade loss was borne by higher income groups and profits." After the failure of central negotiations, the government availed itself of this extraordinary authority to impose an award that featured flat payments, awarded a higher increase to minimum wages, and prohibited dividends and professional incomes from exceeding recent levels.[136]

In 1973, the OECD noted the recent emergence of a "formally announced union goal of striving for settlements which will tend to reduce differentials in income distribution." While praising the ethical objectives involved, "it must be recognized that its attainment could

134. Albeda, "Recent Trends," pp. 323–24.

135. Peper, "The Netherlands," p. 138; Economist Intelligence Unit, *Quarterly Economic Review: Netherlands*, no. 3 (1973), pp. 2–3.

136. OECD Economic Surveys, *Netherlands*, May 1973, pp. 17, 20; Economist Intelligence Unit, *Quarterly Economic Review: Netherlands*, no. 1 (1974), p. 2.

contribute something to inflationary pressures."[137] In fact, the compression of wage differentials caused by flat absolute increments, "price compensation" varying inversely with income level, relatively large increases in minimum wages, and also, on a net basis, fiscal drag have been held to contribute to the shortages of skilled labor referred to earlier in connection with social security increases. According to a Central Planning Bureau analysis, wage drift has tended to restore differentials, but, as in Sweden, any such local reactions are almost automatically neutralized at the next round of central negotiations.[138] (But recall the low negative *WD* coefficients in our *WN* equations.)

Did increases in white-collar salaries fuel subsequent increases in blue-collar wages? The positive coefficients on the *DIF* variables in our drift equations show some tendency in this direction. These coefficients are well below unity and not strongly significant, indicating less than complete compensation for salary increases. Our measure probably underestimates the magnitude of this reaction, however, since the *DIF* measure is restricted to changes in hourly wage rates of adult male office workers, whereas the higher-income salary earners seem to have been a more important target of egalitarian policy. Judging both by the organized reaction of those groups and by the hostility with which white-collar organization was received by the blue-collar organizations, that was certainly the case.

In the Netherlands, as in Sweden and elsewhere, income egalitarianism cum inflation has generated growth in white-collar organization. White-collar organization has long posed a problem in the Netherlands. At the end of the war, the central union federations subscribed to the principle of comprehensive industrial unionism, emphasizing that white-collar employees should be organized in the same unions that represented blue-collar workers. This meant that existing white-collar organizations could not be affiliated with the federations, although some were affiliated with the NKV, nor could they be represented either on the Foundation of Labor or on the Social and Economic Council, membership in which was restricted to "organized," or affiliated, labor bodies. Yet there were more than 250 "independent" organizations, and they increased in membership more rapidly than did the major union groups. Between 1947 and 1975, the independents' membership increased from 147,000

137. OECD Economic Surveys, *Netherlands,* May 1973, p. 39.
138. Ibid., March 1979, p. 9, n. 4; March 1980, p. 28.

144   THE NETHERLANDS

to 438,000, and their share of total union membership rose from 19 to 26 percent.[139] Originally, being unrepresented on the foundation and the SER did the independents no harm: they did not have to share responsibility for restraining their members' incomes, while postwar shortages of professionals assured the maintenance of satisfactory relative levels of remuneration. But at the end of the 1950s, the professionals, led by the university professors, petitioned for recognition and representation on the SER. In 1966, shortly after effective wage restraint had been blown up by the wage explosion of 1964, organizations of executives, technicians, scientific workers, and controllers in the private sector, especially in the giant firms, banded together to form the Nederlandse Centrale van Hoger Personeel (NCHP), the Dutch Federation of Managers' Unions.

Within a decade, the membership of the NCHP had grown from 5,000 to 35,000. Its potential membership was estimated to be 80,000. In 1967, the NCHP also petitioned for a seat on the SER, arguing that it had satisfied the criterion of reasonable coverage. But the central federations boycotted the application, fearing that the entry of the NCHP would mean the transfer of a vote from the labor side to the management side. At their bidding the SER raised the entry requirement to 120,000. After the formation of the FNV—the confederation of the NVV and the NKV—in 1976, however, two white-collar organizations left the NKV. They teamed up with the NCHP, which then joined forces with the unaffiliated Center for Higher Civil Servants and some smaller organizations to form a "master organization." This group, with a membership of 125,000, was able to clear the higher hurdle and was grudgingly admitted.

Union demands for income-graded cost-of-living indexation and for the inclusion of salary determination in the central negotiations for 1973 served as an organizing catalyst for the NCHP. Within a year its membership jumped from 10,000 to 30,000. The leaders of the NCHP rejected the claim of the FNV that the interests of salary earners are identical with those of their employers, and indeed the union attempt to cover the salaried workers with their own bargaining blanket seems inconsistent with that argument. The NCHP also questioned the motives behind the egalitarian incomes policies of the FNV. The FNV's defense

139. This growth included some instances of secession from the federations. See Windmuller, *Labor Relations in the Netherlands,* pp. 169–71, 183–86; Albeda, "Changing Industrial Relations," p. 141.

has been that income differentials can be justified only by "differences in effort and unpleasantness of function," but, according to the NCHP, "the true reason was that the economic situation permitted no real increases [other] than those achieved at the expense of better paid employees."[140] Yet the NCHP also likes to claim that the more highly skilled and more highly paid blue-collar workers have been made unhappy by relative increases in minimum wages and other low-wage categories; this implicitly acknowledges that the motivation of the blue-collar organizations is genuinely egalitarian. When such disputes over principle involve inconsistencies on both sides, they end by dramatizing an underlying inflation-generating clash of interests. It is clear that in the Netherlands, as in Sweden, the egalitarian thrust of union wage policies and government tax policies has aroused a white-collar backlash in the form of a "growth of membership among a group of workers which is generally regarded as being much less union-minded than other categories of workers."[141]

Demands for Jobs and Power: "Nonmaterial" but Not Irrelevant

Further strain on the centralized system of wage determination, and on Dutch labor relations in general, has been generated by a set of so-called nonmaterial demands by the union federations, which combine the objectives both of employee and union representation in management and of direct job protection. In recent years, these demands have been in the context of a social contract—as compensation for forgoing increases in real wages—but they grew out of earlier policies that had been developed when the unions could still regard job protection as supporting wage increases. Before unemployment had climbed back to its postwar levels, it manifested itself most prominently in the form of localized plant closings. It could plausibly appear as a structural phenomenon calling for local antidotes rather than systemic medicine. Industrial concentration had replaced general capital shortage as the villain of the piece, while growing insistence on decentralized industrial relations weakened the feasibility of general wage restraint as a remedial policy.

The unions' first reaction came in 1968 and consisted of pushing

140. NCHP, "Senior Staff on the Social-Economic Scene" (n.p., 1977), p. 5.
141. Ibid., p. 1.

demands for severance pay to displaced employees. But this was not preventive medicine, and, after the 1970 wildcats, some prior restraint was attempted. The new Works Council Act of 1971 required management to consult with the works council before closing or relocating plants or making changes in production or in corporate control.[142] In 1973, this policy was supplemented by another new law that required all medium-sized and large companies to establish supervisory boards of directors, which are empowered to approve budgets, mergers, and major layoffs and which, in addition, appoint management boards. The members of these supervisory boards are co-opted—that is, they are nominated by both works councils and shareholders, each side being given the right to veto the other's nominees.[143] These two important pieces of legislation provided potentially important restraints on managerial authority. The consultative obligation, however, was made contingent on absence of opposition from "important interests"; the unemployment problem itself, moreover, grew steadily more acute. Hence jobs became the principal issue in labor disputes during the 1970s.[144] In some instances these disputes took the form of plant occupations to prevent closing. The most spectacular such dispute occurred in 1972 and brought about cancellation by the multinational concern AKZO of plans to close down two synthetic-fiber plants in the Netherlands in addition to others in Belgium, Switzerland, and Germany.

But as unemployment increasingly assumed the dimensions of a general problem and was seen to be bound up with cost inflation and international competitiveness, it became apparent that the solution could not be found simply in a series of ad hoc attempts to force individual employing units off their demand curves. Therefore, the union federations were prepared to accept freezes on real wages and increases in investment and even in profits as necessary conditions for reduced unemployment. But they were not willing to regard wage restraint as a sufficient condition as well, as they seemed to have done in the late 1940s and the early 1950s. They accepted that wage restraint could increase profits and hence the ability of firms to hire more Dutch labor, but they professed little confidence in the strength of the incentive provided by wage restraint to do so. They argued instead that increased ability to hire more Dutch labor also meant increased ability to hire foreign labor

142. Peper, "The Netherlands," p. 147.
143. Ibid., pp. 147–48; Albeda, "Changing Industrial Relations," p. 139.
144. Akkermans and Grootings, "From Corporatism to Polarisation," p. 173.

instead by investing abroad, especially by multinationals, or increased ability to invest in more labor-saving equipment. And so the FNV has not found it unreasonable to insist that social-contract policy should provide some means of ensuring that the intended employment consequences of wage restraint be realized.

This was the context in which the FNV began to advance its nonmaterial demands, which have included the establishment of joint industry committees to discuss plans for future investment and employment, accepted by the employers after the 1977 strikes;[145] the VAD plan for channeling future "excess" profits into union-administered funds to help defray the costs of social security; extension of codetermination; and, most recently, demands for a shorter workweek. Considered as a package, these demands were obviously intended to provide compensation, together with fiscal and social security measures, for a real wage standstill. Negotiating for employment outcomes becomes especially desirable when wage bargaining is severely circumscribed; as a prominent leader put it, "We can't bargain over real wages, but we can bargain over jobs." And with opportunities in collective bargaining restricted, it became important to gain compensation for the members—for wage gains forgone—through political bargaining. The VAD scheme for channeling future excess profits into social security funds was at least intended to minimize future tax burdens on the active working population. Strengthening and extension of codetermination would also provide compensation in the form of greater control over employment decisions at the level of the enterprise. In addition, extension of the concept from "worker participation" to "worker control" and the transformation of works councils into "workers' councils" would presumably constitute nonmaterial compensation of a high order.

Finally, the package promised something for the central federations themselves. Statutory encouragement of works councils and of codetermination, combined with restraint on wage bargaining, exerts a decentralizing influence on the trade-union movement. Job control at the local level could either supplement or substitute for wage drift. Since part of the objective of the FNV was to substitute job bargaining for more centralized wage bargaining, it might seem institutionally desirable that some job bargaining take place at centralized levels. Intentionally or not, establishment of joint industry committees would have that effect;

145. Albeda, "Changing Industrial Relations," pp. 143–44.

they would permit the national unions to elevate the domain of job bargaining to the industrywide levels at which they have traditionally conducted wage bargaining, and they would also contemplate an active coordinating function for the FNV and the CNV. VAD would go further in the direction of centralization: in funneling part of enterprise profits into a union-administered national fund, it would funnel some authority from the works councils and the supervisory boards to the federations.

But union opposition and other opposition as well have prevented a new social contract from materializing out of these nonmaterial elements. The CNV and its Protestant members have regarded "workers' control" not as compensation for wage restraint but as a social cost in itself. They favor profit sharing and representation by works councils on boards of directors, but they regard both innovations as serving the ends of cooperation and "mutual responsibility." Disagreement over this issue helped to prevent the CNV from joining the NVV and the NKV in the new confederation, FNV; and, as Albeda wrote, "The old differences between Socialist and Christian (especially the Protestant CNV) unions have resurfaced in a new context. . . . The future may see less cooperation between the CNV and FNV; thus the old ideological gap—which had been greatly reduced during the immediate postwar years—is opening up again."[146] At the same time exponents of adversary unionism, even within the militant and left-influenced Industriebond, entertained serious reservations of their own about participation and codetermination, fearing that it would make their members more responsive to company management and to local groups of workers.

Opposition to VAD by employers and large segments of public opinion has been similar to criticism of the Meidner Plan, which VAD resembled, in Sweden: too much authority and power to the union movement. Notwithstanding its prewar acceptance of union-administered unemployment insurance, the contemporary Dutch community seemed unwilling to accept a union-administered fund destined for social security as a quid pro quo for wage restraint. In 1978, a new, nonlabor government issued a new version of VAD which omitted the diversion of excess profits into a central fund.[147]

The other union demands—job bargaining and the shorter workweek—threatened to gobble up cost savings that might be realized by

146. Ibid., pp. 139 and 142.
147. OECD Economic Surveys, *Netherlands*, March 1979, p. 49.

wage restraint. If nonwage but cost-increasing demands can be called "noneconomic" in the United States, job bargaining and shorter hours can be called "nonmaterial" in Holland; but they are poor compensatory material for social contracts and central negotiations just the same. In the first place, they are likely to be most valuable to the worker when they are costly to the employer. Under work sharing, unit costs need not rise if unions and employed workers observe a real wage freeze and accept a reduction in weekly earnings. But if work sharing entails compensatory increases in hourly pay rates and if the latter exceed increases in productivity, unit costs will be increased—and unemployment, the object of the exercise, could remain. Under job bargaining, it was contemplated that hours of work and real wage rates would both remain unchanged, but, where job-security agreements had bite, they would increase costs by obliging the employer to produce the output demanded with more labor than he would have preferred to employ. Thus, as noted, job-security bargaining can produce the equivalent of a make-work rule under which the individual employer is forced off his labor-demand curve. (This is depicted by the combination of the real wage rate $0R''$ and employment, $0S$ or $0S'$, which yields a point such as S or S' above the demand curve $K'K'$ in figure 3-3. In the extreme case the unions might be regarded as having compensated SS' of unemployment by having helped increase transfer payments in relation to wages and as having eliminated $S'N$ with job-security arrangements which increased employment from $0N$ to $0S'$.) Should this type of agreement be generalized under central bargaining, however, it would require a more extensive subsidy program.

Attempts by the unions to generalize job bargaining and work sharing—in 1977 and 1978, respectively—failed. They failed in part because the minister of social affairs wrote the Foundation of Labor that reduction of working hours could be regarded as an admissible way to reduce unemployment only "so long as the cost level of enterprises remains unaffected."[148] They also failed because the cost to the employer and the value to the employee of these demands can vary significantly from one sector to another. Thus, although some job-security agreements were concluded in 1978, they were made in the more prosperous sectors, where they were less restrictive and, possibly, of less value to the employees involved. Elsewhere, poststrike agreements to study in-

148. Ibid., p. 50.

vestment and employment ran into the inability of firms to guarantee employment during a recession. And in 1979, an attempt to cut the workweek to thirty-five hours split the union movement; the metalworkers were forced to abandon it and the FNV, whose support had not been very strong, decided against renewing the demand under prevailing circumstances.[149]

In short, the price of nonmaterial innovations—measured in terms of shifts in power to the unions (with respect to worker-control proposals) and in economic terms (with respect to work sharing, and so on)—seemed to be steep. And the returns to the community seemed to have depreciated in value in the late 1970s for two reasons. In the first place, the goal of full employment may not have been valued so highly as it had been during the two preceding decades. After observing that unemployment was widespread and had reached its highest level in more than a quarter of a century—4.4 percent in 1976—an OECD report observed that "public concern has been less than would have been expected only a few years ago."[150] This reduction in the community's employment target was attributed to the generous levels of unemployment compensation—as well as to the other transfer programs for which the unions had been pressing as another part of their social-contract packages. In the second place, as noted earlier, to a growing extent prevailing levels of unemployment were associated with labor shortages, and the latter gave rise to the apprehension "that it may be more difficult to encourage faster growth of non-energy export industries by means of further wage moderation."[151]

But instead of abandoning wage restraint the government proposed in effect to call a halt to the increase in transfer-payment programs as a way to overcome labor shortages and increase labor-force participation. In 1981, it contemplated a reduction in unemployment benefits—a step that in principle could make for a reversal of the rise in the ratio of benefit payments to wages while continuing the attempt to subject the latter to direct restraint. Although it was to be balanced by some increased spending to increase employment, the general thrust of the new policy, as set forth in Blueprint 1981, was to increase international competitiveness and profitability by reducing the exploitation of natural gas reserves—and its currency-appreciating effects—and simultaneously to

149. "Dutch Wage Talks: Watershed," *The Economist*, April 28, 1979, p. 94.
150. OECD Economic Surveys, *Netherlands*, February 1977, p. 15.
151. Ibid., March 1980, p. 6.

restrain government spending, especially social security payments and increases in pay in the public sector. And this deflationary program—which would, however, include various tax incentives for investment and employment—was to be accompanied, as noted earlier, by a zero target for real contractual wage increases.[152] Thus was contemplated a return to uncompensated incomes policy; indeed, the unions were offered negative compensation in the area of social welfare in exchange for wage restraint. But whether such a policy could be implemented by tacit acceptance of government wage decrees was highly speculative. An uncompensated policy compounded of both wage restraint and deflation might require more complete consensus on the union side than a compensated policy that holds out more immediate prospects of expansion.

Conclusion

For both economic and institutional reasons the Dutch have experimented with formalized incomes policy to a greater extent than has any other country included in this study, with the possible exception of Austria. The Dutch economy is small and extremely exposed to international competition; yet its wages and prices have reflected the operation of powerful domestic forces as well as external forces that have limited the effectiveness of policies of demand management. Traditions making for a combination of organizational pluralism, based on political and confessional associations, and cooperation, combined with a corporatist legacy of union involvement in public administration and of government authority in the domain of collective bargaining, created a general predisposition in favor of incomes policy. These policies initially took the form of centralized wage negotiations that were guided by official forecasts and targets; the latter were incubated in an independent body containing influential public representatives, the Social and Economic Council, and they were underpinned by both legal authority and an independent agency, the Board of Government Mediators. Wage restraint was also supported by price restraint, which was intended primarily to stiffen the backs of the employers in central bargaining by prohibiting price increases from reflecting wage increases.

For nearly two decades, the system worked well and was credited

152. Ibid., March 1979, pp. 29–32, 50; March 1980, p. 69.

152   THE NETHERLANDS

with being a decisive factor in the economy's strong postwar recovery in output and employment, its high rates of growth, and the maintenance of domestic labor costs below levels prevailing abroad. But the ability of the "social partners" and their Foundation of Labor to produce central settlements that were both satisfactory to their respective constituents and responsive to overall economic requirements soon began to weaken as labor markets tightened, as the heritage of wartime cooperation eroded, as large-scale firms sought greater bargaining independence, and as union members and other workers grew restive. As the central bargainers became less effective, the role of independent agencies and of government increased. Originally they were intended to supplement and strengthen the central bargaining policies and institutions—as they had done during the experiment with nationwide job evaluation during the early 1950s. Subsequently, however, they became more of an alternative to central bargaining. An ill-fated, although not ineffective, experiment (1959–62) with wage guidelines based on increases in sectoral productivity was supposed to replace centralized wage setting with decentralized bargaining; instead it brought on more government intervention into specific bargaining situations. The successor policy (1963–68) was designed to restore the authority of the central federations of unions and employers in the Foundation of Labor and to relegate the Board of Mediators and the government to standby roles, but the private parties failed to rise to the occasion and the government had to step in and issue its own wage norms.

In fact, the union federations have always been prepared to accept the necessity for such policymaking by the government in the event of deadlocks between the parties at high levels; what they have objected to—and successfully opposed—is "unbinding" agreements at industry and company levels. Their objective, especially after widespread rank-and-file unrest and wildcat strikes at the end of the 1960s and the beginning of the 1970s, was to avoid being compromised with their bargaining affiliates and their members by supporting a wage policy that the government was empowered to administer in detail. The leaders were willing to lead only if the followers could be persuaded to follow— because in fact the followers had been growing ever more restive and self-assertive.

Their restiveness, and the resultant decentralization, was partly the product of incomes policy itself and the restraints to which it subjected the unions, although the Dutch have consistently sought to minimize those institutional strains by accommodating central policies to market realities. But factors that have generally been independent of incomes policies have also made for restiveness, decentralization, social divisiveness, and cost inflation. In addition to the decline of the postwar consensus, the growth of large-scale enterprise and a more competitive international economic environment, they included the "burden" of increased taxes and government transfer payments, which the unions pushed for but failed to accommodate to completely in wage bargaining; egalitarian wage and salary policies, which helped to provoke a backlash in the form of widespread organization among salaried employees; and recent bargaining emphasis by the unions on reduced hours and job security. These factors exacerbated the inflationary and deflationary potentials of the rise in the prices of oil and of internationally traded commodities, and they contributed to the reputation of the rise in natural gas exports as a "curse in disguise" instead of an unalloyed disinflationary blessing. Thus Dutch unionism contributed to an acceleration of wage inflation, to a relative rise in unit costs (in world currency terms), and to a decline in profitability during the first half of the 1970s, and it has been held to contribute to an increase in structural unemployment as well.

To counter these tendencies the Dutch attempted to introduce a new generation of incomes policies—the social contract—under which union members would be compensated for wage restraint with tax reductions and increased transfer payments and employers would be compensated for certain cost increases with subsidies. Later, as increasing unemployment, inflation, and international competitiveness greatly reduced the authorities' ability to compensate, the unions sought to include increased codetermination, profit-sharing, and employment guarantees as a quid pro quo for a standstill in real wages. On the basis of economic performance, it cannot be maintained that these policies have been notably successful. The social-contract experiments, moreover, were attended by continued breakdowns in central negotiations. Still, the breakdowns were followed by officially announced wage policies that appeared to be tacitly accepted in the context of social-contract bargaining. And wage increases, both nominal and real, began to decline during the late 1970s, while a long decline in profitability came to at least a temporary halt. This may reflect the rise in unemployment—although not to the extent that it might be regarded as a wage-induced phenomenon. But it may also reflect the effectiveness of the makeshift form of compensated incomes policy to which the Dutch perforce resorted during the 1970s. What remains to be seen at this writing is whether wage restraint can survive a withdrawal of compensation by the government and whether the unions will be willing and able to assent to a policy that combines wage restraint with deflation.

IV

Norway

Norway, along with Austria, provides a leading example of attempts to formulate a consensus approach to wage and price restraint. During the past thirty years, Norway has evolved from a system of largely voluntary restraint in the immediate postwar years to increasingly formal consultations involving the government, culminating between 1973 and 1977 in multilateral negotiations between the government and the main economic interest organizations over the development of real income. Then, quite suddenly, in September 1978, the government imposed a comprehensive freeze on wages and prices.

The pressure for an institutionalized consensus is a by-product of three conflicting goals of economic policy and the fact that incomes regulated by negotiated agreements constitute almost three quarters of factor income. The first goal is to maintain the country's share of international markets. The second is full employment, which is pursued with an extremely accommodative fiscal and monetary policy. The third is an income-redistribution goal, which receives unusually large weight in Norwegian policy formulation. Each of these goals can be threatened by inflation, yet the active pursuit of the objectives has come to be an important source of Norwegian inflation. The conflict has grown even more acute and is at the root of the growth and increasing formalization of Norwegian incomes policy.

The development of a formal consensus approach was made easier by the presence of centralized collective bargaining institutions that limited the number of voices in a potential consensus. At crucial points, moreover, the development of incomes policy was informed and aided by the development and general acceptance of sophisticated analyses of the inflation process and the nature of distributional conflicts in Norway. Indeed, Norwegian economists have argued that the determination of wage rates is an instrument of economic policy that should be subject to government influence. Forecasts generated by an econometric formalization of one model of the international transmission of inflation have been a significant part of the consensus discussions and negotiations. In this respect, the Norwegian procedures differ sharply from incomes policy institutions in Austria and most other countries, where technical analyses of some of the underlying issues, such as income distribution, are not a primary factor in policy implementation.

Throughout a period of fifteen years, the government moved from the role of an interested observer to that of an active participant in wage negotiations. As in Austria, however, the multilateral negotiations were not mandated by legislation, and adherence was voluntary. Faced with the opposition of several unions, moreover, the government rejected a more formal statutory approach to incomes policy that was proposed by a government commission in the early 1970s. Yet it was drawn by the complexity of its economic goals, and an unwillingness to sacrifice them, into direct negotiations with the interest organizations. These negotiations were conducted, however, in the context of a rather permissive attitude toward traditional general economic constraints—most notably, the balance of payments—that had been conditioned by optimistic forecasts of the probable earnings from oil discoveries in the North Sea. As these expectations proved incorrect, the government abandoned the consensus arrangements and adopted the wage and price freeze in an effort to force an adjustment in real earnings.

Economic Background to Norwegian Incomes Policy

The study of Norwegian incomes policy involves a central paradox. Although almost 75 percent of factor incomes are determined in the short run by organized negotiations, the most important, widely accepted model of inflation and long-run income distribution stresses the fundamental importance of largely exogenous developments in world prices and the secular growth in the productivity of domestic labor. While the prevailing analysis of Norwegian inflation assesses the influence of domestic factors as limited, considerable policy attention has been devoted to the outcome of income negotiations throughout most of the postwar period. We shall begin our examination of this paradox with a discussion of the general economic developments, particularly with respect to inflation, that formed a background to Norwegian incomes policies during the 1970s.

The Inflationary Mechanism

With a trade sector accounting for some 40 percent of gross national product (GNP), discussions of inflation in Norway frequently emphasize the influence of world prices, the exchange rate, and the international transmission of inflation. The discussion has been facilitated by the development of a two-sector model of inflation by the Norwegian economist Odd Aukrust to provide a more rational basis for discussions of the economic issues involved in income negotiations.[1]

The Aukrust model not only provides a link between world price movements and domestic inflation, but also traces the implications of alternative price and wage movements for the income distribution. Because of these features, it has been used extensively to forecast the consequences of alternative wage settlements before each round of collective bargaining negotiations since its development in the mid 1960s. The short-run version of the model, moreover, yields an important insight into the nature of the distributional tensions underlying income determination in Norway. In Aukrust's words:

Incidentally, one has to give up the popular belief that the struggle over income shares may be viewed simply as a confrontation between wage earners and employers. Instead, wage earners and owners of enterprises in the sheltered industries may well have a common interest in rising wages since, according to the model, a rise in wages will lead automatically, by means of price adjustments, to a proportionate increase in profits of the sheltered industries. Together these groups may be able to obtain a (short-run) gain in real incomes at the expense of other groups (farmers and owners of enterprises in the exposed industries). The parties confronting each other in the struggle over income shares, therefore, may be said to be (1) the farmers, (2) the owners of enterprises in the sheltered industries and the wage earners, and (3) owners of enterprises in the exposed industries.[2]

1. The basic references on the short-run and long-run versions of the model, which is discussed in more detail in chapter 1, are Odd Aukrust, "PRIM I: A Model of the Price and Income Distribution Mechanism of an Open Economy," *Review of Income and Wealth,* series 16, no. 1 (March 1970), pp. 51–78; Odd Aukrust, "Inflation in the Open Economy: A Norwegian Model," in Lawrence B. Krause and Walter S. Salant, eds., *Worldwide Inflation: Theory and Recent Experience* (Washington, D.C.: Brookings Institution, 1977), pp. 107–66. For a discussion of the applicability of the model to Sweden, see Gösta Edgren, Karl-Olof Faxén, and Clas-Erik Odhner, *Wage Formation and the Economy,* tr. by Margareta Eklof (London: Allen & Unwin, 1973).

2. Aukrust, "Inflation in the Open Economy," p. 125.

Table 4-1. *Development of Real Income, Norway, Selected Periods, 1951–76*

Average annual percentage increase

Item	1951–57	1957–63	1963–65	1951–65	1970–73	1973–76
Net domestic product[a]	3.6	3.6	6.2	4.0	4.6	4.6
Net domestic product per man-year[a]	3.4	3.3	5.4	3.6	n.a.	n.a.
Total factor income	3.4	3.2	6.5	3.8	4.8	4.7
Wages per man-year	3.8	4.3	2.6	3.9	3.6	4.3
Agricultural income per man-year	4.7	1.6	7.8	3.8	6.7	15.6
Fishing income per man-year	−1.7	0.3	35.2	3.8	13.7	−6.4
Entrepreneurial income[b]	1.5	−0.2	10.7	2.0	. . .	. . .
Sheltered industries	3.1	4.4	4.4	3.9	−1.3	2.1
Exposed industries	−0.4	−7.7	25.1	−0.4	0.1	−14.9
Import-competing	1.8	4.9	17.5	5.2	n.a.	n.a.
Export-oriented	−1.2	−11.2	31.4	−1.7	n.a.	n.a.

Sources: Royal Norwegian Ministry of Finance, *The National Budget of Norway, 1967*, p. 90; Norges Offentlige Utredninger (NOU), *Om grunnlaget for inntektsoppgjørene, 1977* [On the background for income settlements, 1977], NOU 1977:17 (Oslo: Universitetsforlaget, 1977), p. 14.
n.a. Not available.
a. Figures for volume.
b. Excluding agriculture and fishing.

The model is most susceptible to criticism as a general theory of inflation because of its neglect of the demand side. As developed, the model assumes that demand is perfectly accommodating to changing cost pressures but is not an independent source of inflationary pressure. While this assumption seems too strong for many economies (see particularly the discussion in the chapter on Denmark), it seems reasonably descriptive of the Norwegian economy, at least until the early 1970s. In a recent study, for example, the Aukrust model provided an explanation of Norwegian price changes superior to the demand-oriented alternatives of the quantity theory and the Phillips curve.[3]

Data on the development of incomes in the exposed and sheltered

3. See William H. Branson and Johan Myhrman, "Inflation in Open Economies: Supply-determined vs. Demand-determined Models," *European Economic Review*, vol. 7 (January 1976), pp. 15–34. On the basis of their empirical analysis for Norway and Sweden the authors conclude that market-demand forces are important in determining price changes unless the demand side is rendered passive through an accommodating macroeconomic policy. Not only did the Aukrust model outperform the alternatives, but the presence of an accommodating demand policy seemed descriptive of Norway; there was negligible variance, for example, in the time series data on the gross domestic product gap.

sectors during the period preceding the formulation of the Aukrust model are consistent with the main results of the model. Table 4-1 contains data on the growth of real income for 1951–76 and for various subperiods. Beginning with the column for 1951–65, the most striking feature of the data is the close similarity in income growth for all groups except entrepreneurial income in exposed industries. The similarities in the various categories of earnings are predicted by the Aukrust formulation. The negative growth rate of entrepreneurial income in the exposed sector, reflecting primarily the experience of export industries, indicates a general tendency throughout the period for costs to increase more rapidly than productivity and world prices, with a consequent squeeze on profits. A review of income development in individual subperiods into the 1970s confirms the prediction of the Aukrust model that the development of entrepreneurial income is more volatile in the exposed sector than in the sheltered sector. The greater interperiod stability of wage income and negative average growth of entrepreneurial income in the exposed sector, moreover, indicate that most fluctuations in international prices or growth in productivity in the exposed sector were more likely to be absorbed by industry than by the collective bargaining institutions.[4]

A somewhat different perspective on the Aukrust relationships—one that emphasizes economic tensions that may be attributable to domestic factors—is offered by the data for the exposed sector in table 4-2. In equilibrium, nominal labor costs in exposed industries will follow the "room" given by the sector's productivity growth and world prices, leaving profits normal and functional shares undisturbed. On the average this is exactly what happened during the 1960s. In fact, wage increases fell short of the room by almost the exact amount of increased nonwage labor costs, such as legislated contributions to social security. During the 1970s increases in average wages and labor costs exceeded the equilibrium rate given by developments in productivity and international prices, with the consequent reduction in entrepreneurial incomes in exposed industries documented in table 4-1. Thus, although the Aukrust model describes a long-run tendency, substantial disequilibrium can be the result when labor costs deviate from their "assigned" path.

---

4. Aukrust notes that the relation between wages and profits in the export industries "is certainly not a relation that holds on a year-to-year basis. At best, it is valid only as a long-term tendency and even so only with considerable slack." Aukrust, "Inflation in the Open Economy," p. 114.

Table 4-2. *Prices, Labor Productivity, Wages, and Labor Costs in the Exposed Industries, Norway, Selected Periods, 1961–76*

Average annual percentage rate of change

Period	Prices[a]	Productivity[b]	"Room"[c]	Wages[d]	Labor costs[e]
1961–70	3.0	5.5	8.5	7.5	8.4
1970–76	6.7	5.6	12.3	13.7	14.4

Source: Computed from unpublished data on the national accounts provided by the Norwegian Central Bureau of Statistics.

a. Deflator for gross domestic product.
b. Gross domestic product in constant prices divided by man-years worked by employees.
c. The sum of the price change plus the productivity change.
d. Wages per man-year.
e. Wages plus nonwage labor costs per man-year.

The sources of the disequilibrium are domestic. During most of the period under study, cost pressures were determined to a large extent by generally uncoordinated decisions in the collective bargaining and legislative processes that establish the path of negotiated wages, taxes, and other charges to employers. When domestic factors are the source of important short-run disturbances, there may be a case for a consensus approach to incomes policy in an open economy.

When the inflationary process is reasonably well described by the Aukrust mechanism, there is a place for a "real" incomes policy, but not for a nominal policy. (See chapter 1 for a discussion of the distinction.) In the long run, under a system of fixed exchange rates, the model predicts that prices in an open economy must follow international prices, so the case for an incomes policy cannot be based on achieving a shift in an inflation-unemployment relation. The function of an incomes policy would instead be to minimize fluctuations in the cost pressures facing exposed industries and to minimize the tendency toward a profit squeeze, a lack of competitiveness, and unemployment in the exposed sector caused in part by a lack of coordination in the making of decisions that affect various aspects of costs. Given the objective of influencing real factors through incomes policy, it is unlikely that any simple guidelines—one based on trends in productivity, for example—will be appropriate. The general goals with respect to prices and income distribution, moreover, may, with given exchange rates, be incompatible.[5]

It would be misleading, however, to suggest that negotiated wages were the only factor in short-run fluctuations in domestic costs and

5. See the discussion in Aukrust, "Inflation in the Open Economy," pp. 124–26.

prices or that collective bargaining was the only source of wage pressures during this period. Given the accommodating nature of monetary and fiscal policy, the economy showed only minor fluctuations around a rather steady growth trend, and Norway did not share in the recession that befell most European countries in the early 1970s. Demand pressure in labor markets contributed to the growth of wages through wage drift (see table 4-3, below). There was also a significant acceleration of the rate of increase in consumer prices, from 3.1 percent in 1969 to 10.6 percent in 1970, which was associated with the introduction of a value-added tax (VAT) on January 1, 1970.[6] This occurred at a time when demand pressures in the economy were intense, and it initiated an inflationary impetus that lasted for several years, propelled in part by periods of price control that will be discussed later.

For the 1970s generally, it is also noteworthy that a larger portion of consumer price movements can be traced to the direct effects of government actions on costs. These actions include the introduction of the VAT, increases in publicly regulated prices, and increases in employers' contributions to social security.[7]

Increasing Labor Costs and International Competitiveness

In order to grasp the scope of an incomes policy and the limitations on it, it is useful to decompose the total change in hourly labor costs into changes attributable to negotiated wage rates, wage drift, and social costs (see table 4-3). When this has been done, the limitations of traditionally designed incomes policies, which are focused on the determination of negotiated rates, become apparent. On the average, increases in negotiated rates made up less than 40 percent of the total increase in Norwegian labor costs during the 1970s. The proportionate importance was much less during the early years of the decade, but it accelerated with the inflation and the decentralized negotiations over two-year agreements in 1974. The remaining increases in labor costs are from wage drift and rising nonwage employment costs. Although wage drift averaged about 3.25 percent a year during the 1960s, it increased with

6. Norges Offentlige Utredninger (NOU), *Om Prisproblemene* [On the price problem], NOU 1973:36 (Oslo: Universitetsforlaget, 1973), p. 43.

7. For example, between 1969 and 1972 employers' contributions were raised from approximately 10 percent to about 16 percent of the wage bill. OECD Economic Surveys, *Norway*, January 1973, p. 18.

Table 4-3. *Decomposition of Increases in Hourly Labor Costs for Adult Industrial Workers, Norway, 1971–77*
Percentage change from preceding year

Wage costs	1971	1972	1973	1974	1975	1976	1977	Average
Total	14.4	10.7	13.2	17.8	19.5	15.6	11.1	14.6
Negotiated rates	3.4	3.0	6.7	9.9	8.6	3.5	5.5	
	(23.6)	(28.0)	(27.3)	(37.6)	(50.8)	(55.1)	(31.5)	(37.7)
Wage drift	6.4	3.8	4.4	6.0	4.7	3.7	4.7	4.8
	(44.4)	(35.5)	(33.3)	(33.7)	(24.1)	(23.7)	(42.3)	(32.9)
Social costs[a]	4.6	3.9	5.2	5.2	4.9	3.3	2.9	4.3
	(31.9)	(36.4)	(39.4)	(29.2)	(25.1)	(21.2)	(26.1)	(29.5)

Source: NOU, *Om grunnlaget for inntektsoppgjørene, 1977*, p. 19. Figures in parentheses are the percentage changes in the total cost of labor.
a. Includes payments for holidays, vacations, and health insurance premiums.

increasing demand pressure to a peak in the early 1970s. The determination of wage drift is an inherently decentralized process, however, and remains outside the direct control of most labor agreements, which basically specify changes in minimum rates. Nonwage employment costs are mandated by legislation and were a particularly important source of Norwegian wage inflation during the 1970s. Yet under traditional wage policies involving the review of bilateral collective bargaining outcomes, there was no mechanism for including the development of social costs within the scope of an incomes policy.

The concern with increases in labor costs arose particularly because of the marked deterioration in the competitiveness of Norwegian products on international markets. Although the current account was in deficit throughout the 1970s, the size of the deficit has grown particularly fast since 1972. Between 1972 and 1977 the trade-weighted average of imported manufactured goods rose 35 percent in Norwegian markets while total Norwegian exports increased only 2.5 percent. (The average increase in exports in ten countries of the Organisation for Economic Co-operation and Development [OECD] during the same period was 22 percent.) There were significant losses of the home market to foreign producers of manufactured products as the share of Norwegian industry in the domestic market fell from 67 percent in 1967 to 57 percent in 1977.[8]

Norwegian unit labor costs accelerated from a combination of increases in labor costs (see table 4-3) and a sharp deceleration in the growth of productivity beginning in mid 1974. Indeed, by 1977 output

8. OECD Economic Surveys, *Norway*, December 1978, p. 19.

per hour in Norwegian manufacturing industry had barely returned to its 1974 level. The particular timing of the slump in productivity is traceable to the onset of an "industrial policy" consisting of a program of subsidies and loans to companies facing economic difficulties. The policy drew the following assessment from the OECD:

From the start of the international recession in 1974–1975 up to the end of 1977 it has been the aim of the authorities to offset as much as possible of the deflationary impact emanating from abroad, partly through selective support to threatened industries. In practice the industrial policy pursued has aimed at maintaining employment in individual enterprises at a high level. . . . With a few exceptions, the subsidies and loans granted were not conditional on steps being taken by the enterprise concerned towards rationalisation, product development or structural change. The support measures may therefore have had the effect of delaying adjustment, and have probably served to maintain a relatively tight labor market with low geographical or occupational mobility.[9]

The net effect of the changes in labor costs, labor productivity, and exchange rates on relative unit labor costs is shown in figure 4-1. Clearly, the overall relative labor-cost position of Norway deteriorated sharply during the 1970s. In relation to those of other countries, Norwegian unit labor costs, including the effects of changes in exchange rates, increased 27 percent between 1970 and 1977. Broader measures of cost provide parallel observations on Norway's declining international competitiveness.[10] Some of the deterioration, however, is attributable to changes in exchange rates, as is clear from a comparison of figure 4-1 with figure 4-2, which illustrates the development of labor costs in local currency units. Cost pressures from collective bargaining and legislation, therefore, are not in all instances the main sources of changing relative costs.

The Influence of Oil and Gas Discoveries

The context of Norwegian incomes policy discussions was significantly influenced by the discovery of important oil deposits in the North Sea and by the policy decisions of the Norwegian government concerning the exploitation of the deposits. The discoveries provoked a fear that rapid depletion of the oil reserves would cause serious disruption of the

9. Ibid., p. 24. A similar, although less drastic, deceleration of the growth of productivity occurred in Sweden during large-scale public investments in industrial policy.

10. See "The International Competitiveness of Selected OECD Countries," *OECD Economic Outlook, Occasional Studies* (Paris: OECD, July 1978), pp. 35–52.

164 NORWAY

Figure 4-1. *Unit Labor Costs in Industry in Selected Countries of the OECD, Adjusted for Changes in Rates of Exchange, 1970–76*

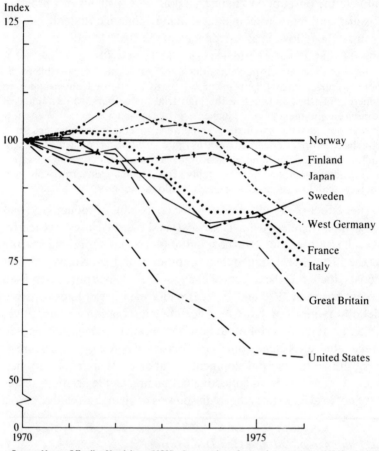

Source: Norges Offentlige Utredninger (NOU), *Om grunnlaget for inntektsoppgjørene, 1977* [On the background for income settlements, 1977], NOU 1977:17 (Oslo: Universitetsforlaget, 1977), p. 45.

Norwegian industrial structure and of macroeconomic policy.[11] In 1974, therefore, before production was initiated on a large scale in the offshore oil fields, the government decided to limit future oil production to a maximum of about 90 million metric ton equivalents (Mtoe) a year. Even this rate was expected to yield huge balance-of-payments surpluses by

11. The OECD noted, for example: "The disruptions could result from an appreciating exchange rate as oil exports rose and the balance of payments improved and/or from a process of inflation and loss of competitiveness if higher oil revenues led to stronger domestic demand." OECD Economic Surveys, *Norway*, January 1980, p. 47.

Figure 4-2. *Unit Labor Costs in Industry in Selected Countries of the OECD, in Local Currency Units, 1970–76*

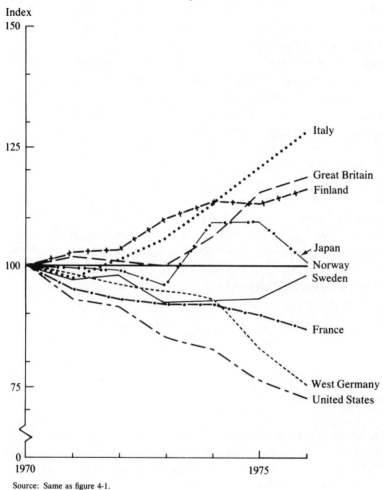

Index

Italy

Great Britain
Finland

Japan
Norway
Sweden

France

West Germany
United States

1970

1975

Source: Same as figure 4-1.

the end of the 1970s. In view of the prospective surpluses from oil revenues, the government was less inclined to treat balance-of-payments deficits during the mid 1970s as significant constraints on economic policy. At the same time, the government attempted to maintain full employment by relying upon traditional demand-management tools and, when faced with a decline in export demand associated with the world recession that followed the oil shocks administered by the Organization of Petroleum Exporting Countries (OPEC), the system of temporary subsidies to individual companies. The effects of imported inflation, moreover, were to be countered by revaluations of the Norwegian krone. Within this general framework, incomes policy was assigned the function of achieving the wage restraint necessary to improve the international competitiveness of Norwegian exports.

So long as the assumptions concerning the future path of oil revenues were tenable, the government had reasonable room in which to maneuver with incomes policy and budgetary policies. Increases in real incomes and consumption that contributed to balance-of-payments deficits could be regarded as advances on the benefits of future oil revenues. By the late 1970s, however, it had become clear that earlier forecasts of future oil revenues had been exaggerated. By 1979 oil output had reached about 40 Mtoe rather than the 90 Mtoe that the authorities had anticipated would be a binding constraint.[12] The retarded growth in oil revenues, along with the world recession, which cut back export demand, produced a sharp balance-of-payments deficit in the very period when substantial surpluses had been expected. The 1977 current-account deficit amounted to 14 percent of gross domestic product (GDP) "instead of the surplus of 7–8 percent expected earlier."[13] These developments led to a radically different approach to incomes policy in late 1978, which will be discussed later.

Institutional Framework for Norwegian Income Determination

The ultimate effects of macroeconomic policies on output and employment depend in part on the nature of the institutional structure of wage and price determination. Of particular importance to macroeconomic adjustment are institutional characteristics that influence the magnitude of wage and price changes in the domestic economy, given underlying real conditions, and the flexibility of wages and prices in response to an external stimulus. We shall attempt to limit our discussion here to features of the Norwegian institutional framework that bear on these issues.

12. Ibid., p. 42.
13. Ibid., p. 47.

Centralized Collective Bargaining Institutions

Beginning with the Norwegian collective bargaining institutions, the dominant characteristic is the centralization of wage determination. Approximately 60 percent of the workers are organized into thirty-seven national unions, organized along industrial lines. These in turn are affiliated with the Landsorganisasjonen i Norge (LO), the Norwegian Federation of Trade Unions, which in most postwar years has had primary responsibility for collective bargaining. Although the LO is the only labor federation, there are a number of largely white-collar unions, representing engineers, shipmasters and mates, and employees in federal and local government, banks, and insurance companies, that are not affiliated with the LO, and a group of LO affiliates in the federal government sector that are represented in collective negotiations by a special association. Nevertheless, fragmentation at the union federation level is not as institutionalized as in Sweden, for example, where conflict between the wage and salary objectives of different labor federations became a destabilizing force in wage determination during the 1970s.

On the employer side, some 8,900 firms, divided into national associations along industry or trade lines, are affiliated with the Norsk Arbeidsgiverforening (NAF), the Norwegian Employers Association. The largest of these associations, such as those covering metal products, contractors, and the pulp and paper industry, join with the central NAF staff in wage negotiations. Although there are also a few employer associations that remain outside the NAF, they do not present an important independent force in collective bargaining.[14] As in Sweden, the federation has strong constitutional authority over the employer side of the collective process. Members of the NAF may not negotiate individually with unions, and the federation can authorize and enforce lockouts.

In principle, the centralization of collective bargaining arrangements can contribute to macroeconomic stability by eliminating the highly imitative and uncoordinated settlements that can emerge from decen-

14. The actual influence of agreements between the NAF and the LO extends beyond organized firms. The extension of terms is automatic for federal government employees, and workers in nonunion firms in the private sector usually obtain increases equivalent to those specified in collective bargaining agreements.

tralized negotiations. When negotiations are spread in time, efforts to maintain a fixed relative wage with respect to other industries or to follow a general wage pattern can contribute to wage inertia in the face of changing external conditions. When there is disagreement over distributional objectives, and hence over "appropriate" wage relationships, decentralized negotiations can also cause explosive wage increases. During the period under study there has been a continuing disagreement between the leaders of the LO and several of the affiliated unions over the appropriate level for collective bargaining negotiations, the pressure for decentralized negotiations coming largely from left-wing members. These unions have argued that decentralized negotiations facilitate the negotiation of larger wage increases. In 1961, and again in 1974, the LO agreed to decentralize negotiations, and the subsequent bargaining was characterized by abnormally intense conflict and wage pressure (see table 4-4).[15] These results, however, may be explained in part by the fact that labor-market pressure was unusually high in each of these years and that there was considerable imported inflation in 1974.

During years of centralized negotiations the LO and the NAF established the guidelines with respect to the principal issues covered by the agreement: the general wage increases, the parameters of the indexation clause, and a solidarity policy of narrowing skill differentials. Each union and each employer association affiliated with the LO or the NAF—about 300 in number—must then revise its agreement in accordance with the national frame agreement. (Separate negotiations covering government employees are always centralized and may in principle differ from the national economic frame agreement established in negotiations between the LO and the NAF.)

If the two parties to collective bargaining are unable to reach agreement, government authorities can block an incipient strike or lockout until the mediation procedures provided for by the Labor Disputes Act

15. When negotiations are centralized, all members of the LO vote on ratification of a draft agreement. When negotiations are decentralized, however, only those union members covered by a particular agreement, usually at the industry level, take part in the vote, and the chance of a strike is greater. Decentralized negotiations also appear to produce pattern-setting wage behavior. Norwegian union membership is highly concentrated, 75 percent of the members of the LO belonging to the ten largest unions. In 1974, the four largest were the unions of ironworkers and metalworkers, municipal employees, building industry workers, and commercial and office employees. The metalworkers' contract tends to set the pattern when negotiations are decentralized to the industry level.

Table 4-4. *Bargaining Level, Wage Inflation, and Strike Activity, Norway, Selected Years, 1961–74*

Year of negotiation	Percent change in hourly earnings of males	Man-days lost through strikes (thousands)
1961[a]	10.0	355
1963	5.4	225
1964[b]	8.3	0
1966[c]	9.0	1
1968	12.1[d]	0
1970	15.3	24
1972	9.0	0
1974[a]	24.8	308

Source: Lars Aarvig, "Incomes Policy in Norway" (Oslo: Norwegian Employers Confederation, June 8, 1976), pp. 3–4.

a. Decentralized negotiations at the industry and branch levels. Negotiations in all other years were centralized (nationwide) with some decentralized adaptation.

b. Settled by binding arbitration.

c. Settled by binding arbitration after union members failed to ratify a proposed settlement.

d. About a third of the increase is compensation for shorter working hours.

have been exhausted. Proposals worked out by the state mediator must be ratified by a vote of union members. Virtually all recent centralized bargains have been negotiated with the assistance of mediation. If a serious strike or lockout threatens, the government also has the authority to use compulsory arbitration.[16]

The duration of collective bargaining agreements and the extent to which the wage provisions of contracts are contingent upon external economic events also influence the degree of wage inertia in an economy. As can be seen from table 4-4, the basic Norwegian collective agreements normally run for two years. Further flexibility, however, is usually provided by interim negotiations conducted in the middle of the contract period to specify the adjustment of money wages to prices during the second year of the contract. Although the indexation of wages to prices has a long history in Norwegian collective bargaining agreements, the actual indexation arrangements are less rigid than those observed in other countries and are adjusted from time to time in the central negotiations. Specific cost-of-living adjustments generally do not apply during the first year of the agreement. The most common arrangement governing the second year of the labor contract during the period

16. Because this authority has been exercised infrequently, it does not appear to have increased the probability that an impasse will develop, as has happened in some arbitration-of-interest situations.

under study is "semiautomatic" indexation, whereby negotiations over the parameters of subsequent cost-of-living adjustments can be reopened after the first year of a contract if the consumer price increase exceeds some threshold.[17] Under traditional bilateral negotiations the Norwegian indexation arrangements usually provided compensation for 60–70 percent of cost-of-living increases. More recent multilateral negotiations have provided for compensation of about 45 percent of the changes in the consumer price index (CPI).[18]

The Norwegian system of indexation thus contains certain institutionally determined lags in the adjustment of wages to prices. There is a lag in the required adjustment of wages, for since 1968 the indexation adjustments have been made once a year. When an adjustment is made it provides partial compensation for price increases. Although it is not entirely clear why the labor movement has accepted all aspects of the indexation system, the arrangement has probably reduced the element of inertia in Norwegian wage changes and, through its flexibility, has facilitated recent bargaining with the government over incomes policies. (This presents a stark contrast to the effects of the considerably more rigid system of wage indexation discussed in the chapter on Denmark.)

The potential conflict between price and distributional objectives referred to in the preceding section reflects in part the fact that negotiations over the determination of income extend well beyond standard collective bargaining arrangements in Norway. Given the location and topography of the country, agriculture, forestry, and fisheries have constituted a relatively large share of the economy and an important element of support for Social Democratic governments. These industries have historically been strongly organized into marketing cooperatives

17. If either party refuses to negotiate over indexation, the contract can legally be dissolved upon one month's notice. See Herbert Dorfman, *Labour Relations in Norway*, rev. ed. (Oslo: Norwegian Joint Committee on International Social Policy, 1975), p. 79.

18. Indexation agreements in most instances specify that wages will be adjusted at a rate of x öre an hour per CPI point, a formula that tends to narrow skill differentials. Unlike indexation systems in Denmark, Sweden, and the Netherlands, wage adjustments are based on movements in the full CPI rather than an index net of the effects of subsidies and indirect taxes. This has permitted the government to attempt on occasion to seek restraint of money wages by increasing subsidies on food and other products. It has also meant that indexation bargaining in Norway has been restricted to the parameters of the indexation system rather than bargaining over the appropriate price index to use in determining wage increases. (See the chapters on Italy and the Netherlands for examples of the latter.) See OECD Economic Surveys, *Norway*, January 1965, pp. 15–16.

of producers, and during the postwar period, producer organizations in these sectors have regularly bargained with the government over their incomes through negotiations over the prices of farm products and the size and conditions of government subsidies to each sector.[19] The government, moreover, has adopted a policy of gradually raising agricultural incomes to the level of workers in manufacturing. Since these negotiations ultimately affect key elements of the consumer price index, which in turn influences wage increases through indexation arrangements, the potential role of the government and of consensus institutions is great.

Development of Incomes Policy Institutions

Nevertheless, while the government initiated several institutional changes to coordinate negotiations and improve the economic information available to negotiators, its movement toward a formal "consensus" in the form of multilateral bargaining arrangements was gradual and was not fully realized until the mid 1970s. Before the 1970s, direct government involvement in wage negotiations was resisted by both the LO and the NAF. The LO, however, was inclined to support less far-reaching institutional changes proposed by the Social Democratic party, which held political power in Norway from 1936 to 1965. The first of these, begun in 1956, was better coordination in the timing of the various negotiations in the primary sectors to avoid potentially explosive income competition among the economic interest groups and to permit each group to negotiate with similar economic expectations. The government also encouraged the centralization of collective wage negotiations for similar reasons.

Following a sharp acceleration of prices in 1962, the government established the Contact Committee, presided over by the prime minister and consisting of the ministers of finance, of consumer affairs, of agricultural affairs, and of fisheries, and representatives of the LO, the NAF, the Farmers' Union, the Fisherman's Union, and the Union of Smallholders and Farmers. The Contact Committee, which was the center of Norwegian incomes policy discussions for a decade, was similar in purpose to the concerted-action discussions in Germany. Until

19. The central government negotiates with the Fisherman's Union, the Farmers' Union, and the Union of Smallholders and Farmers.

1974, the purpose of the committee was to exchange information on income objectives in advance of the bilateral income negotiations and to discuss economic forecasts, the assumptions on which those forecasts were based, and the implications of the forecasts for income growth. The committee had no review authority over the ultimate outcome of wage and price negotiations.

With the advent of the conservative government in 1965 came a series of efforts to develop a more formal approach to incomes policy, although none of the efforts or proposals reached the degree of stringency (in the form of controls or guidelines) observed in incomes policies adopted in most other countries. The first action was to create a committee of three prominent, nonpartisan economists, with Odd Aukrust, the research director of the Central Bureau of Statistics, as chairman, which formulated a model in which the implications of alternative wage settlements for prices and income shares could be studied. The result of this committee's work was the short-run version of the two-sector "Scandinavian" model of wage inflation in an open economy discussed in chapter 1. This represented a considerable advance in the analysis of international transmission of inflation, but the immediate interest within Norway was in the implications of the model for the room for wage increases in collective bargaining. From the perspective of the biennial wage negotiations, the model enabled analysts who began with the prognosis for the rate of growth of labor productivity and world prices to trace the implications of alternative wage settlements for domestic price inflation and income shares. It was hoped that this exercise in itself would contribute to greater agreement over the "appropriate" scale of wage increases.

The government wished to present an analysis based on this model before each round of negotiations. With so much riding on the assumptions and the outcome of a fairly technical economic analysis, the employer and labor organizations asked to participate. The government regarded their participation as a way of narrowing disputes over the economic context of negotiations and changed the original committee to include representatives of the negotiating parties, the corresponding ministries, and the same neutral chairman, Aukrust. The reconstituted committee is known as the Technical Reporting Committee on the Income Settlement (TRC; also known in English as "Technical Calculating Committee" or "Technical Expert Group") and has been an important element in the consensus institutions for more than ten years.

The operation of the TRC presents an interesting contrast to the consensus institutions in Austria, where technical analysis by professional economists is minimized. Committee members do not dispute the structure or mechanisms implied by the Aukrust model, which forms the technical basis of their computations. To the extent that disagreement occurs between members of the LO and the NAF, it is likely to be over the forecasts for growth in productivity and world prices that are provided by the Central Bureau of Statistics and the Ministry of Finance. The NAF forecasts, which are based on information received from affiliates of the NAF, at times differ from the forecasts of government agencies. At this point a certain amount of bargaining may enter into the forecasting process, and on rare occasions reports are issued with the reservations of individual members noted. Nevertheless, as an institution of consensus the TRC appears to have been effective in providing an agreed economic base for collective negotiations and in eliminating the sort of suspicion of government economic forecasts that has surfaced in the course of incomes policy experiments in other countries.

Pressures for Multilateral Income Determination

Although the Norwegian government has moved toward greater coordination of income determination with economic policy in order to pursue the economic policy goals discussed in the introduction to this chapter, the shift to a consensus or multilateral bargaining format in 1973 can be traced to three interrelated elements: the failure of experiments with direct price controls to provide a long-run reduction in the rate of inflation and the consequent emphasis on the restraint of the underlying cost pressures; the nature of the distributional conflicts underlying the wage inflation process; and the contribution of government policy actions to the acceleration of cost pressures and price inflation in the early 1970s.

Price Controls

Aside from the regular negotiations with the agricultural and fishing organizations, the Norwegian government made no direct intervention against price formation from the mid 1950s until 1969. With growing demand pressures, the introduction of a value-added tax scheduled for January 1, 1970, and an upward drift in prices already under way, the government in September 1969 imposed "a temporary prohibition of any rises in producer fixed prices and a price stop for certain durable consumer goods" in order to "counteract price hikes in anticipation of the tax changes."[20] The freeze apparently accomplished its main objective of preventing a widening of profit margins and was abolished in 1970.[21] Inflation immediately accelerated in subsequent months, and a freeze was again imposed on November 20, 1970. The freeze was enforced strictly until the summer of 1971, when a series of exceptions was granted. On November 15, 1971, the freeze was discontinued because in the view of the government the action would favor "the negotiation of responsible wage increases in the Spring of 1972."[22] (This may have been influenced by an unusual clause in the collective bargaining agreement between the LO and the NAF that apparently protects NAF members against a profit squeeze from increasing labor costs during a price freeze. The clause provides that the NAF accept only negotiated increases in money wages that can be passed on as price increases; otherwise negotiations may be reopened.) Following a further acceleration in prices, a comprehensive price freeze was introduced on September 7, 1972, but was gradually relaxed, then abolished on January 1, 1973.

The behavior of consumer and wholesale prices during the period is traced in figure 4-3. Prices appear to follow a fairly conventional path, the rate of increase declining during at least the first two freeze periods and accelerating with the removal of the regulations. The Norwegian government's own evaluation of the succession of price freezes concedes that they simply postponed the adjustment of prices to cost pressures that developed in 1970 with the implementation of the VAT during a period of rising import prices and an expansive fiscal policy.[23] With the failure of direct price controls in the early 1970s policy attention shifted to elements of cost pressure that were in principle susceptible to government influence—wages, taxes, and employer contributions.

20. Royal Norwegian Ministry of Finance, *The National Budget of Norway, 1970* (Oslo, 1969), p. 7.

21. According to the OECD, "excluding the mechanical impact of VAT estimated at 5.8 per cent, the annual rate of increase of consumer prices was reduced to 2 per cent, suggesting that at least a part of the initial rise in indirect taxation had been absorbed by profit margins." OECD Economic Surveys, *Norway*, January 1973, p. 7.

22. Royal Norwegian Ministry of Finance, *The National Budget of Norway, 1972*, p. 53.

23. For an official discussion, see *The National Budget of Norway, 1973*, p. 67.

Figure 4-3. *Percentage Changes from Preceding Quarter
in Consumer Prices and Wholesale Prices, Norway, 1969–73*

Percentage change

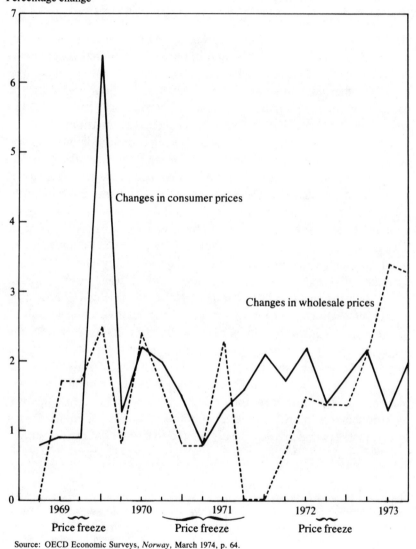

Source: OECD Economic Surveys, *Norway*, March 1974, p. 64.

Distributional Conflicts

The redistribution of income and wealth has received considerable emphasis as a policy objective in Norway. On the other hand, fundamental disagreements over the appropriate distributional goals apparently remain, for most direct efforts to achieve redistributional objectives have become independent sources of inflationary pressure. With the passage of time, the failure to achieve certain goals has forced the government to reconsider the methods of securing redistribution.

REDISTRIBUTION THROUGH COLLECTIVE BARGAINING. For most of the postwar period, considerable emphasis has been placed on the "solidaristic" wage policy of the trade unions in collective bargaining negotiations. As in Sweden and Denmark, the policy amounts to an effort to narrow the wage structure (largely skill and sex differentials) by negotiating relatively large wage increases for low-wage workers. Yet one of the most consistent findings in studies of Norwegian wage determination is that although the central negotiations unquestionably narrow the wage structure that existed before the negotiations, wage drift tends to reestablish the original differentials.[24] None of the studies, however, arrives at a conclusive interpretation of the relative contribution of market and institutional forces to these findings. If, for example, the wage structure is originally in equilibrium, given the skill structure of supply and demand, then the solidaristic policy will yield a disequilibrium wage structure, and wage drift will simply reestablish equilibrium—in response to skill shortages, for example. Alternatively, the compensatory movements in drift may reflect notions of fairness or equity among skilled workers that are not closely related to market patterns of supply and demand.

24. In a 1969 study by Professor Tor Rødseth, commissioned by the Norwegian Ministry of Wages and Prices, no significant tendency toward the equalization of labor incomes during the preceding ten to fifteen years was found; this was attributed to the fact that wage drift was largest for highly paid workers. The conclusions of the study are discussed in Royal Norwegian Ministry of Finance, *The National Budget of Norway, 1970*, p. 54. Subsequently, in an extensive official study of wage drift by a commission including economists from the government, the LO, and the NAF, similar factual conclusions were reached. See NOU, *Om Lönnsglidningen* [On wage drift], NOU 1977:26 (Oslo: Universitetsforlaget, 1977), p. 46. For evidence on the relation between wage differentials and the timing of collective bargaining negotiations, see OECD Economic Surveys, *Norway*, 1973, pp. 16–17.

Whatever the exact interpretation, the solidaristic policy has become an independent source of wage inflation. In an econometric study by the OECD the relation between redistributional efforts and subsequent wage inflation was documented.[25] After estimating separate models for negotiated wage changes and wage drift, the OECD concluded that "egalitarian wage policies were found to push up both contractual wage increases and wage drift, on average contributing more than 10 per cent to the total rise in wages" during the period 1954–73.[26]

Whichever interpretation of the relation between relative wages and drift is correct, the compensatory behavior of drift renders collective bargaining a relatively ineffective tool for achieving the redistribution of labor incomes. Exclusive reliance on collective bargaining, moreover, would overlook the question of transfers between the economically active and inactive segments of the population. By late 1969 the government noted publicly that "it would seem necessary to take into use other instruments than previously for facilitating the solution of the low-wage problem."[27]

GOVERNMENT DISTRIBUTION POLICY. In fact, the government had begun a major expansion in transfer programs during the mid 1960s. In particular, with the introduction of the National Insurance Scheme at the beginning of 1967, the basic income allowance to pensioners was increased substantially and was subsequently adjusted for price increases. At the same time, children's allowances, financial aid to students, and certain price subsidies were also increased. These adjustments were particularly large in 1970 as a result of changes in the tax system (see table 4-5). Beginning with the introduction of the National Insurance Scheme, the increase in transfers substantially exceeded the increase in earned income (see table 4-5, columns 1, 5, and 6), thereby contributing to a significant equalization of income conditions between the economically active and inactive segments of the population. The differences in the development of real disposable income for the two groups is even more striking, since basic social insurance payments are

25. OECD Economic Surveys, *Norway*, January 1975, annex 1, pp. 41–54.
26. Ibid., p. 18. The regression for wage drift also contained the unemployment rate, the rate of change of consumer prices, and the rate of change of export prices as explanatory variables. The regression for negotiated wage changes included the marginal income tax rate and the rate of change of consumer prices as additional explanatory variables.
27. Royal Norwegian Ministry of Finance, *The National Budget of Norway, 1970*, p. 55.

Table 4-5. *Transfers from the Public Sector to Private Consumers, Norway, 1966–78*

Percentage change from preceding year

Year	Social security sector			Total transfers (4)	Hourly earnings (5)	Transfers minus earnings (6)
	Family allowances (1)	National Insurance Scheme (2)	Total (3)			
1966	7.3	13.8	10.6	11.0	8.5	2.5
1967	19.4	25.2	19.6	16.7	6.2	10.5
1968	12.6	17.7	16.2	15.1	12.1	3.0
1969	5.0	17.4	17.0	15.5	6.0	9.5
1970	225.6ᵃ	33.2	44.6	33.9	15.3	18.6
1971	0.5	25.2	21.3	21.3	9.3	12.0
1972	2.8	17.6	16.5	17.3	9.0	8.3
1973	7.2	18.1	15.8	15.9	12.2	3.7
1974	1.5	13.6	12.6	12.1	24.8	− 12.7
1975	2.3	20.5	19.0	18.2	13.2	5.0
1976	14.3	19.5	19.3	18.5	15.2	3.3
1977	2.4	5.6	6.3	5.4	. . .	. . .
1978	−0.7	15.5	14.3	13.9	. . .	. . .

Sources: Royal Norwegian Ministry of Finance, *The National Budget of Norway, 1969*, p. 64; *1970*, p. 54; *1972*, p. 51; *1975*, p. 42; and *1978*, p. 60.

a. Largely attributable to tax changes.

not taxed. The development of gross and disposable real income for a couple receiving a minimum pension and an industrial worker is graphed in figure 4-4. Adjusted for changes in consumer prices, the basic pension rate increases about three times as rapidly as industrial wages. The divergence is greater when the taxation of earned income and insurance premiums of workers, required in part to finance the transfers, are accounted for in the calculations. Indeed, from 1970 to 1972, the disposable real income of industrial workers remained virtually flat, as the retardation in the advance of real consumption in the economically active sector was achieved through increased taxation, but it then rose steeply.

In the process of increasing reliance on the budget to achieve redistribution of income, the government produced further tension between its objectives in distribution and price stability. Redistribution to the inactive population required greater taxation of the active population. Yet so long as the active population did not fully share the distributional goals and continued to bargain over disposable real incomes, money

Figure 4-4. *The Growth of Disposable Real Income Received
by a Pensioned Couple and an Industrial Worker, Norway, 1965–76*

Percent

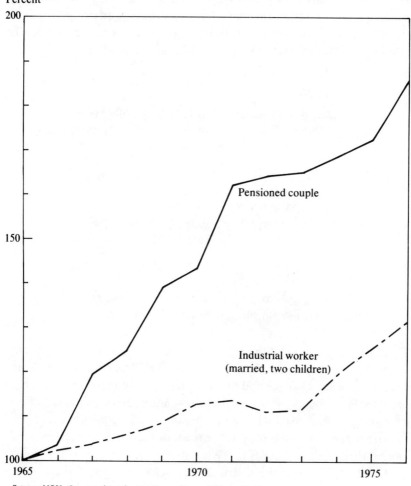

Source: NOU, *Om grunnlaget for inntektsoppgjørene, 1977*, pp. 36–37.

wages would adjust in response to changing tax rates, and wage inflation
would be the consequence of attempting to satisfy mutually incompatible
distributional goals.

As the marginal tax rate faced by the average Norwegian worker
increased substantially during the period, negotiated wages appeared to
be somewhat responsive to the tax structure. Three negotiated wage-

change regressions from the OECD study referred to earlier are reproduced below. The independent variables are identical for each (the rate of change of consumer prices lagged one quarter, $\dot{P}_{t-1}$, the change in relative wages in settlement years, $DIFF$, and the lagged marginal income tax rate, TM_{t-1}), so the only difference is for the period covered. The results are as follows (with standard deviations given in parentheses):

1954–73

$$\dot{W} = 0.40 + 0.43\dot{P}_{t-1} - 0.15DIFF + 0.028TM_{t-1}$$
$$(0.67)\quad(0.13)\qquad(0.06)\qquad\quad(0.015)$$
$$R^2 = 0.68$$

1954–63

$$\dot{W} = 0.23 + 0.78\dot{P}_{t-1} - 0.16DIFF + 0.018TM_{t-1}$$
$$(0.13)\quad(0.13)\qquad(0.05)\qquad\quad(0.010)$$
$$R^2 = 0.90$$

1964–73

$$\dot{W} = 0.46 + 0.27\dot{P}_{t-1} - 0.11DIFF + 0.060TM_{t-1}$$
$$(1.65)\quad(0.10)\qquad(0.14)\qquad\quad(0.037)$$
$$R^2 = 0.49$$

From the perspective of the relation between direct taxation and wage behavior, the important findings are the significant relation between negotiated wage changes and the marginal tax rate faced by an average industrial worker and the fact that the magnitude and significance of that relation have increased with the progressivity of the tax structure. It is also true, however, that only 1.5 percent of the 1954–73 wage increase can be attributed to changes in the tax structure.

By late 1972, both the distributional achievements of the transfer policies and their inflationary consequences were recognized, and the 1973 national budget notes that "in view of the level reached in the social benefits offered, it seems natural henceforth to favor a more equal progression in the incomes of the two population groups."[28] From this point on, discussions of proposed increases in public expenditures and of fiscal policy generally were centered on the implications for the growth of real disposable income for the working population, a development that contributed to the broadening of participation in incomes policy

28. *The National Budget of Norway, 1973*, p. 65.

institutions beyond the traditional parties to collective bargaining. The reorganization of the incomes policy institutions will be discussed in the following section.

The "Consensus" Approach to Income Determination

The acceleration of inflation in the early 1970s, despite the existence and activities of the Contact Committee, led to the appointment of a committee under the chairmanship of Hermod Skånland, deputy governor of the Norges Bank, to study the sources of the inflation process. In June 1973, the committee, consisting of representatives of the various economic interest groups, issued a report that provides an unusually coherent discussion of the intellectual case for the use of consensus institutions for the formulation of incomes policies. The case rests on the observation that the distributional conflicts underlying the inflationary process go well beyond the conflicts addressed in labor-management disputes on which more traditional incomes policy institutions focus their attention.

The Skånland Committee Report

In its analysis of policy objectives, the Skånland Committee Report notes at the outset that literal price stability is not feasible, since it would require the sacrifice of targets set for other economic objectives, such as employment, growth, and distribution.[29] The primary objective of the report is therefore to suggest methods of achieving some reduction in the rate of inflation experienced in the early 1970s. The appropriate policy approach is complicated, however, by the fact that in line with the data reviewed earlier, the committee's analysis identifies multiple causes of Norwegian inflation (including world price movements, domestic demand, distributional conflicts, and so on) and hence multiple solutions, and there are constraints on many of the policy solutions that prevent their being pursued to the point at which complete price stability would be achieved.[30]

29. This discussion draws heavily from "Fresh Approach to Prices and Incomes Policy," *Norges Bank Economic Bulletin,* vol. 44, no. 3 (September 1973), pp. 116–26.
30. In a world of generally fixed exchange rates, for example, domestic inflation in an open economy will depend importantly on world prices, as the Aukrust model demonstrated. The only way to eliminate this source of inflation would be to make

182   NORWAY

With respect to distributional conflicts, the committee's fundamental
point was that many of the most potent mechanisms for redistribution
lie beyond the control of income negotiations as traditionally constituted:

If no change takes place in taxation rules, an increase in incomes will provide
greater revenue for the public administration. Since direct income taxes are
progressive, public tax revenue will increase relatively more than private income,
and disposable income of wage earners will show a relatively smaller increase
than pre-tax income. If the public sector uses its higher revenue for purchasing
more goods and services than previously, it will absorb an increasing share of
the greater production and there will be correspondingly less room for an increase
in the private sector's purchases of goods and services. Only if the greater
revenue is used for increasing transfers or subsidies will it form the basis for an
increase in private consumption, and the economically active will normally
benefit from only part of that increase.

Because of the circumstances outlined above, the traditional view that the
wage negotiations are a question of distributing real resources between two
opposing parties is actually not true. . . .

The public sector's purchases of goods and services put limits on consumption
by the private sector. In addition, the ability of the economically active groups
to finance their own consumption is being curtailed by the transfers to the
inactive groups and by the financing of the health services which is imposed on
them through the National Insurance Scheme.[31]

The committee regarded income developments during 1970–72 as an
example of this process. Although nominal wage increases averaged
10.9 percent a year, about 60 percent of the increase was matched by
price inflation and more than 40 percent of the increase went into higher
direct taxes. Although workers attempted to increase their real earnings
through income negotiations,

the public authorities had made plans for an increase both in the inactive groups'
share of total income and in the proportion of the gross domestic product to be
used for public sector purchases of goods and services. This could be financed
through higher taxes, but then there would be no room for greater consumption
by the economically active groups. . . . The conflict had to be "solved" by price
increases.[32]

exchange rates a more flexible tool of economic policy. Norwegian membership in the
"Snake"—an alliance of eight European countries designed to stabilize the dollar value
of their currencies—from 1973 to 1978 would have precluded the degree of exchange-
rate flexibility that would be required to insulate Norwegian inflation from external
influences. In part the limitations on exchange-rate policy modify the practical price-
inflation target for Norway.
   31. "Fresh Approach to Prices and Incomes Policy," pp. 119, 121. The complexity
of distributional conflicts has also been emphasized along somewhat different lines by
Odd Aukrust. See footnote 2.
   32. Ibid., p. 120.

The report therefore argues that there is a fundamental economic conflict in modern economies between the distributional goals of the public authorities and those of the private economic interest organizations, as well as the more traditional conflicts within the latter group over distribution among participants in the labor force. As various groups pursue mutually inconsistent distributional goals, no single group is likely to attain its objective, but the process will generate inflation.

The case for a consensus is thus the case for an institution in which the distributional objectives of public authorities and private interest organizations can be reconciled, and the Skånland Committee Report proposed the establishment of such an institution as an alternative to existing Norwegian incomes policy arrangements. Specifically, the report suggested that the Contact Committee be supplanted by a Council for Prices and Incomes Policy to which the Technical Reporting Committee would report. The council, which would be somewhat larger than the Contact Committee, would be charged with negotiating guidelines for the development of wages, prices, price supports, social security payments, tax rates, and subsidies, and membership would constitute an obligation to honor the guidelines.[33]

The fundamental task of the proposed council would be the determination of the division of public and private consumption and the fiscal policies and increases in money income that the division implies. The report indicates that the future jurisdiction of the Norwegian collective bargaining institutions would be over the distribution of the (predetermined) total increase in value added between profits and wages and among groups of workers. The report acknowledges that "it would be difficult to incorporate definite obligations regarding wage drift,"[34] although as noted earlier, this is an important element of Norwegian inflation. There are at best moral sanctions against breaking the guidelines for nominal wage increases, and the report recognizes that guideline agreements may not be ratified. In these instances it suggests an accommodation by fiscal policy, subject to its review by the proposed council. This procedure would be quite consistent with the accommodating fiscal-policy stance characteristic of postwar Norway, but would also seem to dissuade the rank and file from compliance with the guidelines.

33. The Skånland Committee Report does not itself offer examples of such guidelines, but it does consider several issues in implementation, including the functions and jurisdiction of several Norwegian economic and political institutions.
34. "Fresh Approach to Prices and Incomes Policy," p. 122.

The scope of the proposed Council for Prices and Incomes Policy also raised questions concerning the jurisdictions of the executive and legislative branches of government in the formulation of the budget and economic policy. The Skånland Committee Report notes, in fact, that "the Storting may or may not sanction the guidelines" established by the council, depending on the consistency of the guidelines with long-term plans and the number of general consultations with the Storting (the Norwegian parliament) during the development of the guidelines.

Post–Skånland Committee Developments

Although much of the official reaction to the Skånland Committee Report was negative, developments during the subsequent four years indicate a widespread acceptance of both the analysis of the distributional conflicts underlying the inflationary process and the implication of the analysis that income determination should move into a multilateral forum. Some would say that the committee's fundamental ideas slipped in by the back door.

In the debate that followed issuance of the report, opposition was directed at the proposal for a formal incomes policy organization and the development of binding guidelines. Within the Skånland Committee, both the LO and the NAF supported the proposal for a Council on Prices and Incomes Policy. Although this action represented an important modification of each organization's views favoring free collective bargaining without government intervention, the proposal also appeared to increase the authority of the central federations over their constituents. The guidelines for nominal income growth would be established through multilateral negotiations in the proposed council, and while the distribution of the increase would be left to bilateral bargaining, the ultimate distribution was to be consistent with the guideline, which required central coordination. Although the implications for the bargaining structure were not discussed explicitly, the Skånland proposal appeared to offer greater institutional protection to the NAF and the LO by leaving no real place for decentralized bargaining. With the publication of the proposal, the same analysis predictably placed the constituent member unions of the LO in opposition to the proposal and brought to the surface a periodic difference of opinion between the LO and the national unions concerning the appropriate level of collective bargaining. In the end, under pressure from the left wing of its membership, which, as noted earlier, prefers the greater autonomy permitted by decentralized bargaining, the LO opposed the proposal in public.[35] Subsequently, the LO and its affiliates agreed that the 1974 wage negotiations would be decentralized to the industry level.

The government's response to the Skånland Committee Report did not appear until the spring of 1975.[36] Although sympathetic to the committee's view that future approaches to incomes policy would need a broader focus than traditional bilateral bargaining relationships, the Social Democratic government argued against a system of binding guidelines and a permanent formal institution along the lines of the proposed council on the grounds that any single guideline would be unlikely to coincide with differing opinions over the appropriate distribution of income, or changes through the years in distributional objectives. As a result, the government favored a more flexible, even an ad hoc, approach that could be adjusted to the distributional needs of a particular set of circumstances. By implication, the government did not necessarily believe that multilateral negotiations would be appropriate in each round of income determination. A majority of the Storting supported this position, although the nonsocialist minority held the NAF view that a long-run solution was needed.

In fact, the government had expanded Norwegian incomes policy in the direction suggested by the Skånland Committee—without adopting the formal structure proposed in the report—two years before its official response was announced. For the 1973 mid-contract negotiations over indexation, the government established a working group that included the main economic interest organizations to develop "a combined settlement of wages, farm product prices and Government policies. . . . Parallel to the discussion in this working group, the organizations started their bilateral negotiations on the wage regulations, based on alternative assumptions with regard to Government measures."[37] Forecasts with the Aukrust model established alternative combinations of fiscal measures and nominal wage increases that would permit a certain growth in disposable real income. With the potential function of fiscal policies

35. In addition, the labor federation opposed expanding the membership of the Contact Committee to include the Norwegian Federation of Industries and the two largest trade associations.

36. Parliamentary Report no. 82 (1974–75).

37. Lars Aarvig, "Incomes Policy in Norway" (Oslo: Norwegian Employers Confederation, June 8, 1976), p. 8. This paper provides a useful review of the coordinated incomes settlements in Norway for 1973–76.

clarified, the government proposed a "package solution" in which it would initiate anti-inflationary fiscal measures in exchange for a lower degree of price compensation in the index settlement. The government then moved to increase disposable real income by increasing subsidies and raising the minimum standard income tax deduction by 10 percent and the lower income limit for computing tax in some brackets by 11 percent; the LO and the NAF ultimately accepted an official mediator's proposal for adjustments in money wages providing compensation for 45 percent of price changes. (Previous indexation arrangements had provided 60 to 70 percent compensation.)[38]

The decision of the LO to conduct decentralized negotiations in 1974 undermined the possibility of a multilateral negotiating arrangement. Although the government sought to influence the outcome indirectly by announcing further tax relief and subsidy increases just before the negotiations, the ultimate settlements caused a wage explosion that substantially influenced the course of labor costs during the next three years (see table 4-4 and the analysis later in the chapter).[39]

The outcome of the decentralized negotiations of 1974 renewed interest in the development of consensus arrangements as a method of achieving negotiated wage restraint. A variety of factors made it easy for the government to propose and the economic interest organizations to accept multilateral bargaining arrangements. First, it was clear that under the existing structure of tax rates government tax policy provided more leverage over the growth of real income than increases in money wages. Nevertheless, reductions in the progressivity of the tax structure imply a loss in normal tax revenues that would conflict with public expenditure objectives, including a redistribution of income to the economically inactive population. In the case of Norway, the income tax reductions that would constitute the principal government contribution to a consensus agreement could be financed by current and prospective taxes and royalties from discoveries and extraction of oil in the North Sea. Without the foreseeable availability of these revenues, it is unlikely that the government would have been able to offer substantial concessions in the multilateral negotiations.[40]

38. With the loss of tax revenues the government withheld NKr 100 million of scheduled appropriations from the 1973 fiscal budget. Royal Norwegian Ministry of Finance, *The National Budget of Norway, 1974*, p. 20.

39. In the judgment of the OECD "the 1974 settlement has been the most important single factor behind the acceleration of inflation in recent years." OECD Economic Surveys, *Norway*, January 1978, p. 34.

40. More generally, the relatively high current-account deficit was not considered a

Second, the principal economic interest groups had strong incentives to participate. For the LO, participation restored the authority of the central hierarchy of the organization following the decentralized wage determination of 1974. Given the historical ties between the LO and the Social Democratic party, moreover, the labor federation was assured an important influence on the formulation of the economic objectives of the government. On the employer side, dissatisfaction with the results of traditional collective bargaining and a concern with government-determined cost pressures led to a shift in the historical opposition of the NAF to government involvement in the collective bargaining process.

In September 1975 the government members of the Technical Reporting Committee suggested that economic policies and income settlements during the following year should attempt to advance real disposable income more by limiting the growth of taxes than by use of the indexation arrangements, which would continue to generate cost pressures. The government suggested further, and the economic interest organizations ultimately agreed, that it would be easiest to achieve these objectives through a comprehensive, multilateral income settlement. This occurred first with the autumn 1975 indexation negotiations. With an expected price increase of 10 percent, the government's plan proposed an 8 percent increase in money wages to yield a 3 percent increase in real disposable earnings. Employers objected to the 80 percent compensation for price increases during a period in which the combination of international recession and cost increases caused by the decentralized settlements of the previous year was exerting a substantial squeeze on profit margins in the exposed sector. In the final agreement some of these objections were met by replacing 5 percentage points of the 8 percent nominal wage increase by fiscal measures.[41] Although the negotiated indexation formula provided only 30 percent compensation for price increases, the settlement also provided for increased family allowances, a temporary reduction in the withholding tax rate, and higher producer

---

constraint on economic policy by the Norwegian government during the mid 1970s. In early 1974, for example, the OECD was predicting a shift in the current account from a deficit of 2 percent of GDP in 1971–73 to a surplus of 7–8 percent in 1977, with revenue from oil royalties and taxes in the latter year amounting to about 13 percent of estimated 1974 tax receipts. In fact, the oil sector continued to contribute to the current-account deficit through 1977 as imports were swollen by investments in drilling equipment while the extraction and export of oil was delayed by technical problems and government policies to control the rate of exploration and exploitation. OECD Economic Surveys, *Norway,* March 1974, p. 32; ibid., January 1978, p. 6.

41. For details, see Aarvig, "Incomes Policy in Norway," pp. 10–11.

prices and state subsidies for farmers. There was also a price freeze for the last four months of 1975 to prevent price increases from offsetting wage increases. According to official estimates the settlement restrained price and cost increases by 2 percentage points more than a solution with no fiscal measures would have done.[42]

The first set of multilateral negotiations over a full contract revision occurred in the spring of 1976 within the Contact Committee, which was transformed for the purpose of this particular negotiation into a decisionmaking body. As in previous negotiations the government announced a target for the growth of disposable real income—3 percent— as well as more general objectives concerning costs, employment, and taxes. In the background, however, were certain cost pressures mandated by legislation. The standard workweek was scheduled to be reduced on April 1, 1976, from 42½ to 40 hours without loss of income. This factor alone implied a 6.25 percent wage increase. In autumn 1975, moreover, the Storting had endorsed a policy goal of gradually increasing average agricultural incomes to equality with average income in industry within six years.

In the preliminary discussions, alternative combinations of nominal increases in income and income tax changes were developed to clarify the choices available. Tripartite negotiations were focused on the relation between government measures and wage increases. Subsequently— following the procedure suggested in the Skånland Committee Report— the LO and the NAF negotiated over the distribution of the nominal wage increase, and the government conducted separate negotiations with public employees and the farmers' organizations. A general proposal by the government formed the basis for the settlements, although the assistance of the state mediator was required in the negotiations between the LO and the NAF. In the final step, the government secured the approval of the Storting for increased allowances and a reduction of income tax rates, a reduction in social charges to employers from 16.7 to 15.5 percent of wages and salaries, an extension of food subsidies, increased family allowances, and larger social security payments to increase the real disposable income of pensioners. Interestingly, there was no proposal for an indexation of the tax system—as there is in Denmark, for example. With such indexation, the government would

42. Royal Norwegian Ministry of Finance, *The National Budget of Norway, 1976,* p. 14.

lose some of its ability to trade in the tripartite negotiations over the rate and mechanisms of increases in real disposable income.

A similar accord was reached in multilateral negotiations over the midterm contract revisions in March and April 1977. After preparing the way with a slight devaluation of the krone to ease the plight of export industries, the government entered the negotiations prepared to contribute to its objective of an average increase of 2.5 percent in disposable real income in 1977 by offering income tax reductions. Employers opposed any wage increase on the grounds that the competitive position of export industries had been weakened by the growth of labor costs. The unions demanded a wage increase of 9 percent, including wage drift. (With the proposed tax reductions this was expected to yield a 2.5 percent increase in disposable real income.) With the assistance of the state mediator and a devaluation of the Norwegian krone at the beginning of April, which reduced some of the pressure on the export industries, an agreement was reached without open conflict. The agreement provided for a wage increase of 2.9 percent, which included special increases to poorly paid workers and income tax reductions. The government also reduced the employers' contribution to social security by 0.5 percent of wages in an effort to achieve agreement over the size of the wage increase. With expected wage drift, the package was projected to produce the 2.5 percent target increase in disposable real income.[43]

The Collapse of the Social Contract

The remainder of the 1970s saw a growing conflict in labor relations—parallel to developments in Denmark and Sweden—and a gradual breakdown of the consensus arrangements, as the government moved to adopt measures to resolve conflict between the LO and the NAF unilaterally. The NAF and the LO were no closer together at the beginning of the 1978 negotiations. Noting that Norwegian labor costs continued to increase more rapidly than those of Norway's principal trading partners, the NAF continued to oppose any wage increase. Wage drift accounted for about two thirds of the increase in earnings in 1977, moreover, and employers sought an agreement with the LO to bring drift under control. In a situation similar to one prevailing in Denmark, where

43. For further details on the settlement, see OECD Economic Surveys, *Norway*, January 1978, p. 34; John T. Addison, *Wage Policies and Collective Bargaining Developments in Finland, Ireland, and Norway* (Paris: OECD, 1979), p. 85.

similar demands were being introduced by employers into the central negotiations, it is doubtful that the LO had sufficient authority over the local unions to gain control over drift. In any event, the demands of the LO included compensation for groups that did not normally receive wage drift as well as a continuation of the gains in real disposable income received during 1977 and a minimum earnings guarantee for poorly paid workers. In principle, both parties continued to support the multilateral bargaining arrangements that had been used during 1975–77.

By now the government was aware that the economic forecasts for the late 1970s had been too optimistic and that the expansion of domestic demand, fueled in part by growth in real income and the government's industrial policies, had been too rapid. Domestic demand pressure had contributed to the development of labor shortages and an acceleration of wage drift. At the same time, revenues from production of oil and gas from the North Sea were well below earlier estimates, and exports continued to be depressed by Norway's growing relative cost disadvantage along with the general world recession, which was more protracted than had been expected. The strong domestic expansion was threatening the viability of Norway's traditional export and import-competing industries. As a result, the government had little to give in multilateral negotiations and argued that economic developments would not support further gains in real disposable income.

The government did not enter the negotiations directly but in February 1978 devalued the krone 8 percent within the European Snake and imposed a "temporary" price freeze. Shortly thereafter, the LO and the NAF reached an impasse and the state mediator entered the negotiations. With the failure of mediation the unions declared a general strike of 260,000 workers that was halted by a statute that referred the conflict to arbitration. The arbitration award in May 1978 provided for a 1.8 percent wage increase loaded slightly in favor of poorly paid workers. Although earnings were expected to increase 8 percent with wage drift, no advance in disposable real income was expected. Revisions in a sickness-benefit scheme, however, added about 2 percent to employer's labor costs.[44]

This settlement and subsequent increases in wage drift did little to rectify the general economic situation, and on September 12, 1978, the

44. For further details on the 1978 negotiations, see Addison, *Wage Policies*, pp. 85–86; OECD Economic Surveys, *Norway,* December 1978, pp. 14, 34–35; Norwegian Employers Confederation, "Wage Settlement in Norway by Arbitration Award" (June 2, 1978).

government, in a radical change in its approach to incomes policy, instituted a general wage freeze and extended the price freeze that had been introduced in February. The combined wage-and-price freeze was in effect through the end of 1979. With respect to wages, the freeze prevented the revision of collective bargaining agreements that normally would have been made in central negotiations during April 1979 and prevented the alteration of local agreements, which was a frequent source of wage drift. With the effect of negotiations that had not been completed when the freeze was announced and provisions from the 1978 settlement, the increase in earnings for 1979 was expected to be 4 percent—about half the 1978 increase. Since changes in import prices could be passed through into domestic prices, consumer prices were expected to increase about 4 percent during the freeze.

Policy Effects

Evaluation of the effect of Norwegian incomes policy is impeded by a methodological problem noted in the discussion of Austria: incomes policy institutions have existed throughout most of the years studied; it is thus not possible to make an informative comparison between policy-on and policy-off periods. It is clear, however, that there was a significant change in the Norwegian approach to incomes policy in 1973 with the shift to multilateral bargaining over the mixture of nominal wage increases and fiscal measures that would be used to achieve a real disposable income growth target set by the national government.

The Multilateral Negotiations

The shift toward a more overt government presence was motivated by a desire to relieve the distributional tensions underlying wage and price pressures. It is therefore worthwhile to see whether the realization of a consensus approach in the form of multilateral bargaining was associated with smaller wage and price increases than would have been predicted on the basis of prior structural relationships. The pre-1972 wage and price relations do, of course, include the effects of the incomes policy institutions of that period—the Contact Committee and the TRC—so our analysis will constitute a test for any *additional* restraint that was achieved with the shift to multilateral negotiations. Limitations in the data require an examination of the period in two stages. In the first we shall estimate the Aukrust model relations for 1956–72 and test for their stability during the period 1973–76. In this analysis we shall use data from the Norwegian national accounts for the exposed and sheltered sectors. Although the results of the analysis indicate that a closer analysis of the wage-determination process would be valuable, the national-accounts data are not further decomposed into negotiated rates, wage drift, and nonwage labor costs. In the second stage of the analysis, therefore, the stability of economywide negotiated rates and wage drift during 1973–76 is tested.

Estimates of "pure" and "amended" specifications of the Aukrust model are reported for 1956–72 in table 4-6. The amended specifications typically incorporate variables that represent potential domestic sources of inflation which are not stressed in the strict formulation of the Aukrust model, although they have been known to influence the inflationary process in some countries. One important purpose of the analysis is to examine the relative importance of external and internal factors in the inflationary process in Norway.

Inflation in an open economy is purported to begin in the export sector. For the period 1956–72, regression 1 in table 4-6 provides support for the Aukrust proposition that prices in the export sector must follow world prices, since producers in the exposed sector are price takers on world markets. The coefficient of world prices is essentially unity, as predicted, and the constant term is not statistically significant. Nevertheless, the R^2 and standard error of the regression indicate considerable variation around this average relation. The residuals from the regression indicate that most of this variation is attributable to unusually large positive deviations in 1956 (6.70) and 1970 (7.71)—the year of the large increase in the VAT—and negative deviations in 1958 (-9.74) and 1972 (-7.84). Some statements of the Aukrust mechanism imply that short-term fluctuations in domestic costs will be absorbed by firms in the exposed sector, and evidence presented in table 4-1 indicated that profit margins are more volatile in the exposed sector. The substantial variation around the pure Aukrust relation suggests the possibility that firms adjust to some cost pressures by raising prices, even in the short run, despite the jeopardy to world market shares. It is appropriate, moreover, to test the proposition contained in the model that domestic demand pressure has a negligible effect on price movements in the exposed sector. In regression 2 in table 4-6, therefore, cost variables (the rate of change of indirect taxes and the rate of change of unit labor costs) and a demand variable (the gap between actual and predicted real gross domestic products) are added.[45] The results confirm the negligible effect of domestic demand pressure and changes in unit labor costs during the period. Indirect tax changes, however, are significantly correlated with both world and Norwegian exposed-sector price changes. For the period 1956–72 the tax variable actually dominates the world price variable, suggesting that legislative actions may influence exposed-sector pricing and profit margins.[46]

The labor-cost relations of the Aukrust model are tested in regressions 3–8. In the exposed sector, labor costs must follow the room provided by the growth of world prices and productivity if world market shares are to be maintained. The collective bargaining objectives that ultimately influence wage movements in the sector are assumed to be formulated on the basis of this concept of room—that is, the maintenance of existing functional shares that it implies—rather than domestic labor-market pressure. Whatever the tendency for labor costs to follow this pattern in the long run (see table 4-2), the regression analysis indicates that it is not the primary determinant of year-to-year movements in labor costs (see regression 3, table 4-6). Although there appears to be some tendency for labor costs to follow world price changes when the components of the room are specified separately (see regression 5), the addition of the ratio of the number unemployed to job vacancies indicates that the real short-run influence is from domestic labor-market pressure (see regressions 4 and 6). This amendment erodes the price influence but improves the statistical properties of the exposed-sector labor-cost regressions. It also indicates the potential for a profit squeeze in the exposed sector when labor markets are tight, as they were until policy changes were made in late 1977 and early 1978.

Under the assumptions of the Aukrust model, labor costs in the

45. The data for indirect tax changes and real GDP gap are for the entire economy. The latter variable is the residual from the regression: $\log GDP = 10.48 + 0.045TIME$; $R^2 = 0.996$, calculated from data for 1956–76. The source is OECD, *National Accounts of OECD Countries, 1950–1979* (Paris: OECD, 1981), pp. 58–59. All other data are for the exposed sector only and were provided by the Norwegian Central Bureau of Statistics.

46. In unreported regressions estimated for each of the dependent variables in table 4-6, lagged values of the dependent variable were added to several specifications in an effort to capture the significance of expectations. The variable never attained statistical significance.

Table 4-6. Price and Wage Relations, Exposed and Sheltered Sectors, Norway, 1956–72

Regression number	Dependent variable	Constant	Independent variable					Summary statistic		
			$\dot{P}_t^w$	ULC_t^e	$\dot{T}_t$	GDPGAP		R^2	Durbin-Waton	Standard error
1	$\dot{P}^e$	0.40 (0.32)	0.98 (2.65)	...	...	...		0.32	1.84	4.19
2	$\dot{P}^e$	0.80 (0.57)	0.60 (1.50)	−0.089 (0.29)	0.91 (2.25)	67.76 (1.15)		0.55	2.08	3.79

Regression number	Dependent variable	Constant	Independent variable					Summary statistic		
			$(\dot{P}_e^w + \dot{Q}_e^t)$	U/V	$\dot{P}_{t-1}^w$	$\dot{Q}_t^e$	$\dot{L}C_t^e$	R^2	Durbin-Waton	Standard error
3	$\dot{L}C^e$	5.76 (4.01)	0.32 (1.72)	...	...	...	...	0.16	1.98	2.65
4	$\dot{L}C^e$	11.49 (5.42)	−0.026 (0.14)	−0.49 (3.20)	...	...	...	0.52	2.53	2.09
5	$\dot{L}C^e$	5.47 (4.01)	...	...	0.86 (3.52)	0.23 (1.02)	...	0.47	2.38	2.18
6	$\dot{L}C^e$	8.79 (4.37)	...	−0.31 (2.08)	0.49 (1.71)	0.11 (0.52)	...	0.61	2.97	1.96
7	$\dot{L}C^s$	2.74 (2.59)	...	...	...	...	0.70 (5.60)	0.68	2.09	1.41
8	$\dot{L}C^s$	2.83 (1.28)	...	...	...	...	0.70 (3.73)	0.68	2.08	1.46

Independent variable

			$\dot{T}_i^s$	$U\dot{L}C^s$	$\dot{L}C^s$	$\dot{Q}^s$	GDPGAP			
9	$\dot{P}^x$	1.80	0.39	0.51	...	...	...	0.87	1.95	0.82
		(3.77)	(4.71)	(6.85)						
10	$\dot{P}^x$	1.99	0.39	0.49	...	...	17.76	0.89	2.22	0.78
		(4.83)	(4.83)	(6.83)			(1.56)			
11	$\dot{P}^x$	2.14	0.37	...	0.49	−0.58	...	0.87	1.96	0.85
		(2.36)	(4.40)		(5.46)	(3.37)				
12	$\dot{P}^x$	2.48	0.37	...	0.46	−0.59	18.66	0.89	2.23	0.80
		(2.82)	(4.49)		(5.33)	(3.61)	(1.59)			

Sources: The rate of change of prices ($\dot{P}^i$), labor costs ($\dot{L}C^i$), and output per man-year ($\dot{Q}^i$) in the exposed and sheltered sectors ($i = e,s$) were computed from unpublished national-accounts data provided by the Norwegian Central Bureau of Statistics. The rate of change of world prices was computed from the index of export prices for industrial countries; International Monetary Fund, *International Financial Statistics*, 1977 supplement (May 1977), pp. 64–65. The rate of change of indirect taxes is from OECD *Economic Surveys, Norway*, January 1975, pp. 48–49. The ratio of unemployed workers to job vacancies (U/V) is from OECD, *Main Economic Indicators, 1960–79* (Paris: OECD, 1980), pp. 471–73; *GDPGAP*, actual GDP minus predicted GDP, generated as described in footnote 45; GDP data are from OECD, *National Accounts of OECD Countries, 1950–1979*, vol. 1 (Paris: OECD, 1981), pp. 58–59. Numbers in parentheses are *t*-statistics.

sheltered sector follow labor costs in the exposed sector, either because of imitation in collective bargaining or because of the operation of competitive forces. The former mechanism implies a shorter lag between wage movements in the two sectors (and a truncation in the allocative function of relative wages). The regression analysis of sheltered-sector labor costs confirms the existence of the spillover (see regression 7). Unreported regressions that lagged $\dot{L}C^e$ performed less well, suggesting the presence of important institutional elements in the spillover. Labor-market pressure beyond that already embedded in $\dot{L}C^e$, moreover, does not influence sheltered-sector labor costs (regression 8). Only the fact that the coefficient of $\dot{L}C^e$ is significantly less than unity is at variance with the Aukrust hypothesis. Given the overall structure of the regression, the coefficient implies declining relative wages in the sheltered sector when $\dot{L}C^e$ exceeds 9 percent, as it has since 1971.

The final component of the model consists of pricing in the sheltered sector, which is postulated to follow a simple cost-markup scheme. The results, reported in regressions 9–12 of table 4-6, are consistent with this view in most respects. The rates of change of both indirect taxes and unit labor costs are statistically significant, although the coefficients are significantly different from unity. Domestic market demand does not attain statistical significance as an independent determinant of sheltered-sector prices.[47]

Regressions 1, 6, 7, and 9 were used to predict values of their respective dependent variables for 1973–76, under the assumption that the 1956–72 regression structure remained stable throughout the period of multilateral bargaining and international price upheavals.[48]

Clearly the central objective of the multilateral negotiations aimed at wage restraint should be to influence the growth of labor costs in the exposed sector, since these determine labor-cost increases in the sheltered sector, which in turn influence prices in that sector through a cost-

47. Estimates of the more general form of the sheltered-sector price equation

$$\dot{P}^s = \dot{P}^w + (\dot{Q}^e - \dot{Q}^s)$$

did not yield significant results.

48. Data on indirect tax changes are not yet available for 1973–76. Only changes in unit labor costs, therefore, were used to predict sheltered-sector price changes during these years. The prediction equation, estimated on data for 1956–72, is

$$\dot{P}^s = 1.64 + 0.60 \; U\dot{L}C^s.$$
$$(2.21) \quad (5.39)$$

$R^2 = 0.66$; Durbin-Watson $= 2.02$; standard error $= 1.28$

Table 4-7. *Actual and Predicted Labor Costs and Price Changes, Norway, 1973–76*

	Exposed sector			Sheltered sector				
Year	P	A	A − P	P	P*	A	A − P	A − P*
				Labor costs				
1973	13.0	13.7	0.7	12.4	11.8	11.8	−0.5	0.1
1974	19.2	15.7	−3.5	13.8	16.2	13.0	−0.8	−3.2
1975	21.5	18.9	−2.6	16.0	17.8	17.6	1.6	−0.2
1976	15.2	12.8	−2.4	11.7	13.4	13.0	1.3	−0.4
	Standard error = 1.96				Standard error = 1.41			
				Prices				
1973	19.4	10.6	−8.8	7.6	8.7	8.6	1.0	−0.1
1974	25.7	2.3	−23.4	8.7	11.4	14.3	5.6	3.0
1975	11.9	15.1	3.2	10.5	12.3	7.0	−3.5	−5.3
1976	0.9	7.1	6.2	7.6	9.7	9.3	1.7	−0.4
	Standard error = 4.19				Standard error = 1.28			

Source: Computed from regressions 1, 6, 7, and 9 in table 4-6.

A Actual; P Predicted; P* Predicted on the assumption that labor costs in the exposed sector are equal to their forecast values.

markup process. Prices in the exposed sector, on the other hand, must follow world prices. The "consensus" arrangements of 1973–76, moreover, were not focused directly on pricing and profit-margin decisions, with the exception of negotiations over subsidies to agriculture and fishing. We shall therefore begin our analysis of 1973–76 with the determination of labor costs in the exposed sector.

Actual and predicted values of labor costs and prices are reported in table 4-7. Labor costs in the exposed sector grew less rapidly than predicted during 1974–76. Although generally consistent with the notion that the tradeoffs achieved in multilateral negotiations were associated with some restraint in nominal wage increases, the prediction errors should be assessed in the context of the standard error of the regression (1.96). The largest prediction error occurs in 1974, moreover, when the fledgling consensus approach gave way to decentralized collective bargaining. Some clues as to the nature of the structural changes behind the prediction errors for the labor-cost equations is available from a comparison of the prediction equations in table 4-6 with their counterparts estimated on the basis of data for 1956–76, as reported in table 4-8. With the addition of data for 1973–76, it is clear that the responsiveness of labor costs in the exposed sector to world price changes declined

Table 4-8. *Price and Wage Relations, Exposed and Sheltered Sectors, Norway, 1956–76*

Regression number	Dependent variable	Constant	$\dot{P}_i^w$	ULC_e	$\dot{T}_i$	GDPGAP	R^2	Durbin-Watson	Standard error
				Independent variable				*Summary statistic*	
1	$\dot{P}_e$	2.14 (1.61)	0.333 (2.02)	...	...	...	0.18	2.05	5.14
2	n.a.								

Regression number	Dependent variable	Constant	$(\dot{P}_i^w + \dot{Q}_i^e)$	U/V	$\dot{P}_{i-1}^w$	$\dot{Q}_i^e$	$\dot{L}C_i^e$	R^2	Durbin-Watson	Standard error
				Independent variable					*Summary statistic*	
3	$\dot{L}C^e$	6.69 (6.17)	0.27 (3.29)	...	...	...	...	0.36	1.59	3.28
4	$\dot{L}C^e$	11.23 (8.10)	0.14 (1.96)	-0.56 (4.03)	...	...	...	0.67	2.34	2.44
5	$\dot{L}C^e$	6.72 (6.64)	...	...	0.48 (6.76)	0.10 (0.58)	...	0.73	1.96	2.18
6	$\dot{L}C^e$	9.98 (7.81)	...	-0.35 (4.71)	-0.35 (4.71)	0.05 (0.35)	...	0.83	2.94	1.81
7	$\dot{L}C^s$	2.45 (3.23)	...	...	...	...	0.74 (9.91)	0.84	2.19	1.34
8	$\dot{L}C^s$	2.61 (1.55)	...	-0.011 (.10)	...	...	0.73 (6.07)	0.84	2.19	1.38

Sources: Same as for table 4-6. Numbers in parentheses are *t*-statistics.
n.a. Not available.

during the mid 1970s; this contributed particularly to the finding for 1974. The negative errors of prediction are also attributable to a decline in the constant term, and since this term includes the average effect of unspecified determinants of labor costs—distributional factors, for example—the decline may reflect the results of the development of a multilateral approach to income determination.

Any restraint in the growth of labor costs in the exposed sector should ultimately influence labor costs and prices in the sheltered sector. Standard predictions for labor costs in the sheltered sector that are based on *actual* changes in the exposed sector, however, will miss this element of restraint and test only for *additional* effects of consensus policy beyond those attributable to the slower growth of $\dot{L}C^e$. Therefore, separate predictions based on actual changes (P) and forecast changes (P^*) in exposed-sector labor costs are reported in table 4-7. The difference between P and P^* reflects the effect of the prediction errors for exposed-sector labor costs. With the exception of 1974, labor costs in the sheltered sector have not moved much differently from predictions based on *forecast* changes in labor costs in the exposed sector ($A - P^*$). The latter were, in fact, lower than predicted, however, and the spillover relation between the two sectors remained stable (compare regression 7 in tables 4-6 and 4-8). In 1975 and 1976, therefore, $P < P^*$ and actual increases in labor costs in the sheltered sector exceeded expectations, given the cost restraint in the exposed sector. Thus, the policy achieved no additional restraint on sheltered-sector wages beyond that transmitted through the spillover process, and even the latter tended to be canceled by autonomous developments in the sheltered sector.

Although the behavior of the Aukrust mechanism during the mid 1970s is important, given its influence on Norwegian thinking about the inflationary process, the direct objective of the multilateral bargaining experiments was to restrain negotiated wage increases by providing alternative mechanisms for advancing real incomes. Paramount among these were changes in the structure of the income tax. The policies therefore raise several issues for evaluation: whether the income tax relief was in fact translated into negotiated wage restraint; whether any negotiated wage restraint achieved in multilateral bargains is simply nullified by higher wage drift; and whether other economic consequences of the multilateral bargains influenced the subsequent behavior of negotiated wages and drift.

With regard to the first question, the intellectual and empirical foundations for a tradeoff between tax rates and negotiated wage-rate increases in Norway are provided, respectively, by the report of the Skånland Committee and the relation between tax rates and money wage changes—as examined, for example, in the OECD wage analysis reported earlier. While the Skånland Committee Report argues that negotiated wage demands were influenced by the taxation required to finance transfers to the inactive population and other government programs, the OECD analysis indicated that the influence of the tax structure was statistically significant but small in magnitude. During the period 1954–73, the twenty years preceding multilateral negotiations, changes in the income tax structure accounted for 0.6 point of the 39.1 percentage-point increase in contractual wages (or 1.5 percent of the total increase).[49] The relation between the income tax structure and negotiated wage changes, however, apparently *disappeared* during the period in which multilateral negotiations were conducted, for when the regressions reported earlier were extended to include data for 1974–77, the income-tax-structure variables were no longer significant! (It is possible that the relation was disturbed by the "wage explosion" associated with decentralized negotiations in 1974, but even if this is so, the basic point of the original OECD analysis was that there was relatively little room for wage restraint by means of manipulation of the tax structure.) Generally, the tax aspects of the multilateral bargains do not appear to have exerted a directly restraining influence on negotiated rates during the mid 1970s.

In fact, there appears to have been a significant structural change in the negotiated wage models beginning with 1974, the year of the decentralized negotiations, but continuing into 1976 and 1977. The OECD regression estimated from data for 1954–73 significantly underpredicts contractual increases in each of these years.[50] The principal structural change associated with the addition of the 1974–77 data is a heightened sensitivity of negotiated wages to price changes at a time when the acceleration of world prices was having a strong effect on inflation in Norway.[51]

A secondary but significant structural change, given the egalitarian

49. OECD Economic Surveys, *Norway,* January 1978, p. 21.

50. Ibid., p. 20.

51. The coefficient of consumer price changes increases from 0.47 to 0.83 in the contractual-rate regression with the addition of 1974–77 data, and the OECD argues that "recent developments seem to have pushed the compensation rate to 100 percent for wage drift and contractual increases combined." Ibid., pp. 21, 42.

objectives of the labor movement, was an increase in the importance of changes in skill differentials in negotiated rates. Interestingly, the multilateral bargaining arrangements had very little effect on prices except indirectly through wage restraint. (The main direct influence on prices was through government subsidy policy toward agriculture and fisheries.) In the attempt to influence prices indirectly by negotiated wage restraint, the government's main instrument for concessions, tax policy, did not have an effect of sufficient magnitude on rates to exert much leverage on prices. Furthermore, the consensus arrangements failed to control the development of wage drift.

This leads to consideration of the behavior of wage drift during the recent period of multilateral negotiations. For the period 1954–73, an OECD analysis indicates that wage drift was significantly related to labor-market pressure, domestic and export price increases, and changes in wage—or skill—differentials.[52] These regressions tracked the data for 1974–77 extremely well, and, unlike the negotiated-rate equation, they did not show a significant structural change. There was, however, an increased sensitivity of drift to changes in consumer prices and reduced sensitivity to labor-market pressure during the period. The fact that the behavior of wage drift was in accordance with predictions, *despite* the structural increase in negotiated rates beginning with the decentralized negotiations in 1974, indicates that there was no significant compensatory relation between rates and drift during the period of multilateral negotiations, with the result that overall wage pressures increased substantially. This merely underscores the fact that one weakness shared by consensus approaches with traditional guideline approaches to incomes policy is a lack of control over wage drift.

In part the failure of wage drift to decline despite the unusually large contractual increases during 1974–77 reflects some of the broader, second-order effects of the consensus agreements. In particular, the income tax reductions, by contributing to the overall economic stimulus, increased labor-market pressure and hence wage drift. A multilateral bargaining approach that involves trading tax concessions for negotiated wage restraint, therefore, may ultimately be nullified by induced wage drift when employment is relatively high. As a mechanism of wage and price restraint it may be most fruitful during recession when the stimu-

52. Ibid. Although skill differentials are generally narrowed in official negotiations as unions pursue their egalitarian objectives, the structure tends to be restored by subsequent wage drift, which is proportionately greater for skilled workers.

lative effect of tax reductions has relatively little effect on wage drift. The provisional evidence from Norway suggests that it may not be a viable anti-inflation policy throughout a sustained period of full employment.

The Freeze

The general price and wage freeze that began in 1978 achieved the immediate deceleration of wages and prices associated with such policies, despite pressures from notable "self-inflicted wounds." While wage and price increases did not fall to zero, inflation decreased to about the 4 percent rate forecast by the government after taking account of certain slippages in the freeze.

In the case of Norwegian wage behavior during the late 1970s, it is not possible to separate the influences of the freeze, the 1978 arbitration award, which was made four months before the wage freeze, and possible changes in expectations generated by the more restrictive stance of fiscal and monetary policy. From 1977 through 1979 there was a clear deceleration in both contractual rates—from 2.9 percent to just over 1 percent—and wage drift—from 10 percent to just over 4 percent (see table 4-9). The freeze was only in effect during the last three and a half months of 1978, however, and some of the deceleration in negotiated rates may have started earlier with the arbitration settlement.

An analysis of the forecast errors in the late 1970s for predictions of contractual rates and wage drift from the regression equations discussed in the preceding section confirms that the deceleration was more rapid than would have been predicted from historical wage relations. (Note that all the forecast errors reported in table 4-9 are negative.) When the results for negotiated rates and wage drift are combined, the impression is one of a striking shift in wage behavior. Yet it is difficult to attribute this result to the arbitration award and the freeze when the forecast errors for 1977—a year before the changes in incomes policy—are negative and larger (in absolute value) than the errors for 1979, the only sample observation that falls almost entirely within the freeze period. The data for both contractual rates and drift are therefore consistent with the possibility that some more general influence on wage determination preceded the developments of 1978 and altered the historical wage relationships throughout the period.[53] On the other hand, the

53. The OECD commented that "it is likely that even without the freeze, wages would have increased less than previously because of changed expectations and attitudes

Table 4-9. *Negotiated Wage Rates and Wage Drift, Actual Increases and Forecast Errors, Norway, 1977–79*

Percentage change from first quarter of one year to first quarter of following year

Item	1977	1978	1979
Negotiated rates			
Actual increase	2.9	2.1	1–1.5
Actual increase minus predicted increase	−5.9	−5.3	−2.5 − 3
Wage drift			
Actual increase	10.0	6.0	4–4.5
Actual increase minus predicted increase	−4.8	−8.2	−4 − 5

Source: OECD Economic Surveys, *Norway*, January 1980, p. 18.

influences responsible for the 1977 prediction errors might not have been sustainable without reinforcement from the 1978 freeze. Unfortunately, beyond cautioning against automatic attribution to the freeze of effects such as those reported in table 4-9, a definitive discrimination between alternative projections is not possible with the available data.

Prices in Norway were frozen at their predevaluation level following the devaluation of the krone against the Snake currencies in February 1978—seven months before the freeze was extended to cover wages. The freeze was followed by a prompt deceleration in consumer prices from 12 percent to 6.5 percent during the first and second quarters, respectively, of 1978.[54] During the third quarter, however, prices reaccelerated to 9 percent from a self-inflicted wound. Since 1975 the government had been implementing the parliamentary decision to equalize incomes in agriculture and manufacturing through a combination of agricultural price increases and subsidies to farmers that were established in the social-contract negotiations. The goal had been pursued with sufficient vigor that between 1974 and 1978 there had been a 75 percent increase in real incomes in agriculture in contrast to a 12.5 percent advance in the private sector generally. The agricultural incomes settlement for 1978 amounted to Kr 5 billion, of which 55 percent was in the form of agricultural price increases, including a 17 percent increase between prices in the second and third quarters of 1978 that was allowed as an exception to the freeze.[55] Nevertheless, the general deceleration

in the wake of the reorientation of economic policy." OECD Economic Surveys, *Norway*, January 1980, p. 18.

54. Ibid., December 1978, p. 15.
55. Ibid., p. 35.

Table 4-10. *Consumer Price Increases, by Sector of Origin, Norway, 1977–79*

Percentage increase over preceding year

Sector of origin	1977	1978	1979
Farm products of domestic origin	3.3	6.9	6.8
Other consumer goods of domestic origin	9.0	8.7	4.3
Imported consumer goods	11.0	6.9	6.1
Rent	5.9	7.4	4.7
Services	12.9	9.6	2.8
With important wage element	12.1	9.0	4.6
With other price elements	13.4	9.8	2.4
Total consumer price index	9.1	8.1	4.8

Source: OECD Economic Surveys, *Norway*, January 1980, p. 15.

of prices continued into 1979, when prices almost reached the government's 4 percent target (see table 4-10).[56]

Table 4-10 also indicates the sectors in which the freeze appeared to have the strongest effects on prices—services, rents, and nonagricultural, domestically produced consumer goods. A more extensive deceleration of the CPI was apparently prevented by the government's policy toward agriculture, which prevented any decline in the prices of Norwegian farm products, and toward oil price increases, which influenced import prices. By the end of the decade, it remained to be seen whether these short-term influences would be followed by a sharp acceleration of wages and prices once the freeze had been lifted.

Conclusions

The Norwegian experience of the 1970s provides the most interesting observation on the intellectual case for and limitations of a social-contract approach to incomes policy in an environment of sharp distributional conflicts. (It also compels comparison to the Austrian experience, in which a more durable set of social-contract institutions emerged from a similar economic environment.) Domestically there is considerable evidence of the influence of distributional conflicts in the inflationary

56. Consumer prices actually increased only 3.5 percent from the third quarter of 1978 to the third quarter of 1979, but an acceleration in the last quarter of 1979 raised the average for the calendar year. Ibid., January 1980, p. 15.

process. Disputes over the appropriate wage structure have fueled increases in contractual wages and wage drift, as in other Scandinavian countries. Conflicts over the appropriate distribution of the national income between the economically active and inactive segments of the population generated further pressure on labor costs as wages increased in response to efforts to raise through taxation the share of resources allocated by public authorities. Efforts to reduce disparities in income between agriculture and the industrial sector by raising the price of agricultural products also fed wage increases through indexation arrangements.

The combined effect of these pressures on money wages, along with increases in contributions by employers for legislatively mandated social costs, threatened Norway's international market position. At the same time, Norway was a member from 1973 to 1978 of a European currency alliance, the Snake, which was intended to limit fluctuations in exchange rates. The latter factor amounted to accepting a "hard-currency option"—as, for example, Austria had—and the policy pressures and constraints that went with it. In particular, tying the Norwegian krone to an appreciating basket of currencies made imports more attractive in Norwegian markets and placed pressure on export industries to keep costs in line with those of Norway's principal trading partners. Incomes policy arrangements that were developed during the 1960s removed one potential source of wage instability by coordinating the timing of negotiations and establishing a general economic framework for negotiations, but it remained to establish an institutional mechanism within which distributional conflicts could be resolved more effectively.

The multilateral negotiations discussed in this chapter, in which the government announces a target increase in real disposable income, then coordinates negotiations over the size and distribution of changes in wages, taxes, and public expenditure that will cause this target to be reached, are one such mechanism. For several reasons, however, this mechanism has not proved to be an apt solution.

First, within the context of Norwegian income-determination institutions, which exhibit considerable heterogeneity, the prospective revenues from oil and gas discoveries in the North Sea may have been the key factor that permitted the social-contract negotiations during 1975–77 to reach closure. In the absence of these prospects, the government would have been able to give much less and would have been forced to advance much lower targets for growth in real disposable income. Thus, the Norwegian experience does not provide strong evidence of the viability of multilateral negotiations as a mechanism for achieving adjustment to external supply shocks or other sources of economic austerity. Indeed, the failure of the social-contract approach in the face of a need to adjust to greater austerity during the late 1970s and the consequent adoption of a more traditional approach to incomes policy indicates that this approach may be more appropriate to spreading plenty than to sharing burdens.

Second, there are inherent macroeconomic limitations on the social-contract approach to incomes policy. The key to multilateral negotiations is the ability of the government to contribute to the resolution of distributional conflicts by reducing taxes and—at times—increasing certain government expenditures. But both these actions expand demand and stimulate wage drift. Whatever restraint in official wages is induced by tax changes will tend to be offset by increased wage drift. From this perspective, the Norwegian experience of the mid 1970s provides another example of the futility of incomes policy in a climate of excess demand.

Third, the foregoing observation is compounded by the fact that a statistical analysis of Norwegian wage determination indicates that changes in tax rates, the only real leverage that the government has in multilateral negotiations, are not a primary element of wage push. It is also the case that income tax reductions do not generally produce a uniform gain in real disposable income for all workers. In a progressive income tax system, tax reductions may yield the largest gains to highly paid workers. Because of this tendency to counter the general egalitarian objectives of the unions, the instrument may prove less acceptable to labor in the course of time.

Fourth, the main target of the social-contract arrangements, negotiated wage increases, were not a principal element of Norwegian labor cost increases during the 1970s. The behavior of wage drift and statutory social costs was largely independent of the multilateral negotiations. Wage drift is particularly responsive to labor-market pressure—hence the consequences of the social contract, as noted earlier—and to changes in the skill structure of wages. But even the latter factor is left to bilateral negotiations between the employers and unions. In sum, the government brought to these negotiations a relatively weak instrument to apply to a relatively small component of labor costs, and that instrument could induce offsetting movements in other components of labor costs. By the end of the 1970s wage drift remained the principal challenge to Norwegian wage policy, and it was clear that the social-contract approach to incomes policy was no more successful in restraining drift than its predecessors had been. In the end it did not make a fundamental contribution to the restoration of Norway's international competitive position.

The parallel political investments in social-contract arrangements in Norway and Austria invite comparison because the outcomes, as of 1980, were so different. Both countries initially seemed committed to a hard-currency option but each has responded differently to the domestic economic pressures that follow from this policy. Austria has placed virtually the entire burden of maintaining its position in international markets while tied to an appreciating currency on the restraint of earnings through the social-contract institutions. In particular, it has largely resisted pressures for measures to protect or sustain companies most threatened by international competition. Norway has been less willing to accept the domestic consequences of the hard-currency option. Rather than resist protectionist measures, the Norwegian government in the mid and late 1970s allocated large amounts to an industrial policy that sheltered Norwegian industries from competitive pressures. This removed the burden of adjustment from the income-determining, and incomes policy, institutions, but it also contributed to a striking decline in the productivity of Norwegian industry. With only two observations no definitive explanation of these different policy choices is possible. One striking difference between the income-determination institutions in the two countries, however, is the extent to which distributional conflicts are channeled into the collective bargaining process. The inability to resolve issues of wage structure in either bilateral collective bargaining or multilateral negotiations with the government has prevented progress in reconciling the restraint of money wages required to maintain international competitiveness with full employment. In contrast, Austria has managed to keep significant distributional conflict out of the collective bargaining process.

V

The Federal Republic of Germany

In most countries, trade unions and collective bargaining have been seen as contributing to difficulties in meeting one or more important macro-economic policy objectives, and incomes policies have been considered for their effectiveness as correctives. In the Federal Republic of Germany, however, unions, collective bargaining, and related public policies have been seen—at least by outsiders—in a setting of outstanding economic success. By 1973, a little more than a quarter of a century after the defeat and partition of Germany, the Federal Republic had reached levels of gross domestic product (GDP) and private consumption per capita that were equaled (or marginally exceeded) only by Sweden, Canada, and the United States among the twenty-five countries in the Organisation for Economic Co-operation and Development (OECD).[1] This plateau was reached, moreover, by balanced performance at high levels in employment, prices, and external balance as well as in economic growth.

The Dimensions of Success

The long period 1960–77 reveals some of the dimensions of the German "economic miracle" as well as certain aspects of the performance of its labor market. To begin with, the average rate of unemployment in Germany was the lowest in the group. Its average rate of price inflation was also lower than that of any of the other European countries; only the United States had a lower rate of inflation, and that of Canada was as low as Germany's. In the countries in which unemployment was comparable to that in Germany—Sweden and Japan—inflation was much greater; and in the North American countries, where rates of inflation were comparable, unemployment was much higher. In figure 5-1, in which average inflation rates of prices and wages are plotted, respectively, against average unemployment rates for the eight industrial

1. Organisation for Economic Co-operation and Development, *Basic Statistics: International Comparisons* (Paris: OECD, 1975).

208

countries, Germany's generally superior performance in these two dimensions is revealed graphically. Germany's "discomfort rate," obtained by adding the rates of unemployment and inflation together, has been distinctly lower than that of every other country in this group. Indeed, the German discomfort rate was lower than that of every other country in every single year between 1960 and 1977, with the exception of Japan in 1972.

Germany's rates of growth of manufacturing productivity and real GDP per capita, on the other hand, have not been outstanding. Germany ranked no higher than sixth in this field of nine countries. Real GDP per capita grew less rapidly in Germany than in France and the Netherlands, although more rapidly than in Italy, Sweden, and the United Kingdom. On the other hand, the growth of German manufacturing productivity was associated with notably less discomfort than elsewhere during most periods, except in Japan. This is portrayed in figure 5-2, in which the sum of unemployment and consumer price inflation appears on the vertical axis as a rough and ready (but popularly used) indicator of welfare.

In addition, the growth of productivity might be taken in conjunction with the rate of increase in real wages. The rate of growth of real wages was higher, in relation to that of most other countries, than the rate of growth in productivity: Germany ranked third or fourth in the former category and, as noted, sixth in the latter. While real wages tended to rise as rapidly as productivity in Germany during the long period, moreover, this was not the case in the other countries, with the strong exception of Italy. During the 1960s, real hourly compensation rose less rapidly than productivity in Germany, but during the 1970s, the former outpaced the latter.

When the growth of productivity and the rise in money compensation are taken together, the rate of increase in unit labor costs in manufacturing is shown to have been significantly lower in Germany than in Italy, the Netherlands, and Sweden throughout the entire period. During the 1960s and early 1970s, however, inflation of unit costs in Germany did not differ greatly from cost inflation in the other European countries. Germany ran approximately parallel with France in both productivity and hourly compensation until after 1973. The differences came after the oil crisis in 1973, and they were of sufficient magnitude to affect the ranking during the long period 1960–77. On the other hand, the hourly compensation component of the changes in unit labor costs exhibited

210 THE FEDERAL REPUBLIC OF GERMANY

Figure 5-1. *International Comparisons of Rates of Inflation and Unemployment, 1960–77, 1960–70, 1970–73, and 1973–77*

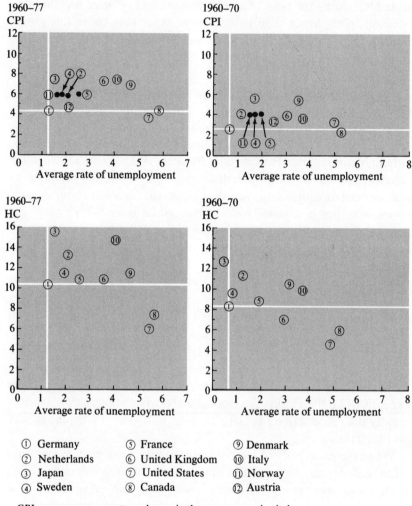

① Germany   ⑤ France   ⑨ Denmark
② Netherlands   ⑥ United Kingdom   ⑩ Italy
③ Japan   ⑦ United States   ⑪ Norway
④ Sweden   ⑧ Canada   ⑫ Austria

CPI = average percentage change in the consumer price index
HC = average percentage change in hourly compensation

Sources: Mean annual percentage change in consumer price indexes, Organisation for Economic Co-operation and Development, *Main Economic Indicators* (Paris: OECD, various issues); OECD, *Economic Outlook,* various issues; annual rate of change in hourly compensation of production workers in manufacturing, computed from the least-squares trend of the logarithm of the index numbers, *Monthly Labor Review,* various issues; mean annual average unemployment rate, adjusted for international differences, OECD, "Methodological and Conceptual Problems of Measuring Unemployment in OECD Countries," report no. SME/CA/75.28 (Paris: OECD, January 1976); OECD, *Economic Outlook* (Paris: OECD, various issues); OECD, *Main Economic Indicators: Historical Statistics, 1960–1979* (Paris: OECD, 1980); OECD, *Labour Force Statistics, 1968–1979,* and earlier issues (Paris: OECD); U.S. Bureau of Labor Statistics, Division of Foreign Labor Statistics; OECD Economic Surveys, *Netherlands,* March 1978; annual rate of change in real GDP per capita, computed from the least-squares trend, OECD, *Main Economic Indicators,* various issues; OECD, *National Accounts Statistics* (Paris: OECD, various issues).

Figure 5-1 (*continued*)

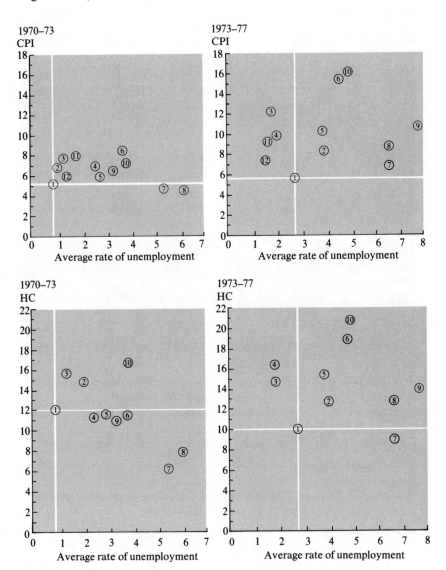

Figure 5-2. *International Comparisons of Discomfort and Growth,*
1960–77, 1960–70, 1970–73, and 1973–77

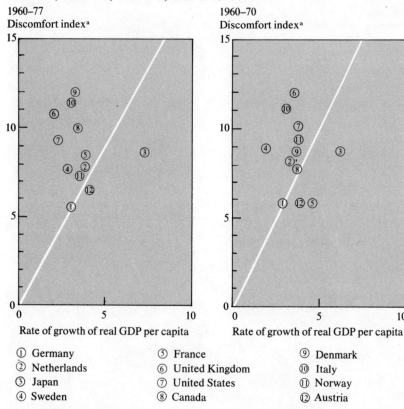

1960–77
Discomfort index[a]

1960–70
Discomfort index[a]

Rate of growth of real GDP per capita

Rate of growth of real GDP per capita

① Germany	⑤ France	⑨ Denmark
② Netherlands	⑥ United Kingdom	⑩ Italy
③ Japan	⑦ United States	⑪ Norway
④ Sweden	⑧ Canada	⑫ Austria

Sources: Same as for figure 5-1.
a. The discomfort index is equal to the percentage change in the consumer price index plus the unemployment rate.

lower annual rates of change than all the other European countries except France during the 1960s and the mid 1970s.

Finally, the balance-of-payments performance of Germany has been at least as outstanding as that country's employment, price level, and growth records throughout the long period, although its welfare implications have been less unambiguous. Until the 1980s Germany's external account tended to be in surplus, and the shares of exports in both world markets and gross national product (GNP) rose sharply.[2] The authorities

2. German exports rose from 4.6 percent of world exports during 1950–53 to 11.2 percent during 1970–73; the greater part of this growth occurred in the 1950s, however, following Germany's postwar re-entry into the world market. The share of exports in

Figure 5-2 (*continued*)

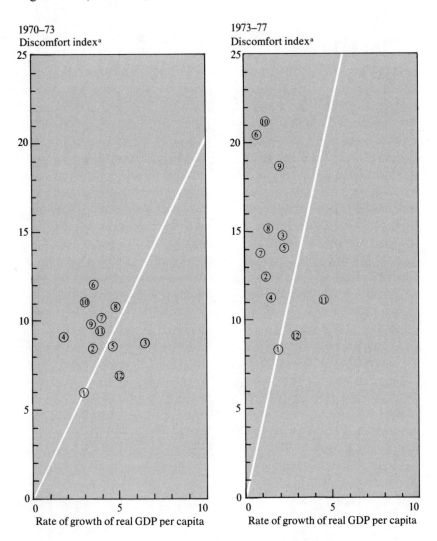

1970–73
Discomfort index[a]

Rate of growth of real GDP per capita

1973–77
Discomfort index[a]

Rate of growth of real GDP per capita

GNP stood at 28 percent in 1975; it had been only 17 percent during 1952–57. See
Michael Kreile, "West Germany: The Dynamics of Expansion," in Peter J. Katzenstein,
ed., *Between Power and Plenty: Foreign Economic Policies of Advanced Industrial
States* (Madison: University of Wisconsin Press, 1978), p. 192; Otmar Emminger, *The
D-Mark in the Conflict between Internal and External Equilibrium, 1948–75,* Essays in
International Finance, No. 122 (Princeton: Princeton University Press, 1977), pp. 7, 20.

Table 5-1. Wage-Change Regressions, West Germany, 1958–76

Equation	Dependent variable[a]	Constant	PW_{t-1}	CPI_{t-1}	Q_{t-1}	UR	$CHEM_{t-1}$	DL	SS_{t-1}	R^2	Durbin-Watson	Standard error
							Independent variable[b]				Summary statistic	
1	WR	9.43 (3.03)	0.62 (2.9)	-0.48 (-0.86)	-0.0033 (-0.010)	-1.79 (-2.70)	0.026 (2.21)	0.00087 (1.45)	-0.024 (-0.22)	0.85	2.47	1.32
1a	WR	7.08 (4.78)	0.45 (5.60)	...	0.19 (0.77)	-1.40 (-2.94)	0.025 (2.19)	0.0010 (1.79)	-0.052 (-0.50)	0.84	2.40	1.30
1b	WR	1.70 (0.82)	...	1.03 (3.76)	0.65 (1.97)	-0.21 (-0.44)	0.022 (1.50)	0.0016 (2.24)	-0.13 (-0.98)	0.74	2.33	1.68
2	WD	-0.43 (-0.14)	-0.13 (-0.63)	0.059 (0.11)	0.34 (1.02)	0.21 (0.33)	0.00054 (0.047)	-0.0012 (-2.06)	0.017 (0.16)	0.59	1.18	1.28
2a	WD	-0.14 (-0.10)	-0.11 (-1.43)	...	0.32 (1.33)	0.16 (0.37)	0.00060 (0.055)	-0.0012 (-2.78)	0.020 (0.21)	0.59	1.19	1.23
2b	WD	1.18 (0.77)	...	-0.26 (-1.26)	0.20 (0.83)	-0.11 (-0.33)	0.0013 (0.12)	-0.0013 (-2.59)	0.039 (0.40)	0.57	1.30	1.25
3	BCE	9.00 (1.80)	0.49 (1.44)	-0.42 (-0.47)	0.34 (0.61)	-1.58 (-1.49)	0.026 (1.40)	-0.00033 (-0.34)	-0.0071 (-0.040)	0.63	1.74	2.11
3a	BCE	6.94 (2.99)	0.34 (2.71)	...	0.51 (1.29)	-1.23 (-1.66)	0.026 (1.43)	-0.00020 (-0.23)	-0.032 (-0.20)	0.63	1.72	2.04
3b	BCE	2.88 (1.06)	...	0.77 (2.15)	0.86 (1.97)	-0.33 (-0.52)	0.024 (1.21)	0.00022 (0.24)	-0.091 (-0.52)	0.56	1.70	2.20

a. WR, percent change in hourly wage rates in manufacturing, from Organisation for Economic Co-operation and Development, *Main Economic Indicators: Historical Statistics, 1960–1979* (Paris: OECD, 1980), and OECD, *Main Economic Indicators* (Paris: OECD, various issues); BCE, percent change in average hourly earnings of workers in industry, from *Statistisches Jahrbuch 1976 für die Bundesrepublik Deutschland* (Stuttgart: W. Kohlhammer, 1976); WD, wage drift = BCE − WR.

b. PW, percent increase in export prices for manufactured goods from market economies, used as proxy for world prices, from United Nations, *Yearbook of International Trade Statistics* (New York: United Nations, various issues); Q, percent change in the ratio of real GDP to civilian employment, from OECD, *National Accounts Statistics* (Paris: OECD, various issues), and OECD, *Main Economic Indicators: Historical Statistics, 1960–1979*; UR, level of registered unemployment as a percentage of the civilian labor force, from OECD, *Main Economic Indicators: Historical Statistics, 1960–1979*; DL, level of days lost in industrial disputes, from *Arbeits- und Sozialstatistik des Bundesministerium für Arbeit und Sozialordnung* (Bonn: Bundesministerium für Arbeit und Sozialordnung, various issues); CHEM = E_t − E_{t-1}, where E is civilian employment, from OECD, *Labour Force Statistics* (Paris: OECD, various issues); SS, percent change in the ratio of employers' contributions to social security schemes to total wages and salaries paid, from OECD, *National Accounts Statistics*; CPI, percent change in the consumer price index, from OECD, *Main Economic Indicators: Historical Statistics, 1960–1979*. Numbers in parentheses are *t*-statistics.

regarded the surpluses as a source of "imported inflation"—under a regime of fixed exchange rates and, in the 1970s, of "dirty" floating— and concern has been expressed that the growth in exports might cause the German economy to be excessively dependent on world trade. Some support for the imported-inflation hypothesis can be found in equations 1 and 3 in table 5-1, which are estimates of changes in wage rates in manufacturing and average hourly earnings, respectively, insofar as the coefficients of the explanatory variable *PW*, which is a measure of past changes in world prices, are positively signed, whereas the coefficients of the *CPI* variable, a measure of changes in domestic consumer prices, have the wrong sign and are of less significance. In the wage drift equation 2, on the other hand, the signs on these two price-change coefficients are reversed, although neither result is significant. It should also be noted that the coefficients of both variables are positive in equations 1a, 1b, 3a, and 3b, in which these two variables are dealt with separately.[3] Clearly, equilibrium in the external account would have been preferable to a tendency to surplus, which had persisted despite five currency revaluations before 1973 and which subsequently weathered even the oil price increases. Nevertheless, inflation imported through external surplus at least meant avoidance of ultimately importing unemployment through external deficit, a prospect with which other countries have been confronted. Instead, Germany may be said to have imported full employment through export-led upswings in activity and growth. And although Otmar Emminger has claimed that "in no other major country has imported inflation played such an important role as in the Federal Republic of Germany,"[4] it is also true that in no other European country has domestic inflation been so low.

Thus the German economy has been more successful than its neighbors in attaining the employment objective stressed by the Keynesians, the price-stability objective stressed by the monetarists, and the objective of international competitiveness stressed by the Scandinavians. As pointed out by Romanis, the exchange rate of the mark was originally (at the end of the war) pitched at a level that was designed to promote the independent recovery of the devastated German economy through expansion of exports, and it was understandable that the domestic authorities should seek to perpetuate their initial advantage.[5] But their

3. See table 5-1.
4. *The D-Mark*, p. 1.
5. Anne Romanis, "Balance of Payments Adjustment among Developed Countries," *IMF Staff Papers*, vol. 12, no. 1 (March 1965), p. 17.

success was remarkable, and the postwar performance of the German economy was duly hailed as a miracle and later presented as a miracle that had played too long. It was certainly a bit mysterious. The coexistence of low rates of inflation and unemployment with a surplus on external account would not ordinarily represent a state of equilibrium. Under a regime of either flexible or fixed rates of exchange, the surplus would be expected to liquidate itself. In the former case, of course, it could do so through appreciation of the currency, with disinflationary results, although realistically at the cost of "temporary" increases in unemployment. On the other hand, in a world of fixed exchange rates, in which the deutsche mark was "undervalued," equilibrating tendencies could be manifested in inflationary tendencies—in either a pull or a push on domestic costs in response to increasing demand for and profitability of exports. (Indeed, the Aukrust model posits a combination of domestic inflation and equilibrium on external account, in the absence of continual appreciation.) Attempts to hold the line on domestic costs and prices through restrictive monetary policy would only raise the domestic rate of interest above the world rate and thus attract an inflow of foreign capital—a condition about which the frustrated officials of the Deutsche Bank complained eloquently and at length. Under these conditions, unemployment would tend to be held below its "natural" rate and, according to the monetarist theory, the inflation thus imported should accelerate until domestic costs had risen sufficiently to eliminate the export surplus at the prevailing rate of exchange. The alternative would be to revalue the currency. The Germans, as noted earlier, did have recourse to revaluation on five occasions, and they certainly avoided both accelerating inflation and heightened unemployment during the 1950s and 1960s. But the tendency to surplus survived, at least through the 1970s. How did developments in the German labor markets—demographic, institutional, and policy developments—affect this economic performance?

Labor in Excess Supply and in Increasing Supply

Extensive employment in Germany of migrant labor from outside the national boundaries has been regarded as one of the secrets of its economic success, and it undoubtedly contributed an important element of elasticity and flexibility to the labor supply. On the other hand, this potential cost advantage was not unique to Germany; recourse to immigrant labor in Germany, moreover, was made possible in part by the cooperation of a cost-conscious trade-union movement. The standard reference model, which rejects the proposition that price stability, external surplus, and full employment can exist simultaneously in stable equilibrium, posits clearance in markets—notably including the labor market. That assumption clearly did not hold in the case of West Germany at the end of the war. Much of Germany's capital stock had been destroyed or damaged in the war, and part was separated from the Federal Republic by the postwar partition. The partition also contributed both a reduction in potential domestic demand and an increase in labor supply. The separation of East Germany meant the loss of an important segment of the domestic market by the western sector, in which the bulk of German industrial capacity was located. Hence, wrote Wilhelm Hankel, "The former (but now lost) internal labor markets for West German industry had to be replaced by foreign markets."[6] Certainly demand management abetted this development. The currency reform of 1948 drastically contracted the money supply, and an ensuing bout of price inflation—14 percent in the last half of that year—was ended by a policy of monetary restraint. Unemployment rose, prompting the government to adopt some expansionary measures, including a work-creation program. But then came another and more prolonged inflationary spell, which lasted from the second quarter of 1950 to the second half of 1951, during the Korean boom, together with a sharp deterioration in the balance of payments. So restrictive credit and fiscal policies were imposed, along with some import restraints, and the external account swung sharply into surplus.[7]

An increase in the labor supply accompanied the early restraint in home demand and continued until the beginning of the 1960s. It was provided by a large-scale influx of refugees, which increased the labor force by 7 million between the end of the war and the erection of the Berlin Wall in 1961. These refugees came first from Eastern Europe and subsequently from the Communist German Democratic Republic. The latter group was characterized by relatively high labor-force participation,[8] and since their migration was not primarily determined by demand,

6. Wilhelm Hankel, "West Germany," in Wilfrid L. Kohl, ed., *Economic Foreign Policies of Industrial States* (Lexington, Mass.: D. C. Heath, 1977), p. 107.

7. Henry C. Wallich, *Mainsprings of the German Revival* (New Haven: Yale University Press, 1955), pp. 68–106; Emminger, *The D-Mark*, p. 4.

8. Charles P. Kindleberger, *Europe's Postwar Growth: The Role of Labor Supply* (Cambridge, Mass.: Harvard University Press, 1967), pp. 30–31; Wallich, *Mainsprings*, p. 282.

it was held largely responsible for the persistence of high rates of unemployment—about 6 percent between 1949 and 1954—in the face of steadily increasing employment during the first half of the 1950s.[9] On the average, moreover, the refugee labor was highly skilled, well educated, strongly motivated, and easily assimilated. Since these workers were good potential substitutes for members of the existing labor force, the unemployment of the time could be regarded as constituting a true excess supply of labor.

The substitutability of the refugees is also indicated by the fact that, when unemployment did fall during the second half of the 1950s, neither the numbers nor the rates of vacancies increased appreciably until after 1959.[10] (Note the vertical scatter of observations between the 1.0 percent and 1.4 percent vacancy rates in figure 5-3.) The immigration of refugee labor, moreover, is credited with retarding the rate of increase in money and real wages.[11] Both developments helped to keep unit labor costs from rising as rapidly as manufacturers' prices.[12] With labor in excess supply, output could respond more elastically in response to export demand, and a strong position of external surplus could be maintained.

After the late 1950s refugee labor was replaced as an important source of incremental supply by foreign "guest workers," mainly from southern and eastern Europe and the Middle East. These foreign workers differed from the earlier refugees in two respects: they were, on the average, less highly skilled, less well educated, and less acculturated, and they were admitted primarily in response to increased demand for unskilled labor. (The difference in qualifications may be reflected in figure 5-3, which shows that, whereas the unemployment rate was reduced from relatively high levels without a large increase in the vacancy rate during the 1950s, later and further reductions in the rate of unemployment—to extremely low levels, it must be admitted—were associated with disproportionately great increases in the vacancy rate.) Yet, at the end of the 1960s, 20 percent of the male foreign workers—although only 3 percent of the female—were in skilled manual occupations and 36 percent were semi-

9. Employment increased by 3 million (or 20 percent) between 1949 and 1954, while unemployment declined by 300,000. See Wallich, *Mainsprings*, pp. 292–94, data from table 36.

10. The unemployment rate declined from 5.6 percent in 1955 to 1.3 percent in 1960. See Hans Günter and Gerhard Leminsky, "The Federal Republic of Germany," in John T. Dunlop and Walter Galenson, eds., *Labor in the Twentieth Century* (New York: Academic Press, 1978), p. 156.

11. See especially Kindleberger, *Europe's Postwar Growth*, pp. 28–36.

12. Wallich, *Mainsprings*, p. 301.

Figure 5-3. *Unemployment and Vacancy Rates, Germany, 1955–78*[a]

Sources: OECD, *Labour Force Statistics, 1956–1966* (Paris: OECD, 1968); ibid., *1954–64* (Paris, 1966); OECD Economic Surveys, *Germany,* December 1965, April 1968, June 1971, July 1977, and June 1979; Bundesministerium für Arbeit und Sozialordnung, *Haupterergebnisse der Arbeits- und Sozialstatistik* [Highlights of employment and welfare statistics], 1973/1974 (Bonn, 1974).

a. Data for 1955 and 1956 do not include West Berlin or the Saar.

skilled; 63 percent were employed in the manufacturing sector.[13] Although immigrants from other countries of the European Economic Community (EEC) contributed disproportionately to the ranks of the skilled workers, the process of absorption seems to have been highly efficient.

And there is no doubt that the supply of these newcomers has been highly elastic; their numbers increased from 279,000 at the beginning of the 1960s, when they represented 1.4 percent of the employee labor force, to 1.8 million, or 8.1 percent, in 1970, and to 2.5 million, or 11 percent, in 1973, when further immigration from countries outside the EEC was discontinued.[14] Thus, wrote Gerhard Fels, "the supply of labor remained ample even after full employment was achieved."[15] Herbert

13. Stephen Castles and Godula Kosack, *Immigrant Workers and Class Structure in Western Europe* (Oxford: Oxford University Press, 1973), pp. 71, 73, 82.

14. Günter and Leminsky, "The Federal Republic," table 3.5, p. 160.

15. Gerhard Fels, "Inflation in Germany," in Lawrence B. Krause and Walter S. Salant, eds., *Worldwide Inflation: Theory and Recent Experience* (Washington, D.C.: Brookings Institution, 1977), pp. 591–92.

Giersch refers to "a surprising elasticity of labour supply, mainly from foreign sources" as one of the causes of a characteristic lag of wages behind productivity during upswings in activity—which, in fact, tended to be led by export demand.[16] The lagged and limited influence of productivity on contractual wages and earnings is suggested by the small and positive coefficients on the PW_{t-1} and Q_{t-1} variables in equations 1 and 3 (see table 5-1). The fact that periods of expansion preceding serious contraction in the 1960s were longer in Germany than in either France or Italy is also consistent with Giersch's observation, and, therefore, so is the fact that average yearly increases in money wages and unit labor costs were lower in Germany than in these other two countries during the prerecession upswings and during the 1960s as a whole (see table 5-2).

Nevertheless, the explanatory value of the elastic-labor-supply hypothesis is quite limited. To begin with, it cannot readily be squared with the apparent influence of what was called "labor market pressure variables" on money wages in an OECD regression analysis. Through this analysis, which covered the period from 1958 through the second quarter of 1970, it was found that the lagged reciprocal of the difference between the unemployment rate and the job-vacancy rate and the ratio of unemployment to employment were significant determinants of the year-on-year changes in employee compensation.[17] The large and negatively signed coefficients of the unemployment variable, UR, in equations 1 and 3, which cover the longer period 1956–76, are consistent with these findings, although changes in employment, $CHEM$, apparently exerted no appreciable influence on wages.

A strong association between the rates of wage inflation and of employment is consistent with a model that is characterized by increased demand, a virtually fixed labor supply, and a declining export surplus. If, however, as was noted in a Canadian analysis, "variations in the level of demand are reflected in the labour market mainly through variations in the rate of inflow of industrial workers rather than in the rate of

16. Herbert Giersch, *Growth, Cycles, and Exchange Rates: The Experience of West Germany,* Wicksell Lectures, 1970 (Stockholm: Almquist and Wicksell, 1970), p. 18.

17. OECD Economic Surveys, *Germany,* June 1971, pp. 46–48, 52–53. The rates of change in an index of industrial capacity use and in real GNP per employee were less satisfactory as a combination of alternative predictors. Additional explanatory variables were changes in income from property and entrepreneurship (which was significant when used with the labor-market pressure variables) and in the GNP price deflator (also significant).

Table 5-2. *Movements in Compensation, Productivity, and Unit Labor Costs in Germany during and after Periods of Expansion in the 1960s*

Percentage rate of change

Country and period	Hourly compensation in manufacturing (national currency)[a]		Productivity[a]	Unit labor costs[a]
	Nominal	Real		
Germany				
1961–66	8.52	5.58	6.03	2.49
1967–69	7.33	5.11	6.44	0.39
France				
1960–63	9.40	5.12	4.57	4.83
1964–67	7.13	4.53	5.92	1.21
Italy				
1960–63	13.24	8.61	5.76	7.48
1964–67	6.06	2.73	6.57	−0.51
United Kingdom				
1960–65	6.23	2.88	4.02	2.21
1966–68	4.62	1.08	4.86	−0.24

Source: Arthur Neef, "Unit Labor Costs in the U.S. and 10 Other Nations, 1960–71," *Monthly Labor Review,* vol. 95, no. 7 (July 1972), pp. 3–8; OECD, *Main Economic Indicators: Historical Statistics, 1960–1979.*
a. Computed from the least-squares trend of the logarithm of index numbers.

unemployment,"[18] a strong relation between wage changes and unemployment ought not to be expected.

Nor is it obvious that the rather general tendency of labor costs to increase more slowly in Germany than elsewhere in Europe during the 1960s and 1970s—and to do so at lower levels of unemployment—is attributable solely or even primarily to the availability of foreign sources of labor. Germany's greatest relative decline in hourly compensation and unit labor costs occurred after new immigration from countries that were not members of the EEC had been stopped in 1973. (This measure was taken in response to a sharp rise in unemployment, but unemployment nevertheless remained lower in Germany than elsewhere, except in Sweden.) And it is not apparent that labor-force elasticity has been significantly greater in Germany than in some other countries. During 1967–69, immigrants accounted for 7 percent of the German labor force, but immigrants accounted for 6.3 percent of the work force in France

18. Ronald G. Bodkin and others, *Price Stability and High Employment: The Options for Canadian Economic Policy* (Ottawa: Economic Council of Canada, 1966), p. 253. Their own wage-adjustment equation, covering the period 1954–65, implies a virtually horizontal Phillips curve; see p. 251.

and 6.5 percent in Britain.[19] Italy, a net exporter of labor, has drawn extensively from domestic pools of underemployed in the agricultural south.

It may nevertheless be true that Germany drew more efficiently, with respect to demand, or extensively on foreign labor reserves or that its guest workers, while of lower productive potential than the refugees of the 1950s, were better qualified or more strongly motivated than foreign employees in other countries or than southern Italians in northern Italy. But even if this be admitted for the sake of argument, it might be asked why the other countries did not avail themselves of labor from the same places and as extensively and efficiently as the Germans did. Herbert Giersch may have supplied a partial answer to this question when he wrote: "Right from the start the trade unions have always accepted the competition of immigrant labour."[20] In making labor-supply elasticity in part a function of institutional discretion, Giersch implicitly distinguished Germany from other countries in which comparable union power or comparable union restraint was lacking. France might be classed as a country in which the power was lacking; Britain—where union opposition once blocked the importation of Polish coal miners—as a country in which power existed but without discernible restraint.

Restraint under Bargaining

Thus other factors, in addition to conditions of labor supply, would have to be invoked in an attempt to explain why German compensation and labor costs have been rather sensitive to levels of unemployment and why they have tended to increase less rapidly than compensation and costs elsewhere. The German system of collective bargaining is one such additional factor; it has, to a greater extent than the availability of incremental labor, been cast in a dual role of villain and hero in the economic miracle play. Those who have emphasized inflationary tendencies in the economy and the limitations of monetary policy in curbing those tendencies have blamed the unions for bargaining excesses—as well as the government of the day for profligacy. Emminger claimed that the price increases which forced the 1961 revaluation had been "aggra-

19. Castles and Kosack, *Immigrant Workers*, p. 61.
20. *Growth, Cycles, and Exchange Rates*, p. 10.

vated since early 1961 by excessive wage demands,"[21] and he assigned "cost inflation" a goodly share of the blame for threatening international competitiveness and, in effect, forcing the Bundesbank's hand in producing the deflation of 1966–67. This diagnosis, in which increased vacancies and other manifestations of reduced elasticity of supply were routinely ignored, rested implicitly on the assumption that the German trade unions were endowed with market power, which enabled them to make costs, and therefore prices, accelerate more rapidly in response to increases in export demand than prevailing supply conditions would otherwise have required. On the other hand, observers who have concentrated on the comparative performance of Germany—its success in restraining costs and prices while achieving high levels of performance and growth during the postwar period as a whole—have imputed exemplary restraint to the bargainers.

In principle, the two interpretations are not inconsistent with each other. Restraint, like pushfulness, implies the possession of power. The exercise of restraint obviously does not imply bargaining outcomes that are less inflationary than wage movements which would be produced in the absence of collective bargaining. But restraint under bargaining could produce wage movements that are more sensitive to levels of unemployment than wage changes which would be produced by unorganized markets with plentiful supplies of foreign labor available on demand at going wage rates. The downward-sloping Phillips curve implicit in our estimating equations, and in those of the OECD as well, are consistent with the operation of bargaining restraint, whereas either all-out cost-push or demand-determined immigration has been taken to imply the horizontal variety.[22]

Germany's relatively moderate movements in wages and unit labor costs have frequently been ascribed to a restrained bargaining performance. The significance of the coefficients of the world price-change variable, PW, in equation 1 (as well as in 1a) suggest that international competitive forces have exerted a strong influence on contractual wage determination in this large European economy. The fact that the sum of the PW coefficient and the coefficient of changes in economywide productivity, Q, is less than unity, especially in the contractual-wage equation, is also consistent with bargaining restraint, for it suggests a

21. The D-Mark, pp. 16–22.
22. For the cost-push implication, see Bodkin and others, Price Stability, p. 26.

Figure 5-4. *Movements in Labor Productivity and in Real Average Hourly Compensation, Earnings, and Wage Rates, Germany, 1961–76*

Percentage change

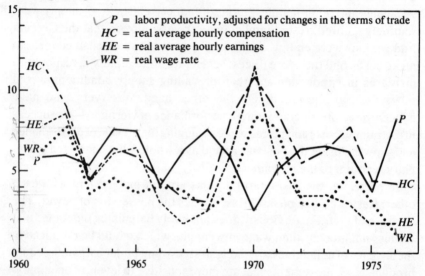

Sources: Manufacturing labor productivity, compensation, and earnings, U.S. Bureau of Labor Statistics, *U.S. Handbook of Labor Statistics, 1978* (Washington, D.C.: BLS); consumer price index, manufacturing wage rate, and data for terms-of-trade adjustment, OECD, *Main Economic Indicators: Historical Statistics, 1960–1979*.

tendency for increases in wages—as distinct, however, from total compensation—to rise less rapidly than the "room" allowed them in the Aukrust model. The same tendency is shown in figure 5-4, where real wage rates are seen as rising less rapidly than productivity between 1963 and 1970 and again after 1972, although real total hourly compensation, inclusive of social security tax payments by employers, rose more rapidly than productivity during the 1970s. And during the period 1972–76, adjustment to the oil price shock of 1973 was characterized by a lower rate of increase in real wages (net of employer tax payments) in Germany than in France, Italy, the United Kingdom, and its smaller neighbors, Austria and the Netherlands. Unemployment increased sharply, which tended to depress real wages, but it remained at relatively low levels in Germany; and, as Schelde Andersen pointed out, productivity rose strongly.[23]

23. Palle Schelde Andersen, "Recent Wage Trends and Medium-Term Problems," in *Collective Bargaining and Government Policies* (Paris: OECD, 1979), pp. 194–95.

Table 5-3. *Germany's Strike Record Compared with Those of Six Other Countries of the OECD: Days Lost, Workers Involved, and Duration of Industrial Disputes, 1961–75*
Thousands

Period and category	Germany	France	Italy	United Kingdom	Nether-lands	Sweden	United States
1961–65							
Days lost per employee	0.018	0.147	0.654	0.127	0.080	0.004	0.285
Workers per dispute	0.55	1.11	0.80	0.62	0.22	0.13	0.38
Days lost per dispute	3.13	1.30	3.50	1.30	0.61	0.93	5.39
1966–70							
Days lost per employee	0.006	1.61[a]	0.954	0.226	0.014	0.033	0.595
Workers per dispute	0.84	1.16[b]	1.19	0.51	0.43	0.35	0.52
Days lost per dispute	0.99	1.39[b]	5.40	1.91	1.22	3.04	8.76
1971–75							
Days lost per employee	0.048	0.185	1.13	0.536	0.037	0.065	0.437
Workers per dispute	0.40	0.61	1.73	0.53	2.31	0.36	0.44
Days lost per dispute	2.14	1.07	6.09	5.17	18.95	3.88	6.81
1961–75							
Days lost per employee	0.024	0.164	0.575	0.296	0.044	0.034	0.440
Workers per dispute	0.60	0.94[b]	1.24	0.56	0.99	0.29	0.45
Days lost per dispute	2.08	1.23[b]	5.00	2.79	6.92	2.62	6.98

Sources: Number of days lost because of industrial disputes and number of workers involved in industrial disputes, International Labour Organisation, *Yearbook of Labour Statistics* (Geneva); civilian employment, OECD, *Labour Force Statistics;* numbers of industrial disputes, ILO, *Yearbook of Labour Statistics,* and Bundesministerium für Arbeit und Sozialordnung, *Arbeits- und Sozialstatistik* (Bonn, various years).
a. The 1968 estimates of days lost is from Walter Kendall, *The Labour Movement in Europe* (London: Allen Lane, 1975), p. 130.
b. Not including 1968.

It is not possible to find a simple, unambiguous indicator of relative bargaining pressure, let alone restraint. Germany's frequently cited record of industrial peace, however, might be taken as a rough and ready indicator. Table 5-3 supports a familiar comparison; since the end of World War II, Germany has had the lowest level of strike activity of any large non-Communist industrial nation. Since the positive coefficient of the *DL* variable, signifying days lost in work stoppages in equation 1, suggests the existence of an independent (although weak) relation between strike activity and the rate of increase in negotiated wages, the fact that little time was lost by the Germans is consistent with the notion that relatively few strikes are an indication of a fairly high degree of restraint.

But if a low incidence of strikes is taken as an indicator of bargaining restraint, it does not indicate the nature or the sources of that restraint. According to the discussion in the first chapter, restrained bargaining conduct and outcomes mean that the "actual" bargaining power of unions is restrained, but this can come about in various ways, including the following:

• The potential, or maximum, bargaining power of the unions may be held down by strong employers or by self-restrained or inhibited members.

• The demands or desired bargaining power of the unions may be depressed below their potential by self-restrained unions, which possess sufficient authority to impose restraint on their members to whatever degree is required.

• Potential or desired bargaining power, or both, may be restrained by a political-social climate that—whether through public policy, politics, or informal consensus—may contribute to the resistance of employers, depress the militancy of the employees, or otherwise incline union organizations to policies of restraint.

The Cool Climate: Unionism as a Social Counterweight

In Germany, the political and social environment has included injection of certain structural elements into the collective bargaining system by the American and British occupation authorities after the end of the war and assignment of high priority to domestic price stability as a goal in its own right. Aversion to inflation was the moral that virtually all sectors in German society drew from the national nightmares of the past, including not only the hyperinflation of the early 1920s, but also the subsequent depression and the Nazi dictatorship, for which the earlier inflation has been held partly responsible. And because aversion to inflation reflected revulsion from totalitarian control, the Germans proved selective in their choice of policies. They were for a long time reluctant to pursue price stability and full employment by a combination of budgetary expansion and incomes policy, because that combination was associated with the dirigisme of the Third Reich—notwithstanding the fact that Hjalmar Schacht's policies had apparently been an important factor in reducing unemployment in the 1930s.[24] Instead, the so-called social market economy (soziale Marktwirtschaft) school of thought predominated; it emphasizes both fiscal and monetary restraint, competition, and external balance. In monetarist fashion it prescribes direct

24. Bent Hansen, with Wayne W. Snyder, *Fiscal Policy in Seven Countries, 1955–1965* (Paris: OECD, 1969), p. 228.

targeting only for the objective of price stability. The extent to which the employment objective can be met depends on the extent to which the requirements of meeting domestic and international competition hold employers' feet to the fire and stiffen their resistance to wage demands and also on the extent to which domestic price stability can elicit restraint on the part of employees and unions.[25]

Indeed, the establishment of a system of collective bargaining in an otherwise pure social market economy might seem to be an anomaly; it suggests a parallel to the awkward exempt status accorded to American unions with respect to the antitrust laws. In the United States, legislated support for collective bargaining can be placed in historical perspective as a second-best alternative, adopted in consequence of the limited ability of antimonopoly laws to translate the competitive ideal into reality in the marketplace. American unionism won a wary and almost grudging acceptance along with big business, to which it has been regarded as a social counterweight. The German experience obviously diverges from the American in important respects. Postwar support could be regarded as the resumption of a tradition of strong and independent unionism before the 1930s; it owed much to the identification of important business sectors with the Hitler regime; and it reflected, as noted earlier, the direct influence of both the American and the British occupation authorities. Antimonopoly policy in Germany was also inspired and encouraged by the same wartime and postwar influences, but it lacked significant historical roots and instead had to contend with traditional acceptance of cartelized enterprise as fully compatible with managerial efficiency and international competitiveness. Germany's postwar antimonopoly laws have therefore been characterized by significant exceptions, and

25. This view was promptly contested by the unions and the Social Democrats in the downswing of 1949–50, and, as we have noted, the Christian Democratic government and the Bank Deutscher Länder (the predecessor of the Bundesbank) were ultimately obliged to announce tax reductions and a job-creation program to reduce unemployment, which had reached 10–12 percent (Wallich, *Mainsprings,* pp. 79–87). The Korean boom supervened, however, the foreign-exchange position deteriorated, and a policy of credit stringency was reinstituted. Subsequently, as Emminger points out, Germany became "an extreme surplus country within the EPU (European Payments Union)" and was rewarded by an export-led *Mengenkonjunktur,* or "expansion without inflation," in 1952–54 (Emminger, *The D-Mark,* pp. 4, 5). This policy was adopted at the insistence of the EPU, which made it a condition of an extension of credit, whereas an American suggestion for rationing and price controls, which had been dismantled at the time of the currency reform, was not accepted. The conservative choice was vindicated by the outcome, when, "despite the absence of major stimulating measures, business turned up in the second half of 1952" (Wallich, *Mainsprings,* p. 99).

the Germans have been regarded as more readily disposed than the Americans or the British to accept oligopolistic arrangements within industry.[26] Nevertheless, the second-best analogy does hold to the extent that, in Germany as in the United States, the community has supported unionism and collective bargaining for their properties as a social counterweight, while restraining them in the interest of economic performance, among other things. This offers some contrast both to France, where collective bargaining has generally lacked effective public support, and to the United Kingdom, where the social counterweight has at times threatened to overbalance the economic mechanism itself.

German unions, for their part, have also implicitly accepted their status in the community as a second-best expedient, as have their American counterparts. In each country, the unions have naturally chafed under various restraints that have been laid upon them, but neither union movement has displayed any discernible enthusiasm for thoroughgoing trustbusting, with the economic and policy risks to which such a course of action would expose them. German unions and workers in particular have valued large-scale enterprise for the job security that it has traditionally provided, they held attempts by the Allied occupation process to break up the big companies as partly responsible for high postwar levels of unemployment, and they have opposed domestic attempts to invigorate anticartel policy in the 1970s and 1980s when unemployment has been reaching and exceeding levels recorded in the 1950s.[27]

The counterweight was heaviest at the beginning of the postwar period, when, as Folke Schmidt wrote, "the trade-union people were made welcome to organize the workers in the shops, whereas in the first few years the employers, because of the denazification programme, were not allowed to engage in organizational activities."[28] Subsequently, membership in the Deutscher Gewerkschaftsbund (DGB), the German Trade Union Confederation, whose affiliates account for about four

26. The exceptions, especially in the case of mergers, were defended in part on the grounds that Germany's entry into the Common Market made it less important to approximate competitive conditions within domestic industry. See Geoffrey R. Denton, Malcolm C. Maclennan, and Murray Forsyth, *Economic Planning and Policies in Britain, France, and Germany* (London: Allen & Unwin; New York: Frederick A. Praeger, 1968), pp. 58–61.

27. *Wall Street Journal,* August 21, 1979.

28. Folke Schmidt, "Industrial Action: The Role of Trade Unions and Employers' Associations," in Benjamin Aaron and K. W. Wedderburn, eds., *Industrial Conflict: A Comparative Legal Survey* (New York: Crane, Russak, 1972), p. 37.

fifths of the German trade unionists, rose less rapidly than total employment, until the mid 1960s. On the other hand the DGB gained a million members between 1950 and 1965. As a result of the ensuing recession and attendant circumstances, the DGB lost 200,000 members in the next three years, 1965–68; still, membership remained constant as a fraction of both total and dependent employment—26 percent and 30 percent, respectively.[29] Since the 1970s, about 40 percent of the country's wage and salary earners have been members of the DGB, with about 7.5 million members, and of three other federations—the Deutsche Angestelltengewerkschaft (DAG), the German Salaried Employees' Union, with about 500,000; the Deutscher Beamtenbund (DBB), the Association of German Civil Service Officials, with about 700,000; and the very small Christlicher Gewerkschaftsbund (CGB), the Christian Trade Union. This degree of organization in Germany is lower than the membership density in the United Kingdom, which began to exceed 50 percent in the 1970s, but it is considerably higher than densities in the neighborhood of 25 percent, which are found in France and the United States. By international standards, it appears that German unionism has been equipped with a fair allotment of potential bargaining power, to the extent that bargaining power can be measured by density of membership.

In addition, the level of market power associated with a given degree of organization may be affected by application of the principle that conditions negotiated by unions apply to nonmembers as well as to members. This principle has found two applications. In the first place, provision has been made for the extension of collective agreements to firms that are not members of the signatory association of employers, provided that at least half the employees in the industrial sector involved are employed by member firms and provided further that extensions be approved by both the union and the employer federations covered and that it is found by the federal or state minister of labor to serve the public interest.[30] In the second place, in organized establishments negotiated

29. Between 1951 and 1955, the membership of the DGB fell from 40.5 percent of civilian employment to 35.7 percent. By 1960 it had fallen to 31.7 percent, and in 1965 it stood at 24.9 percent. By 1970, however, membership in proportion to employment had increased a bit, to 25.7 percent. It should be noted that the decline in membership in relation to dependent employment was less than its decline in relation to total civilian employment in the 1960s: from 31.3 percent to 29.9 percent in the former case, and from 31.7 percent to 25.7 percent in the latter. For DGB membership data, see Günter and Leminsky, "The Federal Republic," table 3.6, p. 165; see also p. 164.

30. Hans Reichel, "Recent Trends in Collective Bargaining in the Federal Republic of Germany," in International Labour Office, *Collective Bargaining in Industrialised Market Economies* (Geneva: ILO, 1974), p. 258.

terms and conditions of employment are often extended to union members and nonmembers alike. The extension of union conditions to unorganized firms and employees can increase union bargaining potential at any given degree of organization when it limits competition by nonunion firms, including new entrants, in product markets or when it limits the incentive of employers to substitute nonunion workers for union members.[31]

On the other hand, extension may also retard or prevent an increase in the degree of organization and of union bargaining potential by obviously reducing the incentive of employees to join unions and swell their treasuries. Symmetrically, but considerably more worrisome to the unions, extension can threaten to make free riders out of present union members. Thus extension can cut either way: its net effect can be either to protect or to erode union positions. Under conditions of high employment and high use of capacity, which generally prevailed between the mid 1950s and the mid 1970s, the potential for protection was not very great, and extensions of collective agreements were not frequently resorted to. But the unions have been made uneasy by the threat to their members and, therefore, to their potential bargaining power by the ability of employers to apply union-negotiated conditions to nonunion employees.

This suggests another, more nearly contemporary parallel with U.S. experience: American employers have frequently maintained their relative wages at levels designed to discourage organization (although this has not necessarily entailed a close tracking of union settlements in the short run).[32] In Germany, as in the Netherlands, some unions attempted to negotiate benefits exclusively for their members in separate contracts. This members-only attempt was made by the unions in textiles and garments and in construction—the latter having been one of the few industries in which contractual provisions were extended to nonsignatory firms. But the employers, who had always extended negotiated conditions to unorganized employees, contested this, and the Federal

31. Indeed, the striking power of a union could be greater under conditions of extension than under industrywide bargaining in a completely organized market. In both cases, the unionized employer's propensity to resist is weakened by the knowledge that all his competitors will be obliged to settle on the same terms as he does; but in the former case, he is also faced by the prospect of loss of a share of his market to his nonunion and nonstruck competition.

32. Robert J. Flanagan, "Wage Interdependence in Unionized Labor Markets," *Brookings Papers on Economic Activity, 3:1976,* pp. 635–81.

Labor Court buttressed their custom by invalidating the members-only contracts.[33] (American unions have not been noticeably interested in bargaining for members only, but if they were to change their minds, they too might run afoul of certain laws—the law setting forth the union's duty to represent all employees in the bargaining unit equally, and prohibitions against domination of a union by an employer, for example, and the law against discrimination against employees in order to encourage union membership.)

A more direct way for unions to solve the free-rider problem in organized establishments is to negotiate closed-shop agreements, but this remedy is also precluded by law in the Federal Republic.[34] In making the closed shop illegal, Germany offers a further parallel with American treatment of unions. And it stands in marked contrast to the United Kingdom, where the unions successfully resisted a law—the Industrial Relations Act of 1971—which would have outlawed the closed shop and ultimately forced its repeal.

The German propensity to impose legal restraints on unionism extends to strikes. This raises a further parallel with American mores, in that both countries have made it illegal to violate a no-strike agreement, as it is called in the United States, or the "peace obligation," as it is called in Germany. Indeed, in both countries an obligation not to strike during the term of the collective agreement has been inferred in the absence of an explicit clause in the agreement. In the United States a no-strike agreement has been inferred from the existence of a provision for grievance arbitration in the contract. In Germany—where disputes arising out of the interpretation or administration of collective agreements come under the jurisdiction of official tripartite labor courts unless the parties have provided for private arbitration—the peace obligation

33. Thilo Ramm, "Labor Courts and Grievance Settlement in West Germany," in Benjamin Aaron, ed., *Labor Courts and Grievance Settlement in Western Europe* (Berkeley and Los Angeles: University of California Press, 1971), p. 90; Reichel, "Recent Trends," p. 258; Joachim Bergmann and Walther Müller-Jentsch, "The Federal Republic of Germany: Cooperative Unionism and Dual Bargaining Systems Challenged," in Solomon Barkin, ed., *Worker Militancy and Its Consequences, 1965–75: New Directions in Western Industrial Relations* (New York: Praeger Publishers, 1975), p. 253; Walther Müller-Jentsch and Hans-Joachim Sperling, "Economic Development, Labour Conflicts, and the Industrial Relations System in West Germany," in Colin Crouch and Alessandro Pizzorno, *The Resurgence of Class Conflict in Western Europe* (New York: Holmes & Meier, 1978), vol. 1, pp. 276–77.

34. Walter Kendall, *The Labour Movement in Europe* (London: Allen Lane, 1975), p. 124.

is simply regarded as an implicit quid pro quo in the collective contract.[35] But the close parallel ends with the treatment of strikes during the term of an existing contract, for the Germans have tended to circumscribe the right to strike more narrowly than have the Americans—and a fortiori, than their European neighbors. The Americans have indeed prohibited not only those strikes conducted by specific unlawful means—sit-down strikes, for example, or strikes marked by purposeful recourse to violence—but also those conducted for certain unlawful purposes; the latter include notably exertion of pressure on neutral, or "secondary," employers, who may be involved in commercial relations with "primary" employers who are directly involved in a labor dispute, or who may be caught in a crossfire between rival unions contending with each other over the assignment of work or for the right to represent a particular group of employees. But in general, the right of "any employee" to strike in furtherance of "any current labor dispute," whether "for the purpose of collective bargaining or other mutual aid or protection," is asserted, and the status of the striker as an employee may in various cases be protected under the National Labor Relations Act.[36]

In Germany, the legal scope for striking—and locking out—has been considerably greater than it had been during the Weimar Republic, when compulsory arbitration of disputes over the terms of new collective bargaining agreements existed. Nevertheless, the postwar legal system rests on a historical foundation that is paternalistic as well as liberal in nature. It originated in the late nineteenth and early twentieth centuries, when governments of the time attempted to compensate for the bargaining weakness of the early Socialist unions by establishing labor courts. Thus, public policy sought to reduce the market power of the employers by building up the power of the state and not necessarily by increasing the power of the trade unions. The deep misgivings of liberal critics of the system of labor courts under the Weimar Republic were subsequently confirmed by the Nazi experience; they were not completely allayed by the postwar elimination of compulsory arbitration, moreover, which they regarded as a paternalistic dispensation under Adenauer's "chancellor democracy." Even the legal enforceability of collective bargaining contracts—a feature of the American system but absent in Britain—

35. Charles J. Morris, George E. Bodle, and Jay S. Siegel, eds., *The Developing Labor Law* (Washington, D.C.: Bureau of National Affairs, 1971), pp. 534–35; Gino Guigni, "The Peace Obligation," in Aaron and Wedderburn, *Industrial Conflict*, pp. 147, 151; Ramm, "Labor Courts," p. 135.
36. 29 U.S.C. 154.

could be considered to confirm the view that, as Ramm put it, "unions and employers' associations [are] lawmaking agents of the state, thus performing a function that is otherwise reserved to the state."[37]

The right to strike is recognized and protected, and strikers are exempt from the requirement that employees must give their employers prior notification of intent to terminate contracts of employment, an exemption which, technically, was not extended in the United Kingdom. But protection of the right to strike is not necessarily intended to redress a presumed de facto inequality in bargaining power between an employer and his employees, as it is in France and Italy. In those countries, employers do not possess a parallel legal right to lock out, on the grounds that lockouts, especially of the "offensive" variety, negate the right to strike; indeed, this view was widely held in the United States under the National Labor Relations Act until the mid 1960s. But in Germany—as in the United Kingdom, in Sweden, and now in the United States—the lockout is treated on a legal basis of parity with the strike.[38]

A legal doctrine known as *soziale Adequanz* (social adequacy, or appropriateness), moreover, has been of obvious concern to liberal scholars of the law; it certainly presents the unions with an unsubtle reminder of the limits that an unsentimental social and political climate can impose on their bargaining potential. According to this doctrine, the right to strike, while protected, is modified by the requirement that the strike be consistent with the "moral social order of the society as it developed historically."[39] The courts are thereby granted wide discretion. And while it is not necessarily the case that social inappropriateness is presumed until rebutted, a strike is an inappropriate violation of the right of enterprise if it cannot be followed by a collective agreement between the parties involved. This means that, to be appropriate, a strike must be directed against the legally recognized bargaining party and must be over bargainable issues. Hence sympathy strikes and political strikes would be illegal in Germany.[40] In contrast, American employers may replace sympathy strikers only when it is necessary to do so to

37. Ramm, "Labor Courts," pp. 84–85, 88, 156.
38. Xavier Blanc-Jouvain, "The Effect of Industrial Action on the Status of the Individual Employee," in Aaron and Wedderburn, *Industrial Conflict*, pp. 194–96, 223–24; Morris and others, *Developing Labor Law*, pp. 539–56.
39. Bergmann and Müller-Jentsch, "The Federal Republic," p. 254.
40. K. W. Wedderburn, "Industrial Action, the State and the Public Interest," in Aaron and Wedderburn, *Industrial Conflict*, p. 328; Thilo Ramm, "The Legality of Industrial Actions and the Methods of Settlement Procedure," in Aaron and Wedderburn, *Industrial Conflict*, pp. 276–77, 266–68.

maintain—in the language of the National Labor Relations Act—"efficient operation," and American employees have the right to strike "for the purpose of collective bargaining or other mutual aid or protection" in "any current labor dispute."

In Germany, where collective bargaining has been typically carried on between industrial unions, each of which possesses roughly a monopoly over its jurisdiction, and regional or national associations of employers, secondary disputes may present less of a problem than in the United States and Britain, and even less than in some continental countries where jurisdictions are more fragmented and may be more in dispute. For this reason tying the right to strike to the direct collective bargaining relationship might not seem particularly likely to restrict union bargaining potential. In Germany, however, the direct bargaining relationship itself has been truncated by law as well as by custom. Although, as in the United States, the collective agreement is legally binding and must be reduced to writing, the union may be barred from direct participation in a dispute that arises under the terms of the contract that it has negotiated. The union may represent an aggrieved member in proceedings before a labor court, but it cannot be a party itself, because collectively negotiated conditions become part of the individual employment contract. If a union believes that the terms of a collective agreement with an association of employers have been violated by a member firm, moreover, it can address a complaint only to the association, which is then supposed to persuade the employer to honor the agreement.[41]

Management must deal with employee works councils, which have been given the "right of codetermination" on questions that involve the administration of collective agreements. Yet the works councils are organizationally independent of the unions whose contracts they administer. By law they are supposed to be set up in all establishments that have at least five employees, and they are elected by all employees, whether they are union members or not. They are not supposed to negotiate matters that are covered in union agreements, and—not being legally recognized as unions—they do not have the right to strike or, for that matter, the right to levy dues. The idea behind the Works Council Act of 1952—which revived an old German tradition of employee codetermination—was to assure employees the right to participate in the determination of their own immediate conditions of employment

41. Ramm, "Labor Courts," pp. 89–90.

without restricting the bargaining activities of the unions or managerial efficiency. The law anticipated the establishment of a "dual system" of industrial relations in Germany, on the basis of a division of labor performed and respected by two distinct and autonomous types of labor organization. In fact, the union movement has always sought more codetermination—which includes representation of employees on supervisory boards of directors as well as the prerogatives of works councils—than governments have been willing to offer; and, at least until the end of the 1960s, the unions did not regard the works councils primarily as rival organizations. The unions were not given an express or exclusive right to nominate candidates in works council elections, and union shop stewards do not enjoy distinctive legal status in the plants, as do works councilors. But shop stewards and other union officers actually do draw up lists of union candidates in works council elections, and about four fifths of all works councilors are union members. Union stewards also frequently represent employees in an early stage of plant grievance procedures, before grievances are referred to the works council. But the works council is well regarded by German workers as a representational institution, and the inevitable interaction between the councils and the unions has produced a flow of influence from the councils to the unions as well as in the opposite direction. While union councilors help indirectly to determine how works councils function in plants, the works councils may also exert considerable influence on the unions at the regional level, sometimes as elected officers, and some of them are even reported to have championed moderation in union bargaining in order to allow more room for locally determined components of pay.[42]

But the influence of the works councils on union policy is most effectively deployed in securing clauses in collective agreements that permit the negotiation of supplementary agreements between councils and individual employers; such waivers are permitted under the law and allow the works councils to enter what would normally be part of the contractual preserves of the unions. Assent by the parties is not strictly necessary, however, because the employer could in any event unilaterally dispense benefits to his employees in excess of those that are

42. See Adolf Sturmthal, *Workers Councils: A Study of Workplace Organization on Both Sides of the Iron Curtain* (Cambridge: Harvard University Press, 1964), pp. 59–60, 65–66, 70–73; Müller-Jentsch and Sperling, "Economic Development," p. 282; Bergmann and Müller-Jentsch, "The Federal Republic," pp. 250, 262.

contractually negotiated on his account. On the other hand, the unions were legally prevented from encroaching on this local turf when they proposed that the increases negotiated with employer associations apply to the actual pay levels prevailing in the firms and plants.[43] At least until recently union attempts to negotiate "effective wages" and "opening clauses," which would permit the unions to negotiate with plants and companies within the context of the industrywide agreement, have run counter to the legal model of a union as a minimum-wage-setting institution.

Nevertheless, such restrictions on the activities of unions do not necessarily minimize the total bargaining potential of employees in the dual system that prevails in Germany. If, for example, locally generated wage drift contained a substantial "push component" as a result of pressure exerted by strong works councils, this would not be the case. Less scope for union bargaining would simply mean more scope for the works councils, just as, in Great Britain, slack left by the national unions in industrywide bargaining was at times more than taken up by the autonomous and aggressive shop stewards. In such an event, a dual system could even make for a greater sum total of potential bargaining power than a unitary and centralized system, with powerful local units generating variations in drift in accordance with variations in employers' "ability to pay," as if guided by an unseen discriminator. But since German works councils, unlike British shop stewards, are not legally allowed to strike and therefore are not supposed to do so, the circumscription of the union bargaining domain seems to be implicitly regarded as inherently minimizing the potential bargaining power of employees.

But even if the unions could not increase the bargaining potential of employees at the local level, could they not compensate in their own area of allowable economic conflict by raising contractual rates to levels that would minimize local drift? Not if the employers, their local fronts secured against strikes, could concentrate sufficient bargaining power of their own to hold down contractual increases at the industry level and thus protect the scope for unilaterally determined drift. And not if union members were reluctant to support compensatory claims by the national organizations. Could the effectiveness of the works councils as representative institutions—and the German councils have been regarded as

43. Ramm, "Labor Courts," p. 92; Müller-Jentsch and Sperling, "Economic Development," p. 277; Günter and Leminsky, "The Federal Republic," p. 175; Kendall, *Labour Movement*, p. 127.

more powerful than their French or Italian counterparts[44]—contribute to such reluctance, either by providing a partial substitute for pecuniary returns or by imparting a cost-conscious turn of mind to the employees in the enterprise, as is indeed prescribed by the Works Council Act? In the next two sections, we shall consider briefly whether the behavior of employers and the attitudes of the workers reflected the literally restrained welcome extended by the posttotalitarian democracy to its trade unions and to collective bargaining.

Tough Employers

There is reason to believe that the restrained performance of the two-tiered German system of industrial relations owes something to the determination of employers to control their costs and to keep their international competitive positions strong. To begin with, the structure of collective bargaining in Germany is conducive to resistance on the part of the employers. Bargaining is typically conducted on an industrial basis, although also on a regional basis. About 80 percent of all firms, employing 90 percent of all employees in the private sector, belong to some 44 national and 385 state (or *länder*) and regional associations, which in turn are affiliated with the Bundesvereinigung der Deutschen Arbeitgeberverbände (BDA), the Central Federation of German Employers' Associations. Thus, as has been commonly observed, the employers are more thoroughly organized than the wage earners.[45] Industry-level bargaining can enable employers to avoid the obvious drawbacks both of American-style company-level bargaining, which affords the national union a potential whipsaw advantage, and of Swedish-style economywide, or total private-sector, bargaining, which, by threatening a countrywide strike, threatens to invoke forced mediation by public authorities. And since industrywide bargaining reflects the influence of smaller and less profitable firms within the employers' associations, the contractual settlements could accommodate their relatively low "ability to pay"; this would leave room for drift to be paid by the more profitable firms at the bottom tier, where they need deal only with domesticated and legally fangless works councils.

44. Kendall, *Labour Movement*, p. 126.
45. William Fellner and others, *The Problem of Rising Prices* (Paris: Organisation for European Economic Co-operation, 1961), p. 318; Bergmann and Müller-Jentsch, "The Federal Republic," p. 247.

Yet an industrywide structure affords only a certain potential for employer resistance. It provides no assurance that the potential will be realized; in fact, it offers a certain disincentive to resist by assuring competing firms that wage settlements will be identical, or nearly so, and that interfirm cost structures will be left unaltered. Exposure to international competition should offset this disincentive to resist union demands; yet industrywide bargaining exists in other, equally open, but more inflation-prone economies. In addition, the regional basis of German bargaining might provide unions with some of the advantages of decentralized bargaining if they could make pattern setters out of regions in which industry happens to be more prosperous or employees more militant than the average. At the same time, even regional bargaining could threaten to create a public "emergency" in the event that an impasse was reached and thus invite official intervention and high settlements in the interest of industrial peace. Thus under bargaining with regional associations German employers are not immune from the drawbacks to which their foreign colleagues are exposed under either more or less decentralized systems.

But the wage policies of employers in the open sector of the economy were constrained by restrained price policies that permitted them to maintain or expand their shares of international markets; the fact that the coefficients of the world price change variable, PW, in equations 1 and 3, while positive, are considerably less than unity might be interpreted as a reflection of such pricing policies (see table 5-1).[46] So, instead of following the path of least resistance to the unions, many employers sought to exploit the opportunities for resistance held out by their bargaining structure. They have also attempted to compensate for one of its bargaining deficiencies, as they would regard it, by designating a single "core commission" of representatives of large enterprises in the heavy (or "metal") industry sector to join management teams in the various regional negotiations with the multi-industrial union IG Metall.[47] The employers' associations have been granted a good deal of influence

46. Lloyd Ulman and Robert J. Flanagan, *Wage Restraint: A Study of Incomes Policies in Western Europe* (Berkeley: University of California Press, 1971), pp. 182–83; Fels, "Inflation in Germany," p. 192.

47. Bergmann and Müller-Jentsch, "The Federal Republic," p. 247. During the mid 1960s, American experience provided a mirror image of the German core commissions when a "coalition committee," composed of representatives of eight national unions, which had bargaining status in various plants of General Electric, sought successfully to represent the union side in the various plant negotiations.

and authority over member firms. The latter are protected by strike and lockout funds, to which they must contribute; the availability of significant compensation, which may cover fixed costs, salaries, and even damages claimed by customers or suppliers during shutdowns, sets the German employers' association apart from its counterparts in France, Italy, and Britain. The member firm nevertheless retains the decision to take a strike or to lock out; this is in contrast to the authority possessed by the Swedish employers' organization, which also provides for strike benefits. (However, the Swedish system of collective bargaining is so centralized that it affords employers little scope for resistance through shutdowns.) The German association also seeks to protect members involved in strikes or lockouts from loss of market share to other member firms: the latter may not hire the struck or locked-out firm's employees, may not solicit its customers, and may not transfer its own custom away from the former.[48] Naturally, no such protection is extended to nonmember firms that are struck; it thus constitutes an incentive to join or remain in the association. And outsiders may be more vulnerable to strikes than members because they are not covered by the peace obligation in association contracts. Thus in 1965, when the Ford Motor Company was threatened with a strike by IG Metall, the metalworkers' union, which sought to force it into a separate enterprise agreement, it decided to break with its American tradition by joining the employers' association and taking refuge in its current no-strike clause. This episode confirmed an earlier general judgment that "considerable pressure can be brought to bear on employers who do not follow the agreed line."[49]

Although the central federation itself, the BDA, does not conduct negotiations, it too wields considerable influence over the bargaining policies and strategy of employers. In 1954 the BDA concluded an agreement with the DGB on the union side, as a result of which the various parties to direct bargaining established bipartisan procedures for impasse mediation in so-called settlement agreements. (These agreements provide for strike-free cooling-off periods, in some cases for the appointment of neutral chairmen to settlement boards, which in turn may recommend terms of settlement.) Both sides preferred self-govern-

48. Murray Edelman and R. W. Fleming, *The Politics of Wage-Price Decisions: A Four-Country Analysis* (Urbana: University of Illinois Press, 1965), p. 96; Schmidt, "Industrial Action," p. 44.

49. Reichel, "Recent Trends," pp. 257–58; Fellner and others, *Rising Prices*, p. 318.

ment by "the social partners" themselves to a return to the Weimar system of compulsory arbitration.[50] But in accepting the obligation of an employer to promote industrial peace, the BDA did not propose to sacrifice the bargaining power of employers. On the contrary, it insisted that "a state of balance of the two forces must exist; if it does not, the weaker party will be the victim of the stronger and partnership will be replaced by its mortal enemy, the claim of power."[51] To that end, the BDA urged its members to create "risk [-pooling] communities" with the funds and protective regulations referred to above. And the central federation itself has access to the strike funds that are established at the regional, industrial, and multi-industrial levels.

The predisposition of the German business community to resist economic pressure from the unions resembles the long-prevalent attitude of American businessmen, but the German approach differs from the American in two respects. In the first place, acceptance of social partnership as an equilibrium relationship suggests that there may be less disinclination to "recognize" and maintain a permanent bargaining relationship with unions in Germany than in the United States or, for that matter, in Italy and France. (In the United States the nonunion alternative is nurtured, somewhat paradoxically, by provision for employee representation and "decertification" elections run by the National Labor Relations Board.) It might be noted that employer resistance through hard bargaining can sometimes produce less inflationary wage movements than resistance through bribery of unorganized employees to remain unorganized. In the second place, the strategy of united employer resistance contemplated by the German associations is in contrast to the practice and preference of employers in a large sector of American industry, in which company-level bargaining is prevalent. (About a third of the collective agreements in the Federal Republic have been at the enterprise level; most of these, however, cover firms that remain outside associations in their respective industries.)[52] United employer resistance, like resistance cum recognition, could also prove more effective than the corresponding American alternative—if the threat of lockouts, as personified by the coalition core committees, is indeed credible.

In view of Germany's record of peaceful industrial relations, one

50. Ramm, "Legality of Industrial Actions," pp. 297–98.
51. Schmidt, "Industrial Action," p. 44.
52. Reichel, "Recent Trends," p. 257.

cannot expect to find evidence of repeated recourse to extended employer resistance, including lockouts. But the record does contain enough evidence of such resistance to suggest that the prevailing condition of industrial peace and, by international standards, restrained settlements has reflected the existence of demonstrable bargaining power on the part of the employers. The latter was revealed in the early 1960s, after unemployment had fallen to a plateau of less than 1 percent, and it followed a period, in the second half of the 1950s, when unions had begun to develop symptoms of increased militancy while unemployment was still higher than 3 percent. The key jurisdiction was the bellwether metals sector, in which the militancy of the workers had manifested itself in strike referendums in 1954 and 1955 and in a four-month strike in Schleswig-Holstein in 1956. The multi-industrial union IG Metall refused to subscribe to the general mediation agreement of 1955, and disputes in this sector tended to elicit ad hoc intervention by state and federal ministers, with consequences generally favorable for the union side. In 1954, a "pattern-plus" settlement was made when a mediation award made by the minister of labor in Bavaria was higher than an earlier mediated settlement made by *Land* (state) officials in Baden-Württemberg. And the wage increases in 1956–57, which followed the Schleswig-Holstein strike, were blamed by the Central Bank for precipitating a recession and condemned by Economics Minister Erhard for exceeding the increase in productivity.[53] Then, in 1961, when the mark was revalued, the BDA issued more detailed guidelines for the establishment of strike funds and supportive behavior by nonstruck firms, and during the next two years the employers moved over to the counteroffensive. In 1962, Gesamtmetall, the employers' federation in metals, replied to contract termination notices by IG Metall in three regions by posting lockout notices in two others. This dispute was mediated by the prime minister of Baden-Württemberg, but in 1963, actual strikes in that state were followed by actual lockouts. The latter had not been resorted to since 1928, and Otto Brenner, the militant president of IG Metall, charged that "with the lockout class warfare waged from above is again in full swing." But one man's idea of class warfare was another's idea of social partnership. "There were no political grounds for the decision," replied the federation of employers, and its purpose was "not to teach the metal union a lesson." The purpose was simply to drain the unions' strike

53. See Fellner and others, *Rising Prices,* pp. 336–45.

funds by widening the area of conflict. The effect was to arouse fear of a nationwide shutdown, which elicited the mediation efforts of Ludwig Erhard, later chancellor of the Federal Republic; but this time the mediated settlement, although it split the difference between the announced positions of the parties, was not greatly in excess of estimated growth in productivity.[54]

The 1963 stoppages were followed by a spell of industrial tranquillity, which lasted until 1969–70, when the wave of grass-roots strikes that had been sweeping over much of the continent reached Germany. The period of calm may well have reflected the chilling effect of the sharp recession of 1966–67 as well as of the earlier lockouts, while the wildcats, as we shall suggest later, were not amenable to the lockout strategy. Nevertheless, the employers saw no reason to deviate from their course. In 1970, the BDA issued another policy statement ("The Solidarity of Members in the Event of Wildcat Strikes"), which reiterated its rules of etiquette for employers and urged the member associations to make stronger provision for mutual aid.[55] The following year the metals industry returned to do business at the same old stand. The automobile employers rejected a settlement, suggested by a mediator, which the union had accepted. Armed with a special emergency fund, they countered IG Metall's selected strikes with a series of lockouts that left as many as half a million workers idle and was responsible for the greatest number of man-days lost in the postwar period. A union official branded these tactics as "brutal behavior on the employers' side"; the latter defended it as "in the interest of shortening the strike." The dispute lasted about three weeks, and the settlement was less than what the mediator would have awarded and only slightly in excess of the relevant rise in the cost of living.[56]

In 1974 a rather sharp acceleration of contractual wage increases occurred. It was associated with a relaxation of fiscal policy following the oil crisis in October of the preceding year, with continuing high export demand after a period of great appreciation of the currency, with Germany's second wave of wildcat strikes, and with widespread strikes in the public sector. On the other hand, appreciation of the currency had

54. Schmidt, "Industrial Action," pp. 45–46; New York Times, May 2, 8, 13, 1963.
55. Schmidt, "Industrial Action," pp. 44–45.
56. New York Times, November 23 and 25, 1971; "Locking Them Out," The Economist, November 20, 1971, p. 101; Müller-Jentsch and Sperling, "Economic Development," pp. 262, 263.

caused a pronounced increase in Germany's relative unit labor costs (in dollars) and export prices.[57] In any event, the propensity of the employers to resist at the association level remained strong. The first evidence of this occurred when the unions struck the prosperous shipyards in Bremen, seeking thereby to set a pattern for the then less profitable automobile industry and, in general, to avoid wider negotiations. The employers' federation in Baden-Württemberg promptly voted to support a lockout, and Volkswagen threatened to take a long strike rather than "be smashed to pieces by totally outrageous demands." A second manifestation of the will to resist came in connection with the public-sector settlements—following strikes in rail and road transport, postal service, garbage disposal, and other public services—which were deplored by Chancellor Brandt as excessively high. The employers in the engineering association announced that they would not accept "any such yardstick," and, while their own settlements—at 11 to 11.5 percent—also broke the chancellor's double-digit barrier, they proved to be 1.1 to 1.6 points lower than the public settlements.[58]

The strikes and settlements in the public sector marked a departure from Germany's version of the Aukrust mechanism, whereby the metals and chemicals branches in the internationally competitive sector of the economy tended to set the pattern for the rest, including the sheltered sector.[59] Not only did the sheltered sector move ahead on its own in 1974, but the public settlements were approximated in the chemicals industry. The latter, however, is the smallest major branch in terms of employment, accounting for 3 percent of the dependent labor force, whereas the metal industry, accounting for 21 percent, is the largest. And metals at least prevented the Aukrust wage-transmission mechanism from going into reverse, not only because it did not accept the public settlements as a pattern for itself, but also because it continued to serve as a pattern setter for retail trade and construction, which are predominantly sheltered industries in the private sector.[60] But this did not mean that Gesamtmetall had secured its leadership for all time. In

57. OECD Economic Surveys, Germany, May 1974, pp. 14, 28–31; ibid., July 1975, pp. 8–10.

58. Le Monde, March 20, 1973; The Times (London), September 5 and 12, October 16, November 12, 1973; January 25, February 11, 1974; Financial Times, October 21, 25, 28, 1973; January 25, 29, 30; February 11, 13, 19, 1974; OECD Economic Surveys, Germany, July 1975, table 1, p. 7.

59. Reichel, "Recent Trends," p. 264.

60. OECD Economic Surveys, Germany, July 1975, table 1, p. 7.

1978, the engineering settlement exceeded the government's less than 5 percent guideline, while the public sector, chemicals, and even IG Metall's own members in steel did settle for "a 4 in front of the decimal point." Even so, the engineering employers granted an increase just equal to 5 percent, after taking a three-week strike and resisting a union effort to set a pattern with a 7 percent rise won by the longshoremen.[61]

The militancy of employers was not confined to the engineering sector nor was it reserved for issues about pay. In 1976, for example, the printing industry countered a newspaper strike with a lockout in a dispute in which the union nevertheless managed to exceed the officially approved settlement in engineering and in the public sector.[62] Less than two years later, the same parties locked themselves into a prolonged and bitter strike and lockout over technological change in the newspaper industry. As a result, the employers won the right to have reporters type copy directly into typesetting computers and to reclassify typesetting as a clerical job, subject to provision for attrition of the skilled typesetters.[63] In 1978, the engineering settlement referred to in the preceding paragraph also dealt with the subject of technical change: it provided that technologically displaced workers be allowed to transfer to or be trained for other jobs at comparable pay or, if such are unavailable, that they receive a compensatory bonus.[64]

In Germany job security and technological change came to the fore as issues in collective bargaining during the 1970s, after unemployment began its steep rise. That rise was interpreted by unionists—and, indeed, by others as well—as in good part a structural phenomenon. The principal bargaining demands that the structural emphasis appeared to support were demands for work sharing, in particular a shorter workweek. This implied much more significant cost increases than the compensatory arrangements granted by the engineering employers. And so, when IG Metall demanded a phased reduction in weekly hours to thirty-five in November 1978, in addition to a 5 percent increase in hourly rates, the employers countered with an offer of a two-week increase in vacations,

61. "Will the Ruhr Follow Suit?" *The Economist,* April 8, 1978, p. 90; "Five Weak Excuses for Not Reflating," ibid., April 29, 1978, p. 95.

62. "Bad Time to Strike," ibid., May 15, 1976, p. 90; *New York Times,* May 19, 1976.

63. "Solidarity Is as Solidarity Does," *The Economist,* March 4, 1978, p. 82; "Typists Take Over; Craftsmen Retreat," ibid., March 25, 1978, p. 81.

64. "Will the Ruhr Follow Suit?" p. 90.

and when the union struck the steel plants that supply the automobile industry, the employers' association locked out the rest. The stoppage—the first in the industry in fifty years—lasted six weeks. It was settled largely on the employers' terms, the basic workweek being kept intact, although extra days off were awarded and the vacation period was to be increased from four to six weeks by 1983.[65] The union claimed that the lockouts constituted a move "to bleed our union funds"; in fact the stoppage consumed "50 million marks' worth of strike funds." IG Metall had joined forces with the printers' union in filing more than 40,000 individual lawsuits that challenged the constitutionality of the lockouts that arose out of the earlier engineering and printing strikes. But the steel industry was not deterred from recourse to this weapon, and when the president of the miners threatened to call his members out in a sympathetic strike against the lockouts in steel, the employers threatened to take reprisals against the union if it violated the peace obligation in its collective agreements.

The demand for a shorter workweek, which precipitated the stoppage in steel, had been developed earlier by the DGB as a bargaining objective for the entire labor movement. Ultimately it elicited a characteristic response from the BDA, the central federation of employers, which had reacted to disputes in the past with guidelines for secondary tactical action and financial support. During the steel strike and lockout, the BDA issued a "taboo catalogue" of certain union demands—including reduction in the workweek and reduction in the duration of wage agreements below twelve months—which individual member firms might not accede to without first obtaining permission from their respective associations.[66] IG Metall, frustrated by the outcome of the 1976 strike and worried by the hostile reaction of its members to the settlement and by the local activists in its ranks, sought to counter these tactics by calling "warning strikes" at the expiration of wage agreements and before the conclusion of new ones. Warning strikes were not uncommon abroad—in Italy and the United Kingdom, for example—and in Germany they had been called in public transport, in 1977, and even in metals, in 1977 and 1978. An arbitration agreement in the latter jurisdiction, however, forbade striking as long as mediation was in progress, and IG

65. "Steeling the Workers for Defeat," ibid., January 13, 1979, p. 64; "IG Metall Forges a New Weapon," ibid., June 9, 1979, p. 94.
66. "IG Metall," p. 96.

Metall proposed to eliminate this ban.[67] The union demand amounted to a limited legitimization of local strikes, for these would be sanctioned by a recognized union in furtherance of collective bargaining agreements and only during periods when the peace obligation was not in effect. Taken at face value, the warning strike would not appear to be an effective countermeasure to sympathetic action by employers, since nonstruck employers would presumably be free to impose lockouts— although the simultaneous occurrence of a sufficiently large number of such strikes might reduce the efficiency of the employers' roving commissions. Nevertheless, the demand of IG Metall was intended to remind the employers that the exercise of their bargaining power in official centralized negotiations could ultimately frustrate individual union members to the point at which they would turn to unofficial and decentralized channels of recourse—as they had done in 1969 and 1973, to their undeniable advantage.

The metalworkers' warning shot was also, therefore, an implicit acknowledgment by the largest union in the country of the effectiveness of centrally directed employer resistance and of its own inability to outflank social partners of its own choosing. Table 5-3 lends some support to this view. Although, as we have seen, consistently far less time has been lost because of industrial disputes in the Federal Republic in relation to the size of its employed work force (days lost per employee) than in any of the other Western European countries of comparable size, it does not rank proportionately as low with respect to the average number of striking workers per strike. Thus, throughout the entire period 1961–75, the average number of workers per strike in Germany actually exceeded the number in the United Kingdom and even the United States, while far fewer days were lost per strike in Germany than in the other two countries, and in the rest as well. These comparisons are consistent with the view that strike size in Germany, while smaller than in the other large countries—and in the Netherlands too—was held up by the united resistance of employers under association bargaining and, further, that relatively widespread strikes may have acted as a disincentive to frequent strikes or to strikes lasting for long periods.

But the ability of employers to impose the costs of strikes and lockouts on unions did not imply that the unions could obtain no returns from striking. The positive coefficients of the strike variable, DL, in equation

67. *International Herald Tribune,* supplement, April 1977; "A 7% Minimum?" *The Economist,* February 11, 1978, pp. 94, 96; "IG Metall," p. 94.

Table 5-4. *Contractual Wage Increases and Wage Drift, Germany, 1965–77*

Percentage change from preceding year

Year	Hourly earnings of adults in industry[a] (1)	Hourly wage rates of adults in manufacturing[b] (2)	Drift (column 1 − column 2) (3)
1965	9.8	7.1	2.7
1966	6.6	7.5	−0.9
1967	3.2	5.3	−2.0
1968	4.4	4.4	0.1
1969	8.9	6.5	2.4
1970	14.8	12.4	2.4
1971	11.0	13.4	−2.4
1972	8.9	8.5	0.5
1973	10.4	9.8	0.6
1974	10.2	12.0	−1.8
1975	7.9	9.1	−1.2
1976	6.4	5.6	0.8
1977	7.1	7.5	−0.4

a. From *Statistisches Jahrbuch 1976 für die Bundesrepublik Deutschland.* Figures are rounded.
b. From OECD, *Main Economic Indicators: Historical Statistics, 1960–1979;* OECD Economic Surveys, *Germany,* June 1979, statistical annex.

1 and also in equations 1a and 1b suggest that time lost in industrial disputes was one of the determinants of increases in contractual wage rates (see table 5-1). On the other hand, the negative coefficients of DL in the wage-drift equation, 2, and also in equations 2a and 2b, suggest that any returns to militancy were net of reductions in extra contractual earnings.

Table 5-4 shows that the sharply increased raises in contractual rates in 1970 were both preceded by and associated with negative drift and also that a jump in contractual raises in 1974 was associated with and followed by negative drift. It might also be noted from figure 5-5 that the strongly positive residuals from equation 1 in 1970 followed a marked negative residual from equation 2 in the preceding years. Of course, reductions in local extracontractual earnings would include net reductions in overtime and incentive earnings, which would come about automatically as the result either of the stoppages themselves or of economic recession, which occurred in 1966–67 as well as in 1971 and 1974–75. The effects of recession, however, should have been controlled for by the unemployment and the change in employment variables in the

Figure 5-5. *Residuals*[a] *from Equations 1–3, Table 5-1*

Equation 1: Changes in the wage rate (*WR*)

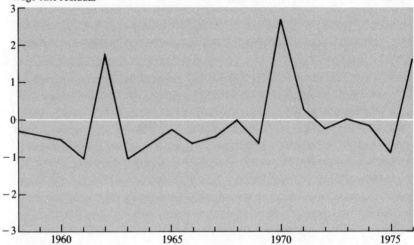

Wage-rate residual

Equation 2: Wage drift (*WD*)

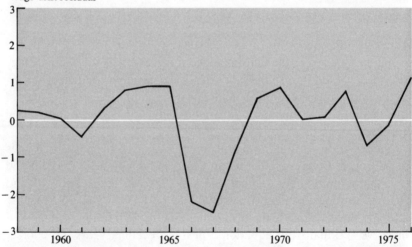

Wage-drift residual

a. Residual = actual − predicted. Residual measured in standard error units.

Figure 5-5 (*continued*)

Equation 3: Changes in hourly earnings (*BCE*)

Earnings residual

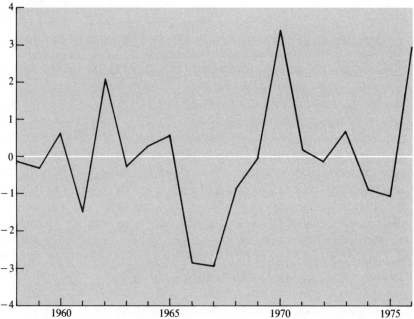

estimating equations—which, incidentally, indicate little influence on drift. Negative drift has also included reductions in local noncontractual bonuses, moreover, which indeed helped to touch off an early outbreak of strikes in 1966–67 and prompted the unions to march under the banner of "No negative wage policy."[68] Thus, negative drift could give rise to strikes as well as the other way around. But in neither event could it be concluded that the resistance of employers to the unions under industry-level and multiemployer bargaining merely caused a transfer of labor bargaining power to the grass roots. On the contrary, by holding down contractual settlements, such resistance may have contributed to autonomy for the employers in wage setting in the plants, thereby allowing the firms a greater opportunity to minimize unrest and discourage strikes when they felt it advisable to be more positive in their drift policy. That

68. Müller-Jentsch and Sperling, "Economic Development," p. 263; Ulman and Flanagan, *Wage Restraint*, pp. 190–91.

brings up a new question and leads us away from a consideration of the attitudes and behavior of employers to a consideration of the motivation of the workers.

Docile Workers?

In attempts to explain the model performance—comparatively peaceful and noninflationary—of the German collective bargaining system, it has been ascribed mainly to worker docility and union restraint rather than to employer firmness. Of course the three phenomena are not necessarily mutually exclusive; they could even all emerge as products of the same environment. Some examples can be cited. In the first place, Edelman and Fleming imputed to the German workers a tendency, which they discerned in the 1950s, to accept a subordinate position in the social and economic hierarchy, and they traced this to an old and strong tradition of social stratification, which was reinforced by "a highly stratified educational system."[69] The same pervasive influence would be invoked in accounting for the speedy postwar comeback of the German employer class, which could be regarded as a return to a historical social equilibrium. A highly specific example of acceptance of a tradition of social inequality was supplied by Ramm when he noted that

German employees generally do not go to the labor courts while their contract of employment is still in effect. Evidently, they are afraid of repercussions. . . . It seems . . . that the German system fails . . . to protect the employee against repercussions by the employer.[70]

In contrast, although in a somewhat different context, the American National Labor Relations Act makes it an unfair practice for an employer to discriminate against an employee because the employer has availed himself of the protection of the act. In Britain, where the tradition of class inequality survived into the postwar period but became subject to serious challenge by members of the lower orders, similar protection was written into the Industrial Relations Act of 1971 by a Conservative government.[71]

Another example might be found in the popularity that the independent

69. Edelman and Fleming, *Wage-Price Decisions,* pp. 83 ff.
70. Ramm, "Labor Courts," p. 155.
71. A. W. J. Thomson and S. R. Engleman, *The Industrial Relations Act: A Review and Analysis* (London: Martin Robinson, 1975), p. 47.

but company-bound works councils have commanded within the postwar work force. Sturmthal classed as "joint paternalism" a system in which "the works council has become a partner in a management team which administers the labor force of the enterprise with authority and benevolence."[72] Finally, a powerful example of common causality is provided by the general revulsion from, rather than acceptance of, another postwar heritage—the heritage of inflationary excess, followed by unemployment, followed by the collapse of the democratic social order. That negative consensus would be capable of jointly producing firmness in the employer, passivity in the wage earner, and restraint in the union in the determination of wages. And it was initially reinforced by consensus on an ordering of economic objectives by which clear priority was assigned to the rebuilding of the economy and subordination of consumption to the requirements of investment and growth.

But have these potential influences really made—or kept—the German worker significantly more nearly content with his lot and less militant than his colleagues elsewhere? It is no more feasible to measure the worker's level of satisfaction directly than to isolate the employer's propensity to resist wage claims. In the case of the employer, however, the conclusions drawn from all our behavioral and structural comparisons pointed in the same direction—that is, of aggressiveness—whereas, in considering the case of the worker, two international comparisons that we have attempted yielded only qualified conclusions.

In the first of these we may note that in other countries—notably the Netherlands—where a postwar consensus on the priority of growth and the need for wage restraint initially existed, it had pretty well dissolved by the 1960s. The consensus was eroded as the growth that took place under its sway generated impatience in the wage earner and also as a younger generation of workers with shorter memories progressively replaced the veterans. It could hardly be denied that similar corrosive agents have been at work in Germany, where managers expressed concern over the passing of the works council leader who was described (in Sturmthal) as "a man in his late fifties or early sixties, who has worked in the plant for twenty years or more, a solid family man, who is well known to a large segment of the personnel and well respected by both his colleagues and his superiors. . . . They usually have a long record of trade union membership, which reaches back to the unions of the Weimar

72. Sturmthal, *Workers Councils,* p. 68.

Republic, and in some cases even to imperial days.''[73] The prospect of a line of such stalwarts being replaced by an infusion of latter-day Jusos, or young radicals, has apparently made many a German manager's flesh creep. Nevertheless it is arguable that the corrosive process has been a relatively slow one in the Federal Republic—that good Dutch memories of shared wartime adversity created a less potent and durable incentive to postwar restraint than German nightmares about prewar inflation, which were reinforced by a second postwar inflationary experience that preceded the currency reform.

The second comparison involves Germany's participation in the European wave of shop-floor unrest, which began at the end of the 1960s, as well as a second outbreak of such illegal strikes in Germany in 1973–74. Although the German strikes followed the French and Italian series, they gave occasion for almost as much surprise as the dramatic events of May 1968 in France, precisely because the German worker had been regarded as more self-restrained and subject to discipline than his neighbors. It is true that the German wildcat was pretty small beer, internationally speaking. Table 5-5 shows that time lost in stoppages, in relation to the size of the work force, in the Federal Republic was only a fraction of time lost in France, Italy, and the United Kingdom in their respective years of peak strike activity during the period 1968–71. And it might be noted that 1971, which was the peak year in Germany during this period, was not primarily a year of wildcat strikes; the data reflect lockouts as well as strikes, most of which were official, and thus the militancy of the employers as well as of the workers. It might also be noted that the Germans did not stand alone at the bottom of the wildcat league. Strikes were comparably few in Sweden and the Netherlands; yet Swedish and Dutch workers have never been regarded as particularly docile. What all three of these countries have had in common is systems of collective bargaining and industrial relations that are better developed than those in France and Italy, and this may have provided the three with safety valves that enabled them to respond somewhat better— although still imperfectly—to worker dissatisfaction during the preceding decade.

In any event, there is no evidence that standards of pay and security found by workers to be minimally acceptable were lower in Germany

73. Ibid.

Table 5-5. *A Comparison of Days Lost because of Strikes in Germany, Selected Years, 1962–75, and Days Lost in Six Other Countries of the OECD*

Days lost (thousands)/civilian employment (thousands)

Year	Germany	France	Italy	United Kingdom	Nether- lands	Sweden	United States
1962	0.017	. . .	1.14	. . .	. . .	. . .	. . .
1963	0.070	0.31	. . .	. . .	. . .	. . .	. . .
1968	0.001	7.59[a]	. . .	. . .	. . .	. . .	. . .
1969	0.010	. . .	2.05	. . .	. . .	. . .	. . .
1970	0.004	. . .	. . .	. . .	0.057	. . .	0.845
1971	0.170	. . .	. . .	. . .	. . .	0.217	. . .
1972	0.003	. . .	. . .	0.995	. . .	. . .	. . .
1973	0.021	. . .	. . .	. . .	0.128	. . .	. . .
1974	0.041	. . .	. . .	0.60	. . .	. . .	. . .
1975	0.003	. . .	1.44	. . .	. . .	0.090	. . .

Sources: Days lost because of industrial disputes, International Labour Organisation, *Yearbook of Labour Statistics,* various issues; civilian employment, OECD, *Labour Force Statistics,* table 2, various issues.

a. Estimate of days lost in 1968 is from Kendall, *Labour Movement in Europe,* p. 130.

than elsewhere. Real wages may not have risen as rapidly in Germany as in Italy and the two smaller countries during the 1960s or the entire period 1960–77; but they did match the growth in France and they outpaced real wages in Britain. And the record certainly does not point to an exceptionally high tolerance of unemployment: Germany could boast the lowest rate of unemployment in the group throughout the entire period, except during the post-OPEC recession—and even then the unemployment rates in Germany remained lower than those in Italy, France, and Britain. Nor is there any evidence here to suggest that the German worker has been subject to money illusion notably less often than anyone else and therefore more willing to put up with smaller increases in nominal wages. German wage earners enjoyed as good a run for their money as the French and the British in the 1960s and maintained their standing in the double-digit club in the first half of the 1970s. They have not armed themselves with wage indexation, as workers have done in Italy, Denmark, and the United States, for example. It is sometimes possible to exaggerate the importance of this contractual form, however, as we suggest in the chapters on the Netherlands and Italy. In the case of Germany, the contract period was reduced to a year from eighteen months or longer, after the first batch of wildcat strikes in 1969.[74] The German practice of negotiating one-year contracts for wages and salaries, which are distinct from multiyear agreements covering other subjects, such as hours of work, holidays, incentive systems, and wage structures, is analogous to annual wage reopenings under some American long-term agreements. In short, while it is possible that German workers may have been better satisfied with less, the fact is that they have not had to make do with less; on the contrary, they have tended to enjoy a bigger bundle of pay, security, and progress than workers in most other lands. And if the German worker's bundle of benefits has been larger, his lower strike record need not be ascribed to greater docility.

If, as Ramm alleged, German workers have been relatively unassertive in pressing individual grievances against management on the shop floor, they have been as supportive of demands and as critical of settlements negotiated by their unions as workers anywhere else. As early as 1954 an arbitration award had been preceded by a strike vote in which the demands of the metalworkers had been supported by more than 80 percent of the members in a demonstration of solidarity that was attributed to the employers' "misjudgment of worker psychology."[75] In 1956 members of the same union rejected a settlement negotiated by the leaders, in an attempt to settle the strike in Schleswig-Holstein, by nearly as large a margin—a vote of no confidence, which was described as "an event without precedent in the history of unionism."[76] In 1962–63, strike activity was sufficiently intense to provoke government intervention as well as widespread resistance on the part of employers, and from figure 5-5 it can be seen that the positive residuals from equation 1, estimating changes in contractual rates, was almost as strong as those for the wildcat years of 1969–70. The second half of the 1960s was generally a period of industrial peace, but in 1971 an OECD survey claimed that

a growing alienation between trade union leadership and members seems to have developed during the past decade, and emergence of phenomena such as the wildcat strikes in the autumn of 1969 may reflect a more active attitude on the part of the rank and file of more than temporary significance.[77]

Some would regard the second outcropping of rank-and-file strikes in 1973 as speedy confirmation of this OECD hypothesis, although all

74. *Financial Times*, November 28, 1973.
75. Fellner and others, *Rising Prices*, pp. 337–38.
76. Quoted in ibid., p. 344.
77. OECD Economic Surveys, *Germany*, June 1971, pp. 15–16.

would agree that it was provoked by high rates of inflation.[78] It can be argued that in 1973 the inflation had taken the unions by surprise, whereas the unrest earlier might be traced back to deliberate union policy, which will be discussed in the next section. Developments in 1977–79, however, furnished further evidence of divergence of outlook between the members and the leaders. In 1977, the leaders of IG Metall negotiated wage increases that they themselves were reported to regard as excessive. In 1979, fewer than half the steelworkers involved in the 1978 strike voted in favor of the terms of settlement. Only a 25 percent vote in favor was required to end the strike, but the outcome, as in 1954, was regarded as a vote of no confidence.[79]

Recurrence of dissatisfaction on the part of the members does not imply disenchantment with either trade unionism or the method of collective bargaining in general. The members pay dues that are in excess of an hour's pay a week—very high by international standards—and for the most part they do so without checkoff.[80] The dissatisfaction of the members does imply, however, a belief that the unions in question could have secured more for their members, and this belief is consistent with the view that the low strike record can be ascribed to the exercise of restraint by the unions as well as to policies of the employers and to various constraints created by public policy and the judiciary. But why should the unions have followed a course of action that exposed them to the risk of disaffection even if, by so doing, they may have minimized the risks involved in striking and being locked out?

The Unions: Structural Bases for Restraint

In their unsuccessful attempt to reserve some of the gains from collective bargaining for their own members, German union leaders resembled Dutch unionists who sought in members-only bargaining some protection from the consequences of their participation in highly institutionalized incomes policies. But if the German system cannot offer union members special economic incentives to remain in good standing, neither does it provide them with some opportunities for

---

78. See Bergmann and Müller-Jentsch, "The Federal Republic," p. 267–78; Müller-Jentsch and Sperling, "Economic Development," pp. 263–64; "Survey," *The Economist,* December 1, 1973, p. 31.

79. *International Herald Tribune,* supplement, April 1977.

80. "Steeling the Workers," *The Economist,* January 13, 1979, p. 64.

defection that are found elsewhere. On the contrary, as we have suggested, unions in Germany may well have been more secure in their relations with employers than unions in other European countries—in Italy, for example, or even in Britain—as well as in the United States. And while the structure of collective bargaining may have lent itself to vigorous resistance by employers to specific union demands (within the context of "mature" bargaining relationships), the structure of German unionism has tended to narrow the range of alternatives available to the members.

In certain respects, union structure is more centralized in Germany than in France, Italy, and the Netherlands, and it is more centralized than union structure in Britain and Denmark in other respects. At the end of World War II, the labor leaders in West Germany broke away from the French and Italian pattern and from their own Weimar tradition of plural and parallel organization, which was based on political and confessional differences, in favor of "unitary organization." But partly at the urging of the British and American occupying authorities and of union leaders who feared the possibility of Communist control, they refrained from vesting formal authority over collective bargaining in the central federation in the East German manner and established autonomous national unions instead in sixteen industrial jurisdictions. In establishing the principle of autonomy for the national unions, the West German union movement became decentralized along contemporary British and American lines, but in virtually wiping the slate clean of small craft unions they did not. In 1949 more than a hundred separate organizations—there had been twice that number under Weimar—were merged into the sixteen industrial unions that originally formed the central DGB.[81] The Germans were able to accomplish at one stroke a structural streamlining that is not yet in sight for the British, with some 450 autonomous organizations, or for the Americans, with 170, after a generation of piecemeal amalgamations. The German industrial unions are vertical with a vengeance, moreover, for they include salaried employees as well as production and maintenance employees. More than a quarter of the 7.4 million members of DGB-affiliated unions are salaried employees and civil servants,[82] which exceeds the combined membership of the German Salaried Employees' Union and the Association of German Civil Service Officials.

81. Fellner and others, *Rising Prices,* p. 315; Kendall, *Labour Movement,* pp. 112–13.
82. Günter and Leminsky, "The Federal Republic," pp. 164–65.

The avoidance of organizational fragmentation in the structure of German unionism has been conducive to cost restraint in three ways. First, widening the range of employment alternatives potentially available to members threatened by displacement has facilitated acceptance of changes in working conditions—at least as long as job loss remains small in relation to the size of the jurisdiction in question. A hitherto prevalent practice of demanding increased compensation for adverse changes in working conditions rather than seeking to obstruct the changes themselves was consistent with this approach.[83] So was the rejection by the unions of a suggestion once made by the chairman of the DGB that the unions agree to a reduction in the workweek without a compensating increase in hourly pay, as a response to unemployment that was believed to be largely structural and technological in origin.[84] Second, narrowing the range of organizational alternatives available to members has removed one incentive to engage in competitive wage bidding. Finally, the existence of extensive occupational and geographic jurisdictions has made it possible for union negotiators to take the central perspective of the price setter rather than the worm's-eye view, with the narrowly defined occupational (or departmental) group facing a relatively inelastic demand curve for the services of its members.

But a broader perspective entails a policy of wage restraint only if, as noted earlier, the union is believed to possess considerable bargaining power and if its members are subject to some restraint. If the first condition did not prevail, restraint by the union would be unnecessary; protection of employment opportunities could be left completely to the resistance of employers to union wage demands. And if the members were not under control, restraint by the national union would be futile or politically dangerous to the leaders. In fact German unions have equipped themselves with an asset that has tended to build up both their bargaining power in relations with the employers and their organizational power in relations with the members. The asset is financial, consisting of large union funds, which are accumulated by high dues. We have seen that the employers devised their secondary lockout strategy partly in order to counter the bargaining power that this financial system conferred on the unions. The latter, for their part, adopted strong central controls over striking, which have had the effect of making it difficult for local groups to untie national purses and to keep them open. Under most

83. Müller-Jentsch and Sperling, "Economic Development," p. 267.
84. *International Herald Tribune*, supplement, April 1977, p. 135.

union constitutions, a strike cannot be called unless the national executive has decided to conduct a referendum of the members and unless 75 percent of the potential strikers vote in favor, and after a strike has been called, only 25 percent need approve of a negotiated settlement for the union to call off the strike.[85]

Grumbling is invited by a system under which the will of a militant majority can be thwarted. But where could they find an effective alternative outlet for their militancy? Not normally in their various works councils, which can neither raise revenues on their own nor call strikes. And not normally in their local shop stewards, although left-wing and more militant elements in the unions had pinned on these locally elected officials their hopes for making the works councils less dependent on the employers and more militant than the national unions. The net flow of influence so far, however, seems to have been from the works councils to the shop stewards and the unions, rather than in the opposite direction. Although the winners in works council elections frequently have been nominated by the union stewards, the shop steward elections, which are restricted to union members, are often controlled by the works councilors, on whom the stewards depend for necessary information as well as released time, in connection with their duties. And, as noted earlier, the works councils have tended to exert a moderating influence on the bargaining policies of the national unions, usually at the regional level, in order to keep their own economic room for maneuvering. Shop stewards—and works councilors as well—did help to lead some of the wildcat strikes in 1969, and shop stewards were among those giving voice to discontent with various negotiated settlements in subsequent years. But while the unions, like the employers—and like the Dutch unions in 1970—promptly acceded to on-the-spot settlements, they subsequently attempted to impose discipline on the stewards and to limit their autonomy.[86] Not having incorporated grievance handling into the collective bargaining relationship, the German unions may not be able to integrate the stewards into the union hierarchy to the degree achieved by industrial unions in the United States. On the other hand, the contrast between the position of the German *Vertrauensleute* (people of confidence) and the British shop stewards—whose authority has until recently been virtually unchallenged by either management or their unions—is

85. Müller-Jentsch and Sperling, "Economic Development," pp. 271, 278; Kendall, *Labour Movement*, p. 116.
86. Müller-Jentsch and Sperling, "Economic Development," pp. 282–83, 293–96.

sharp enough. The German unions, with precedent, may find it useful to conjure up the specter of revived militancy when they feel that the employers have been pressing them too hard; and indeed they may post a ghost watch of their own when formulating their contractual wage policies and demands. Nevertheless, they have been in a stronger position than unions in Britain and most other places to follow policies of restraint.

The national unions themselves are autonomous, and collective bargaining is decentralized and is not synchronized. There was strong support in the immediate postwar period for centralization at the federation level, but, as we have seen, this idea was rejected. Both the small number of national unions and their distribution by size, however, accommodate the adoption of wider perspectives and more centralized influence on bargaining than are usually found either in countries such as the United Kingdom and the United States, where the authority of the central federation is weak, or in such a country as France, where federation authority is strong within the union movement, but where the movement has not made collective bargaining its principal concern.

More than three out of every ten union members in the DGB and one of every eight employees (wage and salaried) in the country belong to a single trade union, IG Metall—which, with 2.6 million members, lays claim to the title of "the largest single trade union in the world." According to the leaders of IG Metall, the economic weight of the institution, represented by the number of its members as well as their strategic location in the export and import-substitute sectors of the economy, dictate that its bargaining policies be formulated with their macroeconomic consequences in mind. The relative size, financial resources, and jurisdictional breadth of the metalworkers' union have made it into something of a cross between a national industrial union and a central federation: it takes on the broader perspective of a federation, but its resources ensure its autonomy and its independence of the DGB.

The DGB, on the other hand, is not without influence on collective bargaining, especially where the smaller affiliates are concerned. While bargaining is decentralized, the great activity displayed by the BDA, its opposite number on the employers' side, in collective bargaining has been conducive to some comparable activity by the DGB. After the DGB adopted its Düsseldorf program of 1963, in which it formally abandoned a Marxist program calling for industrial nationalization in favor of a Keynesian program for full employment, growth, and a stable currency, attempts were made to endow the confederation with explicit bargaining authority. These attempts failed, but the DGB does have constitutional authority to issue guidelines on wage policy to its affiliates and to require prior notification of intended strikes. Following the founding congress of the DGB in 1949, in which the autonomy of the national unions was firmly established, the latter reduced the proportion of their dues revenues that they paid to the central federation, but the DGB maintains extensive research and training services. It was IG Metall, a substantial contributor to the income of the DGB, which was instrumental in blocking the attempts to endow it with more authority.[87] IG Metall, together with a few other large unions—in public service, chemicals, and construction, for example—"can afford to steer a course fairly independent of the DGB . . . [whereas] the smaller unions . . . are more in need of aid, counsel, and in the end, support, from the DGB."[88]

Thus the national unions with narrower jurisdictions are subject to influence by the federation, while IG Metall, although less dependent on the DGB, shares its central outlook. While collective bargaining is decentralized and sequential in Germany, the structure of unionism is conducive to an articulated process of wage determination. The DGB lacks the authority possessed by the Swedish LO or the Austrian confederation, but the Germans have assembled an alternative mechanism for transmitting wage impulses from the open to the sheltered sectors of an economy, which, while much larger than that of Sweden or Austria, is almost as much exposed to international competition.

Sensible Unions?

When asked why their unions have tended to behave with restraint by international standards, even critical Germans quite often reply, "Because they are sensible." How does the sensible-union hypothesis square with other capsule explanations of Germany's economic success, such as the alleged docility of the workers, elasticity of the labor supply, and firm (or sensible) monetary policy? To begin with, it can be advanced as an alternative to the worker-docility hypothesis. Sensible union policy does not presuppose especially tractable members: the unions in question

87. Bergmann and Müller-Jentsch, "The Federal Republic," pp. 243, 245; Fellner and others, *Rising Prices,* p. 317n.
88. Kendall, *Labour Movement,* p. 116.

may be able to satisfy a normally demanding body of members without fully exploiting their bargaining potential or they may possess sufficient authority over the members that they are able to bargain within a zone of discretion.

On the other hand, the availability of an elastic supply of labor does not necessarily rule out the exercise of bargaining restraint by the unions. This is especially true when increments to the domestic labor supply show up promptly as increased employment, at existing wage levels, rather than as increased unemployment, which tends to reduce union bargaining power and to depress wage levels. As noted earlier, German unions have been credited with contributing to the elasticity of the German labor supply by accepting "the competition of immigrant labour,"[89] but it was always stipulated that immigrant labor be paid standard wages—although the immigrants have been disproportionately concentrated in low-wage and otherwise unattractive occupations. Since the late 1950s, this has made for demand-limited migration, as revealed in reduced migration into the country and in backflows during downswings in activity in the mid 1960s and mid 1970s. Other things being equal, migration that is not demand-limited would tend to reduce the amount of bargaining power left unexploited by the unions, since it would reduce their bargaining potential, through increased unemployment, without necessarily reducing their desired goals. In figure 5-6, such an inflow would be depicted by a downward displacement only of the curve of maximum potential bargaining power, *MNW,* since any given level of employment, along 0*E,* would be associated with a larger volume of unemployment. Demand-limited migration, however, would not reduce unexploited bargaining power because it would not reduce maximum bargaining power, although of course it could prevent both potential and unexploited power from increasing in response to increasing demand. Therefore, it would not preclude the existence of a zone of bargaining discretion that is assumed in the sensible-union hypothesis, so Giersch could attribute a lag of nominal wages behind productivity in cyclical upswings to "trade-union policy" as well as to an elastic labor supply.[90] In figure 5-6, *EW* represents the average real wage level at which the supply of labor to the economy is perfectly elastic, at least to the point *D* at which *MPL* = *EW.* Above *EW, MNW* remains in place.

The sensible-union hypothesis may also be invoked in explanations

89. Giersch, *Growth, Cycles, and Exchange Rates,* p. 10.
90. Ibid., p. 18.

Figure 5-6. *Representation of Bargaining Restraint*

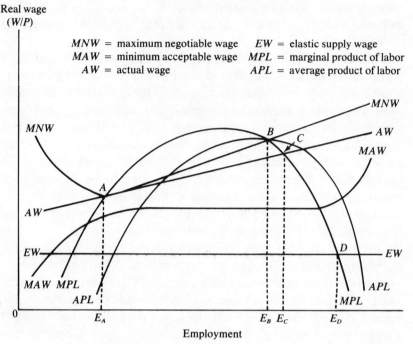

Real wage
 (*W/P*)

MNW = maximum negotiable wage	*EW* = elastic supply wage
MAW = minimum acceptable wage	*MPL* = marginal product of labor
AW = actual wage	*APL* = average product of labor

Employment

of Germany's economic performance that stress the importance of
monetary policy but also take its limitations into account. These limitations may include inability by the monetary authority to restrict the
money supply and the inflation rate under a regime of fixed exchange
rates and to determine the level of employment under a regime of flexible
exchange rates. In the former case—with fixed exchange rates—unions
could be blamed, as noted earlier, for a "cost inflation" that is prompted
by the effort of employers to reduce real wages when they would exceed
marginal productivity beyond the point of optimum use of capacity—if,
for example, the employers wished to reduce the real wage from *B* to *C*
in order to move from E_B to E_C in figure 5-6. Such an inflation is proof
against restrictive monetary policies if the latter raise domestic interest
rates in relation to world rates, thereby attracting an influx of foreign
funds. On the other hand, if during an export-led upswing in activity the
bargained real wage remained below productivity at full use of capacity—
as traced out by the line *A W* in figure 5-6—the unions might be credited

with exercising a restraining influence on the rate of inflation—and, ultimately, on the money supply.

It is more likely, however, that even a union movement whose wage policy was guided by a central perspective would err on the high side rather than on the low side, and it is unlikely that the monetary authority would always be lacking in control over the money supply, especially when, as during the recessions of 1958 and 1967, interest rates abroad were rising or the demand for exports was falling and the current account was in deficit.[91] Under these circumstances, an effective monetary contraction might be followed by an upswing, with money wages at first rising less rapidly than the room created by the sum of increases in world prices and domestic productivity, although somewhat more rapidly than consumer prices, and with real wages rising less rapidly than productivity and profits (see figure 5-6). Subsequently, money wage increases would tend to exceed their room and real wages would rise in relation to productivity, as productivity declined in relation to trend, profits fell, and price inflation accelerated.

Three explanations for the wage lag during the upswing are suggested. The first follows from the monetarist hypothesis of adaptive expectations, the second has to do with institutional inertia, and the third mainly with a sensible union policy of restraint. The hypothesis of adaptive expectations, apart from its theoretical failure to explain the recurrence of cyclical wage lags, is unnecessarily restrictive in the face of rising real wages and productivity in the expansion. Institutional inertia has been inferred from the existence of fixed-term contracts and also from the time taken by union negotiators to satisfy themselves that the cyclical trough was safely behind them—time provided by the existence (not the illusion) of constant or rising real wages.[92] But contractual wage setting alone does not suffice to explain the cyclical wage lag. The usual term of the contract is only twelve months, and, more important, contracts have proved to be "living documents," to apply Walter Reuther's famous definition, on more than one occasion. They were reopened under duress during the wildcat strike episodes in 1969, as noted earlier, and also in 1973. And in 1954 and in 1967–68, they had been extended beyond their termination dates, when they could have been "denounced," in some

91. Emminger, The D-Mark, pp. 10–11; Giersch, Growth, Cycles, and Exchange Rates, p. 25.

92. Fels, "Inflation in Germany," p. 599; Giersch, Growth, Cycles, and Exchange Rates, p. 19.

cases and renegotiated at what proved to be low rates of increase for longer periods in others, such as iron and steel in 1968.

Forecasting error was certainly a factor in 1967–68, and in 1959 the unions had held back partly because of "uncertainty . . . as to whether the recovery was sufficiently well based to affect employer bargaining attitudes."[93] But in both instances, caution in bargaining risked unrest among the members. In 1957, the metalworkers of Schleswig-Holstein had registered their disapproval of the terms of their strike settlement, and bargaining restraint in 1967–69 terminated in the outbreak of wildcat strikes—as did a subsequent period of relative restraint in 1972–73. It is unlikely that the German unions would have persisted in sailing close to the wind solely to avoid confrontation with the employers. Greater union militancy in the early stage of an upswing could modify the attitudes even of employers whose reluctance to raise export prices could be translated into united resistance at the bargaining table. Or, if employer resistance remained stubborn, it could be used by the union leaders to dampen the expectations of the members, thereby depressing the level of the *MAW* curve in figure 5-6—an option that, according to some observers, was exercised during the steel dispute in 1978.

Indeed, institutional inertia might be ascribed not so much to union delay in exploiting an upswing in bargaining potential as to a conscious policy of refraining from exploiting it fully. The stability of unit labor costs during the *Mengenkonjunktur* in the first half of the 1950s was attributed by Emminger to "moderate wage policies," which the unions followed because, according to the OEEC study, they were "conscious of the necessity to avoid wage increases which might diminish the number of jobs available, and were satisfied to accept a slowly increasing level of real income."[94] The Düsseldorf program of the DGB in 1963, which endorsed a stable currency along with full employment, ratified union subscription to the community's aversion to inflation and the implication that maintenance of price stability be accepted as a prior constraint on all policy instruments. The program emphasized equity in the distribution of wealth and income, but it also repealed support of Marxist socialism and it emphasized the need for continuous growth. As Giersch put it, "Inequality of income distribution . . . was in fact accepted for a surprisingly long time."[95] The Düsseldorf program re-

93. Fellner and others, *Rising Prices*, p. 347.
94. Ibid., p. 336.
95. Giersch, *Growth, Cycles, and Exchange Rates*, p. 10.

placed Marx with Keynes and favored countercyclical demand management; but support for a stable currency meant that achievement of the employment objective was seen to depend primarily on growth of exports. Hence a philosophy of restraint survived into the 1960s, after the passing of the period of capital shortages and unrestricted immigration of refugees. It may have survived less strongly than the Bundesbank and perhaps the general public might have wished, but it survived more strongly in the German union movement than in most other union movements. And toward the end of the decade the propensity toward restraint exhibited by union officials was even greater than desired by the Council of Economic Experts—strange bedfellows, on this occasion, of discontented members of the rank and file.

By inference the academic economists in the council—and others as well—drew a distinction between a restrained union policy and a sensible one and showed that failure to appreciate the limitations of monetary policy in a regime of fixed exchange rates could lead to restraint being carried to excess. They claimed that a 4 percent wage target, which was urged by a Social Democratic minister for economic affairs and accepted by the unions for 1968, was too low because it would induce an excessive lag in real wages and consumption, which would be succeeded by a surge of cost inflation. Their preferred solution was a revaluation of the currency, but since that was politically unattainable at the time, a second-best solution lay in a modest but early wage inflation, which would retain more resources in the domestic sector and prevent the development of a lopsided, export-led boom. The prognosis behind this backfire strategy was not falsified by subsequent developments: the rates of increase in consumer prices, money wages, and real wages more than doubled in the upswing of 1969–72; it was widely believed that the wildcat strikes had ushered in permanently higher levels of employee and union militancy; and an influx of foreign funds frustrated attempts at stabilization by the Bundesbank as German interest rates rose higher than world levels.[96]

But the idea of building an early backfire never caught on. It was an ingenious approach to the problem of international cost disequilibrium under fixed exchange rates, which was mentioned at the outset of this chapter, but its academic sponsors in the Council of Economic Experts

96. Ulman and Flanagan, *Wage Restraint*, p. 190; *Wall Street Journal*, March 9, 1970; OECD Economic Surveys, *Germany*, June 1971, p. 24; ibid., June 1972, p. 15; Emminger, *The D-Mark*, pp. 22–23, 30–32; Fels, "Inflation in Germany," p. 594.

also happened to be participating actively in an experiment in incomes policy at the time. Those who criticized the unions for having contributed to domestic inflation during the 1960s were not likely to place great confidence in a policy the most immediate and foreseeable consequences of which would be to increase cost inflation. Those—sometimes the same people—who, looking abroad, praised the unions for having contributed both to the relative price stability of Germany and to its relatively long and sustained expansion during the first half of the 1960s were not likely to welcome a policy that offered less restraint.

Under a regime of freely floating exchange rates, the council would not have had to consider early wage inflation as an alternative to appreciation of the currency. The Bundesbank could not be prevented by international market developments from determining the money supply and hence the rate of inflation, in which case collective bargaining would affect the level of real wages and hence of employment. This went by the name of "reprivatization" of the unemployment risk. But it did not have to work to the net disadvantage of the unions. A restrictive monetary policy that caused an appreciation of the currency sufficient to prevent a neutralizing influx of foreign funds could enable the unions to maintain real wages at levels higher than employers would wish. Employment in the economy would be lower than it might be otherwise, but the burden of unemployment might be borne disproportionately by new entrants to the work force and other "marginal" groups still outside union jurisdictions. Profits and price inflation would also be lower, which would mitigate discontent among the members and reduce the probability of wildcat strikes. Finally, reduced profitability would reduce the bargaining potential of the unions by increasing the resistance of employers and, in this respect, permit the unions to exercise less discretionary restraint. Of course, this happy outcome would depend on the validity of the three assumptions that we have introduced. In the first place, it would not obtain if the float were not free, so that the differences between the international and domestic rates of inflation were less likely to be offset by variations in the exchange rate. Second, it would not obtain if the monetary authority were to gain independence of external influences only at the expense of its internal authority, so that negotiated increases in labor costs would force accommodation of the money supply and increases in the rate of domestic inflation in relation to world inflation would be offset by depreciation of the currency. And, finally, the happy conclusion would not be reached if the authorities and the unions were not reasonably near accord on employment targets or their relation to real wages.

In some respects things worked out according to plan in the 1970s but not in other periods. A sharp deceleration in contractual wages at the end of 1971 and the first quarter of 1972 was attributed to the floating and appreciation of the deutsche mark that had begun in May and was to terminate with the Smithsonian realignment in December. The average rate of wage increase fell from 15 percent to 9 percent, although unemployment rose only slightly and remained well below the level of job vacancies. But strikes and lockouts in the export sector (metals and chemicals) had preceded the lower settlements, so it was believed that the stronger resistance of employers was generated by "companies [which] may have seen little prospect of passing excessive wage costs on to export or domestic prices."[97] But this period could be regarded as only a hiatus. Although inflation, excluding oil prices, did not accelerate sharply in the 1972–73 upswing, wages reacted more rapidly than during past upswings, as the outbreak of wildcat strikes in the autumn of 1973 brought additional wage increases and as union settlements increased in the course of the year.[98] This second wave of wildcats confirmed the general impression that Germany had been suffering from increased cost inflation caused by heightened labor militancy ever since 1968. This view was strengthened in 1971, when the floating of the deutsche mark was taken to mean that "price increases can no longer be blamed on imported inflation."[99] It was thus implied that the monetary authority had not been completely free to determine the rate of domestic inflation even though the appreciation of the mark might have made it feasible to do so.

In May 1973 the government introduced a set of restrictive fiscal measures, but it relaxed them at the end of the year, and it increased government spending to minimize the deflationary effects of the oil price increases and of the appreciation of the mark in relation to the dollar.[100] Meanwhile, the unions were seeking to protect the real wage incomes of their restive members against the inflationary effects of the same oil price increases, and they were led on this occasion by the public workers,

97. OECD Economic Surveys, *Germany*, June 1972, pp. 20, 22.

98. Ibid., May 1974, p. 20.

99. Economist Intelligence Unit, *Quarterly Economic Review: Federal Republic of Germany*, no. 4 (1971), p. 5.

100. OECD Economic Surveys, *Germany*, May 1974, pp. 9–10, 40–44, 73–74.

who had less reason than others to fear loss of their jobs. The employers, although reluctant to match the pay increases in the public sector, were also made apprehensive by the rank and file. At the same time, they were reassured by fiscal policy: they counted on being able to pass wage increases along into price increases and to protect their own real incomes that way. Both sides expected inflation to be at least 10 percent in 1974 and discounted official projections of 8 to 9 percent inflation when they were negotiating settlements that averaged more than 12 percent. But they reckoned without the Bundesbank, which, "in pursuance of the agreed monetary targets, but contrary to widespread expectations . . . did not accommodate the higher nominal wage increases by an easing of credit conditions. Consequently, businessmen were on average unable to fully pass on cost increases resulting from the high wage settlements and the upsurge in raw material prices."[101] In fact, the rate of increase in consumer prices did not accelerate in 1974 but held at only 7 percent, so the growth of real wages accelerated from 3 percent to 5 percent. Profits were squeezed, the unemployment rate increased from 1.2 percent in 1975 to 2.6 percent in 1979, and contractual wage increases fell sharply in late 1974 and 1975. Although a recovery began in 1975, contractual wage increases fell to 9 percent, down from 12 percent the year before, and real wage increases dropped from an average of 3.1 percent to 1.1 percent. In 1976 and 1977, contractual wage increases continued to decline—to 4.5 percent and 3.9 percent, respectively— while gains in real wages, after falling to 1 percent, increased to 3.6 percent in 1977. The rate of price inflation declined throughout—from 7 percent in 1973–74 to 4 percent in 1977—and it was significantly lower than in all the other OECD countries in the years after the beginning of the float and the oil price increase. This performance was consistent with an earlier episode, which, according to the head of the Bundesbank, "effectively refuted the assertion that no country can insulate itself against worldwide inflation."[102]

The break with the past, however, was not complete. This was not the first time that Germany had had comparatively low rates of inflation. The rise in the unemployment rate after the upswing had got under way presented a contrast to its rapid decline in 1968 and 1969, but unemployment remained notably lower than in most other countries. Exports were

101. Ibid., July 1975, p. 7.
102. Emminger, The D-Mark, p. 38.

an even stronger factor in the upswing of 1975 than they had been in 1967–68, and despite appreciations in the exchange rate between 1973 and 1979 that exceeded 40 percent, "the current account surplus . . . failed to show the desired decline."[103] It could be argued that adjustments in the exchange rate failed to eliminate the external surplus because of the limitations placed upon the monetary authorities by formal arrangements, notably the "tunnel," and by ad hoc cooperative efforts by central banks to avoid destabilizing currency movements. These limitations were accepted—in part because they protected employment and investment in export industries, but in part also because it was recognized that other countries would not find it feasible to counter the inflationary effect of unlimited appreciation of the deutsche mark on their own domestic cost levels. This could thus tend to perpetuate the German surpluses. If wages could have been as responsive to monetary contractions in the deficit countries as they were in Germany, the surpluses would have been less stubborn, exchange rates could have been more flexible, and control by the Bundesbank over the domestic price level less constrained. But because the German unions were more sensible than others in responding to changes in monetary policy, the monetary authorities were obliged to rely to some extent on the continued discretion of the unions in controlling inflation.

Indeed, union discretion could not have been dispensed with even if exchange rates had become completely flexible, endowing the monetary authority with maximum control over the price level while leaving real wages and employment to be affected by collective bargaining. Privatization would not be acceptable as a steady diet because the government—if not the Bundesbank—cannot be indifferent to the outcome of bargaining and also because it cannot be assumed that union wage policies would always be constrained to government specifications. If the unions and their members should choose a collision course, as they did in 1974, the heads that got banged might not always be their own; they could prefer a combination of a higher real wage, lower profitability, and a higher unemployment rate than the authorities would find acceptable. Thus the unions were not likely to be strongly deterred in their choice of a wage policy by potentially adverse output or substitution effects on the employment of such groups as foreigners, college graduates, women

103. OECD Economic Surveys, *Germany*, July 1977, pp. 7–8, 17; ibid., June 1978, p. 20.

seeking part-time employment, school leavers seeking apprenticeships, or even workers past the age of fifty whose share in unemployment was reduced after the 1967 recession by a lowering of the legal retirement age in 1973 and by contractual provision for greater job security. The government could take steps to reduce the intake of foreigners, as it had in 1973, but it had to be more actively concerned with the welfare of the domestic groups. Between 1973 and 1977, the unemployment rates among these demographic groups were substantially higher than the total unemployment rate and, with the exception of unemployment among older men, increased more rapidly. (The unemployment rates for apprentices and graduates remained lower than the overall average, but also increased more rapidly throughout the period.) Many individuals in these groups, moreover, were not classed as unemployed, because they were deterred from entering the labor force by lack of job opportunities. The *stille Reserve,* or "potential labor force," which includes voluntary job changers, numbered between 300,000 and 400,000 in 1976, when registered unemployment was 1,060,000.[104]

In fact, the unions were greatly concerned by the behavior of unemployment. The unemployment rate of prime-age workers—those between the ages of twenty-five and fifty-four—to which most of their members belong, increased no less rapidly than the overall total, and the latter rose from 1.2 percent of the dependent labor force in 1973 to 4.8 percent in 1975; by 1979 it had fallen to only slightly less than 4 percent. The rates in excess of 4.5 percent in the second half of the 1970s, while not excessive by international standards, had not been equaled in Germany since the latter half of the 1950s. Although output increased steadily from the 1975 trough, unemployment remained virtually steady at its new high plateau. The embarrassing restraint shown by the unions after the recession of 1966–67 had at least been accompanied by a quid pro quo, since the unemployment rate fell from 2.1 percent to 0.7 percent. There was no such happy result after the 1974–75 recession, despite the fact that the rate of increase in real wages declined more steeply and to lower levels than it did after 1966. The unions were told that real wage levels were nevertheless too high, which meant that profitability was too low, which meant that investment was too low. Increasing wages in relation to the price of capital (as well as other prices) could contribute

104. Ibid., June 1978, p. 11, table 3, p. 16; ibid., June 1979, table 3, p. 14; ibid., July 1977, p. 23.

to investment in labor-displacing equipment, but this would simply aggravate the unemployment problem by reducing the amount of labor required to operate a given stock of capital at normal rates of use. (The trend of capital–labor ratios apparently accelerated after 1969; and in 1977 it was estimated that half the total unemployment, or half a million people, was of such a "medium-term" nature, caused by a shortage of physical capacity.[105]) The fact that restraint of real wages was not being rewarded by reduced unemployment simply meant that more restraint was needed—to stimulate capital-widening investment by increasing profitability and to discourage capital-labor substitution. And, given the condition of domestic price stability—and the improved ability of the Bundesbank to enforce that condition—more real wage restraint meant more bargaining restraint.

The unions countered with remedies of their own, which had the aim of attacking the unemployment problem directly, both by reducing the supply of labor and by increasing the demand. On the supply side, the DGB argued—and IG Metall later struck—for a shorter workweek. The original proposal of the DGB suggested an uncompensated reduction of one hour in the week—or, more generally, the promise of wage restraint in exchange for such a reduction—but this was given a cold shoulder by individual union negotiators in favor of the standard demand for offsetting increases in hourly pay. Both versions were rejected by the Council of Economic Experts, the latter on the usual grounds that increasing costs would be self-defeating and the former because even it would increase personnel costs and because rationing of work at the original wage could raise the marginal utility of income above the marginal utility of leisure! In fact, the bargaining demands for a compensated thirty-five-hour week did arouse the usual suspicion that the unions were interested at least as much in increasing wages for their employed members as in reducing the ranks of the unemployed.[106] This concretely illustrates the limitations of the privatization approach to the problem of unemployment.

The union remedies were not entirely procrustean, since the unions have naturally supported the case for more expansionist management of demand. They rejected the view that reducing real wage rates and

105. Ibid., June 1978, p. 16; ibid., June 1979, p. 74; ibid., July 1977, pp. 23–24; ibid., June 1978, pp. 39–40.

106. *International Herald Tribune*, supplement, April 1977, "Survey," p. 13; OECD Economic Surveys, *Germany*, July 1977, p. 29; "Limited Partnerships," *The Economist*, July 1, 1978, p. 86.

increasing rates of return are the way to reduce unemployment. In the first place, reducing real wages would reduce consumer demand, or purchasing power, as well as costs, and if demand were depressed, reducing costs and increasing rates of return would be ineffective in stimulating investment. In the second place, increasing demand and real wages need not increase unit costs as long as cyclical increases in productivity and capacity utilization can be realized. This purchasing-power approach is not analytically incompatible with a wage-restraint approach, which, as noted earlier, approves of real wages rising as long as they rise less rapidly than productivity—along the path traced by AW in figure 5-6. (The equilibrium model of the international monetarists would rule out rising real wages because it excludes the possibility of a cyclical rise in productivity by the assumption that the labor market is continually in equilibrium, so unemployment must be voluntary, but German economic analysts have always stressed cyclical swings in the utilization of capacity and labor.)

The question is empirical—whether the demand effects or the cost effects of a given wage increase predominate at any time—and the results are sensitive to the assumptions used in the estimating models. Thus simulations by both the Council of Economic Experts and the OECD Secretariat implied that lower money wage settlements would yield increased employment and higher rates of growth in GNP; but the OECD estimate of the increased growth was only a fifth as high as that of the council. The unions, however, could point to estimates showing the elasticity of demand for labor at less than unity as evidence that any increased employment attributable to wage restraint would be less than an induced reduction in wage earners' incomes, so on distributional grounds they might prefer an alternative path toward increased employment. Employers pointed to a continuing decline in profits, the net rate of return on capital having followed a downward trend at a cyclically adjusted annual rate of 0.3 percent, from 16.75 percent in 1960 to 9 percent in 1976.[107] In the recession year 1975, however, there was an unusually large difference between the trend and the observed rates—between 10 percent and 7.5 percent—so it could be argued that reflationary measures could increase profit margins significantly. It could also be argued, along the lines of the open oligopoly model described in chapter

107. OECD Economic Surveys, *Germany*, June 1978, p. 38; annex 1, pp. 63–64; July 1977, p. 31n.

1, that even if real wages rose more rapidly than productivity, or if they rose while productivity and therefore profit rates declined, output and employment could continue to rise, as long as profits remained positive.

The German unions were not disposed to go that far, however. They did not seriously challenge the thesis that increased growth of potential output—that is, capacity-increasing investment—was essential to what the OECD called "a durable return to full employment in the medium run," and they did not dissent from the general view that the necessary investment required increased profitability and reduced inflation.[108] They continued to accept responsibility for moderating inflation, but they insisted that the authorities continue to assume responsibility for securing full capacity levels of employment. Thus, in a period of greater exchange-rate flexibility and appreciation of the currency, the unions continued to receive approbation from the outside for

responsible . . . attitudes—reflected in wage settlements consistent with a high degree of price stability—[which] have been a decisive factor in the achievement of better economic performance as the deceleration of inflation has enabled more expansionary demand management. And this, in turn, has meant that *real* wages and incomes generally have increased at a higher rate than in many other countries where high *nominal* wage increases have necessitated restrictive demand management and slow *real* economic growth.[109]

The unions were apprehensive lest unemployment supplement or supplant inflation as a source of discontent among the members in the 1970s, especially since issues involving job security and work effort have strong local characteristics. We have seen that some long and bitter disputes were caused by these issues, and in one of them, the steel strike of 1978, discontent of the members with the union leaders was made evident in the hostile reception to the negotiated settlement. This episode, however, also illustrated the attempt by the unions to forestall grass-roots activity by taking these issues up at the national level and at the same time attempting to establish greater disciplinary control; to the extent that this could be done, the outcomes would remain subject to a greater measure of restraint. The economic climate was conducive to the success of this strategy, since the combination of persistent unemployment and appreciation of the currency that characterized the upswing after 1975 made for increased resistance by employers to any increase in militancy on the part of the workers. These conditions were

108. Ibid., July 1977, pp. 11–12; ibid., June 1978, p. 24.
109. Ibid., June 1979, p. 59.

not conducive to successful local wildcat activity—wage drift was slightly negative in 1975, 1977, and 1978 (see table 5-5)—and they thus helped to channel discontent into official bargaining, where the authority of the national union was in effect reinforced by the extended opposition offered by the association of employers.

The economic climate may ultimately have tended to dampen the propensity to militancy in two ways. First, by contributing to a steady reduction in consumer price inflation, from 7 percent in 1974 to 2.6 percent in 1978, the appreciation of the currency helped real wages at least to increase at an average rate of 3 percent a year between 1976 and 1979 and thus to maintain the incomes of wage earners at or near minimum levels of acceptability, as the quotation above suggests. Second, unemployment, in persisting at historically high levels—actually declining gently from 4.7 to 4.3 percent of the dependent labor force between 1975 and 1978—may have reduced employment expectations and standards of acceptability; the OECD took note of "a process of getting accustomed to the relatively high level of unemployment."[110] Müller-Jentsch, who had interpreted the grass-roots strikes of 1969 as the reaction of a "new wage consciousness," or "rise in workers' levels of expectations," to the profit boom following the 1966–67 recession, later opined that the new wage consciousness failed to survive the " 'pacifying' effects of mass unemployment and reduced hours," as a result of which "job security alone seems to have become the workers' primary concern."[111]

Neither of these two interpretations is implausible, but they suggest divergent lines of speculation regarding future behavior. Müller-Jentsch's interpretation suggests that, even if unemployment should return to very low levels, workers might remain insecure and adverse to risk for some time and hence less militant in their demand for pay as well as other conditions. The OECD observation suggests that, even if unemployment should remain at higher levels than prevailed before 1975, growing familiarity could breed a return to the higher levels of militancy formerly associated with lower levels of unemployment and to a more clearly delineated gap between the explicit employment targets of the public authorities and the lower targets implicitly acceptable to the unions. In either case, the probability of greater militancy and pushfulness would

110. Ibid., p. 9.
111. Müller-Jentsch and Sperling, "Economic Development," pp. 297–302.

be increased by the disappearance of current-account surpluses and the end of currency appreciation. They could also be increased by a period of slow growth, which could bring disillusionment with policies calling for wage abstention in favor of higher profitability. In that event there might be greater concentration on the distribution of income, which the Düsseldorf program did make an object of union policy and which, along with the level of employment, a system of more flexible exchange rates made, at least potentially, more susceptible to influence by wage negotiation than it had in the past. These eventualities do not appear highly probable at the time of writing, although the trade surplus declined sharply in 1978 and 1979, but neither can any be excluded out of hand. The ability of the German union leaders to follow sensible and restrained bargaining policies in the future may be no less constrained by a prudent regard for the sensibilities of the rank and file than it was between 1969 and 1975. And therefore the need for incomes policy, German style, is also likely to remain.

Incomes Policies, German Style

Incomes policy has played a modest role in Germany's miracle play, partly because the roles assigned to monetary policy and to the social partners have been major ones. Commitment to monetary discipline has received the highest priority "in a country where the Central Bank has a high degree of autonomy and where the views of the Bank on the appropriate conjunctural policies do not always and necessarily coincide with those of the Government."[112] The German system of collective bargaining was also devised as an autonomous institution charged with social responsibilities. In 1950, the two newly established central federations urged a policy of self-government through joint conciliation and, in rejecting the Weimar system of compulsory arbitration, warned that government intervention and regulation of wages were not consistent with this approach. Chancellor Konrad Adenauer subsequently subscribed to a hands-off policy, as long as the parties could conduct bargaining "without disruptions of the economy and disturbance of the community caused by serious labor conflicts."[113]

112. Hansen, *Fiscal Policy,* p. 224.
113. Schmidt, "Industrial Action," p. 37.

Still, a case for government intervention could be made out of the inability of the Bundesbank and the social partners, between them, to deliver politically acceptable levels of price stability and employment. The limitations placed on the ability of the bank to secure price stability under fixed rates of exchange and high-level employment under floating rates of exchange have been well advertised by the bank itself. The social partners, moreover, could not be counted on to deliver the requisite cost restraint. Folke Schmidt classified Germany along with Sweden as a country in which structural centralization, originating in "a unified front of employers," was sufficient to permit the operation of a system of industrial self-government; in Sweden the social partners were able to assume a goodly share of the responsibility for macroeconomic stabilization along with industrial peace. The German system of industrial relations, however, has remained less centralized than the Swedish system, while the economic standards by which the performance of the social partners is evaluated have been more exacting in Germany than in Sweden. German union and bargaining structures have been sufficiently centralized to permit the exercise of bargaining restraint by large national unions, but the two-tier system of industrial relations has exposed the unions to competition from works councils, plant-level management, and spontaneous action by the rank and file of the members. The German system has been sufficiently decentralized to permit more effective employer resistance, but an adversary relationship, even if it is based on mutual recognition, is not conducive to reaching the kind of joint consensus on national economic requirements that the Swedish social partners used to generate. Meanwhile tolerance of domestic price inflation seems to have been appreciably higher among Swedes than among Germans, who in addition are alleged to have been more reluctant to settle simply for balance on the current account. And the Germans have been more prone to blame inflation on the unions, while the Swedes, especially employers and unions, have tended to regard it as primarily of external origin. For a long time the Swedes seemed to accept—or wished to accept—the Aukrust-EFO model as providing almost a complete explanation of inflation, in which case incomes policy could be rejected a priori as ineffectual. The Germans, on the other hand, have believed—or, as Giersch put it, "were made to believe"—that the domestic price levels were entirely determined by a markup model. In fact, world price movements have affected domestic wage movements to some extent, as the positive coefficients of the PW variable in equations

1 and 3 in table 5-1 suggest, so wages have not been autonomously determined. Nevertheless, the persistence of the cost-push stereotype has helped to create a potential function for incomes policy—specifically, for an incomes policy confined to wage restraint.

While wage controls would be inconsistent with either industrial self-government or the social market economy, a milder form of guidance need cause no more embarrassment in Germany than in other industrial democracies. Wage restraint could even be accepted more easily in Germany, a country in which unions have been subject to extensive legal restraints and where their behavior is ultimately subject to the test of "social adequacy." And where a legally established system has limited the potential helpfulness of unions to members at the work place, an official policy on pay could even be found helpful by the unions in justifying restraint to the members in the unions' own area of competence.[114] Incomes policy could help the unions to follow sensible policies when it might be difficult to initiate them explicitly. As for the other social partner, the employers could find little to object to in a policy that applied principally to wages and less cause for concern that it would have to be extended seriously to prices in a country in which conservatives rather than Social Democrats, as in Sweden and Britain, were in office right after the war. Finally, the Bundesbank could find a place for incomes policy, provided that it could help rather than hinder it in its central task of "safeguarding the currency." Indeed, the Bundesbank, which enjoyed from the outset an exceptional degree of autonomy and authority as "a kind of macroeconomic super-institution,"[115] has participated actively and overtly in the formulation of incomes policies.

Incomes policy in a mild but revealing form surfaced with the emergence of the surplus problem after the end of the noninflationary expansion of 1952–54. The rate of growth decelerated and the rate of inflation accelerated during the next three years. The minister of economic affairs, Ludwig Erhard, favored revaluation, but he was successfully opposed by Chancellor Adenauer, the Bundesbank, and the business community, who were concerned about the long-run consequences for business activity. (The budgetary policies of the central government did not turn notably expansionary until the recession year 1958.) Meanwhile, the DGB announced a new policy on the first of May, 1955, which

114. Reichel, "Recent Trends," p. 259.
115. Kreile, "West Germany," p. 208.

favored wage increases in excess of increases in productivity, in order to increase the share of labor in the national income. Against this background, the ministers of economics and finance, the president of the Bundesbank, and representatives of the employer associations held a meeting of their own and declared that

private business and the public sector should take every opportunity of lowering prices where this can economically be done. The view was unanimously expressed that in wage negotiations, the parties should be moderate in claims and grants. Wage increases which lead to price increases are not acceptable.[116]

But only the wage policy was meant to bite, and the following year the government bared a tooth. After the DGB had rejected the proposal of the BDA that any negotiated wage increases and reductions in hours be limited to the economywide increase in productivity, IG Metall concluded an agreement in North Rhine–Westphalia that provided for a reduction in hours, a wage increase of 8 percent, and a reopening clause to be activated if prices rose in excess of 3.5 percent between November 1956 and the end of 1957. The member firms objected, Erhard denounced the reopening clause as endangering the stability of the currency, and the contract was revised, excluding the reopener and reducing the other benefits. This was followed by the long strike, the settlement of which drew a vote of no confidence from the union members, but which was followed in 1957 by denunciations of cost-push inflation by both the Bundesbank and Erhard. The leaders of the metalworkers continued their left-wing drumfire in support of a redistributional wage policy, but this time, instead of striking for a cost-of-living reopener, the union cautiously extended its contracts in the early phase of the upswing in 1959. That upswing, however, made the authorities even more anxious than they had been before, as unemployment fell to very low levels, the cost of living reaccelerated, wage drift increased sharply to overcompensate for the decline in the rate of contractual increase, and the persistence of external surplus made it impossible for a restrictive monetary policy to succeed. The government ultimately, in 1961, decided to revalue the mark, but it did so reluctantly and belatedly. Earlier, Chancellor Adenauer had elicited a statement on wage policy from the Bundesbank, the Blessing Memorandum, which was issued in 1960 and which warned against wage increases in excess of gains in productivity, which it estimated to be about 3 or 4 percent.

116. Fellner and others, *Rising Prices,* p. 340n; see also p. 339; Emminger, *The D-Mark,* pp. 6–10; Hansen, *Fiscal Policy,* p. 235.

Like the earlier exhortations, this policy was judged ineffective but it was nevertheless popular. It was criticized on economic grounds; if effective, it would indeed have tended to exacerbate the balance-of-payments problem. And it seriously underpredicted the rise in productivity, which turned out to be more than 6 percent, just as a more ambitious Dutch policy forecast subsequently did. Nevertheless, insistence on a redistributionist wage policy had been waning within the union movement, and on this occasion the chancellor consulted with union leaders as well as the employers and coupled a plea for wage restraint with an appeal to employers to reduce prices in response to increased productivity.[117] The unions were naturally averse to wage norms that would have tended to redistribute income away from wages, and they were critical when in 1962 Economics Minister Erhard issued an appeal for *Masshalten* (moderation) of wages alone and after consultation only with management.

But the DGB supported the establishment of an independent agency. The business community, which was developing its lockout strategy at the time, was also in favor of such an arrangement, believing that it would inevitably lend support to wage restraint. In the government, Erhard had originally supported the creation of an independent agency for forecasting and analysis, although Adenauer had not. What emerged was the establishment in 1963 of an independent Council of Economic Experts, appointed by the government and charged with making recommendations for the maintenance of full employment as well as price stability and external balance.[118] The council was to operate in the context of the free-market economy and was forbidden to take positions on specific measures; Erhard soon fashioned an ad hoc instrument of incomes policy out of the social partners' institution of mediation, however, when he personally intervened in the metalworkers' strike in

117. Emminger, *The D-Mark,* pp. 13–17; Edelman and Fleming, *Wage-Price Decisions,* pp. 138–39; Bergmann and Müller-Jentsch, "The Federal Republic," pp. 256–57; Fellner and others, *Rising Prices,* pp. 342–43, 350. Presumably, the inclusion of price reduction in the policy statement was intended to meet an earlier complaint by the Bundesbank that wage increases tended to be uniform and pitched to the increases in productivity in the most rapidly growing sectors—just as was aimed for in the Scandinavian model. Price reductions in these sectors would be consistent with a policy that pitched general wage increases to the economywide average growth in productivity, along the lines of the later American and British policies.

118. Andrew Shonfield, *Modern Capitalism: The Changing Balance of Public and Private Power* (London: Oxford University Press, 1965), p. 294; Edelman and Fleming, *Wage-Price Decisions,* pp. 139–40.

1963 and triumphantly announced a settlement that corresponded to the going rate of increase in productivity.

While these origins of German incomes policy can be linked to the limitations of monetary policy in curbing inflation, subsequent development occurred as part of a Keynesian reaction to the effectiveness of monetary policy in contributing to the sharp recession of 1966–67. In 1967, the passage of the Law for the Promotion of Stability and Growth, which envisaged the purposeful adoption of countercyclical budgetary measures, placed incomes policy in the Keynesian context in which it had originated elsewhere. The new law required the government to initiate "concerted action" among the unions, employer associations, and public authorities, which included the Bundesbank, and to provide them, through the office of the Council of Economic Experts, with quantitative guidelines and other relevant economic information.

The influence of the Sozialdemokratische Partei Deutschlands (SPD), the Social Democratic party, which had just entered the government as a junior partner in a grand alliance with the Christlich Demokratische Union–Christlich Soziale Union (CDU-CSU), the Christian Democrats, was reflected in two ways. In the first place, the law, as a statement of policy, stressed the importance of full employment in its own right; at the same time, it did not do so at the expense of price stability as a prior objective—notwithstanding subsequent protestations by Social Democratic leaders to the effect that they would prefer a higher rate of inflation to a higher rate of unemployment. Incomes policy could help the bank and the government together to operate a tight monetary policy in conjunction with an expansionist fiscal policy. By holding down labor costs it would help minimize any adverse effects of the former on investment and on exports and of the latter on cost stability. Under a regime of flexible exchange rates, which materialized later, an incomes policy that maintained or reduced relative costs in Germany's favor could reap the gains from a heavy or appreciating currency through a benign feedback on domestic prices and costs.

In the second place, the new concerted-action procedures bore the Social Democratic imprint, and they seemed to make it more feasible for the unions, in the wake of the Düsseldorf program of the DGB, to follow sensible wage policies. It placed the unions in a position of institutional equality with the employers and it permitted them to appeal to the independent authority of the Council of Economic Experts. In 1967, one attempt was even made by Karl Schiller, the Social Democratic minister of economic affairs, to accommodate the continued—post-Düsseldorf—concern of the DGB with distributional equity; if wage restraint became associated with a disproportionate increase in profits in the upswing, the unions would be allowed subsequent wage increases to catch up and restore "social symmetry."[119]

The strategy appeared to work, not wisely but too well. As in 1957, the unions delayed reopening their contracts, and throughout the first two and a half years of operation of the new policy, the negotiated wage increases remained within the official guidelines. But like Governor Blessing in 1963, Minister Schiller in 1967 seriously underpredicted the short-term expansion that began that year, and a gaping social asymmetry which was the result of an unexpectedly sharp rise in profits (see table 5-6) was rectified only after the occurrence of the sort of rank-and-file uprising that the concerted-action approach was supposed to head off. Instead, the grass-roots rumblings seemed to crack the foundations of the policy. The authorities tried to maintain the policy in 1971 by publishing a new set of norms and "orientation data," but the unions, while attempting to restrain their base-rate increases, negotiated various profit-sharing and bonus schemes, as well as compensation for shorter hours and holidays, which brought increases in total compensation well above target levels. It was feared that, the members having shown the way to redistribute—or re-redistribute—income through accelerated wage increases, the unions would have to follow. It was also feared that they would be encouraged to do so by the commitment of the policy—and the newly elected (1969) Socialist-led coalition government—to full employment: instead of wage moderation making full employment feasible, high-level employment would underwrite wage inflation. So in 1971 the government published a supplementary report in which alternative rates of wage increase were related negatively to increases in output and employment.

At the same time it was denied that the policy itself had been responsible for the profit-wage explosion on the grounds that it could never have substituted for the currency revaluation which, in 1969, came too late. But if exchange rates are sufficiently flexible, why bother with a policy that could be upset by forecasting error, distributional shifts, and expectations of high-level employment? In any event, the floating and appreciation of the deutsche mark that occurred in the second half

119. Bergmann and Müller-Jentsch, "The Federal Republic," pp. 258–59.

Table 5-6. *Changes in Real GNP, Income from Property and Entrepreneurship, and Compensation of Employees, Germany, 1968–72*

Percent

Year	Changes in real GNP		Changes in income from property and entrepreneurship		Changes in compensation of employees	
	Projected	Actual	Projected	Actual	Projected	Actual
1968	4.0	7.3	11.8	17.5	4.7	7.4
1969	4.5	8.2	1.0	6.6	8.5	12.7
1970	4.0–5.0	5.8	4.0–5.0	9.7	12.5–13.5	17.7
1971	3.0–4.0	2.7	3.0–4.0	3.7	9.5–10.5	13.3
1972	2.0–3.0	2.9	6.0–7.0	7.1	7.0–8.0	9.7

Source: *Jahreswirtschaftsberichte* [Annual report on the economy], cited in OECD Economic Surveys, *Germany*, May 1973, p. 7.

of 1971 was accompanied by a marked deceleration in the rate of contractual wage increases whereas a concomitant downswing in activity and rise in unemployment were slight. This could justify a retreat from incomes policy, especially since it was feared that the spirit of militancy among workers had not yet subsided from levels that concerted action had been unable to contain. So, although inflation remained at historically high levels, the OECD reported that, in 1972,

the Government has refrained from direct intervention into the price/wage formation process, not only because of political inopportunity [*sic*], but also because this approach is not regarded as tackling the problem at its roots. It is rather seen as postponing the problem, and indeed aggravating it in the future. The burden of stabilisation policies lies therefore with demand management.[120]

But neither the government nor the Bundesbank was content to keep its hands off, notwithstanding either increased tensions in industrial relations, which militated against the effectiveness of incomes policies, or the increased effectiveness of demand management—after the deutsche mark was allowed to float against the dollar in 1973—which was supposed to lessen dependence on direct intervention into wage formation. The government, which since 1969 had been a coalition of the Social Democrats and the Free Democrats, having responded to the oil price increase in 1973 with fiscal relaxation, appealed to the unions to hold wage

120. OECD Economic Surveys, *Germany*, June 1971, pp. 13–17, 30–31; ibid., June 1972, pp. 20, 22; ibid., May 1973, p. 5; Emminger, *The D-Mark*, pp. 26–27.

increases to a maximum of 10 percent, despite the second outbreak of wildcat strikes. The Bundesbank continued to limit the growth of the money supply in order to achieve the same end,[121] and President Klasen said, "I know exactly the stabilising factor they represent in industry and that their leaders are fighting with their backs to the wall."[122] The subsequent acceleration of negotiated wage increases, especially in the public sector, contributed to Chancellor Willy Brandt's decision to resign from office. The Bundesbank, as we know, reacted by holding firm and refusing to validate the cost increases in 1974. Finally, in November of that year, the government and the bank agreed on a new set of stimulatory fiscal and monetary measures; but

these moves towards a more expansionary policy stance were accompanied by explicit warnings to both sides of industry that this policy could only be maintained provided wage settlements in 1975 were substantially below the previous ones. This message was taken seriously by employers and unions as wage increases fell drastically compared to the preceding round.[123]

A commitment to high-level employment on the condition of the achievement of a target level of price stability obviously assigns less importance to direct wage restraint in the policy mix than does a commitment to price stability on the condition of the achievement of a target level of employment. The conditional commitment to high-level employment, however, may also be distinguished from an unconditional commitment to price stability. The latter could presumably be implemented without any policy of direct wage or price restraint, under a regime of completely flexible exchange rates, but it could require price restraint if exchange-rate flexibility were limited. The German approach has been a compromise between the Bundesbank—whose explicit commitment to price stability sometimes conflicted with its explicit commitment to exchange-rate stability—the government, with its legal obligation to pursue contracyclical budgetary policy in the interest of high-level employment, and the unions, with their own formal commitments to full employment and against acceptance of the distributional status quo.

This approach to stabilization policy has been implemented through

121. *Financial Times*, December 20, 1973; January 25, 1974; February 11, 1974; February 13, 1974; *The Times* (London), February 18, 1974; OECD Economic Surveys, *Germany*, July 1975, p. 26.
122. *Financial Times*, October 25, 1973.
123. OECD Economic Surveys, *Germany*, July 1975, pp. 7–8.

three devices, all of which were brought into play in 1974. They are publication of monetary targets by the Bundesbank, alternative forecasts by the Council of Economic Experts relating nominal wage increases negatively to growth in real GNP, and formal concerted-action meetings at which these and other data are presented to and discussed with the social partners. At least formally there is a natural division of labor between the monetary targets of the bank and the Phillips curves of the council. The targets, which were introduced for the first time in 1974, after the establishment of the currency Snake—or joint float of the currencies of the European Monetary System—and were intended to obviate short-run changes in monetary policy, are derived from projections of growth rates in potential GNP, expected changes in use of capacity, and estimates of "unavoidable" price increases. The target increases in the money supply thus derived set limits to the growth of nominal GNP, and the council's projections help to form the basis of wage guidelines that are consistent with the realization of the employment levels that help to determine potential output. It was acknowledged, on the basis of past experience under fixed exchange rates, that the relationship between year-to-year changes in nominal GNP and in the Central Bank Money Stock (CBM) was a loose one, so velocity was unstable. But it was hoped that, under floating rates, the relation would become more stable. It was also hoped that, by influencing the wage and price decisions of the social partners, publication of the targets and associated norms under the auspices of concerted action would have the same effect and thus help to make monetary policy more effective. In fact, publication of monetary targets has been credited with contributing to wage and price moderation after 1974; but the targets themselves were overshot, especially in 1978, because of exchange purchases that dirtied the float, and in 1979 a wide range—6 to 9 percent—replaced the single figure of 8 percent that had served as the target since 1976. And while the extra liquidity thus created tended to make an expansionist fiscal policy effective by keeping interest rates down, the overshooting "raised doubts about the credibility of monetary targets."[124]

Meanwhile, the persistence of unemployment during the upswing weakened incomes policy from another direction. The unions, as we know, believed that their restraint had been unrequited and that it justified settlements that exceeded guidelines in 1976, in printing, and

124. Ibid., June 1979, pp. 31, 39–40, 46–48; ibid., July 1975, pp. 26–27, 41–43.

THE FEDERAL REPUBLIC OF GERMANY

1977, in engineering. Their disenchantment, together with the deteriorating state of industrial relations, also underlay their decision, in July
1977, to pull out of the concerted-action sessions. Earlier, President
Vetter of the DGB had said that the "honeymoon was over," after ten
years, as far as concerted action was concerned, adding that "if the
social market economy isn't capable of re-establishing full employment,
one must wonder whether such a system will remain defensible in the
future."[125]

In fact, the importance of concerted action as an institution can be
exaggerated, although it has been a distinctive and highly visible characteristic of German incomes policy, much admired by foreigners in
search of importable solutions. The concerted-action meetings have
been largely ceremonial and informational—too short, sometimes lasting
less than a full day, too infrequent, held only two or three times a year,
too unwieldy, sometimes attended by more than a hundred people, and
too understaffed, having no permanent secretariat, to function as policymaking sessions. Concerted action has provided an effective public
forum for the government and the Bundesbank to present their views
and their findings, to generate discussion, and to mobilize public support.
But it has not served directly to integrate monetary and fiscal policies
with wage and price setting, notwithstanding efforts made by the unions
to secure some de facto abridgment of the autonomy of the Bank. It has
not been associated with any significant increase in the overall political
and economic status of the unions. This was dramatized when the unions'
withdrawal was triggered by the decision of the employers (the BDA) to
contest the constitutionality of the Codetermination Law of 1976, which
certainly was intended to enhance the socioeconomic importance of
organized labor in the community.

Thus, as Fels wrote, "It would be an exaggeration to maintain that
concerted action has fulfilled the coordinating function originally intended."[126] Its greatest apparent success came at the outset, when wages
lagged behind profits and productivity in 1967–68.[127] The residuals from
equation 1, however, which estimate changes in contractual rates, were
not strongly negative in that period, whereas the wage-drift residuals,

125. *L'Express*, January 10–16, 1977, p. 43; see also *The Times* (London), July 2,
1977.
126. Fels, "Inflation in Germany," p. 619.
127. The residuals for 1967 and 1968 are negative and exceed the standard error of
estimate for equation 1 (see table 5-1).

from equation 2, were strongly negative (see table 5-1). The policy may have been more effective at the level of the firm than in the domain of collective bargaining. The unions rebounded strongly in 1970 after the wildcat strikes in 1969, moreover; note the large positive residual from equation 1 in figure 5-5. This, however, does not imply that incomes policy did not make for wage restraint after the mid 1960s, because, as noted earlier, there had been continuing efforts at persuasion and intervention by the government and by the Bundesbank before incomes policy had become more highly institutionalized. And afterward the policy may have been effective in offsetting a more militant disposition on the part of the rank and file, assuming that the two waves of wildcat strikes did signify a change in mood.

In this connection it might be noted that the standard statistical test for structural stability, which consisted in comparing the goodness-of-fit of equations 1–3, which covered the period 1958–76, with that of the same equations estimated for the subperiod 1958–68, which antedated the wildcat strikes at the end of the 1960s, presented no evidence to reject the null hypothesis—that is, that both sets of observations were generated from the same model (see appendix to this chapter). While too much importance should not be attached to such a test, it agrees with the German experience, which differed from that of various other European countries that did, according to a variety of evidence, experience "structural breaks" or more inflationary wage-setting proclivities during the 1970s. If it could be assumed that concerted action was the only change not subject to our statistical controls in the 1970s, the conclusion that this form of incomes policy added nothing to the restraint that had previously characterized the German system of industrial relations would not be unwarranted by this evidence. But if in fact Germany shared in a heightened sense of worker militancy that in other countries seems to have been translated into more inflationary wage behavior, it is possible that concerted action plus what followed might have supplied some offsetting extra restraint.

The actors themselves carried on in their traditional roles, although with some new lines, both before and after the unions' withdrawal in 1977. Both the Bundesbank and the government discovered, after 1973, that there were both economic and political limits to the privatization of unemployment. The bank found out that the difference between life under a dirty float and the old life under fixed exchange rates was a difference of degree and not of kind and that, in consequence, its innovative experiment in incomes policy through the setting of monetary targets grew more unreliable just as the need for restraining costs increased. The government, having participated in incomes policy through conditional reflation in 1975, announced a tax-reduction package two years later without conditions but in the hope that it would create a climate favorable to moderate bargaining settlements. The Council of Economic Experts continued to support wage restraint, but now it did so—through the device of alternative projections—to help reduce persistently high unemployment, which was associated with sluggish growth in exports, which in turn reflected a relative rise in German labor costs in 1976 and 1979. The last, to be sure, reflected the effects of appreciation, which was then in excess of international inflation differentials; measured in local currency, German unit labor costs had been declining since 1973. Nevertheless, profits were being squeezed, and data showing high relative levels of German hourly labor costs were interpreted as a threat to the country's competitive position. Restraint by the unions in the past was grudgingly acknowledged by independent experts, but more was insisted on.[128]

The unions, on the other hand, were seeking shorter hours and talking about rationalization and purchasing power theory, but although purchasing power was at least consistent with the official objective of reducing the share of the foreign balance in GNP, they did not turn a deaf ear to arguments for restraint in the interest of maintaining international competitiveness.[129] In 1978 contractual hourly rates rose 5.7 percent; the council had earlier agreed to a target of 5.5 percent, although they had opened hopefully with 3.5 percent. That occurred the year after the unions had quit the formal multilateral meetings, and it was associated with the steel strike settlement that was unpopular with the rank and file. Thus, while the trappings of the new incomes policy were gone, the

128. *Wall Street Journal*, September 14, 1977; OECD Economic Surveys, *Germany*, June 1978, pp. 4–7; ibid., June 1979, pp. 19–22, 61; Economist Intelligence Unit, *Quarterly Economic Review: Federal Republic of Germany*, no. 1 (1977), pp. 14–15; no. 4 (1977), pp. 2–3.

129. An opinion survey in 1978 revealed that most employees attributed high unemployment to technological displacement but also that 31 percent of them accepted that firms must rationalize in order to maintain their international competitiveness. See Economist Intelligence Unit, *Quarterly Economic Review: Federal Republic of Germany*, no. 4 (1978), p. 12.

substance seems to have remained. Certainly the authorities continued to work hard; Chancellor Schmidt remarked,

I have been talking to trade unionists and the leaders of industry and banking 200 hours a year on an average. It has been an enormous undertaking in a Keynesian sense and in terms of moral suasion. There is no way to get out of economic difficulty without shouldering the difficulties.[130]

But if bargaining restraint could be said to remain at traditional levels, employment did not. Had the German unions been offered any inducements—not necessarily as a quid pro quo—that could help to account for bargaining restraint in the absence of concerted action and full employment? We can discuss in this connection four developments, two of which date at least from the early postwar period, while the other two are relatively recent arrivals. The first consists of Germany's extensive system of *social security*, which originated under Bismarck in the 1880s and which, in the postwar period, has been regarded as an integral part of the contemporary social market economy. Its recent development in the postwar period is reflected in the more rapid growth (in real terms) of total hourly compensation (which includes the contributions of both employers and employees) and earnings (which includes the contributions of employees but not those of employers) than of wages and salaries, net of tax and employee contributions (see figure 5-7). In addition, the share of employers' contributions in both total compensation and gross domestic product have increased—the former from 13.6 percent in 1965 to 21.8 percent in 1977 and the latter from 7 percent to 10.4 percent.[131]

It might appear that increases in payments by employers to social security exerted more of an inflationary push than the negotiated components of labor costs during the 1970s, since, as figure 5-4 shows, real hourly labor costs rose more rapidly than productivity between 1972 and 1976, while both wage rates and earnings rose less rapidly than productivity. But it cannot be assumed that total compensation would have increased less rapidly if the social security tax payments had increased less rapidly: on the contrary, the former might have increased more rapidly if the increased taxes and benefits had indeed been keeping union bargaining militancy down or increasing the resistance of employ-

---

130. "Schmidt's Lesson," *The Economist*, September 29, 1979, p. 49.
131. *National Accounts of OECD Countries, 1960–1977* (Paris: OECD, 1979), vol. 2; ibid., *1950–1978: Main Accounts* (Paris: OECD, 1980), vol. 1. The contributions of employers include contributions to private pensions.

Figure 5-7. *Developments in Real Compensation and Earnings per Employee, Germany, 1960–78*[a]

Thousands of deutsche marks

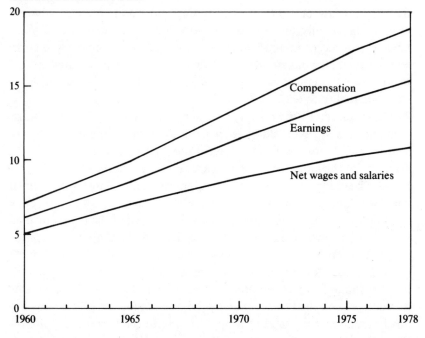

Source: OECD Economic Surveys, *Germany,* June 1979, tables C, I, J.
a. Compensation = earnings + contributions of employers to social security. Earnings = net wages and salaries + wage tax + contributions of employees to social security.

ers to union demands. The case a priori for reduced militancy on the part of the employed work force, in response to transfer payments to inactive individuals, is certainly not unambiguous, although the case for increased resistance by employers in the face of higher contribution rates is straightforward. In any event, our attempted inclusion of a social security variable in the equations estimating changes in contractual rates (equations 1, 1a, and 1b) and total earnings (equations 3, 3a, and 3b) revealed no strong evidence of the hypothesized negative relation, although the coefficients of the lagged SS variable are negative.

Mitbestimmung (codetermination) of enterprise policy is another German social innovation that could be regarded as potentially offering an inducement to bargaining restraint. The instruments of German codetermination have been the works councils and employee-elected directors to the supervisory boards of firms. The supervisory board appoints and oversees the managing board, which includes the manager of employee relations. Codetermination at the top level was first introduced, in a law of 1951, in coal mining and iron and steel, where it remains most fully developed. In those industries there are as many labor directors as shareholders' directors on the supervisory boards, and a specified number of the labor directors are nominated by the majority union in the company—usually three of eleven are on the labor side—including at least one who is not an employee of the company. The labor directors have been allowed by custom to designate a neutral member to cast tie-breaking votes—the chairman is nominated by the shareholders' directors—and have a de facto veto power over the selection of the labor relations manager on the three-member managing board. The unions, whose interest in codetermination dates from Weimar and earlier, have been trying to have this system of "parity representation" in coal and steel extended by law to the rest of the economy ever since it was introduced under the auspices of the British occupation authorities, but they have not yet succeeded. In 1952, a Works Constitution provided for one-third labor representation on supervisory boards in other industries and required that all worker directors be nominated by the works council rather than by the trade union. In 1976, a new law finally mandated parity, but it applies only to the larger companies— those having more than 2,000 employees—and it provides that a managerial white-collar employee be included among the labor directors, that the chairman of the board cast a double vote in case of a tie, and that the labor relations manager be chosen by a simple majority of the supervisory board. The employers fought the steel-coal system, or *Montanmitbestimmung* (mining settlement), throughout: the 1951 act was passed only after the metalworkers and the mine workers had threatened a political strike against the Adenauer government, and the 1976 act was promptly subjected to constitutional challenge on the grounds that it abridged constitutionally guaranteed property rights and the right of free collective bargaining. The challenge was thrown out—but primarily because the Constitutional Court found that the law does not establish true representational parity.[132]

In fact, the worst fears of the opponents of *Mitbestimmung* failed to

132. Economist Intelligence Unit, *Quarterly Economic Review Special*, no. 20: *Worker Participation*, January 1975, p. 9; *Jenkins Work Report*, February 1979, pp. 9–10.

materialize, even in coal and steel. The labor directors, although they have turned out to be almost all union members, have readily complied with their legal obligation to, in effect, assign highest priority to the profitability of the enterprise. Wages in coal and steel advanced no more rapidly than elsewhere; they did not break out of the annual pattern of wage rounds. The labor directors did not take a negative approach to employment problems: on the one hand, they supported investment and technological change as a way of creating and protecting jobs; on the other hand, they supported a consolidation of the hard-coal industry in the Ruhr, which halved the mining work force between 1958 and 1968. There have been complaints about delays in decisionmaking in such employment-related problems as plant layoffs and closings and, in the case of Volkswagen, on direct foreign investment (in the United States).[133] But the works councils, which negotiate over many plant-level issues that involve employment security, might have forced at least as much delay in the absence of the labor directors, who are their institutional partners in codetermination. And, to look on the positive side, most employers would probably not dissent from the general consensus that codetermination has been an effective democratic response to whatever appeal the system of industrial nationalization as practiced in the Communist East German state might otherwise have held out to West German workers.

Nevertheless, German managers remember that the unions originally supported codetermination as a *socialist* alternative to nationalization, and they have not forgotten that the Social Democratic party, at the behest of the DGB, attempted, unsuccessfully, to couple the extension of parity in 1972 with a union-administered profit-and-asset-sharing scheme, as the union movement in Sweden subsequently did. They argue further that a new generation of left-wing union staff technicians could attempt to implement this socialist objective—unlike the present generation of labor directors, whom some of their juniors denounce as industrial Uncle Toms for their moderation. They also point out that codetermination, with equal representation, under conditions of more

133. Spiros Simitis, "Workers' Participation in the Enterprise—Transcending Company Law?" *Modern Law Review*, vol. 38 (1975), pp. 1–22; James C. Furlong, *Labor in the Boardroom: The Peaceful Revolution* (Princeton: Dow Jones Books, 1977), pp. 40–43; Herbert J. Spiro, *The Politics of German Codetermination* (Cambridge: Harvard University Press, 1958), pp. 144–45; "Survey," *The Economist*, February 26, 1977, p. 24.

unemployment and greater uncertainty could yet produce those adverse consequences for managerial efficiency, technical change, staffing, and competitiveness that largely failed to materialize when parity was the exception rather than the rule and when a decline of employment in one industry could be accommodated by an abundance of alternative employment opportunities in expanding sectors. And they fear above all those provisions of the new law that, in the spirit of *Montanmitbestimmung* (in coal and steel), reserve between a quarter and a third of the labor seats on the supervisory board, depending on its size, for outside union representatives. Some firms even reorganized their operations or corporate structure to escape from being subject to codetermination law.[134]

Yet the consequences need not be as the employers anticipated them. While the extension of parity codetermination on the supervisory board could strengthen the relative power of the labor side, the inclusion of outside representatives of the national unions could exert a moderating influence. (In both the coal and steel reorganizations of the 1960s, the union directors sought to overcome the "plant egoism" of the employee directors—for example, in arguing for the closing down of high-cost and inefficient units. And on one occasion the president of IG Metall, as vice-chairman of the Volkswagen board, argued, unsuccessfully, against a price increase on the grounds that it could have inflationary consequences.) By extending the authority of the national union at the company and plant levels, codetermination might make possible the exercise of a greater degree of restraint than would otherwise be forthcoming.

Such downward extension of their authority might also make it less difficult for the national unions to participate in concerted action—which since Weimar times has been regarded as codetermination at the highest—the federal—level. The unions have resented being pressured publicly into accepting wage targets that they have felt could expose them to the risk of repudiation by the members—especially when they have had reason to believe that the employers would grant to their members as drift what they, together with the Bundesbank and the government, had denied to the unions under legal bargaining in the upper tier of the two-tier system. Their resentment and apprehension, together

134. Spiro, *Politics of German Codetermination*, p. 36; Simitis, "Workers' Participation," p. 14; Rudolf Meidner, "Employee Investment Funds and Capital Formation," *Working Life in Sweden*, no. 6, June 1978, p. 2; Furlong, *Labor in the Boardroom*, pp. 63, 78; *Wall Street Journal*, June 28, 1980; "Steely Clashes," *The Economist*, August 16, 1980, p. 39.

with the persistence of unemployment, might well have led the unions to pull out of codetermination, even if the employers had not chosen to take the 1976 law to court. The court challenge did serve as more than a convenient pretext for the unions, however. It implied that the employers were unwilling to assent to a grant of institutional protection to the unions as a quid pro quo for concerted action. It could signify that the extra degree of union restraint to be so obtained was not worth compromising the existing level of autonomy enjoyed by the firm in making employment decisions, investment decisions, and certain pay decisions under the two-tier system. Or else it could signify a belief of employers that the unions could be induced to continue in their traditional ways of restraint, with or without the resumption of concerted action.

We have already discussed tax cuts, which constitute the third and most direct inducement to wage restraint—a relationship that policymakers made most explicit during the second half of the 1970s. As part of a reflationary fiscal-monetary package, an income tax cut should outperform negotiated wage increases in increasing output and employment, since it could increase "purchasing power" without directly increasing labor costs in relation to capital costs or labor costs abroad. And it offers the individual wage earner direct compensation for gross wage income forgone as the result of bargaining restraint. On the other hand, the tax instrument is alleged to have suffered from certain deficiencies as an incentive to union restraint. Offered as a public good, the general tax cut might not offer much of an incentive to restraint under decentralized bargaining; the centralist properties of the German bargaining system were sufficiently strong, however, for the types of conditional reflationary package of tax cuts and spending increases that were offered in 1975 to have been effective in securing restraint. But the compensation that the individual worker receives for his union's wage restraint may be regarded as incomplete if others benefit more; thus in 1979 "fiscal policy . . . supported the redistribution of income towards profits," which indeed rose more rapidly than wages during the second half of the 1970s. And third, the tax cuts and other elements of a generally expansionist policy seemed to be more effective in increasing profits and sales than in increasing employment until the end of the decade—and even then the vigorous increase in fixed investment that occurred, while strong, was primarily capital-intensive in nature.[135] While the tax cut offers compensation to the individual member, unlike *Mitbestimmung*

135. OECD Economic Surveys, *Germany,* May 1980, pp. 8, 20, 21.

with outside union directors it does not offer any institutional protection to his union, which receives little credit if any for the tax cut while it is seen to hold back in wage negotiations. Some German unionists have argued against linking tax cuts to wage increases on the grounds that the integrity of collective bargaining would thereby be impaired.

Finally, the Social Democratic party, which has been the senior partner in a governing coalition with the Freie Demokratische Partei (FDP), the Free Democrats, between 1969 and 1983, has been cited as a moderating influence on the unions. Its influence has been exercised both indirectly and directly. It has been responsible for either introducing or strengthening the other institutional incentives to restraint, although not always with that end primarily in view. Concerted action was, as noted earlier, a Social Democratic innovation, introduced shortly after the SPD first entered the government in the Grand Alliance with the Christian Democrats in 1966. It was under Social Democratic–led governments that the great increase in social security transfer payments occurred in the 1970s, that representation of workers and unions on supervisory boards was increased under the Codetermination Act of 1976, and that tax cuts and other reflationary measures were linked to wage restraint. But above all the government has been credited with directly inducing the unions to go along with an economic policy that assigned priority to the reduction of inflation and the revival of private investment in the face of a sluggish recovery of employment. In this context, fiscal stimulus was restrained, and the government encouraged the Bundesbank to publish its monetary targets as a guide to wage moderation. Furthermore, Chancellor Helmut Schmidt maintained his unofficial and intensive contacts with the union leaders, and his efforts were widely regarded as having been effective. The employers, while unsympathetic to deficit spending and *Mitbestimmung* and cool to concerted action, applauded these efforts. One of their number bestowed this accolade: "There is no better capitalist chancellor than Schmidt. He handles the unions and leaves the rest to us."[136]

The chancellor's influence with the unions was enhanced by the fact that the SPD has been less dependent on union support than, say, the British Labour party or the Swedish Social Democrats. Coalition government—first with the CDU and later with the FDP—contributed to the independence of the German party. The unions could not expect to

136. *San Francisco Chronicle,* July 8, 1980.

call the tune: they could not demand too high a price for their economic cooperation, and if they withheld cooperation at a realistic price, they could have contributed to the replacement of an SPD-FDP government with a CDU-FDP government. Thus the small but strategically situated Free Democrats could block or dilute Socialist concessions to their trade-union allies. The limitations on parity codetermination written into the 1976 law, for example, as well as the abandonment of the asset-sharing plan, were the work of the Free Democrats. Neither the moderate Social Democrats among the union leaders nor the moderate Social Democrats in the government, moreover, were unhappy with the party's dependence on a conservative coalition partner, because it strengthened the position of each moderate group in its relations with its respective left-wing colleagues. Furthermore, the SPD itself is a coalition in which the interests and objectives of its union constituents had to be balanced against those of its middle-class and white-collar constituency, and it has courted the latter since the end of the 1950s.[137]

There are limits also to the attachment of the German union movement to its political ally. A sizable proportion of union members are not members of the SPD; estimates at the end of the 1960s ranged from 30 to 60 percent. Ever since the "unitary" union movement was formed by amalgamating the postwar survivors of the Catholic and liberal federations with those of the Socialist federation, German labor leaders have been sensitive to this diversity of political citizenship within their ranks. They demonstrated the limits of their willingness to cooperate with their Social Democratic colleagues in the government when they refused to hold to Chancellor Brandt's wage line in 1972, although this did not lead to a change in government. Conversely, they had previously demonstrated their willingness to support Christian Democratic governments on specific policy issues.[138] They did not turn a deaf ear to Erhard's *Masshalten* or to the Bundesbank.

It may have been easier for the unions to appear responsive to official pleas and warnings before the wildcat stoppages. For them to exercise the same moderation after those events as they had beforehand—and in the face of persistently high unemployment—may well have required the help of relatively new and positive policy incentives. In the German

137. Richard J. Willey, "Trade Unions and Political Parties in the Federal Republic of Germany," *Industrial and Labor Relations Review*, vol. 78 (October 1974), pp. 52–53.
138. Ibid., pp. 42, 43.

296 THE FEDERAL REPUBLIC OF GERMANY

setting, an expansionist fiscal policy had to be cautious and had to be linked to a tight and effective monetary policy, and this mixture in turn required the resumption of restraint under collective bargaining. During the second half of the 1970s the unions seemed willing to accept the need for restraint, obviously not because it appeared to constitute a sufficient condition for reattaining full employment but because it appeared to be a necessary condition for securing both diminished inflation and increased employment, in that order. That seemed sensible—especially by the end of the decade, when unemployment declined to 2.1 percent of the total labor force.[139]

Conclusion

It is reasonable to assign the West German brand of industrial relations and trade unionism a share of the credit for that country's strong overall economic performance—that is, in employment, prices, growth, and international competitiveness. The restrained behavior of collective bargaining, which can be measured by both industrial peace and the outcome of negotiations, is not simply a reflection of the bargaining power of German employers, nor can this bargaining power be explained simply as reflecting an elastic supply of foreign labor or of monetary discipline. Germany's access to foreign labor has been in part the result of a union policy of acceptance; it has been limited by demand since the late 1950s; and foreign labor has not been used more extensively in the Federal Republic than in other countries in which the record of inflation has been worse. Monetary policy has been effective in restraining inflation in organized labor and product markets as well as in others, but it has not been consistently effective because of the inflexibility of the exchange rates. When, after the early 1970s, exchange rates did become significantly more flexible, monetary policy could be more effective in controlling price levels, thereby contributing to the relatively high levels of resistance to union demands offered by German management.

But other factors have also contributed to the bargaining strength and aggressiveness of German employers under given conditions in the labor market. First, there is a set of legislated and judicial restraints on union activity that seems generally to have reflected a design to encourage the

139. OECD Economic Surveys, *Germany*, May 1980, p. 13.

development of trade unionism as a democratic social counterweight to big business while stunting its development as an economic heavyweight. It has nurtured a truncated system of collective bargaining under which works councils at the plant and company levels are denied the right to strike, while unions, which negotiate mainly with employers' associations, are denied the right to negotiate directly with member firms or to apply contractual increases to actual pay levels of the firm. Second, instead of choosing the path of least resistance under industrywide bargaining, German employers have armed their associations with strong disciplinary authority and large financial resources, which have countered many union attempts at pattern setting with secondary lockouts. Employers' aggressiveness in industrial relations can be traced in part to their aggressiveness in international product markets, in which German firms are reported to have submitted to the discipline of world prices with comparative alacrity in the interest of expanding and maintaining their shares of the market. While the aggressiveness of large-scale German management is consistent with rational, long-run maximization of profits, it is also exceptional by international standards, and therefore it is said to be tinged with special nonrational values or preferences. The international pricing behavior has been held symptomatic of a generalized neomercantilist thrust, although this proposition has been strongly contested. And the willingness of employers to invest in a public good, such as sympathy lockouts, has been ascribed to a strong communal preference for internal price stability in the ordering of policy alternatives. This is a preference that is readily traceable to unique and traumatic historical circumstances.

It has also been alleged that the strong German employer was the mirror image of a characteristically docile German worker, who limited the potential bargaining power of his trade union. The willingness of workers to defer increases in consumption in favor of investment at the end of the war was not confined to West Germany, however, and in Germany as elsewhere, notably in the Netherlands, that spirit had shown clear evidence of wear and tear by the mid 1950s, when members in large numbers began to vote against settlements negotiated by union officials. German workers participated in the wave of wildcat strikes that swept through much of Western Europe at the end of the 1960s; they staged another outbreak in 1973, and as late as 1978 they demonstrated discontent with a settlement in steel after a long strike. There is nothing in the record of gains in real wages and levels of employment to indicate that German workers have been prepared to settle for less than workers elsewhere, and there is evidence that strikes, while called infrequently by international standards, have paid off in higher contractual settlements.

The unions themselves, moreover, have been well organized in the big industrial sectors of the economy—and in the public sector as well—into a small number of industrial bodies. The union market is no longer divided among competing political and confessional groups, as it was before the war; like the organizations of employers, the unions are well financed and pay generous strike benefits, and they are ably staffed. Under the German two-tier structure, with its works councils, the shop steward is neither autonomous, as in Britain, nor a bargaining functionary of the national union inside the company gates. On the other hand, there is a good deal of interaction and overlap among works councilors, union officials, and stewards. Impatience among the members, when it did occur, reflected a widespread belief that their unions were wont to exercise restraint and to refrain from the full use of the bargaining potential that government policies, labor-market conditions, and the attitudes of employers had helped to delimit.

The German unions have been able to bargain with restraint partly because their own structure has been so centralized that leaders were confronted with an economywide perspective, partly because the leaders shared the prevailing policy predilections for internal price stability, high-level employment, and growth, partly because they could plausibly claim that policies of restraint that strike them as only sensible have paid off in economic progress for their members. The channel through which sensible unionists have had to navigate, however, has been a tricky one; they have had to steer a course between what significant rank-and-file elements have considered minimally acceptable levels of incomes and security and what official authorities have regarded as maximum acceptable rates of increase in labor costs.

The authorities have never been reluctant to communicate their views to the unions and their social partners in collective bargaining, the employers. Incomes policy has been part of the policy scene in Germany since the 1950s. It was regarded as a handy adjunct to demand management, at first under fixed exchange rates, when monetary policy was unreliable, later under partly flexible rates, when the Bundesbank and the government felt that real wage rates and the level of employment were things too serious to be left to the unguided hands of collective bargainers. During the 1970s the channel open to sensible unionism narrowed considerably, when it appeared that wage restraint failed to pay off in reduced unemployment and insecurity. At the same time a policy of wage restraint received heightened emphasis from a government led by the Social Democrats, who sought to combine monetary stringency with deficit spending, the latter including notably increased government expenditures and transfer payments. In Germany, as in other countries, this second generation of incomes policies—which were aimed at real-wage restraint—offered compensation to the members in the form of tax reductions and to the union organizations in the form of formal concerted-action sessions. But the German version of incomes policy was characteristically stern. The tax reductions were accompanied by a warning of unpleasant alternatives. The concerted-action meetings put the unions uncomfortably on the spot as the Bundesbank trotted out monetary targets for wage guidance and official economists interpreted the existence of unemployment as evidence that collective bargaining, however restrained, produced excessively high real wages. The unions, moreover, have been unable to secure a full extension of the type of codetermination that has prevailed in the coal and steel industries since the early postwar period and that, by providing for the inclusion of "outside" union representatives on corporate boards of directors, would enable the unions to establish a formal institutional presence inside factory walls. Nevertheless, the performance of collective bargaining remained restrained, and with unemployment declining at the end of the 1970s to less than 4 percent of the total labor force, sensible unionism rode out the storm and facilitated a recovery fueled by an expansionist domestic policy.

In the future, processes for bargaining restraint are likely to be at least maintained, if unemployment is to remain lower and inflation no higher than during the latter half of the 1970s. If other countries took a leaf out of Germany's national book and turned to more restrictive monetary and fiscal policies, West Germany's export prospects would dim, while conservative criticisms of its new expansionist fiscal policies might be intensified on the grounds that, in combination with monetary restraint, they are inimical to private investment and economic growth. Under such conditions more bargaining restraint could be called for, and the leeway for sensible unionism could be narrowed further.

Appendix

Table 5-7. A Test for Stability[a]

Dependent variable	Independent variable								Summary statistic			
	Constant	PW_{t-1}	CPI_{t-1}	Q_{t-1}	UR	$CHEM_{t-1}$	DL	SS_{t-1}	Sum of squared residuals	R^2	Durbin-Watson	Standard error
1958–76 ($n_1 = 19$)												
WR	9.43 (3.03)	0.62 (2.91)	−0.48 (−0.86)	−0.003 (−0.01)	−1.79 (−2.70)	0.026 (2.205)	0.0009 (1.45)	−0.024 (−0.22)	19.07	0.85	2.465	1.32
WD	−0.43 (−0.14)	−0.13 (−0.625)	0.059 (0.108)	0.34 (1.02)	0.21 (0.33)	0.0005 (0.05)	−0.001 (−2.06)	0.017 (0.16)	18.02	0.58	1.18	1.28
BCE	9.00 (1.80)	0.49 (1.44)	−0.42 (−0.47)	0.34 (0.61)	−1.58 (−1.49)	0.026 (1.40)	−0.0003 (−0.34)	−0.007 (−0.04)	48.99	0.63	1.74	2.11
1958–68 ($n_2 = 11$)												
WR	11.52 (3.75)	0.99 (2.60)	−1.42 (−2.19)	−0.52 (−1.43)	−0.37 (−0.285)	0.04 (3.185)	0.001 (0.95)	−0.53 (−1.60)	3.07	0.91	2.87	1.01
WD	2.63 (0.60)	−0.08 (−0.15)	−1.02 (−1.1)	−0.13 (−0.245)	1.00 (0.54)	0.02 (1.025)	0.0001 (0.085)	−0.35 (−0.75)	6.27	0.66	1.35	1.445
BCE	14.15 (4.34)	0.91 (2.24)	−2.44 (−3.55)	−0.65 (−1.68)	0.63 (0.46)	0.06 (4.38)	0.001 (1.01)	−0.88 (−2.51)	3.46	0.95	1.83	1.07

Sources: See footnotes to table 5-1.

a. Null hypothesis: the structure does not change. Degrees of freedom: 8.2. The critical value of $F_{(8,2)}$ at the 95 percent level is 19.4. The test statistics for the three equations are WR, 1.30; WD, 0.47; BCE, 3.29. The test statistic for all three equations is considerably less than the critical value of $F_{(8,2)}$ at the 95 percent level. There is thus no evidence to reject the null hypothesis that both sets of observations—those for 1958–68 and those for 1958–76—are generated from the same model. Numbers in parentheses are t-statistics.

VI

Sweden

By the mid 1960s the Swedish economy had come to be characterized as "an inflationary, full employment economy";[1] and this reputation survived into the steep international recession that began a decade later. Money wages and unit labor costs have been subjected to one set of forces that has exerted upward pressure on labor costs in this small open economy, and they have been subjected to another set that has exerted downward pressure. Among the cost-raising influences have been inflationary movements in world prices, strong institutional and political support for equality in the distribution of income, and a high degree of union bargaining and political power. Downward pressures on labor costs have been exerted by periodic declines in international demand for Swedish exports, and, at least until recently, a high degree of managerial discretion in matters affecting labor productivity at plant and company levels.

Institutional Self-Restraint

In this environment Swedish collective bargaining seems to have functioned as an imperfectly restrained system, tending to exert less pressure on labor costs than it might have done but frequently more than finance ministers and central banks, among others, found comfortable. Evidence of a high degree of potential bargaining power may be found in the exceptionally high degree of organization in Sweden, where about 95 percent of blue-collar employees and 70 percent of white-collar employees in manufacturing are organized.[2] The exercise of restraint might be inferred in part from the peaceful climate of Swedish industrial

1. Bent Hansen, with Wayne W. Snyder, *Fiscal Policy in Seven Countries, 1955–1965* (Paris: Organisation for Economic Co-operation and Development, March 1969), p. 357; Assar Lindbeck, *Swedish Economic Policy* (Berkeley and Los Angeles: University of California Press, 1974), p. 2.
2. Gunnar Högberg, "Recent Trends in Collective Bargaining: Sweden," *International Labour Review*, vol. 107, no. 3 (March 1973), pp. 223–38.

relations, at least until the end of the 1960s, which was in marked contrast to Sweden's own prewar experience when, other things being equal, much higher levels of unemployment should have made for fewer strikes. Sweden's postwar record was outstanding in comparison with the records of other countries, moreover, at least through the 1970s. Thus Sweden, with an average of 40 days a year per thousand employees lost during the period 1960–71, ranked second lowest in a comparison of eight industrial countries; Japan, which came in third, had an average of 147. Germany was lowest, with 23 days lost, so Sweden has been closer to Germany than to Japan.[3]

Restraint seems to have been reflected in the development of labor costs and shortages in the sectors exposed to international competition. Even during recessions the number of unfilled jobs has been very high in relation to the number of unemployed. In 1971, when unemployment reached 101,000, there were 36,000 vacancies; and in 1972, with unemployment at 107,000, the number of vacancies stood at 31,700.[4] The competitive private sector has recruited foreign labor heavily—fully 14 percent of the manufacturing labor force is foreign—but this has not eliminated shortages, especially of more highly skilled labor.

The persistence of shortages has meant that the unions did not raise the wages of labor in short supply as much as they might have. But to have raised them in the same proportion as other wages would have violated the labor movement's policy of wage equalization, or "solidarity." Thus to have raised the wages of labor in short supply more rapidly would have meant raising the general level of all wages more rapidly, and this would have meant increasing the costs of Swedish exports and import substitutes more rapidly in relation to world prices and productivity and hence eliminating shortages by reducing profits and the demand for Swedish products rather than by increasing labor supplies. Sweden's central labor and management negotiators sought to rein in the Metal Workers' Union and the firms in the open, or "competitive," sector because they were well aware of the importance of accepting external price movements as a constraint on domestic wages. They were early and enthusiastic subscribers to the Aukrust model when it appeared in the early 1970s, because they felt that it described what they had been trying consciously to do all along. They believed that in Sweden

3. The Conference Board, *Resolving Labor-Management Disputes: A Nine-Country Comparison,* no. 600 (New York: Conference Board, 1973), table 2, p. 12.

4. OECD Economic Surveys, *Sweden,* April 1977, table E, p. 55; diagram 13, p. 39.

institutional restraint was both necessary and forthcoming, although the model itself stresses the disciplinary role of competitive market forces. In a book that emerged from a remarkable collaborative research project sponsored by Landsorganisationen i Sverige (LO), the Swedish Confederation of Trade Unions, the Tjänstemännens Centralorganisationen (TCO), the Central Organization of Salaried Employees, and the Svenska Arbetsgivareföreningen (SAF), the Swedish Employers' Confederation, the joint authors wrote:

> The primary task of the unions is to negotiate as large a share of the production result as possible for their members. But with the strength that these organisations have nowadays in Sweden, they must sense a responsibility for the economy which goes far beyond this primary task. It is true that they have often been accused of demanding too much in wage negotiations and, consequently, of having caused price increases. . . . But in negotiations the unions have been aware of the risk of making such heavy inroads into profitability that the basis for future development in business enterprises deteriorates. The negotiators have long ago become aware of the existence of a point beyond which no claim should be pushed lest it impairs the prospects for future wage increases.[5]

Centralized Bargaining as an Alternative to Incomes Policy

Institutional restraint was made possible by Sweden's highly centralized system of collective bargaining. This system began to evolve at the beginning of the century, when employers, who had been resisting unionism and strikes with lockouts and mutual strike insurance, formed a central organization, the SAF, to deploy these weapons more effectively. They were prepared to cede great authority to the SAF, which ultimately came to have exclusive power to authorize, order, terminate, and pay compensation for lockouts and to order member firms to avert or end strikes.[6] But it soon became their purpose to negotiate from strength rather than to avoid union recognition, so they took the initiative in proposing a stable bilateral relationship to the unions. They preferred this approach to a relationship imposed and regulated by the government, partly because "business interests never carried as much weight in

5. Gösta Edgren, Karl-Olof Faxén, and Clas-Erik Odhner, *Wage Formation and the Economy* (London: Allen & Unwin, 1973), pp. 222–23.

6. T. L. Johnston, *Collective Bargaining in Sweden: A Study of the Labour Market and Its Institutions* (London: Allen & Unwin, 1962), pp. 75–76.

Swedish politics as in most of the great European industrial nations and in the United States."[7] On the union side, impetus toward centralization was provided by proponents of two time-honored Socialist causes—the assignment of priority to the bargaining requirements of low-wage workers and the establishment of industrial unions. The national craft unions resisted, however, and effectively guarded their bargaining autonomy until the depression of the 1930s. But then, when union bargaining power weakened and when legislation was proposed (by a Social Democratic minority government) to protect the interests of neutrals in labor disputes, the LO was able to respond to an invitation by the SAF to establish bilateral machinery.[8] Following the recommendation of a government-appointed commission, the so-called Basic Agreement of 1938 established a bilateral Labor Market Council to settle disputes involving essential public services—if necessary, with the aid of a jointly appointed impartial chairman. It is significant, however, that, under this agreement—and indeed under a law of 1928—recourse to secondary boycotts and sympathetic action remain permissible;[9] this is essential to the operation of a system that depends on strong central organizations. (This balance-of-terror approach is in contrast to the American approach, which, in relying extensively on regulation and intervention by the government, outlaws most secondary activity, although lockouts in multiemployer bargaining units are lawful.)

During and after World War II and the advent of a high-employment economy, the public interest in containing inflation and maintaining balance-of-payments equilibrium effectively supplanted the public interest in peaceful industrial relations as an incentive to the parties to centralize their collective-bargaining arrangements. Traditional support by employers was increased as their bargaining power grew weaker in the new economic environment and as their political influence declined. The SAF was particularly interested in centralized bargaining as a way

7. Swedish Information Service, "Labor Relations in Sweden," *Fact Sheets on Sweden* (Stockholm, n.d.).

8. Peter Jackson and Keith Sisson, "Employers' Confederations in Sweden and the U.K. and the Significance of Industrial Infrastructure," *British Journal of Industrial Relations,* vol. 14, no. 3 (November 1976), stress the absence and the threat of legislated restraints on unionism and bargaining as an explanation of the rise of centralized bargaining in Sweden (pp. 310–13).

9. Johnston, *Collective Bargaining,* pp. 34–35, 146–47, 171–85.

SWEDEN 305

of holding down domestic costs in relation to world prices in the interest of the smaller, less profitable firms, which were increasingly threatened by the expansion of large-scale enterprises during the rapid growth of international trade in the postwar period, because "employer associations are naturally disinclined to grant wage increases of a size and structure that would put many affiliated firms out of business."[10]

Support for centralized bargaining was also strengthened within the labor movement, where it came to be regarded, first, as an alternative to a government-imposed incomes policy and, second, as a necessary institutional device to implement an egalitarian wage policy.

During the early postwar period, the SAF and the LO had cooperated in a government policy to secure wage restraint in the face of full employment and excessive demand, only to be rewarded by widespread discontent among workers, extensive wage drift at the plant level, and ultimately a "wage explosion" triggered by the Korean War. Wages jumped 20 percent in 1951 and another 20 percent in 1952.[11] In the latter year, a plea for further restraint by the finance minister (a Social Democrat) was rejected by the LO, which then accepted a proposal by the SAF for central bargaining—although only as an emergency measure. Further pressure from the finance minister for restraint, however, led, in 1956, to the regularization of economywide bargaining—a process in which the government's responsibility has usually been limited to providing the parties with economic forecasts that they can take into account "in making their own estimates before the start of negotiations."[12] (Yet the constitutent unions, at a meeting of the LO's representative assembly, must approve the agreements reached through central negotiations; and, indeed, these agreements are formally regarded only as recommendations to the national unions.) Thus, while some other countries have attempted either to build or to shore up centralized bargaining institutions in order to implement official incomes policies, in Sweden central bargaining was adopted, at least in part, in order to avert such policies, but at the same time to serve the national interest in economic stabilization at high levels of employment.

10. Swedish Information Service, "Labor Relations."
11. Lindbeck, *Swedish Economic Policy,* pp. 28–30, 70–74; Edgren, Faxén, and Odhner, *Wage Formation,* pp. 30–31.
12. Edgren, Faxén, and Odhner, *Wage Formation,* p. 31.

The Objective of the Central Bargainers: Employer Resistance or Union Restraint?

Union opposition to incomes policy was based on objection not only to government intrusion into the domain of collective bargaining but also to what the union representatives regarded as the excessive and one-sided demands made on them to restrain their constituents. They wanted the burden shared. Accordingly, they came to favor two different approaches, which are alleged to rely on external restraining forces to generate some effective employer resistance to union wage demands without necessitating an increase in unemployment above very low target levels. In addition, both approaches tend in principle to restrain labor costs indirectly by operating in a manner consistent with the requirements of economic efficiency and growth in productivity. In fact, under each approach, the bargaining system is supposed to outperform an unorganized market system by dispensing with temporary, short-run changes in wage differentials by means of which labor resources are theoretically reallocated in response to relative changes in the demand for or supply of labor in an unorganized market, a reallocation that would be difficult to realize where organized groups of workers sought to protect their relative wages. The first approach was associated with the names of Gösta Rehn and Rudolf Meidner, the two leading labor-movement economists of the 1950s, and the second was associated with Odd Aukrust's theory of the international transmission of inflation, as adapted and modified in the light of Swedish experience by Gösta Edgren, Karl-Olof Faxén, and Clas-Erik Odhner (or EFO, as their book came to be known).

The Rehn-Meidner approach followed Keynes in maintaining that inflationary pressures at less than full employment are associated both with labor bottlenecks in particular occupations and regions and with increased union bargaining power. This analysis provided a case for "active labor-market policy," or a set of government programs to subsidize and train unemployed workers who could thereby be moved, at unchanged relative wages, to jobs in expanding firms and sectors in which labor shortages existed. In principle, policies with such specific objectives would simultaneously reduce both inflation and unemployment, whereas expansion of overall demand could reduce unemployment only by increasing inflation. In so doing, such policies would not only tend to reduce wage drift by eliminating local bottlenecks but might also induce restraint in collective bargaining, in two ways. In the first place, unions would not feel called upon to extend wage increases generated in pockets of excess demand to sectors in which labor was still in excess supply. Second, the use of selective labor-market instruments might allow the economy to reach high-level employment without generating as much of an increase in aggregate profits as would a general expansion of aggregate demand, and this might serve either to increase employer resistance or to damp down union militancy.

To the extent that active labor-market policies permit expansion to be concentrated in low-cost, dynamic firms and sectors, they obviate the need to raise prices and profitability sufficiently to permit the expansion—or even the survival—of high-cost units. As a result employer bargaining resistance might be increased, especially since, as we have observed, the profitability of smaller, high-cost affiliates has strongly influenced policymaking in the employers' associations. Under a regime of economywide bargaining, however, the employers' disposition to resist might be relatively unimportant, since widespread strikes and lockouts rapidly assume the character of national emergencies in which the public authority is drawn into a three-handed game holding the weakest hand. The substitution of active labor-market policies for general reflationary measures, therefore, could not suffice to reduce aggregate levels of profitability at given levels of unemployment; the latter would require reducing incentives to union militancy. In any event, while labor-market policies have been employed extensively in Sweden, they did not prevent the inflation-unemployment tradeoff from growing worse during the second half of the 1960s.[13]

The Aukrust model calls attention to the restraint on Swedish labor costs originating outside the country in the form of world prices. But this is a long-run theory, which postulates a constant share of profits in the distribution of the income of a firm. While the employer always has an incentive to resist granting wage increases in excess of the "room" created by changes in international prices and sectoral productivity, there is no reason to believe that, under centralized collective bargaining,

13. Rudolf Meidner and Rolf Andersson, "The Overall Impact of an Active Labor Market Policy in Sweden," in Lloyd Ulman, ed., *Manpower Programs in the Policy Mix* (Baltimore: Johns Hopkins University Press, 1973), pp. 117–58.

the resistance of employers would be more effective against union pressures to exceed that allowance than it would be under other circumstances, including those discussed earlier in connection with the Rehn model. While a wage change that originates in the tradables sector is supposed to be reproduced exactly in the sheltered sector of the economy in a new equilibrium, moreover, the theory does not allow for any competitive lags in the adjustment process—such as might be associated with a transfer of additional labor into the tradables sector, for example. Self-restraint by the central labor federation is therefore needed in order to ensure that wage increases in the competitive sector do not exceed the room created for them and to ensure that wage increases in the sheltered sector do not exceed wage increases in the competitive sector. These were the tasks which EFO claimed that, in fact, the central bargainers performed throughout the 1960s.

Economic Performance in the 1960s and Early 1970s

To judge by the performance of the economy, the collective bargainers did quite well. Unemployment averaged 1.7 percent between 1960 and 1970. Inflation was not low; consumer prices rose an average of 4 percent a year during that period, and the average annual increase in hourly compensation was 9.4 percent. But increases in productivity were also large, so the average increase in unit labor costs was only about 2 percent in kronor, or 3.5 percent in U.S. dollars, while real hourly compensation rose at an average annual rate of nearly 5.5 percent.[14] The trade account was periodically in deficit, but with a pronounced tendency toward balance, which, after a reversal in the second half of the decade, seemed to have resumed in 1970–73. The current account tended to be in balance from the mid 1950s to the mid 1960s.

Yet danger signs appeared during the second half of the 1960s. Unemployment increased somewhat during that period. This has been attributed in part to structural factors on both the supply and the demand sides—strong increases in participation by women in the labor force,

14. OECD, *Main Economic Indicators* (Paris: OECD), various issues; U.S. Bureau of Labor Statistics, *Monthly Labor Review,* various issues.

induced partly by tax changes and improved day-care services, and "continued structural rationalisation in industry, with a movement of labour and capital towards high productivity sectors and bigger firms."[15] The increase in unemployment also reflected a European "growth recession" in demand, in which Sweden participated in 1966–67. In addition, persistent deficits appeared in the current account; while this, too, reflected the recession, the authorities feared that it also indicated that Swedish export costs and prices had been rising too rapidly. A downward trend in profits was consistent with this explanation, for it was in evidence early in the decade (see figure 6-1). The association between increased concentration and declining profit margins, moreover, might suggest that rising costs could have contributed—along with increasing international competition and the constraint of world prices— to both developments.

In part, EFO noted a tendency for hourly labor costs to outrun the combined increases in product prices and productivity, so that "operating surplus" in the internationally competitive sectors declined by about two thirds of 1 percent a year. This occurred in both the 1950s (1952–60) and the 1960s (1960–68). In the 1950s, however, the decline was concentrated in the raw-materials sector, whereas in the 1960s it appeared in the finished products sectors as well, although the greatest squeeze continued to be in raw materials. In the sheltered sector, excluding government, on the other hand, the average operating surplus increased slightly.[16] While the results for the sheltered sector are consistent with the cost markup model of pricing contained in the Aukrust theory, the results for the competitive sector, where output prices are set in the world market, suggest that the Aukrust-EFO model does not tell quite the whole story as far as short-run variations in Swedish wage changes are concerned. Attempts by the central bargainers to exercise discretionary restraint, therefore, while effective during most of the 1960s, are found not to have been completely effective when they are judged by the criteria of international competitiveness and export profitability.

That conclusion can also be inferred from some of the econometric work of Lars Calmfors, who tested the Aukrust model in a series of

15. OECD Economic Surveys, *Sweden,* March 1969, p. 12; April 1970, p. 32.
16. Edgren, Faxén, and Odhner, *Wage Formation,* table 1.1, pp. 16–17; pp. 20–21.

Figure 6-1. *Profits before Depreciation as a Percentage of Turnover in Large Manufacturing Enterprises, Sweden, 1955–79*

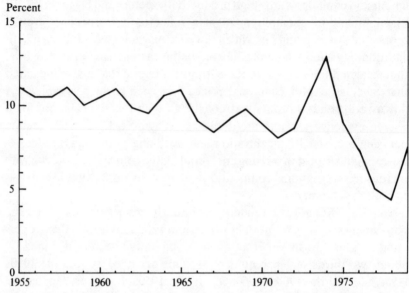

Percent

Source: National Central Bureau of Statistics, *Företagen, 1979* (Stockholm: NCBS, 1981), table E, p. 42.

regression equations covering the period 1958–73.[17] He found some support for that model in his wage-change equations (as well as in his price-change equations). Wage changes in tradables are related significantly to price changes plus productivity changes in that sector. Wage changes in the nontradables sector are related significantly to wage changes in tradables on a one-to-one basis; since the tradables variable is not lagged, we interpret the relation as evidence of institutional linkage through the LO-SAF central negotiations. The same evidence of an institutional linkage is found in the case of Norway.

At the same time Calmfors concluded that the international influence on wages has not been as strong as the Aukrust model would have predicted, at least in the short run, since the coefficients of his price-change and productivity-change variables in the tradables sector seem to be well below unity. He also concluded that wage increases in the

17. Lars Calmfors, "Inflation in Sweden," in Lawrence B. Krause and Walter S. Salant, eds., *Worldwide Inflation: Theory and Recent Experience* (Washington, D.C.: Brookings Institution, 1977), pp. 502–20.

open sector have reflected both changes in the level of domestic demand (included in the difference between vacancies and unemployment) and "a strong element of autonomous wage-push" (impounded in a large constant term), as well as the international price and sectoral productivity influences referred to above. And he interpreted the underestimates by the equations of the large wage increases of 1970–73 as evidence of an increased degree of institutional push.[18]

Calmfors's results are consistent with the results obtained in Franz Ettlin's quantitative estimates of wage levels, although Ettlin infers that the effect of a given change in the rate of unemployment on the rate of change in wages dwindles in time. This tends to support the interpretation of the Aukrust-EFO model as a long-run explanation of wage and price inflation.[19]

Our own wage-estimating equations, which are reproduced in the appendix to this chapter, suggest that the primary effect of changes in international prices and domestic productivity was on the central negotiated wage settlements, while conditions of labor demand, as measured by vacancy rates, and changes in the cost of living more directly affected wage drift. Obviously no great claims can be made on behalf of an equation—equation 1—that seeks to estimate average annual negotiated wage changes with the aid of only nine observations (during the period 1959–75) and a single complex explanatory variable—that is, the sum of changes in world prices and domestic productivity minus wage drift. The latter makes collective bargaining into a residual claimant, something that was once, in 1967, specifically proposed by the SAF economists but rejected by the union side, on the grounds that it would tend to increase drift and diminish the importance of the central negotiations.[20] On the other hand, the central settlements have included extra compensatory payments to groups of wage earners who have little or no opportunity to secure drift, and this obliges the negotiators to anticipate drift when calculating the total cost of their agreements. Roughly, these results tend to confirm the hypothesis of effective institutional restraint, although

18. Ibid., p. 517; see also p. 516.

19. Franz A. Ettlin and Johan A. Lybeck, "The International Dependence of Swedish Wages and Prices" (1974); Franz A. Ettlin, "Wage Determination in the Step 1 Quarterly Model of Sweden" (December 1978).

20. Lloyd Ulman and Robert J. Flanagan, *Wage Restraint: A Study of Incomes Policies in Western Europe* (Berkeley: University of California Press, 1971), pp. 105–07.

without excluding the presence of elements of institutional push—as
suggested by the underestimates of negotiated increases in 1971 and 1975
as well as in the first half of the 1960s and also by the responsiveness of
wage drift to increases in the cost of living (equation 2).

When judged by the Aukrust criteria of international competitiveness
and profitability, the existence of "autonomous wage push" could mean
that the Swedish union movement failed to exercise sufficient restraint
in pursuit of certain bargaining or political objectives. Two of these
objectives were to protect real wages from erosion by the increasing
cost of living and to alter or protect relative wages. Although competitive
theory predicts that a rise in consumer prices will sooner or later induce
an equivalent rise in money wages even in the absence of collective
bargaining, no explicit allowance is made for this feedback in the
Scandinavian model. Statistical evidence has, moreover, been lacking:
Calmfors, like Jacobsson and Lindbeck before him, found that lagged
consumer price changes proved to lack significance as a predictor of
change in money wages,[21] although the coefficients have the expected
positive sign. World price increases have accounted for an important
part of consumer price increases in this small open economy, however,
and our results suggest that negotiated wages succeeded in capturing
much of that component of increases in the cost of living. They also
suggest that part of any rise in consumer prices has found its way into
wage drift—which, according to equation 3, is unaffected by increases
in either world prices or negotiated wages. Since cost-of-living compensation is divided between negotiated settlements and wage drift, the
consumer price coefficient on a wage-drift equation—equations 2 and
3—would be expected to be significant and positive but well below unity.
(It is actually +0.22.) The combined cost-of-living increase (from the
two sources) could yield an increase in total earnings in excess of the
room generated in the open sector.

Equality, Centralization, and Wage Drift

Another potentially inflationary union objective has been the narrowing of wage differentials, or what has been termed the "solidaristic"
policy of the LO. There have been two versions of this policy. The first
policy called for equal pay for equal work. It required the narrowing of

21. See Lars Jacobsson and Assar Lindbeck, "Labor Market Conditions, Wages
and Inflation—Swedish Experiences, 1955–67," *Swedish Journal of Economics*, vol. 71

intraoccupational wage differentials, which included geographic and intraindustrial differentials, but not necessarily of interoccupational wage differences. It underlay Rehn's presumption of active labor-market policies that would substitute more efficiently for short-run changes in occupational wage differences and that would increase both levels and growth of productivity by squeezing out less efficient firms. The SAF regarded active labor-market policy as a way of holding down wage increases in the more profitable firms in an industry and consequently of avoiding severe profit squeezes in the others.

But espousal by the LO of the policy of equal pay for equal work soon gave way to its support of a broader policy that permits equal pay for unequal work and the narrowing of wage differences among as well as within occupations, industries, and regions. At the end of the 1950s, the central negotiations provided that low-wage regions were to be granted extra wage increases through special negotiations by the national unions affiliated with the LO, and in 1964 provision was made for low-wage supplements to be paid on an individual-by-individual basis, the average wage of male industrial workers serving as the basis for calculation.[22] This increasingly comprehensive and detailed egalitarian policy offers a strong contrast to the assumption implicit in the Aukrust theory of an invariant equilibrium industrial wage structure. In fact, the Swedish policy of compression generated a two-part mechanism of wage push, the first part taking the form of wage drift in high-wage industries and occupational categories and the second taking the form of incremental increases in the central settlements that have been designed to neutralize that drift.

From the mid 1950s to the end of the 1960s wage drift exceeded the total of negotiated wage increases and amounted to nearly half the increase in wage costs, including fringes and benefit payments by employers. It is often regarded simply as a phenomenon of excess demand and can be generated when, according to Aukrust, negotiated increases are restrained by an incomes policy below the room for wage increases.[23] But, according to EFO, drift reflects, in addition to short-

---

(June 1969), pp. 64–103, and "On the Transmission Mechanism of Wage Change," ibid., vol. 73 (September 1971), pp. 273–93. See also Calmfors, "Inflation in Sweden," pp. 511–15.

22. Edgren, Faxén, and Odhner, *Wage Formation,* pp. 32, 42–44; Derek Robinson, *Solidaristic Wage Policy in Sweden* (Paris: OECD, 1974), pp. 17–24.

23. Odd Aukrust, "Inflation in the Open Economy: A Norwegian Model," in Krause and Salant, *Worldwide Inflation,* p. 115.

ages, changes in job composition and "increased intensity of work and improved piece work skills," and also "increases in productivity through rationalisation which is not accompanied by the recalculation of piece rates or by incomplete recalculations." It includes, moreover, "elements in the application at the national union level that go beyond the central agreement recommendations issued by SAF and LO" as well as "extra concessions and 'generous' interpretations of the agreements in the negotiations at plant level which follow immediately upon the central agreements"; and these in turn reflect "the contagion effect of applying agreements in individual enterprises, both 'horizontally' by extending them to other groups not included in the first place, and 'vertically' through the effect of minimum wage increases on the higher wages." And it further includes extra payments made during the contract period, not only to attract and retain labor but also "to secure the cooperation of the labour force during changes in production."[24]

Some elements of drift, therefore, have served the interests of efficiency and growth through wage flexibility at plant level; in this respect wage drift might be regarded as complementary to centralized wage bargaining, just as in the United States local plant agreements are explicitly "supplemental" to companywide collective agreements. On the other hand, drift has sometimes represented the informal exertion of bargaining power by local groups seeking to protect or advance their relative wage positions in reacting to particular provisions of the central agreements. Finally, drift has emerged from the reaction of management to centralized wage policy, as when the result of wage compression was either problems of employee morale or specific labor shortages. In Sweden drift was especially pronounced in the sectors in which wages are relatively high and those that are internationally competitive. In those sectors restraint seems to have been motivated by the desire to reduce relative wages in the interests of egalitarian wage policy—as well as by concern over the relative cost position of the competitive sector. Thus the Organisation for Economic Co-operation and Development (OECD) reported that during the second half of 1969 a slowdown in the vigorous postrecession expansion and a deterioration in the current account was caused by capacity constraints in key industries, notably shortage of skilled labor—"as well as by tighter monetary conditions" and, according to Calmfors, a profit squeeze in the export sector.[25]

24. Edgren, Faxén, and Odhner, *Wage Formation*, pp. 144–45.

25. OECD Economic Surveys, *Sweden*, April 1970, p. 5; ibid., April 1971, pp. 6, 27–28.

The inflationary effects of wage drift have been augmented by determined and ingenious efforts made to counter drift and to anticipate it at the central negotiating level. These have included the negotiation of higher percentage increases for hourly workers than for pieceworkers and for special catch-up allowances to be paid in the second and third years of long-term agreements to poorly paid workers receiving below-average drift. How has this tug-of-war come out? Until recently it was believed that the efforts of the LO to reduce wage differentials through central negotiations had been stymied by locally generated drift. The high-wage industries had pretty well maintained their relative positions in the 1960s. There was some slight compression in the interindustrial wage structure after a period of widening in the early 1950s, however, and wages in low-wage areas tended to rise more rapidly than wages elsewhere during the life of each multiyear contract.[26] And Faxén has recently presented evidence which shows that hourly earnings of the high-wage construction workers did decline significantly in relation to manufacturing earnings during the period 1963–75 (as the LO negotiated smaller percentage increases in building); women's wages in manufacturing have risen in relation to those of men since 1969, which Faxén ascribes primarily to low-wage protective provisions in the central agreements; wages of manual workers rose in relation to salaries of certain classes of engineers as comparable skill levels in both groups decreased; and shortages of skilled workers remained greater than shortages of nonskilled labor from 1961 onward.[27] A recent analysis by the OECD shows that the coefficient of variation in earnings in the private sector, weighted by shares of employment, declined steadily and by about a third between 1963 and 1976.[28]

The Growth of the Government Sector

The task of reconciling an egalitarian wage policy with the maintenance of international competitiveness was complicated by the very rapid growth of the public sector. This development assumed heightened

26. Lindbeck, *Swedish Economic Policy*, p. 157; and Edgren, Faxén, and Odhner, *Wage Formation*, pp. 45–48.

27. Karl-Olof Faxén, "Wage Policy and Attitudes of Industrial Relations Parties in Sweden," paper delivered at the Fourth World Congress of the International Industrial Relations Association, September 6–10, 1976.

28. OECD Economic Surveys, *Sweden,* April 1978, p. 28.

significance in the 1970s, although it had been growing in importance throughout the previous decade. In the 1960s the trend rate of increase in employment in the public sector was 5.4 percent a year; the rate for the total economy was 0.4 percent, and there was a decline of 0.4 percent in the manufacturing sector.[29] Between 1950 and 1970 employment in the public sector increased 141 percent.[30] By the end of the 1960s Sweden, with 40 percent of its GNP devoted to public expenditures, headed a list of twelve industrial countries in this respect. During the 1970s the government share grew much more rapidly in Sweden than in any other OECD country; by 1977 it had reached 59 percent, whereas in the Netherlands it was only 53.4 percent, and the unweighted average for all OECD countries combined was 39.4 percent. In 1980 the government share stood at 64 percent.[31] Employment in the public sector rose from about 21 percent of total employment in 1970 to about 28 percent in 1978.[32]

Growth of the public sector was originally supported by the Social Democrats, including trade-union leaders, not primarily as a means of expanding aggregate demand and employment, but as a means of extending economic egalitarianism by removing from the market system a growing array of services that had been in increasing demand but inelastic supply—typically because of relatively low rates of growth in productivity.[33] Total tax revenue increased from 40.5 percent of GNP in 1970 to 53.4 percent in 1977; Sweden became the only OECD country in which the tax burden exceeded half of GNP.[34] Thus, rising public expenditures were covered by rising taxes. In particular, they were financed by sales taxes, later changed to a value-added tax, because, while the LO was determined to press on with both solidaristic wage bargaining and increased public spending, the Swedish tax-and-subsidy structure was already steeply progressive.

But while progressivity was thus limited, and while the effect of increasing sales taxes was to dampen aggregate demand, "certainly there were repercussions on wages and salaries," as Hansen wrote in the early 1960s.[35] A "tax push" on wages presumably came about

29. Ibid., June 1973, diagram 8, p. 17.
30. *Population and Housing Census, 1970*, part 10, table 3.
31. Preliminary National Budget, 1981.
32. OECD Economic Surveys, *Sweden*, April 1980, pp. 38–40.
33. Rudolf Meidner, *The Trade Union Movement and the Public Sector* (Stockholm: Landsorganisationen i Sverige, 1974), pp. 30 and 33.
34. OECD Economic Surveys, *Sweden*, April 1980, p. 40.
35. Hansen, *Fiscal Policy*, p. 371.

because, just as the preference of the leaders of the LO for solidaristic pretax wage policy found significantly less than unanimous acceptance within—and outside—the ranks, so too did their preference for public consumption—insofar as the latter entailed willingness to forgo increases in private consumption. Many Socialist members of the Riksdag, therefore, after voting for increases in public spending and for increases in taxation to finance them, withdrew to the bargaining table, where, in their roles as trade-union representatives, they negotiated extra money wages to compensate their members for the higher taxes that they had earlier levied in a display of fiscal responsibility.

The relative expansion of the government sector interacted with the solidaristic wage policy of the LO in three respects. First, to the extent that any tax push to which it contributed raised the average marginal tax rate by increasing the proportion of wage earners in the higher brackets of the heavily progressive tax structure, it tended to exacerbate problems of shortage, especially through absenteeism. Second, shortages in the open sectors were increased on the demand side as well as on the supply side by a combination of contracyclical and trend increases in public-sector employment. The public sector tended to hold onto workers whom it had taken on during periods of slack in the private sector. "When [according to EFO] later in the upswing, industry required labour, it was anchored in the sheltered sector and had no wish to leave it, in favour of a less safe livelihood in the competing sector. It was replaced to some extent by foreign workers, but the shortage of labour nevertheless meant a decisive brake on industrial expansion" in 1966–68.[36]

A similar increase in employment outside the competitive sector was contributed by a housing boom, which was stimulated by government subsidies and rent controls and much of which was concentrated among the municipalities. This development, together with increased demand for purely public services, tended per se to increase relative wages in the sheltered sector, which by the mid 1960s had begun "to share the role as pace-setter for wage developments."[37]

Finally, the growth of public employment implied a relative increase in the size of the sheltered sector of the economy and also an increase in the proportion of the combined wage-earning and salaried work force outside the joint SAF-LO bargaining unit. Thus, in addition to domesti-

36. Edgren, Faxén, and Odhner, *Wage Formation*, p. 203.
37. OECD Economic Surveys, *Sweden*, April 1972, p. 21; Lindbeck, *Swedish Economic Policy*, pp. 186–89.

cally generated demand pressures, the increase in employment in the public sector created the potential for a greater institutional push on costs originating in the sheltered sector. None of these developments, of course, diminished the tendency for international prices to generate wage and salary increases throughout the economy, but they did constitute a purely domestic source of wage and salary increases, and they helped to make wages and salaries respond more sluggishly to any decelerating influences emanating from abroad.

In the 1970s: Waiting Out the World

While labor costs were subjected to ever stronger, internally generated upward pressure during the 1960s, the performance of the economy remained quite satisfactory. In the 1970s, however, domestic pressures on the bargaining system intensified, and they were joined by increased pressures from abroad. The external pressures—the rise in world commodity prices during the upswing of 1972–73, followed by the oil price explosion—were of course felt by Sweden's competitors as well, but Swedish policymakers did not march in lockstep with their opposite numbers. The difference is revealed first by the fact that in 1971–72 Swedish unemployment rose to a level more than 30 percent higher than the average in the OECD countries and then by the fact that it plunged abruptly below the average—nearly 50 percent in 1976—and remained lower throughout the balance of the decade. Output suffered its greatest decline, moreover—both absolutely and in relation to output abroad—during the latter half of the decade, when unemployment was relatively low.[38]

In 1971–72, the Swedish authorities responded to a prior deterioration in both current and capital accounts by adopting restrictive fiscal policy measures which, at the cost of higher unemployment, were promptly rewarded by a sharp swing of the current account into surplus. Inflation of money wages did accelerate between 1970 and 1973—from an average annual rate of 9.4 percent during the 1960s to 11.6 percent—but this reflected international inflationary developments. In fact, Sweden's response to these developments was on the whole restrained. Hourly compensation and unit labor costs rose less rapidly in Sweden than in any other European industrial country. Real wages rose less rapidly only

38. OECD Economic Surveys, *Sweden*, April 1980, diagrams 17 and 18, pp. 50–51.

in France, and, whereas both real and money wages had, on the average, risen more rapidly in Sweden than in Germany during the 1960s, now they—together with unit labor costs—rose more rapidly in Germany.[39] And while money wages rose more rapidly than productivity during the early 1970s, they rose less rapidly than did productivity and export-sector prices—or the Aukrust room—combined.[40]

Thus the deflationary medicine appeared to work, but an unemployment rate that averaged 2.3 percent in 1970–73 was generally regarded as too high a price to pay for a policy intended as a response to a decline in net external demand by effecting a relative reduction in domestic costs. Accordingly, when the oil crisis of 1973 combined a much more severe decline in external demand with a relative rise in Swedish costs,[41] the authorities adopted a set of measures that compensated for the decline in the demand for labor but, in so doing, tended to increase domestic costs further. This "bridging" strategy of keeping unemployment low while waiting for external demand to revive featured the adoption of such selective measures as the release of investment finance from the investment funds, sharply increased expenditures on traditional "supply-oriented" labor-market programs designed to improve occupational and geographic mobility, and also a set of "demand-oriented" measures directed at firms rather than individual workers. The latter included inventory subsidies which increased from SKr 113 million in 1972–73 to a peak of SKr 954.5 million in 1976–77; government orders to firms, which increased from SKr 49.4 million in 1972–73 to SKr 299.3 million in 1977–78; "in-plant training to avoid layoffs," which rose from less than SKr 1 million in 1973–74 to SKr 483 million in 1977–78; and temporary jobs for older workers in the clothing and textile industries, which varied from a low of SKr 1 billion in 1974–75 to a high of SKr 3 billion in 1977–78.[42] These and other subsidy measures—including cash

39. OECD, *Main Economic Indicators* (Paris: OECD, various issues); U.S. Bureau of Labor Statistics, *Monthly Labor Review*, various issues.

40. Calmfors, "Inflation in Sweden," table 4, p. 526.

41. Important export industries such as forest products and steel are energy intensive, and the energy component of the consumer price index is reported to have risen more rapidly in Sweden than in the OECD as a whole after 1972. See OECD Economic Surveys, *Sweden*, April 1980, p. 33.

42. The Expert Group for Labour Market Research (EFA), *Labour Market Policy in Transition—Studies About the Effect of Labour Market Policies* (Stockholm: Departmentens Offsetcentral, 1978), table 1, pp. 8–9. This is a summary in English of the report of the Expert Group at the Swedish Ministry of Labour.

grants to the unemployed—increased from about 1.5 percent of gross national product at the beginning of the decade to 3 percent in 1977–78.

These policies greatly reduced recorded, or "open," unemployment. As figure 6-2 shows, the proportion of people in the labor force affected by labor-market measures more than tripled between the early 1960s and the late 1970s. This proportion nearly equaled the unemployment rate in 1972, and by 1977–79 it averaged nearly twice the unemployment rate. Workers undergoing training as well as those employed in subsidized temporary jobs and on projects for the disadvantaged are included in this measure. Those receiving in-plant training to avoid layoffs are also included—and their number increased from 419 in 1975 to 41,319 in 1977. These subsidy measures, moreover, have been supplemented by legislation—the Promotion of Employment Act and the Security of Employment Act, 1974—that obliges an employer to give one month's advance notice of general layoffs and notice varying from one to six months, determined by age, of dismissals. "The purpose . . . is to give the union organizations . . . an opportunity of demanding consultations with the employer, e.g., concerning the possibility of alternative solutions, the postponement of the measure he has planned, etc."[43]

These various employment-protection policies contributed to a gap between actual employment (net of labor market measures) and employment estimated on the basis of past changes in gross domestic product and real wages and salaries, which opened up dramatically in 1974.[44] Unfortunately, the implicit reduction in open unemployment also meant a reduction in productivity, as employment rose in relation to potential output. The older, supply-oriented measures were designed to increase productivity by promoting mobility; thus, while they could restrain aggregate demand in relation to employment, they would do so by helping to hold down inflation and increasing the growth rate of output. The demand-oriented measures, however, tended to keep excess supplies of labor (in relation to unsubsidized demand) in place. As a temporary expedient, this was defensible: short-term reductions in the productivity of labor would give way to upswings when the economy returned to "normal" use of capacity with the recovery of world demand for Sweden's cyclically sensitive exports. But the world let Sweden

43. Ministry of Labour, International Secretariat, *Swedish Laws on Security of Employment, Status of Shop Stewards, Litigation in Labour Disputes* (Stockholm, May 1977), p. 16.

44. OECD Economic Surveys, *Sweden,* April 1976, p. 20.

Figure 6-2. *Proportion of the Labor Force Involved in the Labor-Market Measures and Proportion Unemployed, Sweden, 1963–79*

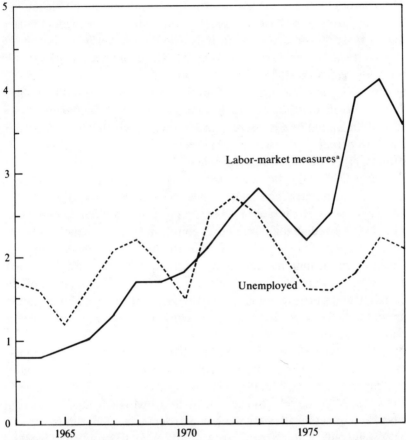

Percentage points

Sources: National Labour Market Board, *Labour Market Statistics*, no. 3 (Stockholm: NLMB, 1982), tables 24, 27, 30, 31, and 33; National Central Bureau of Statistics, *Yearbook of Labour Statistics, 1981* (Stockholm: NCBS, 1981), tables 2.2.4 and 2.13.3.
a. Labor-market measures include training (such as in-plant training to avoid layoffs), relief work, sheltered employment, home work centers, semisheltered employment, archive work, and aid for musicians.

down by staging a hesitant recovery in mid 1975; the gap proved wider than the bridge builders had anticipated. The decline in foreign demand, moreover, was seen to exhibit important "structural" components as reduced market shares in shipbuilding, iron, and steel products reflected increased competition from low-cost producers in Asia and South America.

Prolongation of the bridging policy was reflected in a sharp decline in yearly growth of output per man-hour in manufacturing—from 5.8 percent in 1970–73 (and 7.3 percent in 1960–70) to 1.3 percent in 1973–77. Whereas by this measure the growth of productivity in Sweden had exceeded growth in Germany, France, and the United Kingdom during the early 1970s—and growth in Italy and the Netherlands during the 1960s—it was lower than in any other OECD country except Britain in the bridging period, 1973–77.[45]

The collapse in the growth of productivity was mirrored in a sharp acceleration in unit labor costs. Between 1973 and 1977, unit labor costs rose at an annual rate of more than 15 percent, which was exceeded in Italy (18 percent) and Britain (19 percent) but was much higher than in France (10.4 percent) and especially higher than in Germany (4.6 percent). During the 1960s and the early 1970s, the rate of increase in unit labor costs had been significantly lower in Sweden than in Germany, although the Swedish rate of domestic price inflation had been higher. The rise in Swedish unit labor costs contributed to a decline in international competitiveness, an increase in the deficit on current account, and declining profit margins and investment. In 1977, the bridging policy gave way to a stabilization program that featured devaluation of the currency and a drastic reduction in inventory subsidies, although labor-market policies were continued and open, or recorded, unemployment remained at very low levels.[46]

The rise in unit labor costs need not have been relatively so great had the decline in the growth of productivity been offset by a corresponding decline in the rate of increase in hourly labor costs, both wage and nonwage. Alternatively, the decline in the growth of productivity might have been offset by allowing the krona to depreciate, but this might well have triggered a faster rise in wages. In any event this route was blocked by a decision to maintain the value of the currency in relation to the deutsche mark. In fact, the rate of increase in real hourly compensation sharply accelerated between 1973 and 1977, when, at 6.9 percent a year, it was much greater than in any other OECD country. Thus, real hourly costs accelerated sharply while the growth of productivity was sharply decelerating, so the difference between the rate of increase in the former

---

45. U.S. Bureau of Labor Statistics, *Monthly Labor Review*, various issues.
46. OECD Economic Surveys, *Sweden*, April 1978, passim; ibid., April 1979, pp. 44–45.

and the latter—what the OECD called the "real wage gap"—was positive.[47]

The increase in the real hourly cost of labor during the period, however, substantially exceeded the increase in real hourly earnings; indeed the average increase in earnings was only 1 percent a year, which was much lower than the OECD average of 2.9 percent[48] and in line with the (unadjusted) rise in output per man-hour in manufacturing. The difference was attributable mainly to rapid increases in social security taxes paid by employers, which contributed greatly to the growth in Sweden's tax burden, discussed earlier. Thus, in at least a proximate sense, the inflationary villain of the piece was the government, which increased transfer payments to the inactive population at the same time that it was subsidizing employment to a growing extent in the active population, rather than the social partners in collective bargaining. The latter, of course, contributed a largely discretionary component to the rise in unit costs, and their contribution exceeded any room left over for wage increases after the increases in nonwage labor costs had been subtracted from the increases in productivity (adjusted for changes in the terms of trade).

Policymaking and Bargaining Failure

From the foregoing discussion it can be seen that the relative rise of unit labor costs in Sweden and the deterioration of its international competitive position after 1973 have been associated, first, with exogenous shocks that may have impinged with exceptional severity on the Swedish economy and, second, with exceptionally ambitious public policies designed both to maintain very high levels of employment and to aid the inactive population. Thus if the Swedish system of collective bargaining failed to accommodate itself sufficiently to more straitened circumstances, its failure has not necessarily been greater than the failure of wage-determining institutions in other countries in which total labor costs rose less rapidly than they did in Sweden during the period in question. If the reduced circumstances in which the social partners or

47. Ibid., April 1980, diagram 5, p. 17. The OECD measures divide real compensation and productivity by numbers employed, deflate the former by the private consumption implicit price deflator, and adjust the latter by the terms of trade.

48. Ibid., April 1979, p. 16.

social security policies found themselves reflected the influence of collective bargaining itself or of union political pressure, however, then insufficient adaptation to nonbargained increases in unit labor costs could be regarded as bargaining failure.

In fact, the government itself has been criticized for a sequence of policies in the first half of the 1970s that contributed to subsequent increases in unit costs. First, it was claimed that the deflation of 1971 need not have been so severe—"the idiot stop," some called it—if the authorities had devalued the krona at the peak of the boom of 1969, when the current-account deficit rose sharply, or if they had deflated earlier, or if they had not underestimated the magnitude of the decline in consumption in 1971, which was reflected in a sharp rise in the savings ratio. But the finance minister, an old trade unionist, seems to have been concerned about a tendency for labor costs to exceed increases in productivity and for profit margins to decline in the preceding decade, and he also was concerned about a deterioration in the climate of industrial relations, dramatic evidence of which had been given in the wave of wildcat strikes in 1969–70. Hence devaluation was rejected because of its potentially inflationary consequences, since the central bargaining system could not have been counted on to deliver the requisite degree of restraint of domestic labor cost. Earlier deflation had also been ruled out, it was later claimed, by fear of reviving plant-level discontent. The rise in the savings ratio, moreover, was not unrelated to developments in collective bargaining. In 1970 the central negotiations between the LO and the SAF were held up by militancy among government salaried workers (to be discussed later), and the "protracted wage negotiations seem also to have led to a marked hesitation in consumer spending," as well as contributing to a decline in real disposable income.[49]

It could be therefore argued that the authorities had been constrained by earlier and current developments of costs and labor relations to follow the widely unpopular policy of deflation in the early 1970s and that, in consequence of the unpopularity of that policy, they were constrained to avoid a repetition when confronted by a far more serious surge in costs later on. Thus the authorities, having ruled out devaluation in 1970 because of its potentially inflationary consequences, proceeded to rule out revaluation in 1973–74 because of its potentially deflationary conse-

49. Ibid., April 1972, p. 41.

quences. Revaluation was urged as a way to counter the inflationary consequences of the price rises in energy and other imports and thus to moderate future bargaining settlements. In fact, consumer price inflation accelerated from an annual rate of 6–8 percent in late 1973 and early 1974 to more than 12 percent by midyear, and profit rates (before depreciation and as a percentage of sales—see figure 6-1) continued a steep recovery from a low of about 9 percent in 1971 to more than 13 percent in 1974.[50]

The central bargainers responded to the oil price crisis with a restrained settlement, under which wage-drift guarantees were deferred for a year. That settlement ran for only one year, however, and another outcropping of wildcat strikes occurred. The next agreement, which ran for two years and was front-loaded, has generally been regarded as a disaster. In 1975 and 1976, when labor-cost inflation decelerated abroad (especially in Germany) under the impact of an international recession, it accelerated sharply in Sweden. Total labor costs in industry, which had been rising at an annual rate of 17 percent in 1974, jumped to 25 percent in 1975 and added another 15 percent in 1976. The annual rate of increase in hourly earnings in industry moved up from 11 percent in 1974 to 14 percent and 18 percent, respectively, in the following two years.[51]

This negotiated boost in Swedish labor costs was commonly regarded as having been incited by the earlier jump in profits. Was it an aberration, or did it mean that the Swedish bargaining system had lost its capacity for restraint? Behind the accelerating cost inflation in 1975–76 lay two developments that might charitably be regarded as bad luck. The first of these consisted of a 40 percent rise in social security payments that occurred within the contract period.[52] It helps to explain why total labor costs rose more precipitously than wages in 1975–76, but it does not explain why wages also accelerated sharply at the same time. On the contrary, it might explain why the contractual increases were not even greater than they were: the wage agreement was reached on the understanding that social security payments would subsequently be increased, and the government felt obliged to honor that commitment—as indeed it had done on similar occasions in the past. Thus a public policy that generated cost increases did in this instance reflect the influence of

50. Ibid., April 1976, p. 12; ibid., April 1978, table 5, p. 16.
51. Ibid., April 1978, table 4, p. 15; ibid., April 1976, p. 13; ibid., April 1977, p. 21.
52. Ibid., April 1977, p. 17, n. 18.

collective bargaining in a tradeoff between negotiated wage increases
and increased benefits, but the terms of the tradeoff implied an unsatisfactorily large increase in total labor costs. To that extent, the latter
could not be regarded as simply bad luck, in the sense that relative
increases in nonlabor costs caused by the increases in energy prices
could be so regarded.

Bad timing accounted for the other alleged piece of bad luck. The
international recession caught Sweden in the midst of a two-year fixed-
term labor contract for 1975–76, which prevented negotiated wage
increases and unit labor costs from decelerating more promptly in
response to deceleration abroad. This was not the first time that the
Swedish economy had been caught off base by contract timing. Hansen
observed that, as the result of a contract negotiated at the end of a boom
in 1966, "one year of demand inflation . . . led to three years of
inflationary wage increases."[53] The next contract, which was of three
years' duration and began at the end of the 1969–70 boom, had a similar
effect,[54] and it may have contributed to the exceptionally restrictive
policies associated with the downswing of 1971. The expiration of this
contract, however, was timed fortuitously, and the parties were able to
adjust to the oil price crisis during their regular scheduled negotiations.
They did so by concluding a moderate one-year agreement for 1974. This
in turn enabled the LO to negotiate a new agreement on much more
favorable terms before the 1973–74 upswing gave way to recession and
to accept a duration of two years. Following the termination of the
critical 1975–76 agreement, the parties concluded another one-year
contract for 1977, as a result of which the annual rate of increase in
contractual wage rates fell from 8 percent to 3.5 percent.[55]

In the context of conventional collective bargaining, the downturn in
activity in the 1975–76 contract period might be regarded as a piece of
bad luck. When strong unions can negotiate satisfactorily large contract
gains, they wish to do so for longer periods than when they negotiate on
less satisfactory terms. Conversely, they will negotiate a long-term
contract only on favorable terms. (This may present a contrast to those
implicit-contract theories that have workers willing to trade away income
levels for stability, but we are here in the world of explicit contracts.)
The LO and the SAF indeed demonstrated their capacity to negotiate

53. Hansen, *Fiscal Policy*, p. 375.
54. Lindbeck, *Swedish Economic Policy*, p. 78.
55. OECD Economic Surveys, *Sweden*, April 1978, pp. 15–16, n. 20.

one-year contracts in 1974 and again in 1977; both contracts, however, provided only moderate increases. But it was consistent for the 1975 settlement, which was a "rich" one, to be of longer duration. Nor might that settlement have been expected to be broken into and renegotiated on less favorable terms after it had begun to pay off like a good insurance contract. On the contrary, the longer agreements concluded in both 1975 and 1978 provided for reopening in the event that changes in external conditions rendered the negotiated terms *less* favorable than originally contemplated. The 1978 agreement afforded partial protection to real wages by permitting two reopenings to occur in the event that consumer prices increased by more than specified threshold amounts in each subperiod. And the 1975–76 agreement protected the relative incomes of wage earners by permitting the LO to reopen if groups of salaried employees, in separate negotiations, secured more favorable conditions. In addition, reopening was permitted in the event that "substantial derangements in the economy" should occur.[56]

The union perspective under the highly centralized Swedish system of collective bargaining, however, has been broader than the perspective offered by conventional collective bargaining. It has obliged the LO negotiators to assess and assume a considerable amount of responsibility for the economywide repercussion of their economywide bargaining and hence to bargain responsively and with self-restraint. In 1975–76, the situation called for increased bargaining flexibility to offset the employment rigidity promoted by government policy after external and private demand had fallen off—and especially since the negotiated increase had been so large. It was the government, like a risk-averse employer, that wanted a two-year contract and that sought to "buy" one on moderate terms by scheduling the increase in social security benefits and also two income tax cuts.[57] The unions signed a two-year agreement but on stiff terms. Thus the long-term agreement, like the rise in social security costs, bound the government, rather than the unions, as the international position of the economy grew worse. A situation that called for greater bargaining restraint, flexibility, or both failed to elicit either. By Swedish standards, this must be considered a case of bargaining failure.

In fact, there is reason to believe that the Swedish bargaining system was caught in a weakened condition in the early 1970s by events that made extraordinary demands on it. Weakening of the bargaining system

56. Ibid., April 1976, p. 35.
57. Ibid., June 1975, pp. 37–38.

was induced by persistence of egalitarian wage and salary policies and also by a related tendency for wages to be determined at the local level. The weakening of the bargaining system was manifested in some uncharacteristically dramatic developments, which included two waves of wildcat strikes and rupture of institutional linkages between the determination of pay in the private and public sectors and between the determination of wages and of salaries, which touched off a leapfrogging process in 1975. These developments will be discussed in the next two sections.

The Wildcat Strikes and the Weakening of the SAF

We have noted that the outbreak of wildcat strikes in 1969–70 is alleged to have helped inhibit policymaking, and another outbreak in 1974 had the same effect. Fear that increased unemployment would add fresh fuel to the fires of rank-and-file discontent militated against the adoption of earlier—and arguably milder—deflationary policies in the first instance and against revaluation of the currency in the second. Yet in Germany also there were two outcroppings of plant-level unrest, which coincided roughly with the Swedish disturbances, and the German authorities were not dissuaded from following either course.

Furthermore, wages were a more important issue than unemployment. Unemployment was relatively high during both strike periods and, except in 1970, exceeded the number of job vacancies.[58] As in other countries, therefore, the wildcat strikes were not a reflex of excess demand in the labor markets. Strikers did respond, however, to the decline in the growth rate of real disposable income and in the share of labor in the national income that occurred in 1969–70 and, later, to the abnormally large rise in profits that followed the moderate settlement in 1974. (The latter is reminiscent of the role played in producing the first German strike wave by the bulge in profits and the restrained wage settlements in Germany in the upswing of 1967–69.)

Three other issues were raised in the course of the wildcat strikes, however, and they appear to have assumed a special importance in connection with Swedish collective bargaining and industrial relations because they were related closely to differentiating characteristics of that system. The first was the discontent of more highly paid groups of

58. See, for example, ibid., April 1970, p. 11.

workers with the solidaristic wage policies as enacted in the central agreements. Wage issues were raised by strikers in small firms and in subbranches in which wages were low in relation to regional averages;[59] most of the strikers in 1969–70, however, were highly paid workers.[60] In these years, according to Edgren, Faxén, and Odhner, most of the strikes in engineering were "by groups which considered themselves unfairly treated by the levelling nature of the agreements."[61] Faxén pointed out that in 1970, 1974, and 1975, more than 70 percent of the wildcat strikes occurred within four months after the conclusion of the national agreement, which he regards as evidence of a reaction against special provisions for the low paid that compressed wage differentials.[62]

The second issue consisted of alleged rank-and-file dissatisfaction with the centralized bargaining organizations, especially the LO, as an outstanding example of remote and authoritarian bureaucracy. This issue was stressed by younger, left-wing observers, who accused the LO of locating decisionmaking far from the grass roots without raising wages enough to restrain profits in the large firms in the private sector. In the nine-week miners' strike at LKAB, the nationalized iron mines in the northern community of Kiruna, the strikers' demands included withdrawal of their employer from the central negotiations. They were represented by an unofficial group of leaders that included radical elements, some of them Communists.

The third issue, also advanced by the left, had to do with an alleged deterioration in working conditions. Associated with increasing industrial concentration, "rationalization," and cost control were, it was argued, increasingly less tolerable levels of physical effort, monotony, and job insecurity imposed on the workers.[63] The predominant importance of wage issues among the reasons advanced for unofficial strikes might be regarded as inconsistent with an explanation that lays considerable stress on the "quality" of working life. It really is not, but it does implicitly belie the assumption of a starkly dichotomous relation between pecuniary and nonpecuniary issues upon which the radical criticism of the centralized union bargainers has in part been based. This is so for

59. Walter Korpi, "Shop-Floor Bargaining and Industrial Democracy: Unofficial Strikes in Sweden" (Stockholm: Institut för Social Forskning, n.d.).

60. Swedish Information Service, "Labor Relations."

61. Edgren, Faxén, and Odhner, Wage Formation, p. 56.

62. Faxén, "Wage Policy," p. 8.

63. See, for example, Casten van Otter, "Sweden: Labor Reformism Reshapes the System," in Solomon Barkin, ed., Worker Militancy and Its Consequences, 1965–75 (New York: Praeger Publishers, 1975), pp. 208–09.

two reasons. In the first place, many of the wage issues concerned piecework problems, and problems concerning the operation of incentive pay systems, such as the determination of standards and effort, are closely related to disputes about the exercise of managerial authority on the shop floor. These disputes, according to a survey in the metals industry, were regarded as constituting another important set of grievances leading to rank-and-file strikes. In the second place, the solidaristic wage policy, an independent cause of concern among better-paid workers, which furthered the concentration of employment in more efficient firms and sectors, "has also [induced] the more profitable industries to step up their cost reduction programs."[64]

Some of these developments had been weakening the central negotiating structure and, in particular, the authority of the employers' federation, the SAF. When, at the turn of the century, the employers originally vested considerable authority over wage bargaining in a central federation, they firmly retained control over personnel management—an important determinant of productivity—at the company and plant levels. They insisted that all collective agreements contain what Americans would call a management rights clause, known originally as Article 23 and later as Clause 32, which guaranteed the employer freedom "to direct and distribute the work of his enterprise, to engage and dismiss workers at his own discretion, and to employ organized or unorganized workers as he sees fit."[65] Collective contracts were made legally enforceable, and the Labor Court, which was established in 1928 to settle disputes arising out of the interpretation of these contracts, upheld Clause 32 as a legal right of management.[66]

After World War II, however, the functional division of labor between the SAF and the individual firm became more and more blurred by the payment of wage drift by the firm, both as a reaction to the solidaristic central settlements and as part and parcel of the incentive systems installed by the larger firms. Whether initiated by management itself or by pressure from the local unions, local wage setting reflected weakness on the part of the SAF—as well as of the LO—for the SAF supposedly had the authority to discipline firms for paying wages higher than rates specified in the national agreement. This weakness became dramatically

64. Swedish Information Service, "Labor Relations."
65. Johnston, *Collective Bargaining,* pp. 78–79, 125, 205–06.
66. Ibid., p. 158.

obvious in the wildcat episode of 1970, for the SAF could not prevent struck firms from settling with the unofficial strike leaders. Volvo, which had invariably been granting "customary drift" to its union in what really amounted to separate settlements, settled in 1970 without even consulting the SAF.[67] Toward the end of the year the employers' federation did fine a shipyard for granting increases beyond what was allowed in the engineering industry agreement, but the firm subsequently went bankrupt and was merged into a shipping company. That was the first time in fifteen years that the SAF had levied a fine; it also proved to be the last time until after the highly restrained settlement of 1978.[68] The availability of SAF strike insurance, moreover, did not provide a sufficient incentive to induce firms—especially large, capital-intensive firms—to take local strikes in order to avoid paying drift; after 1970, the threat of wildcat strikes sufficed to deter resistance.[69]

Finally, the SAF found itself unable to play its trump card—the sympathetic lockout. During the mid 1970s it became apparent that member firms were not disposed to support lockouts within the context of central bargaining. Firms in the sectors in which financial balances and self-financing ratios were being squeezed particularly hard pressed the federation to resist the LO more vigorously,[70] and there was some talk of a lockout led by the firms that were near bankruptcy. But these firms declined the honor, offered on various occasions by the chairman of the SAF, because of their need to maintain cash flow. This reflected the dominance of the liquidity constraint over the incentive to resist, which was imparted by declining sales and profits—and hence by the costs of shutting down a plant. The hook of a J-shaped curve relating union bargaining power to the level of economic activity, on which many British employers were said to have been impaled for some time, became visible in Sweden during a period when declining profitability and liquidity were confronted by the maintenance of employment and labor incomes through extensive subsidy. Because settlements must be uniform under central negotiations, the existence of important pockets of illiquidity tended to make the central settlements conform to the inability

67. Economist Intelligence Unit, *Quarterly Economic Review: Sweden,* no. 1 (1970), pp. 7–8.

68. Faxén, "Wage Policy," p. 7.

69. Ibid.

70. OECD Economic Surveys, *Sweden,* April 1976, pp. 26–29; ibid., April 1977, p. 35.

of the least profitable and liquid sectors to resist, rather than according to their ability to pay, and it made them conform to the ability to pay of the more profitable and liquid sectors rather than to their ability to resist.

Since individual firms were less often capable of resisting demands for local drift while the SAF was less often able to prevent large central settlements, the demands made on self-restraint by the LO increased. But when, in 1976, the employers pressed for a low central settlement, the LO negotiators argued that a low central settlement would make the individual firms less willing and more often unable to resist local demands for correspondingly higher drift—although it might be recalled that, according to equation 3 in the appendix to this chapter, the level of drift did not appear to be systematically related to changes in the employer's ability to pay net of centrally negotiated wage increases. As it happened, the 1977 contract did turn out to be moderate. Indeed, when Volvo subsequently refused to offer any increase in excess of the central frame agreement, the local union sued management in the Labor Court, claiming that this departure from what had been a traditional practice of drifting above the central settlement constituted a breach of contract. Had the Volvo union won its case, the central bargaining framework might have been dealt a mortal blow. The local did not win, but the suit itself revealed that the system was in trouble.

The LO Response: Worker Participation, Job Security, Co-ownership, and "Politicization"

The LO did not respond to growing militancy and autonomy on the shop floor by retreating from the egalitarian wage policy that had helped to increase that militancy. It addressed itself instead to the nonwage issues that surfaced in 1969–70: feelings of resentment over the monotony of work, lack of involvement in decisionmaking, and job insecurity. In Sweden as elsewhere, the wildcat phenomenon concentrated minds wonderfully on participation by workers in company decisionmaking and even ownership. By addressing these problems, however, the LO hoped to save its egalitarian wage policy and to reduce wage inflation in the process. In 1971, the Metal Workers Union, which had been obliged to restrain its members' wages in the more profitable competitive sectors in the interest of solidaristic overall settlements, raised these issues in the hope that devices could be found that might substitute for wage increases and at the same time siphon off the alleged excess profits that they had been obliged to tolerate. Less wage restraint would then be required on the union side if worker participation could somehow succeed where an active labor market had failed—to stiffen the resistance of employers without reducing investment and employment.

Some large-scale employers had also been interested since the mid 1960s in forms of worker participation, but in the interest of increasing productivity as well as worker satisfaction. They emphasized experimentation with "job enrichment," including rotation and redesign of jobs, with the object of enhancing the worker's autonomy and, they hoped, his interest in his work. The interest of management was well accommodated in the Agreement on Rationalization, which the SAF and the LO concluded in 1972 and which widened the scope of rationalization "so as to cater not only [to] the traditional demand to develop the technical and economic determinants of production, but also and in equal measure [to] the demands concerned with a good working environment and improved job satisfaction."[71]

But the unions' objectives obviously encompassed some much more ambitious social engineering. In 1971 both the LO Congress and the TCO, a white-collar federation, called for a strengthening of the consultative workers councils, which had been established by the SAF-LO Agreement of 1946, and also for "joint determination," which meant, among other things, representation of employees on company boards. The SAF declined to enter into an agreement that would bind stockholders' meetings. Therefore, the LO resorted to the legislative route, as the Germans had done. In 1972 an act was passed that entitled employees in joint stock companies having at least 100 employees to appoint two board members. The object was to increase the influence and the responsibility of employees with respect to decisionmaking, but in a survey made in 1975 it was found that until then board membership was not regarded as enhancing the influence of employees very much, that most employees seemed to have little interest in the work of their representatives on the boards, and that, in any event, the boards had relatively little decisionmaking power.[72]

The joint-determination program adopted by the LO in 1971 had also called for the elimination of Clause 32, the management-rights clause, which had so long symbolized the absence of an effective union presence

71. SAF-LO Agreement on Rationalization (Stockholm, 1972), p. 6.

72. National Swedish Industrial Board, *Board Representation of Employees in Sweden: A Summary from a Survey* (Stockholm: NSIB, 1976), pp. 27, 30, 33.

on the shop floor. But the SAF was unwilling to go much beyond issuing a call for "good collaboration" with "the directly affected employees, the union representatives and the joint bodies" (the works councils). So the LO once again turned to a Social Democratic government for legislation. In 1976, the Riksdag unanimously passed the Law on Codetermination in Working Life, which nullified Clause 32 and instead made it mandatory for management to negotiate on any and all aspects of the employment relationship, including the direction of the work force and the allocation of work, as well as on matters outside this relationship, notably investment decisions. Under this law unions are free to strike in pursuit of such demands, even while central collective agreements are in force. Not only must an employer negotiate over these issues, upon request, before making a desired change; in matters of particular importance—especially in which layoffs are threatened—he must take the initiative and notify the union before proceeding. And he must furnish the union with all information relevant to negotiations, although union negotiators are bound to keep secret certain information of vital importance to the enterprise. Finally, in questions of contract interpretation, the onus is now on the employer to initiate judicial proceedings (before the Labor Court) within ten days; otherwise the union's view will prevail. Thus, having eliminated a wide area in which the union had had no right of intervention, the Swedes have moved beyond the American rule of "management moves and the union grieves" to a condition characterized by prior restraint on employer movement. And they moved beyond the Germans, who, while legislating "codetermination" rights for local works councils, withheld from the councils the right to strike.

Indeed, prior restraint on management had been legislated in two substantive areas before the passage of the 1976 Law on Codetermination. In 1973 an amendment to the occupational safety and health legislation of 1949 empowered union safety stewards in plants to stop any work that they regarded as dangerous until the issue had been resolved by a government inspection.[73] And in 1974, the Security of Employment Act and the Promotion of Employment Act were passed, requiring advance notice of mass layoffs and individual dismissals.

Management was resentful of what it regarded as "the politicization

73. Steven Kelman, "Occupational Safety and Health in Sweden: The Politics of Cooperation," Swedish Information Service, *Working Life in Sweden*, no. 2 (December 1977); and Andrew Martin, "From Joint Consultation to Joint Decision-Making: The Redistribution of Workplace Power in Sweden," Swedish Institute, *Current Sweden*, June 1976.

of the labor market," but while the legislated restrictions required greater managerial concern with plant-level industrial relations, Swedish firms had already been moving in that direction after 1970. While the legislation offers clear disincentives for firms to hire additional workers, moreover, especially for the short or uncertain term, it may not have altered practice very much. Ever since 1938, when the Basic Agreement was concluded between the LO and the SAF, management has been obliged to give up to four months' notice in contemplation of dismissal of more than a hundred wage earners; under the new laws maximum prior notification has been extended to six months. Dismissal compensation has been provided for under the national collective agreement since 1964, and these agreements are legally enforceable. As a result of informal social and union pressures, according to Delamotte, "collective dismissals are rare in going concerns, and are mainly caused by a firm's closing down or becoming unprofitable."[74]

But if, in fact, the managers could learn to live with codetermination, they nevertheless feared that a profit-sharing plan put forward by the LO in 1976 would be the death of private enterprise in Sweden. This plan embodied an annual transfer of 20 percent of company profits, after depreciation but before taxes, through the issuance of new shares of stock and their transfer into union-controlled employee funds, which are supposed to remain in the company as working capital for a minimum of ten years. It was devised by the LO economist Rudolf Meidner, who adapted it from an early German proposal, and was addressed directly to the metalworkers' drift-versus-profits dilemma. It was supposed to maintain the self-financing capability of firms in the competitive sector and thus stimulate investment, while diverting incremental assets and profits from the private owners. Unions in less profitable industries and firms, however, complained that their 20 percent slices would come out of smaller pies—in some instances, no pie at all—and they are the natural supporters of wage solidarity. It is interesting that a group of Swedish industrialists, formed in 1974, came up with a plan that addressed this problem by basing employee funds on payrolls, rather than company profits, and by building funds on an industrywide—even on an economywide—basis as well as on a company-level basis.

The LO later came out with a new version of the Meidner plan, which, like the businessmen's proposal, provided for three levels of funds, including a central "equalization" fund. The LO plans differed from the

74. Yves Delamotte, *The Social Partners Face the Problems of Productivity and Employment* (Paris: OECD, 1971), p. 65.

industry plan, however, in failing to vest ownership or the right to dispose of the stock or the right to receive dividends in the individual employee. Thus it was criticized as essentially a way of increasing the power of the unions over the companies and, incidentally, over the rank and file at the plant level. (Certainly it was the object of the unions to prevent the highly paid rank and file from securing drift, although local unions would be given part of the voting rights in the funds.)

The revised profit-sharing plan of the LO became an issue in the Swedish election of 1976, which was lost by the Social Democratic party. The Center-Conservative-Liberal coalition, which succeeded the Social Democrats, announced in favor of greater decentralization of Swedish institutions. They submitted a plan in March 1978 that called for investment funds to be run by wage earners collectively but to be financed by private savings subsidized by tax reductions. The LO and the Social Democratic party came out with still another plan, which moved them closer in some respects to the position of the conservatives and the employers. It stressed the need for more investment; it restricted coverage of the proposed appropriation of profits to larger firms; and it provided for two payroll taxes—one, of 1 percent, on the uncovered private firms, to build up a "codetermination fund" to finance union activities in furtherance of codetermination, and another, of 3 percent, on all firms, to provide resources for research and development in the competitive sector. Resources for the development fund were, according to Meidner, to be "made available by a reduction in the future wage increases."[75] This would appear to offer acceptance by the LO of an incomes policy in exchange for extension of codetermination and capital sharing. At the same time it would offer institutional protection to the LO, to the central frame agreement, and to wage solidarity by reducing the ability of individual employers to pay drift.

Weak Links: White-Collar Employees in the Public and Private Sectors

At the beginning of the 1970s the LO-SAF central frame mechanism and the egalitarian policies of the LO were challenged from the outside as well as from within. The militancy of highly paid blue-collar unionists

75. Rudolf Meidner, "Employee Investment Funds and Capital Formation: A Topical Issue in Swedish Politics," *Working Life in Sweden*, no. 6 (June 1978), p. 7.

in the LO was matched, if not exceeded, by the militancy of more highly paid members of the salariat. But while the former have sometimes been in short supply, growing demand for white-collar labor in relation to the demand for blue-collar labor, attributable primarily to the growth of the services and government sectors, has been more than matched by a long-continuing increase in relative supply, with the expansion of higher education; shortages of salaried workers have been much less acute than shortages of manual workers, especially of skilled workers. And associated with this long-term phenomenon has been the lack of opportunity to secure pay increases in the form of drift, mainly because of a much lower incidence of incentive pay systems among salaried groups. During the twelve-year span 1963–64 to 1974–75, average annual wage drift, 4.78 percent, was three times as large as salary drift, which averaged 1.58 percent. These market influences have been associated with a decline in the relative pay of salaried workers. Between 1956 and 1976, the ratio of salaries to wages, before taxes, in industry declined from nearly 2.5 to 2, and the average annual rates of increases in salaries averaged 1 percentage point less than the rates of increase in wages (see table 6-1).

This lagging of salaries behind wages occurred through the institutional "linking" of wage and salary increases for all occupational groups to the wages of male adult workers.[76] The LO-SAF agreement was to set the pattern for salary increases in both the private and public sectors. The government as an employer is represented, not by the SAF, but by the Statensavtalswerk (SAV), the National Collective Bargaining Office, and the national firms are represented by a Bargaining Organization of Swedish State-Owned Enterprises (SFO), in separate negotiations. But while the relatively great increase in the salaried labor force might have facilitated the steady process of institutionalized compression of the salary-wage ratio, the latter could also have generated a steady buildup of resentment not unlike that experienced within the ranks of the more highly paid blue-collar workers, who were quite often in short supply. The increase in the size of the white-collar force, moreover, made possible an extremely rapid growth of organizational strength, both absolutely and in relation to the size of the LO. The TCO, which was formed in 1944 as an amalgamation of federations in the private and public sectors, had grown from fewer than 200,000 members to more than 800,000 by 1973. The Sveriges Akademikers Centralorganisation

76. Edgren, Faxén, and Odhner, *Wage Formation*, p. 32.

338   SWEDEN

Table 6-1. *Differences between Percentage Increases in White-
Collar Salaries and Blue-Collar Wages, Sweden, 1956–76*

Year	Difference	Year	Difference
1956	-1.68	1967	-1.09
1957	-0.10	1968	-0.71
1958	-1.00	1969	-3.68
1959	-0.59	1970	-2.64
1960	-0.25	1971	-1.03
1961	3.13	1972	-2.49
1962	-1.23	1973	0.53
1963	-1.02	1974	0.82
1964	-1.96	1975	1.87
1965	-2.72	1976	-5.36
1966	0.59		

Sources: Average monthly salaries of employees in manufacturing, Central Statistical Office, *Löner*, 1967:1; hourly wages of adult workers in industry, Svenska Arbetsgivareföreningen, *Statistiska Byrå, 1977* (Stockholm: SAF, 1977).

(SACO), the Swedish Confederation of Professional Associations, established in 1942 as an association for graduate professionals, had reached 120,000 members fifteen years later. The growth of both these white-collar organizations can be regarded in part as a reaction to blue-collar unionism and the egalitarian policies of the LO, in conjunction with the redistributional effects of Sweden's relatively high rate of inflation on its steeply progressive income tax structure. Thus, although the relative growth in numbers of salaried workers might have facilitated a process of relative decline in their pay, the latter in turn furnished an ever stronger incentive to have itself arrested or reversed, while their growth in numbers presented the salary earners with a potentially powerful institutional instrument for doing so. The institutional linkage could be weakened as the blue-collar dog found it increasingly difficult to wag its lengthening white-collar tail.

The white-collar idea of linkage has implied, if not widening of salary-wage differentials, at least maintenance of them. In place of the male industrial wage criterion for linkage devised by the LO, the TCO has urged its affiliates to demand salary increases equal in percentage to the economywide growth in productivity; this would maintain the share of salaries, before taxes, in the national income. At the same time, however, the TCO has shared the concern of the LO over low-income groups and has coordinated its bargaining for poorly paid civil servants with the

LO.[77] The TCO has been able to ride both horses, because—except in 1956 when the SAF invited both the TCO and the LO to participate in parallel central negotiations—salary increases have been negotiated by the affiliated national associations in the TCO rather than by the central federation itself. These affiliates had objected to the uniformity imposed by the 1956 settlement. But one of them, Svenska Industritjansteman-naförbundet (SIF), the Clerical and Technical Employees in Private Industry, with 200,000 members, broke away from its linkage with the LO, and in 1969, together with two other affiliated unions, negotiated a five-year agreement with the SAF. It was based on trends in productivity in the industrial and—contrary to sound Aukrust doctrine—the building sectors.[78] This settlement, moreover, was reached before the LO-SAF central frame agreement, which was supposed to set the pattern. The salaried unions did agree, however, to increases lower by 1 percent a year than increases in blue-collar earnings.

In contrast, the SACO, which represents upper ranges of the salariat, principally in the public sector, was more dynamic and less inhibited in its opposition to the LO. It has objected to the leveling effect on disposable incomes exerted by inflation in conjunction with the progressive income tax structure, and it has couched its demands in terms of "real wages after taxes."[79] And it was involved in two significant strike episodes—the first in 1966, in defense of an agreement including greater increases than those negotiated earlier by the LO and the SAF, and the second in 1971. On both occasions, however, the Social Democratic government offered effective resistance, responding, as the SAF had sometimes done in the private sector, to small strikes with large-scale lockouts and, in 1971, by having the Riksdag pass a law ordering the strikers back to work—just six years after it had legislated the right of government workers to strike. In both instances the government acted in support of demands by the LO for repudiation of the SACO's claims— or, as in 1966, actual agreements; in 1971 the LO refused to settle with the SAF until after a settlement had been reached with the public sector. In a real sense the government acted as the political arm of the labor movement in enforcing its function as pattern setter. The majority of

77. Ibid., pp. 53–54.
78. Ibid., pp. 38–40, 34, 56.
79. It has also justified differentials in current income on the grounds that they are needed to achieve parity in "life income," since university graduates invest heavily in human capital before entering the labor market, which they do at a relatively late age.

public opinion, however, was also opposed to these strikes by relatively well paid public officials, notably educators.

Nevertheless, while both market and institutional pressures made for a compression of salary-wage differentials, the latter persistently provoked countervailing moves by salary earners.

The problem promised to intensify when the salariat in the private sector began to stir, and their new organization, the Privattjänstemannakartellen (PTK), the Private Sector White Collar Workers' Syndicate, has proved more effective than the SACO. The PTK was formed in 1973 as a bargaining alliance between the Graduate Engineers, a SACO affiliate, and two TCO affiliates, Sveriges Arbetsledareförbundet (SALF), the Foremen's Association, and the SIF. The formation of the PTK reflected dissatisfaction with the TCO and the 1969 agreement, which had provided for annual increases lower than the wage increases negotiated by the LO. In 1975 the SIF demanded that the salaried employees receive "100 percent drift compensation"—that is, the same compensatory payments that the central frame agreements have provided automatically where drift is low and which frequently involve low-wage groups. The SALF broke with the SIF on this demand at the time, on the grounds that 100 percent compensation would restore differentials to an extent not warranted by the relative increase in the supply of more highly educated workers and also that it would not furnish an effective incentive for unemployed white-collar workers to enter skilled blue-collar trades where shortages existed. Nevertheless, the PTK called a strike in 1975 (over a pension issue) and was able to power its way into the high-level bargaining arena. (It represents more than half a million salaried employees.) In the agreements negotiated that year, wage earners in the LO received an average increase that was 1 percentage point higher than the increase received by salaried employees in the private sector.[80] But the difficulty in resolving the wage-salary tussle was reflected in the so-called control station proviso, which was inserted in all agreements and which allowed the employee side to reopen if other employee groups negotiated more favorable conditions after their own had been concluded. The failure of the LO and the PTK to come to terms over wage-salary differentials caused a leapfrogging of demands, which helped make it impossible to restrain the critical 1975 central frame agreement.

In contrast with the SACO, however, the PTK seemed to accept,

80. OECD Economic Surveys, *Sweden*, April 1976, p. 41.

first, that it should not outrage public opinion by generating national crises; second, that it should not oppose equalization of income in principle;[81] and finally, that its principal negotiating target had to be the LO rather than the employers. In negotiations that preceded the one-year 1977 agreement, the PTK renewed the demand for 100 percent drift compensation, turned down a mediators' proposal for a settlement 0.5 percent higher than the proposed LO settlement (which the LO had accepted), declared a ban on overtime, and finally called for selective strikes. The PTK took care, however, to shut down activities that did not present the public with an emergency. And after the SAF had joined the LO in opposing 100 percent drift compensation, on the grounds that it would cause a resumption of leapfrogging and another highly inflationary set of increases, the two employee federations agreed on an "80 percent rule." But the astute and dynamic chairman of the PTK managed to broaden the base to which the 80 percent multiplier was to be applied, so that it included not only the estimated wage drift in the LO sectors but also the wage drift "guarantee" paid out centrally to industries in which drift was less than 80 percent of the all-industry average. Unions in the public sector received the same compensation as the PTK. Thus the agreements provided for greater increases in salaries (3.8 percent) than in wage rates (3.1 percent).[82] Nevertheless, the absence of leapfrogging helped to moderate the 1977 agreements.

The agreements for 1978–79 appeared to reestablish egalitarianism. The 80 percent rule of drift compensation won renewed acceptance, but this time the contractual wage-rate increases, 1.9 percent in 1978 and 3.1 percent in 1979, were slightly greater than the salary increases, 1.6 percent and 2.6 percent, respectively.[83] The difference was justified with reference to the fact that the PTK sector does not contain as many low-

81. The leadership of the PTK has included Social Democrats, in contrast to the general political identification of the SACO with non-Socialist parties. The chairman of the PTK, however, was not a true believer in distributional egalitarianism.

82. When the carryover effects of the 1975–76 agreement are added, the difference between the two rates of total contractual increase becomes even greater—7 percent for salaries as against 3.4 percent for wages. OECD Economic Surveys, *Sweden*, April 1978, pp. 15–16, n. 22.

83. Ibid., p. 48. Provision was also made for reopening the agreements in both 1978 and 1979 in the event that consumer prices should exceed specified threshold increases. In 1978, actual price increases (5.2 percent) did not reach the threshold (7.4 percent). (See ibid., April 1979, p. 13.) The January–October 1979 threshold (5 percent), however, was exceeded, as the result of oil price increases, and resulted in reopening and ultimately exceeding an arbitration award of wage increases of 1.5 percent, effective in November of that year. (Ibid., April 1980, p. 16, n. 25.)

income employees as the LO sector. But the centrally negotiated
compromise did not win acceptance at the grass roots. PTK locals
secured local supplements that were greater than those which the LO
locals were allowed under the central frame agreement, and this provoked wildcat strikes in protest by LO groups.[84]

Further disorganization set in in April 1980, when the white-collar
unions in the public sector, joined by the LO blue-collar unions in that
sector, staged a series of selective strikes that closed airports, the
customs service, the Stockholm subway, television and radio broad-
casting, and all but emergency hospital services.[85] Their purpose was to
secure under the new contracts then being negotiated pay increases that
would be equal to the forthcoming wage increases in manufacturing,
including drift. At the same time, a joint study by the LO, the PTK, and
the SAF revealed that, because of an upward drift in salary classifications, the average salary of PTK members had risen nearly as rapidly as
the average wage of LO members throughout the decade. Hence the
white-collar employees were receiving the equivalent of salary drift in
addition to the partial compensation for wage drift, which by itself was
intended to lag salary increases behind wage increases 1 percent a year.[86]
These two developments contributed heavily to the collapse of the next
round of negotiations and the ensuing general strike and lockout.

The Events of May 1980

On May 1, 1980, 110,000 workers in LO unions went out on strike,
and another 600,000 were locked out by 20,000 SAF-affiliated firms. The
massive stoppage lasted ten days and was widely regarded as the
spectacular collapse of a unique system of highly centralized but voluntary pay determination, which had been attended by more than four
decades of exemplary industrial peace, social reform, and, at least until
recent years, national economic health. The "spirit of Saltsjöbaden"—

84. Sven-Ivan Sundquist, "LO Wins the Zero-Sum Game," *Dagens Nyheter,* May
11, 1980; English translation by the SAF, June 1980.
85. *Wall Street Journal,* April 28, 1980.
86. Sundquist, "LO Wins the Zero-Sum Game." The average annual wage increase
during the period 1970–79 was 10.4 percent and the average salary increase was 9.4
percent after standardization for the distribution of salary earners by grade level. The
effect of an upward drift in salary classifications, however, was to raise the nonstan-
dardized salary increase to 10.2 percent.

a resort town that was the birthplace of the original Basic Agreement of 1938 and the site of subsequent negotiations between the LO and the SAF—was epitomized by an occasion in the early postwar period on which two men, the chairman of the LO and the chairman of the SAF, rowed out to the middle of the lake and rowed back with a new contract. But it would be a misleading oversimplification to depict the breakdown of central negotiations in 1980 as simply the failure of the current representatives of the LO and the SAF to resolve their differences—as the collapse of bipartisan negotiations under straitened economic circumstances. Certainly such differences existed: a demand of the LO for an 11.3 percent wage increase had been countered by an SAF offer of only 2.3 percent when the stoppages were called. From the viewpoint of the SAF and the government, the economic distance between the negotiating parties was not as wide as it seemed, since the employers' offer was supplemented by a proposed price freeze and a tax cut—which will be discussed later. Nevertheless, it symbolized a difference in objectives. The union's battle cry was "real wage protection" for its industrial members after the last hike in oil prices; real earnings in manufacturing had declined 4 percent in 1977 and 3 percent in 1978 and had barely held their own in 1979.[87] The employers wanted to improve profit margins together with productivity, which had indeed risen sharply in 1979, but profits were still lower than the recession levels recorded in 1967 and 1971, and the nonfinancial corporate sector as a whole was still in the red at the end of 1979.[88] They also wanted to increase their international competitiveness; although unit labor costs in manufacturing had actually been decreasing, absolutely and in relation to the OECD area, export volume had risen less than anticipated in 1979, and the current external balance had fallen sharply as a result of the increase in oil prices.[89] The employers' view was that increases in energy prices should not be passed on in increased wages. An earlier attempt to defend this position had prompted the LO to call a ban on overtime in October 1979, after the oil price increase had raised the consumer price index by more than the threshold increase in the consumer price index specified in the 1978–79 agreement and had triggered a reopening. The mediators obtained a compromise by which the unions were awarded half the oil price increase.

87. OECD Economic Surveys, *Sweden,* April 1980, table 4, p. 15.
88. Ibid., pp. 17, 18.
89. Ibid., pp. 19–23.

Nevertheless, the LO agreed on the need to maintain profitability, if not to increase it,[90] and to increase international competitiveness—especially in view of their opposition to the currency devaluations that the new "bourgeois" government, a coalition of nonsocialist parties, had effected in 1977. Since complete restoration of real wages could not be obtained from the employers, therefore, it had to be secured at the expense of some group or groups outside the "central frame" of collective bargaining. The choice, as far as the LO was concerned, could be determined by an application of the social welfare and egalitarian ethic that the LO shared with its political allies in the Socialdemokratiska Arbetarepartiet (SAP), the Social Democratic party. It precluded focusing on the elderly and disabled in the inactive population—especially since transfer payments and the contributions of employers had increased much less rapidly in 1979 than in previous years.[91] It indicated a renewal of the tussle with the salary earners and with both the salary earners and the largely driftless wage earners in the public sector. To begin with, the LO demanded protection for or restoration of real wages after taxes. (This was an echo of the original demand of the SACO early in the decade; by now even many blue-collar workers faced a marginal tax rate in excess of 50 percent.) In addition, it originally demanded that the PTK, in its separate negotiations with the SAF, receive 4 percentage points less than the approximately 11 percent demanded by the LO.[92]

In subsequent negotiations the PTK rejected this demand and reinstated the rule for 80 percent drift compensation. But the LO succeeded in modifying this rule in two respects. First, the multiplicand of PTK's 80 percent was restricted to the LO's wage drift; it no longer included the wage-drift guarantee. Second, the LO received separate compensation for "individual increments for qualifications, etc." in lieu of in-grade salary increments for advancement in professional qualifications and age. (Tit for tat: the salaried earners got payment in lieu of the wage earners' drift; the wage earners would get payment in lieu of the salaried earners' individual career increments.) The combined result of the

90. Sven-Ivan Sundquist, "Zero Sum Game Can Begin," *Dagens Nyheter,* May 4, 1980.

91. OECD Economic Surveys, *Sweden,* April 1980, pp. 15–18. This is reflected in the fact that, whereas total hourly labor costs in manufacturing had risen more than half again as rapidly as earnings in 1977 and 1978—11 percent versus 7 percent—the two rose at virtually the same rate in 1979—7.8 percent versus 7.4 percent.

92. Sundquist, "Zero-Sum Game Can Begin."

subtraction from salaries and the addition to wages was a 10 percent average increase in LO wages and an 8 percent increase in PTK salaries. In the public sector, where separate negotiations covered equal numbers of wage and salary earners, the average pay increase came to 8.8 percent.[93] The LO thus won only half the 4 percent premium over the PTK settlement that it had originally demanded. On the basis of the estimated results of a freeze on prices on the one hand, however, and an announced schedule of progressive tax reductions on the other, the LO's settlement was expected to maintain average levels of disposable real wages.[94] Finally, the LO-SAF agreement contained a clause similar to the earlier "control station proviso," which was intended to guarantee that the SAF's agreement with the PTK would contain the same rules for wage drift compensation as the public-sector agreement of the LO. Ultimately, the PTK concluded an agreement with the SAF that did cost less in percentage terms than the LO agreements, but the establishment of a new formula for drift compensation was deferred until the next bargaining round at the beginning of 1981.

The outcome was interpreted as a victory for the LO in what was called Sweden's zero-sum game; but why did the LO have to go out on strike? The SAF had stiffened its spine by changing its leaders in response to the dissatisfaction of its smaller affiliated firms with the 1975 agreement; hence its very low "final offer" to the LO and, subsequently, its rejection of the final mediation proposal and its extensive and successful recourse to lockouts by some 20,000 individual firms. On the other hand, it was known that a stoppage would be without cost to the striking and locked-out LO members, whose strike benefits averaged half their normal income and whose reduced tax burden, thanks to the highly progressive income tax structure, could take care of the other half. But the SAF was not the only target of the LO; the SAF was cast partially in the role of a "secondary," or neutral, employer who was supposed to transmit pressure to the "primary" union target. The latter consisted of the salaried employees, who, like the wage earners, were represented in separate negotiations in the private and public sectors. The SAF may have had no serious quarrel with the LO's demand for a redistribution

93. Sundquist, "LO Wins the Zero-Sum Game."
94. Ibid. Since the pay increase was negotiated in absolute terms across the board, the real incomes of low-wage groups would rise slightly, while real incomes of wage earners above the average would decline. Thus the LO continued to implement its internal policy of wage compression.

of labor income away from salary earners, who were in abundant supply. But its member firms might feel strongly about the morale and well-being of their own salaried employees, and, while the confederation had regained sufficient authority and influence to initiate lockouts, it had been unable to prevent its affiliates from making the local side deals with units of the PTK in 1979 that helped to erode the 80 percent rule. Hence the efficiency of the SAF as a conductor of LO pressure on salaries in the private sector was low.

Similarly, the LO lacked authority over its own affiliates in the public sector, the Statsanställdas Förbundet (SF), the State Employees, with 190,000 members, and the Svenska Kommunalarbetareförbundet (SKAF), the Municipal Workers, with 490,000 members. In the public sector, the authority of the LO was not buttressed by support from the employer side, as it was in the private sector. During the 1960s, employer solidarity helped to hold the restive metalworkers within the central frame agreements when there was considerable feeling in that union that solidaristic bargaining was preventing it from more fully exploiting its own sector's current ability to pay. During the 1970s, the SAF refused to bargain separately with a Communist-led breakaway union of dockworkers, and it withstood a strike by this strategically situated group in June 1980, after the general lockout had ended.[95] But in the public sector, bargaining on the employer side has been conducted by three agencies representing respectively the central government (the SAV), the counties, and the municipalities. These representatives of public employers have not had the same immediate interest as the SAF in constraining settlements within limits set by international competitiveness and profitability in the exposed private sector or, for that matter, in minimizing costs in their own sector. On the other hand, they do have a strong immediate interest in avoiding the interruption of essential public services. Hence they had no great incentive to support the LO in its demand for a restrained and egalitarian wage policy in the high-wage public sector, where equal absolute general increments, combined with reduced drift compensation, might entail a relatively low degree of reduction in real pay.

95. But it should be noted that, while the resistance of employers strengthened the LO transport workers in their jurisdictional struggle with the breakaway harbor workers, the LO union did threaten to call out its truck drivers if the employers attempted to negotiate separately with the harbor workers (see *Dagens Nyheter*, May 25, 1980). The LO occasionally struck a reciprocal blow for the jurisdictional integrity of the SAF, moreover, as when the LO pressured a multinational subsidiary into joining the SAF and accepting representation by it in central bargaining.

Rejecting their parent federation's initial demand that drift compensation be confined to the manufacturing (SAF) sector, the two LO unions in the public sector entered into a coalition with the two salaried TCO affiliates in the public sector—the Statstjänstemannaförbundet (TCO-S), the Sector for State Salaried Employees, and the Kommunaltjänstemannakartellen (KTK), the Federation of Local Government Salaried Employees—and conducted the selective strikes in April that preceded the LO-SAF stoppages. Total membership represented by this "Gang of Four" came to about 1,210,000. Added to the 150,000 in the SACO-SR (the professionals' organization in the public sector), the organized wage-earning and salaried workers in the public sector almost equaled the number of LO wage earners in the private sector, about 1.4 million. This long sheltered-sector tail ultimately wagged the LO dog: this was the SAF interpretation of the final settlement of the general strike and lockout. After the LO had rejected a "final bid" which was submitted jointly by the mediators in the private and public sectors and had gone out on strike, the mediators returned with a new and improved final bid, which added 2.5 percent to their earlier proposal. The SAF, which had approved the first offer as consistent with the ostensibly agreed-upon objectives of both improved international competitiveness and real wage protection for the majority of LO wage earners, accepted this one only under protest. "LO never wanted this," the chairman of the SAF told the press; "LO was trapped by the public sector."

Thus it appeared that the LO could do little to maintain the real disposable income of its average wage earner through central bargaining with the SAF in the golden spirit of Saltsjöbaden. The increased militancy of the SAF precluded bilateral negotiation of a wage increase at the expense of profits, which the leaders of the LO were disinclined to do anyway. And the continued militancy of the PTK, fortified by growing militancy of both salary and wage earners' organizations in the enlarged public sector, precluded bilateral negotiation of a wage increase at the expense of salaries. Only pressure from the government might hold salaries or profits back. Government pressure might be induced through the exercise of political influence, or it might be induced through the exercise of brinksmanship at the bargaining table. Before 1976, when the Social Democrats (SAP) were in office, political influence would have been a more realistic possibility for the LO, whose influence over the SAP has been great—as revealed, for example, in the Meidner plan episode—although subject to limits imposed by the requirements of macroeconomic policy and international competitiveness, as revealed by the government's deflationist reaction in 1970–71. But with the SAP no longer in control of the government, the LO responded to increased resistance from the SAF at the bargaining table by pushing its bargaining partner to—and ultimately beyond—the point of impasse in order to confront the government with a public emergency and conscript the bourgeois neutrals on its side. The SAF responded to such induced, publicly applied government pressure by acceding to a mediation proposal that it had at first rejected. But the PTK was a more important object of the exercise in brinksmanship than the SAF, and whether the LO could trap the PTK between the SAF and a nonsocialist government remained undecided after the 1980 stoppage. The private-sector jurisdiction of the PTK made it less vulnerable than the SACO to public pressure not to strike. What seems to have been demonstrated is that once wage bargaining becomes a three-player game, the government is drawn in to make a fourth—especially when the attainment of bargaining objectives is predicated on the reduction of relative and real incomes of groups that are not represented in wage bargaining in the private sector.

Although the bargaining behavior of the LO together with the SAF may have carried the economy to the brink, government intervention was blamed by some for shoving it over. The government was accused of dictating the terms of the mediators' first final offer, which was congenial to the SAF but was rejected by the LO. Since the ensuing stoppage ended with acceptance by both sides—although by the SAF only under duress—it was argued that the great shutdown could have been avoided if the mediators had not originally been constrained by the government in their pursuit of a peaceful settlement. The government felt itself constrained downward by considerations of economic policy, whereas the LO was to some extent constrained upward by relative and real pay pressures emanating from its already restive public-sector membership. The episode could be interpreted as a dramatic example of a conflict between industrial relations policy and incomes policy. And it will be recalled that ever since 1950 the Swedish system of collective bargaining had been regarded as a voluntary alternative to incomes policy—or at least it was regarded as an alternative to government intervention in the determination of wages: critics of the 1980 mediation presumably had not been critical of the handling of the SACO episode by the labor government at the beginning of the decade, nor presumably did they object to the prospective application of government pressure by the PTK.

Incomes Policy and the 1980 Shutdowns

Incomes policy implemented through intervention, however, can be distinguished from incomes policy based on compensation for wage restraint, and a case for union acceptance of the latter won increasing support in the 1970s. As early as the 1950s, Erik Lundberg showed that disinflationary effects of a heavily progressive income tax system, through fiscal drag, can be outweighed by its inflationary effects as nominal incomes rise in a cyclical upswing.[96] It became ever more difficult for negotiated increases in money wages to yield increases in real disposable income for the average LO member, as high rates of inflation forced more and more workers into higher marginal tax brackets and, recently, as sharp reductions in the growth of productivity magnified the price-raising effects of wage increases. Even before the OPEC price increases, Lundberg, assuming a constant markup on unit labor costs in the sheltered sector and a 4 percent annual rate of growth in productivity, showed that a money wage increase of 10 percent could not yield a real wage increase of 3 percent; later, Calmfors produced another example, assuming a 3 percent increase in productivity in the sheltered sector, which yielded an absolute reduction of 1.6 percent in real disposable wages.[97]

Lundberg resigned himself to the fact that "union leaders will not be reasonable and accept the theoretical conclusion that by demanding less in nominal terms . . . they would make a better bargain in real terms."[98] But he held out hope for "a policy of concerted moderation in wage demands" if it were to be associated with a policy of currency appreciation that would hold down profit margins. Other possible avenues of compensation to the unions lay in tax reductions and also in price controls and subsidies. In 1970–71, the government chose the latter course. It accompanied a deflationary policy—characterized by increases in the contributions of employers to social insurance, a value-added tax (VAT), and a wage-bill tax—with the imposition of a general price freeze. The freeze was imposed (for the first time since 1956, when

96. Erik Lundberg, *Business Cycles and Economic Policy,* tr. by J. Potter (Cambridge: Harvard University Press, 1957).

97. Erik Lundberg, "Incomes Policy Issues in Sweden," in Walter Galenson, ed., *Incomes Policy: What Can We Learn from Europe?* (Ithaca, N.Y.: Cornell University Press, 1973), pp. 54–55; Calmfors, "Inflation in Sweden," pp. 531–34.

98. Lundberg, "Incomes Policy Issues," p. 55.

the last of the wartime controls had been dismantled) in order to halt a developing increase in profit margins in services and the distributive trades and thereby to exert a moderating influence on the coming round of wage negotiations.[99] It was an extraordinary response to an extraordinary event—the wildcat strikes of 1969–70—and also an attempt to minimize the effects of developments in the sheltered sector on the movement of the general level of money wages.

The next attempt to influence wage negotiations came in 1973, in anticipation of the expiration of the current front-loaded, three-year agreement and in conjunction this time with a mildly expansionary policy. Accordingly, the basic pension charge on wage earners was eliminated, while the employers' contribution to social security was raised once again. In addition, a price freeze on food staples that had been introduced in December 1972 was extended, together with a subsidy to farmers, and the VAT was subsequently reduced. The ensuing settlement for 1974 was moderate, thanks in part to the tax measures that increased real disposable wage incomes by 6 percent while raising employers' labor costs by 3.3 percent. But while it was believed that the tax reductions did help to moderate the wage settlement, it was stressed that no deal had been struck, and indeed the government announced its measures before negotiations began.[100] The unconditional nature of the government's incentive became painfully apparent after the 1975 negotiations. As noted earlier, two reductions of marginal tax rates in the middle brackets had been announced—one went into effect in 1975 and the other was scheduled for 1976—in addition to an increase in social security benefits. The income tax reductions were necessary to offset fiscal drag and thus helped to maintain employment. But they failed as adequate wage incentives, although it could be argued that the settlement would have been even greater than it was in the absence of these and other measures.[101] On the other hand, the LO's subsequent quasi offer of wage restraint in exchange for the establishment of an asset-sharing fund, made during its party's losing election campaign in 1976, could be regarded as an acceptance in principle, however faint, of incomes policy.

99. OECD Economic Surveys, *Sweden*, April 1971, pp. 31–32.

100. Ibid., July 1974, p. 21 and n. 3; p. 23 and n. 2; p. 43.

101. The government also established two so-called investment funds in 1974, which reduced stated net profits by requiring firms to pay a total of 35 percent of their net profits into blocked special deposit accounts. See OECD Economic Surveys, *Sweden*, June 1975, pp. 54–55; see also pp. 37–38.

The conservative coalition, which succeeded the SAP in government following the 1976 election, desired incomes policy at least as ardently as its predecessor had. Its objective was to improve international competitiveness and reduce an extremely high deficit on current account while maintaining employment at traditionally high levels. It pursued the former objective by depreciating the krona by 17 percent during the course of 1977, but its commitment to high-level employment required the adoption of expansionist rather than restrictive demand management in view of the decline in industrial output in 1977–78. Since fiscal expansion financed substantial hoarding of labor, an expansion of export demand induced by the depreciations could generate a sharp cyclical upswing in productivity, which in fact did occur, and could thus contribute to a corresponding relative reduction in unit costs. The combination of depreciation and increased central government deficits, however, militated against restraint in money wages, so the government tried in various ways to encourage a return to restraint in bargaining. It set the tone in April 1977 when it attempted only a limited devaluation of the krona—6 percent—because central negotiations were going on. (By August another and larger devaluation was required, but by this time the moderate 1977 agreement had been concluded.)[102] Beyond that, the bourgeois government followed the script written by its predecessor, although with a few variations of its own. In both 1977 and 1978, personal income tax rates were reduced as before, in the hope that wage moderation would be induced while fiscal drag was being reduced, and in 1978, income tax rates were automatically indexed for the first time. In 1977, as earlier, the income tax reduction was partly financed by increased contributions by employers to social security, and in conjunction with the devaluations, a general payroll tax was reduced and the VAT was increased. The 1978 tax cut was not accompanied by an increase in the employers' social security tax, and the payroll tax was eliminated.[103] In addition, an attempt was made to soften the inflationary effect of both 1977 devaluations with the imposition of temporary price freezes, the first of which ended in May, when the new contract was signed. In 1978, a partial price freeze was accompanied by a system of general compulsory advance notification of price increases.

The effectiveness of these price measures was doubtful: while consumer price inflation fell from 13.6 percent in the first quarter of 1978 to

102. Ibid., April 1978, pp. 20–21.
103. Ibid., April 1978, pp. 46, 48; ibid., April 1979, p. 44.

7.6 percent in the final quarter, the rate of increase in domestic demand also fell. But an immediate object of the exercise was achieved when price inflation in 1978 did not exceed its January level by the amount required to reopen the agreement, although the oil price increase in 1979 did force a reopening in October, after the second contractual subperiod.[104] Thus, while a moderate one-year agreement in 1974 had been followed by a highly inflationary two-year agreement, the moderate 1977 settlement was followed by an equally moderate two-year agreement, and the increase in hourly earnings in the total economy kept decelerating through 1979. Indeed, real disposable wages declined 4.5 percent between 1977 and 1978.[105]

In general, therefore, a favorable correlation could be observed between bargaining outcomes and government intentions during the last three years of the decade. To what extent this was due to the compensatory policies that were followed is impossible to determine; it is possible that the LO would have attempted moderation in the wake of the 1975 settlement in any event. Nevertheless the LO did bargain with restraint after the unfortunate 1975–76 agreement, and it did so with a conservative coalition in office. The latter, for its part, furnished various incentives that at least were calculated to contribute to bargaining restraint, and these included, incidentally, the continuation of the employment policies of their predecessors. On the other hand, these policies were not without cost, either to the government itself or to the union movement. The moderate wage settlements did contribute to a sharp increase in exports and the elimination of the deficit on current account in 1978, and they permitted a reduction in the discount rate. The compensatory measures by which the government sought to encourage bargaining restraint, however, contributed to the steep increases in government deficits that appeared in 1978 and especially in 1979, when a new round of oil price rises caused a reduction in private activity. The more unfavorable budgetary position induced a tightening of monetary policy and a sharp rise in the discount rate in 1979, in order to stimulate borrowing abroad. Meanwhile consumer price inflation, having fallen from an annual rate of 10 percent in 1977 to about 6 percent in the first half of 1979, turned up sharply in the second half, when it triggered the cost-of-living reopener under the prevailing LO-SAF agreement.[106] The

104. Ibid., April 1979, pp. 13–14.
105. Ibid., April 1979, pp. 44, 13; ibid., April 1980, p. 16, n. 25.
106. Ibid., April 1980, pp. 5–6, 15, 28–32, 58.

fuel price increases thus exerted their two-edged, deflationary-inflation-
ary effect. At the outset of a new set of wage negotiations, the government
found itself more than ever in need of a restrained wage settlement but
with less leeway to offer fiscal inducements to obtain one.

In the meantime the governing coalition's stabilization program had
been going against the egalitarian grain of the LO. The income tax
reductions and indexation, while compensatory, tended to make the
system less progressive than it otherwise would have been. Elimination
of the wage tax by a conservative government contrasted with the
introduction of this tax earlier by a Socialist government in the deflationary program of 1970–71. The increase in the VAT in 1977 found a Socialist
precedent in a prior increase in 1970, but the latter was followed by a
Social Democratic reduction in 1973. Even price freezes had to be
regarded warily: earlier freezes received part of the blame for the sharp
increase in inflation that had occurred during the term of the restrained
settlement of 1974. Devaluation promptly stimulated an increase in
exports and an improvement in external balance, but it worked by raising
profit margins and depressing real wages, which made restraint in
bargaining more difficult to achieve. Revaluation, on the other hand,
offered an incentive to wage restraint. It had been advocated by assorted
economists in 1973 as a way to head off the inflation that followed, but it
was rejected in the tripartite EFO study, in which West Germany was
cited as an example to be avoided because of the "great political and
economic problems" that revaluation could entail.[107] Now, however,
Clas-Erik Odhner, the LO co-author of that book, reopened the possibility of substituting revaluation for depreciation in a policy designed to
reduce the relative costs of production in Sweden. Finally, criticism of
depreciation of the currency was joined to Socialist concern over the
growth and scale of the budget deficits and foreign borrowing that
financed industrial subsidization and nationalization under a bourgeois
government.

But it was of course recognized that appreciation required vigorous
wage restraint if Sweden, unlike Germany, were to maintain its strong
commitment to full employment and that tax reduction was, realistically,
essential to both wage restraint and high employment. Accordingly, the
LO and the Social Democratic party proposed a new stabilization
program in January 1980, which linked revaluation with a freeze on

107. Edgren, Faxén, and Odhner, *Wage Formation*, p. 228.

prices and rents, a 1974-style compulsory investment reserve fund, and an income tax reduction in order to facilitate a noninflationary wage agreement. And as an additional incentive to wage restraint the two Socialist partners revived the Meidner plan in altered and scaled-down form. It would consist of a central fund, which would be financed by a 0.5 percent payroll tax, thereby reviving a variant of the wage tax that the nonsocialist government had eliminated, as well as a tax on profits, and that would acquire company shares.

Thus did the LO announce its readiness to engage in policy bargaining over real wages with a nonsocialist government. If protection of the real wages of the bulk of its members required the LO to reach or force an agreement with the PTK over salaries, however, it also required bargaining with the PTK over the shape of a tax cut that might elicit a noninflationary wage agreement and thus a relative reduction in Swedish costs. Accordingly, three of the parties to collective bargaining in the private sector—the LO, the PTK, and the SAF—held a series of wage-salary-tax negotiations among themselves. The government was happy to be excluded, preferring to await a joint proposal rather than continue the practice of announcing its measures unconditionally and in advance of negotiations. But the LO had always preferred to be a follower—first of the SACO and later of the PTK—and when it failed to reach agreement with the PTK in these three-party, two-level negotiations, it called on the government to come out with the kind of wage incentives that it had in mind. The SAF tried to counter this by proposing that taxes as well as wages be subject to mediation. The LO rejected this suggestion by scheduling a ban on overtime. The government gave way on both points. It appointed conventional mediation commissions in the private and public sectors, and it announced a new stabilization program.

This package accommodated the demands of the LO for vigorous price controls with food subsidies and a rent freeze. Establishment of an investment fund into which firms would be obliged to deposit 25 percent of their pretax profits in 1980 was also proposed; as in 1974, however, this measure really amounted to a business tax credit, since firms would be allowed to draw on their special deposits for investment in new capital.[108] The LO-SAP proposal for a payroll tax and stock-acquisition plan did not find its way into the government's program, but local union participation in the administration of the investment funds was provided

108. Sundquist, "LO Wins the Zero-Sum Game."

as a gesture in the direction of codetermination. Most important was the announcement of an income tax reduction, which was concentrated in the lower and medium income range—the so-called LO bracket. But on the other hand, the government announced that its package was offered on the condition that nominal wages and salaries would be maintained at substantially unchanged levels. And it was silent on the financing of the tax reductions and on revaluation.

The SAF was satisfied with the package, especially with the near-freeze proposal on wages and salaries, and therefore dropped its opposition to conventional mediation. It could also be claimed that the requirements of the LO for protection of real wages in the private sector were satisfied by the proposal. But the PTK and the Gang of Four in the public sectors did not fare so well: whereas more than 40 percent of the members of the LO were in the tax range most favored by the scheduled reductions, the PTK and the public-sector unions each had only about 2 percent of their respective members in those brackets.[109] The LO, faced with unrest among its public-sector affiliates, refused to postpone its ban on overtime, and subsequently, on April 21, the organizations of wage earners and salaried workers did stop working overtime, then staged their selective strikes. At the end of April the mediators made their first final offer, which called for a nominal wage increase of 2.3 percent. But the government was not able to hold to this position after the strike. The second proposal added 2.5 percent to the cost package. The government, as we know, prevailed on the SAF to accept this, which it did only after protesting that it would inflate the costs of tradables and domestic prices and would risk future tax increases. Subsequently, the government announced that it would not be able to enact certain marginal tax reductions in 1981, as scheduled, and later it increased the VAT. It also replaced the price freeze with a milder monitoring scheme.

Thus, in 1980, the LO moved against the government on the tax front as well as against the PTK on the salary front. It won a slow bicycle race against the government by obliging the latter to show its hand before the conclusion of wage negotiations, and it won a similar race against the PTK by making its own agreement with the SAF contingent on acceptance by the PTK of drift compensation on the public-sector model. But in neither case was the victory decisive: the agreement of the PTK with the SAF left open the question of principle, or criterion, and the

109. Ibid.

356 SWEDEN

subsequent tax measures of the government seemed to reduce the amount
of progressivity implied in the tax measures that formed part of its May
package, while its relaxed price control also favored profits.

A way out of the impasse was suggested—implicitly, but not too
subtly—by the Social Democrats: since the LO had become convinced
that improvement or even maintenance of their members' average real
income depended on appropriate tax changes, could not policy bargaining go forward more smoothly if the LO could bargain with a Socialist
government rather than a bourgeois one? But while it might be argued
that the LO would be likely to make a deal with a Socialist government
without striking, could the same be said of the PTK? Furthermore, the
bourgeois coalition granted almost as much as the LO and the SAP had
jointly indicated they could agree on. (The government did not agree to
an asset-acquiring fund, opposition to which is intense in the business
community, while support for it among the rank and file of the LO did
not seem very active.) So it is difficult to attribute the strike to the
prevailing political balance of power; the strike could not be called a
political strike, although the Socialist opposition tried to capitalize on it.
A future decision by the electorate, however, might persuade either the
PTK or the LO, depending on the outcome, to moderate its relative-
income objectives. Otherwise, under prevailing economic circumstances, the LO seems called on to modify its real wage aspirations, its
employment policy, or both, as well as to continue in its posture of
reluctant consent to incomes policy.

Conclusions

Until recently Sweden provided an example of bargaining restraint
and industrial peace under a highly centralized system and in the absence
of government incomes policy. Restraint was reflected in an economic
record that, until the mid 1970s, was rather well characterized by the
Scandinavian model: high levels of employment, adequate international
competitiveness, and satisfactory levels of economic growth, combined
with high rates of domestic inflation. The structural centralization that
underlay Swedish bargaining restraint was motivated on both the employer and the union sides by a strong desire to minimize government
intervention into collective bargaining, but each side had an additional
reason of its own for supporting a strongly centralized bargaining

structure. For the employers, organized into a strong central federation (the SAF), centralized bargaining was seen as essential to strong resistance to union demands, although in an impasse centralized resistance by employers would have to be—and ultimately was—neutralized by the inability of the government to sustain a general shutdown. For the union movement, on the other hand, a strongly centralized structure of collective bargaining was required to implement a solidaristic or egalitarian wage policy. The effect of wage solidarity, however, was to generate certain decentralizing and destabilizing tendencies; it stimulated local wage drift by groups of highly paid workers that the union federation, the LO, sought to neutralize by negotiating supplemental "drift guarantees" for other groups.

There were additional decentralizing or destabilizing forces at work. A growing tendency on the part of firms, especially large enterprises engaged in international competition, to increase their control over costs by determining various pay components locally and in conjunction with standards of work contributed to wage drift. The relatively strong growth of the sheltered sectors—especially the government and housing construction—enabled them to exert a growing influence on wage determination: wages were increased both by the pull of increased demand and employment and by the push of organizational growth. Finally, high rates of inflation combined with a highly progressive tax structure to reduce real disposable salaries in relation to wages. This development was favored not only by the LO on grounds of equity but also by the SAF as an efficient market response to an increase in the relative supply of more highly educated workers. But it was not appreciated by the salary earners themselves, whose growing numbers made for greater organizational influence.

The Scandinavian model, which the LO and SAF negotiators have tried to translate into practice, does not explicitly encompass distributional shifts such as those mentioned above, nor does it contemplate pattern-setting wage behavior arising in the sheltered sectors of the economy. And as the room for negotiated wage increases became compressed by the slowdown in growth that began during the latter half of the 1960s and by the sharp deterioration in the terms of trade and the accelerated growth of the government sector and its transfer payments that occurred in the 1970s, the destabilizing tendencies in the Swedish system came increasingly to the fore. They were manifested first in Sweden's wave of wildcat strikes in 1969–70, in which groups of disaffected highly paid workers played a prominent part. Hard on their heels came a display of bargaining militancy and strikes among highly paid salaried employees, which began mainly in the public sector and which spread subsequently to their colleagues in the private sector and ultimately to wage earners in the public sector. These groups were afflicted by relative lack of opportunity to secure drift payments and by the heavily progressive tax structure. But the LO was not willing to lower its egalitarian standards in response to these developments, especially since inflation and tax progressivity were making it ever more difficult, if not impossible, to increase or even maintain the average real disposable income of its own members through negotiated wage settlements.

Nor was the LO willing to retreat from its commitment to full employment after the oil price increases in 1973–74. This commitment was shared by both the Social Democratic government at the time and the Center-Liberal-Conservative coalition that succeeded it in 1976. They had to honor it by pursuing various policies of subsidization, since increased transfer payments and a three-cornered tussle between wages and salaries—which involved the SAF in separate negotiations with the LO and the PTK—precluded sufficient flexibility of domestic costs. Finally, since the "bridging policies" of its predecessor had reduced productivity and international competitiveness, in 1977 the conservative government resorted to depreciation of the currency, which stimulated an increase in exports but threatened to destabilize wage negotiations through "imported inflation."

The LO did soften its traditional hostility to incomes policy in the 1970s, however. It did not do so because it found incomes policy to be either a necessary or a sufficient condition for securing gains in nonwage areas. When the Social Democrats were in office, the LO could secure legislative benefits in the fields of working conditions, occupational safety and health, and job security without the need to make any concessions at the bargaining table. And after the Socialists had been replaced by their "bourgeois" opponents, the LO was unable to secure the establishment of a union-administered codetermination fund for the acquisition of equity shares, although labor spokesmen hinted at acceptance of wage restraint as a quid pro quo. But the union leaders did become more receptive to official attempts to secure restrained increases in money wages as they came to realize that they would not be giving up much of real value in the process, since roughly half of any negotiated increase in money wages could be subtracted by higher taxes while the other half could be eaten up by an induced price increase. Governments attempted to capitalize on these relationships by using tax reductions and price freezes as inducements to the union negotiators to moderate their wage demands. These and other inducements were offered unilaterally, since the negotiators did not relent in their opposition to government intervention in the bargaining process and also since income tax reductions were required to maintain demand and employment anyway. Nevertheless, union negotiators as well as those representing management did take earlier tax and related measures into account; in any event the LO returned, after a damagingly inflationary settlement in 1975, to the traditional pattern of responsiveness and restraint that they had last practiced when their Social Democratic allies were in power.

Limits were imposed on the LO's restraint, however, by three considerations. In the first place, insistence by the LO on a continued reduction in salary-wage differentials encountered strong resistance from the PTK, the salaried employees' organization in the private sector, and even from LO affiliates, as well as from other unions of salaried employees in the public sector, where the demand for drift compensation was popular. In the second place, as mentioned earlier, the LO failed to secure the adoption of a union-administered codetermination fund supported out of profits; this scheme had been devised after the wildcat strikes as both a response to discontent among the workers and a means of reducing the room for pay increases in the then profitable export sector. And in the third place, the LO was opposed to redistributive aspects of the conservative coalition's "stabilization program," which included, at various times, indexation of the income tax, increases in the VAT, and depreciation of the currency.

Things came to a head in 1980, after the oil price increase in 1979 had raised both labor and nonlabor costs—through an extra negotiated cost-of-living wage increase—and had also increased the budgetary costs of any new tax concessions. The ability of the employers to grant pay increases and of the government to grant tax reductions were both tightly circumscribed; so the SAF offered only a nominal increase, while the government tried to make its compensatory package contingent on the adoption of the employers' offer. The LO seemed willing to accept a moderate wage increase and, together with the SAP, it proposed a social-contract package to go with it. But the LO also sought to deny the payment of drift compensation outside the SAF sector as a way of protecting the average real wage of its members. Its public-sector affiliates, however, and the various organizations of salaried employees as well, opposed this; furthermore, the LO and the PTK could not agree on a schedule of tax reductions. The impasse was resolved only after a settlement within the competitive sector's "room" had been rejected in favor of a larger settlement that accommodated demands raised in the sheltered sector and that exceeded the wage increase on which the government's tax package was based. The strikes and the lockouts in the private sector seemed to demonstrate that even united resistance on the part of employers, strengthened by inadequate profitability, could not prevail against stoppages that, under a highly centralized system of collective bargaining, inevitably threatened the entire economy and the public at large. On the other hand, the salaried employees and the wage earners in the public sector have demonstrated the capacity to inflict the same kind of damage. And the government's subsequent deflationary tax measures showed that it too could force a stalemate with the union movement. Ultimately, the distribution of income must be resolved by the electorate.

Postscript

Unfortunately, this conclusion appears to have been warranted in the light of subsequent events. In February 1981—early in the negotiating season—the LO and the SAF concluded a new two-year agreement to succeed the one-year agreement that had emerged from the general shutdown of 1980. The LO rejected a proposal by the SAF for a three-year agreement that would have left room for both devaluation of the currency and a rise in indirect taxes—a "reversed incomes policy." Nevertheless, the settlement was moderate—calling for total increases of only about 3.5 percent in each year and for threshold cost-of-living compensation excluding increases in the price of oil. While low-wage categories received higher percentage increases, the package also included a three-stage reduction in marginal tax rates to 50 percent for the majority of fully employed recipients of income. In a joint press release note was taken of the need to increase productivity and profitability and it was stated that "the labour market organizations are fully aware of their responsibility." There was really no news in that, in the light of Sweden's postwar record, but the white-collar ghost continued to haunt the old central bargaining table. The PTK was offered the usual 1 percent discount below the central frame agreement, on the usual grounds that their ranks contained a high proportion of highly paid employees, and they rejected this deal on the usual grounds of lack of opportunity to recoup in drift. Within three months about 150,000 white-collar members of the PTK went out in selective strikes that affected some of the larger concerns in the competitive sector and the banks, and employers countered with lockouts that affected 250,000 white-collar workers. This labor dispute was superimposed on a sharp dispute over proposals to reduce tax progressivity immediately, which the LO opposed. The labor dispute was mediated, but the government fell.

Appendix: Wage-Change Estimating Equations, 1959–75

(1) $WN = -0.77 + 1.02\,(\overline{P_w + LP} - WD) + 2.91Dl;$
         $(-0.60) \quad (6.85) \qquad\qquad\qquad (2.49)$
         $R^2 = 0.90$; Durbin-Watson = 2.63; standard error = 1.28

(2) $WD = -0.36 + 0.09VAC + 0.22CPI + 0.01(\overline{P_w + LP} - WN);$
     $(-0.66) \quad (6.80) \qquad (4.15) \qquad (0.23)$
     $R^2 = 0.89$; Durbin-Watson = 1.40; standard error = 0.49

(3) $WD = -0.34 + 0.09VAC + 0.23CPI.$
         $(-0.65) \quad (7.05) \qquad (4.66)$
         $R^2 = 0.89$; Durbin-Watson = 1.35; standard error = 0.50

Definitions and Sources

$WN\,(WD)$:   Annual percentage increase in negotiated wages (wage drift) for adult workers in industry. Sources: 1956–69, Gösta Edgren, Karl-Olof Faxén, and Clas-Erik Odhner, *Wage Formation and the Economy* (London: Allen & Unwin, 1973); 1970–76, Swedish Employers Federation.

P_w: Rate of change of export prices for manufactured goods from market economies, used as a proxy for world prices. Source: United Nations, *Yearbook of International Trade Statistics*.

$\overline{P_w + LP}$:   Refers to "room" for labor cost increases.

LP: Rate of change of labor productivity. Source: U.S. Department of Labor, *Handbook of Labor Statistics*.

*D*1: Dummy variable taking the value 1 for 1960, 1962, 1964.

VAC: Vacancies. Sources: OECD, *Main Economic Indicators: Historical Statistics;* and *Statistical Yearbook for Sweden*.

CPI: Rate of increase in the annual consumer price index. Source: *Statistical Yearbook for Sweden, 1977*.

Numbers in parentheses are *t*-statistics.

VII

The United Kingdom

As in the other countries in our study, there was a wage explosion in the United Kingdom at the end of the 1960s, followed by increases in the international prices of commodities and energy, then a deep international recession, which began in the mid 1970s. As elsewhere, rates of inflation increased sharply in the 1970s over those that had prevailed during the 1960s, while unemployment rose also. In other respects—especially the rate of growth in productivity—comparative performance has been bad. The highest rate of inflation—nearly 30 percent for retail prices in the first half of 1975—was capped only in Italy. Before an interpretation of these phenomena is attempted, some of the main institutional and economic developments must be considered.

Levels of Bargaining

"The study of British industrial relations today is to a considerable extent the study of how a system of industrial relations fashioned at a time of unemployment . . . has reacted to a long period of full employment," an observer noted in 1970.[1] The inheritance of the interwar years was a system in which basic rates of pay were negotiated at the industry level between employers' federations and national unions. Full employment after World War II added a second tier. Throughout much of manufacturing industry, bargaining over pay and conditions developed on the shop floor, where individual shops—or work groups, departments, or gangs—negotiated through their shop steward—that is, their union representative—with supervisors or foremen. For the most part this fragmented bargaining was confined to the private sector; it was characterized by informality, by the use of custom and practice, and by the threat of unofficial strikes, and it was often associated with systems of payment by results, which afforded frequent occasion to renegotiate piecework prices.

1. Hugh Armstrong Clegg, *The System of Industrial Relations in Great Britain* (Oxford: Basil Blackwell, 1970), p. 39.

From the late 1960s to the early 1970s most large companies moved to more formalized, plantwide bargaining, where senior shop stewards, or convenors, negotiated with higher management, and where piecework gave way to measured day work as a basis of pay. Through the 1970s the bargaining level slowly shifted upward to companywide bargaining. At the same time—in the private sector—industrywide negotiations became less important and the focus of these negotiations is now more on minimum-earnings guarantees than on basic rates.[2] Within the public sector, on the other hand, the industrywide or "national" level has been the most important level of negotiations throughout the postwar period; since most public-sector industries have a single employer (outside local government), companywide bargaining by the second half of the 1970s had become the standard model for large concerns in both public and private sectors of the economy, but with one difference: in the public sector negotiating has been the prerogative of national union officials; in the private sector companies have generally negotiated with panels, or "combines," of senior shop stewards from different plants.[3] The United Kingdom is unique in our sample of countries (apart from Italy in the 1970s) for the importance of the shop, plant, or company bargaining role of shop stewards. Shop stewards, while acting as agents of the national union in the plant, have seen themselves primarily as work-group representatives. Their ability to behave independently of national unions is the result, in large part, of their ability to call unofficial strikes, which, as will be shown later, could prove more cost-efficient to unionists—and less so to employers—than official strikes called by national unions after the completion of fixed-term contracts.

The leaders of the national unions have tolerated and defended this division of power for much of the postwar period. But the role of national union officials in private-sector negotiations appears to have been increasing as unemployment rates in the United Kingdom during the early 1980s rise to levels approaching those of the 1930s.[4] Thus, from the perspective of 1981, it may be that the study of industrial relations is the study of the way a system of industrial relations fashioned in the

2. William Brown and Michael Terry, "The Changing Nature of National Wage Agreements," *Scottish Journal of Political Economy*, vol. 25 (June 1978), pp. 119–33.

3. For details of some of these developments, see William Brown, ed., *The Changing Contours of British Industrial Relations: A Survey of Manufacturing Industry* (Oxford: Basil Blackwell, 1981).

4. "Business This Week," *The Economist*, April 11, 1981, p. 69; see also figure 7-1.

postwar era of full employment is reacting to a prolonged period of growing unemployment.

Productivity

British productivity was the least impressive in our sample of countries. Table 7-1 shows British performance in relation to that of its principal European competitors. The existence of comparatively low levels of productivity in the United Kingdom in the 1950s might have generated the expectation that subsequent rates of growth would be relatively high. Denison attributed Britain's low productivity in part to "the lag of average practice behind the best known"[5] (in addition to a lower capital–labor ratio), and this presented what Caves termed "a greater opportunity for residual growth"[6] as well as a corresponding competitive incentive. But competitive convergence to European levels has yet to occur, at least in the aggregate. Growth could, in fact, continue to be low for the same reasons that growth was low in the past if the length of lags behind best practice can be attributed to such things as "how hard [the workers] work . . . the skills and initiative of managers and entrepreneurs . . . and . . . legal and other institutional obstacles to the efficient use of resources."[7]

Such obstacles have been manifested in a considerable variety of restrictive arrangements or practices, such as excessively stringent apprenticeship requirements in some sectors; overmanning of equipment, of new equipment in particular; enforced overtime or restriction of output under incentive pay systems, both of which may be responsible for underuse of capacity; and restrictive work assignments, which may cause overmanning or, through delays in maintenance, underuse of capacity. In addition, informal procedures that have prevented management from installing new equipment or procedures without prior negotiation and that have been buttressed by recourse to local stoppages and slowdowns tend to reduce the rate of industrial growth. Such restraints

5. Edward F. Denison, assisted by Jean-Pierre Poullier, *Why Growth Rates Differ: Postwar Experience in Nine Western Countries* (Washington, D.C.: Brookings Institution, 1967), p. 281.

6. Richard E. Caves and Associates, *Britain's Economic Prospects* (Washington, D.C.: Brookings Institution, 1968), p. 12.

7. Edward F. Denison, "Economic Growth," in Caves and Associates, *Britain's Economic Prospects*, p. 260.

Table 7-1. *Comparative Growth of Productivity in the United Kingdom, Italy, France, and Germany, Selected Periods, 1955–78*
Average annual rates of growth in national income per person employed

Country	1955–64	1965–70	1970–74	1974–78
Italy	5.4	6.1	3.7	0.8
France	4.7	4.9	3.8	3.9
Germany	4.3	4.6	3.5	3.5
United Kingdom	2.3	2.6	2.0	1.6

Sources: 1955–64, Richard E. Caves and Associates, *Britain's Economic Prospects* (Washington, D.C.: Brookings Institution, 1968), p. 232; 1965–78, Organisation for Economic Co-operation and Development, *Economic Outlook* (Paris: OECD, 1979).

have existed elsewhere, of course, especially in the United States, but, it has been claimed, neither as extensively nor as intensively as in Britain, where the greater autonomy of shop stewards and of bargaining at plant level were particularly conducive to the imposition and retention of restrictive practices.[8] This hypothesis is supported by a large number of case studies which show that manning is higher or productivity lower in British-owned or British-managed plants than in technologically similar foreign situations. It also receives some confirmation from R. E. Caves's quantitative analysis of the determinants of British-American differences in productivity levels and growth rates within various industries, insofar as such differences may be negatively related to differences in the frequency and duration of strikes and in the extent of collective bargaining coverage in the older industrial regions.[9] It might also be noted that Caves's study fails to show a positive relation between size of plant or firm or the degree of industrial concentration and the relative productivity of British plants; on the contrary, the relations are weakly negative, which Caves regards as consistent with the findings of Prais and others of a positive relation between plant size and strike frequency, partly because of the greater potential for dispute over work assignments and work rules in larger plants.[10]

8. Lloyd Ulman, "Collective Bargaining and Industrial Efficiency," in ibid., pp. 324–80.

9. Richard E. Caves, "Productivity Differences among Industries," in Richard E. Caves and Lawrence B. Krause, eds., *Britain's Economic Performance* (Washington, D.C.: Brookings Institution, 1980), pp. 160–74.

10. S. J. Prais, "The Strike-proneness of Large Plants in Britain," *Journal of the Royal Statistical Society*, series A, vol. 141, pt. 3 (1978), pp. 368–84.

Inflation, Real Wages, Unemployment, and Profitability

A watershed in U.K. performance with respect to inflation and unemployment took place in the late 1960s. From 1950 until 1966 the average rate of unemployment was 1.75 percent, rising above 2 percent in only five of the seventeen years (see table 7-2 and figure 7-1). From 1967 until 1974 unemployment averaged 2.85 percent, fluctuating between a low of 2.5 percent and a high of 3.9 percent; then unemployment jumped to between 5.3 percent and 6.8 percent during the second half of the 1970s and to more than 10 percent in 1981.

Inflation was moderate during the 1950s and 1960s. Between 1953 and 1969, the gross domestic product (GDP) deflator rose at an average annual rate of 3.3 percent. During the 1970s, in contrast, the average rate of inflation was 13.5 percent. British performance with respect to unemployment and inflation during the 1950s and 1960s, especially 1953–66, was successful: inflation was only slightly higher than the Western European average, while no large country enjoyed a more prolonged period of very low unemployment.

The growth of real wages divides into three periods. During the 1950s and 1960s real wages grew at 2.5 percent a year, but during the four years 1970–73 the growth rate increased to 3.9 percent a year. From 1975 to 1979 the average growth rate fell to 0.6 percent; this was the result of a decline in 1976 and 1977 and increases in 1978 and 1979. There is evidence of a further decline in real wages beginning late in 1980.

The real wage growth in the 1950s and 1960s, though low, still exceeded the growth of productivity. Cumulatively this produced declines in international competitiveness and profitability. The latter was exacerbated during the first half of the 1970s by the rapid growth of real wages. By 1975 the pretax real rate of return had fallen from 12.3 percent in 1961 to 5.2 percent (see table 7-3). There was a recovery thereafter, but further declines in 1979 and 1980 led to a rate of 2.7 percent in 1981.

Incomes Policies and Industrial Relations Legislation

Our period divides into two halves with respect to government involvement in the labor market. Between 1951 and 1964, under the first

368 THE UNITED KINGDOM

Table 7-2. *Unemployment, Wage Inflation, and Price Inflation, United Kingdom, 1950–81*

Annual percentage rate of change (except ratio)

Year	GDP deflator	CPI	Unemployment rate	Average weekly wage earnings	Ratio of private-sector earnings to public-sector earnings
1950	0.7	3.2	1.6	5.8	101.5
1951	7.5	9.2	1.3	10.2	100.4
1952	9.1	9.1	2.2	7.5	99.3
1953	3.0	3.0	1.8	5.4	101.3
1954	2.0	2.0	1.5	7.4	102.8
1955	3.7	4.4	1.2	9.0	103.5
1956	6.2	4.9	1.3	7.3	102.1
1957	4.1	3.7	1.6	5.8	100.8
1958	4.5	3.1	2.2	2.3	100.8
1959	1.6	0.5	2.3	5.1	101.3
1960	1.9	1.1	1.7	6.6	103.3
1961	3.3	3.4	1.6	5.4	104.3
1962	3.3	4.3	2.1	3.2	103.9
1963	2.2	1.9	2.6	5.3	101.6
1964	2.5	3.2	1.7	8.3	103.7
1965	4.3	4.8	1.5	8.5	103.0
1966	4.0	3.9	1.6	4.2	102.5
1967	2.7	2.5	2.5	5.8	101.3
1968	3.5	4.7	2.5	7.8	103.1
1969	3.7	5.4	2.5	8.1	103.1
1970	7.9	6.4	2.6	13.5	100.0
1971	10.3	9.4	3.5	11.1	99.0
1972	10.2	7.1	3.9	15.7	96.5
1973	9.0	9.2	2.7	15.1	97.2
1974	15.4	16.0	2.6	20.0	96.0
1975	28.4	24.2	3.9	23.4	87.9
1976	14.3	16.5	5.3	13.2	89.4
1977	14.0	15.8	5.7	8.6	91.2
1978	10.6	8.3	5.7	13.8	92.8
1979	14.6	13.4	5.4	16.0	93.4
1980	19.2	18.1	6.8	20.7	89.0[a]
1981	11.6[b]	11.9	10.6	12.9	88.4[a]

Sources: GDP deflator, Wynne A. H. Godley, "Inflation in the United Kingdom," in Lawrence B. Krause and Walter S. Salant, eds., *Worldwide Inflation: Theory and Recent Experience* (Washington, D.C.: Brookings Institution, 1977), table 1, pp. 454–55, for 1950–75; Central Statistical Office, *National Income and Expenditure* (London: Her Majesty's Stationery Office, 1980), for 1976–79; CSO, *Economic Trends*, no. 347 (September 1982), for 1980 and 1981. CPI, Godley, "Inflation in the United Kingdom," pp. 454–55, for 1950–75; *Department of Employment Gazette*, vol. 89, no. 1 (January 1981), for 1975–80; *The Economist*, various issues for 1981. Unemployment rate, Department of Employment and Productivity, *British Labour Statistics: Historical Abstract, 1886–1968* (London: HMSO, 1971), for 1950–68; idem., *British Labour Statistics Yearbook, 1973* and *1974* (London: HMSO, 1974 and 1975), for 1969–74; *Department of Employment Gazette*, vol. 87, no. 12 (December 1979), and vol. 90, no. 10 (October 1981), for

Figure 7-1. *The Rate of Unemployment in the United Kingdom,*
1935–81

Unemployment
(percent)

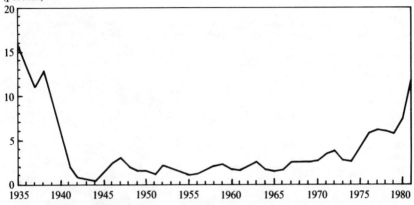

Sources: 1935–68, Department of Employment and Productivity, *British Labour Statistics: Historical Abstract,*
1886–1968 (London: Her Majesty's Stationery Office, 1971), tables 160, 161, and 165; 1969–74, idem., *British Labour*
Statistics Yearbook, 1973 and *1974; 1975–80, Department of Employment Gazette,* vol. 87 (December 1979), and
vol. 90 (January 1981); 1981, *The Economist,* various issues, 1981.

postwar Conservative government,[11] there was no industrial-relations
legislation and only a minimal attempt at an incomes policy—Selwyn
Lloyd's public-sector pay pause—in 1961–62. After 1964, successive
Labour and Conservative administrations had frequent recourse to
incomes policies. Wilson's Labour government from 1964 to 1970 had,
in one form or another, a continuous policy; the Conservative government of Edward Heath, 1970–74, was initially hostile to incomes policy
before executing in 1972 its celebrated U-turn, which led to collision

11. The Conservative prime ministers were Winston Churchill (1951–55), Anthony
Eden (1955–57), Harold Macmillan (1957–63), and Alec Douglas-Home (1963–64).

1975–81; the data relate to the number of unemployed not including school-leavers. Average weekly wage earnings,
CSO, *Economic Trends,* no. 347 (September 1982), table 40, col. 4; *Department of Employment Gazette,* vol. 88,
no. 5 (May 1980), table 125, col. 1, p. 567; ibid., vol. 76, no. 6 (June 1968), table 126, col. 1, p. 525; *Ministry of*
Labour Gazette, vol. 74, no. 6 (June 1966), table 126, col. 1, p. 359; ibid., vol. 60, no. 8 (September 1952), p. 303;
the data for 1980 and 1981 are average earnings throughout the economy of Great Britain; the data for 1953–79 are
average weekly wage earnings of all full-time manual workers in the United Kingdom; the data for 1950 and 1951
are average weekly earnings of all workers in the United Kingdom; the data are for October of each year. The ratio
of private-sector earnings to public-sector earnings, Andrew Dean, "Public and Private Sector Pay and the Economy,"
in J. L. Fallick and R. F. Elliott, eds., *Incomes Policies, Inflation, and Relative Pay* (London: Allen & Unwin,
1981), table 3.1, p. 47, for 1950–79; *Department of Employment Gazette,* vol. 90, no. 10 (October 1982), table 5.3,
p. 546, for 1980 and 1981.
　　a. Data on earnings in the private and public sectors for 1980 and 1981 are not available; the ratios for these two
years are 93.4 times the percentage change in the ratio of average earnings in the whole economy to average earnings
in public administration, for 1980 and 1981, respectively.
　　b. Because of industrial disputes, data for the third quarter of 1981 are unavailable; the figure given is based on
an average of figures for the other three quarters.

Table 7-3. *Real Wages, Profits, and Strikes, United Kingdom, 1961–81, and Average, 1950–60*

			Strike behavior		
Year or period	Annual rate of change in real earnings (percent) (1)	Pretax real rate of return (percent) (2)	Number of stoppages beginning in year (3)	Number of strikes known to be official (4)	Number of work days lost in all stoppages in progress during year (thousands) (5)
Average, 1950–60	2.7	n.a.	2,181	n.a.	3,231
1961	3.1	12.3	2,686	60	3,046
1962	0.0	11.2	2,449	78	5,798
1963	2.4	11.4	2.068	49	1,755
1964	3.6	11.9	2,524	70	2,277
1965	1.5	11.2	2.354	97	2,925
1966	1.9	9.9	1,937	60	2,398
1967	3.4	10.0	2,116	108	2,787
1968	2.4	10.1	2,378	91	4,690
1969	2.0	9.9	3,116	98	6,846
1970	5.8	8.6	3,906	162	10,980
1971	1.6	8.9	2,228	161	13,551
1972	4.8	9.3	2,497	160	23,909
1973	3.2	9.1	2,873	132	7,197
1974	3.3	6.0	2,922	125	14,750
1975	2.9	5.2	2,282	139	6,012
1976	−3.0	5.5	2,016	69	3,284
1977	−4.8	6.9	2,703	79	10,142
1978	5.5	7.2	2,471	90	9,405
1979	2.5	5.2	2,080	82	29,474
1980	2.6	3.6	1,330	67	11,964
1981	2.0	2.7	1,338	34[a]	4,266

Sources: Annual rate of change in real earnings, CSO, *Economic Trends*, annual supplement, 1981, no. 6 (London: HMSO, 1980), for 1961–79; CSO, *Economic Trends*, no. 347 (September 1982), for 1980 and 1981; real earnings are calculated as total wages before tax, divided by the number of employees in employment and by the retail price index; pretax real rate of return, *Bank of England Quarterly Bulletin*, vol. 22, no. 2 (June 1982), table A, p. 243, for 1963–81; and vol. 18, no. 4 (December 1978), for 1961 and 1962; strike behavior, *Department of Employment Gazette*, vol. 89 (January 1981), vol. 80 (January 1972), and vol. 67 (January 1959).

n.a. Not available.

a. First eight months only.

with the miners; Labour under Wilson, 1974–76, and Callaghan, 1976–79, had again a continuous incomes policy. The period from mid 1975 to mid 1978 is widely regarded as the only long period of effective incomes policy. In contrast, the Conservative government of Mrs. Thatcher, from mid 1979, firmly resolved to eschew its use.

Each government since 1964 has involved itself in industrial-relations legislation. Wilson, in 1968–69, and Heath, in 1971, each attempted legislation to diminish the power of shop stewards (*In Place of Strife*, 1969; Industrial Relations Act, 1971); both attempts were thwarted by union opposition. The Labour government of 1974–79, as its part of a social contract, embarked, by contrast, on an ambitious series of pro-union laws designed to restore the legal status quo ante, to bolster rights of organized workers, and to facilitate the organization of unorganized workers—especially through the Trade Union and Labour Relations Act, 1974, and the Employment Protection Act, 1975. The successor Conservative government returned to union-restrictive legislation, of a mild sort, in the Employment Acts of 1980 and 1982.

Strikes and Union Membership

Measured by strike statistics, militancy rose dramatically during the period from the late 1960s to the mid 1970s; since then it has abated somewhat (see table 7-3, column 3). This reflected a sharp rise between 1968 and 1970 in the total number of strikes and an increased number of official strikes (see table 7-3, column 4), to which the large number of days lost in the 1970s is primarily attributable. The rise in the number of strikes during 1968–70, especially during the second half of 1969, was the British version of the European strike-wave phenomenon of the late 1960s; as elsewhere, this took the form of an increase in unofficial strikes.

In Britain the increased strike activity was accompanied by a marked increase in unionization—from 43 percent of the labor force in 1968 to 48 percent in 1971 and 52 percent in the middle of the decade. Higher degrees of organization were reached in many traditional blue-collar sectors of industry—metals and engineering, for example—where employment had been stagnant or declining, but new organization was especially pronounced in such growing areas as the public sector and professional, technical, and other white-collar occupations.[12] Thus new organization was part of a general "upsurge of labour militancy between 1969 and 1974," thereby furnishing an example of the analytic equivalence between the effects of a change in the degree of organization and a change in bargaining intensity, referred to in chapter 1.

12. Robert Taylor, *The Fifth Estate: Britain's Unions in the Modern World*, rev. ed. (London and Sydney: Pan Books, 1980), pp. 24–40.

Differentials between the Public and Private Sectors

Until the late 1960s the earnings differential between the public and private sectors remained at roughly the level of the early 1950s. As a result of incomes policy, public-sector pay suffered in the late 1960s, although this does not emerge clearly from the aggregate figures. The immediate result was an unprecedented series of unofficial strikes in the public sector in late 1969 and early 1970. The long-term consequences were increased militancy in many public-sector unions, greatly increased unionization, especially of less well paid workers in the public sector, and a significant shift of pay differentials in favor of the public sector until the late 1970s (see table 7-2, column 5).

Differentials between Skilled and Semiskilled Workers

The other significant shift of differentials, from skilled to semiskilled and unskilled in certain industries, of which engineering is the clearest example, also occurred between the early and late 1970s, after relatively little change in differentials during the 1950s and 1960s. The shift was partly associated with the policies of the two largest unions in the private sector, the Transport and General Workers' Union (TGWU) and the Amalgamated Union of Engineering Workers (AUEW), which—particularly in the 1970s—sought to compress differentials within manufacturing industries.[13] In the late 1970s, however, reaction by the skilled groups led to a change in leadership and a change in policy within the AUEW and to an abandonment of an egalitarian incomes policy under a Labour government.

How can these events be interpreted? A widely held monetarist view is that unanticipated inflation of international origin during the late 1960s and early 1970s caused both the strike waves and the increase in unionization, as a result of which both real wages and unemployment increased. The jump in price inflation was interpreted as unanticipated,

13. While we frequently refer to the Transport and General Workers' Union as a private-sector union, it has several important jurisdictions in the public sector, especially in the docks and in road transport.

since expected price inflation was measured as a weighted average of past inflation, and various measures of lagged price inflation have been employed as explanatory variables in econometric models seeking to explain changes in both union membership and strike behavior. The most recent and careful work along these lines was done by David Smith, but he, like others, noted that the quantitative historical evidence is not strong or unambiguous, especially in the postwar period.[14] It might be noted from table 7-2 that jumps in consumer price inflation which occurred in 1950–52 and 1959–62 were at least comparable to the nearly fourfold increase between 1967 and 1971 but without producing growth in membership or comparable strike activity.

Obviously, interaction occurred between strikes and organizing activity, the rate of inflation (whether expected or unanticipated), and unemployment during the first half of the 1970s, but we prefer a story that began well before the initial and simultaneous occurrence of both the jumps in strikes and organization and the jump in wage and price inflation. In our view, the main propulsive force behind the sharp acceleration in both wage and price inflation was a rise in worker militancy; this marked the culmination of a process in which rising expectations of workers encountered a slowdown in the rate of increase in real wages together with increased work intensity—production standards—which marked "shakeouts" of labor and industrial "rationalization" during the sharp recession of 1966–67 and the subsequent weak recovery and slowdown in growth. Official incomes policies also contributed to the slowing of real wage growth during the period. As this complex process wore on in the second half of the decade, individual grievances accumulated and terms and conditions of employment were pushed below minimum levels of acceptability for an increasing number of people until something like a critical mass was reached. Groups whose pay had been lagging felt a particularly keen sense of inequity; notable among these were semiskilled workers and especially poorly paid workers in the public sector. Discontent engendered by lagging real and,

---

14. David C. Smith, "Trade Union Growth and Industrial Disputes," in Caves and Krause, *Britain's Economic Performance*, p. 107. In the course of this thoughtful analysis, Smith extends and modifies the work of George Sayers Bain and Farouk Elsheikh, *Union Growth and the Business Cycle: An Econometric Analysis* (Oxford: Basil Blackwell, 1976); John H. Pencavel, "An Investigation into Industrial Strike Activity in Britain," *Economica*, new series, vol. 37 (August 1970), pp. 239–56; and John Shorey, "Time Series Analysis of Strike Frequency," *British Journal of Industrial Relations*, vol. 15 (March 1977), pp. 63–75.

in some cases, relative wages and by rising production standards was generally manifested in an eruption of strike activity; in unorganized or lightly organized sectors, an extension of unionism was a necessary intermediate step between the buildup of discontent and its expression in collective action.[15] The increased militancy generated a wage explosion in 1969–70, markup pricing produced a sharp jump in price inflation in 1971, real wages rose because domestic prices were partially constrained by world prices, and official attempts to moderate this growth in real wages by demand management increased unemployment.

Public policy contributed to conditions that fostered the buildup of workers' grievances during the second half of the 1960s. The theme which runs through this chapter is that of the attempts of successive governments, Conservative and Labour, to control the growth of real wages in relation to the growth of productivity. Until the mid 1960s tacit cooperation between the Conservative government and the national unions did help produce a slow rate of growth of real wages, and the small excess of this over growth in productivity was paid for by declining international competitiveness, which tended to cheapen the price of imports, thus keeping inflation low. In implied exchange for self-restraint by national unions in industry negotiations, the Conservative government followed a broad policy of noninterference in labor markets and maintained unemployment at a low level. But this situation, although it was prolonged, proved ultimately unstable. The wage restraint and the full employment appear to have created a large gap between the potential bargaining power of semiskilled workers in manufacturing and the wages that they actually received through negotiation. Some craft groups were able to protect their relative wages within independent craft unions— and there were still nearly 600 separate national unions in the country in the mid 1960s—but the bulk of them could be represented by highly

15. Union growth has been found to be a determinant of strike activity in econometric estimates of strike frequency. So have changes in real wages lagged by only one year. Smith, "Trade Union Growth," pp. 117, 118, 123. Smith also ascribes increased unionism and strike activity to various policy developments in the late 1960s and early 1970s. Included, in the former case, are the report of the Commission on Industrial Relations in 1969 and the establishment of the Advisory, Conciliation, and Arbitration Service (ACAS) and, in the latter, the possibly perverse effects of incomes policies. At the same time it might be noted that the increase in militancy was strong enough to frustrate the attempt of a Labour government in 1969 to enact industrial relations legislation and to force the repeal of the Industrial Relations Act passed by a Conservative government in 1971.

autonomous shop stewards under fractional bargaining in the plants. The wage gap generated both an economic response and an institutional response. The economic response was wage drift, roughly equal to the excess of real wages over growth in productivity, producing steadily declining competitiveness. The institutional response was to swing the leadership of both the TGWU and the AUEW behind a more militant approach on wages.

The Labour government of 1964 thus inherited a situation of substantially reduced international competitiveness—real wages too high in relation to productivity—in which the two largest unions in the private sector were hostile to wage restraint. The Labour government analyzed the economic malaise as attributable in large part to fragmented bargaining by shop stewards: this was seen both as responsible for low growth in productivity through the constraints imposed on management and as inimical to wage moderation. It therefore developed an incomes policy designed to reduce the incidence of fragmented bargaining and, as far as possible, to secure wage restraint and also improved productivity, but the burden of restraint fell heavily on poorly paid workers in the public sector, with little history of militancy, because of difficulty in securing moderation in the private sector.

The Labour government generally increased the militancy of the national unions. To make incomes policy and growth in productivity more effective it had had to increase unemployment during 1967–70. It had attempted, moreover, to legislate concerning unofficial strikes in 1969. The 1970s opened with a union movement less moderate than it had been earlier, and, in particular, the conjunction of the more militant public-sector unions concerned with improving the lot of the poorly paid and large private-sector unions biased toward the semiskilled imparted a strong egalitarian impulse to the unions.

The 1970s divide into three parts: in 1970–72 and 1979, Heath and Thatcher, respectively, rejected cooperation with the unions; in 1973–78, first Heath, then Labour governments under Wilson and Callaghan developed policies in cooperation with—or designed so as not to alienate—the unions. Because of the high level of union bargaining intensity in the early 1970s, this period was marked by a rapid growth of real wages in relation to productivity; this produced sharply declining profitability and competitiveness. The subsequent reversal of antiunion policies, from 1973 on, was a result of this experience; it was also, for the Labour government, a reflection of the need to rebuild with the unions bridges that had been damaged in the late 1960s. Between 1973 and 1978, therefore, industrial relations legislation favored the unions. Their egalitarian goals, moreover, bore fruit in the reduction of skill differentials and the increase in the public and private earnings differential. This was made possible, first, by the use made by the unions of the continuous incomes policies during this period; second, within the private sector, it seems likely that it was aided by the move away from fragmented bargaining toward plantwide bargaining under senior shop stewards, who were frequently more responsive to the semiskilled and unskilled than to the smaller number of skilled workers.

There is considerable evidence of real wage moderation during the period 1973–78; real wages fell spectacularly, by more than 10 percent, between mid 1975 and mid 1977. But in 1973 and 1974 such moderation as there was was insufficient to offset the deteriorating terms of trade. In 1973 this was caused by an effective devaluation designed to correct competitiveness as well as rising relative commodity prices and in 1974 by the energy price increase. The result was a sharp acceleration of inflation in each of the two years.

The difficulty of securing sufficient moderation in 1973–74 stemmed partly from the inheritance of the late 1960s and partly from the antiunion legislation and deflationary policies pursued by Heath between 1970 and 1972. Yet policies similar to those of Heath were adopted, with greater success, by Mrs. Thatcher from 1979 on. Mrs. Thatcher's approach, although strongly motivated by economic libertarianism, was consistent with the view that the best that cooperation, as in 1973–78, could provide was moderation in real wages; that, if anything, this aggravated the problem of growth in productivity, since moderation depended for its successful implementation upon senior shop stewards, while growth in productivity was seen as requiring the restoration of managerial discretion and tough employers; and that a really high rate of unemployment was necessary to weaken the organized semiskilled workers and bring about the desired changes on the shop floor.

Tacit Cooperation under the Conservatives: The 1950s and Early 1960s

Although the Trades Union Congress (TUC) had preferred compulsory arbitration to direct government control over wages during the war, it lent support to a nonstatutory incomes policy promulgated by a Labour government's chancellor of the exchequer, Sir Stafford Cripps, early in 1948. It supported this policy for nearly two and a half years, until increasing dissatisfaction among union members, reflected in extensive and uneven wage drift, forced it to withdraw its support in mid 1950.[16] Nonetheless, the thirteen years of Conservative rule, from 1951 until 1964, were marked by deliberate moderation on the part of most national unions. The General Council of the TUC continued to support "the observance of reasonableness in the formulation of wage claims" explicitly until 1956; from then on—when the leadership of the Transport and General Workers' Union passed to Frank Cousins, who was left-wing and opposed to moderation—the "reasonableness was less publicly stated but vigorously pursued." Motions from leftist unions, especially the then Communist-dominated Electricians, sought at successive congresses to make the TUC "support efforts of the Unions to defend the living standards of their members by the submission of wage claims."[17] Such formulas for the abandonment of moderation were generally defeated by large majorities.

This moderation makes comprehensible the economic performance of the United Kingdom during this period. With the benefit of hindsight, the record of an average level of unemployment of 1.8 percent and an average inflation rate of 3.8 percent was a considerable success. It did not appear so to contemporary economists, whose criticisms concerned slow growth and the "stop-go" business cycle. But *growth* has been slower since 1964, and fluctuations in unemployment have increased.

Not only have economic conditions subsequently grown worse: since the mid 1960s successive governments, Labour and Conservative, have imposed almost continuous incomes policies, have used deflationary policies to control both real and nominal wage inflation, and have attempted to pass antiunion labor legislation. By contrast the 1951–64 Conservative government eschewed all three—a high rate of unemployment, incomes policies (with a brief and not very serious exception in 1961–62), and labor laws—as serious policy instruments.

16. Murray Edelman and R. W. Fleming, *The Politics of Wage-Price Decisions: A Four-Country Analysis* (Urbana: University of Illinois Press, 1965), pp. 180–83. The authors cite John Corina, "Wage Drift and Wage Policy," *Economics*, vol. 17 (Spring 1963), pp. 284–93.

17. Leo Panitch, *Social Democracy and Industrial Militancy: The Labour Party, the Trade Unions and Incomes Policy, 1945–1974* (Cambridge: Cambridge University Press, 1976), p. 42.

There are no compelling statistical arguments to prove that the national unions exercised moderation. But aside from the institutional evidence to be discussed below, certain facts—while hardly conclusive—are suggestive.

• In two periods after 1964—namely, 1970–72 and 1979–80—it would be generally agreed that the unions were using no discretion; in the first the average increase in real wages was 4.1 percent and unemployment was 3.3 percent; in the second, real wages rose 2.4 percent a year on the average and average unemployment was 7.6 percent, and if, as some econometricians persuasively argue, unions are concerned with net of tax real wages, the latter rose 3.9 percent in 1979.[18] In contrast, real wage growth averaged 2.6 percent between 1951 and 1964 and unemployment 1.8 percent. There is a counterargument, namely, that the cause of higher growth in real wages during the early 1970s was not increased bargaining intensity but changed worker attitudes; we shall argue later that the latter phenomenon applies to certain parts of the public sector, and even there there was substantially increased bargaining intensity.

• In no other country with strong unions in our sample was there a performance similar to that of the United Kingdom during this period in the absence of tacit or explicit wage restraint on the part of the unions.

• Restrained union behavior provides an explanation for the econometrically observed lack of sensitivity of wage inflation to the pressure of demand and to price inflation. Unions did not maximize their bargaining advantages when unemployment fell or inflation rose, seeing these as situations in which moderation was especially needed to head off strong government counterinflationary measures that they might find damaging.

The notion of a tacit agreement between the Conservative government and the unions provides a rationale for the moderation with which each behaved toward the other. The Conservatives came to power in 1951 determined to erase memories of unemployment and antiunion policies of the interwar years. Churchill's minister of labour, Sir Walter Monckton, was appointed as a conciliator, and he went to some lengths to avoid serious official strikes in the early 1950s. "I must, in all honesty, say how impressed I have been . . . by the wisdom, the moderation and the

18. S. G. B. Henry, "Incomes Policy and Aggregate Pay," in J. L. Fallick and R. F. Elliott, eds., *Incomes Policies, Inflation, and Relative Pay* (London: Allen & Unwin, 1981), pp. 23–44. Data for 1980 are not yet available.

sense of responsibility of the great bulk of the trade union movement and the great bulk of their leaders, certainly of the TUC itself," was how he summarized his experience in 1954.[19] Deakin, the general secretary of the Transport and General Workers, had made clear the position of the TUC Council in the first Congress (1952) after the election of the Conservatives:

My submission to Congress is that the guidance offered by the Council last year remains equally valid in present circumstances. It was then made clear that the Council was not opposed to applications for wage increases. We recognize that with a steadily increasing cost-of-living wage claims are justified. Council nevertheless urged, as it does now, the observance of reasonableness in the formulation of wage claims and the exercise of good sense.[20]

Two years later the TUC spelled out to the government the conditions for continued moderation:

Trade unionists have shown that they are aware that the problems of Britain are their problems and that their own living standards depend on increasing industrial efficiency. Trade unionists have shown too that given a square deal, they are willing to accept obligations for the sake of this objective. If, however, the Government or the industrialists by their actions cause trade unionists to reject these obligations, this will do more than turn the clock back in industrial relations: it will jeopardise our whole future.[21]

They were serious obligations: as one trade union leader put it: "If we say 'hands off our voluntary machine', surely that carries with it a corresponding obligation on our part to show that wage questions can properly be left to be dealt with in a customary way without endangering the national economy."[22]

The unions attached great importance to noninterference by the government. Interference was seen as regulation of union activity on the shop floor; their reasons for opposing such regulation will be discussed later. They also saw incomes policy as interference: in the absence of strong political support for a government that imposed it, the administration of such a policy would subject the national unions to intolerable strain. The unions also feared a return to the use of unemployment as a regulator of wage inflation and labor-market conditions. The strong two-way ties between unions and the Labour party were fixed in a compromise such that, except in extremes, a Labour government would respect such

19. *Conservative Party Conference Report, 1954*, p. 106.
20. *Trades Union Congress Report, 1952*.
21. Trades Union Congress, *Economic Report, 1954*, p. 300.
22. L. Evans, *Trades Union Congress Report, 1952*, p. 482.

noninterference and would preserve full employment.[23] But while a Labour government was preferred by the unions, it was understood—as part of the compromise—that the return of Labour to office was of subsidiary importance to the preservation and development of their collective bargaining functions.

How were the national unions able to pursue wage restraint, when many workers and some unions opposed it? The answer lies in the structure of wage bargaining. On the shop floor workers negotiated, through their shop stewards, earnings increases greater than the increases in basic rates of pay (see table 7-4). But it was through the latter, which were determined in industrywide negotiations, that the national unions could have a restraining effect. The econometric evidence suggests that wage drift did not increase to compensate the shortfall in wage rate increases fully.[24]

The other problem faced by the national union leaders who sought moderation was the opposition to restraint within the national unions, notably the TGWU after 1956, when Frank Cousins became general secretary, and also in some of the smaller unions. Here the restrainers were aided by the existence of wage rounds of industrywide negotiations, in which the rough size of increases was frequently set by two or three key settlements. The heyday of these wage rounds was in the 1950s;[25] they disappeared as a clearly observable phenomenon in the 1960s, though key settlements remained of importance. These rounds provided a lever with which to exert pressure. "We must frankly admit," said a leader of the Electricians, "that these decisions [by the TUC] have never stopped affiliated organizations from prosecuting wage claims on behalf of their members, but at the same time those of us who engage in day to day negotiations know full well the advantage that the employers take from any TUC decision aimed at curbing wage claims."[26]

Frank Cousins presented a more serious threat. When he became general secretary of the TGWU the union's "decision to fight for higher wages became a priority. It was seen by Frank Cousins and his closest

23. Lewis Minkin, "The British Labour Party and the Trade Unions: Crisis and Compact," *Industrial and Labor Relations Review*, vol. 28, no. 1 (October 1974), pp. 7–37.

24. J. C. R. Dow, *The Management of the British Economy, 1945–1960* (Cambridge: Cambridge University Press, 1965), pp. 351–56.

25. William Fellner and others, *The Problem of Rising Prices* (Paris: Organisation for European Economic Co-operation, 1961), pp. 432–36.

26. Walter C. Stevens, *Trades Union Congress Report, 1954*, pp. 479–80.

Table 7-4. *Wage Inflation: Annual Rate of Change in Wages,*
United Kingdom, 1951–64

Percentage change

Year	Average weekly earnings	Basic weekly wage rates
1951	10.2	8.5
1952	7.5	8.2
1953	5.4	4.7
1954	7.4	4.3
1955	9.0	6.7
1956	7.3	7.9
1957	5.8	5.1
1958	2.3	3.6
1959	5.1	2.6
1960	6.6	2.6
1961	5.4	4.1
1962	3.2	3.6
1963	5.3	4.7
1964	8.3	4.4

Sources: Average weekly earnings, *Employment and Productivity Gazette*, vol. 76, no. 6 (June 1968), vol. 74, no. 6 (June 1966), vol. 60, no. 8 (September 1952); basic weekly wage rates, ibid., vol. 76, no. 6 (June 1968), table 130, p. 531; data are for manual workers.

advisers . . . as the starting point for a change in policy. . . . Wages in British industry were far too low, especially among the majority of workers represented by the TGWU: the semi-skilled and unskilled workers."[27] But Cousins was outmaneuvered by the majority in the TUC. When Cousins led a long and unsuccessful bus strike in London in 1958, other leaders privately urged the government not to concede and gave Cousins no aid. And when the TGWU had to negotiate in concert with others, as it did with the AUEW during the 1957 strikes in engineering and shipbuilding, it could not count on their support in pressing its demands.[28] An interesting contrast may be drawn between the failure of the TGWU in the late 1950s and the success of the miners in 1973–74; in each case the union involved was opposed to wage restraint under a Conservative government, but in the latter the other unions— although they did not strike—helped the miners with moral authority, financial aid, and secondary action.

The Swedish union movement also supported an incomes policy

27. Geoffrey Goodman, *Cousins: The Awkward Warrior* (London: Davis-Poynter, 1979), p. 115.

28. Clegg, *Industrial Relations*, p. 339.

during the early postwar period that ended in a wage explosion, and it also followed this traumatic experience with a bargaining policy characterized by considerable self-restraint. In some respects, however, the British effort, while less effective when judged by the criterion of international competitiveness and balance-of-payments performance, was more remarkable than the Swedish. Conditions favoring the latter included a high degree of centralized authority in collective bargaining on both the management and union sides; the absence of autonomous unionism in the plants, although Sweden has always had extensive wage drift; and the continuance in office of the union movement's political allies, the Social Democratic party.

These conditions did not exist in Britain. To begin with, bargaining between national unions and employers' federations was at the industry, not the national, level, though industry negotiations are called national negotiations in the United Kingdom. The British Employers' Confederation—which was to merge with the National Association of British Manufacturers and the Federation of British Industry in June 1965 to become the Confederation of British Industry—and the TUC never engaged in collective bargaining with each other. The various employer associations did not possess authority over their affiliated firms comparable to the powers of the Swedish Employers Confederation—power to order its members either to initiate or terminate or refrain from lockouts, for example, or to fine firms for paying wages higher or lower than centrally negotiated levels. Nor did the TUC possess comparable authority over its respective affiliates, the national unions. The British unions, like the Swedish unions, possessed little authority at the plant level; but, as noted, in Britain, unlike in Sweden, groups of union workers at the plant level tended frequently to be actively engaged in fragmented bargaining. Their bargaining militancy, furthermore, grew apace with the moderation exercised by the leaders of the national unions. Why, then, were the national unions so much concerned to preserve the autonomy of shop stewards?

In the first place, national unions saw their own activities, which included political activities and participation in governmental consultative bodies as well as collective bargaining, as complementary to, rather than competitive with, the work of the shop stewards, which included grievance handling, contract administration, and bargaining. They regarded bargaining at the top and bottom tiers, moreover, as complements rather than as substitutes for one another, each contributing independently to total increases in wages. Thus, as traditional unionists, they found no grounds for objecting to any "extra" increases in pay secured by shop stewards under "fragmented bargaining." As a consequence, when the national leaders wanted to moderate the total rates of increase, they felt that they were in a position to do so by letting up on the component negotiated at the industrywide level. In the United States, especially when company-level, rather than formal industrywide, bargaining has been more prevalent and has been associated with contractual and frictional linkage between national and "local supplemental" bargaining, the relationship between the two tiers has been regarded as partly competitive, and wildcat strikes in violation of national agreements have often been seen as inimical to the interests of the national union. Not so in Britain; as Clegg sees it:

Although trade unions have no reason to relish a growth of unofficial strikes, this arrangement has many advantages for them. It is cheap. Shop stewards recruit members, collect the funds and handle workshop grievances at little or no cost to the union. In many instances no full-time official visits a plant from one end of the year to the other. The shop stewards man up the branch, district, divisional, regional and national committees and conferences of the unions and thereby give the leaders the impression that they are still in touch with the workshops. Workshop bargaining exploits favorable opportunities without the unions having to exert themselves, and the unions can then try to extend these gains to the members elsewhere.[29]

A second reason for lack of national opposition to shop steward autonomy lay in the relatively democratic structure of union government. In many unions, lay officials, generally shop stewards, played important roles within the union, whether on national or regional executive committees or in policymaking conferences.

The autonomy of the shop stewards and their influence within the national unions reflected the economics of wildcat strikes, which, as suggested earlier, could prove more cost-effective to unionists and less cost-effective to employers than official strikes called or sanctioned by the national union. More than 90 percent of British stoppages were unofficial, and proneness to flash shutdowns earned many an exporter the reputation of being an "unreliable supplier" and caused him a loss of market share. Firms obviously had a strong incentive to eliminate this source of uncertainty and disruption by offering increased resistance to

29. Hugh A. Clegg, *How to Run an Incomes Policy* (London: Heinemann Educational Books, 1971), p. 63.

unofficial shutdowns, but the costs of such resistance could be higher than costs of resistance to official strikes. They could include higher capital costs associated with the stocking of extra inventories of parts or products throughout the entire term of the official agreement (and not just prior to official negotiations). Alternatively, higher costs of resistance could also be the result of an employer's customary obligation to provide his employees with minimum periods of notice—at least one week—before removing them from the payrolls. Hence nonstriking workers, either in the struck firms themselves or in the employ of their customers, would have to be paid during all or part of a flash strike, even when the latter unbalanced inventories.[30] This is in contrast to the situation in the United States, where the employer's obligation was usually limited to a half or a single day's pay when specified by a collective agreement. It also contrasted with experience on the Conti-nent, where advance notice of dismissal was also required but where, before the 1970s, there was little effective organization at the plant level and where the "peace obligation" sometimes had statutory backing. While wildcat strikes can alienate nonstriking workers, moreover, when the latter suffer loss of work and pay, as has occurred in the United States, requirement of notice could underwrite sympathetic support for striking groups. And officers of national unions would not find themselves under internally generated pressure to discipline wildcat strikers, for the latter, while pressing their own claims, would not be imposing sacrifices on others that could ultimately reduce the negotiating strength of the entire national organization. Indeed, the latter would itself be in a position to help a local group of unofficial strikers at no cost to itself. If an employer threatened to dispense with the customary notice to groups

30. The employer's obligation to provide due notice, as well as the length of such notice, or to pay wages in lieu of notice, was expressed or implied in the individual contract of employment, sometimes stipulated in collective agreements (which have not had contractual status) and, after 1963, stipulated in the Contracts of Employment Act. That act provided a statutory basis for advance notice, which was made to vary directly with tenure of employment. Employees must also serve notice on their employers; and when such notice is given in the case of official strikes, employers have time to serve notice on their nonstriking employees. Employers have rarely sued for damages when unofficial strikers failed to give notice, however. It might also be noted that the layoff issue was not addressed by the Employment Acts passed in 1980 and 1981. See K. W. Wedderburn and P. L. Davies, *Employment Grievances and Disputes Procedures in Britain* (Berkeley and Los Angeles: University of California Press, 1969), pp. 23, 27, 33–35; Arthur Marsh, *Industrial Relations in Engineering* (Oxford: Pergamon Press, 1965), pp. 160–63, 314–15; *The Times* (London), November 24, 1981.

of employees made redundant by the strike, the national union might be able to threaten retaliation by declaring the strike official and further extending the area affected by economic conflict.

These considerations made for extension of the influence of shop stewards within the national unions as well as for the preservation of local autonomy, although wider economic and political developments were more important—and more widely discussed. In the 1950s bargaining autonomy and opposition to government constraints was an objective adopted by national unions in which the shop stewards exerted considerable political influence.

The decision to implement this objective by bargaining restraint in industry negotiations, on the other hand, reflected more of an independent input of the national unions, because the shop stewards were not noticeably anxious about the wage-inflation problem. Hence, the situation was unstable: restraint on the part of the national unions in the interest of keeping the government at bay helped to increase both the bargaining militancy of the shop stewards and their political power within the unions, which in turn tended ultimately to increase the probability of government intervention and of the substitution of defiance and militancy for moderation by the national unions themselves. The two dimensions of instability became clear as the period progressed.

The institutional instability caused by national union moderation manifested itself in leftward movements within the unions, where the gap between the potential bargaining power on the shop floor and the existing situation was greatest. This was true among the increasingly important semiskilled workers, particularly in the assembly-line industries, such as automobiles, but it was also true more generally in engineering and other manufacturing industries. The two unions most affected were the two largest, the TGWU and the AUEW. In 1956 the change to a leadership more responsive to the bargaining potential of the shop floor had come about in the TGWU. Within the AUEW the change of leaders was delayed until the 1960s but the process was in operation earlier.

The economic instability was revealed in a wage drift that ran counter to the restraint in the development of wage rates. The overall effect was that real earnings grew about 1 percent a year faster than real productivity. This was made possible without accelerating inflation by an improvement of the terms of trade, an improvement with two components: the small relative decline in the world price of raw materials in the 1950s, which then reversed itself, and a decline of U.K. competitiveness in manufactures. In the early 1960s, as U.K. businesses became more conscious of international competition, increases in real wages also had a counterpart in reduced profitability.

In the mid 1950s, the Conservative government began moving tentatively in the direction of incomes policy. In 1956, the government sought voluntary price restraint from the employers and wage restraint from the unions. After the TUC rejected the proposal, it appointed an independent, nonpartisan Council on Prices, Productivity, and Incomes to report on price and wage developments; this council ultimately suggested that movements in pay should be related to movements in productivity—but not necessarily with precision in each individual case. In 1961–62, the chancellor of the exchequer, Selwyn Lloyd, responded to a balance-of-payments crisis by appealing for a "pay pause," which was effective in curtailing wage increases in the public sector but not elsewhere. The TUC opposed the pay pause. It was followed by a white paper, which did set forth a specific target for wage increases, and by a National Incomes Commission (NIC), which, like the earlier council, had no partisan membership, because the TUC refused to volunteer.[31] The NIC, it should be noted, had sought to substitute the cooperation of employers for that of the unions: it encouraged employer resistance to policy-breaking union pay claims in the private sector in 1956–57.[32] In both instances, however, the government backed away from these initiatives when they were made aware of the degree of TUC displeasure.

Meanwhile, the unions and the TUC were following an even-handed policy, for they declined to provide the Labour opposition with specific commitments to future wage restraint. Indeed, they insisted that the party, which the TUC had helped to establish early in the century in order to secure the enactment of legislation that would remove legal obstacles to trade-union bargaining and political activity, reject recourse to new restraints on bargaining in the postwar period. At the same time, the leaders in the union movement, who were moderates, mobilized their considerable influence within the party behind the leaders of the party, also moderates, led by Hugh Gaitskell, against the party's left wing.[33] The left supported and found support among militant trade

31. David C. Smith, *Incomes Policies: Some Foreign Experiences and Their Relevance for Canada* (Ottawa: Queen's Printer, 1966), pp. 106–12.

32. H. A. Clegg and R. A. Adams, *The Employers' Challenge* (Oxford: Basil Blackwell, 1957); claims were broken in the public sector as well in 1962.

33. Minkin, "British Labour Party," pp. 7–17.

unionists, although the bargaining militancy of the latter was not motivated by a desire to support the left wing of the party by discrediting the
moderates. On the other hand, to the extent that the bargaining moderation of the unions furthered the opposition's electoral prospects, it
tended to strengthen the party's moderate leaders against its left wing.

It was widely believed at the time that union moderation would help
Labour electorally. A record of de facto cooperation with official wage
restraint under a past Labour government, followed by policy opposition
cum bargaining moderation under the Conservatives, held out the
prospect for resumption of policy cooperation under a future Labour
government. As the 1964 election approached, moreover, the TUC
softened its position on incomes policy by accepting it as part of a
comprehensive system of economic planning, which was supposed to
realize the economic growth that had eluded the Conservatives, whose
"expansionist" policies had been frustrated by the prompt emergence
of deficits in the balance of payments. Thus Labour could campaign with
the promise of official union support for a program of wage restraint
based on union cooperation.

At the same time, the leaders of the party and of the TUC were aware
of the limitations imposed on national union cooperation by the mood of
the members in the plants and the motivation and independence of the
shop stewards who led them. Thus James Callaghan saw the task as "a
gigantic essay in persuasion and cooperation . . . to secure the assent
of the whole nation," because while "trade union leaders can agree with
the Government to try to restrain incomes . . . there is no union leader
in this country who can, in the end, override the basic wishes of those
who elect him to his job."[34] And while George Woodcock, the general
secretary of the TUC, envisioned a situation in which the British labor
movement would ultimately substitute policy bargaining with the government for pay bargaining with employers, he later made it clear that,
to be acceptable, an incomes policy must be voluntary, with no sanctions
imposed for violating its pay norm.

Toward Militancy under Labour, 1964–70

Labour won the election in 1964 and, with Harold Wilson as prime
minister, plunged vigorously into an attempt to keep faith with both the
electorate and the unions. But the task that faced the new government

34. Panitch, *Social Democracy*, p. 57.

was of a different order from that which had confronted the Conservatives a decade and a half earlier. The economic adjustment required was now appreciably greater, just as the ability and desire of the unions to deliver— paradoxically, given TUC-Labour ties—was appreciably less. Confronted at the outset with a serious deterioration in the balance of payments, Labour forswore recourse to either deflationary demand management or compulsory wage controls; in addition, it determined to avoid depreciation of the currency, instituting instead a set of temporary import charges. At the same time, the government relied heavily on a policy of voluntary wage restraint, which it proceeded to develop in close consultation with the General Council of the TUC and sought to embed in a long-term economic plan that called for a rise in the annual growth of productivity from 2.3 percent, in 1955–64, to 3.2 percent. The interrelation between wage restraint and growth in productivity was made explicit when the 1965 white paper, *Prices and Incomes Policy,* provided that "exceptional" pay increases above the norm—of 3–3.5 percent—could be justified "where the employees concerned, for example, by accepting more existing work or a major change in working practices, make a direct contribution toward increasing productivity in the particular firm or industry. Even in such instances some of the benefit should accrue to the community as a whole in the form of lower prices."[35]

The policy also provided that above-norm settlements could be paid "where there is general recognition" that wages and salaries are "too low to maintain a reasonable standard of living" or "where there is widespread recognition that the pay of a certain group of workers has fallen seriously out of line with the level of remuneration for similar work and needs in the national interest to be improved." The white paper also provided a zero norm for price increases to accompany the 3–3.5 percent wage norm and established rigorous conditions for exceptions in the case of low growth in productivity and "unavoidable increases" in nonlabor or unit capital costs by stipulating that they were to apply only where "no offsetting reductions" in costs could be made. Finally, the new Labour government, unlike its predecessor, was able to establish a tripartite administrative agency for its voluntary wage

35. *Prices and Incomes Policy,* Cmnd. 2639 (London: Her Majesty's Stationery Office, 1965). It should be noted that the Conservatives' white paper of 1962 also provided for exceptional increases in such cases, among which it indeed listed "renunciation of restrictive practices," but they made no comparable attempt to implement this criterion through administrative machinery.

policy—and for its price policy as well—the National Board for Prices and Incomes (NBPI).

Nevertheless, the wage norm was not widely observed. Between May 1965 and July 1966, when the voluntary policy was in effect, wage rates and hourly earnings rose at an annual rate of about 7.5 percent, and by the second quarter of 1965, new wage increases were being negotiated every six months. As table 7-2 shows, the percentage increase in average weekly earnings indeed declined between 1965 and 1966 as unemployment increased, but according to David Smith's econometric analysis, the rate of increase in earnings was nonetheless greater than expected, although the increases in weekly and hourly rates were not.[36] Local drift, together with a reduction in the standard workweek from forty-two hours to forty, now outweighed apparent restraint by the national unions in negotiating rates.

In September 1965, the government departed from its commitment to voluntarism by announcing its intention to require, through legislation, advance notification to the NBPI of intended wage and price increases. The TUC moved to head off this requirement by setting up its own internal vetting system—a move reminiscent of the national unions' individual attempts at moderation under the previous government. The government then drew up plans for a nonstatutory "early warning system," whereby unions would give advance notice of "impending claims" to the TUC committee, which would have five weeks in which to react to such demands, if they wished to do so at all, and which would keep the government informed of union compliance with these early warning requirements. Appropriate government departments would have to be informed of intended price increases and would then review them in the light of the pricing criteria in the white paper *Prices and Incomes Policy*.[37] Prospective increases in both pay and prices that raised questions of compliance with the white paper's criteria would be referred by the government to the NBPI, which would have up to two or three months to report.

The NBPI, therefore, could not determine which cases it would consider. There was, moreover, no guarantee that all pay claims—

---

36. Smith, "Trade Union Growth," pp. 133–34.

37. The white paper justified price increases only where productivity increases were relatively low, where materials or capital costs rose, or where sufficient capital would otherwise be unavailable—and only in cases where it proved impossible to effect offsetting reductions in costs.

especially those initiated by shop stewards at the plant level, which accounted for much of the drift—would be brought to the attention of the TUC committee, although in July 1966 the government finally secured legislation providing penalties for uninformative unions and companies. Thus, the Labour government moved toward a "compulsory" early warning system—and it did so with the endorsement of the TUC, although the engineering workers voted against it. But even this legislation could not have required shop stewards to inform their unions of their local claims. The TUC, moreover, had refused to adopt a numerical wage norm for the guidance of its vetting committee, and the latter never requested the Ministry of Labour to refer a single case to the NBPI.[38]

In fact, the statutory early warning system never got started, for, in response to another sterling crisis in July—and, it was reported, to pressures from international bankers[39]—the government instituted a twelve-month freeze on wages, prices, and dividends, which accompanied a severely deflationary set of fiscal and monetary policies. For the first six months all wages and fringe benefits, prices, and dividends were to be at a complete standstill; and for the balance of the period, there was to be "severe restraint," in which prices could be raised only to cover increases in taxes and costs over which the firm "cannot exercise full control," while the only exceptions to the zero pay norm were pay increases directly related to improved performance, which should not raise average unit labor costs in the firms.[40] The policy was backed by statute—the Prices and Incomes Act of 1966. It was a law of only one year's duration, however; its enforcement powers, which related primarily to early warning, were held in reserve, and in fact the government invoked these powers on only a few occasions. The freeze was explicitly intended to rely on voluntary cooperation, and despite the fact that the deflationary measures and the rise in registered unemployment—1.3 percent to 1.8 percent of the civilian labor force between July 1966 and June 1967—suppressed earnings, the record suggests that voluntary compliance was indeed forthcoming. Hourly wage rates increased only 2.8 percent during the twelve-month period, whereas the increase had been 7.4 percent during the preceding twelve months, and, while earnings increased only 1.7 percent, the rise in rates was concen-

38. National Board for Prices and Incomes, *General Report, April 1965 to July 1966*, Cmnd. 3087 (London: HMSO, 1966), p. 34.
39. *New York Times*, July 25, 1966.
40. *Prices and Incomes Standstill*, Cmnd. 3073 (London: HMSO, 1966).

trated entirely in the second six months of "severe restraint."[41] The rise
in rates was matched by the rise in consumer prices—2.5 percent—but
this meant that real earnings declined.

The period of severe restraint was followed by a period of moderation,
which lasted from July 1967 to March 1968. The norm remained zero,
although the prefreeze exceptions were allowed, and the government
could delay increases in prices and pay up to seven months if they were
referred to the NBPI. But hourly rates rose 9.2 percent and earnings 8.8
percent, while the rate of registered unemployment increased to an
average of 2.3 percent, from 1.8 percent during the preceding twelve
months, during this period.

In November 1967, the Wilson government devalued the pound; as a
result, a fourth stage of incomes policy was announced, which lasted
from April 1968 to the end of 1969. The zero norm was continued,
although increases up to 3.5 percent were allowed in cases of "productivity bargaining," which included elimination of restrictive work practices, of major revisions of internal wage structures, and of the presence
of poorly paid workers. A new Prices and Incomes Act (1968) extended
the government's power to delay price or wage increases to a maximum
of twelve months and also empowered it to order price reductions upon
recommendation of the NBPI. During this period, unemployment remained high, at more than 2.3 percent, but so did the rate of increase in
earnings. Hourly rates rose at an annual rate of more than 4.5 percent
between April and December 1968 and another 5.5 percent in 1969. This
represented a considerable reduction from the period of moderation.
But earnings rose at an annual rate of nearly 7.6 percent during the first
eight months of 1968 and 8.3 percent in 1969. According to Fels, "In the
third quarter of 1969, the Government, without reference to the NBPI,
sanctioned a series of much publicised above-norm pay settlements . . .
and largely abandoned any pretence that the policy was being applied."[42]

Finally, in the first six months of 1970—its last six months in office—
the Labour government reacted in a new white paper to the recent
increases by setting a range of 2.5–4.5 percent for pay increases and
dropping a 3.5 percent norm for dividends that had been instituted after

41. Data on unemployment and wages taken from Allan Fels, *The British Prices and Incomes Board* (Cambridge: Cambridge University Press, 1972), table 3.1, p. 29; table 3.2, p. 31.
42. Ibid., p. 28.

the period of moderation.[43] Wage rates and earnings exploded, with annual rates of increase of 12.6 percent and 13.6 percent, respectively, although unemployment rose in 1970 to 2.6 percent.

The detailed history of attempted wage restraint by the Labour government through its successive incomes policies between 1964 and 1970 makes depressing reading. But their apparent ineffectiveness raises two problems. If these policies were completely ineffective, why did the period end with an unprecedented strike wave and wage explosion? Equally, why had relations between the trade-union movement and the Labour leaders sunk by 1969 to arguably the lowest level in the party's history? The answers to these questions stem in part from the economic and institutional inheritance of the Conservative government, as discussed earlier. But they also reflect the facts that the wage restraint was less ineffective than it appeared and that the government's policies were directed toward other objectives in addition to wage restraint.

The Labour government inherited severe economic problems, including low international competitiveness, lower profitability than in the 1950s, and a low growth rate of productivity. The system of fragmented bargaining was held partly responsible for these difficulties, particularly by the NBPI. The incomes policy therefore had at least three separate objectives. The first was wage restraint, the second was growth in productivity, and the third was reorganization of the system of plant bargaining along the broad lines recommended by the Donovan Commission, which had been set up by the Labour government to inquire into the industrial relations system—and which had informal intellectual links with the NBPI. The Donovan Commission held that the way forward from the two-tier system of simultaneous industrywide and shop-floor bargaining was to formalize bargaining at the plant or company level. The power of shop stewards was too strong to allow abolition of the lower level. Instead, both the commission and the board sought an institutionalization of the lower tier by developing plantwide (or companywide) bargaining, thus placing senior, full-time shop stewards at the center of the stage. Parallel to the institutional shift there was to be a change in the system of payments. Payment-by-results—used increasingly in manufacturing in the 1950s and 1960s—with incentives linked to individual output, was seen as conducive to fragmented bargaining. In its place the commission advocated measured day work, where certain

43. *Productivity, Prices and Incomes Policy after 1969*, Cmnd. 4237 (London: HMSO, 1969).

minimum levels of performance were required. This would make it possible to reduce or contain wage drift by "cut[ting] down on the opportunity for fragmented sectional bargaining and concentrat[ing] on general increases throughout the whole of the undertaking."[44] But the change in the locus of power—from shop stewards to senior shop stewards—and in the type of payments system was not a simple improvement in organization that would leave all the participants in a better position. The change was designed to moderate growth in real wages in the future by increasing managerial control. It was, moreover, envisaged as necessary to make a future incomes policy effective. Clegg, as a member of the NBPI, noted in 1971:

The first objective of an incomes policy must be to control pay in the two thousand or so large undertakings, since the smaller establishments may generally be supposed to follow the larger in their pay decisions. . . . However, the truth is that many of the two thousand or so British undertakings under discussion do not settle their pay at plant level, but at the level of the department, or the section or the workshop or the gang. . . . The problem of control for a British incomes policy is not how to regulate pay in two thousand plants, but how to cope with two hundred thousand or more workshops, sections and groups, each having considerable autonomy to negotiate for themselves.[45]

There was a conflict between the short-run aim of direct wage restraint and the long-run approach through reorganization of bargaining systems. Reorganization required substantial wage increases to be palatable to well-organized work groups whose shop stewards stood to lose power. The encouragement given to wage realignment in 1968 and 1969 provoked strikes and substantial wage increases.[46] It has been suggested that other plants in turn may have struck in an effort to obtain comparable increases, though they were not subjected to wage realignment.[47]

A second impetus to strikes in the private sector in the late 1960s came from the deflationary policy of the government. In each of the years 1967–70 unemployment was well above 2 percent. This facilitated attempts by employers to recoup profitability. Among these was rationalization in the form of a "shakeout" of surplus labor. Coincidentally, there was a large increase in the number of mergers. As did wage realignment, it seems likely that these measures contributed to the increase in private-sector strikes in 1968 and 1969.

The TUC had been prepared, without enthusiasm, to cooperate in a

44. Clegg, *How to Run an Incomes Policy*, pp. 64, 83.
45. Ibid., pp. 82–83.
46. Ibid., p. 64.
47. Ibid., pp. 64–65.

voluntary incomes policy in 1964. This had been presented as an integral part of the economic planning exercise that occupied a large part of the government's energy between 1964 and 1966. The National Plan held out the possibility of faster growth and full employment within a framework that involved a substantial expansion of the public sector. But the plan was effectively abandoned in the external crises of 1966 and 1967, incomes policy was given statutory form, and the goal of full employment was given up. By 1967 the trade unions were hostile to the government and suspicious of it. At successive union conferences, motions now began to be passed against its policies. But it was the attempt in late 1968 and early 1969 to legislate on unofficial strikes that brought relations between the TUC and the government to their nadir.

Partly employing the recommendations of the Donovan Commission, the secretary of state for employment and productivity, Barbara Castle, had issued in 1968 a white paper, *In Place of Strife,* which contained proposals for substantial benefits for the unions in addition to others which required strike votes and conciliation pauses in certain circumstances.[48] In general, the function of white papers is to spell out proposed legislation. But the bill placed before Parliament in early 1969 bore little relation to the white paper and was directed, without sweeteners, at the problem of unofficial strikes. It was seen as a political move by an unpopular prime minister who sought to make a scapegoat of the unions. The unions were heavily opposed, and the parliamentary Labour party and the cabinet, in which Home Secretary James Callaghan was the main opponent of the bill, were deeply divided. The bill was withdrawn in March 1969, but it left a legacy of bitterness between the unions and the prime minister.

Both the strike waves, however—especially that in the public sector—and the state of TUC-government relations are difficult to understand fully if it was in fact the case, as is generally assumed, that—apart from mid 1966 to mid 1967—the incomes policies were unsuccessful in restraining wages. This assumption is typically justified in one of two ways. First, increases in money wages greatly exceeded the norms laid down in the successive policies. But such a test depends on the realism of the norms and does not settle the question whether the wage increases were less than they would have been had the unions exercised no restraint. Econometric tests avoid this difficulty and also show the

48. *In Place of Strife,* Cmnd. 3888 (London: HMSO, 1969).

policies to have been unsuccessful; but in econometric work it has been assumed that no restraint was exercised between 1951 and 1964 and hence—if we are correct in believing there was significant restraint during that period—this work is equally invalid.

The record and reputation of the policy notwithstanding, it might have proved temporarily effective. The period 1964–69, or mid 1967 to mid 1969, shows up as restrained when it is compared to the subsequent period, 1970–74. This is still true if the year 1970 is dropped from the comparison on the ground that the wage explosion in 1970 represented a catch-up after the incomes policy of the Labour government—though, of course, to say that the wage increases of 1970 were a catch-up as a result of the policy is close to accepting the existence of effective prior constraint. Real wages increased on the average 3.0 percent a year between 1967 and 1969, down from 5.5 percent a year between 1970 and 1974 or 5.1 percent a year between 1971 and 1974. In the early 1970s, moreover, economic conditions—profitability and unemployment—were on the average worse than in the late 1960s.

A possible counter to this argument that there was effective restraint from mid 1967 to mid 1969 stems from the effect on real wages of the sterling devaluation of November 1967. The short-run effect of devaluation is to reduce the real wage, since import prices have risen by the amount of the devaluation and domestic prices have risen by a proportion of that amount equal to the import content of final output. But such devaluation-induced restraint operates only for as long as it takes unions to reestablish the negotiable real wage. Apart from the very short run, restraint in the real wage could not have been due to devaluation. Indeed, the increase in the rate of inflation caused by the 1967 devaluation explains to some extent why the low money-wage norms of the post-1967 policies were unrealistic.

Also, the overall restraint on wages was felt more strongly by some groups than by others. One possibility is that the late 1969 strikes in the public sector were caused by the fact that the incomes policies in 1967–69 fell particularly heavily on the public sector. Against this, as Dean and others have pointed out, the aggregate statistics of differentials between public and private earnings moved only slightly toward the private sector during the period (see table 7-2, column 5).[49] The change becomes somewhat more significant when it is noted that periods of

49. Andrew Dean, "Public and Private Sector Pay and the Economy," in Fallick and Elliott, eds., Incomes Policies, Inflation, and Relative Pay.

Table 7-5. *Wage Increases of Selected Groups of Workers, United Kingdom, 1967–69*

Period	Average weekly earnings in manu- facturing	Railway workers[a]	London bus crews[b]	Miners[c]	National Health Service	
					Adult males[d]	Adult females[e]
October 1968 on October 1967	8.3	10.3	8.8	5.2	2.1	1.0
October 1969 on October 1968	8.4	10.4	8.8	4.1	5.9	4.8

Sources: Average weekly earnings in manufacturing, Department of Employment and Productivity, *British Labour Statistics Yearbook, 1976* (London: HMSO, 1978), table 44, p. 110; all other data from ibid., table 39, p. 103.
a. British Rail, male adult rates.
b. London Transport, male road staff.
c. Adult males.
d. Men, 21 and over, hospital employees.
e. Women, 21 and over, hospital employees.

increased unemployment had previously favored the public sector (see table 7-2, column 3). Nonetheless it is difficult to make a strong case from the aggregate data of a shift in differentials sharp enough to have provoked the unprecedented wave of unofficial public-sector strikes in late 1969.

Disaggregated statistics reveal, however, that, while some groups of employees in the public sector moved ahead rapidly, others were indeed held back. Earnings data by industry group in manufacturing show that earnings in different manufacturing industries grew at broadly the same rates between 1967 and 1969.[50] But significant divergences are shown in the earnings of manual workers in different public-sector groups in table 7-5; unfortunately these are the only groups for which earnings information is readily available for the 1960s.

As can be seen, the earnings of miners in a nationalized industry and manual workers in the National Health Service (NHS) deteriorated sharply in relation to average earnings in manufacturing. Two of the largest groups involved in the unofficial strikes in the latter part of 1969 were the Yorkshire miners and local government refuse collectors, to whose rates of pay those of manual workers in the NHS have traditionally been linked. On the other hand, neither railway workers nor London

50. Wynne A. H. Godley, "Inflation in the United Kingdom," in Lawrence B. Krause and Walter S. Salant, eds., *Worldwide Inflation: Theory and Recent Experience* (Washington, D.C.: Brookings Institution, 1977), p. 462.

bus drivers, whose earnings did not fall in the same proportion, were involved to any significant extent in the wave of unofficial strikes of late 1969.

The public sector was vulnerable to incomes policy because the government was the employer and because bargaining was carried out in industrywide negotiations.[51] Where unions either felt too weak to resist the government, as did the General and Municipal Workers Union when representing many poorly paid public-sector groups such as the refuse collectors, or supported the government out of loyalty, as did the National Union of Mineworkers—though they were split on this issue—low settlements were the result. But the consequence of the strike waves of late 1969 was to transform many previously quiescent unions in the public sector into militant ones.

Public-Sector Bargaining, Unemployment, and Labor Legislation: Conservative Strategy, 1970–72

When the Conservatives formed a new government, in June 1970, money wages were exploding at an annual rate of 15 percent; unemployment was high by postwar standards—2.6 percent—and it was continuing a rise that had begun in the mid 1960s, when it had been as low as 1.5 percent; incomes policy had not been seriously applied since the last quarter of 1969, and an attempt to introduce labor-relations legislation in the hope of reducing the excesses of fragmented bargaining on the shop floor had failed. The new government, led by Prime Minister Edward Heath, pushed ahead with labor legislation and secured the passage of the Industrial Relations Act of 1971. It made no attempt, however, to revive formal incomes policy during its first two years in office, relying instead on hard bargaining by government agencies to wind down the rate of increase in wages in the public sector—the so-called $n - 1$ strategy—and on free collective bargaining in the private sector.

According to the Organisation for Economic Co-operation and Development (OECD), "The choice of strategies reflects the present administration's conviction that private initiative should be left as unhampered as possible, while still checking the abuse of market

51. The bargaining structure in mining had been centralized in the mid 1960s.

bargaining power by suitable legislative action."[52] Indeed, proceeding with industrial relations legislation was sufficient to preclude the revival of incomes policy based on union restraint and thus revealed Conservative predilections for laissez faire. In any case, the recent debacle of incomes policy had foreclosed that option for the short run. A policy of purposeful deflation was designed to ensure that free markets and free collective bargaining would operate under conditions of sufficiently great slack—in unemployment and excess capacity—to generate more tolerable rates of wage inflation. Unemployment increased from 2.6 percent in 1970 to 3.5 percent in 1971. The rise was much steeper and the level reached much higher than under the previous government. In fact the rise of nearly 50 percent in unemployment was greater than planned, but, though it prompted some measures of demand reflation, unemployment went on rising in 1972 to 3.9 percent.

In summary, the new government hoped that a lower rate of wage inflation would be compatible with free collective bargaining in the private sector, as a result of the more moderate settlements that it hoped to secure in the public sector, the operation of the new Industrial Relations Act, and the disinflationary influence of higher unemployment.

The "n − 1" Strategy in the Public Sector

The government, as employer, proposed to obtain successively smaller settlements in the public sector. Though the policy did not literally work thus, the tag "n − 1" captured the idea that each settlement would be 1 percent lower than its predecessor. The logic of the policy was rooted in the institutional importance of comparability in British pay bargaining. Its importance, both within the public sector and between public and private, ruled out the imposition by the government of a significant cut in the rate of wage increases in the public sector. A significant cut—even had it been possible to impose—would have disrupted differentials within the public sector between the groups on which it was imposed and those that had secured increases earlier, as well as between public and private sectors. In addition, comparability allowed the government to hope that private-sector wage setting would follow public-sector experience. It was in reality a disguised incomes policy, but the government could argue to the contrary that it was simply

52. OECD Economic Surveys, *United Kingdom*, December 1971, p. 17.

free collective bargaining with a readiness to sit out strikes if necessary. However, $n - 1$ could not be so easily squared with that other expression of economic libertarianism, the monetarist theory of inflation. For if the $n - 1$ policy was seen as affecting the rate of increase in money wages not only in the public sector but, with the example set by the government, in the private sector as well, the model upon which $n - 1$ was based regarded union settlements in the public sector as an exogenous determinant of the level of expectations in private markets and hence of inflation. In contrast to the monetarist professions to be found in the government, $n - 1$ reflected a Keynesian view of what generated inflation. It was also in contrast to the Aukrust model of inflation in an open economy, according to which wage increases originate in the exposed, private sector and are transmitted to the sheltered, government sector.

The $n - 1$ policy resembled the type of incomes policy that the Conservative government had introduced in 1961–62, when the government attempted to implement a pay pause by denying pay increases in the public sector. In that episode, the government had refused to accept an award by an industrial court—a tribunal of voluntary arbitration— for the first time since the passage of the Industrial Courts Act in 1919.[53] This time the government attempted to withhold its conciliation services in disputes unless it was understood that the settlements would be within the limits set by the government.[54] The government believed, moreover, that it had acquired an additional enforcement mechanism in the power, granted to it in the new Industrial Relations Act, to declare a cooling-off period of up to sixty days and to take strike votes in disputes threatening the national economy. The American rationale of the cooling-off period, however, has been to provide an opportunity for conciliation and mediation to be employed, whereas on this occasion the government was essentially trying to rule out the possibility of compromise in pay disputes.

The $n - 1$ policy met with some success in 1971, the first year of operation. A long strike by the postal workers at the beginning of the year was settled with a 9 percent pay increase, terms very close to the Post Office's offer of 8 percent. This set a precedent for other groups— including more than half a million nurses and ancillary workers in the National Health Service and local authority administrative employees—

53. Fels, *British Prices and Incomes Board,* p. 11.
54. Clegg, *Industrial Relations,* p. 465.

who negotiated increases in 1971 of 8–9 percent, which were less than the increases in their earlier settlements. Two significant exceptions to the $n - 1$ rule, however, were provided by the manual workers in local government and the electricity supply workers. In the former case, some strikes were called after the government had refused to make its conciliation services available, whereupon the local authorities, many of whom were controlled by Labour, and the unions set up their own Independent Committee of Inquiry, which expressly repudiated the $n - 1$ criterion in making its award. In the case of the electricity workers, a ban on overtime and working to rule persuaded the government to convene a court of inquiry. These two groups received increases of 15–16 percent.

In 1972, it became apparent that the government could neither persuade nor compel powerful unions to follow the policy. A strike in the coal mines, with effective mass picketing at the docks and power stations, produced another court of inquiry, which awarded the miners a 20 percent increase—after the government had offered 7.5 percent—on the grounds, in principle excluded by $n - 1$, that the miners' relative wage had been considerably reduced. This strike caused cuts in electric power, the government declared a state of emergency, and industry was put on a two- to three-day week. The next and last test of $n - 1$ occurred in the spring of 1972, when the railway workers refused to accept an arbitration award and fired the usual warning shot by working to rule and refusing to work overtime. The government ordered a cooling-off period, which was unproductive, then conducted a strike vote under the Industrial Relations Act, but after the members voted overwhelmingly in favor of striking, the dispute was settled with an increase of 13 percent. The 1971 settlement, which British Rail offered in 1972, was just over 9 percent. After this episode, the $n - 1$ strategy was dropped.

The experience under $n - 1$ did not invalidate the hypothesis of public-sector wage autonomy on which it was based, but it certainly lent little support to the inference that wage modification could be secured by hard bargaining in the public sector. The autonomy hypothesis is based on the view that employment in the public sector is sheltered from market influences by virtue of inelastic demand—the essential nature of many public services—and the susceptibility of public-sector employment to political influences. While inelastic demand may be highly conducive to wage autonomy, however, it also makes for union bargaining strength and thus militates against the effectiveness of an incomes policy based on the resistance of public employers. In fact, $n - 1$ proved ineffective against the big battalions based in the energy and transportation jurisdictions. To be effective, an incomes policy applied to the public sector would have had to rely on persuasion, rather than on resistance or legal coercion—in short, it would have had to resemble more conventional policies. But persuasion would have been difficult in part because Labour's incomes policies had already proved more effective in some parts of the public sector than in the private sector, where there was greater opportunity to secure local wage drift. So now the public-sector unions, primarily the coal miners, felt that they had some catching up to do, and they did not feel inhibited by political considerations. Thus the susceptibility of public-sector employment to political influences also worked to the disadvantage of $n - 1$: the political forces playing on the unions made for noncompliance. Another example of perverse political influence was referred to in connection with the manual workers employed by local governments, when their Labour employers joined forces with their unions in circumventing the attempt of the government, first to constrain, then to withhold mediation. The policy was unable to restrain the big well-organized unions in the public sector. It is arguable that this was responsible for the lack of effect of $n - 1$ on the private sector—that it was precisely the unions which could break through $n - 1$ that made key bargains with economywide consequences. The burden of the policy fell instead on the weaker public-sector unions, converted to militancy as a result of the previous administration's incomes policy, but unable to withstand the $n - 1$ policy. Thus a consequence of the policy was to increase the militancy of these unions further, and they withheld moderation from the Labour government in 1974. The immediate effect was to make the public-sector unions support the opposition to the Industrial Relations Act, although its impact fell largely on the private sector.

The Industrial Relations Act of 1971, or Fighting the Last War

Although the Conservatives enacted their Industrial Relations Act in the absence of an incomes policy, it was hoped that the changes it would bring about in the structure and conduct of bargaining would be conducive to less inflationary outcomes. If the act could increase the authority of the national unions at plant level, the incidence of wildcat strikes and wage drift would be reduced, the nationals could afford to conclude more moderate settlements, and the latter would not be supplemented by militant local groups and their shop stewards. In other words, the act was intended to validate the assumption of the 1950s that wage restraint could be secured through the moderation of the national unions. It was supposed to "create strong, but responsible unions."[55] The act followed the American National Labor Relations Act in broad outline, setting forth "unfair practices" proscribed to employers and to unions, safeguarding the rights of individuals to join or not to join unions, thereby outlawing the closed shop, and facilitating recognition of unions by employers. But the unions, while protected, were required to register their rules with a Registrar of Trade Unions and Employers Associations, who could withhold registration if the union rules failed to guarantee free and open elections and otherwise provide for democratic government (in ways reminiscent of those specified in the U.S. Landrum-Griffin Act). And registration was an important protection because only registered unions and their authorized agents—listed with the Registrar, who, it was assumed, would refuse registration if unions sought to include shop stewards as authorized agents—were exempted from a prohibition against inducing breach of contract in a labor dispute. Finally, contrary to previous law, collective agreements were presumed to be legally enforceable contracts unless the parties agreed in writing that they should not be. An unregistered union could be sued for damages arising out of a strike in breach of contract; a registered union could not. In these ways the act sought to minimize the incidence of wildcat strikes and thus bolster the authority of national unions over the shop stewards.

In protecting the individual employee against unfair dismissal, however, and allowing him independent access to judicial remedy, in the form of industrial referrals, the act was not consistent with the objective of strengthening the authority of the national union at the plant level. In thus protecting the right of the individual worker, the act followed the practice of Continental countries with labor court systems. In the United States, on the other hand, the individual is guaranteed only the right to present a grievance independently to his employer; under collective bargaining, the individual has recourse to a grievance procedure that usually provides for impartial arbitration as its final step, but whether and how far his case will be taken up is up to the union representatives. Under this system, "owning the grievance" reinforces the authority and

55. Brendon Sewill, "In Place of Strikes," in *British Economics Policy, 1970–74: Two Views,* Hobart Paperback no. 7 (London: Institute of Economic Affairs, 1975), p. 30. Sewill was an adviser to the Heath government.

influence of the national union at the work place and at the same time makes the officials of national unions more intimately acquainted with and responsive to sentiment among the members than would otherwise be the case.[56]

In any event, we know that the union leaders generally had no wish to have greatness thrust upon them in the form of increased authority over their shop stewards, and now that the influence of the latter had been reflected in the election of "left-wing" administrations in the two largest unions, the Transport Workers and the Engineers, there was little disposition to support an act that, in the process of conferring unwanted authority, restricted activities of the unions while offering largely unneeded protection.[57] With inadequately staffed national offices, moreover, many unions felt that if the act were successful it would adversely change the balance of power on the shop floor, at least in the short run: shop stewards would be deprived of the strike weapon, but no effective system of grievance resolution would take its place. After massive demonstrations, the TUC, in a special meeting, recommended against registration and cooperation with the Industrial Relations Court established under the act. Some unions—notably the Electricians, the General and Municipal Workers, the Local Government Officers, and other public-sector unions—in which the national officers in fact enjoyed a goodly measure of control over the shop stewards and where local bargaining was of less importance, were less strongly opposed to the act. But the extreme hostility aroused in the public sector by the $n - 1$ strategy, and then an episode in which five dock workers were jailed for contempt by the Industrial Relations Court in April 1972, prompted these unions to come off the register. In two instances, in 1972 and 1974, the Engineers refused to pay fines levied by the court; the response of the court was to sequester union funds, thereby touching off protest strikes. In the 1974 case, a nationwide engineering strike was threatened, but a group of anonymous donors paid into the court the sum awarded to the employer in question! In 1972, the National Union of Railwaymen aborted the government's cooling-off powers under the act, as noted earlier. In short, the unions successfully defied the law and the government.

Management, furthermore, especially in large-scale enterprises, was

56. Lloyd Ulman, "Connective Bargaining and Competitive Bargaining," *Scottish Journal of Political Economy*, vol. 21 (June 1974), pp. 97–109; A. W. J. Thomson and S. R. Engleman, *The Industrial Relations Act* (London: Martin Robertson, 1975), p. 67.

57. Clegg, *Industrial Relations*, pp. 463–64.

not eager to buckle on its new legal armor. A research team found that only three of the seventy-seven large companies that it surveyed even considered using the provisions of the law on strikes—and none did use them.[58] None of the companies surveyed that operated under closed-shop arrangements was willing to upset the status quo, although the status quo was now clearly illegal. And, although some small firms were willing to seek injunctions against stoppages by unions or shop stewards, firms with established bargaining relationships generally refrained from running the obvious risks involved in seeking to alter the balance of power on which those relationships had been erected.[59]

The movement in the direction of formal, institutionalized plantwide or companywide bargaining, moreover, to which we have already referred, had been advancing rapidly even before 1971, when the Industrial Relations Act was passed. In the United Kingdom, as elsewhere, this development was associated with moves by larger enterprises to control unit costs more effectively with the aid of such instruments as job evaluation and measured day work. The incentive to do so was especially great in Britain, where unit labor costs were rising more rapidly than in competing countries and where, under fixed rates of exchange, profitability was declining. Looser labor markets, characterized by higher unemployment after the mid 1960s, especially in 1971–72, provided a relatively favorable opportunity for management to make these moves. Thus the incidence of job evaluation doubled between 1968 and 1975–76,[60] and the number of measured day-work systems increased fourfold between 1968 and 1973.[61] At the same time, the incidence of single-employer bargaining rose throughout the 1970s and was regarded as the most important level of bargaining in three quarters of the companies included in a 1975 survey.[62] As single-employer bargaining became more important, so too did formal plantwide bargaining, which tended to replace fragmented bargaining on the shop floor. (As a result, base pay has been increasing in relation to earnings, while rates negoti-

58. Brian Weeks and others, *Industrial Relations and the Limits of Law* (Oxford: Basil Blackwell, 1975).

59. Ibid.

60. National Board for Prices and Incomes, *Job Evaluation*, Cmnd. 3772 (London: HMSO, 1968); William Wentworth Daniel, *Wage Determination in Industry* (London: Political and Economic Planning, 1976); Manab Thakur and Deirdre Gill, *Job Evaluation in Practice* (London: Institute of Personnel Management, 1976).

61. Office of Manpower Economics, *Measured Daywork* (London: HMSO, 1973).

62. Daniel, *Wage Determination in Industry*.

ated by industrywide associations have declined in relation to earnings.)[63] Thus the emergence of plantwide and companywide bargaining was associated with the relative decline of industrywide bargaining, on the one hand, and fragmented bargaining, on the other. But this convergence was not associated with an increase in the importance of national unions at plant level, as in the United States. Rather, it was responsible for an accrual of power by senior and full-time shop stewards, who owed their increased authority to the need both to operate under the new, broader systems of wage determination and to coordinate bargaining locally when more than one union is represented on the shop floor. For these reasons, management found less potential gain in a piece of legislation that was designed in good part to eliminate the lack of control produced by fragmented bargaining, which was already in decline, and to strengthen the authority of the national union, which was regarded as unrealistic, in view of the influence of shop stewards in the national unions, and unnecessary.

Deflation as a Policy

The third leg of the government's economic policy was a looser labor market. Already under the Labour government unemployment had risen from an average of less than 2 percent to around 2.5 percent in the late 1960s. The Labour government saw this, at least publicly, as regrettable, but outside the immediate control of economic policy. Heath, on the other hand, argued at the time that somewhat looser labor markets were a necessary condition of successful economic management.[64] The subsequent rise in unemployment, from 2.6 percent in 1970 to 3.5 percent in 1971 and 3.9 percent in 1972, had an effect on the rate of money wage increases. The rate of increase in hourly earnings declined from 14.9 percent in 1970 to 12.7 percent in 1972, and the rate of increase in wage rates in newly negotiated settlements fell from 12 percent in the first quarter of 1971 to 10 percent in the first quarter of 1972.[65]

But reliance on deflation highlighted its disadvantages. In the first place, the high level of unemployment reached in 1971 and maintained

63. Brown and Terry, "The Changing Nature of National Wage Agreements."
64. Colin Crouch, *Class Conflict and the Industrial Relations Crisis* (London: Heinemann, 1977).
65. OECD Economic Surveys, *United Kingdom,* January 1973, table 6, p. 19. The data quoted refer to wage-rate increases for the least well paid males and are unadjusted for change in the settlement period.

through the first half of 1972 appeared insufficient to insulate private-sector wage claims from public-sector key bargains. Following the coal and railway agreements early in 1972, the average rate of increase in new settlements rose from 10 percent in the first quarter of that year to 11.7 percent in the second quarter and 13.3 percent in the third quarter.

Second, while unemployment moderated increases in money wages in 1971, it failed to have a strong effect on the growth of real wages. With the benefit of hindsight the increase in the growth of real wages is seen to have been the most striking feature of the first half of the 1970s. The average growth rate of real wages, deflated by the CPI deflator, was 2.3 percent a year between 1961 and 1969; during the four years 1970 to 1973 it rose to 3.9 percent (see table 7-3).

While productivity grew more rapidly during this period, moreover, it did not offset the increase in real wages; between 1960 and 1969 GDP per capita grew at an annual rate of 2.5 percent, and between 1970 and 1973 (leaving out 1974, when productivity fell 1.0 percent), at 3.5 percent; in the three years 1970–72, productivity grew at 3.2 percent and real wages at 4.1 percent.

How was this strong wage pressure—in the face of increased unemployment—to be explained? Unemployment had been rising in relation to job vacancies since 1966, when earnings-related unemployment benefits and redundancy, or severance, payments were introduced; this has been interpreted by monetarists as indicating a rise in the equilibrium rate of unemployment, which made the economy more inflation-prone at higher levels of unemployment. An equation by Gray, Parkin, and Sumner estimated money wage increases on the basis of a cubed ratio of unemployment compensation to after-tax wages, as well as the inverse of unemployment squared and the expected change in prices. The results seem to have overproved the case, however: according to this specification, increased unemployment compensation doubled the "natural" rate of unemployment and increased wage inflation 50 percent between 1967 and 1974.[66] MacKay and Reid found a positive and statistically significant relation between duration of unemployment and amount of unemployment benefit (not of redundancy pay), but the relation was a weak one, implying that the introduction of the benefits would have accounted for about 12,000 out of 500,000 male redundancies in 1968.[67]

66. Comments by Michael Parkin and by Wynne A. H. Godley in Krause and Salant, *Worldwide Inflation*, pp. 480–81, 483, 485–88.

67. D. F. MacKay and G. L. Reid, "Redundancy, Unemployment, and Manpower Policy," *Economic Journal*, vol. 82 (December 1972), pp. 1268–69.

The rise in the unemployment–vacancy ratio, moreover, was also attributed to an alleged tendency of employers to "shake out" labor that was in excess of operating requirements.[68] While both the increase in benefits and the shakeout of labor tend in principle to increase unemployment in relation to job vacancies, they should exert opposite effects on the rate of wage increase, under competitive conditions. The increase in benefits should induce a withdrawal of supply, because it enables workers to prolong their search for better jobs—or to quit and search more frequently; this in principle exerts an upward influence on wages. But the shakeout, since it decreases the probability of finding any job in the relevant wage range, should induce workers to abandon their searches and accept employment sooner, or to quit less frequently, and thus tends to depress wage rates. Thus any inward shift in labor supply imparted by increased benefits is to some extent offset or outweighed by an outward shift imparted by the shakeout. The shakeout is also associated with an inward shift in demand which, since it reduces the probability of obtaining a job, is in fact responsible for the outward shift in supply; taken together, the two effects imply an increase in the excess supply of labor, at the going real wage. The countercyclical rise in the growth of labor productivity during the early 1970s suggests that the shakeout was a phenomenon of importance.

A more plausible explanation of the simultaneous rise in unemployment and increased growth in real wages attributes the former to the shakeout, together with insufficient aggregate demand, and the latter to the strength of union bargaining for real wages in the first period since the war in which the unions—outside the public sector—have engaged in "gloves-off" free collective bargaining. It had paid the unions to be moderate under the Conservatives during the 1950s and early 1960s, for in exchange the Conservatives forswore deflation, labor legislation, and incomes policy. But no such deal was available in 1970; instead, the unions had to react as best they could to a high rate of unemployment, the Industrial Relations Act, and $n - 1$. In the climate of the 1950s, moreover, moderation by the unions was widely believed to favor Labour's electoral chances; in the early 1970s the alternative argument, that only a Labour government could deal with militant unions, gained ground.

This left the Conservative government with two choices: increase unemployment or impose an economywide incomes policy. But unem-

68. OECD Economic Surveys, *United Kingdom,* January 1973, pp. 27–28.

ployment greater than 3 percent was politically unacceptable to many in the government; it is indeed arguable that the Treasury had not foreseen so substantial an increase in any case. Those politicians who favored expansion were joined by influential voices in industry. The main employers' body, the Confederation of British Industry (CBI), had already, in July 1971, undertaken an independent initiative. It obtained a written promise from 179 of its 200 largest affiliated firms in the private sector not to raise prices for the coming twelve months except when it was unavoidable and in no case in excess, of 5 percent. In return, the CBI expected the government to adopt reflationary policies, and it hoped that a combination of reduced unemployment and price moderation would elicit wage restraint from the unions. The voluntary approach of the CBI to incomes policy did not prove particularly effective, however, in inducing wage moderation. The confederation and its signatory firms did hold the line, and the rate of price increase did in fact decline, at both wholesale and retail levels, during 1971–72. But the CBI action affected only the prices of industrial goods; retail prices, to which wages would respond most sensitively, did not decline as much as wholesale prices, and, by the autumn of 1972, had begun to reaccelerate.[69]

The Conservative U-Turn: Incomes Policy, Reflation, and the Miners' Strike, Mid-1972 to February 1974

With the failure—or insufficiency—of voluntary price policy and the reacceleration of wage inflation, the government turned to a policy of direct wage restraint. In July 1972 it held a series of talks with the TUC and the CBI that linked a faster rate of growth of output, 5 percent, and real incomes to wage and price restraint—about 8 percent and 5 percent, respectively—together with a relative improvement in pensions and low-wage incomes.[70] Predictably, the talks failed to generate a voluntary consensus. The growing militancy through the 1960s of the two largest unions, the Transport and General Workers and the Engineers, and, of more recent origin, of the public-sector unions was greatly intensified by Conservative policies between 1970 and 1972. Explicit agreement involving wage restraint was thus not politically possible for the unions,

    69. Wyn Grant and David Marsh, *The CBI* (London: Hodder and Stoughton, 1977), p. 193.
    70. OECD Economic Surveys, *United Kingdom,* January 1973, p. 21.

whatever their leaders might have wanted. Indeed, what was surprising at the time was that the TUC was prepared to meet with the government at all.

The TUC was, however, aware of a growing flexibility through 1972 in the government's behavior, which modified the most important argument noted at the end of the preceding section favoring an uncompromising union attitude. On the other hand, the extent to which the unions could or would compromise was limited. The political opposition to a high rate of unemployment from within the Conservative party and the improvement of the world economy in 1972 made a general policy of reflation inevitable—though its size and duration might have been contingent on wage moderation. Nor did the de facto burial of the Industrial Relations Act—another carrot held out to the unions by the administration—depend on their good behavior: the act was already seen to be ineffective. Generalized union hostility to the government, belief that militancy was not against Labour's electoral interest, and awareness of the gains the unions could make with a Labour administration all combined to limit the natural caution of union leaders. But the government had raised an olive branch; even if barbed by wage control, outright rejection might seem impolitic. The compromise adopted by most unions was passive acquiescence in the statutory policy that the government now proposed.

The government's object, in fact, was not to enlist active and explicit union support: it sought rather, by generally conciliatory policy, to avoid systematic lack of union compliance on statutory wage restraint. Policies were geared to a rapid reflation of the economy. The government quietly discouraged attempts to enforce the collective bargaining provisions of the Industrial Relations Act.[71] And a conciliatory approach was further revealed in the design of the freeze and of the two subsequent stages of the incomes policy that followed it.

The standstill, or stage 1, which lasted from November 1972 until the end of March 1973, froze prices, rents, and dividends, as well as wages—although the freeze on dividends would not prevent profits from rising with the expansion of economic activity. Stage 2, which lasted from April to November 1973, was intended to allow bigger increases for poorly paid workers by giving groups of workers covered by negotiations discretionary authority over the distribution of aggregate increases

---

71. Weeks and others, *Industrial Relations*, pp. 227–28.

averaging up to £1 per person plus 4 percent—which came to about 8 percent—of the straight-time payroll. And it established an individual ceiling increase of £250. While no new increases could go into effect under stage 2 until twelve months had elapsed after the previous settlement, interim increases under agreements negotiated before the November freeze were permitted. Exceptions for increases in productivity, which were supported but abused under Labour's policies, were not permitted, but standard hours could be reduced to forty per week, vacations could be increased up to three weeks, and pension and redundancy plans could be improved. In addition, male-female pay differences could be reduced by as much as a third, although the requirement of the Equal Pay Act of 1970 that women's pay reach 90 percent of that of men by 1973 was suspended. The policy was administered vigorously and with limited discretion by a Pay Board, but the board could and did respect traditional and "equitable" wage differentials.[72]

Stage 3 was designed to run from November 1973 until July 1974, though a Labour government came to office in February 1974. A new maximum of 7 percent a head for the work group, or £2.25, was set, and the ceiling on the annual increase was raised from £250 to £350. In addition, an extra 1 percent "flexibility margin" was allowed for negotiated improvements in holidays or sick leave or "to remedy anomalies" in wage structures caused by the operation of the freeze (stage 1). This time extra increases, up to 3.5 percent, under new productivity arrangements were allowed, and so were premium payments, up to 20 percent of basic time rates, for working "unsocial hours." Sex wage differentials could now be reduced by as much as half. Moreover, wage indexation was introduced in the form of a "threshold" clause, whereby flat increases of forty pence a week would be allowed if the retail price index rose 8 percent during stage 3, and another forty pence for each 1 percent rise thereafter: this was fixed so as to keep the real wage of the average worker constant during stage 3.

There was a noticeable contrast between the conciliatory design of Heath's incomes policy and that of the preceding Labour administration. The latter had collided with a key tenet—comparability—of U.K. collective bargaining: Labour's Prices and Incomes Board had stressed the importance of efficiency, and it had linked allowable wage increases

72. See Crouch, *Class Conflict,* p. 135.

to improvements in productivity on a company-by-company basis; significant divergences had been permitted to develop between wage increases in different sectors. The 1973 policy, on the other hand, emphasized comparability: wage increases were to be the same across the board, with few exceptions. Where there were exceptions, they reflected union concerns—allowing interim increases under previously negotiated agreements, for example—and if the exceptions upset customary differentials these could be restored. The policy also accommodated a more recent concern of many unions, that of improving the position of less well paid workers. This was to be accomplished through the elements of flat-rate increases, union discretion on distribution within the work group, and the possibility of changing the male-female wage differential (of importance on account of less well paid women in the public sector); the evidence suggests that the incomes policy had little overall effect in this respect, except in reducing the sex differential.[73]

Thus the government sought to accommodate its policies to the special concerns of the unions sufficiently to permit it to moderate the growth of real wages, despite the fact that the TUC strongly opposed a statutory policy. Strikes involving the General and Municipal Workers, hospital workers, and civil servants were all resolved by concessions that the stage 2 code was found able to accommodate.[74] Even in the case of the coal miners, in which the strategy was to backfire with fatal results for both the policy and the government, the government had incorporated what it had thought were sufficient concessions—specifically tailored for the miners—into stage 3. And it was to counter the strongly expressed fears of the unions about accelerating price inflation that thresholds were introduced into this stage.

The government's strategy was not the result of an easy choice. Its underlying preoccupation was with the long-run decline in the profitability and international competitiveness of U.K. industry. Both had been made worse by the wage increases of 1970, which had more than extinguished the benefits of the 1967 devaluation. In addition, there was the problem, already apparent in mid 1972, of absorbing a sizable increase

73. See Ken Mayhew, "Incomes Policy and the Private Sector," pp. 72–99; R. Steele, "Incomes Policies and Low Pay," pp. 128–54; and Elliott and Fallick, "Income Policy and the Public Sector," pp. 100–27, and "Incomes Policies, Inflation, and Relative Pay: An Overview," pp. 246–63, all in Fallick and Elliott, eds., Incomes Policies, Inflation, and Relative Pay; and William Brown, "Incomes Policy and Pay Differentials," Oxford Bulletin of Economics and Statistics, vol. 38, no. 1 (February 1976), pp. 27–49.
74. Clegg, Industrial Relations, p. 471.

in the real cost of imported primary commodities. Finally, there was the well-founded belief that—because of real wage push from the public sector, among other factors—real wages would rise faster than productivity in 1972 and 1973 if policies were kept unchanged. In principle there were three possible courses:

1. Maintain unemployment at 3–3.5 percent; but this was inconsistent with union acquiescence in wage restraint; it would have been likely to imply faster growth of real wages than of labor productivity; it was, in any case, politically impossible.

2. Increase unemployment to whatever level was necessary to restrain the growth of real wages sufficiently; a fortiori, this was politically impossible.

3. Reduce unemployment sufficiently to induce union compliance in wage controls, thus moderating the growth of real wages, at the same time exploiting the existence of short-run increasing returns to labor to generate greater growth in productivity.

Figure 7-2 provides a rough idea of the government's argument. The top line represents maximum negotiable growth in real wages and the bottom line the minimum acceptable growth in real wages. The area between these two lines represents the zone of discretion of the union leaders. The reasoning of the government was that only to the left of D, with unemployment held at, say, 3 percent or less, would the unions be prepared to use their discretion, as shown by the dashed line; considerable reflation could with luck elicit considerable discretion; but too much reflation, implying really tight labor markets, and a rapid rise in the minimum acceptable growth in real wages carried the risk of greater growth in real wages. Reflation would also increase the rate of growth in productivity, at least in the short run, though at some point, F, this would turn down again as capacity constraints were encountered.

The government's objective was to choose the rate of unemployment so that the rate of growth of productivity would be higher than that of real wages. Course 1, with unemployment between 3 percent and 3.5 percent, was thus ruled out. In figure 7-2 only two ranges of unemployment rates allowed this objective to be achieved. They are indicated by the shaded areas. The range implied by course 2 was that of unemployment greater than the rate corresponding to point C. But such a policy—while it is economically viable and was the Thatcher strategy of 1979–81—was not even under contemporary political discussion. Course 3 was to reach the other feasible range between A and B. Since

Figure 7-2. *Real Wage Growth and Unemployment in the United Kingdom: The Government's Options in 1972–73*

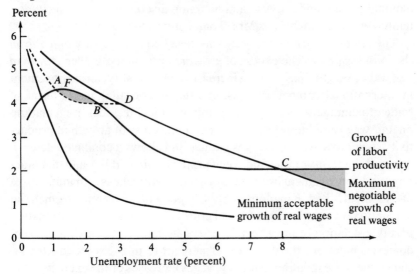

Percent

Unemployment rate (percent)

Growth of labor productivity

Maximum negotiable growth of real wages

Minimum acceptable growth of real wages

the government was uncertain about the shape of each of these curves, the policy was risky. All that was clearly indicated was a substantial reduction in unemployment.

These considerations emphasize the endogeneity of monetary and demand-management policy from mid 1972. Institutional realities demanded rapid reflation as a price of implicit union consent. Monetarist criticism of the "Barber boom"[75] is misleading, therefore, since monetary policy was not exogenous. In addition, British monetarists were overoptimistic in their estimates of the natural rate of unemployment. Their estimation of the natural rate of unemployment, based on data from the 1950s and 1960s, failed to take union discretion in wage bargaining into account. As argued here, the unions exerted moderation—that is, held down the actual real wage-bargaining schedule—for most of the postwar period, formally or informally. Econometrically, therefore, the natural rate of unemployment (in the early 1970s) could seem low—about 3 percent, but to rely on this for policy purposes in 1973 implied that unions would continue to use the average discretion they had used in the past, an implication which, after two years of conflict from 1970 to 1972 between government and unions, was wholly

75. So named after Heath's chancellor of the exchequer.

unwarranted. The true natural rate of unemployment in 1972–73—that is, the level of unemployment consistent with constant inflation, international price competitivity, and no union discretion—was almost certainly very much higher, as Mrs. Thatcher was to discover.

The prices and incomes policy was designed to work *economically* in the following way. The excess of growth in productivity over growth in real wages was to "pay" for an increase of profitability, an improvement in international competitiveness, and the deteriorating world terms of trade of manufactures for primary commodities. If prices are a markup on unit wage and import costs, a 1 percent excess of growth in productivity over growth in real wages implies and allows a combined deterioration of the terms of trade between primary commodities and manufactures and improvement in international competitiveness in manufactures of—in the United Kingdom—about 4 percent. The improvement in competitiveness is the sum of world price inflation less domestic inflation *plus* depreciation of the effective exchange rate. If, at existing rates of domestic inflation, the 4 percent–1 percent ratio is exceeded—for instance, because inflation in money wages increases or the exchange rate is pushed down faster—domestic inflation increases to restore the balance, by reducing growth in real wages or competitiveness.[76]

The overall economic policy of the government in 1972–73 was an important factor in the acceleration of inflation between 1973 and 1974, when the inflation of the GDP deflator rose from 9.0 percent to 15.4 percent and that of the retail price index from 9.2 percent to 16.0 percent. The immediate cause of the accelerating inflation was the substantial depreciation of the exchange rate throughout 1972 and 1973. This, combined with the deteriorating terms of trade, was much greater at existing inflation rates than the minimal excess of growth in productivity over growth in real wages that the incomes policy produced in 1973. Why the excessive depreciation? The government's problem was that a low rate of unemployment appeared to it as necessary to maximize the gap between growth in productivity and growth in real wages; but low unemployment directly caused both the current account and—engineered by an expansionary monetary policy—the capital account to grow worse. Thus the low-unemployment strategy that was conducive to incomes policy also produced a depreciating exchange rate. Within

76. For an explanation of the process, see Rudiger Dornbusch and Stanley Fischer, "Sterling and the External Balance," in Caves and Krause, eds., *Britain's Economic Performance*, p. 71.

limits the depreciation could have been moderated by the government by reducing reserves rather than increasing unemployment, and arguably the real criticism of 1972–73 was that the government's desired effective exchange rate policy was too ambitious. This may in turn have derived from an unrealistic belief in the efficacy of the incomes policy.

How successful was the policy?

Econometric results, as summarized in an excellent survey by Henry, suggest a small though clear effect.[77] The econometric test is unduly severe, however. The incomes policy was imposed during a period of rising inflation in the second half of 1972; insofar as the inflation was generated by factors not included in the econometric models, the dummy variables will be held econometrically responsible: thus incomes policy will appear to have been less effective than it was in fact.

The econometric models, furthermore, do not take into full account the militancy behind union bargaining in the first half of the 1970s. To the extent to which an increase in militancy is included in some of the models it is seen as a real wage catch-up after the incomes policy of the late 1960s. The size of the catch-up is calculated econometrically—very roughly—as the increase needed to return to the trend growth of real wages, when other relevant economic factors are held constant. But—if the argument offered earlier is valid—the unions have exerted a moderating influence on the growth of real wages throughout most of the postwar period; thus the trend growth of real wages is not a guide to union bargaining targets. The militancy of the early 1970s—with the absence of union moderation—may have aimed at higher real wage growth. This is certainly what is suggested by the data in table 7-3, showing growth of 2.3 percent a year in real wages for 1961–69 and 4.1 percent a year between 1970 and 1972. If, in fact, the unions were able to secure average increases in real wages of 4.1 percent a year when bargaining without restraint, what was the effect of the 1973 policy? Unemployment fell sharply in 1973, suggesting that real wages without bargaining restraint would have risen above the 1970–72 average, whereas they did not. A crude estimate of this might be gleaned from the fall in real wage inflation between 1970 and 1971, when unemployment rose by a similar amount. This suggests that real wages might have been moderated by about 3 or 4 percent. Very little reliance can be placed on such a figure, and it should not be taken as an estimate of the effectiveness

77. Henry, "Incomes Policy and Aggregate Pay," especially pp. 32–42.

of the policy; unfortunately, however, the proper way to evaluate the effect of unemployment on wage inflation—through econometric estimation—is vitiated by the moderation of union behavior in the 1950s and 1960s; since, as noted earlier, unions probably moderated wage demands as unemployment declined and price inflation increased, the econometric estimates of unemployment effects are smaller than in periods of unrestrained bargaining.

Case study evidence supports the view that the incomes policy was indeed, within limits, effective. This was the conclusion of William Brown's study of forty engineering factories.[78] In each of the three stages he showed that male grades kept close to the various norms, while women received substantially greater increases in stages 2 and 3, as was permitted. Clegg noted that there were problem industries, of which construction and road haulage were examples, "but the general impression was that the codes were widely followed."[79]

Some of the merits of the policy through 1973 have been mentioned. It was designed, as far as possible, not to conflict with union concerns, it was clearly set out, and there were few loopholes. The Pay Board and Price Commission had limited discretion and did not aim for improvements in productivity and bargaining structures, as had the NBPI, but the increased formalization of bargaining structures, which the NBPI had been instrumental in initiating, greatly aided the administration of the 1973 incomes policy. Finally the strict application of price policy—permitting wage increases to be passed on only if they were consistent with the incomes policy—provided the strong incentive toward compliance by firms, which were increasingly aware of their problems of low profitability.

The policy, however, rested on union acquiescence. While most unions were prepared to accept the incomes policy passively, the miners were not, and the others were not disposed to prod this rogue elephant back into the herd as they had done with the TGWU under Cousins in the late 1950s. Indeed, in 1973–74 the other unions provided both material and psychological aid to the miners.

The National Union of Mineworkers (NUM) demanded a 25 percent raise in the fall of 1973, before stage 3 went into effect. The miners were in a very strong bargaining position, and their top leaders included some

78. Brown, "Incomes Policy and Pay Differentials."
79. Clegg, *Industrial Relations*, p. 470. This conclusion is in part based on an earlier version of Brown, "Incomes Policy and Pay Differentials."

who were politically militant, including Communists and other leftists. In March, a referendum of the members had rejected a strike call by the executive by a two-to-one margin, but that probably led both the moderate president of the NUM, Joe Gormley, and the government to overestimate the moderation of the rank and file. The union had demonstrated its bargaining power in 1972, with the support of the rail and transport workers, the labor movement as a whole, and the general public. And now its position was further strengthened by higher levels of activity among the industrial consumers of coal and, above all, by the oil price increase in the fall of 1973, which drastically increased the importance of the industry in the mind of the general public and its official servants. The government and the National Coal Board were not unaware of these developments, so they attempted to tailor stage 3 to the requirements of the bargaining situation in coal, as they understood them. While stage 3 could not allow an increase in base rates in excess of 7 percent, it did allow for shift premiums for "unsocial hours," for productivity bonuses, for the elimination of "anomalies," and so on. This flexibility permitted the Coal Board to offer a raise of 13 percent plus an additional 3.5 percent contingent on the negotiation of a productivity agreement. It announced this offer proudly—"like a Christmas tree with a lot of presents on it"—but, in so doing, it left itself without a fallback position and it virtually invited the union to hold out for its original demand. This it did by insisting on an above-norm rise in the basic rate. Then the government, led by Prime Minister Heath, dug its heels in. It brushed aside various face-saving alternatives, including an offer from the TUC—but not its autonomous affiliates—to treat the miners as a special case outside stage 3. Following a ban on overtime, the union went out on strike. The government responded by ordering a three-day work week. Heath charged that the strike was a politically motivated effort by "Communists and left-wing extremists" to overturn the statutory policy and the government itself. The union militants were happy to agree with Heath on this point; in fact the Executive Council of the NUM, which was dominated by the left wing, had refused to allow the Coal Board's offer to be voted on by the members. This view won support in various public opinion polls, but when the prime minister called an election in February 1974 and fought it on the question "Who governs Britain?" he lost. The strike, which lasted twelve weeks, was settled under a new Labour government, and the miners, having demanded 25 percent, wound up with 29 percent.

The final failure of Heath's incomes policy suggests that a distinction can be drawn between two degrees of union acquiesence, depending on whether the other unions are prepared to enforce acquiescence on unions ("rogue elephants") that do not follow the policy. In the late 1950s the potential rogue-elephant union was the TGWU under Cousins; the other unions, aware of their overall interest in preserving moderation, went—as has been seen—to great lengths to prevent Cousins from moving out of line, and despite the power of the TGWU, they were broadly successful. The TUC Report of 1958 describes the reaction of the other main union leaders to the TGWU bus strike of that year; the General Council of the TUC

were convinced, as was Mr. Cousins himself, that an extension of the strike whether initiated by the union itself or on the recommendation of the General Council, would transform the strike from an industrial issue into a much wider conflict with political implications. But they disagreed with Mr. Cousins in that they did not think that the wages and standard of living of all workers in all industries depended on the outcome of the busmen's strike. . . . On the contrary, they thought that an extension of the strike, which would necessarily bring the unions concerned into direct conflict with the Government, would end in a failure which would be disastrous for the whole Trade Union Movement.[80]

Social Contracts and Stagflation: Labour in Office, February 1974–May 1979

In one respect at least the new government had less room in which to maneuver than either its Conservative predecessor or the previous Labour administration. Wilson and Heath had each attempted statutory incomes-policy and industrial-relations legislation. But when the new Labour government took office, neither of these options was available, for two reasons. The first is found in the circumstances surrounding the coal strike and the February election in 1974: the miners were seen to have dispatched both birds—the Industrial Relations Act, whose emergency provisions were never invoked during the emergency, and Heath's statutory incomes policy—with one strike. But of greater importance was the one-sided rapprochement between the Labour party and the TUC that occurred after Labour's defeat in the 1970 election.

The 1970 defeat was widely blamed on Wilson, who found himself isolated on the right of the party. His lack of left-wing support had been

80. *Trades Union Congress Report, 1958,* pp. 136–37.

the predictable consequence of the failure of economic planning, the lack of socialist legislation, and support for the United States in Vietnam; more serious was the alienation of the center of the party—and indeed many on the right—as a result of deflation and labor legislation. This alienation was felt in the parliamentary party, in the constituencies, and above all in the unions. The delicate compromise between the industrial and political wings of the party—that a Labour government would guarantee full employment and abstain from interference in collective bargaining in return for union support and noninterference in "political" questions—had collapsed.

Neither the Labour party nor its leaders can easily survive in opposition without the financial and political backing of the unions. Thus Wilson, without power or support, had no real choice but to move toward the unions. As in the early 1930s, the combination of weak party leaders and strong, politically united unions led the latter to impose their authority on the former. The center of equilibrium of the unions by the early 1970s was significantly to the left. This was especially true of the TGWU, under Jack Jones, and the AUEW, under Hugh Scanlon; public-sector unions had also moved in this direction. The degree of union left-wing political activism must not be exaggerated: certainly most union officials and shop stewards were not politically militant. And, although the statement is subject to many qualifications, union leaders moved toward the left for industrial relations rather than ideological reasons. The left within the TGWU and the AUEW in the 1950s had sought their constituency among the shop stewards in the assembly-line industries, because of opposition on the shop floor to the wage restraint that the right-dominated national unions sought to impose; the growth of this constituency had brought Jack Jones and Hugh Scanlon to power in their unions. This constituency grew because it represented the increasing numerical importance of semiskilled workers, and thus to the autonomy of the shop stewards was linked an egalitarian policy on skill differentials. Equally, egalitarian pay policy became important in the public-sector unions after the strikes of 1969 and 1970. The left-wing nucleus in the TGWU and the AUEW, moreover, provided a natural pole around which other more politically moderate unions could gather to express their opposition to government policies from the mid 1960s onward.

In 1972, the growing importance of the unions in Labour policy formation was institutionalized in a Liaison Committee, on which the

TUC was represented equally with the party's National Executive Committee and with its parliamentary leadership. The National Executive was further to the left than the parliamentary leaders, so the balance of the Liaison Committee was left-wing. At the same time, the unions were concerned about Labour electorally, so they were prepared to accommodate—up to a point—the need of the party leaders to present a coherent economic policy. What emerged was the British version of the social contract, whose chief architect was Jack Jones, the general secretary of the TGWU, with its 2 million members. Jones's interest in a social contract included a desire to strengthen both the political and the industrial wings of the labor movement by swapping elements of bargaining autonomy for redistributive public policies and also for increased power of the union over managerial decisionmaking. Statutory control over wages had no part in the agreement: indeed, the union side did not commit itself to any form of government wage policy.[81] The TUC was prepared, however, to instruct its member unions to ensure that, with exception for the poorly paid, real wages did not increase in 1974, and the party was allowed, in its 1974 Manifesto, to "believe that the action we propose on prices, together with the understanding with the TUC on the lines which we have already agreed, will create the right economic climate for money incomes to grow in line with production."[82] Those lines of agreement came to include redistributive measures to help the poorly paid and the poor, including a wealth tax; price and rent control; greater protection against dismissals and layoffs; repeal of the restrictive provisions of the Industrial Relations Act; "democracy in management" through union representation on boards of directors; and further nationalization of industry.[83] It was made clear that a future Labour government would have to maintain full employment, and, as public-sector employer, it would have to be prepared to allow particular leeway to unions that made claims on behalf of the less well paid workers. In seeking to explain why the Labour government of 1974 behaved as it did, it is essential to bear in mind the extent to which it felt that its hands were tied.

Although Labour was able to form only a minority government after the February 1974 election, it promptly began the process of repealing

81. Minkin, "British Labour Party," p. 33.
82. Quoted in Panitch, *Social Democracy*, p. 233.
83. See John Elliott, *Conflict or Cooperation? The Growth of Industrial Democracy* (London: Kogan Page, 1978), pp. 25–32.

those provisions of the Industrial Relations Act that the TUC had found objectionable, including the unfair practices and the prohibition on wildcat strikes, the special court, and the registrar. The new Trade Union and Labor Relations Act, however, strengthened provisions providing recourse and redress for the victims of unfair dismissals; by allowing dismissals for nonmembership under "union membership agreements," moreover, the new act ensured the legality of the closed shop, despite subsequent amendments in the House of Lords to protect against dismissal any employee who refused to join a union on "any reasonable grounds" or because he was a newspaper editor.[84] The following year, the government passed the Employment Protection Act of 1975, which established an independent agency and a union recognition procedure which, unlike the procedure under the defunct Industrial Relations Act, could be initiated only by unions. It provided that particular groups of employees should be entitled to enjoy " 'the general level of terms and conditions' in the industry and region." It also provided that plant-safety representatives, who in turn had been provided for in a health and safety law of 1974, be union appointees.[85]

The Labour government was not able to enact "industrial democracy" legislation, but it was not for want of trying. A committee of inquiry was appointed in 1975,

accepting the need for a radical extension of industrial democracy in the control of companies by means of representation on boards of directors, and accepting the essential role of trade union organisations in this process, to consider how such an extension can best be achieved, taking into account in particular the proposals of the Trades Union Congress Report on industrial democracy.[86]

The majority report of this committee—the Bullock Committee—hewed closely to the TUC line, which, in general, sought to overcome union opposition to the creation of participatory management institutions in the firm by recommending that such institutions be dominated by the trade unions themselves. Thus it recommended that the initiative in proposing a balloting of employees on the question of whether worker directors should be placed on the board of a large company—in numbers equal to shareholder directors—be confined to members of the union or unions in the establishment involved and that, if the requisite majority

84. Clegg, *Industrial Relations*, pp. 479–80.
85. Ibid., p. 487.
86. *Report of the Committee of Inquiry on Industrial Democracy* (London: HMSO, January 1977), p. v.

vote was obtained, the worker directors be nominated only by a Joint Representation Committee of the unions concerned. This was dubbed the "single channel of worker representation," which had been strongly propounded by Jack Jones.[87] The establishment of company joint representation committees, which would be interunion institutions, would have increased the authority of senior shop stewards within their respective national unions and thus would have reinforced the impetus imparted by the development of company-level bargaining. The proposals of the Bullock Committee would thus have ratified the shift in the locus of bargaining power from the shop floor to the senior shop stewards; it would also have given the stewards a measure of institutional protection while carrying the burden of administering a tough real-incomes policy from mid 1975 onward. (The opposition to the Bullock proposals from the Electricians and the General and Municipal Workers reflected at least in part the control that their national officers could exercise over their shop stewards.[88]) At the same time the report would have ratified the downward shift in the locus of bargaining power from the national unions to the company or plantwide level; but the social contract—of which industrial democracy was but one part—was supposed to compensate the national unions for any possible loss of importance in collective bargaining with an enhancement of their political importance. The latter would result from their bargaining with the government over social and economic policies, including policies that would more closely direct the activities of the firms in which the shop stewards would now form part of management.[89] The approach of the Bullock report evoked strong managerial and public criticism for assigning as much power to the trade unions and their designated directors as it did. By 1976 Labour had lost its small majority in the House of Commons as a result of by-election defeats and relied on Liberal parliamentary support. The government had therefore to content itself with a white paper in which, while envisaging legislation, it refrained from committing itself to the Bullock procedures sketched out above.

The white paper on industrial democracy, however, did favor imposing a statutory obligation on employers

to discuss with the representatives of employees all major proposals affecting the employees of the business before decisions are made. These discussions

87. Elliott, *Conflict or Cooperation?* pp. 207–08.
88. See B. C. Roberts, "Participation by Agreement," *Lloyds Bank Review*, no. 125 (July 1977), pp. 12–23.
89. Elliott, *Conflict or Cooperation?* p. 36.

would encompass such matters as investment plans, mergers, takeovers, expansion or contraction of establishments and other organizational changes.[90]

The obligation of management to bargain over investment and employment plans is certainly a key—and highly controversial—substantive characteristic of employee participation in management. But job protection can exist in the absence of participation. The Employment Protection Act furthered job protection by providing for guaranteed pay during layoffs and by extending the mandatory period of notice prescribed in the Contracts of Employment Act to two to three months; this extension, according to Clegg, "comes near to an instruction to bargain over redundancy."[91]

Job protection was implemented by subsidy programs which Britain, like many other countries, instituted during the international recession that began in 1974. The most important of these was the Temporary Employment Subsidy (TES), which was begun in August 1975. Under TES, firms received a weekly subsidy of £20 for as long as twelve months in cases in which redundancies of at least ten workers in full-time jobs were threatened; subsequently, a reduced supplementary subsidy was made available for an additional six months. Between 1975 and 1977, this scheme was estimated to have deterred layoffs of about 200,000 workers. Subsidized firms took business away from others, however, who then required subsidies themselves, so the net gain was "possibly half the recorded figures," according to the OECD. The OECD went on to warn that "if TES was successful in reducing unemployment, in maintaining equipment and manpower during the recession, its extension over a longer period bears the risk of reinforcing distortions in the productive sector by promoting the inefficient use of labour and by supporting inefficient firms at the expense of unsubsidised establishments."[92] This caveat would apply with particular force to those instances in which illiquid enterprises, usually under strong pressure from trade unions and often in declining industries, such as textiles, were granted extensive subsidies under arrangements that ranged from loans to complete government ownership. Through their political influence, unions magnified their ability to secure and protect make-work arrangements. Thus, nationalization, which was included in the unions' social-contract demands, can be said to have been extended in furtherance of job protection under the Labour government—and frequently under

90. *Industrial Democracy*, Cmnd. 7231 (London: HMSO, 1978).
91. Clegg, *Industrial Relations*, p. 485.
92. OECD Economic Surveys, *United Kingdom*, March 1978, pp. 53–55, n. 55.

specific pressures from trade unions. It must be added, however, that this instrument had been deployed by Conservative governments as well.

The last observation raises the question as to whether the adoption of these and other job-protection devices can be regarded as performance by the Labour government under the terms of a social contract. Indeed, the same question can be raised concerning the legislation of institutional protection. A contract requires consideration. Provision by the Labour government of institutional protection and job protection, and also of other types of compensation to be considered later, can be regarded as performance under a social contract only if they were made conditions of wage restraint by the unions. To what extent was there such self-restraint?

The Labour government's attempts at wage restraint can be divided into three periods. The first, marked by limited success, lasted until mid 1975. From mid 1975 until mid 1977, a second period of incomes policy—generally regarded as highly effective—led to a significant decline in real wages, although those who have questioned the responsibility of incomes policy for this decline point to the coincident rise in unemployment from the level of between 2 percent and 3 percent that characterized the early 1970s to between 5 percent and 6 percent. During the third period, from mid 1977 to the demise of the Labour government in early 1979, unemployment remained at this level, and the unions refused publicly to support wage restraint but attempted to do so privately.

The economic debacle of 1974–75 consisted of a sharp drop in profitability—the pretax real rate of return of industrial and commercial companies, exclusive of North Sea oil operations, fell from 9.1 percent in 1973 to 6.0 percent in 1974 and 5.2 percent in 1975—and a further large twist to the inflationary spiral, which rose from 9.4 percent in 1973 to 16.0 percent in 1974 to 24.2 percent in 1975 (see tables 7-2 and 7-3). Competitiveness measured as the relative average value of manufactured exports improved marginally, but this was not true of relative current unit costs, which rose 2.6 percent between 1973 and 1974 and a further 2.0 percent between 1974 and 1975.[93]

Inflation continued to accelerate throughout this period because of the massive decline in the terms of trade. To have avoided inflation would have required a compensating reduction in real wages in relation

93. Dornbusch and Fischer, "Sterling and the External Balance."

to productivity on the order of 3 percent or a compensating decline in U.K. competitiveness by a revaluation or by a faster rise in U.K. prices than in world prices plus the rate of depreciation of the currency. There was arguably a small decline in competitiveness, but real wages rose and productivity fell. Profitability declined, partly because businesses were unwilling to jeopardize competitiveness, partly because of the continuing effect of price controls, and partly because money wages were increased rather rapidly to compensate for price increases.

Much of the blame for the acceleration of inflation and decline in profitability has been laid on the Labour government and the trade unions. The Labour government, however, was a prisoner of the unions at this stage—or believed itself to be—and the union leaders, with whom Wilson was now in close communication, were conscious of the militancy of the union movement. The government believed that the best it could get from the unions was that they would attempt to keep real wages constant. The TUC responded broadly along these lines in a document entitled "Collective Bargaining and the Social Contract." It provided its own guidelines for collective bargaining, according to which wage increases were not to exceed increases in the cost of living, as allowed under the threshold provisions, although in furtherance of its egalitarian approach special allowance could be made for women and less well paid workers in general. The TUC guidelines also provided that the unions continue to observe a decent interval—of twelve months—between negotiations. Given the growth of real wages between 1970 and 1973, the TUC's zero norm for increases in real wages was not an empty gesture.

One criticism of the 1974–75 policy was that it did not envisage a reduction in real wages. Had it been within the government's power to engineer such a reduction, a zero real-wage growth policy would have been mistaken. But in 1974 it was within the power neither of the government nor of the national unions to reduce real wages. A related criticism was that the Labour government retained a controversial feature, the threshold provision, of the previous administration's incomes policy after its stage 3 had statutorily expired in July 1974. The threshold provisions—which gave increases of 40 pence a week for every 1 percent by which the retail price index rose above the initial 7 percent over its level in October 1973 and thus provided 100 percent indexation for the average wage earner—were allowed to remain in force until November. Between May and November 1974, eleven threshold

Table 7-6. *Real Earnings, Unemployment, and Differentials, United Kingdom, 1970–79*
Percent

Year	Growth rate of real earnings per capita, total employees[a] (1)	Retail price inflation[b] (2)	Rate of unemployment[c] (3)	Growth rate of earnings, old series[d] (4)	Growth rate of real earnings based on old series[e] (5)	Private/public pay ratio, male manual worker[f] (6)	Private/public pay ratio, female manual worker[f] (7)
1970	5.8	6.4	2.6	12.1	5.4	100.0	100.0
1971	1.6	9.4	3.5	11.3	1.8	99.0	98.1
1972	4.8	7.1	3.9	12.9	5.4	96.5	94.9
1973	3.2	9.2	2.7	13.5	3.9	97.2	97.0
1974	3.3	16.0	2.6	17.8	1.6	96.0	92.8
1975	2.9	24.2	3.9	26.5	1.9	87.9	87.3
1976	-3.0	16.5	5.3	15.6	-0.8	89.4	90.1
1977	-4.8	15.8	5.7	10.2	-4.8	91.2	93.5
1978	5.5	8.3	5.7	14.5	5.7	92.8	97.0
1979	2.5	13.4	5.4	15.6	1.9	93.4	100.2

a. Table 7-3, col. 1.
b. Table 7-2, col. 2.
c. Table 7-2, col. 3.
d. *Department of Employment Gazette*, vol. 88, no. 6 (June 1980), p. 701; covers mainly production industries.
e. Calculated from cols. 4 and 2.
f. From Dean, "Public and Private Sector Pay and the Economy," p. 53.

payments were made in response to sharply rising retail prices—about 16 percent annually.[94] Here again institutional constraints stayed Wilson's hand. The TUC, conscious of rank-and-file fears of inflation, saw this as the sugar on the pill of wage restraint. Hence union leaders attached importance to the thresholds, and—if they were seen as necessary for union acceptance of zero growth in real wages—the fact that zero growth was guaranteed by the thresholds was not in itself an argument against them.

The more substantive criticism of the behavior of the unions is that they did not deliver on zero growth in real wages, and of the government that it did not follow a deflationary policy: unemployment, at 2.6 percent in 1974, was at its lowest level since the late 1960s. The data on growth in real wages in 1974 have to be interpreted carefully. Economywide real earnings rose 3.3 percent in 1974 (see table 7-6, column 1); real earnings computed from the Department of Employment earnings data (old series), however, show an increase of only 1.6 percent. The latter statistics are based on an inquiry that covers about 40 percent of the work force, primarily in industry (see table 7-6, columns 4 and 5). The former are derived from national income statistics and include the public sector.

A tentative reconstruction of wage developments in 1974 and early 1975 is the following: the strongest pressures for wage increases that confronted the Labour government in 1974 came from newly militant workers in the public sector—such as nurses, local government officers, postal workers, and schoolteachers—whose militancy had been insufficient to counter the $n - 1$ strategy; the unions believed that there would have to be significant concessions to such groups and, through comparability, to much of the public sector. This belief was reinforced by the difficulty of insulating a spillover from the miners' settlement into the rest of the public sector. The large number of poorly paid female workers in the public sector, moreover, made such a strategy consistent with the egalitarian goals of the larger unions. It seems likely that some unions, particularly the AUEW and the TGWU, pursued a policy during this period of compression of differentials in the private sector as well as the public sector. Statistically, the substantial changes in the differentials between the two sectors can be seen in table 7-6, columns 6 and 7. The compression of differentials within the private sector was less marked

94. OECD Economic Surveys, *United Kingdom*, March 1975, p. 12.

Table 7-7. *Skill Differentials in Engineering, United Kingdom, 1963–79*

Ratio of hourly earnings of skilled workers to hourly earnings of laborers

Year	Workers paid according to time spent	Workers paid according to results	Year	Workers paid according to time spent	Workers paid according to results
1963	143	146	1971	144	149
1964	144	148	1972	141	148
1965	143	148	1973	138	143
1966	145	150	1974	137	138
1967	145	152	1975	132	132
1968	144	150	1976	128	131
1969	144	151	1977	128	133
1970	144	148	1978	129	133
			1979	130	131

Source: Ken Mayhew, "Incomes Policy and the Private Sector," in Fallick and Elliott, eds., *Incomes Policies, Inflation, and Relative Pay*, p. 87.

and took place over a longer period—1972–73 to 1975–76 in engineering, as shown in table 7-7.

The suggestion is that the economywide increase of 3.3 percent in real earnings was primarily the result of exceptionally high wage increases in the public sector, which the unions were unable or unwilling to moderate. On the other hand, wage increases in industry were held back to a level much closer to the promised zero growth in real wages. The low increases in industry suggest that there was significant moderation by the unions during 1974–75 and that perhaps some unions, for ideological reasons as well as to cope with internal militancy, bargained higher wage increases for less well paid workers.

The antideflation policy of the government was linked to union wage restraint and more generally to the influence of the unions on Labour policy in 1974. The standard criticism of the low unemployment was that it pushed the real wage higher than it would otherwise have been. But in the government's perception, deflation carried the real risk that the unions would cease to exercise restraint; statistical evidence can throw no light on the risk, but it shows that increases in real wages in industry were minimal at low levels of unemployment. So we suggest that the low-unemployment policy did not produce high growth in real wages; a higher rate of unemployment might have increased real wages because of union withdrawal of discretion, and, in any case, the political influence

of the unions at this stage did not allow the government
deflationary policy.

The high level of aggregate demand was also related to the
wage growth between the public and private sectors. Rapid
public-sector wages can increase inflationary pressures in
through increased taxes, if the budget deficit is unaffected, or through
depreciation of the exchange rate, if an increased deficit spills into the
balance of payments. The government neither increased taxes on the
scale necessary to keep the deficit constant nor allowed a depreciation
of the currency until the last quarter of 1974. Instead, it absorbed the oil
price increases and the low unemployment, in relation to that in other
countries, in a growing payments deficit. This it could do in the short run
because of the increased demand for sterling balances by members of
OPEC. But by early 1975 the contradictions in the government's strategy
were becoming clearer. Inflation was accelerating—to nearly 30 percent
during the first half of the year—because real wages in the private sector
had not fallen to compensate for the decline in the terms of trade, and
additional inflationary pressure came from the depreciation of the
currency. At the same time, the seriousness of the external position
emerged as external holders reduced their sterling balances.

By 1975 the "best" strategy permitted by institutional constraints
during the preceding year had led to the most serious economic situation
of the postwar period. The government now let unemployment rise and
gambled that the external balance constraints would shock the domestic
institutional constraints into permitting an altogether more restrictive
policy on wages.

In July 1975, the government took the initiative in proposing an
incomes policy that was designed to reduce inflation, to restore international confidence in the currency, and to rebuild profitability and
competitiveness. In proposing the new one-year counterinflation policy,
or phase 1, the government anticipated a reduction in the rates of both
wage and price inflation to 10 percent and also, because of the expected
lag of price increases behind cost increases, a decline in real wages
during the first eight months.[95] It was to be enforced through the price
code, under which employers could not pass along above-norm wage
increases in higher prices, and also through the introduction of cash
limits on spending by central and local governments. It was claimed that

95. Ibid., February 1976, p. 30.

the policy would reduce unemployment, but fiscal and monetary policies were not relaxed. It became clear that the government was aiming for a higher level of unemployment, at least in the medium term. Behind this were two considerations. First was the need for external equilibrium in a depressed world economy without resort to protection. In the second place it was now assumed that an incomes policy would be easier to administer in a looser labor market. The unemployment was not to fall on well-organized primary-sector workers, however; they were protected informally by government pressure and formally by the measures described earlier.

The TUC envisaged a different approach from that of the government. It accepted the necessity for wage restraint, but not for unemployment. Attributing the unemployment to the state of the world economy, the TUC proposed a comprehensive system of controls on imported manufactured goods; concurrently, price controls were to be tightened to prevent increased profit margins. This approach conformed more closely to the political orientation of the leaders of the larger unions, who sought a return to the full employment of the 1950s and to whom an unemployment rate of 5 percent was deeply shocking. Yet it is a remarkable fact that the TUC, which had virtually been able to dictate policy to the Labour leaders during the previous five years, not only accepted without serious demur the government's new strategy, but also proceeded for the next two years to implement wage restraint with great effectiveness.

Why was this? The Labour government of February 1974 did not have an overall majority, and although this was remedied in the second General Election of 1974 in November, the margin was paper thin. By 1976, moreover, as a result of by-election losses, the Labour government had to turn to the small middle-of-the-road Liberal party for parliamentary support. During 1974 the government believed that even had pressure on the unions been politically possible within the Labour party, it was not electorally sensible: the oil price increases were held responsible for inflation, and there was considerable public sympathy for the miners and other public-sector groups. But as inflation soared in 1975, the unions were seen, and to a growing extent saw themselves, as the cause. Thus tougher wage restraint was perceived by the unions as necessary to maintain Labour in office.

At this stage the unions had few doubts about their preferences for a Labour government. The Conservative party was in the process of moving to the right. Its monetarist doctrines promised still higher unemployment. And the pro-union legislation of 1974–75, as well as parts of the welfare state, were seen as under serious threat from a future Conservative administration.

The fact or likelihood of Labour dependence on the Liberals gave the government considerable power over the unions. The choice between a strategy of import controls and low unemployment on the one hand and free trade with high unemployment on the other became an argument over a controlled economy. Since the Liberals, who had less at stake in maintaining Labour in office, shared the hostility of the Labour leaders to controls, the TUC had no real choice. Within the unions, moreover, to the chagrin of their left-wing leaders, there was little objection to an increase in unemployment that fell on the less heavily unionized sectors of the economy.

Aside from general considerations, specific factors favored tighter wage restraint. The new policy honored the adherence to egalitarianism of the social contract in that it provided for a flat-rate wage norm—of £6—as well as an income ceiling, £8,500 a year, above which no increases were allowed. This form of policy was especially agreeable to Jack Jones, whose Transport and General Workers included a large proportion of poorly paid workers among its members. This appealed also to some of the public-sector unions. In any case their militancy had much abated as a result of the large change in public-private differences in 1974–75.

The pay settlements in the fall of 1975, covering 3 million workers, generally conformed to the new policy. Weekly base rates declined from 30.5 percent in the first half of 1975 to 24–25 percent in the second half.[96] Unemployment continued to increase throughout the year, but since earnings increased almost as much in the second half of 1975 as they had in the first half, the decline in base rate increases seemed to reflect a strong measure of compliance with phase 1. During the entire phase 1 period, moreover, the annual increase in hourly earnings declined to 14 percent, or about half the rate of increase in the corresponding period in 1974–75.[97]

In the light of the improved inflationary situation and also of an improvement in the current account, the government was considering some easing of fiscal and monetary policy in early 1976. But it also wanted to replace phase 1 with a successor when it expired at the end of July. So the budget introduced by the chancellor of the exchequer in

96. Ibid., table 1, p. 6.
97. Ibid., March 1977, p. 6.

April, while not notably stimulatory on the expenditure side, included a novel feature on the revenue side. It made a reduction in personal income taxes contingent on acceptance by the TUC of a new policy, phase 2, with a pay norm of 3 percent.[98] The TUC, at the April meeting of the General Council, agreed to strive for "a package which would ensure that the tax allowances proposed conditionally by the Chancellor [be] implemented, coupled with an agreement on a pay figure somewhat higher than the three percent mentioned in the Budget."[99] The TUC also insisted that there be "progress on a range of issues such as prices, unemployment, import controls and investment." Nothing was done about import controls, but a new policy was agreed on, phase 2, which allowed maximum weekly increases of 5 percent, between a minimum of £2.50 and a maximum of £4; the maximum had earlier been £6. It was estimated that, after allowance had been made for the maintenance of wage differentials in one form or another, earnings would rise 8 percent—but this would still be substantially less than the rate of increase under phase 1.[100] At the same time, price controls continued to be relaxed in order to encourage new investment, and the old "productivity deduction," which allowed firms to recover only 80 percent of increases in labor costs, was dropped. Food subsidies, moreover, were reduced.

During the second half of 1976, weekly wage rates and average earnings rose at annual rates of 10.6 percent and 11.6 percent, respectively, but during the following half year—the first half of 1977—these rates of increase dropped to 4.1 percent in weekly rates and 8.4 percent in earnings. While wage inflation was decelerating, inflation of consumer prices increased—from 12.8 percent in the last half of 1976 to 17.2 percent in the first half of 1977. At a result, real earnings, which had declined at an annual rate of 1.2 percent in the former period, declined at a rate of 7 percent in the latter. Britain's relative unit labor costs declined, and that helped exports to increase sharply, which in turn helped the current account to move into surplus. At the same time, unemployment continued its climb from 2.6 percent in 1974 to 5.5 percent in the second half of 1976 and remained at that level in the following half year, although employment—in the private manufacturing sector—rose slightly. Thus it appeared that by the beginning of 1977 wages were more restrained

98. The budget also included unconditional tax relief for old people and on child allowances, which in itself was consistent with TUC objectives. See ibid., p. 17, n. 17.

99. Trades Union Congress, *The Social Contract, 1976–77*, para. 11.

100. OECD Economic Surveys, *United Kingdom*, March 1977, p. 26.

than prices, unemployment remained high, and the external danger to the economy had abated considerably.

The social contract—at least in explicit form—did not prove to be a permanent arrangement. In 1977 the TUC passed the following resolution:

This Congress welcomes the continued reduction in the annual rate of inflation which has arisen largely as a result of the T.U.C./Government initiative on prices and incomes. It is further encouraged by the response given by the trade union movement to the Social Contract in 1976–77, and recognising the sacrifice and restraint shown by all workers during the economic crisis of the last 18 months, supports the view that a planned return to free collective bargaining should begin to take place in 1977.[101]

One reason it was decided to return to "free collective bargaining" lay in the dissatisfaction of unions that had greater concentrations of well-paid members—notably the Engineering Workers—with the Jones-inspired flat-rate incomes policies.[102] In addition, union leaders complained that the government had not been able to deliver full employment and, in this regard, to hold up its end of the social contract. Finally, there was a feeling among some union leaders that, even if their political bargaining with the government netted the members a package equivalent in value—or utility—to the pay increases that might have been obtained from employers through collective bargaining, the members would not accord them as much credit for the former as they would have for the latter. This, too, is understandable; a union engaged in political bargaining is involved in a cooperative effort with other unions to obtain a "public good," the benefits of which cannot typically be confined to the particular dues-paying members.

In the 1978 budget, Chancellor Healey again made certain tax reductions contingent on "a satisfactory agreement on a new pay policy," but, since the TUC had renounced the social contract, he subsequently cut the proposed reduction in half. The government also unilaterally announced a 10 percent limit on the increase in "average national earnings," which employers were enjoined not to exceed on pain of loss of government contracts, financial aid under training or subsidy programs, or export credits. Enforcement of the pay guidelines by price guidelines that tied permissible price increases to permissible cost

101. Quoted in Trades Union Congress, *Economic Review, 1977*, para. 244.
102. Ibid., para. 246.

increases was generally abandoned, but the cost of any pay settlements that broke the twelve-month rule would be disallowed.

Yet the government did not abandon all hope of securing at least tacit cooperation from the unions. The latter announced that the collective bargaining to which they proposed to return would be "responsible" as well as "free." The TUC agreed to continue its support of the twelve-month interval between successive negotiations, and the chancellor duly announced that he had taken this pledge into account when settling on the 10 percent ceiling.

Nevertheless, it is widely held that 1978 was the year in which the incomes policy collapsed. Average earnings in 1978 rose 14.3 percent above the 1977 level, and the corresponding increase in retail prices of 8.3 percent implied a rise of 5.5 percent in real wages (see table 7-6). The government's unilateral commitment to a 5 percent pay limit in the summer of 1978, moreover, provoked a winter of severe strikes in the public sector, whose pay awards the government sought to keep beneath this new ceiling. A major strike at Ford, involving 56,000 workers, in October and November converted an offer of 5 percent plus productivity payments into a settlement of about 17 percent, and the consequential sanctions imposed by the government on Ford—cutting public-sector purchases of Ford cars and reducing financial assistance—were revoked after a parliamentary defeat.

But while the incomes policy came to an end, the statistical evidence does not provide strong support for the view that its ending produced a catch-up wage explosion. The annual rate of increase in earnings remained at about 14 percent in the second half of 1978 and the first half of 1979.[103] Real earnings, deflated by GDP deflators at market prices, rose 3.2 percent at an annual rate in the second half of 1978 and 2.4 percent in the first half of 1979, while GDP productivity, similarly deflated, rose 2.1 percent in the second quarter of 1978 and fell 0.5 percent in the first quarter of 1979, the latter the consequence of a decline in domestic output. "Room" for wage increases was thus exceeded, but by a relatively small amount.

A more substantial rise in wages might have been expected. This was at a time not only of rising world demand—which made companies such as Ford vulnerable—but also of pressure on private industry from skilled workers. Skilled workers' hourly earnings, 1.45 times those of unskilled

103. For 1978:2, 14.1 percent and 13.6 percent, and for 1979:1, 15.4 percent and 13.6 percent for the old series and the new series, respectively. Ibid., p. 16.

Table 7-8. *Private-Sector and Public-Sector Earnings,*
United Kingdom, 1968–79

Annual percentage change

Sector	1968–74	1975	1976	1977	1978	1979[a]
Government	12.7	31.7	11.5	8.1	10.4	10
Public corporations	14.4	33.5	15.5	4.5	17.9	13
Total public	13.1	32.1	12.5	7.2	12.8	11¼
Private	12.6	29.9	16.5	11.1	13.7	13½
Total	12.8	30.5	15.3	9.8	13.4	11¾

Source: OECD Economic Surveys. *United Kingdom,* February 1980, p. 16.
a. Provisional, on the basis of the pattern of pay results (New Earnings Survey) in April 1979.

workers in 1967, had fallen by 1978 to 1.19, and while total unemployment rose from about 1.2 million to 1.4 million during 1976–79, the ratio of registered unemployed to vacancies for skilled engineering workers fell from 4 to 2.[104] As table 7-8 shows, moreover, pay in the public sector was squeezed in relation to pay in the private sector between 1976 and 1978; yet the increase in public-sector earnings in the first half of 1979, only 11.25 percent, was still less than that in the private sector.

The 5 percent ceiling adopted by the government for the period mid 1978 to mid 1979 put hard-pressed union leaders in a difficult position. Some saw the measure as a gambit for a September 1978 election, which backfired when opinion polls persuaded the prime minister to wait. Incomes policy was rejected by the Labour party conference on the votes of the big unions, but the leaders of the TUC did not interpret this as a vote for unconstrained collective bargaining. When the Economics Committee of the TUC met with the government in November, it suggested what those constraints might be. "The parties should seek stability in the price wherever possible. . . . Increased productivity and better use of capital equipment should always be considered as a means of combining the objectives of price stability, improved competitiveness and higher living standards for work people. . . . Where firms are in a strong market position they should be pressed to expand output and investment rather than increase prices to the consumer." The document also called for written commitments by employers on price intentions and in a radical step said that "unions should take full account of the information [on the company's situation] disclosed when considering a proper level of settlement."[105] In February, after a meeting with ministers

104. "Skill o' the Wisp," *The Economist,* August 4, 1979, p. 48.
105. Income Data Services, *Focus 12,* February 1979.

on the public disquiet raised by the winter strikes, the TUC issued guidelines on the conduct of disputes in which it said that union rules should "clearly state" which bodies have authority to call, approve, and end strikes; the Income Data Services commented that "this strong recommendation . . . is quite out of the ordinary."[106] As the veteran president of the Miners put it after helping to vote down the incomes policy, "no body of people in the conference hall was more dedicated to the return of 'sunny Jim' and his colleagues to Whitehall than the miners: For God's sake trust us."[107]

But this was no longer a question of trust. The TUC could no longer unite in support of an incomes policy that maintained low skill differentials and reduced the relative pay of public-sector employees. The belated militancy of the semiskilled workers in Britain, which, as table 7-7 shows, generated marked compression of skill differentials in the manufacturing sector during the first half of the decade, subsequently generated a reaction by the skilled workers that brought about a change of leadership in the Engineering Workers and the alignment of that union with the Electricians and others in a bloc which opposed the Transport and General Workers in favoring a widening of differentials. (In the United States militancy among the semiskilled had been awakened with the organization of the industrial unions in heavy industry during the late 1930s, and a reaction by skilled workers began in the 1950s.) Reaction to the reduction of pay in the public sector took the form of the outburst of strikes during the winter of 1978–79—the number of strikers rose from 1 million in 1978 to 4.5 million in 1979, and the number of working days lost jumped from 9.5 million to 29.5 million—which effectively swamped the 5 percent pay norm and the Labour government's electoral chances in the May 1979 election. Labour was hardly in a position to promise the voters a return to industrial peace, as it had been in 1974, or even to full employment, through incomes policy. The Tories were thus able to win the election with a sufficiently large parliamentary majority to enjoy the prospect of a full five years in office.

Margaret Thatcher's Contract with Realism, May 1979–

The performance of the Conservative government that assumed office in May 1979 can hardly be placed in perspective in this study. Yet this

106. Income Data Services, *Brief*, no. 152, p. 2.
107. *The Times* (London), October 4, 1978, p. 4.

government proclaimed a break with the past and declared itself un-equivocally and as a matter of principle in opposition to incomes policy and to accepting the union movement as a partner in policymaking. Not all in the new government were willing to go that far out on this ideological limb. In an interview just before the election, James Prior, one of the leading "wets"—that is, moderates—and employment secretary from 1979 to 1981, had said: "As for the right wing of the party, the fact is that we have to learn to live with the unions." Was he committed against an incomes policy? "We are committed against a statutory incomes policy except in an emergency. Most of us believe that, within a policy of monetary controls generally . . . an understanding of what we can afford to pay out [is needed]." Did that mean some sort of exhortational policy in fact rather like the one Prime Minister James Callaghan had been using? "I don't see a great deal of difference between the policy the [Labour] government is pursuing in terms of monetary policy and cash limits in the public sector and the one that we would follow."[108]

But in fact the government's economic strategy turned out to be significantly different from Labour's. It could be argued that, even if the new government had wanted to revive incomes policy, that course of action was precluded by the experience of 1978 and the hostility of the unions. But the new prime minister was opposed to incomes policy as a matter of principle and on grounds of economic analysis rather than on grounds of political or institutional feasibility. During the last half of the 1970s, as economic conditions failed to recover to earlier levels—profitability in the nonoil sector of industry was lower in 1979 than it had been in 1970, despite some improvement after the mid 1970s—the theory and ideology of monetarism gained in acceptance and influence. Mone-tarists had no use for incomes policy, which at most, they believed, could make possible a temporary reduction in unemployment below its "natural" level until accelerating inflation set in. Prime Minister Thatcher proclaimed and subsequently revealed herself to be a true believer in monetarism, but she also accepted the message of a more ancient and blunter conservative doctrine, which was that more unemployment was necessary to prize open the grip of unionism on the shop floor.

A shift in the balance of power away from the unions was seen as necessary in order both to restrain the growth of real wages and to foster the growth of productivity. The government believed, with some reason, that whether or not the Labour incomes policy had restrained the growth

108. "Britain: How the Tories Would Handle Labor Relations," *Business Week,* April 16, 1979, p. 46.

of real wages, it had restrained the growth of productivity. This was because the more the senior shop stewards had been required to impose wage restraint, the less they were prepared to accept redundancies. (Part of the price paid by the Labour government for the reductions in real wages of 1975–77 consisted of a battery of formal and informal devices for preventing redundancies in large plants.)

This view went hand in glove with a greater spirit of militancy on the part of employers whose spines had been stiffened by low profitability. In 1979 the Confederation of British Industry proposed a strike insurance fund on the German model; this failed to attract sufficient support from the ranks of the big firms, but it was apparent that employers had come some distance from the days of Prime Minister Heath, when they had refused to support the Industrial Relations Act of 1971.

Thus, the new administration's strategy for the economy broke dramatically with the past in rhetoric and substantially in content as well. The rhetoric called for a restoration of a free-market economy. Simple monetarist rules and flexible exchange rates would control inflation. A shift from direct taxation to indirect would increase incentives. A sizable reduction in public expenditure would benefit the crowded-out private sector and make monetary control easier. Union monopoly power would be reduced directly by legislation and indirectly by a tough line toward lame-duck companies whether in the public or private sectors. Incomes policy and social compact were out: it was time, Mrs. Thatcher said, for a "contract with realism."[109] The government disregarded the unions, which in turn went after increases in real wages unrestrained during the second half of 1979. Tom Jackson, the moderate leader of the Postal Workers' Union, told the 1979 TUC Conference, of which he was chairman, that "the movement could not restrain wage demands when the government abandoned all attempts to control prices, withdrew from consensus policies and fostered unemployment."[110] Thus from mid 1979, while real GDP was declining and unemployment rising, real gross earnings were increasing. And, while earnings were increasing in relation to retail prices, retail prices had taken a leap of 4 percent in June 1979 as a result of the budget switch from direct to indirect taxes: the income tax rate was reduced from 33 percent to 30 percent and the value-added tax (VAT) was increased

109. "To Ease the Pain, Breathe Deep," *The Economist,* July 26, 1980, p. 55.
110. "The Unions Retreat into Their Blackpool Tower," *The Economist,* September 8, 1979, p. 29.

compensatorily. Thus in disposable income, those union members who benefited from the income tax cuts were protected against the increases in the VAT. This underlines the point that the unions were bargaining with less moderation than before; for, as econometric work suggests, wage inflation is influenced by the need to meet real net-earnings targets;[111] hence a rise in *net* earnings as a result of income tax cuts would have moderated money wage increases in relation to retail price inflation if union discretion had been constant. A further inflationary push came from the oil price increases in late 1979, which were not canceled by the appreciating pound. In consequence, by June 1980 inflation had risen from 10.3 percent in May 1979 to 21.0 percent; at the same time, the restrictive monetary policy pushed unemployment from 5.4 percent to 6.9 percent.

But in the second half of 1980, as unemployment rose from 6.9 percent in June to 8.3 percent in December, wage inflation dropped sharply. Wage increases appeared at the end of 1980 to be rising at about 10 percent;[112] price inflation fell to around 15 percent. Believers in a unique constant-inflation equilibrium unemployment rate relocated it between 7 percent and 8 percent. Thus one difference from the policy of the Labour government is that it was through the market alone that real wages were reduced and inflation moderated. Enough pressure was created by restrictive demand management to cause redundancies in large plants and to put seriously at risk for the first time the jobs of well-organized workers. The policy worked primarily by changing the attitude of union workers toward the security of their own employment; it is less clear how far the resolve of employers in the private sector to resist wage increases by taking strikes was stiffened as a result of declining profitability, at least initially. In July 1980, the president of the CBI expressed concern that the "financial vulnerability of some companies might prevent them from resisting strikes" and thus from keeping wage increases within the 10 percent target which, he noted, many major companies had adopted.[113] But it appeared that the target was being met and that the number of strikes was greatly reduced from the number in 1979: 431 strikes during May–July 1980, 684 during the corresponding

111. See Henry, "Incomes Policy and Aggregate Pay," p. 41.
112. "Crashing the Pay Barrier," *The Economist*, December 6, 1980, p. 58; this quotes evidence from the CBI's Pay Data bank.
113. "Chronicle: Industrial Relations in the United Kingdom, April–July 1980," *British Journal of Industrial Relations*, vol. 18, no. 3 (November 1980), p. 387.

quarter of 1979; the analogous figures for days lost are 965,000 and 1,760,000 and for numbers of workers involved, 232,000 and 445,000. In addition, certain unions—the Engineers, for example—exercised caution in their demands, while other unions—TGWU at British Leyland, for example—had to back off from militant demands because of lack of rank-and-file support.

The Thatcher government also differed from its predecessors in assigning the task of improving productivity, as well as that of moderating wage increases, exclusively to restrictive demand management. This task consists essentially of increasing the authority and discretion of plant management. It was the lack of such discretion that was seen as impeding industrial rationalization, and in a *wider* perspective as explaining the comparative failure of postwar economic growth. Moderation of real wages was important, but as a necessary—not a sufficient—condition for economic growth. Seen in this perspective, the real incomes policy of the 1975–78 variety is counterproductive, for, with powerful shop stewards effectively administering the policy, the price of moderation of real wages was the preservation of the stewards' power to prevent serious redundancies in large plants and hobble managerial discretion. The new administration made no attempts to prevent companies from creating mass redundancies, and it was loudly rumored that one or two large bankruptcies would not be unwelcome to it. In the belief that financial subsidy for their employer was in the balance, therefore, the work force of British Leyland twice rejected by substantial margins strike calls that the Engineers (reluctantly) and the TGWU had called after the shop stewards had pressured them to do so. (The first occasion, in February 1980, was an attempt to secure the reinstatement of the senior convenor at Longbridge, who had been dismissed for misconduct; on the second occasion, in April 1980, the work force accepted a pay increase of between 5 percent and 10 percent and agreed in principle to a restoration of managerial discretion on the shop floor.)[114]

The desire to bring about more substantial changes in the organization of the shop floor may help to explain the further tightening of monetary and fiscal policy that the government proposed in early 1981. The chancellor of the exchequer announced his determination to stick to a simple monetary target below the current rate of inflation. The argument for this was couched in terms of rational expectations; the occasion for

114. For details of this rather complicated episode, see ibid., pp. 387–88.

it was the failure of the government to keep monetary growth within its previously set target range. Yet according to the ordinary measures of monetary restrictiveness, its policy in 1980 had been fully successful; high interest rates, a high rate of exchange, and a level of unemployment that it could be argued was higher than the natural rate was supposed to be. Indeed, the high rate of monetary growth could be put down in large part to a perverse effectiveness of monetary policy: it was the result of recession-induced increases in unemployment benefits, nationalized industry losses, and bank borrowing by companies to make good their deficits. If it was the aim of the government, moreover, to create rational expectations of lower price inflation by announcing a monetary policy that it was forecast would increase unemployment from 2 million to between 2.5 million and 3 million, it could have supplemented that policy with an official target for appropriate increases in money wages.

A more rational interpretation than rational expectations is that the government proceeded as if in the belief that a rate of unemployment substantially higher than the natural rate was needed to restore managerial discretion in the work place and that such a change would ultimately lower the natural rate itself. This approach can be contrasted with the approach of the Labour government in the mid 1960s, which encouraged managerial efforts to buy out restrictive practices with increases in relative wages, the latter being allowed as exceptions to wage norms. These Wilsonian carrots were not, on the whole, effective incentives, since employers frequently granted wage increases in exchange for future improvements in efficiency that were not realized. The Thatcher stick seemed to be more effective. Between 1979 and mid 1981, output per man-hour rose as output fell—by 17 percent—faster than employment—15 percent—while fixed investment was declining sharply in an untypically—although not unprecedented—contracyclical "shake-out."[115]

A more orthodox way to reduce union bargaining potential was through legislative restraint on union activity. A change in labor law was a further element of the administration's strategy, but there was reported to be much debate within the administration about the degree of change needed. Just before the election, Employment Secretary James Prior had explained that

the changes we propose are comparatively small. . . . Most people recognize

115. "Is Slimmer Fitter?" *The Economist,* July 4, 1981, p. 13; "Are Britain's Big Companies Leaner and Fitter or Just Sadder?" ibid., pp. 73–77.

442   THE UNITED KINGDOM

that there have to be a number of limited changes in the law. But the Conservative Party is not prepared to get itself into a position of trying to pass laws which employers ask us to pass and then don't use. . . . It would be a great mistake if we took certain actions now which merely united the trade-union movement again in an anti-Conservative government posture.[116]

Both the CBI and the Engineering Employers' Federation supported Prior's "piecemeal" approach[117], and instead of the "cover-all" 1971 act, the 1980 Employment Bill dealt with only four areas of concern: secret ballots, picketing, secondary action, and the closed shop. The main provisions of the bill, which was enacted in August, were as follows:[118]

• public money to be made available to unions, if they wish to hold secret ballots on strikes, elections, and constitutional change;

• picketing to be limited to six persons; apart from union officials and dismissed workers, persons who picket at a place other than their own place of work are no longer immune from civil action;

• secondary action no longer immune from civil action (typically inducing a breach of commercial contract) unless taken against an immediate supplier, a consumer, or an employer associated with the employer in dispute by providing substitute goods or services;

• workers cannot be unreasonably expelled from or refused admission to a trade union where a closed shop is in operation; new closed shops must have the support of 80 percent of the workers involved to be immune from unfair dismissal claims if a worker loses his job through operation of a closed-shop agreement.

In 1982, additional legislation was enacted. It further limited union immunity from civil suits by excluding from the definition of "trade disputes" interunion disputes and disputes that are mainly political or personal in nature or that are restricted to foreign issues. It made unions as well as their subordinate bodies or officials liable for illegal acts performed by the latter, unless such acts were repudiated by the National Executive, thereby making union funds attachable for the first time since the passage of the Trade Disputes Act of 1906. It also outlawed contracts between firms requiring the employment of union labor exclusively, and it extended and increased compensation payable to workers dismissed from closed shops for nonmembership.

116. "Britain: How the Tories Would Handle Labor Relations," pp. 46, 48.
117. "Judgement Day." *The Economist,* October 13, 1979, p. 76.
118. For further details, see "Chronicle: Industrial Relations," pp. 381–82.

Proponents of these new laws regarded reduction of the power of unions—and their shop stewards—in the interests of nonunion workers and neutral employers as sufficient justification for their enactment, much as the proponents of the Taft-Hartley Act had done in the United States a generation earlier. But it was also hoped that the legislation would nail down the gains in efficiency and the reduction in the power of shop stewards that had been achieved under severe contraction and unsustainably low levels of economic activity. From the monetarist viewpoint, the legislation is supposed to reduce the natural rate of unemployment and thereby pave the way for a less inflationary expansion. But to what extent can the new legislation be counted on to reduce union bargaining potential at any given level of employment? Withdrawal of immunity from secondary activities is directed to a source of union power which, on occasion, has been decisive; but such restraint depends for its enforcement on a greater disposition on the part of employers to take their bargaining partners to court than has been in evidence so far. Excluding strikes that may be called primarily for political reasons from the protective definition of "trade disputes" presumably is an attempt to address a problem that has been revealed when strike calls issued by national executives or militant shop stewards have been rejected by a majority of the members. But members are normally—that is, at higher levels of employment—more restive than their officers at companywide and, especially, industrywide levels of authority, and they would support politically militant leaders only because the ideological rhetoric of those leaders was accompanied by hard cash demands. In that case even a politically motivated dispute would be wrapped in economic issues.

The heaviest legal artillery seems to consist of placing union funds at risk in damage suits. That could provide national executives with a strong incentive to repudiate wildcat strikes; it could divide wildcat strikers from other dues-paying groups in the national union, and it could even tend to strengthen the authority of the national executive at the expense of the autonomy enjoyed by shop stewards. On the other hand, this legal gun, like the others, must be fired by employers, who have proved gun-shy in the past, when economic activity was at higher levels. The new legislation, moreover, does not make collective contracts legally enforceable—as they have been in Germany, Sweden, and the United States—and hence it does not outlaw wildcat strikes, the basis of the power of shop stewards. Finally, subsidization of union strike ballots and elections rests, like other parts of the legislation, on the premise that the majority of union members would choose lower levels of bargaining intensity than their officers exert, if they were free to make the choice. This is a highly questionable assumption, especially at higher levels of employment and profitability. From a purely economic viewpoint this provision of the new legislation could prove to be self-defeating.

The government's main difficulties in industrial relations came in the public sector. The inheritance of the previous administration was a widened differential between private and public pay, and this had not been corrected by the winter strikes of 1978–79. A commission under the chairmanship of Professor Hugh Clegg had been set up by the Labour government in early 1979 to make recommendations on public-sector pay on the basis of comparability with the private sector; during the 1979 election campaign Mrs. Thatcher committed a future Conservative government to acceptance of its recommendations. As a result, pay in public services and administration rose 27 percent in 1979, while pay in private industry rose 18 percent.[119] This reduced the level of militancy in the public sector, but it did not fit in well with the government's attempt to restrain public-sector spending by confining it within predetermined "cash limits" in order to make room for an increase in private investment. True to form, the government refused initially to announce pay norms for the public sector. The announcement of budget limits left the employees free to choose between higher wages and reduced employment, but when they chose higher wages, as the comparability findings virtually ensured they would do, the government itself was unwilling to accept the consequences for employment. The central government thus came under pressure to disregard its cash limits. It could not, moreover, prevent local authorities from attempting to cover wage increases for their own employees by increasing local taxes, and it came under strong pressure to increase subsidy payments to nationalized industries in order to hold down the loss of jobs in these politically powerful constituencies. (In the case of coal, jobs were protected by economic as well as political muscle. Early in 1981, the NUM struck to prevent the National Coal Board from closing down fifty mines, and, faced with the prospect of another nationwide coal strike—with promised secondary support from the railway unions—the prime minister backed down.) As a result, the government's overall fiscal policy failed to match

119. "Pay Research: Incomparable," *The Economist,* November 1, 1980, p. 68.

its monetary policy in restrictiveness, so private investment was severely depressed, instead of being encouraged, and unemployment was concentrated in the private sector, along with low profits and wage increases. This furnished an example of wage increases in a sheltered, employment-inelastic sector of the economy, forcing up unemployment in the open sector. As a further result, the government began to compromise its principle and to supplement its "cash limits" with "wage ceilings."

Nonetheless, two years after the Thatcher government had taken office, it could claim some elements of effectiveness for its policies. There had been a countercyclical rise in manufacturing productivity; real wages and the rate of price inflation were beginning to decline; and within the manufacturing industry, there had been a significant increase in managerial discretion on the shop floor. Why, in summary, did Thatcher succeed, at least in the short run, compared to her Conservative predecessor, Heath? Three differences stand out.

1. The trade-union movement was less united than it had been in the earlier period and therefore less capable of offering effective resistance to government policies. When the Thatcher government took office, unemployment was already at higher levels than in 1970–71, so when it increased further in 1980, employees in large plants, especially the semiskilled workers, believed that their own jobs were threatened, whereas in the earlier period they had not. Differences between the semiskilled workers and the unions in which they predominated, on the one hand, and skilled workers and their organizations, on the other, had been exacerbated by the egalitarian nature of the incomes policies pursued under the Labour government, which contributed to shortages of skilled workers and lower unemployment in their ranks. In concrete terms, this meant that the two big unions in industry—the Transport and General Workers, in which semiskilled interests predominated, and the Engineering Workers, where skilled workers were more strongly represented—no longer stood together and were not disposed to offer united resistance to the closing of plants, lower manning requirements, and the like. The wage and industrial-relations policies of the new government, moreover, had the effect of perpetuating, if not originating, other divisions among the unions. Unlike Heath, Thatcher refrained from a double-barreled policy that combined legislative restrictions affecting unions in the private sector—as well as the public sector—with an incomes policy, $n - 1$, which bore on the public sector. The Thatcher policy permitted relative wage increases in the public sector, while

unemployment and employer resistance held down wage increases in the private sector. And within the public sector itself, the government resisted claims made by unions of civil servants while giving way to the coal miners.

2. The Thatcher government took the view that the law should consolidate changes in industrial relations that had already been brought about by deflationary policies, rather than attempt, as Heath did, to confront unions with legislation designed to weaken their power.

3. Finally, as a result of a prolonged period of low profitability in the 1970s, the attitudes of employers toward the unions had hardened.

But these changes entailed great economic and, possibly, political cost as investment declined and unemployment approached levels last reached during the Great Depression (see figure 7-1). At issue, within the government as well as in the country at large, was whether activity and employment could turn up and approach satisfactory levels sufficiently far in advance of the end of the government's term of office without the need to abandon its tight monetary policies and also whether, in the event of an upturn, lower rates of inflation and higher rates of increase in productivity could be maintained. The first question is whether private industry has, in the right conditions, a self-starting mechanism; recent moves toward an industrial strategy suggest that the government now shares some of the skepticism of outside observers.

The answer to the second question depends in good part on whether the changes in bargaining behavior and relationships can survive a return to relative prosperity. Advocates of more stringent labor legislation have regarded it as a way of consolidating gains in the bargaining potential of employers realized during a period of activity sufficiently low to make unionists fearful for their own jobs, but it is difficult to specify how such substitution of regulation for unemployment could work. Legislation to outlaw the closed shop would be irrelevant to this purpose—and would be opposed by many firms. Strengthening the authority of the national union at the plant level would strengthen those centralized labor institutions that have been disposed to wage restraint in the past, but attempting to strengthen their authority by making unions liable for breaches of collective bargaining contracts—including wildcat strikes in violation of no-strike agreements—has not proved effective elsewhere and could serve to reunify the trade-union movement and raise the general level of militancy.

VIII

Denmark

For almost two decades, incomes policy discussions in Denmark have been held against a background of high inflation rates—the highest among the countries in this study—a persistent balance-of-payments deficit, and, until the mid 1970s, relatively low rates of unemployment. With the oil price increases of the Organization of Petroleum Exporting Countries (OPEC) Denmark faced a particularly difficult macroeconomic adjustment problem (see chapter 1). Goaded by the external price increases, the rise of Danish prices accelerated, and the unemployment rate almost quadrupled, reaching a plateau upon which it remained for the rest of the 1970s.

These developments intensified concern among policymaking officials over the institutional features of Danish income determination, most notably the systems of collective bargaining and indexation of wages. Yet Danish incomes policy has had a peculiar history. An initial effort in the early 1960s represented one of the earliest social-contract experiments in Europe, but it did not prove to be durable. Since then Danish authorities have tried periodically, although unsuccessfully, to rehabilitate this approach to wage restraint. Their efforts have been frustrated by increasing political fragmentation, which has made it difficult to formulate anti-inflation policy generally, growing instability and conflict in collective bargaining and within the collective bargaining institutions, and the continued and increasing importance of wage drift in the overall growth of earnings.

In the face of these realities, incomes policy has remained an active, if erratic, instrument of Danish macroeconomic policy but has drifted further and further from the social-contract concept. Legislation providing for the direct regulation of prices was in effect, if not notably effective, throughout the 1970s. During the first half of the 1970s, the government took a predominantly laissez-faire position with respect to growth in money wages, but this gave way to increasing intervention into the outcomes of the collective bargaining and indexation systems in

This chapter has benefited from the skillful research assistance of Carsten Kowalscyk and the comments and suggestions of Palle S. Andersen.

the late 1970s without compensatory support for the legislative objectives of the unions. By the end of the 1970s, the strains between potential "social partners" were such that Denmark appeared to be further from a social-contract arrangement than at any time during the postwar period. In this chapter we shall review the developments that led to this situation and analyze and evaluate the effectiveness of recent incomes policies in moderating wage inflation.

Economic Background

With the exception of 1963 the Danish current external account showed a deficit averaging 2 percent of gross domestic product (GDP) in every year during the 1960s and 1970s.[1] Until the early 1960s the deficits were accepted as a transitional price of acquiring the capital imports needed to achieve a reallocation of domestic resources from agriculture to manufacturing and other nonagricultural industries. Yet the imbalance remained long after the reallocation was essentially complete. While the current-account deficit has varied cyclically as the Danish demand for imports has proved to be more income elastic than demand for foreign exports (largely because of the large share of agricultural products), the external imbalance also has a significant permanent component, which has been attributed to labor-cost developments.

Dependence on international trade, which constitutes 25–30 percent of GDP, and particularly on imported oil, which constitutes more than 90 percent of the total energy used, rendered Denmark particularly vulnerable to the oil crises of 1973–74. With the unprecedented rise in the prices of oil and other raw materials, the Danish terms of trade deteriorated by 17.5 percent between the second quarter of 1973 and the third quarter of 1974, raising the external deficit to an average of 3 percent of GDP during 1974–76.[2] The supply shock was accompanied by a rise in inflation and a sharp increase in the insured unemployment rate from an average of 3 percent during the early 1970s to double-digit rates that persisted through the second half of the decade (see figure 8-1). After the initial sharp deterioration in external balance, the subsequent recession brought the current external account close to balance. With the subsequent upswing imports once again increased sharply. But despite an absence of capacity constraints in the export sector, Danish

1. OECD Economic Surveys, *Denmark*, April 1977, p. 10.
2. Ibid., p. 18.

Figure 8-1. *Unemployment and Consumer Prices, Denmark, 1960–78*

Percent

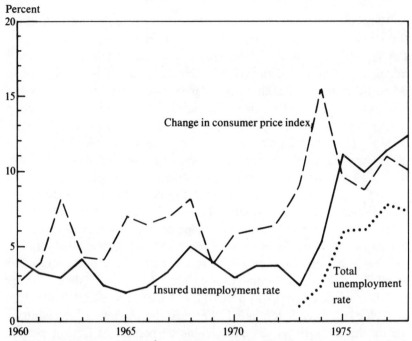

Sources: Danmarks Statistik, *Statistik Årbog* [Statistical yearbook], vol. 82 (Copenhagen, 1978), p. 233; OECD Economic Surveys, *Denmark*, 1965, p. 225; ibid., various issues.

exports grew significantly less rapidly than in 1973, when there had last been an equivalent increase in foreign demand. If the chronic deficit on current account during the 1960s and early 1970s had suggested that domestic factors were important in the continuing imbalance, the sluggish export response to the 1975–76 expansion indicated a further decline in Denmark's competitive position. A subsequent study by the Organisation for Economic Co-operation and Development (OECD) indicated that there was a deterioration in the international competitiveness of Danish industrial exports during the first half of the 1970s that caused a 10 percent loss of foreign market share. The deterioration was associated with increases in unit labor costs more rapid than those experienced by Denmark's trading partners. While there was no further deterioration during the late 1970s, neither was there any improvement in the export performance of industrial goods or restoration of market share, despite the high rates of unemployment in Denmark.[3]

3. Ibid., July 1979, pp. 35, 53–57.

Labor Cost Developments

The deterioration of Danish competitiveness in foreign markets during the early 1970s is generally traced to developments in labor costs. Despite the importance of international trade, much of the Danish inflation that preceded the oil price increases of 1973–74 was tied to domestic economic developments—particularly the pressure on labor markets exerted by growth in the public sector and in construction during the 1960s and early 1970s. In 1962, general government expenditures accounted for 28.8 percent of GDP in Denmark—less than in any other European or North American country at that time. About a quarter of the expenditure was for social security and welfare. During the subsequent decade, the allocation of resources to the public sector grew more rapidly than in any country in this study, and by the mid 1970s the share of public expenditure in GDP, 46 percent, was exceeded only by the Netherlands and Sweden (see table 8-1).[4] Although expenditures on national pensions, unemployment relief, child allowances, and other forms of social security and welfare grew less rapidly than in other OECD countries during this period, the share of Danish GDP allocated to such expenditures continued to exceed the share in other countries during the early 1970s. By 1970, some 60 percent of Danish income transfers and subsidies represented redistributions from the active population to the inactive. At the same time, increased taxation and the automatic effect of a highly progressive income tax system on increasing real resources for the public sector enabled the government to run a surplus into the early 1970s. By the mid 1970s Denmark had the highest ratio of tax revenue to GNP of any country in this study (see table 8-1).

The late 1960s and early 1970s saw a rapid growth of construction in response to an extensive program of housing subsidies and an exemption from the value-added tax for dwelling construction expenses and rent.[5] The rapid growth in these sectors during the 1960s and early 1970s gave rise to an inflationary mechanism that stands the "Scandinavian" model of the transmission of inflation on its head. Strong demand in the

4. Expenditure growth was particularly rapid in education, health services, and economic services, including agricultural subsidies, road construction, and other investments in infrastructure for private industry. See ibid., July 1973, pp. 35–40; Organisation for Economic Co-operation and Development, *Public Expenditure Trends* (Paris: OECD, June 1978), pp. 15–16.

5. For a review of Danish housing policy, see OECD Economic Surveys, *Denmark*, July 1978, pp. 43–46.

Table 8-1. *Public Expenditures and Tax Revenues as Percentages of Gross Domestic Product, Denmark, 1974–76, Compared with Those of Selected Countries of the OECD*

Country	Total public expenditures as percentage of GDP (average, 1974–76)	Total tax revenue as percentage of GNP in 1974	
		Including social security	Excluding social security
Denmark	46.4	46.7	44.0
Norway	46.6	45.3	32.1
Netherlands	53.9	45.2	27.8
Sweden	51.7	44.2	35.7
Austria	39.9	38.1	28.4
Germany	44.0	37.6	24.4
France	41.6	37.5	21.8
United Kingdom	44.5	35.6	29.5
Italy	43.1	31.9	18.6
United States	35.1	28.9	22.3

Sources: Organisation for Economic Co-operation and Development, *Public Expenditure Trends* (Paris: OECD, 1978), table 2, pp. 14–15; OECD, *Revenue Statistics of OECD Member Countries, 1965–1974* (Paris: OECD, 1976), p. 72.

"sheltered" public sector and the construction sector contributed to rapid wage increases, which tended to spread to "exposed" export industries as a consequence of market forces or egalitarian wage policies of the labor unions. Throughout the 1960s, wage increases in construction exceeded increases in manufacturing, but during the early 1970s, manufacturing wages began to catch up, with adverse effects on the Danish competitive position. The catch-up, however, may have been a reflection of a weakening competitive position of Danish manufacturing in labor markets as much as of institutional forces. For example, the OECD noted that

the export industries, faced with slowly rising prices in foreign markets and rapidly advancing wages in sheltered domestic sectors . . . found themselves in an increasingly unfavourable position, unable to attract resources and expand production in line with the growth of export markets. While the export performance can be in part attributed to an unfavorable commodity composition . . . the most severe losses occurred in years of tight labour market conditions and/or larger than average advances in Danish export prices. This suggests that certain exposed industries—with only limited possibilities for passing domestic cost increases on to higher prices—tended to get "squeezed" in periods of excess domestic demand pressure.[6]

6. Ibid., April 1977, p. 10.

452   DENMARK

Table 8-2. *Components of Wage Change and Wage Differentials,*
Denmark, Selected Periods, 1960–79

	Component of wage change				Wage differential	
Period	Wage rate	Index-ation[a]	Wage drift	Total	Female/ male	Semiskilled/ skilled
	Annual average percentage change					
1960–69	3.1	3.1	3.5	9.7	73	81
1970–73	3.1	3.8	5.6	12.5	79	83
1974–79	2.6	6.3	5.4	14.3	86	86
	Percentage distribution					
1960–69	32	32	36	100		
1970–73	25	30	45	100		
1974–79	18	44	38	100		

Source: Danish Employers Federation, Statistics Department.
a. Wage changes attributable to indexation are exclusive of portions frozen by the government during 1975–79.

The determination of wages in Denmark is marked by two central institutional features—a more extensive system of indexation linking nominal wage changes to changes in consumer prices than is found in other countries in this study together with centralized collective bargaining over basic wage rates, and considerable wage drift. The indexation system has contributed significantly to the momentum of Danish inflation and has built the effects of external price shocks such as the 1973 oil price increases into the domestic cost structure more rapidly than elsewhere. With accelerating inflation, indexation payments represented a growing proportion of wage increases during the 1970s (see table 8-2), and one branch of incomes-policy activity came to be focused on possible alterations in the indexation arrangements.

Collective bargaining directly or indirectly influences the base wage of most of the Danish work force. By 1970, about three quarters of all manual workers and more than half of all salaried workers belonged to some seventy unions, which were organized largely along craft lines.[7] Forty-six national unions, representing about 924,000 workers, are affiliated with the Landsorganisation i Danmark (LO), the Danish Federation of Trade Unions, which negotiates a central agreement every two years with its counterpart on the employer side, the Dansk Arbejdsgiverforening (DAF), the Danish Employers Federation. Some 17,000 firms, employing about half the unionized work force, are affiliated with

7. Danmarks Statistik, *Levevilkår i Danmark, Statistisk Oversigt 1976* [Living conditions in Denmark, compendium of statistics, 1976] (Copenhagen: Danmark Statistik, 1976), table 10.15, p. 254.

the DAF directly or through membership in trade associations. The DAF has the authority to order a general lockout with the approval of three quarters of its affiliates and to restrain individual members from negotiating independently on certain issues. Other, smaller employers, usually in small-scale enterprises, are affiliated with other organizations.[8] The central negotiations between the LO and the DAF generally set the pattern for unaffiliated unions and employers.

While the employers seek a bargain that will improve their competitive position in international markets, the LO presses an egalitarian wage policy that is reflected in both the tendency to negotiate equal absolute wage increases for all unions—that is, for all skill levels—and the operation of the indexation system, under which specified movements in an index of consumer prices trigger equal wage increases for all covered workers. During the 1970s this policy was extended to include a concerted effort to negotiate higher relative pay for women (see table 8-2). The egalitarian negotiated wage policy has suited the very large union of unskilled workers more than many of the smaller craft unions, but the latter have often been able to restore their relative pay through compensatory movements in wage drift.[9] As in other Scandinavian countries, however, there is a clear potential for conflict in the differing criteria for wage increases that the employers and the union federations bring to the centralized negotiations.

Danish legislation provides for the involvement of a Board of Mediators whose members are appointed for staggered three-year terms. The mediators have the authority to postpone work stoppages for as long as two weeks and to submit a draft settlement to a referendum of the labor-

8. Allan Rise, Peer Carlsen, and Henning Lindegaard, *Employers and Workers in Denmark*, 2d ed. (Copenhagen: Det Danske Selskab, 1974), pp. 7–11.

9. The central collective bargaining agreement actually establishes two types of base wage rates—nominal wages, which cannot be changed for the duration of the agreement, and minimal wages, which can be raised periodically in response to local negotiations during the term of the agreement. These increases to workers under the minimal wage system are an important source of wage drift and, as will be seen later in the chapter, became an important bargaining issue for the DAF during the late 1970s. The nominal wage system, which generally receives the larger wage rate increases in central negotiations, applies mainly to less highly skilled workers while the minimal system applies mainly to skilled workers. Certain so-called special issues, including overtime payments, the scheduling of work hours, and so on, are also addressed in decentralized negotiations. For details, see Steen Leth Jeppesen, *Lon øg Priser* [Wages and prices] (Copenhagen: NYT Nordisk Forlag, 1975), p. 16; Stig Kuhlmann, *Arbejdsmarkedsforhold* [Labor market conditions] (Copenhagen: NYT Nordisk Forlag, 1976), p. 54.

market organizations. If a mediator's proposals are not accepted, the Folketing, the Danish parliament, can enact them into legislation, and the use of such statutory settlements became more common during the 1970s.[10]

The Elements of Danish Earnings Growth

Although the growth of negotiated wage rates showed no general increase during the 1970s, overall earnings grew steadily in response to indexation payments and wage drift (see table 8-2). The steady growth of earnings raised particularly acute problems for Danish economic policy following the 1973 oil price increases. The subsequent deterioration in both the terms of trade and the growth of domestic output implied an initial decline, then a slower rate of growth in real national income per employed person. At the same time, real wages per employee continued to grow at an unchanged rate into 1975. The ensuing gap between actual real earnings and the "room" for increases in real earnings exceeded that in any other country in the study and posed both a barrier to restoration of Denmark's international competitive position and a serious macroeconomic adjustment problem. In order to understand the principal policy options facing Denmark in this situation, it will be useful to review the growth of each element of money earnings.

THE WAGE INDEXATION SYSTEM. The economic events of the 1970s intensified conflict between the unions, employers, and the government over operation of the automatic wage-indexation system. Introduced in 1918 after a period of wartime inflation, the indexation system covered both the private and public sectors and was seen as a device to maintain a minimum standard of living for groups of wage earners during brief bursts of inflation. By 1930 the system had been abandoned in the private sector at the insistence of the unions in order to avert further wage cuts during a period of falling prices. With renewed inflation in the late 1930s and the prospect of wartime inflation, the system was reintroduced in the private sector in 1939, was subsequently abolished during the German occupation, and was reinstated in 1945.[11]

10. For a more extended discussion and interpretation of the Danish dispute-settlement procedures, see Lloyd Ulman and Robert J. Flanagan, *Wage Restraint: A Study of Incomes Policies in Western Europe* (Berkeley: University of California Press, 1971), pp. 121–22.

11. For a brief history of the early operation of the Danish wage-indexation system, see Walter Galenson, *The Danish System of Industrial Relations* (Cambridge: Harvard University Press, 1952), pp. 151–52.

For wage earners, the indexation system provides a fixed "portion"— 40 öre an hour during the late 1960s and early 1970s—for every three-point change in a special cost-of-living index during a six-month interval.[12] Portions are paid to workers in January and July if there has been sufficient movement in the index, and at the insistence of employers wage portions from indexation are not incorporated into the base wage in order to leave at least some possibility of downward flexibility in wages.

With substantial inflation the wage-regulation index is periodically reset at 100—and the amount of the wage portion is adjusted upward—to stabilize the percentage increase represented by each portion and to reduce the number of portions triggered at any one time. Resetting the index also provides an opportunity to readjust the degree of compensation for price increases, and hence the degree of rigidity in real wages, provided by the indexation system. Since the system does not provide full protection from price increases for most wage earners, the average degree of compensation will rise as the wage-regulation index advances.[13] In principle resetting the wage-regulation index provides an opportunity to bargain over the parameters of the system that govern the extent of compensation for inflation and hence the degree of rigidity in real wages in the economy, but in practice the positions of both labor and management on indexation have been sufficiently well entrenched that the periodic adjustments have been minor.

This has left Denmark with a wage-indexation system that is the most comprehensive and inflexible system followed by any country in this study and that has contributed to both the propagation and the momentum of Danish inflation. By providing for fixed wage portions for all manual

12. The index that currently serves as the basis for Danish wage regulation was introduced in 1963 and is a price index based on the consumption structure of wage and salary earners. (The weights are revised on the basis of a household survey taken every 2–4 weeks.) In computing the index, the Danish Central Statistical Office deducts indirect taxes from market prices and, as would be the case of a more general consumer price index, the effect of direct (income) taxes is excluded. The wage-indexation system thus does not work automatically to alter the effects of tax increases on real disposable income, although, as noted below, Danish personal income taxes have been indexed since 1970. The effect of government price subsidies is also not reflected in the index.

13. Until 1975, however, the system provided that changes in the salaries of civil servants and most salaried workers in the private sector be adjusted on an equal percentage basis to changes in the wage-regulation index on the grounds that these groups were unlikely to gain from wage drift. Over all, wage-index payments averaged about 65 percent of increases in the net price index during the period 1970–75. The degree of compensation ranged from 57 percent for skilled male workers to 68 percent for semiskilled males to 82 percent for female workers.

workers, the system narrows wage differentials by skill and, as will be seen, contributes significantly to pressures for wage drift among skilled workers to restore the original differentials. The system also contributes a considerable element of inertia to wage changes.[14] Indeed, the combined influence of the indexation system and centrally negotiated rates to a considerable extent insulates overall growth in earnings from the effects of demand-management policies on labor-market pressures, while accelerating future wage drift by narrowing wage differentials.

The consequences of the indexation system for macroeconomic adjustment were particularly severe in the period following the oil price increase of 1973–74. Denmark suffered both an unusually large deterioration in terms of trade and an unusually difficult adjustment problem, given the degree of real-wage rigidity. As the large external price increases entered the wage-regulation index, increases in earnings attributable to indexation payments almost trebled in 1974 and 1975 to 9 percent for skilled male workers and around 12 percent for women. Increases in overall earnings exceeded 20 and 23 percent respectively, but as is shown in table 8-2, very little of the general increase reflected an acceleration of negotiated wages or wage drift. External price increases were therefore transmitted directly into domestic costs, bringing about a permanently higher level of costs and prices and a weaker international competitive position. These developments led the Danish authorities to adopt a series of measures intended to blunt the effect of the indexation system on the growth of earnings during the last half of the decade.

NEGOTIATED WAGE RATES. The central negotiations, which occurred biennially during the 1960s and 1970s, have had two general effects on the growth of Danish earnings. First, as is frequently the case with

14. A regression of the annual rate of change of wage-indexation payments, COLA (the cost-of-living adjustment, computed as a percentage of average hourly earnings the previous year), on the unemployment rate, UR, and current and lagged values of the rate of change of the net price index, NPDOT, during the period 1960–76 confirms the absence of a direct influence of labor-market pressure on this element of growth in earnings (t-statistics are in parentheses):

$$COLA = -0.62 + 0.15\,UR_t + 0.38\,NPDOT_t + 0.33\,NPDOT_{t-1}.$$
$$(1.02)\quad(0.87)\qquad(2.99)\qquad\quad(1.87)$$
$$R^2 = 0.87;\ \text{Durbin-Watson} = 2.58$$

Note that the coefficients of the $NPDOT_t$ variables confirm that the indexation system provided compensation for about 70 percent of the increase in net prices during the period.

multiyear collective bargaining agreements, they provide an important element of inertia to wage changes. Regression analyses relating annual changes in negotiated wage rates to current and lagged values of the insured unemployment rate and consumer price changes failed to produce results remotely approaching normal standards of statistical significance. (For an example, see regression 1 in table 8-3.)[15] Thus the direct effects of demand-management policies on this element of labor costs appear to have been negligible during the period under study.

On the other hand, it frequently appears that the bargaining objectives of the LO are dominated by considerations of distribution, and the emphasis on narrowing wage differentials between skills and between men and women increased during the 1970s. A more extended regression analysis that tests for a relationship between changes in negotiated rates and the magnitude of skill and sex differentials confirms the influence of the former differential (see regression 2 in table 8-3) but not the latter (see regression 3). The results indicate, moreover, that the influence of the skill differential on negotiated rates increased significantly during the 1970s.[16] Regression 2, for example, indicates that, other things being equal, an increase of 1 percentage point in the skill differential was associated with an increase of 1.07 percentage points in negotiated rates one year later during the 1960s and an increase of 1.28 percentage points in the 1970s. The response of negotiated wages during the 1970s was sufficient to achieve a sustained reduction in the relative wage of skilled males (from 120 percent of the wage of semiskilled males in 1970 to 116 percent in the mid 1970s) despite the tendency of drift to widen differentials.

A much more dramatic reduction in the male relative wage (from almost 140 percent of the female wage in the early 1960s to about 116 percent in the mid 1970s) occurred with much less inflationary effect, according to the regression results. The difference in statistical results for the two measures of relative wages may reflect the fact that Danish

15. There was no statistical basis for choosing between linear and nonlinear specifications of the unemployment rate in these regressions. The linear specifications performed better in the wage-drift equations reported below in table 8-4, however, and are adopted here for possible comparability.

16. The coefficient of *RWSKILL* describes a change of 1 percentage point in the relative wage of male skilled workers on negotiated wage changes during the 1960s. The coefficient of *RWSKILL70* describes the *additional* effect on negotiated wages during the 1970s. The total influence of the skill differential during the 1970s is described by the sum of the *RWSKILL* and *RWSKILL70* coefficients.

Table 8-3. *Negotiated Wage-Rate Regressions, Denmark, 1960–75*

Regression number	Group covered	Constant	UR_t	$PRICE_t$	POLICY	$RWSKILL_{t-1}$	$RWSKILL70_{t-1}$	$RWSEX_{t-1}$	$RWSEX70_{t-1}$	$\bar{R}^2$	Standard error	Durbin-Watson
						Independent variable[a]				Summary statistic		
1	All workers	4.101 (2.26)	0.351 (1.11)	−0.237 (1.08)	−3.234 (1.98)	...	...	...	...	0.16	2.49	2.82
2	All workers	−20.05 (1.87)	0.600 (1.91)	−0.205 (0.92)	−0.258 (1.74)	1.071 (2.30)	0.212 (1.93)	...	...	0.36	2.17	2.03
3	All workers	−1.26 (0.15)	0.422 (1.15)	−0.168 (0.54)	−3.698 (1.82)	...	...	0.142 (0.69)	0.060 (0.72)	0.06	2.64	2.68
4	Semiskilled males	−22.990 (1.69)	0.484[b] (1.66)	−0.170 (0.60)	−3.092 (1.64)	1.174 (2.03)	0.246 (1.75)	...	...	0.25	2.76	2.12
5	Women	−18.936 (1.31)	0.332 (0.786)	−0.335 (1.11)	−3.223 (1.61)	1.137 (1.82)	0.399 (2.71)	...	...	0.37	2.93	2.13

Sources: Negotiated rates, *RWSKILL*, *RWSEX*, Danish Employers Federation, Statistical Department; *UR*, OECD, *Main Economic Indicators, 1960–79* (Paris: OECD, 1980), pp. 240–41; *PRICE*, International Monetary Fund, *International Financial Statistics, 1981 Yearbook* (Washington, D.C.: IMF, 1981), pp. 158–59. Numbers in parentheses are *t*-statistics; $\bar{R}^2$ is coefficient of determination adjusted for degrees of freedom.

a. *UR* is the insured unemployment rate; *PRICE* is the annual rate of change in the consumer price index; *POLICY* is a variable taking the value 1 during the Danish incomes policy of 1962–64 and zero otherwise; *RWSKILL* and *RWSEX* are, respectively, the proportionate wage differentials between skilled and semiskilled and between male and female workers, defined as 100 (lnW_i − lnW_j); and *RWSKILL70* and *RWSEX70* are interactions between the relative wage variables and a dummy variable taking the value 1 during the 1970s and zero otherwise.

b. Unemployment rate for semiskilled males.

unions are generally organized along the dimension of skill, not sex, and that under the prevailing wage-payment systems, it is easier for skilled workers as a group than male workers as a group to thwart the distributional objectives of the LO during the period between negotiations. The influence of distributional factors can be clarified further by a disaggregated analysis of negotiated wage changes.

Since the stated objective of the LO is to help the least well paid workers, increases in the relative wages of skilled workers should have the strongest positive effect on the negotiated wages of less highly skilled and female workers. This proposition is examined in regressions 4 and 5 in table 8-3, which test for relative wage effects on the negotiated rates of semiskilled males and women, most of whom are in less highly skilled jobs. The pattern of coefficients is consistent with the view that redistributional objectives were an important element in the growth of negotiated wages during the 1970s. Regressions 4 and 5 indicate that during the first half of the 1970s an increase of 1 percentage point in the relative wage of skilled workers was associated with a subsequent increase of 1.4 percentage points in the negotiated rate of semiskilled males and an increase of 1.5 percentage points in the female rate—both considerably higher than the average. The effect on women's rates was particularly strong in the 1970s.

The second effect of negotiated rates on the growth of earnings is also related to distributional tensions. While negotiated rates have themselves been a relatively small component of the total increase in earnings, the egalitarian character of the central agreements has set the stage for future wage pressure in the form of drift. In this significant respect the data on negotiated rates understates the ultimate effect of the central agreement on the growth of labor costs. It is also suggestive of the limitations of an incomes policy that seeks to restrain the outcome of central negotiations without dealing with their distributional implications.

WAGE DRIFT. Throughout the 1970s wage drift continued to contribute significantly to Danish wage inflation, accounting for more than 40 percent of earnings growth. Unlike wage-rate increases from centralized negotiations and wage-indexation payments, drift is inherently decentralized and arises through varied mechanisms. Workers covered by the Danish minimal-wage system, for example, are permitted to negotiate at the firm level for increases above the base wage set in the central negotiations. Since the proportion of workers under the minimal-wage system increases with skill, it is easier for drift to emerge for skilled

460 DENMARK

workers—and the freedom of the LO to pursue a more egalitarian wage structure in negotiations may rest on the existence of the minimal-wage system.[17] A second source of drift is the so-called special or local level of negotiations over piecework and overtime. Finally, workers covered by the "normal wage" system manage at times to obtain more than the central agreement provides.[18]

The importance of wage drift throughout the postwar period has created problems for all parties. For the LO, the fact that a significant element of earnings emanates from decentralized and at times unauthorized bargaining erodes the standing of the federation as a source of workers' well-being. Drift has also tended to thwart the labor federation's egalitarian objectives. For employers, drift constitutes a significant element of uncertainty in the future development of labor costs once a central agreement has been signed. This uncertainty is viewed most negatively by the DAF, which is concerned with the international competitiveness of Danish exports. Among individual employers, there is apparently more ambivalence. The DAF has fined some firms whose pay increases have exceeded the provisions of the central agreement and has told others that it would indemnify them for losses suffered from wildcat strikes that developed from resisting pressures for drift. Nevertheless, employers have usually paid the drift in an effort to avoid losing workers as well as to avoid slowdowns—a response that suggests that a certain amount of drift may have been in response to pressures from excess demand, particularly in the construction and public sectors during the late 1960s and early 1970s. For the government, drift represents the element of earnings that is least subject to institutional control and hence is least subject to policy regulation. More ominous, drift could cancel the effectiveness of incomes policies directed at the central wage negotiations and the indexation system by compensating for wage restraint achieved through such policies.

The fact that drift appears to be beyond the reach of the government or the larger labor-market institutions raises several questions of central importance for macroeconomic policy. We have noted, for example, how centrally negotiated rates and wage-indexation payments appear to

17. According to statistics maintained by the DAF, average annual wage drift between 1961 and 1975 (expressed as a percentage of the hourly earnings from the preceding year) was 5.6 percent for skilled males, 4.0 percent for semiskilled males, and 3.2 percent for women. The average for all workers was 4.6 percent.

18. For a more extended discussion of the sources of Danish wage drift, see Jeppeson, *Lon og Priser*, p. 19.

be beyond the direct influence of demand-management policies. Is the behavior of drift similarly independent of labor-market pressures? Danish wages are indexed to price changes, but the indexation system provides only partial compensation for changes in the net price index and no compensation for the price effects of indirect taxation. Do Danish workers live with money illusion, or does wage drift make up for the shortfall in the indexation system?[19] The LO regularly attempts to narrow wage differentials in central negotiations. Does drift tend to restore the original differentials, as is frequently alleged, thereby contributing to wage pressures in the next central agreement? And if the LO practices wage restraint in central negotiations in an effort to be supportive of the economic policy of the Social Democrats, does this simply trigger an offsetting increase in wage drift?

These questions are addressed in the regression results reported in table 8-4. In these regressions, annual wage drift is initially related to the insured unemployment rate, UR, the rate of change of the consumer price index or the net price index, $PRICE$ or $NETPRICE$, and relative wage measures. Of the latter, $RWSKILL$ and $RWSEX$, respectively, measure the proportionate wage differentials between skilled and semi-skilled male workers and between male and female workers. The first point of interest in the drift regression results is the significance of the unemployment rate. In contrast to the insulation of negotiated rates and wage-indexation payments from the effects of demand-management policies on labor-market pressures, an increase of 1 percentage point in the insured unemployment rate is associated with a reduction of 1 percentage point in drift, other things being equal. The effect of labor-market pressure on overall earnings, however, has been muted by the importance of wage-indexation payments and negotiated rates that have amounted to 60 to 75 percent of earnings during the 1970s. Thus, there have been significant limitations on the effect of demand-management policies on labor costs in Denmark.

A second finding of interest concerns the influence of price changes on the behavior of wage drift. Although the indexation system did not provide full compensation for changes in the net price index, the regression analyses reported in table 8-3 indicated that negotiated wages did not provide the shortfall. In table 8-4, however, it is clear that wage drift is quite sensitive to price movements, and the nature of this

19. It is clear from the insignificant price change shown in table 8-2 that negotiated wages do not make up for the shortfall.

Table 8-4. Wage-Drift Regressions, Denmark, 1960–75

Regression number	Group of workers	Constant	UR	NET-PRICE	RWSKILL	RWSEX	DIFF	WSKILL	WSEMI	RATE	RATE70	R^2	Standard error	Durbin-Watson
1	All workers	2.069 (4.33)	−0.221 (2.16)	0.545 (8.29)	…	…	…	…	…	…	…	0.82	0.780	1.95
2	All workers	7.99 (2.56)	−0.302 (2.96)	0.457 (6.05)	…	…	…	…	…	…	…	0.85	0.710	2.10
3	All workers	0.944 (0.41)	−0.202 (1.82)	0.583 (5.76)	−0.251 (1.91)	0.027 (0.51)	…	…	…	…	…	0.81	0.803	2.05
4	All workers	8.476 (2.62)	−0.303 (2.92)	0.461 (6.00)	−0.281 (2.03)	…	0.132 (0.79)	…	…	…	…	0.85	0.722	2.00
5	Skilled males	13.498 (3.32)	−0.613[b] (3.09)	0.405 (4.06)	−0.447 (2.58)	…	…	…	…	…	…	0.78	0.935	1.56
6	Skilled males	29.96 (3.89)	−0.467[b] (2.61)	0.550 (5.29)	…	…	…	−0.606 (3.76)	0.585 (3.71)	…	…	0.84	0.792	2.43
7	Semiskilled males	7.331 (1.97)	−0.307[c] (3.43)	0.400 (4.35)	−0.189 (1.24)	…	…	…	…	…	…	0.78	0.860	2.74
8	Semiskilled males	11.380 (1.29)	−0.308[c] (3.33)	0.435 (3.74)	…	…	…	−0.238 (1.29)	0.233 (1.30)	…	…	0.77	0.890	2.83
9	All workers	7.438 (2.00)	−0.288 (2.34)	0.455 (5.39)	−0.221 (1.34)	…	…	…	…	−0.039[d] (0.42)	0.027[d] (0.18)	0.82	0.770	2.00
10	All workers	10.215 (3.49)	−0.328 (3.61)	0.373 (4.89)	−0.331 (2.74)	…	…	…	…	−0.056[e] (0.60)	1.53[e] (2.31)	0.88	0.630	1.92

Sources: *NETPRICE*, Danmarks Statistik, *Statistisk Årbog* [Statistical yearbook] (Copenhagen: Danmarks Statistik, 1965), p. 225; ibid., 1978 ed., p. 233; wage drift, *WSKILL, WSEMI*, Danish Employers Federation, Statistics Department; for sources of other variables, see notes to table 8-3. Numbers in parentheses are *t*-statistics.

a. *NETPRICE* is the annual rate of change in the net price index; *DIFF* = *PRICE* − *NETPRICE*. *WSKILL* and *WSEMI* are natural logarithms (multiplied by 100) of the earnings levels of skilled and semiskilled male workers, respectively; *RATE* is a measure of negotiated wage changes, and *RATE70* is the same interacted with a dummy variable that takes the value 1 for the 1970s and zero otherwise. All other variables and statistics are as defined in table 8-3.

b. Unemployment rate for skilled males.

c. Unemployment rate for semiskilled males.

d. Variables constructed using the rate of change of actual negotiated wage rates.

e. Variables constructed using the difference between actual and predicted change in negotiated rates computed from regression 2, table 8-3.

sensitivity has interesting implications for the options that were open to Danish policymakers during the 1970s. First, the size of the price coefficients—in regressions 1-4, table 8-4, for example—is of interest, because in combination with the compensation rate of about 0.70 provided by the wage-indexation system the wage drift results indicate that Danish workers are (at least!) fully compensated for net price increases. Drift removes the money illusion "institutionalized" by the indexation system. But this merely indicates the difficulties confronting Danish efforts to adjust real wages to the macroeconomic realities that followed the oil and raw materials price increases of 1973–74; the combined effect of a long-standing institutional arrangement and the most decentralized and hence least controllable element of the wage-determination system operated to adjust money wages fully to increases in net prices.

The fact that wage drift has compensated for the shortfall of the indexation system has a second implication. Policies that tinker with the indexation system in order to reduce its rate of payout may be futile. Wage drift may simply adjust itself to maintain real wages. This point becomes relevant in evaluating the policy of the Danish government toward indexation payments since 1976.

On the other hand, drift follows the net price index more closely than it follows the full consumer price index. This is seen most clearly in regression 4, table 8-4, which tests for a differential responsiveness of drift to the net price index and to *DIFF*, the difference between changes in the *full* CPI and changes in *net* prices (consisting of changes in indirect taxes and subsidies). The results indicate that drift was not responsive to the excess of full CPI over net price increases: variations in indirect taxes, a frequent instrument of policy in Denmark after 1973, would not provoke wage drift responses. Variations in the willingness of employers to grant drift is likely to account for the differential responsiveness measured in the regressions. Movements in producer prices, which reflect market factors, are more likely to be correlated with changes in net prices than with changes in indirect taxes. Demands for wage drift to offset new indirect taxes may therefore be strongly resisted by employers—a response that may account for the wildcat strikes that followed the announcement of increases in indirect taxes by the Danish government in the mid 1970s.

A third general issue illuminated by the regression results in table 8-4 concerns the interplay between drift and changes in the wage structure.

The results confirm the view that efforts to compress skill differentials in central negotiations will feed the inflationary process by triggering efforts to use wage drift to offset the negotiated changes. Regressions 2 and 4, for example, indicate that a reduction of 1 percentage point in the relative wage of skilled males is associated with an increase in overall wage drift of one quarter of a percentage point in the following year.[20] Changes in the sex differential do not significantly influence drift, however. The interaction between variations in the wage structure and in wage drift are sharpened by a disaggregated analysis of wage drift. In table 8-4 an analysis of wage drift for skilled males (regressions 5 and 6) and semiskilled males (regressions 7 and 8) is reported, based on two alternative specifications of the relative wage effects. A comparison of the coefficients of the lagged relative wage in regressions 5 and 7 indicates that the main source of the effect of relative wage changes on drift, measured in regression 2, is the larger and more significant influence of changing skill differentials on the wage drift obtained by skilled males. The relative-wage coefficient is much smaller and is statistically insignificant in the regression for semiskilled males. Regressions 6 and 8 present an alternative specification of the relative wage variable by entering the log of the earnings level of skilled and of semiskilled men separately. They tell the same story of the relative influence of changes in the wage structure on drift at various levels of the skill structure.[21]

The final issue raised by wage drift concerns its relation to negotiated rates. Two methods of testing for the proposition that drift "compensates" for unusually small or unusually large changes in negotiated rates are reported in regressions 9 and 10 of table 8-4. In the first of these regressions the change in the negotiated wage rate is added as a variable to the basic drift equation by itself (*RATE*) and is caused to interact with a dummy variable taking the value of 1 for the 1970s (*RATE70*). These variables are not significantly related to wage drift (see regression 9). A second view of this process is that drift will only "compensate" for abnormally large or abnormally small negotiated wage changes. From

20. There is some sensitivity to specification. When the rate of change of the full CPI is substituted for the rate of change of net prices in regression 2, the coefficient of the relative wage variable becomes -0.40. On general statistical grounds, however, the specifications using net prices are superior.

21. This specification also provides a check on whether the negative correlation between drift and the relative wage in regressions 5 and 7 was a spurious result of the similarity of the denominator of the dependent variable and the numerator of the independent variable in these equations.

this perspective, drift would respond to deviations from normal behavior of the negotiated wage rate represented by the residuals from a regression describing the average behavior of rates during the period under study. (The *RATE* variable used in regression 10, table 8-4, consists of the residuals from regression 2 in table 8-3; *RATE70* is the interaction of this variable with a dummy variable that is "turned on" for the 1970s.) This specification also shows no significant relation between drift and nego- tiated wage changes during the 1960s.[22] From 1970 to 1975, however, the results indicate that drift was positively correlated with deviations of negotiated rates from their normal behavior. This finding has important policy implications, for it suggests the possibility that an incomes policy that succeeded in restraining negotiated rates below their normal rate of increase (given underlying conditions) would "spill over" into wage drift decisions to produce a further reduction in the growth of earnings. The extent to which this relation held during the late 1970s will be considered further in an evaluative discussion later in the chapter.

Policy Constraints and Options

The foregoing analysis of wage behavior clarifies the role of labor- market developments in the policy dilemma faced by Denmark following the supply shocks of 1973–74. While deteriorating terms of trade implied a slower growth of national income, the growth of real wages remained unchanged initially. Employers generally responded by marking prices up rather than accepting the reduced profit shares implied by these developments. While this temporarily narrows the gap between real wages and real national income per employee, the indexation system provides partial nominal wage compensation to workers and wage drift provides more. These reactions interfere with progress in improving foreign trade. Without a reduction in the profit share, further narrowing of the gap depends either on increased taxation by the public sector to drive a wedge between gross wage income and consumption or on action to mitigate the growth of real incomes. Certain constraints on the use of traditional demand-management policies, however, elevated the prom- inence of the incomes policy option.

Before the supply shocks, Danish policymakers had generally been unwilling to forgo the goal of full employment in the interests of restoring

22. Unreported results using lagged values of negotiated wage changes were also insignificant.

external balance. The result was low unemployment and considerable domestic inflation.[23] At the same time little was done to restore the competitive position of the export sector.

Instead, Danish policymakers have accepted constraints on the flexibility of monetary policy in order to produce an adequate level of foreign reserves. In particular the Central Bank has provided incentives to borrow abroad by keeping domestic interest rates high. The consequent growth in capital imports has kept foreign reserves generally in line with imports, but the high-interest-rate policy has limited the flexibility of monetary policy, and "importantly restrained the use of monetary instruments for influencing the structure and development of domestic demand."[24] This placed the burden of domestic demand-management policy on fiscal policy, but the flexibility of fiscal policy was limited by the long-term efforts to raise living standards through a rapid growth of public expenditure.

Following the oil price increase, the fundamental problem faced by Danish policymakers was to achieve a significant transfer of real resources from domestic demand into the foreign balance subject to the foregoing institutional features and restraints on the use of traditional policy instruments. This implied policies that would reduce the gap between real wages and real national income per employee in order to reduce the claim on resources by private consumption expenditures.

The traditional approach to this problem would have been through exchange-rate adjustment. With the indexation of incomes, however, the initial price increases associated with devaluation would have been transmitted rapidly into the Danish cost structure and threatened the goal of restoring international competitiveness. Thus, before 1979 Denmark de facto accepted a "hard-currency option" similar to that pursued in Austria and has initiated only small adjustments in its exchange rate with respect to countries in the European Snake.[25]

A further consideration facing Danish policymakers was the indexation of the income tax system. Indexation of income tax schedules on

23. The OECD commented that "given the differential cost and price developments at home and abroad, the authorities could only sustain full employment conditions by permitting strong domestic demand pressure to persist and thus accepting the accompanying spillover into imports as an inevitable consequence." OECD Economic Surveys, *Denmark*, April 1977, pp. 16–17.

24. Ibid., p. 15.

25. The effective exchange rate appreciated about 5 percent in 1970–74 and appreciated another 5 percent in 1974–79. Ibid., July 1979, p. 39.

the basis of consumer price developments was introduced in 1970, thereby reducing the amount of fiscal drag associated with domestic inflation. Effective in 1976, however, both tax brackets and basic exemptions were adjusted in accordance with increases in hourly industrial wage rates instead of consumer price increases. This alteration was part of a broader income tax reduction bill that was estimated to reduce the average and marginal tax rates of the average Danish household 5 and 9 percentage points, respectively.[26] In an important respect, however, the tax-indexation system overcorrected for fiscal drag. The linkage to wages, along with the adjustment of current allowances and brackets to past rates of inflation, raised the level of disposable income and price increases. By reversing rather than neutralizing the normal effect of inflation on tax payments (in unindexed tax systems) the Danish system of tax indexation seems to have exacerbated the macroeconomic adjustment problem of the 1970s, for the resultant increase in real disposable income made the shifts of resources from consumption to the foreign sector more difficult.[27] In 1979 this factor was mitigated when Denmark returned to the basis of changes in the CPI.

Faced with a relatively modest restraining effect of unemployment on increases in earnings and the foregoing constraints on other policy tools, the Danes in their fiscal policy since mid 1976 have emphasized the use of indirect tax increases to curb the rate of growth of private consumption. Always an important element of the Danish tax structure, indirect tax increases accounted for about a fourth of the total increase in the CPI in 1977 and 1978 (see table 8-5) and rose to 35 percent of public revenue. These policies succeeded in simultaneously choking off the domestic expansion and raising domestic prices.

Danish Incomes Policies

Given the importance of centralized labor-market institutions in Danish income determination, the influence assigned to domestic wage pressures in the inflation process, and the limitations on demand management associated in part with frequently changing minority govern-

26. Ibid., July 1975, p. 23.
27. On the other hand, the introduction of tax indexation may have mitigated potential "tax push" pressures on wages without formal indexation arrangements, as in Norway.

Table 8-5. *Measures of Consumer Prices, Denmark, 1972–78*
Percentage change from preceding year

Year	Total	Net[a]	Difference
1972	9.3	9.2	0.1
1973	9.3	9.2	0.1
1974	15.2	15.0	0.2
1975	9.6	10.5	-0.9
1976	9.0	8.6	0.4
1977	11.1	8.6	2.5
1978	10.1	7.5	2.6

Source: Danmarks Statistik, *Konjunturoversigt* [Economic trends], various issues.
a. Excluding indirect taxes.

ments, it is hardly surprising that there have been periodic attempts to establish formal concerted-action or social-contract arrangements since the early 1960s. The original arrangement was similar in objective and design to the social-contract institutions developed in Norway during the 1970s. For reasons that will be detailed later, however, the initial Danish arrangements did not prove durable, and the government concentrated on direct price restraint while resisting direct intervention into the wage-determination process until the mid 1970s. In the aftermath of the OPEC supply shock, however, the Folketing assumed a growing responsibility in the determination of incomes policy that left the collective bargaining institutions with a seemingly diminished function in income determination.

First Efforts

In response to an economic crisis brought on by a significant balance-of-payments deficit, the Folketing in 1962 established an Economic Council consisting of some twenty representatives of unions, employers, the civil service, agriculture, and the handicrafts. The ministries of Finance and of Economics and the Danish National Bank participated ex officio. Most important, there was a three-member Board of Chairmen, so far made up of academic economists, which was empowered to meet separately and to issue policy statements independent of the rest of the council. The Board of Chairmen initially recommended that negotiations over wages, over government salaries, and over agricultural subsidies and market prices be concluded simultaneously to avoid the leapfrogging behavior that had sometimes accompanied sequential income determination in the three sectors. (This anticipated by a decade the initial move of the Norwegian concerted-action institutions.) The interest groups represented on the Economic Council agreed to this in principle, but the unions and employers were unable to agree on implementation and the Folketing ultimately legislated the recommendation as part of a general incomes policy package that included a temporary freeze on money incomes.

In the face of the balance-of-payments crisis and a favorable political environment (a government coalition that included the Social Democrats), this policy package appeared to produce some wage restraint in 1963 and 1964, but with subsequent changes in the underlying political and economic conditions it became increasingly difficult for the council to serve as an effective forum for coordinated income determination.[28] Instead, the Board of Chairmen issued guidelines for noninflationary wage increases based on forecasts of growth in productivity and changes in the terms of trade. With this development, the Economic Council acknowledged de facto that it would not be able to serve as a vehicle for multilateral income determination and assumed its present status as a respected independent agency for economic research and short-term forecasts that are generally accepted by both parties.

The "wage norms" that were the result of the council's forecasts were similar to those adopted in first-generation incomes policies in several other countries. They provided a particularly uncertain and unpalatable "norm" to unions, however, in a country in which earnings included wage drift and indexation payments in addition to negotiated wages. If unions saw the guideline as their target, drift and indexation drove earnings well over the norm. If the norm was adjusted for the latter two components of earnings, unions became "residual claimants" of increases in earnings—a position that did not enhance their institutional security. In that event, increases in earnings substantially exceeded the guideline, and all the important issues of income determination that stimulated the formation of the Economic Council continued to face Denmark at the beginning of the 1970s.

The 1970s

Incomes policy discussions and initiatives during the 1970s took place in an environment of sharp conflict among the larger labor-market

28. For details of developments during the 1960s, see Ulman and Flanagan, *Wage Restraint,* pp. 127–46.

institutions over the scope of collective bargaining and the general political instability that was in no small part attributable to the inflation issue. Government incomes policy activity was directed toward the two-year collective bargaining cycle. In anticipation of the spring 1971 contract expirations, the government proposed in 1970 that wage earners forgo three wage portions expected to accrue during 1970 from the indexation system, that the distribution of company dividends be restricted, and that employers' contributions to social security funds be increased. Since each of the larger labor-market organizations could find something offensive in this package, the proposal was quickly rejected on the grounds of protecting traditional freedom to negotiate. Faced with this intransigence, the government adopted in May 1970 a peculiar combination of direct and indirect measures to restrain prices. It established a partial price freeze for services, effective until the expiration at the end of February 1971 of the labor agreements then in force. Rather than alter the indexation system, however, the authorities agreed, in a move that was to be repeated in 1975, to mitigate the effect of the indexation system on labor costs by reimbursing employers for the second two wage portions expected to be triggered in September 1970 by price developments. The Folketing subsequently urged negotiations between unions, employers, and public employees over criteria for the development of incomes.[29] Little came of this suggestion, however, partly because the unions had reservations about cooperating with a conservative government on incomes policy, and by October 1970, the Folketing was willing to approve a government bill for a general freeze of prices and profits at the level of September 1, 1970, until the end of February 1971. When negotiations were protracted, the proposed freeze was extended to the end of March.[30]

The 1971 agreement was concluded without a strike and provided for average wage-rate increases of 4 percent in 1971 and 2.5 percent in 1972. These were not out of line with earlier agreements but exceeded the hopes of the government. The settlement did nothing to ease the more fundamental pressures on labor costs, however. There was no change in the indexation system and no effort to address the wage-drift problem. In fact the distinct egalitarian pattern of the negotiated increases—female and low-wage male workers (about a quarter of union membership) received increases of 9 to 12 percent, while the rates for all others

29. OECD Economic Surveys, *Denmark,* June 1970, p. 29.
30. Ibid., July 1971, p. 24.

remained unchanged—raised the prospect of considerable wage drift for skilled workers during the two years covered by the contract. The settlement also provided for an additional holiday, improved pensions, and reduced hours for shift workers.

With the negotiators unwilling to address the wage-drift problem, the Folketing on April 2 replaced the expiring general price controls with the more limited Prices and Profits Act of 1971, which allowed only the negotiated wage and indexation components of increases in labor costs to be passed through into prices; wage drift was to be resisted by employers or absorbed out of profits. Price increases reflecting increased costs of raw materials and transportation were also permissible. In addition, for six months the prices of public services could be raised only if the increases were warranted by changes in the prices of purchased goods and services.[31] The law was administered by the Monopolies Control Authority, a body with forty price inspectors, whose normal function was to review pricing in certain concentrated industries. Although violators could be fined, the resources for enforcement were too thin to review pricing decisions systematically, and scrutiny was concentrated on larger enterprises. Many firms, moreover, applied for specific exemptions that were included to reduce the distorting influence of the legislation on market signals. In this environment, employers did not offer stiff resistance to wage drift for skilled workers that was stimulated by the negotiated compression of wage differentials. Furthermore, the new law was unable to contain the price explosion that followed the relaxation of the more stringent controls established six months earlier. Between the average for the fourth quarter of 1970 and that for the first quarter of 1971, when the freeze was in effect, the CPI increased at an annual rate of only 2.4 percent, down from a rate of 7.6 percent during the preceding year. But in the first two quarters of the Prices and Profits Act, prices rose at annual rates of 4.3 percent and 8.5 percent, respectively.[32]

The 1973 negotiations took place against a background of widespread labor shortages, high expectations concerning membership in the European Economic Community, and a coalition government led by the Social Democrats. While the Prices and Profits Act of 1971 was still on the books, the rise in consumer prices was accelerating significantly and earnings continued to grow at double-digit rates. Nevertheless, the

31. Ibid., p. 25.
32. Ibid., July 1972, p. 61.

government did not propose an incomes policy to guide bargaining. Despite the importance of the wage issues, conflict over the actual functioning of the tripartite system led to the most severe breakdown in Danish collective bargaining in thirty years, with strikes and lockouts that idled 260,000 workers for four weeks. Since the election of the new Social Democratic coalition in 1971, employers had become increasingly concerned with a breakdown in the traditional spheres of influence between collective bargaining and legislation over labor-market issues. With the Social Democratic government, unions approached the government more frequently for legislation covering items they were unable to obtain through collective bargaining, and the government was willing to make unilateral arrangements with the unions on laws leading to larger contributions by employers without consulting the DAF. The employers argued the importance of being able to forecast future production costs accurately at the conclusion of a collective bargaining agreement, although wage drift rendered this impossible, and in 1973 asked the government for a guarantee that there would be no new bills that would increase labor costs submitted to the Folketing during the course of the next two-year collective agreement. When the government refused, the DAF sought in the 1973 negotiations to obtain a commitment from unions to stay away from the government. The nervousness of employers on the issue was by now heightened by the interest of the unions and Social Democrats in the economic-democracy proposal, which will be discussed in more detail later. The unions also resisted, and a strike and lockout lasted from March 21, 1973, to April 19, 1973.

The ultimate settlement included, as the employers had desired, a protocol indicating that neither the LO nor the DAF would make a political initiative toward the government without first negotiating the matter with the other organization. The agreement also provided for substantial increases in negotiated rates, however, and an improvement in the wage-indexation rate. Flat rate increases in hourly wages and a commitment to equal pay for men and women also continued the egalitarian tone of collective bargaining settlements and provided a continued impetus for wage drift among skilled workers. The agreement therefore promised considerable domestic wage pressure on prices even before the effects of the oil price decisions by OPEC were felt. The oil price increase, as shown in figure 8-1, was followed by increases in unemployment and inflation to double-digit rates.

Against this background, the Social Democrats suffered heavy losses in the December 1973 elections, losses that reflected public disaffection with economic policy. Assuming office in the middle of a two-year collective agreement, the right-of-center Liberal minority government led by Poul Hartling could do little immediately about the growth of earnings. Instead, the government responded to the economic crisis by reviewing arrangements for the direct control of prices and by instituting measures intended to reduce domestic consumption. Given a widespread view that the Prices and Profits Act of 1971 had been ineffectual, an eight-week price freeze, from which only price increases attributable to higher import prices and commodities covered by the European Economic Community market agreement were exempt, was imposed during January and February 1974 while the Folketing discussed long-term economic measures. At the end of the temporary freeze, a new law was passed, which basically removed the exemptions embedded in its predecessor, the Prices and Profits Act, and permitted the Monopolies Control Authority to intervene in the determination of prices and profit margins when it was "considered necessary."[33] With the authority's slim resources for enforcement, however, the legislation could not effect significant additional direct control over prices.

In an effort to reduce the inflationary potential of the deteriorating terms of trade, the Folketing attempted to reduce consumer demand by passing legislation requiring compulsory savings, to be paid into special bank accounts, out of incomes above specified thresholds as well as a package increasing the annual weight tax on automobiles and indirect taxes on tobacco products, alcoholic beverages, and certain durable household goods. The indirect tax increases were limited to final consumption commodities that were predominantly imported and, unlike later increases in the general value-added tax, did not add significantly to the effects of the oil price increase in shifting the aggregate supply curve for domestic production. The indirect tax increases, however, are excluded from the net price, or wage-regulation, index that is used for triggering payments under the Danish system of indexation. Recognizing the effect of these policies on disposable incomes, labor responded with two days of widespread wildcat strikes and local pressures for offsetting wage increases, and wage drift accelerated further (see table 8-6).

By the end of the year, with earnings rising at an annual rate higher than 20 percent, the Hartling government proposed a freeze on wages,

33. Ibid., July 1974, p. 19.

Table 8-6. *Sources of Growth in Earnings, Denmark, 1967–79*

Percentage change from preceding year

Source	1967	1968	1969	1970	1971	1972	1973	1974	1975	1976	1977	1978	1979
Percentage change													
Negotiated rates	1.9	2.7	6.7	1.2	6.4	2.4	2.4	3.0	5.9	1.0	2.3	2.5	1.2
Indexation	3.5	4.5	2.0	3.4	4.5	3.9	3.5	10.3	10.1	7.3	3.7	3.4	3.1
Drift	3.7	2.8	2.3	5.7	4.5	4.5	7.5	9.0	5.5	3.8	4.4	3.9	5.9
Total earnings	9.1	10.1	11.0	10.3	15.4	10.8	13.4	22.3	21.6	12.1	10.4	9.8	10.2
Percentage distribution													
Negotiated rates	21	27	61	12	42	22	18	13	27	8	22	26	12
Indexation	38	45	18	33	29	36	26	46	47	60	36	35	30
Drift	41	28	21	55	29	42	56	40	25	31	42	40	58
Total earnings	100	100	100	100	100	100	100	100	100	100	100	100	100

Source: Danish Employers Federation, Statistics Department. Figures are rounded.

prices, dividends, and profits, a one-year extension of expiring wage agreements, and a termination of the indexation system. The proposal predictably encountered immediate resistance from the labor unions and Social Democrats, who argued in part that it would be inappropriate to impose a freeze while the centralized negotiations for the next two-year agreement were in progress. With a majority in parliament opposed to his proposal, Hartling went to the electorate. But in January 1975, barely thirteen months after it had taken office, Hartling's center-right coalition government was defeated in the general election. Anker Jørgensen now returned as prime minister, leading a minority Social Democratic government.

This transition marked the beginning of a period of increasing government intervention into income-determination decisions as the formal collective bargaining mechanism became less able to produce agreement over wage growth, and, during the latter half of the 1970s, became an ever less important element in the development of earnings. When the biennial negotiations between the LO and the DAF broke down in early March, the Folketing had to legislate a new two-year agreement based on a proposal advanced by the state mediators in an effort to avoid a repetition of the nationwide strikes that accompanied the 1973 negotiations. The legislation came close to simply extending the previous central agreement. It provided for a general wage increase of 1 percent—remarkably low for a period in which total hourly earnings were rising more than 20 percent a year—an increase in the relative pay of low-wage workers, an increase in the rate of compensation provided by the indexation system, and ceilings on profit margins, interest margins, and dividend and bonus payments.[34]

From the perspective of mitigating inflation, the statutory settlement included several contradictory elements. While the settlement produced a significant reduction in negotiated rates in the following year (see table 8-6), the effect of the indexation system was maintained and skill differentials were narrowed further, continuing the pressure on wage drift. The ceilings on profits and interest margins were likely to produce distortions but were considered necessary to encourage union acquies-

34. The ceiling on profits restricted absolute margins in manufacturing, handicrafts, and a variety of services to the level of March 6, 1975, just before the passage of the law. Interest margins charged by commercial and savings banks were limited to the average interest differential during 1972–74, and dividend and bonus payments during 1975 and 1976 were in general to be held to the 1974 levels. For details of the legislation, see OECD Economic Surveys, *Denmark,* July 1975, pp. 27–28.

Table 8-7. *Components of Hourly Wage Increases in Manufacturing and Construction, Denmark, 1974–76*

Percentage change during half year, at annual rate

Period	Wage agreements	Indexation	Wage drift	Total
First half of 1974	4.5	10.5	5.5	20.5
Second half of 1974	5.5	9.5	4.5	19.5
First half of 1975	6.5[a]	9	5	20.5
Second half of 1975	2	4	5.5	11.5
First half of 1976	2.5	7.5	1.5	11.5
Second half of 1976	2.5	3.5	4	10

Source: OECD Economic Surveys, *Denmark,* April 1977, p. 27.

a. The shortening of the weekly working hours, effective December 1, 1974, accounts for 4 percentage points (annual rate), and 2.5 percentage points (annual rate) is attributable to the wage agreement concluded in March 1975.

cence in the low negotiated rate increase. The settlement, in combination with the somewhat delayed effects of the rapid increase in the rate of unemployment, contributed to a sharp deceleration in earnings in the second half of 1975. As shown in table 8-7, the initial deceleration reflected the lower rates established by the agreement and the lower rate of inflation on indexation payments. Wage drift did not show a significant decline until early 1976.

In August 1976 the government took a step toward greater intervention in the collective bargaining process when the Folketing adopted a 6 percent guideline for annual increases in earnings to apply to the central agreement that would run from March 1977 to March 1979. (The particular percentage was chosen because it was the German standard and represented an effort to tie the Danish krone to the Snake currencies.) Since indexation payments were expected to amount to 4 percent a year, the statutory guideline was interpreted to leave "room" for annual increases of 2 percent in negotiated rates. The "guideline" was no more than a political recommendation, however, since there was no mechanism provided to penalize unions or employers who failed to comply.

Wage drift was conveniently ignored in the accounting. It may be that officials of the LO, the DAF, and the government hoped that a statutory guideline would help choke off drift negotiated in local bargaining. In September 1975 the LO and the government had made a joint incomes policy declaration that stated in part that future wage increases should come from central agreements rather than from bargaining at the plant level. Nevertheless, the national unions were not in a cooperative mood. A few had indicated their intention of withdrawing from central negotiations when the 1975 statutory agreement expired, and in December 1976 there were wildcat strikes over wage issues in the oil and transport sectors. In an effort to forestall anticipatory wage and price increases, the government replaced the ceilings on dividends and on profit and interest margins that had been in effect since March 1975 with a temporary freeze on prices, incomes, and rents until March 1, 1977.[35] At that point price regulation reverted to an amended version of the 1971 Prices and Profits Act that authorized wide intervention into pricing activities without significantly expanding the resources for monitoring and enforcement.[36]

Despite the stringent implications of the August 1976 guideline for the growth of negotiated wages, the LO was predisposed to cooperate with the incomes policy of the Social Democrats. Nevertheless, the central negotiations broke down in March 1977 over the concern of employers with wage drift, now the principal element of uncertainty in labor costs.[37] A proposal by the state mediator was accepted by the unions but rejected by the employers, and the Folketing again stepped in to enact the proposal into law, claiming that it was consistent with the August 1976 guideline.[38] As it happened, however, drift averaged more than 4 percent a year during the two years covered by the 1977 settlement (see table 8-6), and as will become clear in the empirical evaluation of the policies, certain features of the statutory settlement and the special indexation legislation contributed to the magnitude of drift.

Although the LO was predisposed to acquiesce in the Social Democrats' incomes policy despite having opposed similar efforts when the right-of-center Liberal party was in power, it expected government support for political initiatives for economic democracy, housing, and tax reform. The spirit of cooperation was shattered in late August 1978,

35. This freeze made wage increases granted as a result of illegal strikes unlawful. It also prohibited the passthrough of any wage increases into prices during the three-month period, although prices could reflect increased fuel and raw materials costs.

36. In the aftermath of these developments, the Social Democrats gained strength, and the Liberals lost, in the February 1977 general election. The results were interpreted as support for the incomes policies of the Social Democrats.

37. Convinced that drift was in part the result of the efforts of skilled workers to restore compressed wage differentials, the DAF opposed the demand of the LO for wage rate increases of 6 percent for low-wage workers. The DAF also sought a two-year halt to local wage agreements—a demand that the LO probably did not have the authority to enforce.

38. Parliament also passed legislation altering the nature of indexation payments, which will be discussed in the following section.

when the Social Democrats sought to increase their parliamentary strength by forming a coalition with the Liberals. The compromise agreement between the two parties removed the possibility of government support for the political objectives of the LO and instituted a new six-month wage-and-price freeze in anticipation of the 1979 round of negotiations.[39]

The breach nullified incipient plans for a prenegotiation tripartite conference to discuss the government's intention with respect to the proposals of the LO along with future criteria for the growth of incomes. Instead, the LO planned to attempt achievement of its economic-democracy objectives through collective bargaining. They were not successful, however. The 1979 negotiations were again concluded by a statutory settlement based on a proposal by a state mediator when discussions between the LO and the DAF were deadlocked. As in 1977, the settlement provided for a negotiated rate increase of 2 percent a year, to which it was expected another 3.5 percent in indexation payments would be added.[40]

The Indexation System as an Instrument of Incomes Policy

The OPEC price increase stimulated a series of efforts to blunt the effect of the indexation system on domestic inflation in Denmark. In January 1974, during the general policy reappraisal that accompanied the temporary wage and price freeze, the government attempted to initiate a social-contract exchange by offering tax cuts as a substitute for wage increases on account of the effects of higher oil prices on the indexation system.[41] That this proposal was rejected by the unions is hardly surprising, since income tax rates and brackets had been indexed to prices since 1970. Indeed, the indexation of an income tax system reduces government leverage in social-contract negotiations by leaving it little to trade. On the other hand, the offer of such a trade could produce conflicts among unions in a system such as Denmark's, in which the wage-indexation system offers the smallest protection from inflation to the workers who are subject to the highest marginal tax rates. Subse-

39. The freeze permitted price increases that were needed because of rises in the cost of energy and imported raw materials or because of pay increases mandated by collective bargaining agreements. Wage drift could not be passed through.

40. OECD Economic Surveys, *Denmark,* July 1979, p. 28.

41. Ibid., July 1974, p. 37.

quently, the Folketing passed instead a temporary program of subsidies that provided partial reimbursement to most private firms for indexation payments, as it had done in 1971.

With no agreement between the employer and labor organizations on fundamental modification of the indexation system possible, the Danish government felt constrained to allow the system to operate according to a new formula established in 1975 while pursuing a series of policies intended to mitigate the effect of indexation on the growth of domestic costs. In legislation passed in March 1975, the Folketing rebased the wage-regulation index at 100 for January 1975, increased the compensation payment from 40 öre to 60 öre for each increase of three points in the index, and shifted salaried and civil service workers from their previous equal-percentage adjustment to the same flat-rate adjustment that applies to all manual workers. The first two adjustments were essentially offsetting, so for manual workers the degree of compensation for inflation remained unchanged.[42] The change in the nature of indexation for salaried workers and civil servants should have modestly weakened the formal connection between prices and wages without changing the system in any essential way. Indeed, the distributional effect of the changes—the implied further narrowing of wage differentials and decrease in the real earnings of better-paid workers—may have been more significant than their contribution to the ability of the Danish economy to adjust to a severe external price increase.

With little change in the institutional determinants of real-wage rigidity, the government turned its hopes to wage restraint through a social contract and, when this proved unsuccessful—to a significant extent because of the behavior of external prices—it turned its incomes policy ingenuity to the development of methods of mitigating the effects of the wage-indexation system on domestic costs. In formulating the social contract embodied in the statutory wage agreement of September 1975, it had been assumed that the wage-regulation index would be slowed so that only one wage portion would be released every six months. When unexpectedly large price increases in late 1975 would have released two portions in early 1976, the Folketing decided to blunt the effect on domestic costs by compensating employers for half the wage indexation costs from January 1976. The subsidy, which amounted to Kr 1.4 billion, merely postponed the effect, however, since it was

42. Ibid., July 1975, pp. 27–29.

allowed to expire in March 1977, "raising average wage costs by 1½ per cent for 1977 as a whole."[43]

The 1976 legislation made formal the assumption underlying the 1975 social contract and restricted direct wage payments from the indexation system to one portion semiannually. When movements in the wage-regulation index triggered additional portions, the amounts were to be paid by the government into blocked individual accounts with the Supplementary Pension Fund. Once two portions had been paid into the account—one each in July 1977 and January 1978—the government was confronted with the question of what to do with them and with any future payments of excess portions into the fund.

By early 1979, the Danish government faced the problem of achieving a domestic adjustment to a new surge of external price increases, which were rooted in the OPEC price decisions of December 1978, with no greater ability to achieve real-wage flexibility than in 1973–75. During the interim the indexation system had not been altered in any way that fundamentally changed the degree of real-wage rigidity. Unlike in the period 1973–75, the prospects for domestic adjustment were now further diminished by the wage-portion disposal problem, which was a direct result of the attempt to mitigate the effect of the indexation system on domestic costs indirectly, rather than seek a more basic change in the system. There was considerable pressure from the unions to release the portions as direct payments to workers, but any possible disposition of the wage portions frozen by the August 1976 legislation was likely to enter the cost structure along with, and in addition to, current wage-indexation payments. These prospects formed a background to the indexation discussions in the spring 1979 wage negotiations.

The disposition of the wage portions, which, with accrued interest, amounted to Kr 10 billion, or 5 percent of private consumption expenditures, by late 1979, was resolved in the resultant statutory wage settlement, in which "it was . . . decided to convert the income equivalent [of the portions] into a gradual increase of the standard annual paid leave by 1 week (to 5 weeks) [annually] as from 1981."[44] Since this arrangement ultimately would transmit gains through indexation into the cost structure, if not into incomes, it hardly provided a long-run

43. Ibid., July 1979, p. 17.
44. Ibid., July 1980, p. 20.

solution for the function of the indexation system in the Danish inflation process.[45]

By late 1979, however, a series of political changes brought about an effort to achieve more fundamental changes in the indexation system itself. In late September the differences between the Liberal and Social Democratic parties over economic policy were so wide that Prime Minister Anker Jørgensen ended his thirteen-month coalition government. A month later, the Social Democrats were returned to office, somewhat strengthened but still a minority government, and shortly thereafter Jørgensen presented a new economic package. The November 1979 measures included a unilateral devaluation of almost 5 percent, which followed by two months a devaluation of 3 percent against the average of the currencies of the European Monetary System (and 5 percent against the deutsche mark). With these devaluations Denmark in effect abandoned its commitment to the hard-currency policy followed during the 1970s.

Faced with a new surge of external price increases and a somewhat stronger political position, the new government also sought to reduce the impact of wage indexation in exchange for increased taxation of wealth and the adoption of a compulsory profit-sharing approach to "economic democracy" that the unions had not been able to achieve in collective bargaining.

In offering the profit-sharing approach to institutional protection, the government also presented the unions with a political problem of their own. The economic democracy issue was of more interest to union leaders and professional staff than to the rank and file. Conversely the rank and file favored the indexation system more strongly than many union leaders, who recognized the limitations of indexation as a device for maintaining and advancing real earnings in the economic environment of the 1970s. Thus, it would have fallen on the union leaders to convince the members that their interests were best served by accepting a weakening of the indexation system in exchange for compulsory profit sharing. In effect, the union leaders, rather than the government, were faced with the task of arguing that economic growth provided better prospects for advances in real earnings than certain features of the wage-determination process.

45. The OECD estimated that this disposition of the wage portions would raise hourly labor costs by about 2.5 percent. Ibid.

The dilemma was short-lived, however, for it soon became clear that there was strong opposition in the Folketing to the economic-democracy proposals from opposition parties on both the left and the right. The government had to withdraw its support of the scheme, but that left little in the package to interest the unions, although the government relaxed the wage guidelines somewhat.[46]

Evaluation

By the end of the 1970s, Denmark had adopted an array of incomes policies that included wage and price freezes, wage guidelines, statutory settlements, and measures to blunt the effects of the wage-indexation system. None of these measures appeared to move the country any closer to the reestablishment of a social contract, which constituted the earliest Danish approach to incomes policy. In this section we shall consider why the social-contract goal proved so elusive and evaluate the apparent efficiency of the piecemeal incomes policies adopted during the last half of the 1970s.

In examining Austrian incomes policy, we suggested that there were diseconomies of scale in negotiating social contracts. The most durable arrangements arise when the number of participants is small, but in order to keep the number of participants small, the principal political and industrial relations institutions must have mechanisms for resolving internal conflicts. In contrast, developments in Denmark during the 1970s indicate a growing instability in politics and labor relations that weakened these institutions and increased the number of voices that would have to be heard in a social-contract arrangement.

Political Instability

The absence of the consensus that would be a prerequisite for a durable social contract is signaled in part by the multiplicity of political parties in Denmark. The number of political parties represented in the Folketing, moreover, increased significantly during the 1970s, from six in 1968 to eleven in 1977. The growing political fragmentation appeared to be related to sharp underlying disagreements in Danish society over

46. For a brief review of the fate of the package, see "Tough Policies Don't Live Long," *The Economist*, January 5, 1980, p. 51.

DENMARK 483

Table 8-8. *Political Parties Represented in the Folketing, Selected Years, 1957–79*

Percent

Party	1957	1960	1964	1966	1968	1971	1973	1975	1977	1979
Social Democratic	40.0	43.0	43.4	39.4	35.4	40.0	26.3	30.3	37.1	39.4
Radical Liberal	8.0	6.3	5.7	7.4	15.4	15.4	11.4	7.4	3.4	5.7
Conservative People's	17.1	18.3	20.6	19.4	21.1	17.7	9.1	5.7	8.6	12.6
Liberal Democratic	25.8	21.7	21.7	20.0	19.4	17.1	12.6	24.0	12.0	12.6
Single-Tax	5.1	...	...	...	...	...	2.9	...	3.4	2.9
Socialist People's	...	6.3	5.7	11.4	6.3	9.8	6.3	5.1	4.0	5.7
Communist	3.4	...	...	...	...	...	3.4	4.0	4.0	...
Centre Democratic	...	...	...	...	...	...	8.0	2.3	6.3	3.4
Christian People's	...	...	...	...	...	...	4.0	5.1	3.4	2.9
Slesvig	0.6	0.6	...	...	...	...	...	...	...	...
Independent	...	...	3.4	2.9	...	...	...	...	...	...
Left Socialists	...	...	...	...	2.4	...	...	2.4	2.9	3.4
Progress	...	...	...	...	...	...	16.0	13.7	14.9	11.4
Total	100.0	100.0	100.0	100.0[a]	100.0	100.0	100.0	100.0	100.0	100.0
Total number of seats (excluding representatives from Greenland and the Faeroe Islands)	175	175	175	175	175	175	175	175	175	175

Sources: *Levevilkår i Danmark, Statistisk oversigt 1976* [Living conditions in Denmark, compendium of statistics, 1976] (Copenhagen: Danmarks Statistik, 1976), p. 250; *Politiken,* October 24, 1979, p. 3. Figures are rounded.
a. In the 1966 election 2.4 percent of the seats in parliament were won by the Liberal Central party. This party did not win representation in 1968 and did not nominate candidates thereafter.

economic policy, and the formulation of policy became increasingly difficult, provoking frequent changes in government. These changes are summarized in table 8-8, which describes representation by political party in the Folketing.

Throughout the 1950s and 1960s the Social Democratic party was the dominant force, averaging 40 percent of the seats in the Folketing. As a minority party, however, the Social Democrats had to maintain the support of the Socialist People's party as well as of their own left wing, which generally opposed any slowing in the growth rate of social expenditure. During the same period the main opposition, the Liberal Democratic party, held between 20 and 25 percent of the seats. During the late 1960s and early 1970s, however, both parties began to lose standing, while smaller parties, representing more extreme economic and political views, gained support.

The most remarkable gains were made by the Progress party, from its first appearance in the December 1973 election. Under the leadership of Mogens Glistrup, who campaigned on a tax-limitation platform, the Progress party secured the second largest vote in the election, with 16 percent of the seats in the Folketing. In the January 1975 election, the Progress party retained most of its electoral support despite the fact that Glistrup, in his capacity as a highly successful tax lawyer, had been accused of some 2,400 cases of tax evasion. The 1973 election also produced gains for the new Centre Democratic party, which had been started by a disaffected Social Democrat. Most of these gains appeared to come at the expense of the Social Democrats, whose representation plunged in the 1973 election from 40 to 26 percent of the seats in the Folketing as voters reacted against high taxation, inflation, and the continued growth of public expenditures. At the same time, however, there was growing support for the left of the political spectrum as the Communist party won seats for the first time since the late 1950s.

With the declining representation of the major parties, it became increasingly difficult to formulate economic policies that would gain sufficient support to sustain a particular government. When the Social Democratic party lost heavily in the December 1973 election, a minority Liberal party government was formed, with Poul Hartling as prime minister. When the government's policy package, consisting largely of increased indirect taxes on tobacco, alcoholic beverages, automobiles, and durable household goods was passed by the Folketing in May, it was greeted by widespread opposition from labor, culminating in strikes, demonstrations, and pressure for offsetting money wage increases. By December 1974, with the LO and a majority of the political parties opposed to the plans of the minority Liberal party government for a new wage and price freeze, the prime minister called for a general election over his policies in January 1975, only to be defeated after holding office for barely thirteen months.

The successor Social Democratic government was able to win the acquiescence of the LO in an incomes policy that was only slightly less stringent than that proposed by the Liberal government, but continued cooperation appeared to depend upon the government's political support for an economic-democracy, or capital-sharing, proposal. When it became expedient to strike a compromise with the right-of-center Liberal party in an effort to form a coalition strong enough to take decisive economic policy measures, however, the Social Democrats were willing to abandon economic democracy and other policy objectives of the unions. The effort to develop a stronger political configuration caused a loss of government influence with the unions.

Nevertheless, the differences between the Social Democrats and

Table 8-9. *Work Stoppages in Denmark, Selected Periods, 1968–78*

Item	Annual average, 1968–72	1973	Annual average, 1974–78
Number of disputes[a]	42	205	205
Number of workers involved	26,839	337,100	76,870
Number of working days lost	46,840	3,901,200	170,620
Days lost per worker	1.7	11.6	2.2

Source: International Labour Office, *Yearbook of Labour Statistics, 1970* (Geneva: ILO, 1970), p. 790; ibid., *1979*, p. 596.

a. The data include lockouts but exclude political strikes and disputes in which fewer than 100 working days were lost.

Liberals remained too great to facilitate progress toward a major new economic policy, and thirteen months later Jørgensen dissolved the government and called for new elections. The 1979 elections also failed to bring a new political alignment, however, although parties representing extremes of the political spectrum lost ground (see table 8-8).

Labor Relations Malaise

The Danish system of industrial relations also appeared increasingly unstable during the 1970s. Tensions within the labor movement did not cause the formation of new federations conducting independent negotiations, as in Sweden. The Danish LO possessed less authority over affiliated national unions than did its Swedish counterpart, however, and attempts to increase the authority of the LO during the 1970s—by acquiring control over a central strike fund, for example—were rebuffed by the national unions. The limitations on the LO's control over the actions of individual unions may have reduced the impetus to form new federations that specialized in the interests of particular groups of workers, as were formed in Sweden, but as the 1970s progressed the tensions within the national unions began to be released through frequent wildcat strikes.

As table 8-9 indicates, strikes before 1973 were quite subdued. The breakdown of collective bargaining during the central negotiations in 1973 produced a dramatic stepwise change in the frequency, duration, and economic scope of work stoppages.[47] The figures are particularly

47. In the case of the frequency of disputes, the 1974–78 average marks a steady increase in the number of stoppages, from 134 in 1974 to 314 in 1978.

revealing because of the decline in official strikes during the last half of the 1970s. The breakdown of negotiations in 1973 marked the last round of official strikes, since the statutory settlements of 1975, 1977, and 1979 precluded legal work stoppages. As a result, the data signal an increase in unofficial and illegal strikes, despite the fines imposed on participants by the Labor Court. As noted earlier, some of the wildcat strikes represented spontaneous protests against government economic packages that included large indirect tax increases whose price effects would fall outside the scope of the wage-indexation system. Others were more directly aimed at local working conditions. In sum, however, the rise in unofficial strikes added to the pressures for increased wage drift and moved the determination of large parts of the compensation package further from the control of the employer and labor federations in the central negotiations. This reduced the authority of the LO over its affiliates further—a situation that was probably exacerbated by the LO's cooperation with the negotiated wage-growth norm of 2 percent in the 1977 and 1979 rounds of collective bargaining. The DAF, having tried unsuccessfully to encourage its affiliates to stop paying drift, tried to get the LO to exert control over individual unions by making an issue of decentralized wage determination in the 1977 negotiations. The result, however, was a statutory settlement that left the basic tensions unresolved.

Policy Impact on Wages

Earlier we reviewed the direct measures that the Danish government took during the last half of the 1970s to restrain the growth of earnings. These included increasing interventions into the collective bargaining process through statutory settlements in 1975, 1977, and 1979, which were intended to produce smaller increases than would have been negotiated freely in the threatened strike situations in each of those years, supplemented by wage guidelines which formed the basis for statutory settlements in 1977 and 1979. Negotiations were also preceded by increasingly long periods of wage and price freeze in an effort to strengthen the resistance of employers to drift, presumably a factor that contributed to the greater frequency of strikes, and to prevent anticipatory price increases. The government has also tinkered with the indexation system continually since 1975, first subsidizing employers for the payment of certain "portions," then placing all but one portion every

Table 8-10. *Actual Changes minus Predicted Changes in Components of Earnings, Denmark, 1976–79*

Component of earnings	1976 Pre-dicted	1976 Actual minus predicted	1977 Pre-dicted	1977 Actual minus predicted	1978 Pre-dicted	1978 Actual minus predicted	1979 Pre-dicted	1979 Actual minus predicted
Negotiated rates	4.7	−3.7	4.9	−2.6	2.6	−0.1	3.2	−2.0
Wage indexation	a	a	6.9	−3.2	6.0	−2.6	5.6	−2.5
Wage drift								
1	−0.2	3.6	0.6	3.8	4.3	−0.4	1.9	4.0
2	5.4	−1.6	4.5	−0.1	4.3	−0.4	4.7	1.2

Sources: See tables 8-3 and 8-4; predicted values of negotiated rates are from regression 3, table 8-3; wage-indexation payments, the regression in footnote 14; wage drift 1, regression 10, table 8-4; wage drift 2, regression 2, table 8-4.

a. Indexation payments began to be limited in 1977.

six months in a special account in the Pension Fund. These regulations were imposed on an economy in which there was considerable wage drift, however, which, according to our analysis earlier, tended to compensate for price increases not covered by the indexation system and to vary directly with negotiated wages before 1975.

What was the net result of imposing these policies on the wage behavior described earlier? In table 8-10 we compare the actual path of negotiated wages, indexation payments, and wage drift in the late 1970s with the changes predicted on the basis of structural relationships estimated through the first half of the 1970s. It is clear from these computations that the period of the statutory settlements and guidelines was associated with negotiated wage increases that were consistently lower than would have been predicted, given underlying developments in the economy.[48] The same is true of wage-indexation payments during 1977–79, when workers received direct wage compensation for only one portion every six months. In combination, these two policies are associated with reductions in the growth of wage rates and indexation payments that reached almost 6 percentage points in 1977. There are, however, two qualifications. First, the computations in table 8-10 measure short-run effects. This is particularly true of indexation payments, where the disposition of the frozen portions could have considerable influence on future wage growth.

The second qualification concerns the behavior of drift, which was

48. Note, however, the relatively large standard errors of the negotiated wage-rate regressions in table 8-3. For example, the standard error for regression 2 in table 8-3, from which the negotiated rate predictions in table 8-10 are computed, is 2.17.

488   DENMARK

only a direct target of incomes policy during the occasional and limited periods of wage and price "freeze," when drift payments could not be passed through into prices. We compared the actual behavior of wage drift with predictions from two regressions in table 8-10. Statistically, regression 10 in table 8-4 provided the best fit of the data for 1960–75 in our earlier analysis. Predictions from that regression, which had a standard error of only 0.63, are consistently below actual drift during the forecast period, indicating that wage drift tended to cancel some of the restraint in negotiated rates and indexation payments. Much of this appears to be associated with a breakdown in the positive relation between drift and the gap between actual and expected negotiated wage rates, for when regression 2, table 8-4, which omits the rate variable, is used to predict drift, the pattern of prediction errors becomes very different (see the bottom line of table 8-10), and the tendency of drift to "compensate" for the reduction in other components of growth in earnings is not obvious. There was thus no tendency for negotiated wage-rate restraint to spill over into drift. At the same time, wage drift did not increase sufficiently to cancel completely the combined drop in rates and indexation payments below expected growth rates.

In summary, the net effect of the policies was to reduce the growth of earnings below expected rates during 1976–79. There are at least two reasons, however, to doubt the sustainability of this result in future years. The first, discussed earlier, concerns the growing pressure to dispose of the accumulating unpaid indexation portions. The second concerns the willingness and ability of the LO to cooperate by scaling down its money-wage objectives. Such restraint as has been shown has been offered in the expectation of a quid pro quo in the form of government support for political and nonpecuniary objectives of unions, but this support has not been forthcoming. This is seen most clearly in the efforts of the LO to establish economic-democracy arrangements.

Economic Democracy

Although the Danish LO, with its other Scandinavian counterparts, had demonstrated a strong egalitarian commitment, it had also encountered sharp limitations on its ability to alter the distribution of income and wealth substantially through traditional collective bargaining and legislative means. As we have seen, before the 1970s the behavior of wage drift tended to nullify efforts to negotiate a more egalitarian wage structure. During the 1970s negotiated agreements and, to a certain extent, the indexation system achieved some narrowing of wage differentials by sex and, less dramatically, given the role played by drift, by skill. Under the Social Democrats, moreover, the personal income tax system had become one of the most progressive in the world, and as noted in table 8-1, tax revenues represented a larger share of GNP in Denmark than in any other OECD country included in this study. Yet changes in the inequality of income and wealth fell short of LO objectives, and the overall burden of taxation and level of public expenditure became a source of political instability that eroded the electoral support of the Social Democrats during the 1970s. Faced with these limitations on its traditional egalitarian objectives, the LO, with support from some Social Democratic officials, developed proposals for economic democracy beginning in the late 1960s.[49]

The main proposal, which was introduced as a government bill in 1973, called for the establishment of a wage earners' Profit and Investment Fund financed by contributions from private and public employers. The employers' contribution rate would be 1 percent of the wage bill in the first year of the program and would rise by annual increments of half a percentage point until reaching 5 percent in the ninth year of the program. The egalitarian objective was pursued by the use of different criteria for contributions and ownership. Although contributions to the fund would be based on wages, claims on the fund would depend on employment status, individuals who had worked at least thirty-two full weeks qualifying for one annual share while those having worked sixteen to thirty-two weeks would qualify for a half share. After five or seven years, depending on the proposal, workers could draw the value of shares, including dividends and interest. The share certificates could not be sold or negotiated, however, nor could loans be raised on them. Contributions could remain within the firm, in the form of wage-earner

---

49. The proposals for economic democracy should be distinguished sharply from efforts at industrial democracy. The latter typically include procedures for increasing the representation of workers at certain levels of managerial decisionmaking within an organization. In 1947 and 1970, for example, the DAF and the LO signed agreements that provide for cooperation committees with equal representation by employers and employees and that have codetermination powers with respect to personnel policies, safety, and general conditions of work and have consultation rights with respect to production planning and major economic adjustments by companies. The committees may also discuss the structure and application of wage incentives within the enterprise. See Rise, Carlsen, and Lindegaard, *Employers and Workers in Denmark,* pp. 36, 38.

capital, or the fund could make investments. The operations of the fund would be managed by a council of representatives of unions and the state. Notably absent would be employer representatives. Proponents estimated that after five years of operation the capital in the fund would amount to Kr 5 billion, or 5 percent of GNP, and that after fourteen years the share of GNP would rise to 12.5 percent.[50]

The institutional commitment of the LO leaders notwithstanding, the broader basis of support of the economic-democracy proposals seems to be uncertain. Faced with a declining ability to compete in foreign markets, employers instinctively oppose proposals that will directly increase labor costs. Unless the unions were willing to accept a compensating reduction in negotiated wages, the proposal would increase cost pressures. The LO indicated no interest in such a move, and with negotiated rate increases averaging 3 percent a year in the late 1970s (see table 8-2), there was little scope for it to do so. The DAF also argued that it would be preferable to encourage voluntary increases in saving and investment in industry by altering tax legislation that reduced the returns from industrial investments in relation to the return available from investments in financial institutions, government bonds, mortgage society bonds, or real estate. They also maintained that the overall rate of saving had been lowered as a result of large-scale public investments in various forms of income security supported by the LO and Social Democrats.[51]

There was also little support for this approach to economic democracy among rank-and-file union members.[52] In the first instance, it is not clear that the egalitarian features of the plan would appeal to wage earners whose incomes are relatively high any more than the long-standing efforts of the LO to negotiate a less widely dispersed wage structure. Contributions to the fund would be like a tax on the employer, and the effect on wage earners would depend on the ultimate incidence. One alternative is that Danish employers might simply mark prices up by the cost of contributions to the fund, in which case the program would add to the rate of inflation during its first nine years of operation, in the

50. Ibid., pp. 40–43.

51. For a discussion of the views of Danish employers on alternative approaches to the economic democracy issue, see *Co-worker—Co-owner: Discussion Paper on Economic Democracy* (Copenhagen: Danish Employers Confederation and the Federation of Danish Industries, March 1972).

52. Several opinion polls indicated that at least 75 percent of the work force opposed the economic-democracy proposals.

absence of offsetting gains in productivity by new investments as a result of fund activities. From the government's perspective, this possibility would presumably reduce the value of the proposal in social-contract discussions as a quid pro quo for wage restraint on the part of the unions. The pricing policies of most employers in the Danish industrial sector, however, are constrained by world price developments. The cost of contributions to the fund would therefore have to come out of profits or be shifted onto workers.

If the contributions were made at the expense of profits, as is apparently expected by the proponents of the proposal, then all workers would be better off (in the absence of negative employment effects), although low-wage workers would realize proportionately larger gains. A reduction in profits would probably reduce employment in the long run, however, and the ultimate redistributional effect would also depend on the incidence of unemployment. If instead the incidence of contributions to the fund were shifted onto employees as employers offered greater resistance to negotiated wages or to the payment of wage drift, then the high-wage employees could be worse off.

It is by no means clear that the Danish capital-sharing proposals would provide important incentives for expanded profits through the efforts of workers or owners for greater productivity, for as the proposal is designed the potential incentive offered by ownership is diluted by an important free-rider problem: the benefits of additional profits generated by the activities of workers at any one plant would accrue to the fund and hence benefit all wage earners. The workers responsible for the gains would receive a tiny fraction of the benefits, and the link between action and reward is likely to be too small to provide a powerful incentive.

With the strong opposition of employers and lack of interest on the part of the rank and file, the bill submitted in 1973 was dropped after encountering strong opposition in the Folketing. Nevertheless, the leaders of the LO remained interested in the proposal but did not mount a strong effort to rehabilitate the issue until late 1977. The stringent August 1976 guidelines over negotiated wages and the diversion of half the indexation payments presented the LO with a dilemma over its institutional security. On the one hand, the federation wished to support the Social Democrats, who led a shaky coalition in the Folketing and had shown support in accepting both the guidelines in the 1977 central agreement and the alteration of the indexation payments. On the other hand, this left the LO with little to deliver to its members at a time when some national unions, unenthusiastic about the outcome of the 1977 negotiations, were indicating a preference for independent bargaining.

An obvious solution to the dilemma was to deliver on issues that were not regulated by the incomes policy of the Social Democrats, and by the late summer of 1977 the LO began pressing for an economic-democracy bill in return for its continued cooperation in the incomes policy. In response, the government established a tripartite committee to develop co-ownership proposals. The committee was to report in September 1978 so that the unions could get an indication of the government's intentions with respect to economic democracy before negotiations over the 1979 agreement began.

Government support for a new economic-democracy bill, however, and certain public expenditure objectives of the LO were among the first casualties of the coalition between the Social Democrats and the Liberals in August 1978. The economic package that was part of the compromise underlying the coalition removed the possibility of significant policy concessions from the government in response to wage moderation. As noted earlier, this produced a serious breach between the LO and the Social Democrats, eroded the federation's predisposition to moderate wage demands in the negotiations over the 1979 central agreement, and caused a shift in the pursuit of economic-democracy objectives from the legislative to the collective bargaining arena. In a situation in which the statutory settlement was becoming the norm, however, the determination of legislation could not ultimately be escaped.

Conclusions

Confronted with a continuous external imbalance and certain limitations on the flexibility of traditional demand-management tools, Danish authorities have had a continuing interest in developing incomes policies that would slow the growth of money wages. Yet Danish incomes policy has had a strange history. The earliest efforts, in 1962, achieved one of the first social contracts. Of the countries in this study, only Austria made such arrangements earlier. Within two years, however, this arrangement had weakened significantly, and income determination proceeded as before, with growth in earnings reflecting the outcome of centralized negotiations between the LO and the DAF, semiannual indexation payments, and wage drift. Although the government continued to advance incomes policy proposals, none met with the agreement of the labor-market institutions. The unions had a general antipathy to restraints on their freedom of action, while employers regarded a policy that sought to increase the contributions of employers for social benefits while reducing growth in money wages as a contradictory approach to improving the international competitiveness of Danish exports.

The government therefore resisted intervention into the collective bargaining process, despite the growing conflict between the central labor-market organizations that caused a severe strike and expensive settlement in 1973. Instead, the authorities turned to the more direct restraint of domestic prices with a series of price-control measures that were initiated in 1970 and continued throughout the decade. The price regulations varied in their stringency from period to period, but basically they replicated the history of price-control experiments elsewhere. The longest-running legislation contained significant exemptions, and the resources for auditing and enforcement were sufficiently small that compliance could be seen as voluntary. The more rigid programs, typically calling for a period of general freeze on incomes preceding centralized collective bargaining negotiations, were intended to prevent anticipatory price or wage increases. By the end of the 1970s there was some tendency for the length of these freezes to grow as the prenegotiation freezes themselves came to be anticipated. The relaxation of the more stringent freeze regulations tended to be followed by surges of price increases.

The government's noninterventionist stance toward wages changed in the aftermath of the OPEC oil price crises, which produced a sharp increase in inflation and unemployment. Confronted with a large gap between real earnings and real national income, Denmark faced various choices for reducing domestic consumption sufficiently to release resources to pay for the oil imports at relatively low rates of inflation. In principle there were four approaches to reducing disposable income: increased direct taxation, increased indirect taxation, devaluation, and an incomes policy directed toward wage restraint. The use of the first option was circumscribed by the indexation of Danish income taxes. The second option had an element of perversity about it in that it further exacerbated the aggregate supply shift initially induced by the rise in the world prices of oil and raw materials. A *reduction* in indirect taxation would have produced a counteracting shift in the aggregate supply curve, which, when accompanied by appropriate aggregate demand measures, would have limited the consequences for prices and employment of the OPEC shock. The third option was opposed by the labor-market parties and the government. The fourth option had appeal because of the growing inability of the LO and the DAF to resolve the conflicts between them and the huge indexation payments triggered by the post-OPEC inflation. As it happened, the government adopted the second and fourth options— a somewhat contradictory choice, since the indirect tax increases, which are not included in the price index used to determine indexation payments, induced strikes and possible pressure on negotiated wages and wage drift.

The efforts to formulate an incomes policy were directed at negotiated wages and the indexation system. The efforts to achieve negotiated wage restraint, however, produced two predictable institutional reactions. In initially accepting some restraint on wages in an effort to cooperate with the Social Democratic minority government in the late 1970s, the LO sought compensating gains on nonpecuniary issues. With rates restrained by acquiescence with guidelines, indexation payments determined by legislation, and wage drift beyond the reach of the central labor-market organizations, the LO needed progress on other issues to justify its institutional function. Economic democracy and certain budgetary commitments became the price of LO cooperation in an incomes policy, but when the Social Democrats abandoned these objectives in order to form a broader political coalition, the prospects for some limited form of social contract between the unions and the government evaporated. This was one more example of the observation, first made in the chapter on Austria, that there are diseconomies of scale in negotiating social contracts. In this case political fragmentation, by reducing the parliamentary security of any of the major parties, increases the number of players and interests involved in the bargaining if the main party is to maintain its coalition.

The second reaction involved relations between the LO and its constituent unions. By the late 1970s there was evidence of increased rank-and-file malaise. Although statutory settlements prevented severe disruptions such as the 1973 strike, overall strike activity had risen, unions had refused to give the LO increased authority, and some unions were indicating a preference for moving outside the central framework. While there had been no eruption such as that experienced by Sweden in the late 1960s, by 1980 there was significant evidence of an erosion of the institutional authority of the LO.

These factors made it unlikely that the restraint in the growth of earnings associated with the policies of the last half of the 1970s would be sustained into the 1980s. Nor is it clear that there are alternative policies that would deal more effectively with certain fundamental features of the Danish inflation process. Our analysis of wage drift, for example, suggests that tinkering with the indexation system may be futile—workers will obtain compensation for price increases through drift instead, and unions are likely to insist on more frequent contract negotiations. It is also unclear, after two decades of sporadic experiments, how incomes policy can deal effectively with the distributional motives that relentlessly drive the Danish process of determination of money wages.

IX

Italy

The adverse change in economic performance in the 1970s is more marked in Italy than in the other countries under study, with the partial exception of the United Kingdom. Throughout the 1950s and the first half of the 1960s, real national income per capita increased more rapidly in Italy than elsewhere in Europe, with the notable exception of West Germany, or in North America; and for the 1960s as a whole, the growth of per capita income in Italy was greater than in Germany and was equaled only in France. During the 1960s, the Italian economy was characterized by comparatively high levels of unemployment and comparatively high rates of increase in unit labor costs and real hourly compensation, but its rate of consumer price inflation was not above average, and its growth rate of manufacturing productivity exceeded that of any other major European country. In the first three years of the 1970s, however, price inflation and the rate of increase in unit labor costs were much more rapid in Italy—7.5 and 9.4 percent, respectively—while unemployment rates remained at relatively high levels, and throughout the next four years Italy's growth in productivity fell below growth in Germany and France, while its average rate of increase in unit labor costs doubled, from 9.4 percent in 1970–73 to 18.4 percent in 1973–77. Only in the United Kingdom was there a comparable decline in growth and only there did both inflation and unemployment reach Italian levels by the mid 1970s, but earlier the United Kingdom had occupied last place in the European growth league, whereas Italy had been at the top. Sweden's decline in output per man-hour after 1973 was also dramatic, but it was accompanied by a sharp reduction in unemployment, while the average rate of inflation in Sweden—just under 10 percent in 1974–77—was well below the Italian and British rates of about 16 percent each.

Data are provided in table 9-1 for comparison of Italian inflation and productivity in the 1970s with that in the 1960s, and corresponding data are provided for other major European countries. Also presented are "gap" calculations that show the extent to which growth in real wages exceeded or fell short of growth in productivity; the condition for

496

Table 9-1. *Inflation, Growth in Productivity, and "Gap" Calculations, Italy, France, Germany, and the United Kingdom, Selected Periods, 1961–78*
Percent

Period	Italy	France	Germany	United Kingdom
	GDP deflator, annual rate of inflation			
1961–69	4.3	4.3	3.2	3.9
1970–78	13.1	8.7	5.7	12.9
1970–73	8.0	6.6	6.6	7.7
1974–78	17.2	10.5	4.9	16.1
	Annual growth rate of productivity			
1965–70	6.1	4.9	4.6	2.6
1970–74	3.7	3.8	3.5	2.0
1974–78	0.8	3.9	3.5	1.6
	"Gap" calculations: annual productivity growth less annual real wage growth			
1961–69	0.14	0.29	0.31	0.31
1969–76	− 3.09	− 1.17	− 1.04	− 1.60

Sources: GDP deflator, Organisation for Economic Co-operation and Development, *National Accounts of OECD Countries*, vol. 1: *1950–78* (Paris: OECD, 1980), p. 82; growth rates of productivity, *OECD Economic Outlook, 1979*; "gap" calculations, *Eurostat National Accounts* (Brussels: European Economic Community, 1977), pp. 10–11, 30–31.

constant profitability and competitiveness is (when certain simplifying assumptions have been made) that the two growth rates should be equal. In each of the four countries, performance in the 1970s was significantly worse than in the 1960s; but the size of the Italian negative gap is nearly three times that of France and Germany and about twice that of the United Kingdom. The adverse change in the comparative economic performance of Italy was not the result of the confrontation of different phenomena. As elsewhere in Western Europe, strike waves broke over the economy in the late 1960s, and as elsewhere, the terms of trade declined in 1973–74 and recession followed. The principal differences were two: the strike waves in Italy in 1968–69 overturned the preexisting system of industrial relations, and the inflexibility of the politicoeconomic system prevented adequate adjustment to the resultant increased power of the unions, both initially in the early 1970s and later in response to the change in the terms of trade and the world recession.

The waves of strikes that touched much of Western Europe in the late 1960s took their most dramatic form in Italy. Before 1968 the unions were weak and politically divided; since the early 1950s they had been eliminated from the shop floor by management; they had failed to organize the semiskilled immigrants from the south who came more and more to provide the labor for the assembly lines of northern industry, and while the unions were allowed to participate in industry negotiations on minimum rates, effective collective bargaining scarcely existed. The strike waves from early 1968 to the autumn of 1969 overturned this employer-dominated framework. From a system whose closest parallel was the French emerged a system nearest to that of the British. Semiskilled workers in industry became highly organized; effective shop-floor bargaining became the rule in large plants; and the unions, partially submerging their political differences, began to work more cohesively together. Italian economic history since 1970 has been dominated by generally unsuccessful attempts—by the government, business, the Communist party, and the leaders of the unions themselves—to come to terms with these changes.

Two central questions stand out. Why were the changes at the end of the 1960s so great? And why has subsequent accommodation to them proved so difficult? Before these questions are discussed, some basic features of Italian politics need to be mentioned. It is necessary in Italy, more than in any other European country, to understand the political determinants of the system of industrial relations and the political constraints on economic policy. Politics has been dominated by two parties, the Christian Democrats and the Communists. The strategies of both parties, though different, stem from the same underlying feature of Italian life: the lack of central authority and the widespread diffusion of power.

The Italian Christian Democratic party (DC) has—in fact if not always in name—controlled every government since the end of World War II. Its structure differs from Christian Democratic and conservative parties elsewhere in Western Europe, a difference that reflects the Italian social economy. Italy in 1945 was still largely agricultural. In this respect it was closest, among the countries studied, to France. Unlike France, however, it lacked an effective centralized state apparatus. Thus, power was widely diffused, much of it at the local level, in a society that remained uncoerced by the centralizing disciplines either of national administration or of large-scale industrialization. Because of this diffusion of power, the DC saw itself more as a populist party than one whose main appeal was to the middle classes and business. It thus found itself acting, as it still does, as an aggregate of interest groups—small-holding peasants, the traditional middle classes, small-scale industry, and the

Catholic church, as well as important sections of the industrial working class and big business—mimicking at the national level the "clientelistic," or patronage-based, structure of decisionmaking at the local level. With widespread electoral support, and as the national political expression of the power brokers of local society, the DC has always seen itself as the permanent party of government. As such, it has used the spoils and patronage of office to consolidate and augment its power; it has filled the bureaucracy and the growing public sector with its own appointees. But in so doing it has also found its power constrained. As a result of the fragmented interest-group structure of the DC, these appointees did not give the government a mechanism for central executive control. Instead, patronage provided the various groups within the DC with sources of finance and the ability to block the enforcement of legislation when opposition to enactment had failed.

The Partito Comunista Italiano (PCI), the Italian Communist party, has been denied such patronage. Thrown out of government in the late 1940s, the PCI spent the following two decades in the political wilderness, moving only in the mid 1970s toward a quasi-coalition status. The heterodox strategy of the party has been based intellectually on the same clientelistic diffusion of power and decisionmaking throughout Italian society that is reflected in the fragmented structure of the DC. In a country without an effective civil service to execute government decisions—a situation exacerbated by DC patronage—parliamentary control by itself is of less importance than elsewhere. In a country in which large-scale industry in the 1950s and 1960s was not of dominant economic importance, political power cannot be based solely on the support of the industrial working class. Like the DC, therefore, and unlike Communist parties elsewhere, the PCI has aimed its appeal at many different strata of society, both electorally and institutionally. The specific form of this strategy for most of the 1970s was the "historic compromise"—that the party should aim to share power with the Christian Democrats. In that way it believed it could bargain the insertion of its own cadres into executive positions.

These strategies of the DC and the PCI have been linked by the need for social and economic reform and the failure to realize it. The need for reform—especially the adequate provision of social services and the development of the agricultural south of Italy—has always been of central political significance. Its realization was seen by successive leaders of the DC as a precondition for the maintenance of Christian Democratic electoral preeminence. But the reforms the leaders thought necessary were often bitterly and successfully opposed by conservative interest groups, which had strength in the bureaucracy and the public sector as well as in parliament. Those groups stood to lose by reform in two ways: the administrations required to run reforms threatened the system of *clientelismo,* and the financial cost of reform threatened their public-sector resources. The steady growth of Communist electoral support until the mid 1970s was built upon the failure of reform efforts.

The Labor Market in the 1950s and 1960s

Why were the changes in 1968–69 so great? In the 1950s and 1960s the weakness of the unions created an institutional vacuum in which grievances over wages and conditions could accumulate over long periods. As in France, such accumulations of grievances were resolved by waves of strikes, notably in 1962–63 and 1968–69. The instability of this process was reinforced by the need of industry to maintain sufficient profitability and competitiveness in order to allow rapid growth of output and exports; the need was particularly strong, in the context of increasingly competitive international markets, after a wage explosion in 1963. To industrial grievances in the mid 1960s were added political grievances. Unemployment declined in the north during the 1950s and industry relied increasingly in the 1960s upon immigrants from south and central Italy for its semiskilled labor, but successive governments proved unable to provide the necessary reform of the social infrastructure of the big northern cities. These political and industrial grievances of the mid 1960s produced the massive strikes of 1968–69. The unions were able to use these strikes to transform the system of industrial relations as a result partly of the flexibility allowed them by PCI strategy and partly of the analysis of past mistakes. In contrast to the strikes of the early 1960s, when no such transformation had occurred, the unions helped convert shop-floor militancy into firmly entrenched plant unions, and large companies were unable to eliminate plant-level union activity after the "Hot Autumn," as they had done during the sharp deflation of 1964–65.

Political Strategies: Weak Unions and Intransigent Employers

For most of the twenty years immediately following 1948–49, the unions had only a limited role in collective bargaining. Union weakness

was not a consequence of labor laws. In important respects these have
remained unchanged to the present. The law imposes few sanctions or
obligations on union behavior. The right to strike is embodied in the 1948
constitution. It has been qualified by the courts so as not to apply to
strikes with political objectives, though it is not clear whether this was
an important limitation even before 1970. It is also doubtful whether no-
strike clauses, which were written into a number of contracts in the
1960s, were legally enforceable.[1]

The law has equally little to say on the levels, content, or conduct of
collective bargaining. It imposes no obligations on management or its
representatives to negotiate with the unions. Technically, once signed,
agreements are legally enforceable on employers who are members of
the participating association of employers; in practice, agreements are
widely disregarded, especially by smaller firms.[2] The law, then, was—
and is—permissive. Its effect was to buttress the power of the stronger
side. In Italy in the 1950s and 1960s this strengthened the position of
management.

With important exceptions to be noted, collective bargaining took
place only at the national or industry level in the 1950s and 1960s.
National agreements were "interconfederal"—that is, were concluded
between the employers' confederation, Confindustria, on the one hand,
and the union confederations, on the other. The main agreements
between 1950 and 1960 concerned collective and individual dismissals
(1950); works councils (1953); the *scala mobile* (sliding scale), which
provided for the automatic partial adjustment of wages to changes in the
cost of living (1956); and regional differentials in the minimum wage
(1954, 1960).[3] Minimum industrial wages were also determined by
interconfederal agreement before 1954. From then on, however, industrywide minimum wages for each category of industry were negotiated,
at three-year intervals, between Confindustria and the relevant industry
unions of the three union confederations.

Similar industrywide negotiations still take place in the public sector,

1. Seyfarth, Shaw, Fairweather, and Geraldson, *Labor Relations and the Law in
Italy and the United States,* Michigan International Labor Studies, vol. 4 (1970), pp.
32–34.
2. Arthur M. Ross, "Prosperity and Labor Relations in Western Europe: Italy and
France," *Industrial and Labor Relations Review,* vol. 16, no. 1 (October 1962), p. 67.
3. Gino Giugni, "Recent Developments of Collective Bargaining in Italy," *International Labour Review,* vol. 91, no. 4 (April 1965), p. 283.

in the service sector, and in agriculture. These negotiations establish minimum wage rates and normal hours of work for all workers, divided into a number of different categories and differentiating, until 1969, between regions. These agreements are technically binding on all members within the relevant sector. On occasion before 1969, and generally since, the agreements have dealt with other issues—union rights at the plant level, for example, work conditions, and training. The most important sectoral agreement in the economy has been the Metal Workers' Agreement, covering iron and steel as well as engineering. This has in general set the lead for other sectors with respect both to the level of minimum wage increases and to conditions.

Minimum wages have also been partially indexed to the cost of living. The indexation, the *scala mobile,* is based on a fixed basket, the cost-of-living index for working-class families. In 1956 its base value was set at 100. At the end of every three months, until the system was reformed in 1975, the number of points (*punta di contingenza*) by which the index had increased during the quarter was multiplied by the value of a point, then added, after a month's lag, to minimum wages. The value of a point varied by category of worker and industry and remained constant through the period. Earnings in 1956 for most workers were close to the minimum; this can be seen because the average value of a point in 1974—that is, weighted by the 1974 disaggregation of categories of workers—was 490 lire a month;[4] the figure was 475 lire, 1 percent of monthly earnings in industry, for 1956.[5] The average value of a point in 1956 may be taken to have been somewhat less than 490 on the assumption that a larger proportion of the labor force in 1974 was in higher-category jobs than in 1956. If the cost-of-living index at t is written P_t^c and the minimum wage at t is W_t, the value of a point (assuming no changes in categories) is approximately $W_{56}/100$ (1 percent of W_{56}) or W_{56}/P_{56}^c , since $P_{56}^c = 100$. The percentage change in minimum wages in year t, assuming no time lags in compensation, owing to the *scala mobile,* is then

$$\frac{W_{56}}{P_{56}^c} \times \frac{dP_t^c}{W_t} = \frac{W_{56}/P_{56}^c}{W_t/P_t^c} \times \frac{dP_t^c}{P_t^c} ,$$

where dP_t^c is the increase in the number of points during t. Thus, in year

4. Gino Faustini, "Wage Indexation and Inflation in Italy," Banca Nazionale del Lavoro, *Quarterly Review,* vol. 29, no. 119 (December 1976), p. 368.
5. *Annali di Statistica,* series 8, 27 (Rome: Instituto Centrale di Statistica), table 8.

t, the compensated proportion of the minimum wage is the ratio of the real minimum wage in 1956 to the real minimum wage in t. Similarly, the proportion of earnings indexed is

$$\frac{W_{56}/P^c_{56}}{E_t/P^c_t},$$

where E_t is earnings in t. If $E_{56} = W_{56}$, the percentage of industrial earnings indexed has varied as follows:[6]

1956	100.00
1960	83.95
1965	63.01
1970	44.92

(In February 1975, the degree of indexation was changed as a result of a new agreement between Confindustria and the union confederations, designed to achieve 100 percent indexation by February 1977. This agreement, subsequently at the center of much of the economic debate, will be discussed later.)

Despite the system of partial indexation, national and industry bargaining was ineffective for most of the 1950s and 1960s. Interconfederal agreements on conditions of work were either disregarded by employers, as in the case of dismissals, or used by employers, as were works councils, to cut rather than reinforce links between unions and the work force. In addition, agreements did not have to be signed by all three union confederations. Unanimity was achieved in practice, but it was not a legal requirement and did not always occur.

Industry agreements on minimum wages were imposed by Confindustria, which was dominated by small and medium-sized companies and set minima "at rates which marginal employers could afford to pay."[7] Only in the immediate postwar years and in the early 1960s, under pressure from militant workers in an economic boom, did serious negotiations take place.

---

6. Calculated from data in ibid., table 18, app. 1.

7. Walter Kendall, *The Labour Movement in Europe* (London: Allen Lane, 1975), p. 164. The general idea behind this statement is clear and widely agreed; to put it more precisely raises difficulties. How are prices determined? Why does a higher real wage put a marginal firm out of business as opposed to restricting its scale of activities? How does it take account of the fact that firms can pay less than the minimum wage? And so forth.

These two periods were also exceptional for labor relations in the plant. Otherwise, management was generally free to determine hiring and firing, conditions of work, and actual rates of pay. The formal system of worker representation was through works councils (*commissione interne*), which technically represented workers over grievances.[8] Plant unions began to be set up in a limited way during the 1950s when management permitted, but the few negotiations that took place at plant level were with the works councils, not the plant unions.[9] Not until 1960, when the northern Italian labor market tightened, did serious negotiating take place at the plant level. These negotiations, in which large companies took the lead, were also seldom conducted with plant unions; either the works council represented the work force, or the negotiations were part of an "articulated" bargain and were carried through by full-time district officials of the unions. Articulated bargains had two elements: a framework agreement concluded at the industry level, specifying substantive areas for negotiation at lower levels, and the corresponding plant-level or company-level agreements. This form of contract, however, had a short life. At the end of 1963 severe deflationary measures brought the boom, and the militancy, to an end; from 1964 to the beginning of 1968 industrial relations reverted to the pattern of the 1950s.

The weakness of the unions in the 1950s developed within this collective bargaining framework but was not caused by it. From mid 1944 to 1948 a single union confederation, the Confederazione Generale Italiana del Lavoro (CGIL), united three political factions—Communist, Socialist, and Christian Democratic. Union unity was a reflection of political coalition. Until May 1947, the government, under a Christian Democratic prime minister, included the Communists and Socialists. The exclusion of the latter parties in 1947 put an end to unity within the CGIL. By 1950 there were three union confederations. The CGIL, now Communist and Socialist, mirrored the close, though not always smooth, relation between the two parties. Although the CGIL had lost perhaps 50 percent of its members, it remained the strongest confederation, with the bulk of its strength among blue-collar workers. The Christian Democratic wing of the earlier united CGIL formed the Confederazione Italiana Sindacati Lavoratori (CISL); this was much less well represented industrially than the CGIL, but stronger among white-collar workers

8. Seyfarth and others, *Labor Relations and the Law*, pp. 109–11.
9. Ross, "Prosperity and Labor Relations," pp. 71–72.

and in the public sector. A third, small, confederation was the Unione Italiana del Lavoro (UIL), loosely affiliated with the equally small Social Democratic party, a right-wing group that split off from the Socialists in 1947.

It is difficult to use standard membership data to measure the strength of the various unions. Figures based on union claims—for example, the figure of 6.7 million members in 1950, 1.1 million more than in 1948 after two years of internecine fighting and chaos within the unions—are suspect.[10] In the second place, low membership fees and irregularity in their payment imply an upward bias in international comparisons of active membership.[11] Finally, attempts were probably made, at least in the 1960s, to introduce greater realism into the statistics. If membership figures are taken at face value, average union membership was on the order of 25–30 percent of the labor force during the 1950s and 1960s; a more realistic figure is probably 10–15 percent of the total labor force. In some industries, notably metal manufacturing but also chemicals, the degree of unionization was higher; this was also true of some parts of the public sector—although there the CISL unions often resembled Christian Democratic clientelism in their operation. More reliable figures, for metalworking, are provided in table 9-2. From high membership at the end of the war, the rate for the CGIL and the CISL combined had fallen to between 20 and 25 percent by the end of the 1950s, with some recovery in 1963 and 1964. The big rise in membership occurred only after the Hot Autumn of 1969. In the better organized industries, skilled workers tended to be the most heavily unionized (under the CGIL), while in the public sector this was true of CISL white-collar workers.

What was the basis of union strength between 1944 and 1948? The base of much of the resistance to Mussolini had been on the shop floor. In recognition of the powerful position of workers in the plants after his demise, works councils were set up in 1943 by agreement between employers and unions.[12] These developed into effective plant bargaining

10. Kendall, *Labour Movement in Europe*, p. 156. Kendall offers a good account of the immediate postwar period.

11. Walter Galenson, *Trade Union Democracy in Western Europe* (Berkeley: University of California Press, 1961), p. 2. Galenson estimated that only between 30 and 40 percent of dues were actually paid.

12. Maurice N. Neufeld, *Italy: School for Awakening Countries,* Cornell International Industrial and Labor Relations Reports 5 (Ithaca, N.Y.: Cornell University Press, 1961), p. 450.

Table 9-2. *Union Membership and Strikes, Italy, 1951–59
and 1960–70*

Year or period	CGIL members as percentage of the metalworking labor force	CISL members as percentage of the metalworking labor force	Number of strikes	Days lost through strikes (millions)
Annual average, 1951–55	42.3	7.8	1,578	n.a.
Annual average, 1956–59	18.2	8.8	1,874	5.5
1960	13.8	6.5	2,471	5.8
1961	13.4	6.9	3,502	9.9
1962	13.9	7.2	3,652	22.7
1963	17.6	9.1	4,145	11.4
1964	17.1	9.2	3,841	13.1
1965	15.2	8.6	3,191	7.0
1966	14.9	8.7	2,387	14.5
1967	15.4	9.3	2,658	8.6
1968	15.7	9.9	3,377	9.2
1969	18.2	11.0	3,788	37.8
1970	23.8	13.6	4,162	18.3

Sources: Columns 1 and 2, Alessandro Pizzorno, Emilio Reyneri, Marino Regini, and Ida Regalia, *Lotte operaie e sindacato: Il ciclo 1968–72 in Italia* [Struggles of the workers and the unions: the period 1968–72 in Italy] (Bologna: Il Mulino, 1978), p. 298; columns 3 and 4, Walter Kendall, *The Labour Movement in Europe* (London: Allen Lane, 1975), p. 369.
n.a. Not available.

institutions, and "in practice, during the immediate post-war period, the works councils filled the gaps in activity left by the still non-existent union bargaining."[13] Bargaining took place on the shop floor over layoffs and dismissals, as well as over wages and other conditions of work. Thus works councils—seen by workers as representing unions in the plant—adopted a positive attitude toward collective bargaining and invested time and resources in it. The CGIL made no real effort to restrain such developments, even though suspicious of the potential autonomy of the shop floor. At the national level the CGIL was interested in bargaining with Confindustria over a wide range of questions, including minimum wages, cost-of-living indexation, the status of works councils, unem-

13. Rainer Zoll, "Centralisation and Decentralisation as Tendencies of Union Organisational and Bargaining Policy," in Colin Crouch and Alessandro Pizzorno, eds., *The Resurgence of Class Conflict in Western Europe Since 1968*, vol. 2: *Comparative Analyses* (New York: Holmes & Meier, 1978), p. 133.

ployment insurance, and layoffs. Thus, despite tension between the CGIL and the works councils over plant bargaining, collective bargaining developed at both the plant and the national levels.

Neither Confindustria nor individual employers were able to restrain such developments. Employers looked back nostalgically to the fascist period, but their involvement with Mussolini's regime made their position weak in the extreme. This political weakness of the employers combined with positive union attitudes to make the period one of considerable union bargaining effectiveness.

Union membership was high initially as a result of union activity in the Resistance and the Russian war effort. Union bargaining effectiveness maintained this initial impulse. Most workers join unions out of group interest: if a union bargains effectively at the plant or industry level, those who benefit are generally prepared to meet the cost and other obligations of membership without considering whether it is in their individual interest to do so. Highly effective bargaining in this period, especially at the plant level, was the main reason that the number of members was high. Some workers, however, will act only if it is in their individual interests: benefits negotiated for an entire industry or interconfederally have never been confined to union members in Italy; benefits from plant negotiations, however, especially over layoffs and grievances, tend implicitly, though not explicitly, to be linked to union membership, and sanctions against nonparticipation in strikes and nonpayment of dues develop rapidly with effective plant bargaining. Thus, not only did unions provide benefits, but also the benefits were at least partially privatized.

In contrast to the renaissance of unionism in the immediate postwar years, the decade from the late 1940s to the late 1950s was the nadir of Italian unionism. The decline in unionization paralleled the decline in bargaining effectiveness. The two or three years during which these changes occurred, 1948–50, were crucial to the whole future development of industrial relations. They determined the pattern of economic growth until 1969 on the basis of low real wages, weak unions, and control by employers of conditions in the plant. These changes were the result of strategic choices by the Christian Democrats, by business, and by the Communist party.

Of these choices, perhaps the least important was the strategy of qualified disruption pursued by the Communist party and the CGIL from the late 1940s to the early 1950s. With the onset of the cold war in 1947 and 1948 the PCI was pressured by the Soviet Union into using the CGIL's industrial strength as a political weapon against the Italian government. This had not been the initial response of the PCI to their eviction in 1947 from the postwar coalition government led by the Christian Democrat Alcide de Gasperi. Their initial antipathy to the use of maximum retaliation reflected the PCI analysis of Italian society. At that point, however, it was not easy for the leaders to resist the requests of the Russians, which indeed struck a chord with the "deepest instincts of its cadres and members—faith in Stalin and the Soviet Union, hostility to political, class, and religious enemies at home."[14]

The CGIL acquiesced in this change of PCI policy. In the phase of confrontation, the "Communist leaders [of the CGIL] repeatedly used the federation as a political weapon. Demonstrations, brief strikes, and other forms of agitation were employed in protest against Italian involvement in European defense and economic integration matters and on other major foreign policy issues."[15] The CGIL, at the confederation level, was responsive to the demands of the Communist party because the CGIL was dominated by Communist and, to a lesser extent, Socialist cadres even before the formation of the CISL. (The Socialists remained politically allied to the PCI until the end of the 1950s.)[16] In addition, as CGIL membership declined, the financial dependence of the confederation on the PCI increased.[17] In line with party requirements organizational resources at the plant level were geared toward political agitation within and outside the factory. Neufeld describes how a large concern "soon learned that a deliberate campaign was under way to make orderly procedures and solutions to factory problems impossible" and how "when a tacit agreement had been reached with the grievance committee [works council] on economic matters, factory representatives of the

14. Donald L. M. Blackmer, "Continuity and Change in Postwar Italian Communism," in Donald L. M. Blackmer and Sidney Tarrow, eds., *Communism in Italy and France* (Princeton: Princeton University Press, 1975), p. 53.

15. Donald L. M. Blackmer, *Unity in Diversity: Italian Communism and the Communist World* (Cambridge, Mass.: MIT Press, 1968), p. 265.

16. See Kendall, *Labour Movement in Europe*, p. 157, for a discussion of PSI strategy in the 1940s and 1950s.

17. Pietro Merli Brandini, "Italy: Creating a New Industrial Relations System from the Bottom," in Solomon Barkin, ed., *Worker Militancy and Its Consequences, 1965–75: New Directions in Western Industrial Relations* (New York: Praeger, 1975), p. 85.

union would reply that the proposals were unacceptable to them because they had received instructions to the contrary."[18]

While such disruption certainly occurred in many large plants, its full extent is not clear. The CGIL was neither united in its view of shop-floor bargaining nor fully successful in imposing policies of disruption on the works councils. The works councils "troubled the communists. . . . Instead of acting like lambs, submitting to their bidding, [they] betrayed the possibilities of raging like lions."[19] At the second CGIL Congress, in 1949, Luciano Lama, later to become secretary general, declared himself against institutionalization on the shop floor on the grounds that it led to plant bargaining and thus to corporatist and plant-centered tendencies.[20] But at the same time views stressing the importance of plant negotiations were expressed.[21] In consequence, the CGIL did not on balance aim at maximum disruption. At the national level it held back its more extreme supporters in demonstrations. Moreover, "the major proposal made by the CGIL [in 1949–50] called for a national plan to increase productivity and employment, with the workers accepting certain sacrifices—in the form of a wage standstill."[22] Thus, while it was certainly true that the CGIL moved into an uncooperative posture with respect to bargaining at the plant and national levels, it was not with great conviction and was subject to many internal and some external hesitations.

It was only in part the attitude of the CGIL that caused the collapse of collective bargaining in the early 1950s. From the late 1940s onward, the employers mounted a systematic policy of elimination of union influence from the plants. This paralleled and was posited on a major change of direction by the Christian Democrats. The postwar leaders of the DC, de Gasperi, then Amintore Fanfani, believed that the long-run position of the party depended on its ability to be the government of reform, and they saw the left-wing parties and unions as their main competitors. The 1948 election removed the political threat, since the

18. Maurice F. Neufeld, *Labor Unions and National Politics in Italian Industrial Plants,* Cornell International Industrial and Labor Relations Reports 1 (Ithaca, N.Y.: Cornell University Press, 1954), p. 38.
19. Neufeld, *Italy,* p. 482.
20. Zoll, "Centralisation and Decentralisation," p. 134.
21. Ibid., pp. 133–34.
22. Blackmer, "Continuity and Change," p. 48.

DC gained an overall majority. From then on, the government gave business a framework in which it could proceed to eliminate the unions from the plants, thereby removing the second competitor.

Union weakness was important to the success of DC reformism in three ways. It was seen—correctly—as a central component in rapid industrial growth in both the private and public sectors, which it was believed—incorrectly—would provide the economic resources for reform. It removed an institutional presence that might block, change, or take the credit for DC reformist measures. And, in a country in which institutions are closely linked with elections, it lessened the challenge of a reformist alternative on the left. Apart from these benefits, weakening the unions was a strategy on which most sections of the DC could unite. In the 1970s business would have to compete for public resources with other groups of the DC that were entrenched in the bureaucracy, whereas in the 1950s and 1960s the lobby for industrialization had found support among the conservative and populist groups in the party in opposing the left and reducing the power of the unions.

The framework provided by the government consisted first of placing no obstacle against the methods, legal or illegal, used by business against union sympathizers; in addition, union action was suppressed by the police. "Management was able to dismiss any worker it wanted to, and demands and demonstrations of dissent were dealt with by government action."[23] Of equal importance was an economic policy, based on monetary restriction, that deflated domestic demand, made credit tight, and made access to credit difficult. This policy had three consequences. It forced large companies to orient themselves toward exports; since their shares of the market were minimal at the end of the war—on account of both the war and autarchic fascist production strategies—they required low real wages and high productivity if they were to undercut foreign competitors. The restrictive monetary policy maintained high unemployment in the industrial north. And by increasing the cost of capital, it provided an incentive to increase productivity by "rationalization" at least as much as by capital investment.

The need to hold down real wages and to increase productivity through more efficient use of the labor force made control of the work

23. Ida Regalia, Marino Regini, and Emilio Reyneri, "Labour Conflicts and Industrial Relations in Italy," in Crouch and Pizzorno, *Resurgence of Class Conflict*, vol. 1: *National Studies*, p. 102.

place a primary goal of management. Ample reserves of labor in the south and unemployment in the north combined with the prospect of continued Christian Democratic hegemony to consign to the distant future the need for union cooperation in controlling the labor force. Large-scale business had additional incentives to operate without unions. Low concentration of industry, characterized by a few giant companies and very many small ones, gave added reserves of labor to the giants. In addition, effective collective bargaining would have affected large companies more than smaller, less easily organized undertakings, thus undermining the domestic competitiveness of the large companies. And since the DC was an aggregation of interest groups rather than the guardian of large-scale industry, the government could not have been relied upon to impose unionization on small firms.

Most businesses wanted to be rid of both the CGIL and the CISL. Some businesses, including Fiat and Montecatini, the two largest private companies, made sweetheart deals with the CISL at the beginning of the 1950s, refusing to negotiate with the CGIL.[24] Further, the CGIL suffered more than the CISL from American threats to withdraw contracts from companies with CGIL majorities on their works councils.[25] But although the CISL was not politically disruptive, some of its industrial federation officials wanted to develop collective bargaining at the shop level, thereby threatening the goals of management during this period. Business not only acted, with considerable success, to suppress a union presence in the plant; it was also successful in removing any powers previously enjoyed by the works councils. Plant bargaining thus hardly existed throughout the 1950s. Industry and interconfederal bargaining continued, but they were ineffective. Reorganization of the *scala mobile* in 1956, providing 100 percent indexation for minimum wages, served to "avoid and allay political restiveness among workers."[26] Among large-scale firms such intentions lay behind the use of "planned wage drift. Using this tactic and some related ones the large companies have been able . . . to use wage policy not only to maintain a high measure of control over their labor costs, but also to maximize labor docility,

24. Murray Edelman and R. W. Fleming, *The Politics of Wage-Price Decisions: A Four-Country Analysis* (Urbana: University of Illinois Press, 1965), p. 41.

25. Ibid., p. 42. The threats were transmitted by Clare Boothe Luce, American ambassador to Italy, 1953–57.

26. Ibid., p. 32.

minimize strikes, and even exert considerable control over the development and political complexion of the labor movement."[27]

The decline of effective bargaining, for all the reasons discussed above, led to a serious decline in union membership. The privatization of the benefits of collective bargaining became unimportant as the benefits fell off. As the power of the works councils diminished, moreover, so too did their ability to "privatize" benefits: they could no longer gain more effective redress for the grievances of union members. Equally, privatization in the form of sanctions against nonmembership in unions and nonparticipation in strikes became impossible to enforce in most plants. It was instead employers who privatized the benefits either of nonmembership or of membership in company-approved unions. Access to and retention of Fiat company housing depended upon

managerial judgments of the worker's union affiliation, politics and docility. . . . For some time Fiat systematically transferred all known members of FIOM, its CGIL metalworkers union, to a particular plant which was shortly afterwards shut down. . . . If there are Communists in a man's family, he is not hired. . . . There are no doubt some exceptions, but some such policy is commonly found throughout Italian industry.[28]

It is not surprising that the two largest unions at Fiat during part of this period—UIL and a company union—were also the two perceived by Fiat workers in an opinion poll to be those most favored by Fiat management.[29]

In the 1950s the strategy of union repression produced the economic results that management required. Real wages grew less rapidly than labor productivity, and profitability and international competitiveness increased. On this basis, Italian economic growth was exceptionally rapid during the decade. By the end of the 1950s, however, this apparent stability was beginning to disappear.

Labor Market Instability in the 1960s: The Wage Explosions of 1962–63

Accumulating grievances over both real wages and work conditions combined with tighter labor markets to generate a substantial increase in the militancy of the workers in the early 1960s (see table 9-2, columns 3 and 4). The low unemployment, especially—as table 9-3, column 2,

27. Ibid., p. 36.
28. Ibid., p. 41.
29. Ibid., p. 43.

Table 9-3. *Wages, Productivity, and Employment, Italy, 1960–71*

Percent

Year	Unemployed in the whole economy (1)	Unemployed in the Milan-Turin area (2)	Growth of labor productivity in manufacturing (3)	Share of labor in manufacturing value added (4)	Growth in manufacturing employment (5)	Growth in manufacturing earnings (6)	Growth in nationally negotiated hourly wage rates in manufacturing (7)
1960	5.6	2.5	5.0	58.6	. . .	7.7	. . .
1961	5.1	1.9	2.3	60.2	5.4	6.5	4.4
1962	4.6	1.7	6.6	64.3	3.5	13.6	10.7
1963	3.9	1.7	3.7	67.2	2.9	19.6	14.7
1964	4.3	2.3	1.6	70.1	− 3.5	6.9	14.1
1965	5.4	3.7	8.9	70.0	− 2.4	4.4	8.3
1966	5.9	3.4	8.0	66.4	− 0.2	6.4	3.9
1967	5.4	2.7	4.5	69.2	3.4	10.7	5.3
1968	5.7	2.2	8.5	66.2	2.0	6.9	3.5
1969	5.4	1.8	2.9	67.7	3.3	9.1	7.6
1970	5.4	1.7	6.2	70.4	3.5	18.9	21.7
1971	6.4	1.7	− 1.0	79.1	2.1	11.9	13.5

Sources: Column 1, OECD, *Labour Force Statistics, 1960–71* (Paris: OECD, 1973), and later issues; column 2, Pizzorno and others, *Lotte operaie e sindacato*, p. 298; columns 3–7, *Annali di statistica*, series 7, 27 (Rome: Instituto Centrale di Statistica).

shows—in the advanced sectors in the north (in Lombardy), reflected two separate factors—the external economic and the domestic political. With other countries in Western Europe, Italy shared in the trade-growth boom associated with the early development of the European Economic Community (EEC). In Germany and France unemployment fell from averages of 4.1 percent and 2.1 percent, respectively, for the period 1950–59, to 0.6 percent and 1.6 percent for the period 1960–63 (0.45 percent and 1.4 percent for 1962–63).

The Italian government made no attempt to offset these influences; not until 1964 did it deflate domestic demand. This was neither accidental nor technical, but reflected a significant shift in Christian Democratic strategy toward rapprochement with the Socialists. Through the 1950s the leaders of the DC had believed that they by themselves could provide a government of reform. This they had failed to do, and the electorate had moved to the left in successive general elections: the combined Communist and Socialist share of votes had risen from 31 percent in 1948 to 39.1 percent in 1963; during the same period the share of the DC had fallen from 48.5 percent to 38.3 percent. Reform ran counter to the interests of powerful groups within the DC. Industrialization of the *mezzogiorno,* the poverty-stricken agricultural south of the country, could weaken the hold of the church over a predominantly agricultural population. Provision of adequate social services would lessen the effects of business paternalism. Reform required efficient state administration, and that threatened *clientelismo,* or local patronage. The initial strategy of the leaders of the DC under Prime Minister Amintore Fanfani in the 1950s had been to expand the public sector, in the form of both state agencies and nationalized industries. Fanfani believed that this could give reform-minded leaders direct executive power. In this way the immobility caused by the fragmented interest-group structure of the DC might be circumvented.

But the expansion of the public sector failed to produce a reform coalition. On the contrary, whether intentionally or not, it became a powerful incentive to the fragmentation and clientelization of the state apparatus by the Christian Democratic party, increasingly bent on a policy of spoils to cement its power. . . . Party factions became institutionalized—with their own leaders, headquarters, budgets, and mass media. Their expanding number was not justified by ideological disagreement but by the need to organize in order to control expanding resources.[30]

The failure of the public sector to act as a spearhead of reform promoted the concept of a center-left coalition with the Socialists as the only workable route to reform that would maintain the isolation of the Communists. The Socialist party (PSI) was prepared to move toward a coalition with the DC. Its links with the Communists had weakened during the 1950s, in part as a reaction to the invasion of Hungary in 1956 and the repressionism of Stalin, which became evident at the Twentieth Party Congress of the Soviet Union in the same year. It also mirrored a change of attitude common to other Socialist parties in the late 1950s: a growing acknowledgment that the capitalist system could provide economic growth, even if it was distributionally inequitable from the Socialist viewpoint. The positive benefit to the Socialists of the center-left was the chance that their party could become the pivotal mechanism of reform, thereby capturing votes from the PCI. This required a quid

30. Giuseppi di Palma, "Christian Democracy: The End of Hegemony?" in Howard R. Penniman, ed., *Italy at the Polls: The Parliamentary Elections of 1976* (Washington, D.C.: American Enterprise Institute for Public Policy Research, 1977), pp. 128–29. Much of the underlying argument in reference to the strategy of the DC is taken from this chapter and from Michele Salvati, "The Italian Inflation," 2d draft, Brookings Project on Global Inflation and Recession (1979).

pro quo from the DC. Thus "to facilitate integrating the PSI into the coalition, the DC reconciled itself to giving labor a larger share of the national wealth."[31]

In 1960 . . . the DC was interested in obtaining an expansion of liquidity. It was hoped that such a move would encourage PSI support for the Opening to the Left by holding out the prospect of income redistribution. Guido Carli, the new Governor of the Bank of Italy and himself a supporter of the "Opening," acted to loosen controls. This development helped set the stage for the significant wage increases of 1962. . . . One must conclude that the Bank operates according to criteria that are political and electoral as well as those that are designed to provide a sound business climate.[32]

The economic outcome of the increase in worker militancy was the rapid increase in both earnings and wage rates during the period 1961–64, the increases being most pronounced in 1962 and 1963. The Metal Workers' Agreement in late 1962, and the subsequent industrial agreements in 1963, made for a rate of inflation of wage rates in manufacturing of 10.7 percent in 1962, 14.7 percent in 1963, and 14.1 percent in 1964 (see table 9-3, column 7). Wage drift was 2.9 percent in 1962 and 4.9 percent in 1963, partly as direct concessions to plant militancy, partly as the result of articulated bargains (see table 9-3, columns 6 and 7). The increases in earnings between 1961 and 1964 were not offset by substantial increases in productivity. The annual average increase in productivity was 3.6 percent, so unit labor costs in manufacturing rose at an annual rate of 12.5 percent for 1961–64. These dramatic rises were accompanied by average increases in world prices of manufactures of rather less than 1 percent. Italian industry was thus constrained in the extent to which it could pass on the increased unit labor costs and preserve profitability. Column 4 of table 9-3 shows the share of labor in value added in manufacturing to have risen from 58.6 percent in 1960 to 70.1 percent in 1964. The economic results shown for this period were thus severe declines in both domestic profitability and international competitiveness.

These developments revealed a shortcoming in the policy of the center-left. The price of Socialist cooperation was economic policies directed toward fuller employment and redistribution; after a period during which real wages had grown less rapidly than productivity, some redistribution of income to labor was consistent with continued economic

31. Alan R. Posner, "Italy: Dependence and Political Fragmentation," in Peter J. Katzenstein, ed., *Between Power and Plenty: Foreign Economic Policies of Advanced Industrial States* (Madison: University of Wisconsin Press, 1978), p. 233.
32. Ibid., p. 236.

growth. But limiting the redistribution required a degree of institution-alization of the labor market that did not exist. Without institutionaliza-tion, the unions had no bargaining discretion. In the terms of chapter 1, there was no prior gap between minimum acceptable wages and maxi-mum negotiable wages, and the sharp increase in worker militancy pushed both up together. There was thus no room for a reduction in union bargaining intensity to cushion the effect of increased militancy on the economy.

There were important changes within the unions during this period, although they were insufficient to control the process of redistribution. Since its inception the CISL had been divided between those who, on the one hand, stressed the union's links to the Christian Democrats, were heavily influenced by the Catholic ideology of nonconflictive social cooperation, and were prepared to countenance "sweetheart" deals with employers and those who, on the other hand, sought to develop the CISL into an effective collective bargaining institution. The latter, the so-called innovators, had come to control the policies of the northern industrial unions by the late 1950s.[33] And within the CGIL the losses in membership and electoral support from the works councils in the 1950s led many in the northern industrial unions to move in the same direction as the CISL innovators.[34] With this movement went the realization that cooperation between the CISL and the CGIL was necessary for the development of collective bargaining.

At the same time, the response of the Communist party to the DC-Socialist convergence was to encourage Socialist-Communist links within the CGIL. The PCI was not wholly opposed to the center-left. "If the Socialists continued to collaborate with the Communists and to fight for basic economic and social reforms inside a coalition of the Center-Left, it could serve as an instrument for splitting the Christian Democrats, softening the prejudices of anticommunism."[35] A center-left government, moreover, was a bulwark against the type of right-wing developments of the "July days" of 1960, when the government at-tempted, with the support of the rightist MSI, to change the electoral laws to install, in effect, a permanent right-wing regime. But the danger of the *apertura a sinistra*, the opening to the left, was that the Socialists

33. Peter R. Weitz, "Labor and Politics in a Divided Movement: The Italian Case," *Industrial and Labor Relations Review*, vol. 28, no. 2 (January 1975), pp. 232–33.

34. Blackmer, *Unity in Diversity*, p. 266.

35. Ibid., p. 231.

would succumb to the embrace of the DC and cut their links with the PCI. To safeguard against this, an obvious step was to increase the value to the PSI of joint Socialist-Communist enterprises, which obviously included the CGIL. The CGIL had important links with the Socialists; about a third of its central committee were Socialist, although this proportion fell with organizational level. The PCI thus saw the value of giving the Socialists within the CGIL an increased say in the organization; and at the confederation level, from the late 1950s, the policies of the CGIL moved toward support of center-left policies.[36]

These two changes within the CGIL had divergent implications for collective bargaining. Support of center-left policies required wage moderation at the national level. While this offered opportunities for serious bargaining, it required strong control by the central organization over industrial unions and members in the plants. Organizational policy at the confederation level was thus against autonomy at lower levels. Effective plant bargaining, on the other hand, required increased autonomy. A compromise was to promote "articulated" bargaining; here a framework agreement would be reached at the industry level in which the areas on which further bargaining could take place at the plant or company level were specified. But given the different pressures on the unions at plant and national levels, as well as the militancy of the work force and the lack of institutionalization in the labor market, these changes in the CGIL and the CISL were insufficient to provide the government with bargaining partners with whom incomes policies could be negotiated and put into effective operation.

The serious deterioration in profitability and international competitiveness brought this contradiction home to the government. To deal with these problems the government resorted to deflation in 1964. As can be seen from the employment and unemployment figures in table 9-3, columns 1, 2, and 3, the deflation was severe and prolonged. The resort to deflation to deal with the wage and strike explosion is in contrast to the later policy response to the 1968–69 explosion. Why was the government able to deflate so severely in 1964? First, the unions had not yet established a position of strength within the plants. Instead of building up a shop-floor organization with some autonomy, they concentrated their efforts on the development of articulated bargaining, which they believed they could control. Union bargaining effectiveness certainly

36. Ibid., pp. 270–74.

increased at both the plant and national levels, and as table 9-2 shows, membership rose correspondingly. But the "penetration of the workplace through the establishment of union branches . . . was . . . a failure. . . . The unions themselves . . . hesitated to give these bodies other than organisational functions."[37]

The second reason deflation was feasible was political. Except for its center-left leaders, the DC was not committed to reform, and it opposed organizational strengthening of the unions. This left the Socialists with two alternatives. They could continue to make possible a center-left government, or they could return to the leftist alliance with the PCI. But the latter course gave no hope of their eventually displacing the Communists as the party of the left. The former kept that possibility alive, while at the same time allowing the Socialists a share in the benefits of governmental patronage.

The Buildup of Grievances in the Mid 1960s

In the absence of reasonably well developed and articulated industrial relations institutions, the problems caused by the boom and the wage explosion of the early 1960s led through the mid 1960s to an accumulation of grievances that was the primary underlying cause of what happened in 1968–69. Since waves of strikes occurred in other countries during the late 1960s, however, an explanation that rests entirely on the instability of the Italian system of industrial relations is insufficient. Rather, the instability of the system explains the comparative magnitude of the Italian Hot Autumn; the factors that were common to all European countries were the wage increases generated by the booming conditions in Europe during the early 1960s; the slow rate of growth of world prices during the first half of the 1960s, which stemmed from the relatively high rate of unemployment in the United States and its low rates of price and wage inflation; and policies of deflation, incomes restraint, and plant-level rationalization, which European countries were obliged to adopt in the mid 1960s because of the earlier excessive increases in costs in relation to world prices.

The policies of adjustment pursued by the government and business from 1964 onward were thus an important factor. The deflation enabled employers to disregard the provisions in the 1962 and 1963 agreements

37. Regalia and others, "Labour Conflicts," pp. 140–41.

on articulated bargaining. As can be seen from the difference between columns 6 and 7 in table 9-3, wage drift was sharply negative in 1964 and 1965. The evidence on the growth of productivity confirms the views of many observers that business also used the mid 1960s to rationalize production (see table 9-3, column 3). The average annual growth of productivity during the recession of 1965–69 was 7.1 percent; during the years of low unemployment, 1961–63, it was 4.2 percent. Okun's law predicts a reduction in the growth of productivity as unemployment rises.[38] But this does not take the phenomenon of rationalization, or shakeout, into account. Further evidence concerning rationalization comes from data on capital formation in the mid 1960s. Gross fixed capital formation fell 6.4 percent and 8.6 percent in 1964 and 1965, respectively, and rose only 4.0 percent in 1966, and the share of GNP devoted to investment fell from 23.5 percent in 1963 to 21.7 percent, 18.8 percent, 18.3 percent, 19.0 percent, and 19.7 percent in the five succeeding years. There is also nonstatistical, empirical evidence of intensification of the work process that is consistent with increases in the productivity of labor without an increase in the capital–labor ratio.

If one reads the union press, if one follows case histories of individual factories, one obtains the impression of a general intensification of the work process, which came in different ways and used different methods: reduction in labor-time on a particular machine operation; supervision of an increased number of machines; increased assembly line speeds; spread of incentive payments systems; increase in heavy and onerous work loads.[39]

Statements by Italian sociologists and union leaders are consistent with this impression of a leading Italian economist:

By 1966 businesses had begun to reestablish profits through policies which aimed at reducing unit costs. The method most frequently employed was an increase in assembly line speeds unaccompanied in general by a proportional increase in wages. Similar changes were observed in almost all the factories studied.[40]

38. Okun's law, as originally stated in reference to the U.S. economy, says that for every increase of 1 percent in the unemployment rate there is, other things being equal, a 3 percent reduction in GNP, hence a decline in the growth of productivity. See Arthur Okun, "Potential GNP: Its Measurement and Significance," in American Statistical Association, *Proceedings of the Business and Economic Statistics Section* (Washington, D.C.: ASA, 1962), pp. 98–105.

39. Michele Salvati, *Il sistema economico italiano: Analisi di una crisi* [The Italian economic system: analysis of a crisis] (Bologna: Il Mulino, 1975), p. 45 (our translation). The data on fixed capital formation are from the same source.

40. G. Bianchi, R. Aglieta, P. Merli-Brandini, "Les délégués ouvriers: Nouvelles formes de représentation ouvrière" [Worker representatives: new forms of labor representation], *Sociologie du travail*, vol. 30, no. 2 (April–June 1971), p. 179.

In a discussion of 1968–70, the secretary general of the CISL argued, under the heading "Possible motivation of phenomena of contestation,"

In the years 1965–1967, especially, a process of rationalization in the industries caused serious tensions to arise and was the cause of a new awareness of the problems of working life, this process having taken the form of a balance of forces highly unfavourable to the workers.[41]

The process of work intensification was linked to the phenomenon of migrant workers from the center and south of Italy. The massive migration from the mid 1950s on provided northern industry with the bulk of its semiskilled and unskilled workers by the mid 1960s. With no union background, these workers had remained largely unorganized by the unions throughout the period 1960–64; where there was organization, it was broken by the employers during the subsequent deflation. This is in contrast to the partial reunionization of skilled workers, especially by the CGIL, in the early 1960s. To the very limited extent to which unions had been able to remain established within the plants in the mid 1960s, it was the skilled workers who remained organized. And these constituted the bulk of their membership. Work intensification and wage restraint thus fell disproportionately on the unorganized semiskilled workers.[42] As we shall argue later, the violence of 1968–69, the nature of the egalitarian demands that arose, and the extent to which the unions had to democratize stemmed from the fact that the accumulated grievances were borne predominantly by the semiskilled, who provided the motor force of the strikes—though not always the leadership and organization.

Business was successful in its goal of moderating the growth of unit labor costs. In manufacturing industry the percentage change in unit labor costs in 1963 was 15.4. In succeeding years the changes were 1964, 5.5 percent; 1965, −2.3 percent; 1966, −1.9 percent; 1967, 4.9 percent; 1968, −1.8 percent.[43] Moderation of the growth of unit labor costs does not necessarily lead to increased profitability. Exchange rates were fixed, however, and prices were partially determined by world prices, which were rising more rapidly than the growth of unit labor costs in Italy. Hence, as table 9-3, column 4, shows, some improvement of the

41. Giuseppe Reggio, "Italy: Social evolution with particular reference to the phenomenon of 'contestation' on the part of various groups," in Guy Spitaels, ed., *La Crise des relations industrielles en Europe: Diversité et unité—Les réponses possibles* (Bruges: de Tempel, 1972), p. 112.

42. Regalia and others, "Labour Conflicts," pp. 122–25.

43. Salvati, *Il sistema economico italiano*, p. 96.

share of profits in value added occurred. The share of labor fell from a high point of 70.1 percent in 1964 to 66.2 percent in 1968. With exchange rates fixed, moreover, the extent to which the moderation of unit labor costs was passed on in the form of moderation of prices was reflected in increased international competitiveness. Between 1961 and 1963 the Italian export price index had risen 1.2 percent against the export price index of the EEC; between 1964 and 1968 it fell 5.4 percent. The adjustment was therefore, with respect to both profitability and competitiveness, partially successful.

The strategy of adjustment was pursued not only by employers at the plant level. In national negotiations the union confederations tacitly cooperated in a policy of wage restraint. As noted earlier, the confederated CGIL favored cooperation with the center-left coalition as part of the Communist strategy of maintaining links with the PSI. This was opposed by many within the CGIL industrial unions. While labor markets were tight in the early 1960s, the industrial unions were successful in their opposition. But the mid 1960s deflation had eroded their power bases. The industrial unions, who were the union parties involved in national—that is, industrywide—negotiations, were induced to postpone the reopening of contracts in the key three-year Metal Workers' Agreement from 1965 to 1966. A more serious quarrel between the industrial unions and their centrals took place during negotiations in 1966. "As the political differences between the confederations became increasingly blurred they tended to crop up further down the line in relations between the confederations and their industry wide federations."[44] The industrial unions were not prepared to settle at a low figure, and the government persuaded the confederations to sign the agreement instead;[45] this illustrated the political concern of the PCI to keep the Socialists aware of the benefit of cooperation through the unions.

But the Metal Workers' Agreement of 1966 was a setback for the industrial unions. Wage rates were to rise only 5 percent during the three-year period to 1969. Commitments were made that there would be no strikes in continuous-process industries. Perhaps the consolation prize for the industrial unions was the institution of regulated checkoff of union dues.[46] In addition to rationalization and wage restraint at the

44. Giugni, "Recent Developments," p. 312.
45. Ibid.
46. Ibid., pp. 312–14.

plant and national levels, there was a third significant factor in the increase of the rate of accumulation of grievances during the mid 1960s: the failure of the reform program of the center-left government. The massive scale of migration to the industrial north focused the need for reform on the provision of adequate public services, housing, health, education, and transport, especially in the metropolitan areas of Milan and Turin. The failure to realize these reforms stemmed, as in the 1950s, from the structure of the DC and the lack of executive power of its leaders. The consequence of the failure was to accentuate the difficult conditions in which the greatest number of semiskilled and unskilled workers lived. This increased sense of grievance moved their allegiances electorally leftward and heightened their latent industrial militancy.

The underlying cause of the scale of the strike waves of 1968 and 1969 was the insufficient institutionalization of the system of industrial relations and its consequent instability. Within that framework grievances accumulated partly for the same reasons as in other Western European countries—namely, the response by government and business to the crisis of profitability and competitiveness that the boom of the early 1960s in Western Europe provoked. It was thus not accidental that the Italian strikes in 1968–69 were coincident with strike waves in Germany, the United Kingdom, and France. What was particular to Italy was the size of the internal migration from the south and center to the north and the immobility of the political system. The latter, which had earlier balked at institutionalizing the system of industrial relations, failed to provide the reforms necessary to integrate this migrant labor and thus increased both instability and accumulated grievances.

Transformations of the System of Industrial Relations and the Political Balance: 1968–70

Between 1968 and 1970, waves of strikes produced a transformation in the system of industrial relations: a system in which, although many changes had taken place in them, the unions were weak, centralized, and closely linked to political parties gave way to a system in which unions were strong, much less closely linked to political parties, and with power spread from the shop floor up to the confederations.

A second, related transformation took place during the same period. This was the change in the political system as a result of the successes of the PCI and the Socialist losses in the general election of May 1968.

This changed the concept of the center-left. Its original justification had been as the means of realizing important social and economic "reforms," without Communist support. It was anti-Communist, both in the method of implementation and in the sense that the reforms, once implemented, would reduce the future risk of Communist gains. The 1968 election results were disastrous for the Socialists:[47] they were a reaction against the failure of the coalition to achieve more than minimal reforms. From 1968–69 on, the object of the center-left was regarded by many, including the Socialists, as moving the Communists into the government of the country. As has been seen, these two changes had an important common cause in the failure of reform. And each helped in part to bring about the other: the labor-market transformation of the unions depended in part on government acquiescence, which was a consequence of the political transformation, and this transformation rested in part on the realization by the Socialists of the massive increase in militancy and discontent on the part of the workers. Together, the two transformations set the basic pattern of political and industrial relations until 1980.

The main thrust of the Hot Autumn strikes was provided by the semiskilled workers, of whom a large proportion had entered the industrial labor force only in the 1960s. Although their accumulated grievances were great in early 1968, they lacked strike experience and organization. Despite the tightening labor markets in 1968, the transformation of accumulated grievances into mobilizability of the semiskilled did not come easily. Early strikes in 1968 were led by skilled workers. The "avalanche" of wildcats at Pirelli in the summer of 1968 was started by printers. In fact, the "young, mostly immigrant semi-skilled workers . . . did not begin to establish themselves as autonomous protagonists in important conflicts until the autumn of 1968 and the spring of 1969, finally dominating the scene in the 'hot autumn' of 1969."[48] During 1968 and early 1969, the movement of the semiskilled was not "'spontaneous' in the sense of having originated among workers who had no previous political experience, either in the unions or parties, or in other political

47. The Communists, who had made substantial gains in 1963, increased their share of the popular vote for the lower house by 1.6 percentage points, from 25.3 percent to 26.9 percent. The Partito Socialista Italiano di Unità Proletaria (PSIUP), a left-wing breakaway from the Socialists in opposition to the center-left, gained 4.5 percent of the vote. The Socialists had merged with the more right-leaning Social Democrats in 1966; the aggregate of votes for the two parties in 1963 had been close to 20 percent: in 1968 the share was only 14.5 percent.

48. Regalia and others, "Labour Conflicts," p. 109.

groupings."[49] The work-group representatives who were elected during strikes at this stage saw their role as linking the work force with union representatives outside the plant or the works council inside.[50] Frequently most of the representatives were union activists; where they were not, they sought collaboration and guidance from the unions. Both militant students and unionists associated with parties to the left of the Socialists and Communists were active in this process. By the end of 1968, four types of demands, which reflected the grievances of the semiskilled and the radical influences of some of those associated with their movement, had emerged on the shop floor. These were general wage increases; reduction of differentials, and improvement of working conditions of the skilled workers; greater control over the work place; and participation in the bargaining process.

Until the middle of 1969 there was no coherent involvement or unified strategy on the part of the unions as a whole toward these developments. From 1968 many activists and officials of the industrial unions had been deeply involved. But the representation and demands of the semiskilled posed problems for the CGIL unions, whose strength came from the skilled work force. This was partially annulled by the weakness of the CISL among skilled workers, which enabled the CISL to back the demands of the semiskilled and thus exert competitive pressure on the CGIL. Moreover, the CGIL industrial unions were not in principle against radical change.

By 1966–67 the metalworkers' unions had already related the failure of the unions to capitalize on the favorable conditions of the early 1960s to two weaknesses: first, the need to develop plant-level bargaining autonomy, as opposed to articulated bargaining, and second, the need to organize the semiskilled. This adaptability on the part of the unions related, first, to the strategy of the Communists, which entailed a greater freedom for the CGIL than that allowed the largest French confederation, the Confédération Générale du Travail (CGT), by the French Communist party, and second, to the developments within the CISL, which enabled the "innovators" to come to the fore of the industrial unions. The year 1969 saw the rapid spread of plant conflicts, especially among the semiskilled and the unskilled. "New and infectiously anti-authoritarianism calls for direct control by the workers were made. In this

49. Ibid., p. 142.
50. Ibid.

atmosphere it was very difficult to identify with certainty the attitudes of the militant workers who led the mobilisation and who often took on the label *delegati*."[51]

At this stage, the adaptability of the unions enabled them to regain the initiative. First, they suggested that bargaining demands in the national agreements that were to be negotiated in December 1969 should be determined in consultation with workers on the shop floor. Second, they demanded that plant committees of activists should direct industrial conflict, together with union representatives. The unions had negotiating and organizing skills. Early on, many *delegati* had come to rely on the advice and help of plant-union activists, and in many instances unions put up their own candidates for election as *delegati*. Giugni argued that the unions had gained strategic control of the strikes by the middle of 1969.[52] This was at the cost of accepting the demands for reduced differentials and plant autonomy, including the institutional structure of *delegati* and workers' meetings. Control therefore meant negotiating, bargaining, and organizing in conjunction with—and frequently in the capacity of—*delegati,* rather than controlling the agenda from the top. This cooperative activity involved the negotiation of plant agreements as well as organization of plant activity in relation to national agreements. "In virtually all cases the trade unions joined forces with the delegates' movement during the bargaining stage proper and took over strategic control."[53] In relation to the national agreements, the leaders of the industrial unions typically gave weekly instructions to plants on the total number of hours of strike during that week, while the form and timing of the strikes was left to be determined by delegates, plant-union activists, and workers' meetings at the plant. The process of the formulation of demands in the national agreements was based on the shop floor. It has been estimated that 2,000–3,000 meetings were held in plants to approve the demands.[54]

The culmination of the transformation of the industrial unions was the Metal Workers' Agreement of December 1969, the other industrial agreements based on it, and the Workers' Charter, enacted in mid 1970, which brought the law into line with the transformation of the industrial relations system.

51. Ibid., p. 143.
52. Giugni, "Recent Developments," pp. 315–16.
53. Ibid.
54. Ibid.

The Metal Workers' Agreement was signed first by the state industries at the beginning of December, and by the private sector at the end of that month. It embodied a flat rate increase of sixty-five lire an hour; the workweek was to be reduced progressively to forty hours by the end of 1972; there was to be equal treatment of salaried and hourly staff when sick; overtime was to be limited, but there were to be compensations in pay for the limitation. No limitations on plant bargaining were imposed by the agreement, and, in a significant innovation, ratification on the shop floor was required.

Alongside the negotiations over the Metal Workers' Agreement was the bargaining over the Workers' Charter. The primary element in the charter was that all obstacles to union and *delegati* activity at the plant level were to be removed; in time off work, provision of facilities, and entitlement to hold meetings, unions and *delegati* were given wide-ranging rights on the shop floor. To buttress these rights, a rapid disputes procedure was instituted. These changes were designed to prevent the type of repression of union activity that had prevailed in the 1950s and the period 1964–67.

The role of the industrial unions and the shop floor had been fundamentally changed as a result of 1968–69. The employers by no means accepted these changes. Unions reserved the right to reopen questions in plant bargaining even when they had been settled in national agreements. Moreover,

At shop level the pattern of claims has undergone a remarkable change. Hitherto industrial organization has been the prerogative of management and the unions' task has been to bargain over the consequences of any changes in industrial conditions, especially as regards wages. Nowadays, they question the whole organisation of work within industry. The symbol of this campaign is the assembly line.[55]

The changes reflected the new strength of workers on the shop floor, and the employers were unable to reverse them.

Where did these transformations leave the confederations? The industrial unions controlled the access of the confederations to the greatly increased militancy of the workers. What they required of the confederations was (1) formal autonomy from the political parties; (2) moves toward unification; and (3) concentration on bargaining with the government on social and economic policy—the so-called reform strategy.

55. Ibid., p. 324.

The industrial unions wanted the first two requirements in order to prevent the confederations from returning to the situation of the 1950s and mid 1960s, when they had behaved as creatures of their respective parties, and they wanted the third so that they themselves could retain the exclusive rights in negotiating the national collective bargaining agreements. Also, the need for social reforms was widely held as important in the unions.

The political parties were opposed to unification and autonomy, but both the PSI and the PCI favored the reform strategy. To the PCI the strategy represented an important step toward broad coalitions on the left on questions of common concern; to the PSI it represented a reaffirmation of the new Socialist direction.

At this stage the industrial unions called the tune. The CGIL and the CISL held quadrennial congresses in mid 1969 and accepted the principle of formal autonomy from parties. Both confederations were split on the issue. The secretary-general of the CGIL resigned rather than give up his PCI office, although the party links with the CGIL remained strong in practice. In the CISL, the division was between the "innovators" from the northern industrial unions and northern confederal offices and the southern confederation officials, plus the service-sector and agricultural unions. The leadership of the latter by the CISL was maintained only by accepting the goals of the "innovators," some of whom were included in the CISL secretariat in early 1970.[56] In general, the "conversion" of the confederations marked a tactical retreat.

The strike waves of the early 1960s had been met in 1964 by a sharp deflation, enabling business to eliminate the influence of unions in the plants. But deflation to maintain the status quo ante was not seen as an option by the government in 1969. The government, moreover, was instrumental both in persuading the employers to sign the Metal Workers' Agreement and in passing the Workers' Charter. In part this reflected the reality of shop-floor power in late 1969. It reflected also the second, political, transformation of 1968–70. As discussed earlier, the Socialists now saw their role as aiding the installation of the PCI into the government. While the PCI had cause later to regret the increased autonomous power of the shop floor, its immediate reaction was "in favor of greater reliance on the action of radical social forces."[57] The condition of the

56. Weitz, "Labor and Politics," p. 237.
57. Stephen Hellman, "The Longest Campaign: Communist Party Strategy and the Elections of 1976," in Penniman, *Italy at the Polls,* p. 161.

Table 9-4. *Labor Costs in Industry during Three Triennial Contract Periods, Italy, 1970–79*

Percentage growth rates

Year	Real value added per worker (1)	"Room"— column 1 corrected for changes in terms of trade[a] (2)	Real labor cost per worker (VA deflator) (3)	Real hourly wage earnings (VA deflator) (4)	Real minimum contractual wages (VA deflator) (5)	"Drift" (col. 4 − col. 5) (6)	Real minimum contractual wages (COL deflator) (7)	Real subsidies per worker (col. 4 − col. 3)[b] (8)	"Gap" (col. 2 − col. 3) (9)
1970	6.0	6.0	13.0[c]	13.0	13.4	−0.4	16.6	. . .	−7.0
1971	0.7	0.7	4.1	10.0	6.7	3.4	8.5	5.9	−3.4
1972	5.3	5.3	5.8	7.6	5.0	2.6	4.9	1.8	−0.5
1973	8.9	6.4	14.3	15.4	17.2	−1.8	13.8	0.9	−7.9
1974	2.8	−3.1	7.0	9.5	4.5	5.0	3.0	2.5	−10.1
1975	−9.2	−7.8	2.8	9.3	7.6	1.7	9.5	6.5	−10.6
1976	11.6	11.6	4.0	−0.3	2.4	−2.7	4.4	−4.3	7.6
1977	1.5	1.5	2.1	5.3	9.1	−3.8	9.5	3.2	−0.6
1978	2.8	2.8	0.8	2.7	3.3	−0.6	3.8	2.1	2.0
1979	6.5	6.5	4.3	2.6	4.5	−1.9	3.2	−1.7	2.2

Sources: Column 1, real value added and employment in industry excluding construction, 1971–76, from *Relazione annuale 1976* (Rome: Banca d'Italia, 1977), quoted in Michele Salvati, "The Italian Inflation," 2d draft, Brookings Project on Global Inflation and Recession (1979), p. 42: 1977–78 from OECD Annual Surveys, successive issues; 1979 from *Relazione annuale 1979* (1980), p. 50; 1970 real value added from OECD Economic Surveys, *Italy*, 1971, p. 56; employment including construction, ibid., p. 12; column 2, imports for 1972 from OECD, *Italy*, 1976, table J, p. 64, as a ratio to 1972 GDP at market prices from ibid., p. 52; *i* is measured as the percent change in World Export Price Index of Primary Commodities, *UN Monthly Bulletin of Statistics*, August 1980, table 59, p. 160, *less* the percent change in Unit Value Index of Exports of Developed Market Economies, *UN Statistical Yearbook*, 1978, table 15, p. 58: column 3, nominal labor cost per employee for industry excluding construction, 1971–73, from Salvati, "Italian Inflation." p. 42; for manufacturing only, 1974, from OECD, *Italy*, 1979, p. 21; for industry as a whole, 1975–79, from OECD, *Italy*, 1980, p. 17; employment data, 1971–76, from Salvati, "Italian Inflation," p. 42; 1977–79, from *Relazione annuale 1979* (1980), p.50; GDP deflator in manufacturing, mining, and utilities, 1970–78, from OECD Annual Survey, successive issues; wholesale inflation rate for manufacturing, 1979, from *Relazione annuale 1979*, p. 57; column 4, nominal hourly wage earnings for industry including construction, 1970–77, from OECD, *Italy*, 1980, p. 70; 1978–79 from *Relazione annuale 1979*, p. 54; VA deflator as in column 3; column 5, nominal minimum contractual wage rates for manufacturing, 1970–77, from ILO, *Yearbook of Labour Statistics 1979* (Geneva: International Labour Organization, 1979); 1978 from OECD, *Italy*, 1980, p. 70; 1979, from *Relazione annuale 1979*, p. 55; VA deflator as in column 3; column 7, rates as in column 5; cost-of-living index from OECD, *Italy*, successive issues.

a. Corrections for changes in the terms of trade applied to column 1 for 1973–75 only; real unit costs are $w/\pi + c.t.m.$ and c unit profits are a function of real unit costs, so constant c unit profits require $\hat{w} = \dot{\pi} - [cm t/(w/\pi^t)]$; in the simplified calculations here *cmt* is taken as the ratio of total material imports to GDP in 1972 and measured by categories 1–5 of cost, insurance, and freight (c.i.f.).

b. The difference between columns 4 and 3 is equal to $(\dot{s} + \dot{h})$, where *s* is the ratio of social security contributions paid by employer to earnings and *h* is hours per worker. It is thus equal to a "straight" subsidy, $-\dot{s}$, and a measure of the indirect subsidy, $-\dot{h}$, by way of the Wage Supplementation Fund; the periods when $-\dot{s} - \dot{h}$ has been low or negative—1973, 1976, and 1979— have been years of rising output and increased hours.

c. Because we were unable to obtain labor cost data for 1969 and 1970, we have used real hourly wage earnings here.

Socialists for staying within the coalition was that the government did not frustrate the changes that were taking place in the system of industrial relations.

Strategies of Adjustment in the 1970s

The change in the system of industrial relations in the late 1960s focused attention on three sectors of the economy: large industry, in both the private and public sectors, with a unionized labor force; small to medium-sized firms, able either to employ, to a greater or lesser extent, nonunion—or "irregular" or "unofficial" or "secondary"—labor or to deal with weakly organized union workers; and the nonindustrial public sector, consisting of public services and administration. The gains of 1968–69 were made primarily by semiskilled workers in large-scale industry. There the rise in real wages and the dilution of the control of employers over work processes contributed to declines in profitability and international competitiveness. The main problem of adjustment became that of correcting these downward trends in profitability and competitiveness. The secondary problem, which came to the fore later, concerned differentials between skilled and semiskilled workers.

The history of the 1970s can be divided, as is done to a degree in table 9-4, into four periods corresponding to the triennial wage contracts: 1970–72, 1973–75, 1976–78, and 1979–81. The first two contracts saw real wages rising substantially faster than labor productivity. The "gap" calculations in column 9 show the amount by which the growth of real wages would have needed to be moderated if profitability and competitiveness were to be preserved at constant levels, after taking subsidies and changes in world terms of trade into account. It was only during the third contract period—which coincided with the participation of the PCI in incomes policy—that the growth of real wages was moderated sufficiently to reduce the gap, although, as can be seen from column 1, growth in productivity was lower than even its modest level for the preceding six years. The fourth contract period saw the end of Communist involvement in wage restraint; in its place employers launched a direct offensive against the power of semiskilled workers on the shop floor in an effort to increase growth in productivity. It is too early to assess the consequences of this effort fully.

The Available Strategies

To give a broad idea of the possible strategies, the following list may be of use.

1. *Reduction of union power.* Primarily through deflation, to a lesser extent through the judiciary, the government can create conditions in which employers can reduce union power. To a limited extent, such a policy was pursued in 1970–71—unsuccessfully in large companies. Large companies attempted to reduce plant-level union power directly in 1980–81, apparently with greater success.

2. *Bargaining for moderation in the use of union power.*

a. Bargaining by the government: in 1973–74, an unsuccessful, informal attempt by the center-left government to provide low unemployment, price controls, and reform legislation in exchange for wage restraint; in 1976–78, a concerted attempt to offer participation in government to the Communist party plus developmental reform legislation in exchange for wage restraint, flexibility on working conditions, and union acceptance of deflation; in 1980, an attempt by the government to obtain confederal agreement to a levy of 0.5 percent on wages and salaries in exchange for CGIL and CISL seats on the board to administer funds for development of the south, at the same time helping official unions by tough action against unofficial, "autonomous" unions.

b. Bargaining by Confindustria: an unsuccessful attempt in 1971 to bargain with confederations, swapping guarantees of employment for formal wage-bargaining framework; 100 percent indexation and job-protection measures granted by Confindustria in 1975, hoping for wage restraint in the long run as a result.

3. *Inducing moderation of union power through increased centralization within unions.*

a. Bargaining strategies of Confindustria: the 1975, 100 percent indexation agreement, which was designed to reduce the need to bargain at the shop-floor level and also to establish the confederations themselves as bargaining partners of Confindustria; the confederations were more moderate than plant organizations, because they had to represent weak sections of the work force as well as strong sections and also because they had closer links to political parties.

b. Attempts by the PCI and the confederations to increase the power of the confederations in 1973–77; they were designed directly to produce wage restraint because of PCI fears of a right-wing backlash and also to give the PCI a bargaining lever to gain political power. There were also attempts, especially in 1970–72, by industrial unions to gain control of shop-floor organizations.

4. *Direct and indirect subsidies to industry.*

a. Direct subsidies by the government to help companies in both the private and public sectors that were incurring losses; "fiscalization" of social security contributions by employers, generally financed by increases in value-added tax. Both direct subsidies and fiscalization were resorted to particularly in 1971, 1975, and 1977–78 (see table 9-4, column 8).

b. Government payments to laid-off workers through Cassa Integrazione Guadagni, the Wage Supplementation Fund; from 1975 on, this fund provided 80 percent of earnings lost as a result of short-time working. The reason for regarding such payments as indirect subsidies to industry is that, in the absence of such compensation, the unions would and could simply have refused to allow many companies to lay off workers.

5. *Reduction of costs by resort to the black labor market.* Throughout the 1970s large companies directly and indirectly exploited the secondary labor market, either by subcontracting component production to homeworkers or by purchasing from small companies.

6. *Reduction of unit labor costs through economic expansion.* Effective union opposition to redundancies (and to a lesser extent to short-time working even with 80 percent compensation, because of the effect on the black labor market) made expansion an attractive way of reducing unit labor costs. Table 9-4, column 1, shows how value added per worker rose in relation to employment during the three short periods of expansion, 1973, 1976, and 1978–79. It should also be noted that, by improving the balance of trade, competitive small and medium-sized firms helped make economic expansion feasible and thus contributed to the realization of lower unit labor costs by large firms.

7. *Restoration of international competitiveness by depreciation of the exchange rate.* The government allowed the exchange rate to depreciate in order to restore competitiveness and to rebuild profitability during two periods, 1973–74 and 1976.

These strategies are not, of course, independent. In particular, the three government economic policy strategies, 4, 6, and 7, are severely constrained. Strategy 6, economic expansion, faces two external constraints: if the external balance is initially in equilibrium, an increase in aggregate demand will produce a deficit; it will lead to a loss of competitiveness, moreover, if the real wage depends on the level of output. In the short run, the constraint can be eased by depreciation—indeed, the depreciation may have been provoked by the expansion of output. But competitiveness can only be restored by depreciation if it is accompanied by a positive differential between productivity and real wage growth. This condition (see table 9-4, column 9) pertained in 1976, but not in 1973–74—hence the rapid acceleration of inflation.

Equally, direct or indirect subsidies to industry may increase competitiveness in the short run. But if output is constrained, the effect of subsidies on aggregate demand must be offset by increased taxes elsewhere. If not, the increased output will increase real wages, vitiating some or all of the effect of the subsidy. Thus, though subsidies, depreciation, and economic expansion have all been resorted to, the main efforts of governments and business—as well as of the PCI and the confederations—have been directed toward institutional restraint.

The following subsections are concentrated on these attempts to secure institutional restraint. The power of the semiskilled work force in large plants proved remarkably durable throughout the 1970s. This was because no government was prepared to deflate the economy seriously or aid large companies in attempts at elimination of shop-floor power. In sum, this was because the political position of the Communists was sufficiently strong to block such moves.

Both the government and large businesses were therefore forced into attempts at accommodation with the unions and the PCI. But the necessary rewards for restraint—namely, reforms, which came to be closely linked with Communist participation in government—were not ultimately forthcoming: the conservative wing of the DC proved too powerful. As in the United Kingdom, moreover, effective restraint was confined to real wages; an incomes policy run by senior shop stewards could not permit the redundancies necessary for growth in productivity. Only the small-business sector prospered in the economic environment of the 1970s, unhampered by union restraints and with frequent access to black-market labor.

The reaction to these problems came in 1979–80, when large businesses took matters into their own hands. They were encouraged by the decline in the political power of the PCI, which permitted the government to turn a blind eye.

Return to the Status Quo Ante Frustrated, 1970–72

In 1970, after the turmoil of the Hot Autumn, Italy faced the problems of rapid wage inflation, reduced profitability, a continuing high level of strikes, and balance-of-payments difficulties. The reactions were on various levels. The government was pushed electorally rightward but was compromised in its ability to adopt serious deflationary policies such as it had done in 1964 by divisions among the Christian Democrats. It made no serious attempt, however, to extricate the economy from the recession into which it was falling, thereby, according to one interpretation, giving industry a looser labor market, in which profitability could be more easily recouped. Industry responded by attempting to moderate or destroy union power on the shop floor. But the entrenched position of the work force in larger plants confined the success of such responses to small firms. Large-scale industry developed a dual strategy: when it was possible, indirect recourse to the black labor market; otherwise, acceptance of union power and hence of the need to negotiate with it. At the same time the industrial unions used the period to impose more central authority on union activity within the plant.

By late 1970 three ''democratic'' political directions lay open in principle. The first was a center-right government, sensitive to the needs of a lower-middle-class electorate, with industrial links to small and medium-sized businesses, and aware of the competitive claims of the extreme right-wing party, the MSI. The ideal program of such a government was ''law and order,'' the maintenance of the isolation of the PCI, disengagement from serious reforms, and a return to the status quo ante in industrial relations. The DC faced some temptation to move in this direction. The general atmosphere of social and economic crisis in 1969–70 had elicited a right-wing response among voters. In the local elections of 1971, held only in the South, the neofascist MSI increased its share of the Roman vote from 10.2 percent to 17.2 percent and of the Sicilian vote from 7.2 percent to 16.3 percent; these were significant results in the light of the stability of Italian voting behavior. And these gains were generally at the expense of the Christian Democratic right and center.

The second direction was a center-left government similar to that of the 1960s. This possibility attracted the small center parties as well as many Christian Democrats. By combining limited reform—at least as far as intentions went—with exclusion of the PCI, it could have enabled the DC right to hold its flank against the MSI while keeping a sufficient part of the DC left within the coalition. But such an old-style center-left was ruled out by the Socialists. The latter, rebuffed as they saw it in the 1968 general election for their role in the center-left governments of the 1960s, believed that they now had to collaborate with the unions and the Communist party to legislate reform. Instead, as noted earlier, the Socialists looked in a third direction to a new-style center-left: in this they saw themselves as the informal agents of the PCI and the unions, helping to bring about implicit or explicit involvement of the PCI in government. But just as the electoral concerns of the Socialists blocked an old-style center-left, so those of the DC center prevented the formation of a center-left, new style.

What emerged in 1971 and 1972 was a weak center-right government. Its freedom to maneuver was limited. The Christian Democratic left and left-center refused to accept ministerial office and made governmental restraint a condition of their reluctant support. The power of the DC left was greatly enhanced by that of the CISL, despite the increased autonomy of the CISL. And to the extent that its power rested on the unions, it refused to support any measures, such as major deflation, that threatened the newfound position of the unions.

The result was compromise. There was "no doubt that the [DC took] the [MSI] threat sufficiently seriously to orient its [1973 general] election campaign towards recovering these votes." This implied policies geared toward "the backbone of the MSI [which had come to consist of] the lower-middle and middle classes, with the support of a largish number of minor industrialists unable to adjust to the difficult union situation and rising costs."[58]

On the other hand, no severe recession developed like that which had occurred in the mid 1960s in response to the wage explosion of 1962–63. Measures of credit restriction were taken by the Bank of Italy in 1969 and 1970, and a deflationary fiscal package was implemented in August 1970. This was before the slowdown in world trade that became evident in 1971; moreover, "no real excess demand conditions were present in 1969–70."[59] The intent of the measures, therefore, was probably to act

58. Economist Intelligence Unit, *Quarterly Economic Review: Italy,* no. 1 (1972), pp. 4, 5.
59. Salvati, "Italian Inflation," p. 94.

against cost-push inflation; but if this was so, the measures were too weak.

A sharper, really "lesson teaching" set of monetary credit measures, would certainly have stiffened the resistance of employers against wage concessions, and would probably have choked the *élan* of the collective movement: if a restrictive medicine was chosen, then an overdose of it was necessary in the changed social and political conditions of the late '60's–early '70's. These very conditions, however, were preventing a stabilisation manoeuvre of the same intensity as in 1963–4: no "technical" justification could be alleged for such a policy, and its naked political purpose would have contrasted sharply with the political balance of forces then prevailing.[60]

Such recession as there was combined with the changes of 1968–70 to mark a clear duality of interest between large business and small. Small firms believed that the appropriate reaction to 1968–70 was to eliminate the unions from their plants; in 1971–72 their efforts met with some limited success.[61] Large firms, on the other hand, realized how firmly established unions had become in their large plants. Thus, economic recession did not help them recover lost power; instead—because of short-run economies of scale and their being forced to maintain employment—it implied reduced profitability. At an aggregate level this is borne out by the following statistics for rates of return:

Period	Large private manufacturing companies	Small private manufacturing companies
1965–69	5.0	4.3
1970–73	3.1	5.3
1974–77	2.8	4.9

While some measure of institutionalization of shop-floor power had come about gradually within the industrial unions, moreover, large firms were still faced with unpredictable strikes. Against these developments business had some defenses. To the extent to which shop-floor bargaining power permitted it, capital deepening was a response to higher labor costs.[62] In addition, businesses were prepared to charge workers, through lockouts, the full cost of strikes.[63]

A more serious response was the indirect resort by business to the

60. Ibid., p. 98.
61. Regalia and others, "Labour Conflicts," p. 110.
62. OECD Economic Surveys, *Italy*, November 1972, p. 6.
63. Regalia and others, "Labour Conflicts," p. 116.

"black" labor market, as well as to more "flexible" work assignments in unionized firms in the south. This included subcontracting to small firms that could evade union control of the work force or payment of social security contributions. It also included putting out work on virtually a cottage-industry basis and building new small plants, which employed unionized labor in regions and from work groups, such as women, in which union influence was relatively weak; this gave large companies access to a more easily controlled work force, while placing the unions in an ideologically embarrassing position. Finally, large companies purchased components from medium-sized and small companies that employed more "flexible," albeit unionized, labor.

The black, or "unofficial," labor market existed before the 1970s. (Indeed, such a phenomenon generally exists in countries that are not fully industrialized.) The 1970s, however, witnessed a significant growth in black labor markets. The estimates given below of the numbers of workers in the unofficial labor market are based on calculations in an important recent book on the subject, whose author argues econometrically that the development of the black labor market has been positively related to increases in real unit costs in industry.[64]

Period	Number of workers
1965–69	2,595,000
1970–73	3,548,000
1974–77	3,745,000

The importance of these figures can be gauged by comparison with a total of about 14 million workers in dependent employment in the whole economy and about 6 million workers in dependent employment in industry. Throughout the 1970s the development of the black labor market and also of more flexible work practices in small and medium-sized firms provided large-scale industry with important access to low-cost services and subcontracted components. This has enabled large companies to offset to some extent the rigidities and high costs imposed by the strong plant unions with which they were confronted at the

64. Bruno Contini, *Lo sviluppo di un'economia parallela: La segmentazione del mercato del lavoro in Italia e la crescita del settore irregolare* [The development of a parallel economy: the segmentation of the labor market in Italy and the growth of the irregular sector] (Milan: Edizione di Comunità, 1979). Also, Giorgio Fua, *Occupazione e capacità produttiva: la realtà italiana* [Employment and productive capacity: the Italian reality] (Bologna: Il Mulino, 1976).

beginning of the decade. Smaller firms produced final goods as well as inputs into the production process of the larger firms. In so doing they have tended to exert opposing influences on the profitability of the big enterprises. Where this output competed with the products of big business, it presumably tended to reduce profit margins and market shares, although this possibility has not been discussed in studies of the subject. Instead, emphasis has been placed on indirect beneficial effects of small-scale operation on the profitability of large-scale enterprise, especially in the late 1970s. And as noted earlier, the growth of the small-business sector, by helping the country's balance-of-payments position, permitted the authorities to adopt more expansionist policies and thereby permitted the larger firms to realize short-run economies of scale.

These responses caused relations with the unions to deteriorate. Lockouts and the substitution of capital and black labor for unionized employees did not significantly weaken the organizational positions that the unions had acquired in the large firms as a result of the 1969 strikes. Neither plant unions nor industrial unions were prepared to make concessions on what the employers saw as the key issue at the plant level: binding contracts with peace, or no-strike, clauses. The alternative left to big business was once again to negotiate directly with the confederations. There were two difficulties in this approach. First, Confindustria was still dominated by small and medium-sized enterprises that were not prepared to concede much to reach an agreement with the confederations. Second, the power of the confederations was still quite limited at this stage. Following the Pirelli report in 1970, however, which argued for the need to accept and institutionalize the new power of the unions and to give individual—that is, large—firms a greater say in the policy of Confindustria, a shift toward a more flexible line took place within Confindustria. In late 1971 and early 1972, a series of meetings took place between the union confederations and Confindustria. Confindustria's proposal was to swap guarantees of employment for a framework agreement to regulate collective bargaining, a greater formalization of the structures of worker representation in the factories, and a system of "wage coordination."[65] But the industrial unions would not permit the confederations to go ahead, for they would lose power by such an agreement and, in addition, they did not believe they could sell it to the members and *delegati* on the shop floor. This rejection pushed the large

65. Regalia and others, "Labour Conflicts," p. 151.

companies in two directions: one was to operate through the government; the other was to be prepared to make the offer to the confederations more enticing. They moved in the first direction in 1973, when they helped to bring about the end of the center-right government, supporting a center-left government committed to a formal prices policy and an informal incomes policy. The second direction was taken by Confindustria in 1975, in the agreement to index wages fully against consumer price increases.

Thus, the recession of 1971–72 demonstrated that the *delegati* were firmly entrenched in the plants; large-scale industry began to envisage a long-term modus vivendi with the unions at various levels. The unions were also obliged to come to terms with the *delegati,* when in 1970 and 1971 they formally accepted the system of *delegati* and *consigli*— councils of all the *delegati* in a given plant—as the method of union representation and operation within the plant. Union branches were abolished and union operations within the *commissioni interni* (the old works councils) ended. Although "the delegati [did] not entirely [lose] a basic ambiguity which [arose] from [union and workshop as] dual sources of legitimacy,"[66] the industrial unions were nevertheless generally successful in asserting a broad control over plant-level activity. The main reason lay in control of the *consigli* through their executive committees. In large factories with a *delegato* for every fifty to seventy workers, the *consiglio* was too large to wield an executive function.

The competence of older activists who were specialists in complex aspects of labour relations was again of value. Trade union power within the factory came to be exercised at many different levels, in sharp contrast to the stereotyped image, widespread in 1969, of direct representation based on the mandate of the work group. . . . In practice . . . the executive directed union policy in the factory and was empowered to conduct negotiations with the management.[67]

This process was aided by the negotiation of the *inquadramento unico* by the industrial unions. This was a complex system for reorganization of skill differentials designed to favor semiskilled workers. It worked by reducing the total number of grades and by facilitating the training of semiskilled employees so as to enable them to move into skilled categories. It was a clever move by the unions, spearheaded by the Metal Workers: while it met the aspirations of the semiskilled, it was a sufficiently complex system to give power to those older, loyal union members on the *consigli* with experience in bargaining.

66. Ibid., p. 145.
67. Ibid., p. 146.

A change thus took place in day-to-day control of workers at the plant level. The industrial unions in 1972–73 limited the "maximum degree of intensity" of strikes, for example, and made it a rule that a shop could strike only with the consent and under the control of the *consiglio*.[68] But the change, like that in the United Kingdom from fragmented to formal plant bargaining, was not irrevocable; if the workers in a plant felt strongly and persistently about an issue, the "organizational control" of the union could be insufficient to counter their wishes. The industrial unions, moreover, had been able to make these changes during a period of recession, so there was no guarantee that they could be maintained when labor markets were tighter—unless, of course, the industrial unions were careful not to adopt policies against rank-and-file desires.

The second development in this period was in the role of the confederations. They failed to make serious headway in their bargaining with the government over social policies. In 1973–74 their function was taken over by the industrial unions, which attempted to negotiate social reform directly with individual companies. The confederations had failed for three reasons:

—the politics of a center-right government precluded radical reform;

—the political parties, especially the Socialists, the PCI, and the Christian Democratic left, became seriously concerned for their raison d'etre when policymaking on reform was being conducted between the confederations and the government; and

—as the economy moved into recession, workers and industrial unions became more worried about real wages and employment and were less prepared to strike or demonstrate on social questions.

As a result of this failure, the confederations moved back to a closer relationship with the political parties, thus signaling the temporary failure of the unification movement at the confederal level.

The Failure of the Center-Left, 1973–74, and the Strategy of Confindustria, 1974–75

The resignation of the center-right government of Giulio Andreotti and its replacement by the center-left administration of Mariano Rumor took place in June 1973. The change came about for a number of related reasons. The neo-Fascists had failed to do as well as had been feared in the 1972 general election: this reduced the electoral need of Christian

68. Ibid., p. 120.

Democratic deputies for right-wing policies. At the same time, fascist terrorism increased, possibly to compensate for limited success at the polls; as a result the PCI, fearful of a fascist backlash, indicated that it would support a center-left coalition and advised the Socialists to begin discussions to that end with the DC in early 1973.[69] The Socialist party, with the backing of the PCI and considerable support from the unions, believed that a new center-left could produce significant reform legislation and would thus not compromise its strategy of *revirginarsi* to regain its innocence lost in the coalition with the Christian Democrats in the 1960s. The DC had positive reasons to change position: the DC left was increasingly restless over the lack of any progress toward reform;[70] at the same time, large companies wanted an administration that would combine expansionary economic policies with negotiations with the unions designed to moderate wage increases. Thus, within the DC, a loose coalition was beginning to emerge between industrialists and the center-left.

There was reason to believe that the new administration might be able to gain cooperation from the unions in moderating their wage demands in national contract negotiations in 1973. The industrial unions had regained, during the recession, a substantial measure of control over the *delegati* and the rank and file, so, although the confederations remained relatively weak and still politically divided, the union movement as a whole was more centralized than before. The most militant industrial unions, moreover, those in metalworking and chemicals, had already concluded their negotiations at the end of 1972: the end-of-1973 negotiations included less militant public-sector unions, which were more amenable to the moderating pressure of the confederations. The Communists wanted to contain inflation to buttress themselves, by the continuation of the center-left, against the possibility of a right-wing backlash and the return of the center-right. Finally, there was the belief that the unions would be attracted by an expansionary economic policy and might be able to sell restraint, if it was backed by reform and price controls, to their members.

The new government offered the unions three policies: an expansionary demand policy; a serious move toward reform legislation; and price controls. Prices of staple consumer products were frozen for three months from mid 1973, then made subject to control by the Interminis-

69. Economist Intelligence Unit, *Quarterly Economic Review: Italy,* no. 1 (1973), p. 2.

70. Ibid., no. 4 (1973), p. 3.

terial Price Commission until mid 1974. In addition, companies with turnover of more than 5 billion lire had to declare price increases, which, if approved by the government, could be introduced only after a delay of sixty days. The OECD concluded that "initially, the system proved fairly effective, and during the 3 months of the freeze the prices concerned rose only 1.2 percent."[71] There is slight evidence of a slowdown in the overall consumer price index in the third and fourth quarters of 1973, though it rose sharply in the first quarter of 1974.

With respect to reform legislation, however, the center-left was ineffective. It was hampered not only by the usual problems of the bureaucracy and Christian Democratic conservatism; there was also a sharp division within the government about the appropriateness of embarking on major expansions of public expenditure in 1974. This division mirrored disagreement on the question of whether to deflate: the PSI was unwilling to be seen supporting deflation, and industry and the unions were opposed to it. An unsatisfactory compromise emerged: neither reform nor deflation.

The unions were similarly hamstrung. The confederations had proposed to adopt a position of "benevolent understanding" toward the government, being prepared to use their influence to restrain wage demands, boost productivity, and observe a "social truce" on plant-level disputes.[72] The PCI joined in with the confederal proposals, seeing them as part of a move toward the "historic compromise" that it had just announced as the basic thrust of its strategy. The industrial unions, however, were deeply split on the question of the appropriate line to take. As Brandini wrote,

In the trade union movement there is a leftist orientation strongly represented by the key industrial federations and especially the metal workers federation (FLM), which insist on active shop struggle and reject enduring compromises, binding constraints and the "social truce" found in the "peace obligation" of the agreement. They are opposed to compromises and emphasize fighting aggressively for union remedies and solutions of complaints and grievances and direct achievements through plant and community pressure. The councils of shop delegates are their motor force since they assemble these demands and provide the industrial support to push them.[73]

The strength of such feeling against moderation was forcefully shown in

71. OECD Economic Surveys, *Italy*, January 1975, p. 31.
72. Brandini, "Italy: Creating a New Industrial Relations System from the Bottom," p. 111; see also Economist Intelligence Unit, *Quarterly Economic Review: Italy*, no. 3 (1973).
73. Brandini, "Italy," p. 113.

a national conference of *consigli* in April 1974. The leaders of the industrial unions were aware of the limits of their ability to impose moderation on the rank and file, but they were also concerned about the consequences for employment of failing to do so. Some moderation emerged in the settlements at the national level in late 1973,[74] and the strike figures for the second half of 1973 suggest that the social truce was not without effect during that half year (though not later).

Even if some moderation was observed, however, it was insufficient to prevent the rapid acceleration of inflation. Consumer price inflation was 10.4 percent in 1973, twice the rates in the three years preceding— 5.1 percent, 5.0 percent, and 5.6 percent. And in 1974 it nearly doubled again, to 19.4 percent. Four factors were behind this acceleration of inflation: the maintenance of a high level of demand until late 1974, the depreciation of the exchange rate through 1973 and 1974, the increase in real wages as a result of the national negotiations at the end of 1972 and their insufficient moderation thereafter, and the rise in the price of oil and the world recession. The attempt at an incomes policy came to grief because of the political system, which could not deliver important concessions, especially on reform legislation, to the unions; tight labor markets, which, perversely, the political system could deliver and which reduced the already small degree of discretion that the moderate elements in the union leadership had at their disposal; and the degree of moderation required, which was greater than had been foreseen, on account of the external developments.

During 1974, the growing failure of the attempted incomes policy led to a series of agreements between the industrial unions and major companies. These agreements covered do-it-yourself reform measures, some, for instance, committing companies to undertake a certain amount of investment in the *mezzogiorno,* others to improvements in local transport systems. They also gave what appeared to be substantial money wage increases outside the *scala mobile,* as a result of the sharp acceleration of the rise in the cost of living and in response to a wave of plant strikes. Finally, in late 1974, after the effect of world recession had slashed the order books of large companies, agreements were signed on employment guarantees.

Employers were most unhappy about these company agreements. They felt they had been pressured by the government into the "reforms"

74. Economist Intelligence Unit, *Quarterly Economic Review: Italy,* no. 3 (1973), p. 3.

and later claimed that it was impossible on economic grounds to carry them out. The wage increases were relatively small in real terms, but the declining terms of trade implied a large gap between real labor costs and "room." The large companies, moreover, felt that they were having to bear an unfair share of the burden of employment maintenance as demand began to contract. The experiences of 1973 and 1974 provoked an important new initiative by Confindustria.

This initiative consisted of relocating the center of gravity of bargaining—and therefore of union power—much closer to the confederations. The main aspect of the agreement was 100 percent indexation of the *scala mobile;* a secondary agreement covered guaranteed wages in the event of layoffs and short-time working. Confindustria, under the leadership of Giovanni Agnelli, believed the main proposal so attractive that the industrial unions would be unable to frustrate the desire of Confindustria to deal directly with the confederations. This calculation proved correct. While such an agreement was not really necessary in large, well-organized plants, in which the *delegati* and *consigli* could secure full compensation for price increases with relative ease through company or plant bargains, the industrial unions had had to expend considerable resources on extending such bargains to less well organized plants. From Agnelli's point of view the agreement had a number of advantages besides increasing the importance of the confederations. Agnelli represented the large companies, which generally had to compensate workers for price increases in any event, and little was lost by imposing automatic compensation on smaller companies; whether the net result was a loss or a gain to the large firms depended, as noted earlier, on whether the smaller companies were on balance suppliers or competitors. In addition, Agnelli believed that the removal of disputes over price increases would eliminate a primary source of conflict in large plants, thereby reducing the power of *delegati* and *consigli.*

The agreement was situated, moreover, within an ideological framework that Confindustria had been developing at Agnelli's initiative. This was the long-run goal of creating a class of privileged industrial workers with security of jobs and real wages; such workers would see the benefit, in growth of real wages, of moderate demands, especially concerning working conditions and managerial discretion. The "enemy" of this class was seen to be the public sector, both as an inefficient bureaucracy and as a hoarder of unproductively used resources.

The object of Agnelli's exercise appears to have been the transfer of resources to the industrial sector and away from the public sector, which would be accomplished under conditions of rapid inflation as long as the inflation was offset by depreciation of the exchange rate and as long as the 100 percent indexation was confined to the industrial sector. While the real wages of industrial workers in relation to consumer prices were safeguarded, consumer prices, reflecting smaller economywide wage increases, would fall in relation to industrial prices, and the real cost of industrial labor, in relation to industrial prices, would fall.

Whether the depreciation of the lira in early 1976 was deliberately provoked as part of such an exercise, Agnelli's object ran afoul of reactions by workers in the public sector. Public-sector unions generally reacted vigorously in Italy—as they did in other countries, including Sweden and Britain—to protect their real wages. Where they did not, "autonomous" unions sprang up within the public sector, undercutting moderation on the part of some CGIL unions. As table 9-5 shows, the increase in the number of strikes between 1973 and 1976 was proportionately greater in community, social, and personal services than in manufacturing.

The indexation agreement had three elements. First, it was envisaged that there would be 100 percent indexation for the average wage earner by the beginning of 1977. Second, there were to be staged increases in February 1975, February 1976, August 1976, and February 1977 (the immediate increase in February 1975 gave an average increase of 5 percent on pay). Finally, while in other respects the basic system in operation since 1956 was unchanged, giving all workers the same absolute increase for each point increase in the cost-of-living index added a notably egalitarian emphasis.

The second agreement, made with the implicit assent of the government, provided pay guarantees in the event of partial unemployment. Workers were to receive 80 percent of gross pay—93 percent of net pay—for all idle time from zero to forty hours a week. As a minor disincentive, companies that used the system—the Cassa Integrazione Guadagni—were required to contribute a small part of the compensation—8 percent in the case of large companies and 4 percent for those employing up to fifty workers. More significant, the agreement had provisions for negotiation procedures; these included advance notification to the unions of the number of workers involved, the expected duration of the unemployment, and requirement of joint study of the situation with the union. To the extent that these relatively generous provisions softened the hostility of unions to any reduction in employment or short-time working, the cost was an indirect subsidy from the

Table 9-5. *Strikes in Manufacturing and Community Services, Italy, 1972–78*

Year	Manufacturing			Community, social, and personal services		
	Number of strikes (1)	Workers involved (millions) (2)	Days lost (millions) (3)	Number of strikes (4)	Workers involved (millions) (5)	Days lost (millions) (6)
1972	2,688	2.46	10.20	882	0.53	3.06
1973	1,901	3.98	16.43	872	0.66	2.23
1974	2,906	4.51	11.64	946	1.30	2.79
1975	1,984	7.71	9.52	855	2.20	8.14
1976	1,277	6.55	13.94	623	1.84	3.52
1977	1,943	9.73	9.66	568	1.31	3.15
1978	1,289	5.16	4.95	424	1.12	2.51

Source: ILO, *Yearbook of Labour Statistics, 1979*, p. 651.

government to industry and the acceptance by business of an increased, but also more centralized, negotiating role for the union.

While the pay guarantee agreement might appear to an outside economist more dangerous economically than the 100 percent indexation of the *scala mobile,* the latter has been definitely regarded by Italian observers and participants as the more damaging. Indeed the *scala mobile* has frequently been at the center of political debates since 1977. One problem has been its effect on wage differentials. The belief that it would significantly reduce the skill differential during an inflationary period has been borne out, but it can also be argued that it made an important contribution to the acceptance of wage restraint by semiskilled workers in the large plants during the period 1976–78. A related view at the time—that increased indexation would have severe effects on small companies—has not been borne out;[75] it is widely agreed that small companies were remarkably successful in the second half of the 1970s.

The primary concern was that "the mechanism will cease to be simply a means of defending the purchasing power of earnings and will begin to function perversely as an automatic inflationary mechanism." Underlying this was the feeling that while "negotiations will be conducted within the limits set by productivity," it would not in practice be possible to constrain negotiated increases sufficiently. A more sophisticated view was that, if the inflation rate were to slacken, "owing to a fall in import

75. Faustini, "Wage Indexation and Inflation in Italy," p. 365.

prices or as a result of a sound economic policy, the sliding-scale would automatically generate increases in earnings disproportionate to the increases in the cost of living, thus compromising the efforts to stabilize the economy."[76]

But these arguments are not very persuasive. As noted, the econometric evidence strongly suggests that Italian wages have always been effectively indexed:[77] in the absence of 100 percent indexation through the *scala mobile,* either the policies of employers or union bargaining has recouped the difference. The 1974 company agreements, which provided ad hoc cost-of-living increases, were a case in point. The bulk of the econometric evidence suggests, moreover, that the time lags between wage increases and price increases have been rather shorter than those in most other countries. Further, the unions have had no difficulty in negotiating within the limits set by increases in productivity in the years following the 1975 indexation agreement—in contrast to the situation in the earlier period, 1969–75.

Subsequent attempts to reduce the degree of indexation under the *scala mobile* met with strong and effective resistance. But that testified to the popularity of this institutional device and to the bargaining power of the unions rather than to any inherent automatic effectiveness that might be imputed to it.

Eurocommunism as Incomes Policy, 1976–78: Wage Restraint for Communist Participation in Government

The general election of June 1976 confirmed the increase in electoral support for the Communist party at which a divorce referendum in 1974 and the regional elections of 1975 had pointed. The share of votes cast for the PCI in 1976 was 34.4 percent, whereas its share in 1972 had been only 27.1 percent. In contrast, the Christian Democratic share remained static at 38.7 percent. The period from the middle of 1976 until the end of 1978 was marked by virtually continuous bargaining between

76. Ibid., pp. 370, 372; see also OECD Economic Surveys, *Italy,* March 1977, pp. 14–19, for a similar view.

77. See, among others, Paolo Onofri, "Notes on the Money-Wage Dynamics in the Italian Economy (1960–1970)," University of Bologna; P. Sylos-Labini, "Prices, Distribution and Investment in Italy, 1951–66: An Interpretation," Banca Nazionale del Lavoro, *Quarterly Review,* vol. 20, no. 83 (December 1967); Franco Spinelli, "The Determinants of Price and Wage Inflation: The Case of Italy," in Michael Parkin and George Zis, eds., *Inflation in Open Economies* (Manchester: Manchester University Press, 1976), chap. 8.

the Christian Democratic government, the Communist party, and the unions. The Communist party wanted participation in the government; in exchange it was prepared to use its support and organizational strength within the unions to enforce informal wage restraint. For similar reasons, it was also prepared to support the deflationary economic policies of the government. The Christian Democrats were deeply divided on the extent to which they were prepared to tolerate Communist participation; on the other hand, the new government was more single-minded in its desire to increase profitability and reduce inflation than its predecessors had been. The unions were equally divided; belief in the long-term political benefits of increased Communist participation was confined neither to the CGIL nor to union officials; in addition, the unions advocated maintenance of industrial competitiveness as in the long term a sine qua non for the preservation of the jobs of their members. On the other hand, the democratic structure of the unions and the strength of the shop floor put great difficulties in the way of wage restraint and the voluntary acceptance of redundancies. These tensions within the Communist party, the government, and the unions ruled out a single, clearcut, formal agreement. The continuous bargaining that was substituted for it had all the qualities of bazaar haggling. Nonetheless, the balance in each group was favorable to negotiations, and this represented a change from previous positions.

The 1976 election result was not the only reason for this change. Also of importance was the persistent failure of the economy to adapt to the increased share of the income of labor in value added, the adverse changes in the terms of trade, and the rate of inflation. Table 9-4 shows the extent to which real wages had exceeded room in both 1974 and 1975. In the latter year, the large negative gap reflected a massive decline in productivity. This emphasized the inability, especially of large firms, to dismiss workers, as is shown in the following table for 1976.[78]

Number of employees per firm	Dismissals per 100 workers
10–49	23.73
50–99	18.24
100–199	18.18
200–499	6.71
500–999	3.14
1,000 or more	1.96

78. Confindustria, *Statistiche del Lavoro, 1976* (Rome: Confindustria, 1977).

The deteriorating economic situation, combined with the failure of previously attempted "cures," acted as a catalyst of change within industry and within the Christian Democratic party. In the early 1970s, as was shown in the opening part of this section, the attempt to use deflation to eliminate unions from the shop floor had been thwarted both by the solid implantation of unions within the large factories and by the political balance within the Assembly. From 1974 to 1976 large companies attempted to blunt the militancy of industrial workers with protection of real wages and jobs, but this was not successful in inducing wage restraint and in diverting resources from other sectors of the economy, notably the state sector. Thus, leaders of Confindustria were led to seek a political solution. Corresponding to the two reasons for the failure of the *scala mobile* initiative, there were two requirements for this political solution. The first was that sufficient incentives be given to the unions to enforce wage restraint. The second was that the efficiency of the state sector and control of it by the government be improved so that its resources could be used. It was believed by some that both components could be satisfied by participation of the Communists in the government: this could provide the incentive to unions to deliver wage restraint and could lead to increased efficiency within the bureaucracy. Thus Gianni Agnelli, the former president of Confindustria, could say in July 1976, "The main problem is the working out of an emergency plan in which the Communists absolutely must take part."[79]

Within the DC the support for some form of Communist participation came from the reformist center-left leadership of Aldo Moro and Mariano Rumor and the industrial interest, against the strong opposition of the populist, conservative, Catholic *correnti* of the party. Moro called for a "strategy of attention" to the PCI, and saw a DC whose support would come from "the productive strata in industry and the middle classes."[80] In Moro's analysis, reform required widespread social and political support and a strong economy: political mobilization of the Communists was seen as necessary for the former and a commitment from the CGIL to wage restraint was necessary for the latter. Prime Minister Giulio Andreotti mediated between these two groups, populist and industrialist-reformist, but the strength of the populist group, which represented and held onto power and resources through the clientelistic system, was instrumental in preventing any important concession to the Communist party in exchange for wage restraint.

79. Interview in *The Times* (London), July 6, 1976.
80. Di Palma, "Christian Democracy," pp. 136, 143.

Why did the PCI push at this moment for power sharing? The PCI commitment to the "historic compromise," in the specific form of coalition with the Christian Democrats, dated from the recession of the early 1970s, although its analysis of Italian society, as noted earlier, has always led it to the belief that reform could only be based on a wide alliance of interest groups. The conditions which had at that stage provoked the specific commitment were the fear of a right-wing backlash as a result of 1968–69 and the strength of the Communist electoral position. These conditions applied with renewed force between 1974 and 1976 as the rate of inflation accelerated and the Communist electoral performance improved further; the former increased the fear of reaction by the fascist right, while the latter increased the claim of the PCI to power.

Paralleling these changes in the DC and among the Communists was a significant shift in the locus of power within the unions. The period 1975–76 witnessed a recentralization of authority within the confederations, particularly to the CGIL. How did this come about? After the events of 1968–70, the industrial unions had used the recession years 1971 and 1972 to centralize control of bargaining within the plant. The institutional form in which this control was vested was the executive committee of the *consiglio,* which consisted of senior shop stewards generally with close ties to the industrial unions. This control had been used in 1973–74 by the industrial unions to bargain with large companies on a wide variety of issues. The confederations were excluded from these negotiations, but from 1975–76 the leaders of the CGIL were increasingly able to persuade the industrial unions and the senior shop stewards to use their power in the direction the CGIL wanted them to take.

The reasons were two. The first was the switch in the type of negotiating needed in a period of economic crisis—that is, from late 1974 on. The recession weakened the control of the unions in the smaller plants. Thus the industrial unions needed agreements at the industry and national levels to safeguard the position of less well protected union members. It was the latter negotiating function that the confederations were able to fulfill. Italian commentators have explained this in terms of appropriate organizational level.[81] This is not the entire story: in other countries—the United Kingdom and Germany, for example—industrial

81. Salvati, "Italian Inflation," pp. 69, 70; Regalia and others, "Labour Conflicts," p. 136.

unions have not ceded their power in such circumstances. The switch, in fact, also reflected the ability and desire of Confindustria and the government to confine their bargaining to the moderate and "realistic" confederations, particularly the CGIL.

The second, related, reason was the relationship of the PCI to the CGIL. The confederal leadership of the CGIL remained, even in the turbulent period of 1968–70, closely linked to the PCI. Its strong organizational section, together with that of the PCI, was used from 1974 on as part of a drive to establish influence and control in the plants. This organizational move drew strength from a sequence of PCI electoral successes—the divorce referendum in 1974, regional elections in 1975, and the general election in 1976—and it capitalized on the deeply felt popular desire for a Communist government.

Confederal CGIL control and influence was, however, qualified. The structure of Italian unionism remained democratic; the rank and file, especially in the large factories, could elect new *delegati* and *consigli*. Support of the confederal leaders by the rank and file, and indeed by union officials at all levels, depended upon results of two sorts. The first were economic results: wage restraint and redundancies were acceptable within limits so long as there were clear compensations at the plant or national level. The second were political results: the PCI could maintain its control through the CGIL so long as it could point to significant political advances—not only in an increased share of power but also in an improvement in the content of policies. The increased strength of the CGIL in 1976 was real, but it was fragile and conditional.

What were the aims of the Andreotti government in the two and a half years of negotiations and agreements, formal and informal, with their attendant frustrations, partial realizations, and final demise? First, the government aimed to secure wage restraint, greater flexibility over redundancies, and other measures to increase productivity and reduce unit labor costs. For this the government needed explicit cooperation from the unions. Since the principal industrywide wage agreements had been concluded before July 1976, it could hope to influence company bargains on earnings and labor productivity. It also intended to revise and thus weaken what was seen as the inflationary effect of the 1975 *scala mobile* accord between Confindustria and the confederations. The second aim of the government was to make socially acceptable a further deflation of the economy. The reason for the deflation was that the government believed it would further enforce wage restraint, especially in companies and plants that were less effectively organized, as well as enabling business to have more freedom to increase productivity. The government counted on the PCI to help promote the policy of deflation through its mass organization. Thus Emilio Berlinguer, Communist party leader, formally embraced what he described as the "ideology of austerity" of the PCI. The unions were less enthusiastic. They followed a line of nonopposition to the deflationary policies, however, partly because it facilitated their administration of wage restraint.

The main group of agreements was made in early 1977. A series of measures designed to deflate the economy had been carried out during the autumn of 1976. It was estimated that these measures would reduce demand by an amount equal to 3 percent of GNP.[82] In addition, the government wanted three further sets of measures to reduce unit labor costs: a reform of the *scala mobile,* a union commitment to greater flexibility, and a fiscalization of social security contributions. Of these measures, the first two were to take the form of agreements between Confindustria and the confederations, and the third was to be legislated. Given the policy of overall deflation, the reduction in social security contributions from employers was to be offset by an increase in the value-added tax (VAT), which was to be removed from the *scala mobile* in order to prevent the tax cut from generating an increase in real expenditures and, in general, to reduce the sensitivity of wages to price increases.

In January 1977, the confederations signed the *patto sociale* (social compact), an agreement with Confindustria on greater flexibility. Strong opposition to changes in the *scala mobile* had been expressed within the unions at all levels, and to secure the *patto* the government guaranteed that it would seek no important changes in the modus operandi of the *scala.* Two minor changes in the *scala* were, however, agreed upon and contained in the *patto:* the use of the *scala mobile* in the calculation of overtime pay was eliminated, and privileged indexation systems that had been in force in certain industries, including chemicals, in which productivity bonuses were linked to the *scala,* were brought into line with the rest. These changes signified that details of the *scala mobile* were not sacrosanct to the unions. The provision of practical importance in the *patto sociale* was a commitment by the unions to greater flexibility

82. Economist Intelligence Unit, *Quarterly Economic Review: Italy,* no. 1 (1977), p. 7.

in the use of labor. This commitment covered four areas: withdrawal of opposition to increased shift work, greater use of overtime when it was strictly necessary for the purpose of increasing production rather than as a substitute for increased employment, the ending of restrictions on internal mobility within factories, and agreement to company negotiations to spread holidays through the year in order to reduce their concentration in July and August.[83]

In February 1977 Andreotti announced a partial fiscalization of employers' contributions to social security, the effect of which would have been to reduce labor costs by nearly 5 percent. The fiscalization was to be achieved by an increase in the VAT; this increase was not to count as an increase in the cost of living for *scala mobile* purposes. In addition, it was proposed that the reduction in contributions would be withdrawn from any company that paid wage increases higher than those agreed upon in national negotiations or as a result of the operation of the *scala mobile*.[84] The magnitude of the measures reflected a belief in the inadequacy of the *patto sociale*. It also represented a clever use by the government of pressure from the International Monetary Fund (IMF). Shortly before, the government had asked the IMF for a loan of about $500 million, an insubstantial amount. As a condition of the loan the IMF imposed a series of stringent requirements on the performance of the Italian economy, imposing tight limits on public-sector expenditure and the public-sector deficit. The IMF also demanded government action on labor costs, including the *scala mobile,* and was satisfied by the February measures. To these, however, the unions were adamantly opposed, on the grounds that they caused a serious breach of the *scala mobile* principle. This put the PCI in a difficult position, which was what Andreotti had intended. The party desired an image of respectability, which included acceptance of the obligations of membership in the Western community.

By making it clear that IMF approval can only be forthcoming if certain policies are applied, the government puts the opponents of such policies on the spot. They must either give way or carry the burden of opposing not only the government but also the IMF which in effect represents the Western community of nations. . . . Thereby the policies of a weak minority government can be

83. Incomes Data Services (IDS), *International Report,* no. 42 (February 1977), p. 5.
84. Salvati, "Italian Inflation," p. 67.

carried through because of the power wielded by the IMF and its main creditor nations (particularly the USA and West Germany).[85]

The Communist party agreed to underwrite the IMF requirement on the public-sector deficit; thus it strengthened the hand of the government in maintaining the deflation. The fiscalization, however, with its attendant change in the *scala mobile,* brought the party up against determined union opposition. In fact, "rank-and-file militants [were] so vociferous in their opposition that the leaders of the three main union confederations have had no option but to go along with them."[86] Similarly, the PCI had to follow union opposition to the sanction clause in the fiscalization measure, that employers' contributions would not be reduced in instances in which there was wage drift; this clause would have weakened too explicitly the bargaining power of the *consigli.*

The result, after "a series of frantic negotiations," was a compromise agreement signed with the IMF in April 1977.[87] The unions agreed to allow three items—newspapers, electricity tariffs, and urban transport—to be excluded from the *scala mobile,* while the VAT was still to be included. The fiscalization was otherwise to proceed as before, except that sanctions were to be dropped. In fact, the government agreed to take no "positive measures to interfere with plant bargaining"; in return, the unions agreed informally to maintain their attempts to restrain plant bargaining.

Through 1977 the main form of union support for the incomes policy was in restraining wage demands at plant level, together with tacit approval of the policy of deflation. Unemployment rose from 1.4 million in the first half of 1977 to 1.9 million in the third quarter. This was of sufficient concern to large-scale industry for Guido Carli, president of Confindustria, to call for measures of reflation at the end of 1977.[88] The unions, though divided, refused to join with Carli in this request. Their main activity, however, consisted of attempting to persuade the shop floor of the need for wage restraint. Toward the end of 1976 many large

85. Economist Intelligence Unit, *Quarterly Economic Review: Italy,* no. 1 (1977), p. 7.

86. IDS, *International Report,* no. 43 (February 1977), p. 1.

87. Economist Intelligence Unit, *Quarterly Economic Review: Italy,* no. 2 (1977).

88. Economist Intelligence Unit, *Quarterly Economic Review: Italy,* no. 4 (1977), p. 6.

claims were put in by the *consigli* of metalworking plants in disregard of union policies. These claims reflected a realistic fear that the *scala mobile* would be changed while inflation proceeded at a high rate and that their own bargaining position would grow weaker as unemployment increased.[89] After the confederations had prevented major changes in the *scala mobile,* however, they were able to gain considerable wage moderation in the largest companies. Against claims at the end of 1976 for increases of between 20,000 and 30,000 lire a month for 1977 in small and medium-sized firms, the Fiat unions asked for 15,000 lire a month for 1977 and 10,000 for 1978; similar increases were demanded at Olivetti. The wage restraint was not without cost to the companies or the unions: the companies had to guarantee maintenance of employment—explaining Confindustria's concern for reflation—and rank-and-file goodwill toward the unions was lessened.[90] The claims at Fiat and Olivetti were followed by similar or more moderate claims at IBM, Montedison, Alfa Romeo, and ENI.[91] The large companies were the traditional pacesetters in company negotiations; now that they were being used to influence smaller companies to reduce their demands, however, the pacesetting worked less well. "In smaller engineering companies in the north, the rejection of the national confederations' moderate line—observed in the large-company claims—continues, with strong rank and file pressure for high wage settlements."[92]

An overall assessment of the incomes policy is not easy, because the wage restraint coincided with the adoption of a deflationary demand policy. Whatever the independent role of deflation in restraining wages, however, the acceptance of deflation by the unions and the PCI was itself one part of the incomes policy package. While deflation may have facilitated restraint by reducing levels of activity, moreover, it did not operate by creating unemployment—at least not in large plants. The data on real earnings, shown in table 9-4, column 4, suggest that the policy had strong restraining effects. During the three-year period 1976–78, the average increase in real earnings was 2.6 percent a year; the increases had been 10.2 percent and 11.4 percent, respectively, in the two previous trienniums. There was a productivity cost to the wage restraint, however, because deflation was not allowed to translate into redundancies in large

89. IDS, *International Report,* no. 37 (November 1976), pp. 1–2.
90. Ibid., no. 42 (February 1977), pp. 2–3.
91. Ibid., no. 43 (February 1977), p. 5.
92. Ibid., no. 48 (May 1977), p. 5.

plants. This cost was unavoidable, since the policy was carried out in these plants by the *consigli,* who had a vested interest in maintaining jobs. As in the United Kingdom, marked wage restraint was accompanied by poor productivity (see table 9-4, column 1).

But if the union side was attempting to exercise restraint in bargaining, the Christian Democrats, while involving the Communists explicitly in policymaking, were obviously reluctant to enter into a formal governing coalition with them. In early 1978, the PCI demanded entry into a government of "national emergency." At the same time, the leaders of the CGIL, looking ahead to the expiration of the current contracts at the end of the year, amplified their commitment to interconfederal cooperation and moderation in wage negotiations and to greater flexibility in work assignments in the plants, demanding in return the adoption of structural policies designed to reduce unemployment, mainly in the south and among youth. The other two federations supported these proposals, but many union leaders balked when Secretary-General Luciano Lama of the CGIL characterized the program as one "of sacrifices; not marginal but substantial sacrifices," adding that during the next few years pay "will have to be very restricted" while "we can no longer force firms to keep on a number of workers which is superfluous to their productive possibilities, nor can we expect the *cassa integrazione* to provide aid on a permanent basis to the superfluous workers."[93]

The incomes policy began to fall apart in the second half of 1978. The PCI gained some status by being included in the formal government majority but failed to obtain a national emergency government. The Christian Democrats' tactics paid off as the PCI suffered severe electoral reverses in 1977 and 1978. The Communists moved back into opposition. They voted against the decision to join the European Monetary System (EMS), and they opposed a new three-year program set forth by the government—the so-called Pandolfi Plan—although it bore a close resemblance to the CGIL's own earlier proposals. It called for a freeze on real wages, increased labor productivity, and cuts in overall government expenditures, but with increased public investment in the south and the creation of a half million new jobs.[94] But the unions, who had been lukewarm at best to their own confederation's proposals, opposed the Pandolfi Plan, as they had opposed entry into the EMS, and the

93. Ibid., no. 75 (December 1978), p. 6.
94. OECD Economic Surveys, *Italy,* January 1979, pp. 5–6.

556 ITALY

Communist party, having been unable to lead the unions earlier, now decided to rejoin them. Thus their quest for a "historic compromise" came to an end, as most of the parties in effect felt that the costs involved exceeded the gains. The PCI did not get into the government, whereas it strained its relations with the unions and ran the risk of losing its political personality. The unions faced the risk of estrangement from their members and some of the powerful shop stewards, while dependent employment remained below 1974 levels, although its decline in the large industrial firms was averted.[95]

The Employers Get Tough: 1979–

The withdrawal of the PCI from its quasi coalition with the DC and the relaxation of Communist pressure on the unions to hold back wage increases did not lead to a new period of worker militancy. On the face of it, this was surprising. The official unions had attempted to enforce moderation between 1976 and 1978, although at the cost of growth of "autonomous"—that is, unaffiliated—unions, especially in public services, and of divisions within the unions in industry. Despite these developments during the "incomes policy" period, moderation in union behavior increased during the period following. On the whole, there were less opposition to redundancies, movement away from egalitarianism, and greater acceptance of managerial initiatives at the plant and company levels on conditions and pay. Conflicts emerged between semiskilled and skilled—including white-collar—workers, between some of the industrial unions and the confederations, among the leaders of the confederations, and, finally, between the CGIL and the PCI. Indeed, it is probable that the "realism" of union behavior, while desired by many union leaders, was more a result of increased toughness on the part of employers and—to a lesser extent—the government and of awareness of this toughness on the part of workers than the consequence of a spontaneous change in union attitudes.

Weakness of the Communist party was a considerable factor in inducing the increased toughness of large employers after 1979. The withdrawal of the PCI into opposition in early 1979 came after opinion polls had shown the party to be losing out as a result of its involvement in a government that had imposed deflation and wage moderation but had frustrated major reforms and had engaged in extensive subsidy of

95. Ibid., p. 13; March 1980, p. 11.

inefficient firms and industries. The move into opposition did not, however, help the party. In the general election of June 1979 the Communists' share of the electorate fell by four percentage points, while the Christian Democrats held their share constant. The Christian Democrats were able to capitalize to some extent on the weakness of the PCI. For much of the preceding decade the two reasons for a governmental modus vivendi with the Communist party were, first, to keep the delicate relations between government and unions in balance, and, second, to provide a parliamentary majority. These two reasons were no longer compelling. The unions became less responsive to the PCI. And the Socialist party, in a significant change of direction, provided the DC with its necessary parliamentary majority. In the early 1970s the PSI had repudiated the center-left strategy of the previous decade, acknowledging that it had failed to bring about reforms. Instead it had tacitly allied itself to the PCI; it had seen itself in the 1973–74 center-left government as "representing" the PCI and aimed at its own formula for the PCI in government. Politically this honest-broker role had proved to be a miscalculation. Once the DC and the PCI got together in 1976–78 there was no need for the Socialists. Thus, the Socialists thought increasingly of moving away from the PCI, and the weakness of the PCI in 1979–80, electorally and toward the unions, gave the PSI the opportunity under its new right-wing leader, Bettino Craxi, to revive the old-style center-left. (The DC-PSI governments of 1979 and 1980 were not stable, since significant elements of the DC and the left-wing Socialists continued to believe that, in the long run, reform was only feasible with Communist cooperation; these governments were not continuously threatened from the left, however.)

Employers benefited from the change of government. Indirectly, the government helped the official unions to maintain a more moderate stance by taking a tougher stand against the autonomous unions in the public sector. More generally, in talking of "a new sense of identity and cooperation among employers" in its September 1979 *International Report,* Incomes Data Services (IDS) noted that "there were fewer government pressures and incentives to cajole employers into meeting union requests." In addition, "the judiciary has taken a harder line with unions. Some stiff sentences were recently passed in cases involving disturbances and road blocks."[96]

While the government did not follow a consistent policy toward

96. IDS, *International Report,* no. 104 (September 1979), p. 6.

aggregate demand, it did not attempt to prevent a sharp contraction from the middle of 1980 on. Its resolve was strengthened by the tight monetary policy of the Bank of Italy.[97] The recession mirrored the oil price–induced recession of 1974–75, but in 1980 the government did not react to these developments by putting pressure on companies to hold onto surplus labor, as it had in the earlier period. Although the OECD describes "government transfers [as being] usually handed out with the purpose of avoiding the bankruptcy of large private and public enterprises,"[98] the government in 1980 was content with the tougher line—at least in comparison with the corresponding period, 1974–75—that large companies began to take. Società Italiana Resine, the large chemicals group, claimed that it could not pay the June 1980 salaries of its 30,000 employees and announced that it would close all its plants. Sit-Siemens, the state telecommunications group, announced plans to lay off two thirds of its 30,000 employees after the summer.[99] These layoff plans were made in the context of more restrictive legislation on the use of the Cassa Integrazione Guadagni, the state support system for those laid off or placed on short time. The new legislation distinguished between workers from companies undergoing "reorganization" and those from "lame ducks"; in both cases a maximum period was put on use of the fund—two years in the first case and one year in the second. In addition, workers on long layoffs were to be treated as unemployed and required to accept alternative employment if it was offered through a labor exchange.[100] Thus the government moved toward reduction of this hidden method of subsidizing companies.

The most significant move to assert the right of management to decrease the size of its work force was at Fiat in September 1980. The *Financial Times* described

the confrontation between management and unions at Fiat over the company's drastic plans to slim its workforce [as] potentially the most serious and far-reaching labour dispute in Italy for several years. . . . It is perhaps not too much to say that on the outcome of the negotiations . . . will hinge the ability of big private industry in Italy, ensnared by shrinking competitiveness and low productivity, to carry out the necessary reordering of its affairs. . . . Above all, Fiat does not want to repeat the errors of 1974–75, the last cyclical downturn in the car market.[101]

97. OECD Economic Surveys, *Italy*, March 1980, p. 39.
98. Ibid., p. 41.
99. *Financial Times*, June 27, 1980.
100. IDS, *International Report*, no. 112 (January 1980).
101. *Financial Times*, September 12, 1980.

A strike, lasting thirty-three days, "the single most serious postwar industrial stoppage in Italy,"[102] ended with Fiat gaining substantially what it wanted. The strike exposed serious divisions within the work force at Fiat and in the labor movement outside. It was effectively ended by the "March of the 40,000," a mass demonstration by the so-called silent majority of Fiat workers in favor of settlement on Fiat's terms. Behind the strike had been majorities on union plant committees, strongly supported by the Communist party and by many officials of the Metal Workers. The confederations had, however, taken a more moderate line, and this appears to have been more representative of rank-and-file fears.

Fiat had also broken new ground in its decision in November 1979 to fire sixty-one workers for misconduct. (While Fiat did not release details of the reasons, its problems ranged from intimidation and insulting of foremen to setting fire to cars and to shooting of executives.) Local union attempts to call strikes in support of the dismissed workers were unsuccessful. "Fiat's action," the IDS noted, "has already produced a marked change on the factory floor: the general attitude to foremen has altered, and there has been an end to the insults to which they were previously subjected. It is clear that the Fiat episode has also made a strong impression on workers in some other large companies such as Pirelli, Alfa Romeo, and Italsider."[103]

In addition to acting directly against indiscipline, some large companies, without consulting the unions, began to make payments for good behavior. Michelin in February 1980 gave a bonus worth $300 to every worker with a good attendance record, and Innocenti granted pay raises at the same time on the basis of merit. Such payments would not have been thought possible earlier, but confronted with them in 1980, the unions were virtually powerless. Both independently and in agreements with unions, employers have also stopped paying flat rate increases. They wished to halt the egalitarian shrinking of differentials, and they received considerable support for the idea on the shop floor.[104]

At the national level the new mood of toughness was reflected in the 1979 engineering agreement. The claim that the Metal Workers finally put on the negotiating table in December 1978—after the long arguments within the unions through 1978—had four essential components: demands for more information on more subjects (on production programs, technological information, and commercial policies and on multilateral

102. Ibid., October 24, 1980.
103. IDS, *International Report,* no. 108 (November 1979).
104. Ibid., no. 120 (May 1980); no. 116 (March 1980).

operations abroad); a reduction in working hours; restoration of the public holidays "lost" in 1977; and a wage increase of about 7 percent in the course of three years, with minor concessions on differentials and seniority payments. The employers refused to accept what they saw as the costliest elements of the claim, the demand for increased information in the long run and reduced working hours in the short. Instead they agreed on rather larger wage increases, which in the second and third years would be geared toward an increase of differentials, to which they attached great importance, and sharply limited increases in information rights and reductions of hours. To secure such a settlement from the Metal Workers the employers took a series of strikes, and the agreement was not signed until July 1979. On the basis of the measure of union power suggested by Modigliani and Tarentelli—the shorter the time between anticipated and actual date of agreement, the stronger the union—this delay beyond the anticipated date of January 1979 in the signing of the agreement implied a new low level of union power.

The effect of the changed balance of bargaining strength at the company and national levels was noticeably low growth in real earnings in 1980. Here again there is a contrast with the experience after the oil price increases of 1974. "Taking productivity growth into account," the OECD noted in 1981, the " 'real wage gap' has narrowed progressively despite the negative effects of the terms of trade."[105] In 1980, the change in real compensation per employee was virtually zero, and the share of labor's compensation in GDP fell in both 1979 and 1980.[106]

How did the unions react to these developments? In 1980, when the government proposed a Solidarity Fund for Financial Investments Intended to Develop Employment, the CGIL was ready to join the other two confederations in supporting it.[107] The fund was to be financed by a contribution of 0.5 percent of their monthly earnings from all employees. The confederations were to have seats on the board of management of the fund, and it was envisaged that they would have a significant say in deciding investment policy. The fund was not, moreover, to be another way of financing "lame ducks": initially only "curable" companies in the south were to be aided. This was calculated to appeal more to the confederations, who saw it as a way of helping their wider constituencies

105. OECD Economic Surveys, *Italy,* June 1981, pp. 20–21.
106. Ibid.
107. IDS, *International Report,* no. 123 (June 1980), p. 2; no. 125 (July 1980), pp. 1–2.

and of achieving some of that long-elusive "progress," than to the industrial unions, which had some very lame ducks to protect. It was designed to protect and strengthen the institutional position of the confederations, and the latter accepted the proposal without first consulting the unions. But the Communist party organized a strong opposition to the project, and the confederations, while resentful, backed off. The party, however, was not so influential with the rank and file, for three months later it failed in its support of the Fiat strike over work rules and staffing, which was terminated by the "March of the 40,000." That episode at least left the CGIL less dependent on the PCI, although the PCI had denied it a chance of asserting some authority over the affiliated unions, the plant representatives, and the members.

Summary and Conclusions

The exceptional difficulties encountered by the Italian economy in coping with the deterioration of the international climate in the 1970s and early 1980s can be traced in part to important changes in industrial relations that occurred just before the decade began. Partly as a result of these changes—and also as a result of electoral advances of the Italian Communist party—the government was slow to resort to deflationary demand management to reduce relative labor costs, the responsiveness of wages to price changes was not reduced by higher levels of unemployment, and growth in productivity slumped drastically. Italian industrial relations had always been volatile, characterized by relatively high levels of strike activity, but management had typically been kept in a strong bargaining position by slack labor markets and weakly organized, politically active, and divided unions. High rates of unemployment and union weakness appeared to have been produced by complex interaction between an economic environment characterized by rapid growth and a political environment characterized by a weak central government, a dominant Christian Democratic party in which traditional, rural, bourgeois, and confessional interests have vied powerfully for influence with industrial interests, and a second-largest Communist party, which sought to maintain a dominant relationship with its affiliated trade-union movement (although to a lesser degree than its French counterpart). Communist influence in labor relations was manifested initially by externally inspired efforts to provoke political strikes, which were unpopular and divisive, and later by discouraging plant-level bargaining by works councils and other groups in favor of industrywide bargaining by the central federations, including the Communist-led CGIL. The influence of the Christian Democrats, who were in control of the government, was even more important. Negatively, it was manifested in inadequate investment in social infrastructure and particularly in the development— or "reform"—of the nonindustrialized south, which contributed to excess migration to the industrializing north, labor unrest, capital flight, restrictive demand management, underinvestment, and unemployment during the 1950s and most of the 1960s. Labor-market slack and weak unions were conducive to export-led growth. At the same time, the larger enterprises (as well as smaller firms) pursued aggressively antiunion policies in their plants. The employers, not unlike the Communists, preferred to confine bargaining to the confederation and industrywide arena—and to nominal costs, so that even the *scala mobile,* which was negotiated in the 1950s as a system of partial, and subsequently declining, wage indexation, was designed with a view to strengthening central bargaining and minimizing unrest and activity in the plants.

In the early 1960s labor markets tightened under the combined influence of a boom in external trade and a shift to fiscal-monetary expansionism by the DC, which sought to counter electoral losses by including the Socialists in a center-left government. Declining unemployment was accompanied by greatly increased rises in real wages and unit labor costs and by declining profit margins, and a wage explosion was the direct outcome of an explosion in grass-roots strikes. This had been preceded by a change within the CISL from a traditionally Catholic orientation to an emphasis on militant bargaining, which set the pace for its chief rival, the CGIL. The authorities reacted to the decline in profits and competitiveness by changing from an expansionist to a deflationary policy and also by tacit wage restraint, which was attempted in both the government and the private sectors. In 1965, the industrial unions finally agreed to postpone the reopening of the metal trades agreement for one year, but only after the government had persuaded the central confederations to sign the new agreements when the industrial unions refused to do so. This first generation of incomes policies was not ineffective and indeed served to demonstrate the organizational weakness of the industrial unions in the plants. It complemented demand management, which, in Italy as elsewhere, was associated with investment that was sluggish and employment that was falling in relation to output, increased productivity being generated in part by shakeouts and speedups. The process promoted discontent in the industrial work force that erupted in a second and much more extensive outburst of grass-roots strikes in the Hot Autumn of 1969, shortly after an upswing in activity had begun but while unemployment was still relatively high.

This second explosion of strikes and wages, however, differed from the first in that it caused a sweeping structural transformation of industrial relations in Italy as well as a much more severe squeeze on profits. It was marked by an extension of organization to the semiskilled groups (which included many recent migrants whose grievances were the most acute) and to the plant level. This was in part made possible by the active involvement of the industrial unions at the plant level in response to the emergence of grass-roots leadership—the *delegati*—in 1968–69. This meant that recourse to demand deflation to reduce the bargaining potential of the unions would be less productive than it had been in the 1960s—as the plant organizations dug in with restrictive work practices and work-sharing arrangements—and, therefore, that depreciation of the currency would also be ineffective in securing a durable increase in international competitiveness. But it was also possible that incomes policies, designed to decrease the use of union bargaining potential, might hold out greater promise of success now that organizational issues were more fully resolved and workers' organizations existed and functioned inside the plants as well as outside. In fact, the constraints proved stronger than the opportunities, so government policy was often marked by temporizing. Currency depreciations and subsidy programs, including fiscalization of the contributions of employers to social security and wage supplements to laid-off workers, were not accompanied—for political and bureaucratic reasons—by offsetting reductions in government expenditures or by overall deflation of private demand sufficient to prevent real labor costs per worker from growing more rapidly than productivity in the first half of the decade.

Recourse to deflation was initially attempted in 1970–72, as it had been after 1963, but it was inhibited in part by the political influence of the CISL, the non-Communist confederation, as well as of the PCI and of the Socialists. In the case of the large-scale enterprises, its effect was on output and profits rather than on unit costs, since the union groups could not be dislodged from the plants. The large firms reacted, in a variety of ways, by tapping the "black" or "unofficial" labor force, which enabled them to avoid union pay scales and work rules and also to avoid social security taxes. As a result, this labor force had grown to nearly two-thirds the size of the dependent industrial labor force by the end of the 1970s.

The limitations of deflation and the subsequent adverse movement in the terms of trade following the oil crisis of 1973 also inclined both the large firms and the government to attempt to secure moderation in collective bargaining. In 1973, a new government held out the bait of a short-term price freeze, expansionist demand policy, and a sizable "reform" investment in the south. It was supported by the Communist party and by the union confederations, but the government failed once more to produce the reform measures, and the industrial unions, closer to the plants, adhered to aggressive bargaining and concluded a series of agreements whereby the employers individually were obliged to make "reform" investments and employment guarantees. As in the 1960s, the more militant industrial unions were ranged against the moderate, and politically active, central confederations, and the prospects for wage moderation again seemed to hinge on greater centralization of bargaining. The large-scale employers, now in control of Confindustria, the central employers' association, sought the answer in wage indexation, through the *scala mobile,* the instrument that they had devised nearly twenty years earlier. In 1975, Confindustria concluded two agreements with the confederations. One agreement geared up the *scala mobile* to provide complete indexation at the average wage level by 1977. It was, moreover, to yield equal absolute cost-of-living increases to all categories of skills and industries, thereby tending to compress wage differentials in accordance with the desires of the militant semiskilled groups. A second agreement provided government-financed pay supplements to workers on reduced hours under the Cassa Integrazione Guadagni. The *scala mobile* agreement of 1975 has been generally condemned as an engine of inflation—especially as one that transmitted increases in external costs through the domestic cost structure—and an obstacle to the alignment of real wages with productivity. We regard it more as effect than as cause—as a reflection of union bargaining power and of a general lack of money illusion in the Italian wage-setting process. If it was the intent of Confindustria to raise industrial wages in relation to wages in the public sector, moreover, and thus ultimately to make depreciation of the currency more effective, this aim was frustrated by the militancy of public-sector unions, some of them autonomous—that is, unaffiliated with confederations—operating outside the coverage of the *scala.* On the other hand, both the egalitarian bias of the *scala* agreement and the income guarantees provided by the Cassa Integrazione may have increased the acceptability of centralized bargaining and the influence of the confederations on the union side.

But while the employers preached indexation, wage guarantees, and subsidy, the Communist party promised to deliver wage restraint, increased productivity, and deflation—"the ideology of austerity"—in exchange for a "historic compromise" that would finally admit it into a coalition government. The Italian Communists were by no means the first political party in postwar Europe to dangle their kinship with the trade unions before the eyes of the electorate, but in no other country were the political and, it seemed, the economic stakes so high. By the mid 1970s, the economic and institutional situation essentially required that any incomes policy include acceptance of deflation. Confindustria was agreeable, and the Christian Democratic government, which wished to reduce escalation under the *scala mobile* and to deflate the economy further, began a process of haggling that left both sides short of their respective political and economic objectives. The unions restrained real wages, so that, although management in large plants gained little in the way of greater working flexibility, real wages did not grow as fast as productivity after 1976. But the agreement seemed one-sided: the Communists were unable to gain admission to the government, and the promise of productive public investments once again eluded the unions. The episode drove home a lesson that had been foreshadowed during the early postwar years and again during the mid 1960s: that an agreement which promises a primarily political payoff at a wholly economic cost is likely to strain the institutional fabric of even a highly political union movement.

The lesson was repeated with variations. After the Communists returned to opposition in 1978, the government issued another plan for wage and fiscal restraint and job creation, which it supplemented with a proposal for an employer-financed investment fund that would be administered with the participation of the union confederations. In effect this substituted an offer of institutional protection to the central union bodies for a political payoff to the PCI. The PCI actively opposed and succeeded in blocking the agreement, whereas the union confederations, which had been calling for participation in investment decisions, had been disposed to accept it. The party instead encouraged unions and shop stewards in attempts to protect jobs through the exertion of bargaining pressure on individual firms. But this reversal of party policy encountered an opposite reversal of members' attitudes, which turned more moderate—at least for a while—as the threat of unemployment became imminent and a tight monetary policy combined with deteriorating international competitiveness to stiffen the resistance of employers after the oil price increase of 1979.

It could be that the renewed tender of a government proposal for formal institutional participation by the union federations in more economically efficient investment and employment projects would be received with less timidity by the CGIL. It is even possible that the Italian Communist party would find it expedient to put up with a proposal which, on the face of it, contemplates a weakening of the Christian Democrats' power of patronage and is consistent with the long-elusive objective of "reform" through efficient public investment. Such a proposal would of course improve employment prospects in private industry, and that should appeal to industrial workers and their elected union delegates. Until recently, industrial unionists preferred a combination of worker militancy and government subsidy as a less costly and more direct way to protect their jobs, work rules, and wages. But demonstrations of effective employer insistence on reductions in employment and employer threats to abrogate their *scala* agreements might possibly serve to improve the relative attractiveness—or diminish the relative unpalatability—of future government initiatives.

X

France

Since the late 1960s, the French labor market has sustained three massive shocks: the general strike that followed the student revolt of May 1968, the rise in the price of energy and materials in 1973 and 1974, and the world economic recession that began in 1975. In addition, the recession emphasized the problem of increasing competition in industrial products from less developed countries such as Korea, Mexico, Brazil, and Taiwan. These developments parallel those in other Western European economies.

France differs in important ways, however, from the other countries in this study. Collective bargaining was virtually nonexistent before 1968; it has developed to a limited extent in the interim, but the French labor market is still the most weakly institutionalized in our sample. The structure of production, at least measured by concentration, testifies to an economy that was in 1945 composed predominantly of small-scale industry and agriculture. Finally, until 1981 relations between the government and those officially described as the "social partners" were as close in the case of employers as those with the unions were distant.

The causes of the weakness of the system of industrial relations will be addressed in detail later. The explanation lies partly in the strategies pursued by the main French union, the Communist Confédération Générale du Travail (CGT). These strategies of opposition to involvement in "permanent negotiation" in turn reflected the electoral and organizational needs of the Communist party—namely, control of the CGT, concern that its integration into an effective system of collective bargaining would lead to its independence of the party, use of the CGT to assert the economic contradictions of French monopoly capitalism, and maintenance of belief in the futility of reforms within the system and in the possibility of systemic change only through a Communist government. But equally responsible for the lack of effective bargaining was the antediluvian behavior of employers. Paternalistic, family-controlled companies, which clung to the *immobilisme*—the systematic opposition to innovation—of the 1930s, dominated French industry throughout the

567

1950s and much of the 1960s. Fear and suspicion on both sides of the industrial divide, moreover, were self-reinforcing.

The weakness of industrial relations and consequent low union membership imply, in neoclassical economics, an atomistic labor market. The functioning of the labor market in France was quite different. Its behavior was characterized by periodic instability. The picture is of a market fluctuating between periods of low bargaining power of the workers, generally associated with higher unemployment, when real wages grow slowly and, because of weak institutionalization, grievances accumulate, and shorter periods of frequent strikes, even strike waves, brought about by a sufficient accumulation of grievances, helped by labor-market tightness, and accompanied by rapid growth of real wages. Labor-market tightness has usually been a factor in heightened strike intensity, but not always: the accumulation of grievances in the loose labor markets of the mid 1960s was ignited by the student revolt into the general strike of May 1968 before any reflation of economic activity had taken place.

These structural characteristics largely determined the modalities of government policy, setting French economic policy apart in two ways from that of other countries. First, the close relations between government and industry led to a discretionary style of policymaking. In most countries arm's-length industrial and economic policies, the product of legislative processes, inhibited the ability of governments to differentiate among businesses. French governments have felt, by contrast, little inhibition. The widespread use of price controls, for example, has to be interpreted differently in France from the way it is interpreted elsewhere. The severity of price controls—as well as access to credit facilities in nationalized banks, export subsidies, and investment credits—has been made a condition of appropriate behavior in directions desired by the government. This has not meant state control over private industry; instead, an intimate and delicate bargaining relationship has developed, since the government has been as dependent on business as business has been on the government. These bargains were in general confidential; thus the analysis of the effects of price controls, valid in other countries, has less applicability in France, where the desired effects have not been generally known.

The second factor that set French economic policy apart stemmed from the structure of industrial relations and the labor market. Weak unions and badly organized workers gave the government a policy option, unavailable elsewhere, of ignoring the unions and gambling on the consequences. This option remained after May 1968. Although the May events increased their power, French unions remained the weakest in Western Europe. The threat of the French unions after 1968 was not that they had the power to call serious strikes; it was that there was some likelihood of a strike movement developing if the unions were united in supporting it and if government policies were sufficiently unpopular.

In contrast to other countries, the French government has thus always had available the policy option of ignoring the unions and gambling on the consequences. This was the initial reaction to the May events when the government refused in March 1969 to increase wages in line with rising consumer prices as had been envisaged in the Grenelle Agreement of June 1968. But equally important has been the alternative option of institution building. This was the option followed between 1969 and 1972 by Georges Pompidou, who succeeded Charles de Gaulle as president in 1969. It was a deliberate attempt to create, and entice the unions into, systematic bargaining structures that would eliminate the risks of labor-market explosions implied by the first option. The different policies adopted were not chosen accidentally; it paid at least in part to ignore the unions and gamble in 1968–69, when the unions were divided, just as institution building was later appropriate when the unions were more united and aggressive.

These two institutional characteristics of French policymaking—the style of government-industry relations and the labor market option—are also central to an understanding of economic policy before 1968 and after 1974.

We shall discuss policy in the 1960s to arrive at an understanding of the causes of the general strike of May 1968. Since there were strike waves in other countries in 1968–69, the explanation of the May events is developed primarily within an international economic perspective. All the large Western European countries pursued similar policies in the mid 1960s—incomes restraint, deflation, aid to rationalization in industry—in response to the problems of inflation and profitability that the trade-growth boom of the early 1960s had generated. What differentiated the May events from other strike waves was their massiveness. This differentiation is explained by the combination of the government view that the French economic-industrial problem required deeper changes than were needed in other countries and the institutional characteristics of policymaking noted earlier.

Since the early 1960s the underlying objective of the government has been the creation of large-scale industry, capable of competing in the international economy. This requirement followed from the second structural characteristic noted above, the low level of concentration of French business. It was given force from the opening of the domestic economy in 1958 to competition from the Common Market. And when de Gaulle became president in the same year and established the Fifth Republic, industrialization was central to his ambition for France "to marry her century" and acquire the economic resources to support its claim for great-power status.

To carry through this ambitious program, de Gaulle took the option of ignoring the labor market. Deflation, incomes restraint, and rationalization held down real wages and increased productivity in the mid 1960s, but at the risk that labor would eventually react against accumulated grievances, causing a strike wave and an upward push on real wages. The risk was reduced in the short run, but increased in the longer term, by the effective quiescence of the CGT, for it was in the electoral interest of the French Communist party (PCF) not to challenge, other than verbally, a government that behaved at home as a textbook capitalist government was supposed to, while giving French Communists respectability by a foreign policy of friendliness toward Russia. The risk was increased because the relationship between government and industry enabled the government to have a significant effect, especially through mergers, in a relatively short period.

In making economic policy after 1979 the French government had to react to the rising price of oil, the world recession, and the increasing industrial competition from less developed countries. Policy toward the labor market under President Valéry Giscard d'Estaing, who succeeded Pompidou in 1974, veered from compromise to conflict. Between 1974 and 1976, compromise was imposed by political and institutional considerations. Politically, the 1970s witnessed the end of a clear presidential majority, as a revitalized Socialist party became allied with the Communists. Institutionally, the development of wage bargaining under Pompidou, especially in the public sector, increased the cost of moderating real wage growth through unilateral governmental decision. But, as economic difficulties multiplied, Raymond Barre was appointed prime minister in late 1976 and he took the option of imposing an incomes policy in the absence of any possibility of agreeing on a policy with the unions. With the imposed incomes policy went a more restrictive monetary policy.

Paradoxically, the shift from compromise to conflict at first weakened rather than strengthened the Socialist-Communist alliance and led in 1977 to a break between the two parties. The PCF was already concerned that, in the event of a victory of the left in the 1978 assembly elections, the Socialists would, as dominant partners, control the power of the state while the Communists, through the CGT, would have the burden of imposing wage restraint in a difficult economic situation. So long as Giscard tried to occupy the center ground—politically, economically, and in industrial relations—the electoral benefit to the PCF of breaking with the Socialists was limited; the PCF, moreover, risked long-run isolation and contraction, since the Socialists might then move closer to the center. But when Giscard's policies became tougher, the PCF could break with the Socialists in the comforting belief that this would deny them power, while economic discontent would maintain Communist votes.

The decision of the PCF to break with the Socialists also had repercussions on the system of industrial relations. For with the CGT once again refusing to participate in the development of serious collective bargaining, the second important union, the Confédération Française Démocratique du Travail (CFDT), attempted to go it alone. The CGT could ignore this *recentrage*—or "recentering" activity from political action to collective bargaining—by the CFDT because neither government nor employers gave the CFDT sufficient encouragement. But the election of the Socialist leader François Mitterand as president in May 1981, partially as a result of massive Communist defections, upset such calculations. The Socialists were sympathetic to the aspirations of the CFDT; the new government committed itself to the reduction of unemployment; and the Communists, in both party and union, had to give at least the appearance of cooperating with the government. The commitment of the Socialist-led government to reflation and to income redistribution, moreover, and its sympathy with the bargaining objectives of the CFDT predisposed it to pursue an incomes policy in active cooperation with the unions—and not, as some of its predecessors had, either unilaterally or in cooperation solely with the employers.

The Vacuum of Industrial Relations: Labor-Market Instability in the 1950s and 1960s

In most sectors of the economy collective bargaining did not emerge in developed form until the 1970s. This weakness cannot be attributed to the law regulating collective bargaining and strikes, although its permissiveness may have helped to discourage unions from serious involvement in bargaining. The framework law of 1950 provides for collective agreements at the industry and plant levels in the private sector and in those nationalized companies, notably Renault, deemed to be in competition with the private sector. Any agreement at the industry level must be signed by the "most representative" employers' organizations and trade unions. The agreement covers all employees of member companies of the employer organizations, and it may be extended by the minister of labor to all companies in the industry. Agreements may be made for fixed periods, but if when the time has elapsed the parties cannot arrive at a new agreement, the original continues in force. At the plant level agreements must be signed by the "most representative" unions and may cover wages or other matters if they lie within the framework of a high-level agreement.

The right to strike is constitutionally enshrined, though certain restrictions have been introduced. Blast furnaces and mine pumps, for instance, must continue in operation, special rules govern the police, and since 1963 a notice has been required before a strike can be called in the public sector. In a national emergency, the government can requisition individuals to work.[1] These restrictions, however, have not been of significance.

In practice, therefore, at least in the private sector, the law has obstructed neither bargaining nor striking. The largest unions—including the Communist CGT—all qualify as "most representative." Thus each is capable, irrespective of the extent to which it is actually representative in the industry or plant in question, of signing a collective agreement. For an agreement to be valid, a single union signature suffices. In

1. We acknowledge an intellectual debt in this chapter to Jean-Daniel Reynaud's seminal work on French industrial relations, *Les Syndicats en France*, 1st ed. (Paris: Armand Colin, 1963), and the completely revised third edition, in two volumes (Paris: Editions du Seuil, 1975); in footnotes that refer to the third edition, the volume number is given. The work of Gérard Adam and George Ross is also important.

addition, unions may call or support strikes against the terms of an agreement even if they signed it earlier and it is still in operation.[2]

This permissiveness itself acts, however, to discourage unions from an inclination toward bargaining. There is no compulsion on either side to conclude agreements, since the previous agreement remains in force. If one union signs an agreement, other unions have incentives not to follow: they can accuse the signatory union of giving in too quickly and thus failing to help gain additional concessions, and, since the agreement covers their own members, the absence of their signatures costs them nothing. Workers who are not union members are also covered by agreements, so they have no incentive to join the unions that provide the highest material benefits; unions thus have no need to compete in the provision of benefits.

The effect of the legal system has been to exaggerate the weakness of the unions and divisions among them and to encourage the antiunion mentality of management. But it is incorrect to argue that the law determined the system: the United Kingdom has de facto a similar legal framework, but strong national and local unions have used its permissiveness to their advantage.[3]

Until the late 1960s, collective bargaining was generally ineffective at all levels. At the industry level the lack of serious engagement was in contrast to the formal extent of coverage. By the late 1960s collective agreements covered a wide range of industries at national, regional, and departmental levels.[4] These agreements fixed minimum wages and certain conditions of work, such as holidays and normal hours, but the agreements were in practice dictated by the employers' organization, which could, and frequently would, refuse to negotiate.[5]

During most of this period, bargaining at the plant level was non-existent in the great majority of companies. Unilateral determination of

2. For details, see Reynaud, Les Syndicats en France, chap. 7; Yves Delamotte, "Recent Collective Bargaining Trends in France," International Labour Review, vol. 103 (April 1971), pp. 351–77. The text describes the situation up to 1982; recent legislation has significantly increased union bargaining rights.

3. The argument is that the permissive nature of French labor law was not responsible for weakness of bargaining institutions; different laws—laws similar to those in the United States, for example—might well strengthen bargaining institutions.

4. Jean-Daniel Reynaud, "France: Elitist Society Inhibits Collective Bargaining," in Solomon Barkin, ed., Worker Militancy and Its Consequences, 1965–75: New Directions in Western Industrial Relations (New York: Praeger Publishers, 1975), chap. 8; see table 4, p. 287, for statistics.

5. Delamotte, "Recent Collective Bargaining Trends," p. 356.

wages and conditions was the jealously guarded prerogative of management. Technically, workers have not been without rights of representation. Companies with more than fifty employees are required to have a *comité d'entreprise* (company committee) with a membership elected annually by the work force. Companies are also obliged to arrange for annual employee elections of *délégués du personnel* (employees' representatives). In both instances candidates must be put forward by unions on the first round of the elections. The *comité d'entreprise* is primarily a consultative body with some responsibilities for work safety and social expenditures. The *délégués* are regarded by most workers as the union representative in the plant;[6] their legally established function is to represent workers in grievances that originate from nonobservance of collective agreements by the employer. Both *délégués* and members of the *comité* are allowed time off with pay to fulfill their duties. Further, they have greater legal protection against dismissal than other workers. In practice, these legal rights have had little effect upon the balance of power within the plant. The *comités d'entreprise* have generally been confined to the organization of social functions—canteens and the like— and the *délégués,* frequently faced with arbitrary and paternalistic management, have failed not only to handle grievances but also to develop a say in personnel functions, such as hiring and firing and the distribution of overtime.[7]

The picture of union ineffectiveness in industry negotiations and in the plant is not redeemed by examining the third level at which bargaining took place in the private sector. Interindustry agreements were negotiated between the central employers' organization, the Conseil National du Patronat Français (CNPF), and the principal union confederations. They did not concern wages: the two most important agreements in the 1950s covered retirement pensions (1957) and unemployment benefits (1958), in both instances complementing, for workers in the private sector, the limited state provisions. The same rules governed these agreements with respect to signatures and coverage as applied to industrywide agreements: in particular, the benefits were not for union

6. Reynaud, *Les Syndicats en France,* pp. 212–14.
7. For general references, see ibid., chap. 8; Reynaud, "France: Elitist Society," pp. 295–96; Val R. Lorwin, *The French Labor Movement* (Cambridge: Harvard University Press, 1954), chap. 14; Walter Kendall, *The Labour Movement in Europe* (London: Allen Lane, 1975), pp. 80–94. For case studies, see Maurice Montuclard, *La Dynamique des comités d'entreprise* (Paris: Centre Nationale de la Recherche Scientifique, 1963).

members only but reached to all those employed by member companies of the CNPF. Few agreements were made at this level until the late 1960s.

In the two first postwar decades the public sector mirrors the ineffectiveness of unions in the private sector. The government excluded the unions from any significant role in wage determination. No system of collective agreements existed to parallel that in the private sector.[8] By decree in 1953, the requirement that increases in wages in any part of the public sector have the consent of the minister of finance was made formal. A more flexible procedure superseded this requirement in 1965— the Toutée procedure, which will be discussed later—but government control of overall wage increases remained.

In general, then, in both the private and public sectors, the unions were ineffective, at least with respect to their involvement in collective bargaining. Some qualifications to this generalization are necessary, however. In one industry, printing, systematic bargaining was in operation both on the shop floor and at the national level throughout this period; newspaper printing in the principal towns was a closed shop. In addition, union representatives in the public sector were closely involved at the plant level in personnel functions. This was a legacy of the nationalization statutes of 1945–47, when the Communists were in the coalition government. These statutes provided for decisions on a wide range of personnel questions to be decided by staff committees on which the unions and management were represented equally.[9] "It is the nationalized industries which come closest to the American 'grievance procedure.' "[10]

Two further exceptions may be noted. During the period 1945–47 there was considerable union cooperation at the plant level, in both the private and public sectors, which had the aim of reestablishing productivity.[11] This was in line with the commitment of the Communist party, as part of the coalition government, to economic growth. It seems likely, especially in the larger plants, which were the first to set up *comités*

8. It was noted earlier that nationalized companies, notably Renault, in competition with the private sector are treated here, and in collective bargaining laws, as part of the private sector.

9. Lorwin, *French Labor Movement*, pp. 197–98; J.-M. Verdier, "Labour Relations in the Public Sector in France," *International Labour Review*, vol. 109 (February 1974), 105–18.

10. Reynaud, *Les Syndicats en France*, p. 322.

11. Lorwin, *French Labor Movement*, pp. 266–67.

d'entreprise, that *délégués* or members of the *comités* acquired some power over personnel matters, working conditions, and even earnings.[12] The second exception was the attempt to develop company bargaining initiated by Renault. In September 1955 Renault signed an enterprise agreement covering wages—actual wages, not minimum wages—and holiday pay. Similar agreements followed in fifty other major companies.[13] This movement, however, lost momentum as adverse economic conditions set in in 1958–59.

It would be wrong to conclude from this discussion of the system of industrial relations in France up to the late 1960s that the system was stable. Because of its weak institutionalization, grievances could build up, and there was no safety valve. In the public sector this bottling-up related primarily to macro wage questions—since micro grievances were adequately dealt with—in particular to public-private wage differentials. Grievances in the private sector might be either micro or macro. Under enough pressure of accumulating discontent, waves of shop-floor strikes could develop; these could be channeled by unions into negotiations at whatever level seemed appropriate. The unions, with insufficient strength to call up the waves, thus functioned as skilled surfboard riders. In these terms the general strike of May 1968 was merely the most spectacular wave, although one that sorely tested the skill of the surfers. In the private sector a good measure of plant-level strike movements—as opposed to national, one-day strikes—is given by data on the annual numbers of strikes (see table 10-1). Before 1968 four waves of intensified conflict are apparent—in 1947, 1950–51, 1955–57, and 1961–64. By contrast, column 4 of table 10-1 shows the lower variation around trend of numbers of strikes in the United Kingdom, with its more highly developed system of industrial relations.

It may be objected at this point that two hypotheses, bottling-up (of grievances in individual plants) and bunching together (of strikes in different plants), have been conflated with inadequate explanation. In a weakly unionized system, however, the latter is a natural concomitant of the former. Bottling-up occurs among workers who are badly organized, and because they are badly organized, they lack the confidence and leadership necessary to translate accumulated grievances into strike action. They fear the consequences of ineffective strikes. As a result,

12. Some support for this statement can be found between the lines of Montuclard, *La Dynamique,* pp. 165–66, 266–69, and 296–98.
13. Reynaud, *Les Syndicats en France,* pp. 180–85.

Table 10-1. *Strike Statistics, France and the United Kingdom, 1947–67*

Year	France			Number of strikes in the United Kingdom (4)
	Number of strikes (1)	Number of strikers (millions) (2)	Worker-days lost (millions) (3)	
1947	2,285	3.0	22.7	1,721
1948	1,425	6.6	13.1	1,759
1949	1,426	4.3	7.1	1,426
1950	2,586	1.5	11.7	1,339
1951	2,514	1.8	3.5	1,719
1952	1,749	1.2	1.7	1,714
1953	1,761	1.8	9.7	1,746
1954	1,479	1.3	1.4	1,989
1955	2,672	1.1	3.1	2,419
1956	2,440	1.0	1.4	2,648
1957	2,623	3.0	4.1	2,859
1958	954	1.1	1.1	2,629
1959	1,512	0.9	1.9	2,093
1960	1,494	1.1	1.1	2,832
1961	1,963	2.6	2.6	2,686
1962	1,884	1.5	1.9	2,449
1963	2,382	2.6	6.0	2,068
1964	2,281	2.6	2.5	2,524
1965	1,674	1.2	1.0	2,354
1966	1,711	3.3	2.5	1,937
1967	1,675	2.8	4.2	2,116

Source: Walter Kendall, *The Labour Movement in Europe* (London: Allen Lane, 1975), pp. 365, 371.

bunching together occurs for one or both of two reasons: a tight, or rapidly tightening, labor market, which is some guarantee against failure and subsequent victimization, and a clear external signal, of which the clearest is a strike in a large, high-visibility plant, to allow a worker to believe that his fellow workers will strike if he does.

One or both of these conditions, together with accumulations of grievances, held true for each of the waves of strikes mentioned above, as well as 1968.[14] Apart from 1968, all were periods of tight or tightening labor markets. For 1955–57 and 1961–64 this can be seen from the data in columns 4 and 5 of table 10-2.[15] In 1947, 1955, and 1968, signals were

14. With the exception of 1950–52, about which we have been unable to secure information.

15. For 1947, see Kendall, *Labour Movement in Europe*, p. 353.

Table 10-2. *Prices, Wages, and Labor-Market Variables, France, 1953–68*

Year	Consumer price inflation (1)	Percentage change in hourly wage rates (2)	Percentage change in real wages (col. 2 − col. 1) (3)	Percentage change in labor productivity[a] (4)	ln U/V[b] (5)
1953	. . .	3.0	. . .	3.5	2.93
1954	0.3	6.3	6.0	4.7	2.77
1955	1.1	8.6	7.5	6.3	2.12
1956	4.3	9.1	4.8	4.9	0.97
1957	−0.7	9.2	9.9	4.0	0.48
1958	15.2	13.4	−1.8	2.1	1.16
1959	5.7	7.6	1.9	2.6	2.09
1960	4.1	6.8	2.7	7.4	1.65
1961	2.4	9.2	6.8	4.9	1.13
1962	5.2	9.9	4.7	5.6	0.83
1963	4.9	10.1	5.2	4.8	0.96
1964	3.1	8.8	5.7	5.2	0.95
1965	2.7	6.4	3.7	4.0	1.61
1966	2.6	6.1	3.5	4.6	1.40
1967	2.8	6.8	4.0	4.1	1.86
1968	4.6	11.5	6.9	8.0	. . .

Sources: Column 1, Geoffrey Maynard and W. van Ryckeghem, *A World of Inflation* (New York: Harper & Row, 1975), p. 80 (from International Monetary Fund statistics); columns 2 and 4, Jacques Lecaillon and Brigitte Botalla-Gambetta. "Inflation, répartition [distribution], et chômage [unemployment] dans la France contemporaine," *Revue économique*, vol. 24, no. 3 (May 1973), p. 399; column 5, computed from data in ibid., p. 400.

a. The growth of labor productivity is a measure both of the ability of the employers to pay and of the extent of the tightening of labor markets, since according to Okun's law labor productivity grows faster than trend during an upswing—truer of the 1950s than of the 1960s; the loose labor markets of the 1960s were used to rationalize production.

b. In recent studies by the Institut National de la Statistique et des Etudes Economiques, ln U/V, the natural logarithm of the ratio of number of unemployed to number of vacancies, has been used as a measure of labor-market tightness; see INSEE, *Note "Salaires,"* ref. no. 642/341, September 1975.

clearly in evidence: major initiating strikes at the Renault works in Paris (Boulogne-Billancourt) in 1947,[16] at the great shipyards of Nantes and St. Nazarre in 1955, and at Renault-Cléon and Sud-Aviation-Nantes in 1968. "Renault had for long been the pilot-company of all large movements, particularly in the Paris region, often the first touched by a wave of claims, and where the action was most followed because of its torchlight role." (It was indeed because of this that Renault started the move toward company bargaining in 1955, after the Nantes and St. Nazarre strikes, in an attempt to stabilize bargaining through institutionalization.)[17] In 1968, of course, the success of the student revolt in

16. Lorwin, *French Labor Movement*, p. 116.
17. Reynaud, *Les Syndicats en France*, p. 180; the French ends: "parce qu'elle servait de témoin."

Table 10-3. *Strike Waves and Real Wages, France, Selected Periods, 1946–68*

Annual percentage changes in real hourly wage rates

Nonstrike period		Strike period	
Period	Percentage change	Period	Percentage change
January 1946–January 1947	−20.0[a]	January 1947–April 1947	5.0[a]
		April 1947–October 1947	−19.0[a]
1948–49	−3.0[b,c]	1950–51	4.1[c]
1952–54	4.5[c]	1955–57	7.4
1958–60	0.9	1961–64	6.1
1965–67	3.7	1968	6.9

Source: Table 10-2, except as noted below.
a. Percentage changes throughout period specified, not at annual rates; calculated from data in Val R. Lorwin, *The French Labor Movement* (Cambridge: Harvard University Press, 1954), p. 121.
b. Percentage change only of 1949 on 1948.
c. International Labour Office, *Yearbook of Labour Statistics, 1954* (Geneva: ILO, 1954), table 17, p. 163.

gaining concessions from the government was the primary signal. As in 1936, 1968 showed that, with a strong enough signal, a massive strike wave could be precipitated in a relatively loose labor market.[18]

A readily quantifiable measure of bottling-up of grievances comes from data on real wages. Table 10-3 sets out changes in real wages before and during the strike waves. While statistics before the mid 1950s should be treated with great caution, the data support the idea of constriction of real wages in periods preceding strikes, with the exception of the period 1952–54. Grievances did not accumulate over real wages alone. The discussion below of the causes of the revolt of May 1968 will emphasize two further sources of grievance accumulation in the period 1965–67 that exacerbated the slow growth of real wages: widening pay differentials between the public and private sectors, the result of attempts by the government to keep domestic inflation in line with world prices; and the spate of rationalizations in industry during the same period, designed to realize the profitability and concentration that the government believed was needed if the challenges of the world economy were to be met. In this light, the events of May 1968 can be seen as the response of the chronically unstable system of industrial relations to the policies necessary for international competitiveness and economic growth.

18. The 1936 general strike, which surprised the unions as much as the employers, was precipitated by the Popular Front election victory. Kendall, *Labour Movement in Europe*, p. 43.

The instability of the system reflected the lack of developed collective bargaining and ineffectiveness of the unions. This raises two questions. Why was there no effective bargaining? And what were the economic consequences of the instability?

Weak Unions, Hostile Employers

At the end of World War II there were two general union confederations in France. Very much the larger was the Confédération Générale du Travail, Communist-dominated and with close links to the Communist party. The Confédération Française des Travailleurs Chrétiens (CFTC) was loosely aligned with the Catholic church and the Mouvement Républicain Populaire (MRP), the French Christian Democratic party. A third confederation was formed in 1947, when the Socialist minority, Force Ouvrière, broke away from the CGT because of Communist domination of the latter. Finally a fourth, very small, confederation emerged in 1964 from the opposition in the CFTC when its breaking away from the church was symbolized with a new name, Confédération Française Démocratique du Travail; the new union took with it the discarded name, CFTC. These four confederations organize in each industry and each occupation. The CGT is highly centralized: not much more than a formal distinction exists, with some exceptions, between the central confederation and its industry federations.[19] The others are only somewhat less centralized. Two further centrals are of significance. The Fédération d'Education Nationale (FEN) groups together the teaching unions.[20] And the Confédération Générale des Cadres (CGC) represents white-collar workers.

Data on numbers of union members are not included in official statistics, and the unions do not regularly publish membership statistics. Table 10-4 shows the numbers of members claimed by the two major centrals, CGT and CFTC/CFDT, for selected years. Force Ouvrière probably had fewer members throughout than the CFTC/CFDT.[21] In 1968 the new CFTC claimed 145,000 members, the FEN 450,000, and the CGC 250,000.[22]

19. The CGT has tight control over its paid officials; it has, however, only limited control over its members, something that is true of all French unions.
20. The FEN, like Force Ouvrière, broke from the CGT—of which it was an industry federation—in 1947.
21. Reynaud, *Les Syndicats en France*, p. 127; ibid., vol. 2: *Textes et documents*, pp. 124–25.
22. Kendall, *Labour Movement in Europe*, p. 61.

Table 10-4. *Union Membership, France, Selected Years, 1945–72*
Millions

Year	CGT	CFTC	Year	CGT	CFTC/CFDT
1945	4.50	0.30	1961	1.72	0.47
1946	5.58	0.37	1963	1.77	0.56
1947	5.48	0.38	1965	1.94	0.52
1948	4.08	0.38	1966	1.20	0.50
1949	3.89	0.32	1967	1.94	0.55
1950	3.99	0.33	1968	2.00	0.62
1951	3.08	0.34	1969	2.30	0.68
1952	2.51	0.35	1972	2.33	0.80
1953	1.50	0.34			
1959	1.00	0.65			

Source: Kendall, *Labour Movement in Europe*, p. 339.

Statistics on numbers of members give an idea of changes in membership through the years and some indication of the relative sizes of the several confederations. They should not be given great weight, however. The claims of the CGT and Force Ouvrière, in particular, are generally much exaggerated. In place of a total claimed union membership of 4.5 million in 1968, Kendall suggests a more realistic figure, close to 3 million.[23] Such a figure implies a rate of unionization in 1968 of about 15 percent of the active labor force of 20.5 million. Since 1968 brought an increase in membership, a lower rate of unionization probably characterized much of the 1950s and 1960s. In contrast to the United States, where a comparable percentage of the total labor force is unionized, the average did not conceal a picture of strongly organized and unorganized industries; in France, most industries were weakly organized. Reynaud calculated that, for 1962, even the metalworking industries had a rate of unionization of less than 20 percent.[24] Fewer data are available on union membership at the plant level; Galenson, however, estimated the membership in the large Paris Renault factory of Boulogne-Billancourt, commonly thought of as strongly unionized, at only 10 percent in 1959—though it must be admitted that this was a year in which unionization slumped nationally.[25] It is improbable, therefore, that low average unionization masked a small number of high-membership plants.

Three qualifications to these statistics must be made: First, low

23. Ibid., where it is shown that calculations on the basis of dues paid suggest a CGT membership of 1.2 million for 1969 against the claimed figure of 2.3 million.
24. Reynaud, *Les Syndicats en France*, pp. 127–28.
25. Walter Galenson, *Trade Union Democracy in Western Europe* (Berkeley: University of California Press, 1961), p. 8.

membership was not true for the whole postwar period. In the immediate aftermath of 1945, as table 10-4 shows, unionization was at least twice what it was in the 1950s and 1960s. Second, most of the public sector, and in the private sector the printing industry, were highly unionized throughout.

A third qualification has to do with the fundamental nature of French unionism. The extent of membership does not measure accurately either general approval of unions or the number of workers potentially prepared to strike. Both are very much higher. An analogous contrast exists between the number of members of a political party and the number of those prepared to vote for the party in an election. General approval of unions is shown in the annual elections to *comités d'entreprise*. In these elections, held on a plant-by-plant basis, workers may abstain, vote for a nonunion list, or vote for one of a number of union lists. The results for 1967–68 are shown in table 10-5. The abstention rate was 27.9 percent in 1967 and 26.5 percent in 1968.[26] (The results show, incidentally, the relative popularity of the several unions.) The number of workers potentially prepared to strike is also underestimated by the number of union members. Table 10-1 indicates several years when the number of strikers exceeded 2.5 million. Since it is unlikely that about 80 percent of union members were on strike in each of those years, it may be concluded that many of the strikers were not unionized.

To what extent were the unions able to mobilize union members? In industries in the private sector (with the exception of printing) union mobilizing ability was at a very low level; it was not much greater, despite the large number of members, within the public sector. Writing in the early 1960s, a leading authority on French industrial relations, J.-D. Reynaud, said: "Without strike funds, union federations have few ways in which to exercise influence or control [over strikers]. They can express their approval to a greater or lesser degree, but they only withhold it in extreme cases. They are as little able to control their locals as are the latter able to control their members."[27] Strike activity moves upward from the members to the locals, the federations, and the central confederations, rather than in the other direction. This was not the case in the immediate postwar years. The CGT was then able to mobilize the members, although even then the members also mobilized themselves (against the wishes of the CGT). If the unions

26. Reynaud, *Les Syndicats en France*, vol. 2, p. 106.
27. Reynaud, *Les Syndicats en France*, p. 150.

Table 10-5. *Comité d'Entreprise Elections, France, 1967 and 1968*
Percent

Union or group	1967	1968
CGT	45.0	47.9
CFDT	17.7	19.3
Force Ouvrière	7.5	7.7
CFTC	2.1	2.9
Other unions, excluding the CGC	3.9	5.4
Nonunion	19.9	11.7
Total	96.1	94.9

Source: Jacques Capdevielle and René Mouriaux, *Les Syndicats Ouvriers en France* (Paris: Armand Colin, 1976), p. 85.

were seldom able to mobilize their own members, they were a fortiori unable to mobilize nonmembers, though as noted earlier, the latter were not necessarily opposed either to unions or to striking.

The weakness of the unions was reflected in their lack of resources. Union income from dues in the 1950s and 1960s was minimal in comparison with that in other countries: while low membership was the main cause, the level of dues was small—less than one hour's pay per month—and the average member probably paid dues for less than seven months out of twelve.[28] Little information is available on the extent to which external sources supplemented dues income. Force Ouvrière was financed in the early 1950s, probably by employer organizations, the American Federation of Labor and Congress of Industrial Organizations (AFL-CIO), and reportedly by the Central Intelligence Agency (CIA). No evidence of Communist financial aid to the CGT is available, but it is implausible to suppose that none was given. The shoestring size of the unions, however—the whole CGT had only about eighty full-time employees, including officers and technical assistants—the tiny legal departments, and the virtual nonexistence of strike funds until the late 1960s all testify to extreme union weakness, at least in the field of collective bargaining.[29]

Why was union membership low (and unions therefore financially weak) and why were the unions unable to mobilize members? In some countries the law has been a positive or a negative force both in organizing and in mobilizing. In France few legal obstacles have been placed

28. Ibid., pp. 123–26; Kendall, *Labour Movement in Europe*, p. 64.

29. Lorwin, *French Labor Movement*, p. 169; André Barjonet, *La C.G.T.* (Paris: Editions du Seuil, 1968), pp. 51, 61.

in the way of union membership and mobilization, and positive inducements have been provided. The "checkoff," whereby the employer acts
as agent for the union, deducting union dues from wages, is technically
illegal, as is the closed shop.[30] But as the closed shops of the CGT in
newspaper printing suggest, it is not the law that has prevented closed
shops; and the same is doubtless true of the checkoff.

Aside from legal requirements, two sets of factors are in general
relevant in determining what proportion of a country's labor force is
unionized. Both sets of factors are important in France. The first set may
be described as "direct benefit" factors—those improvements in pay
and conditions brought about by union action. The measures of those
improvements are here called "plant-union effectiveness" when they
occur at the plant level and "national-union effectiveness" at the
regional, industry, or national level.

Plant-union effectiveness is more complex than that at the national
level. First, a formal union presence at the plant is not required; as was
pointed out above, the *délégués du personnel* are generally seen by
workers as "the union." Second, the effectiveness may relate to the
operation of a grievance system and personnel functions, such as the
allocation of overtime or redundancies, or it may include plant or
enterprise bargaining over wages or conditions of work. We assume that
union effectiveness at either level serves to increase or maintain the
number of members. This assumption is based on group self-interest. If
union effectiveness costs money, it is in the group interest for each
worker to pay his dues. And in practice, this is why most workers, most
of the time, in most countries, are reasonably contented to join or remain
in unions. While—and because—the majority behave in this way,
however, there is a "free-rider" problem. If union membership is
voluntary and the benefits of union effectiveness are available to all
workers, individual self-interest is inconsistent with membership. Corresponding to these conditions, individual and group interest can be
equated in two ways. Union membership may be made compulsory,
either formally—through a closed-shop agreement, for example—or
informally—through work-group sanctions, for example. Or benefits
may be confined to members only. The extent to which the inducement
to free riding is eliminated in these ways will be called the degree of
privatization of the benefits.

30. Reynaud, *Les Syndicats en France*, p. 150; Kendall, *Labour Movement in
Europe*, p. 85, n. 1; and Delamotte, "Recent Collective Bargaining Trends," p. 353.

As was argued in the preceding section, practically no direct benefits accrued in France during the 1950s and 1960s from union activity, and most of those that did offered no privatization. Plant-union effectiveness was generally nonexistent. There was little evidence of either effective union-operated grievance procedures or effective plant bargaining. At the national level, minimum, not effective, wages were the subject of negotiations, the outcome was typically dictated by the employers' federation, and such increases as there were were not confined to members only.

To these generalizations three main exceptions were noted above: union effectiveness in printing, union effectiveness in the plants and at the government level at the end of the war, and unions carrying out personnel functions in the public sector.[31] In all three cases, high initial membership was maintained while unions remained effective. When unions ceased to be effective in the plants and at higher levels in the private sector from the late 1940s on, membership and mobilizing ability dropped (see table 10-4). In the public sector, a high level of membership did not go with ability to mobilize.[32] The direct benefits then came from the protection unions could give in grievances and from their personnel function. This was buttressed by privatization. "One could reproach the unions [in the above functions] for discriminating between workers [in the public sector] depending on whether or not they are unionized, which would partially explain the high number of members."[33] Aside from these functions, the unions were ineffective in the public sector. By the early 1950s workers had lost confidence in the ability of the unions to organize and lead strike movements to successful conclusions. So while they remained members because of the unions' plant-level function in the public sector, they could not be effectively mobilized.

Outside the public sector and the printing industry, the virtual lack of union engagement in bargaining explains the low degree of unionization in France. In that explanation the implicit comparison is with other countries. But the number of members at the nadir of union membership,

31. "Union representatives sit on . . . promotion and discipline committees with powers unheard of in most private employment. Grievance handling is more of a joint process." Lorwin, *French Labor Movement,* p. 198.

32. For 1973, an estimate of 75 percent membership in the public sector against 25 percent in private manual employment is cited in Hugh Armstrong Clegg, *Trade Unionism under Collective Bargaining* (Oxford: Basil Blackwell, 1976), p. 12. Estimates of earlier periods could not be found.

33. Reynaud, *Les Syndicats en France,* p. 222.

while comparatively low, was still between 1.5 million and 2 million. We can suppose that at least half these workers were in the private sector. This raises the opposite question: Why were so many private-sector workers unionized? This must be attributed in large part to social factors. In France, as in Italy to a more marked extent, many workers share a class consciousness whose political expression has been the Communist party; this may involve voting Communist and sympathizing with the CGT, or it may go further and include membership in the party or the union. The CGT is seen by many workers as the union that represents the working class: membership is part of a political culture or way of life. A similar argument doubtless accounts for the membership of many in the CFTC, to whom the payment of union dues is an extension of weekly donations to the Catholic church.

Finally, we ask why unions were so ineffective in collective bargaining. As noted earlier, the law has not seriously impeded collective bargaining, but its permissiveness has magnified the weakness of the unions, for no legal barriers have prevented strong employers from dictating their own terms. It is not legal changes, however, that explain the decline, from the late 1940s on, in union effectiveness. The determining factors in understanding this decline—and hence the reflected and reinforcing decline in union strength and membership—were two: the attitude and behavior of the CGT and the juxtaposed hostility of employers.

The policies of the CGT were designed, at least until the mid 1950s, to meet the requirements of the Communist party. Between 1944 and 1947, the PCF was in the postliberation coalition government. The strategy of the party was to move toward a left-center popular front administration. To buttress its leading role if such a move succeeded—and to safeguard its position if it failed—required the development of entrenched positions of Communist strength. Within the private sector this was to be effected through *comités d'entreprise,* within the public sector through parity commissions in the work place and codetermination at board level.[34] In two senses the agency of this development was the CGT. The union, rather than the party, supplied the worker representatives on the various organs (so long, of course, as the CGT won the elections). And it was with the ability of the CGT to deliver on incomes

34. For details, see Lorwin, *French Labor Movement,* p. 103.

and productivity policy that the PCF could buy commitment from the other parties in government to the legislation establishing these institutions.

The ability of the CGT to carry through a tough incomes policy broke down in 1947. Ever more serious wildcatting against restraint led the union to switch from attempted repression to support of the strikers. When the PCF followed suit, it was obliged to leave the coalition. The new French government, now rid of the Communists, followed the American line on the cold war; in retaliation, the Soviet Union told the French Communists to "rely on the masses," and this led to a new phase of extreme CGT militancy. This militancy could count on an accumulation of worker grievances so long as it aimed at improving living standards. But when in 1947–48 the strikes challenged the government directly and with some violence, "the CGT was split (between the PCF-controlled core and the Force Ouvrière), the union rank-and-file was thoroughly intimidated away from direct action, union membership began to decline, and divisions between pro- and anti-Communist workers solidified."[35] From 1949 to 1953 the party mounted a "peace" campaign, and the large part of the resources of the CGT were now devoted to national strikes and demonstrations on this theme. "The CGT was asked to convey a message to its rank and file connecting their immediate material problems with high issues of foreign policy. This message proved too subtle . . . for ordinary unionists to digest."[36] The CGT did not wholly neglect domestic questions. Throughout this period it developed certain policies, in relation to the economy and the labor market, independent of the party. These centered on the possible use of economic planning and taxation in a mixed economy. By 1953, however, the party came to see these developments as against its own interest. The CGT was not to be allowed to make independent moves; "[as] the unique party of the working class the [PCF] alone was qualified to take initiatives."[37] The specific worry of the party was the possibility of a rapprochement between the unions and the reformist government of Pierre Mendès-France. To distance itself from such temptations, the

35. George Ross, "Party and Mass Organization: The Changing Relationship of PCF and CGT," in Donald Blackmer and Sidney Tarrow, eds., *Communism in Italy and France* (Princeton, N.J.: Princeton University Press, 1975), p. 509.

36. Ibid., p. 510.

37. Barjonet, *La C.G.T.,* p. 88.

CGT was required to adopt the "pauperization" theme which Maurice Thorez, the Communist leader, now developed: French capitalism led inevitably to the increasing poverty of the French worker.[38]

As shown above, the behavior of the CGT was conditioned during the Fourth Republic by the needs of the Communist party.[39] The consequence of this behavior was a series of lost opportunities to develop strong and effective union bargaining. Certainly at two points, and possibly at three, a different strategy could have yielded such results. The serious failure of the CGT came during the late 1940s. By 1947 local unions had acquired considerable power in many large plants. The discontent with incomes policy gave an edge to worker militancy that could have been directed toward the establishment or consolidation of effective bargaining at the shop-floor level. Employers were on their "chastened best behavior [and had been] since 1944."[40] Plant bargaining was also on the agenda—of the CFTC metalworkers' union, for instance. But the potential was thrown away by the CGT policies of large-scale political strikes, membership declined dramatically, political differences between unions became insuperable, and with growing confidence "the French *patronat* [management] . . . returned to many of the anti-union, anti-labor practices of the prewar years."[41] Further opportunities occurred in the mid 1950s: as mentioned earlier, the government of Mendès-France held out in principle the possibility of cooperation, and in more direct and practical terms it was offered by the Renault initiative on company bargaining.

Why did the CGT adopt the strategies it did? Directly, as we have argued, it was in response to the immediate requirements of the party. Indirectly, too, the PCF feared loss of control of the CGT: effective bargaining implied the possibility of financial independence for the unions through increased membership and higher dues paid with greater regularity and the consequent danger that the CGT would become more responsive to the economic interests of its members. How was the party able to enforce its will? The CGT is not a completely "closed" organi-

38. Ross, "Party and Mass Organization," p. 512.
39. The Fourth Republic lasted from 1946 until de Gaulle's presidency inaugurated the Fifth Republic in 1958. In contrast to the presidential regime of the Fifth Republic, the Fourth was based on parliamentary government and was dominated by successive coalitions of the center parties, including the Socialists. After the immediate postwar coalition, both the Gaullists and the Communists remained in the wings.
40. Ross, "Party and Mass Organization," p. 510.
41. Ibid.

zation. While partly stage-managed, non-Communists are well represented in the higher echelons of elected union officials, and opposition to both union and party decisions is allowed to exist. Such openness, however, is controlled, and the agency of such control, at least in the short run, is the staffing by party cadres of the organization section of the union.

The CGT apparatus has in any case had its own interest in restraining the growth of local autonomy. The possible danger of such growth was underlined by the anti–incomes policy, anti-CGT strikes by locals in early 1947. The ability to mount such strikes may well have been seen by the CGT as the outcome of the "quasi negotiations" that took place through *comités d'entreprise* during that period. "The new [CGT] line [political strike organizing, no dealings with employers] toward the committees [from late 1947 on] encountered enough resistance in the shops to call for repeated admonitions from higher CGT echelons."[42] Given the permissive legal structure, the development of effective plant bargaining led to the possibility of British-style shop stewards.[43]

On the other hand, the CGT had little to fear from competition. The other centrals were too weak numerically to play a stimulating role. Both the CFTC and Force Ouvrière had sharp internal divisions, which both sapped their strength and prevented collaboration.

In the Fifth Republic, the CGT behaved more recognizably as a trade union, focusing its action on economic issues and moving tactically in response to labor-market conditions. Nonetheless, the CGT policy that emerged in the 1960s—of short, large, high-level protest strikes—was inimical to the development of effective bargaining. In its day-to-day decisionmaking the union operated independently of the party,[44] but its strategy was well tailored to party requirements.

De Gaulle's presidency evoked an ambivalent response from the French Communist party. On the one hand, the economic policies of the regime combined with the shift of the decisionmaking locus from parliament to president to fit the party's hostile analysis of Gaullism as the political expression of "monopoly capitalism."[45] On the other hand,

42. Lorwin, *French Labor Movement*, pp. 115–16, 268.
43. See Clegg, *Trade Unionism*, pp. 64–65, for a general discussion of this point in relation to France.
44. Ross, "Party and Mass Organization," pp. 513 ff.
45. Annie Kriegel, "The French Communist Party and the Fifth Republic," in Blackmer and Tarrow, *Communism in Italy and France*, p. 73.

de Gaulle's policies had much to recommend them to a party which "at its low point in 1962 . . . seemed, like the German Social Democrats before 1914, to have degenerated from a powerful revolutionary movement into a comfortable electoral machine, huge, slow, timid and bureaucratic."[46] Economic policies of wage restraint, rationalization, and concentration meant a growing worker discomfort on which the party could capitalize electorally in the long run. At the same time, the Gaullist rapprochement toward the Soviet Union and Eastern Europe, designed to underline French independence from the United States and NATO, gave added respectability to the French Communists.

More fundamentally, de Gaulle played the PCF game by polarizing French society. His strong center-right presidency ended the centrist compromises of parliamentary coalition government of the Fourth Republic by rendering the center parties impotent. The Socialist party was now forced to collaborate with the Communists if it wished to oppose the Gaullists; because of the weakness of the Socialists in the 1960s, and because the PCF could play a waiting game, collaboration was to be on Communist terms. The PCF could thus sit back and await developments. In doing so, it needed the CGT in two ways. The union had to show the members of the working class how Gaullist policy exacerbated their economic position. But in the process it had to avoid any serious explosion of worker discontent that might have been taken to challenge the regime as a whole; in any situation that might have been construed as revolutionary, the concern of the leaders about the party's survival would exceed their hope for victory.

In the 1960s the CGT acted in line with the needs of the party. The violence of its language calling for "permanent mobilization against the regime, [and] a general CGT-Gaullism conflict" contrasted with the reticence of its behavior. One observer commented, "The gap between the motions of the [1963] Congress and the caution of everyday union action seems a permanent element of CGT strategy."[47] To the CGT the ideal strike was more of a carefully controlled mass demonstration. "The CGT was concerned with promoting movements that would in turn force highly visible bargaining at the industry level in the private

46. Philip M. Williams and Martin Harrison, *Politics and Society in de Gaulle's Republic* (New York: Doubleday, 1972), p. 155.
47. Gérard Adam, "Situation de la C.G.T.," *Revue française de science politique,* vol. 13 (December 1963), p. 971.

sector and between unions and the government at the top of each branch of the public sector. [It placed] lower-level struggles in the perspective of 'building' toward public higher-level confrontations. In 1966 and 1967 . . . [there] were a series of large, often national, one- and two-day protest strikes (with most local union efforts directed toward their preparation)."[48] In the tight labor markets of the early 1960s, the CGT did not attempt to move toward systematic enterprise bargaining. It was opposed to participation in planning and incomes policy. In the 1960s the CGT, cautious lest any actual confrontation with the regime develop,[49] concerned that local bargaining might mean local autonomy, loyally reflecting party anxiety that participation at governmental level was a prelude to integration and CGT independence, and faithfully helping party electoral needs by devoting a large proportion of resources to strikes that were no more than mass demonstrations with little to show as a result, exerted an influence on the development of collective bargaining as adverse as it had had in the postwar period, albeit in more persuasive disguise.

This is not to deny that certain changes were slowly taking place within the CGT. It was less dependent on the PCF than it had been earlier; by 1963 it had relaxed the conditions under which cooperation with other unions could be undertaken; and while its fundamental strategy may have been determined politically, its tactics showed more respect for labor-market considerations than they had earlier. These developments are insignificant, however, in comparison to those that took place in the Communist Confederazione Generale Italiana del Lavoro (CGIL) in Italy during the same period. They are also insignificant in relation to those in the CFTC that caused its change of name to CFDT in 1964.

Since 1944 the Catholic CFTC had been split between two tendencies. The majority of its members (until the early 1960s) "wished to retain its confessional outlook, its stable white-collar membership, and its restricted effectiveness. . . . [It was] close to the MRP, [and] remained loyal to Christian democracy." The minority, with a blue-collar constituency, "sought to emphasize the working-class heritage of the CFTC, to sever all confessional connections, and to attempt to gain members among non–Roman Catholic workers. . . . [Politically it looked to] a

48. Ross, "Party and Mass Organization," p. 523.
49. Adam, "Situation de la C.G.T.," p. 971.

new, non-doctrinaire Democratic Socialism."[50] The fruit of aggressive
organizing of industrial workers by the minority was control of the CFTC
in 1964.[51]

The above description of the goals of the minority also describes the
broad framework within which the CFDT, as it became, has since
operated. Within this framework, however, important differences of
emphasis emerged on a series of related issues. For the left in the CFDT
the commitment to democratic socialism meant workers' control, egalitarianism, societal analysis in class terms, and public ownership of
industry. Reformists, who saw their political home in the Socialist party,
looked to technocratic participation in incomes policy and planning to
influence patterns of investment in private industry and to secure
redistribution of income. Crosscutting both groups were those who saw
in the CFDT the vehicle of effective unionism. For them, workers'
control could be interpreted as bargaining over work conditions at the
plant; egalitarianism, taken as raising the wages of semiskilled workers
in relation to those of skilled workers, was a sensible union organizing
strategy, since the bedrock support of the CGT was among the skilled;
and participation in incomes policy could be worthwhile if the government or industry were prepared to buy it with an effective system for
negotiating wages set up at the industry level or lower.

The reaction of the CGT to these developments was ambivalent.
Workers' control challenged the communist philosophy of democratic
centralism; egalitarianism hit at its support among skilled workers;
participation in incomes policy or planning contradicted its insistence
on the impossibility of improvement under a Gaullist regime; and the
central aim of the CFDT—the establishment of effective bargaining—
threatened its own role as a class union. But at the same time, the
possibility of cooperative action, dormant since 1947, now emerged.
The CFDT sought cooperation with the larger CGT as a necessary
condition of serious pressure at all levels. And in contrast to the Christian
Democratic outlook of the older CFTC leaders, the CFDT regarded the
CGT as a potential ally, albeit with suspicion. The CGT, too, saw the
need for cooperation to make union action effective, and in 1966 a "unity-
in-action" agreement was signed between the two centrals. But the

50. Samuel H. Barnes, "The Politics of French Christian Labor," *Journal of Politics,*
vol. 21 (February 1959), p. 105.

51. For details, see Gérard Adam, "De la C.F.T.C. à la C.F.D.T.," *Revue française
de science politique,* vol. 15 (February 1965), pp. 87–103.

agreement predictably soon broke down. While the CFDT wanted cooperation at the plant or industry level, the dominant CGT desired such cooperation primarily for its national "days of action." During the 1950s the open hostility between the union confederations inhibited cooperation and hence union effectiveness. When the hostility did abate sufficiently to permit joint action, the CGT refused to allow it to be channeled toward the development of effective bargaining.

De Gaulle's Republic: The Industrial Imperative, Wage Restraint, and the Events of May 1968

In 1958 the Fourth Republic met its demise with the accession of de Gaulle to the presidency, which became a more powerful position under the constitution of the Fifth Republic. Economic policy between 1958 and 1968 falls into four periods. In 1958 and 1959 the government followed a policy of stabilization, with unemployment increasing sharply; the growth of real wages was moderated by ending wage indexation and by a de facto devaluation of the currency. From 1960 to 1963 policy was revised and rapid industrial growth was allowed to reflect the trade-growth boom of the Common Market in the early 1960s; attempts to impose wage restraint were unsuccessful, and double-digit wage increases in 1962–63 led to inflation and declining competitiveness and profitability. There followed a brief, abortive flirtation with an incomes policy based on agreement with the unions. And finally, from 1964 to 1968, the economy was run at a higher level of unemployment, wage restraint was imposed on the public sector and, through employers, on the private sector, and a vigorous policy of industrial reorganization was carried out. The result of these policies of the mid 1960s was the general strike of May 1968; this occurred in spite of the highest level of unemployment and excess capacity since 1960.

Several themes underlie this section. The first is the use by the government of the "labor market" option of ignoring the unions and gambling on the consequences. As explained in the preceding section the option existed because of union weakness. During both 1958–59 and 1964–68 the government reduced the short-run gamble by deflation, but the accumulation of grievances to which this led produced strike waves and wage explosions in the long term—in 1962–63 and again in 1968. Neither the option nor its consequences were confined to the private sector: imposition of wage restraint in the public sector during the period 1958–61 and between 1964 and 1968 also helped generate the strikes. A second theme, referred to earlier, is that of the convergence of short-run interest between de Gaulle and the PCF, particularly during the mid 1960s; the CGT did not for this reason seriously exploit the accumulating grievances in the labor market. Third, attention will be drawn through the 1960s to the parallels between French policy and that of other European governments, thus partially explaining the coincidence of the strike waves throughout Western Europe at the end of the decade. That May 1968 was more dramatic than elsewhere was in part attributable to the labor-market instability discussed above. But it was also attributable to a fourth theme of this section, that France had a greater need to change its industrial structure, and the French government had more power to do so, than governments in other countries.

De Gaulle's "industrial imperative" reflected his belief that French political strength must be based on a strong economy. It also reflected the weakness of the private sector of French industry. This weakness was the legacy of the inadequate economic structure and the defensive management mentality of the prewar economy. In 1938 the proportion of the labor force in agriculture, 31.4 percent, was similar to that in industry, 32.3 percent. By 1954 the corresponding figures were 26.1 percent and 35.7 percent. In addition, industry had a low rate of concentration.[52] The small size of French industrial establishments in the early 1960s compared to those of U.S. and German industry can be seen in table 10-6. Much attention was given by policymakers to the fact, noted by Carré, Dubois, and Malinvaud, that "France has few giant industrial groups comparable with those in the United States, or even in Japan, Germany, the Netherlands, or Britain."[53] The policy requirements were two: reorganization and moderation of real wages. The former was needed to change the structure of industry, the latter to provide both incentives and resources to invest. Moderation of the real cost of labor would thus improve international competitiveness; domestic inflation would thus be held back in relation to that of France's

52. J.-J. Carré, P. Dubois, and E. Malinvaud, *French Economic Growth* (Stanford, Calif.: Stanford University Press, 1975), pp. 91, 166. The concentration data for France were comparable only to those for Italy among the countries in this study.

53. Ibid., p. 170. Certain qualifications need to be made about the position in the early 1960s. First, considerable "financial" concentration took place from the mid 1950s, especially among medium-sized companies. Second, the proportion of large, but not giant, companies was not significantly different from that in other countries.

Table 10-6. *Distribution of the Industrial Labor Force, by Size of Establishment, in France (1962), Germany (1961), and the United States (1963)*

Percent

Firm size (number of employees)	France, 1962	Germany, 1961	United States, 1963
10–49	21	16	13
50–99	12	10	10
100–499	34	29	32
500–999	12	12	13
More than 1,000	21	33	32
Total	100	100	100

Source: J.-J. Carré, P. Dubois, and E. Malinvaud, *French Economic Growth* (Stanford, Calif.: Stanford University Press, 1975), table 6.4, p. 166.

competitors, and this in turn would buttress de Gaulle's political desire to strengthen the franc.

The policy adopted in 1958 and 1959 illustrates in a classic way the use a government can make of labor-market instability. Without adequate institutionalization, strike waves or periods of heightened militancy cannot last. Deflating the economy increases the probability that the militancy will collapse. This is indeed what happened in 1958. The number of strikes fell from 2,623 in 1957 to 954 in the following year (see table 10-1). The collapse of militancy implies a reduced equilibrium real wage. The adjustment of the actual real wage to the lower equilibrium level, however, may take time. The government telescoped the adjustment process, first by ending such indexation agreements as were in existence and then by a de facto devaluation of the franc, which allowed prices to rise in relation to wages. The result was a *decline* of 1.8 percent in the real wage in 1958, followed by increases of only 1.9 percent and 2.7 percent during the next two years; in 1957, on the other hand, real wages had risen 9.9 percent.

But policymakers of the early 1960s did not capitalize on these gains, despite the entry of France into the Common Market and the trade-growth boom that ensued. Policy during this period had encouraged industrial expansion by allowing demand reflation from the relatively high levels of unemployment between 1958 and 1960 (see table 10-2). Wage moderation in the private sector was to be secured by attempting to influence employers; in the public sector the authorities were to impose a slow growth rate of wages. In neither sector was any serious attempt made to gain the cooperation of the unions.

During the period 1960–63 output expanded rapidly, but structural change did not occur to any marked extent. The expansion of output, moreover, also contributed to the high level of worker militancy between 1961 and 1964 (see table 10-1). The suggested interpretation is that grievances accumulated during the period of high unemployment between 1958 and 1960; real wages, for instance, rose at an average of only 0.9 percent a year. A tightening of the labor market combined with these accumulated grievances to produce prolonged waves of strikes; the consequence was a high rate of growth of real wages between 1961 and 1964, averaging 6.1 percent a year (see table 10-2).

The analysis of attempted wage restraint is complicated by its differential effects in the public and private sectors. In neither sector were the attempts based on agreement with the unions. In the private sector the government used persuasion on employers' organizations at the industry level to exercise moderation in collective bargaining. While some official statements were made—the prime minister asked the Conseil National du Patronat Français in 1960 to restrict wage increases to 4 percent— the bulk of the pressure was informal. The policy was successful in reducing the incidence of industry bargaining; as Delamotte puts it, "during [1960–64] bargaining slackened and in some industries even came to a halt."[54] This testified to the power of the government over the CNPF and its industry federations. It also emphasized the inability of the unions to back up their demands for industry negotiations, despite widespread worker militancy at the plant level throughout much of the period. The success of the policy was more apparent than real, however. Industry negotiations concerned only minimum wage rates, and these indeed were held back. Earnings at the plant level, on the other hand, rose rapidly, as testified to by the growth of real wages.

In the public sector the government exercised unilateral control over wage increases. Believing that state wage moderation would influence the private sector, it held back public-sector wage increases. "This policy had some success," the Organisation for Economic Co-operation and Development adjudged, "up to 1960, but led to disparities between the increases granted in the private sector and those in the public sector.

54. See Delamotte, "Recent Collective Bargaining Trends," p. 356; see also OECD Economic Surveys, *France,* July 1963, p. 33.

Table 10-7. *Wage and Price Inflation in France, Germany, and the United States, 1960–70*

Percent

| | France | | | Germany, | United States | |
| | Administra- tive sector | Commercial sector | CPI deflator | CPI deflator | CPI deflator | Unemploy- ment rate |
Year	(1)	(2)	(3)	(4)	(5)	(6)
1960	6.7	8.5	4.1	1.3	2.0	5.6
1961	8.7	9.8	2.4	2.4	1.1	6.7
1962	17.0	10.8	5.2	3.0	1.1	5.6
1963	14.6	11.1	4.9	2.8	1.2	5.7
1964	4.5	9.2	3.1	2.4	1.3	5.2
1965	3.8	6.4	2.7	3.1	1.6	4.5
1966	4.8	6.6	2.6	3.7	3.1	3.8
1967	4.9	6.1	2.8	1.7	2.8	3.8
1968	12.5	11.1	4.6	1.5	4.1	3.6
1969	9.0	13.1	6.1	2.7	5.4	. . .
1970	9.6	10.5	5.9	3.8	5.9	. . .

Sources: Columns 1 and 2, Daniel J. B. Mitchell, "Incomes Policy and the Labor Market in France," *Industrial and Labor Relations Review*, vol. 25 (April 1972), table 3, p. 321; columns 3–6, Maynard and van Ryckeghem, *A World of Inflation*, pp. 80, 160.

The result was a prolonged period of unrest in the latter."[55] The accumulation of grievances up to 1961 as a result of widening differentials between the two sectors was aggravated by real-wage developments in the public sector. According to the 1961 OECD survey of the French economy, public-sector wages had still not quite regained their 1957 level by early 1960.[56] The result was a series of strikes beginning in 1961 and culminating in the miners' strike of early 1963. Table 10-7 shows wage increases in the administrative sector and the commercial sector; these correspond roughly to the public and private sectors, respectively, and illustrate clearly the substantial wage increases the government had to accord to the public sector in 1962 and 1963.

Whether or not the public sector affected the private sector—and the government continued in the mid 1960s to think it did—the growth of real industrial wages between 1961 and 1964 compromised both international competitiveness and profitability. A rough measure of the effect upon the former is provided in table 10-7. The two leading countries in world trade, on the basis of export shares of the world market, were the

55. OECD Economic Surveys, *France*, July 1963, p. 33.
56. Ibid., July 1961, p. 16.

598   FRANCE

Table 10-8. *Profit Margins in French Firms, 1951–67*
Percent

Year or period	Joint stock corporations	Publicly owned corporations
Average, 1951–55	8.9	18.5
	(0.36)	(5.65)
1956	8.0	16.0
1957	8.1	20.1
1958	7.9	22.4
1959	8.0	22.0
1960	8.0	13.5
1961	7.3	13.7
1962	6.8	13.1
1963	6.5	12.8
1964	6.7	13.4
1964	6.8[a]	
1965	7.5	
1966	6.9	
1967	6.9	

Source: Carré, Dubois, and Malinvaud, *French Economic Growth*, p. 301; table 9.8, p. 300. Numbers in parentheses are standard errors.
a. Separate figures for joint stock corporations and publicly owned corporations are not available beyond 1964.

United States and Germany. Table 10-7 makes clear how slowly U.S. prices grew during the early 1960s, and both France and Germany lost in relation to the United States during this period (1961–64). But French prices rose faster than German, so France also became less competitive than Germany. Profitability also suffered, as can be seen from table 10-8, where a comparison is made of profit margins in the early 1960s with those of the late 1950s.

Competitiveness declined because French money wages and prices grew faster than world prices in a system of fixed exchange rates. Devaluation would not have been other than a short-run solution, unless money illusion could have been relied on to moderate the growth of real wages. Its success in 1958 required a more rapid adjustment to the lower equilibrium real wage implied by higher unemployment; it was, in any case—even with the rise in unemployment in 1964–65—inconsistent with de Gaulle's aim to establish France as a power within the international monetary system. The increase in real wages caused a reduction in competitiveness insofar as French producers were unconstrained by world prices—that is, to the extent that the increased real wages were paid for by a reduced real cost of imports. And to the extent that world prices did act as a constraint, preventing producers from passing on wage increases fully, the rise in real wages had its counterpart in a fall in profitability. These effects were recognized by the government. "The planners . . . argue that . . . foreign competition restrained price increases in internationally competitive industries so that rising costs could not be passed on in rising prices."[57] In a world of perfect competition, the consequence of increased worker militancy would have been transient: normal profitability would have been restored domestically by those same forces of competition that would have eliminated discrepancies in purchasing power parity internationally. But the French government in 1963–64 did not feel that it could rely on market forces.

The government recognized publicly the need for a substantial increase in profitability. The aim of the fifth plan, formulated in 1964–65, was to increase profits at the rate of 8.6 percent a year between 1966 and 1970, while annual increases in wages per capita were to be held back to 3.3 percent during the same period.[58] The failure of the policies of wage restraint without consensus and industrial change in the expansionary context of the early 1960s led the government in two new directions. The first was an attempt to gain agreement with the unions on an incomes policy; the second, consisting of deflation, imposed wage restraint, and *dirigiste* industrial reorganization, dominated the period from 1964 to May 1968 and followed the collapse of talks on incomes policy.

The attempt to gain an incomes policy through consensus was unsuccessful. Despite prolonged discussions from October 1963 to January 1964, the possibility of agreement was never serious. It was against the interest of the CGT to be seen as cooperating with the government in any event. The strategy of the Communist union was to expose the exploitation of the French worker as a result of Gaullist economic policy. Only a political change, toward which such a strategy was aimed, could provide a framework within which collective agreements, genuinely benefiting the working class, could take place. Gérard Adam quotes a CGT leader as saying in 1966, in the context of other governmental negotiations, "We do not believe that it is possible to reach genuine agreements without a change of regime. It would be

57. Stephen S. Cohen, *Modern Capitalist Planning: The French Model*, rev. ed. (Berkeley: University of California Press, 1977), p. 180. "Rapport sur les principals options du Vᵉ plan," *Journal officiel, lois et décrets*, December 24, 1964, pp. 11406–07, is cited as evidence by Cohen.

58. Cohen, *Modern Capitalist Planning*, p. 186.

different if, after a general election, there was a democratic government."
This clearly states, Adam comments, that "to play the contractual game
with the government would run the risk of upsetting the process of union
demands for political change. It would implicitly be to admit the
possibility of social progress without the Communist Party or even the
Left in power."[59]

The government was not prepared to make political concessions to
the CGT; in place of economic concessions, moreover, the government
wanted real wage restraint, as noted above. The other area in which
concessions might have been made was in the development of genuine
bargaining institutions at the plant or company level. Such concessions
were demanded by the CFDT as the price of cooperation. But they were
bitterly opposed by the CNPF and were not of interest to the CGT. The
government was prepared to make only minor concessions, for two basic
reasons: the unions were weak and had limited control over their
members, so the value of their cooperation was limited, and the available
alternative policy of deflation, imposed wage restraint, and industrial
reorganization was one that the CGT could more easily accept for
political reasons.

A thesis pursued in this book is that the waves of industrial conflict in
Western European countries in the late 1960s were not coincidental.[60] It
is argued instead that they were each the product of similar national
economic policies and business strategies in the mid 1960s—notably of
wage restraint, deflation, and rationalization in one form or another.
These policies in turn were in reaction to the inflation and reduced
profitability that were the result of the European trade-growth boom of
the early 1960s associated with the development of the Common Market.
The form taken by these policies in France in the mid 1960s was deflation,
wage restraint (primarily in the public sector), price controls in the
private sector, and large-scale reorganization of key competitive industries for the purpose of increasing concentration.

The simultaneity of the strike waves in various countries can be
explained in this international economic perspective. The form that it

59. Gérard Adam, "L'Unité d'action C.G.T.-C.F.D.T.," *Revue française de science
politique*, vol. 17 (June 1967), p. 587.

60. For details, see David Soskice, "Strike Waves and Wage Explosions, 1968–
1970: An Economic Interpretation," in Colin Crouch and Alessandro Pizzorno, eds.,
The Resurgence of Class Conflict in Western Europe Since 1968, vol. 2: *Comparative
Analyses* (New York: Holmes and Meier, 1978), pp. 221–46.

took in France in May 1968, however, differentiates it from the strikes in other countries. Four factors explain much of this difference. First, the combination of instability and inadequate institutionalization in the labor market presented the Gaullist regime with a choice in the mid 1960s. On the one hand was a play-safe strategy: institutionalize the labor market to remove its instability, but in the process acknowledge some limitation on the extent of moderation of real wages and industrial reorganization. The alternative was to push through important economic changes during a four- or five-year period and to gamble that a serious destabilizing reaction in the labor market would not occur before the long-run benefits of the policy changes materialized. This same choice, as was stressed earlier, recurred throughout the 1970s.

The government could, and did, minimize the danger of labor-market instability by running the economy at a higher level of unemployment in the mid 1960s than in the period 1960–63. The gamble was also reduced by the broad political strategy adopted by de Gaulle toward the Communist party. As argued above, this second, political, factor was, in effect, an implicit compromise between the two parties. De Gaulle's right-wing economic and social policies and his foreign policy of independence from NATO and rapprochement toward the Soviet Union were in the long-run electoral interest of the PCF. The Communist party was therefore not prepared to challenge the regime or its basic policies.

The "positive aspects" of his foreign policy allowed [de Gaulle] to believe that he held such sway over those "who give prior service to a foreign power" that he no longer had to consider them a threat. . . . The P.C.F. [saw itself as constituting] an *opposing force* without being an *alternative*. Communists and Gaullists opposed but complemented each other; it was a controlled system of mutual aggression. This may explain the feeling of sham abounding in French political life at the time; the hostility which the two adversaries harbored for each other was by no means a pretense, but they were also aware of the need to contain their conflict within the boundaries of the rules of the game.[61]

As pointed out earlier, this implied that the CGT had an electoral function as opposed to a revolutionary or bargaining function.

These factors led the government to believe that it could impose unpopular policies on the labor market. Two further factors made the French situation different from that in other countries: the more pressing need for industrial change in France than elsewhere and the greater

61. Kriegel, "The French Communist Party and the Fifth Republic," pp. 74–75 (emphasis in original).

ability on the part of the French government, because of the particular nature of governmental industrial relations, to impose change upon private industry.

The deflationary measures taken by the government in 1964 slowly pushed up the rate of unemployment from 1.3 percent in 1963 to 1.5 percent in 1964 and 1965, 1.8 percent in 1966, 2.0 percent in 1967, and 2.6 percent in 1968.[62] Column 5 of table 10-2, which shows the logarithm of the ratio of unemployment to vacancies, gives a clearer picture of the loosening of the labor market, showing an increase from an average of 0.91 for 1962–64 to 1.62 for 1965–67.

In these looser labor markets, the government acted to restrain wages in both public and private sectors. In the public sector it used a new method for determining wage increases, developed in the Toutée report of 1964. The government had set up a committee under the chairmanship of André Toutée, a senior civil servant, to devise a method for giving unions a voice in wage determination in the public sector while retaining ultimate control itself. The report recommended that the government set an aggregate figure for wage increases in a particular sector while the precise distribution of those increases among various groups of workers would be the subject of union-management bargaining. While the intent of the report was to improve relations with the unions, "the government ignored those of Toutée's recommendations which aimed at achieving a better negotiating balance between the two sides, and announced without any discussion with them in May 1964 that the system had been adopted in a most restrictive form."[63]

Column 1 of table 10-7 shows the degree of success achieved by wage restraint in the public sector. Wages in the administrative sector rose at an average rate of only 4.5 percent during the four years 1964–67; the rise had been 9.25 percent in the preceding four years and 15.8 percent on the average in 1962 and 1963. Real wages rose 1.4 percent, 1.1 percent, 2.2 percent, and 2.1 percent between 1964 and 1967; they had risen 6.3 percent in 1961, 11.8 percent in 1962, and 7.9 percent in 1968 (column 1 less column 3, table 10-7). In addition, the wage differentials with the private sector (column 2), which had been partially restored by the 1962–63 increases, grew wider. If the ratio between the public and private

62. Organisation for Economic Co-operation and Development, "Methodological and Conceptual Problems of Measuring Unemployment in OECD Countries" (Paris: OECD, January 1976), p. 25.

63. Williams and Harrison, *Politics and Society,* p. 349.

sectors is taken as 100 in 1963, by 1967 it had fallen to 90.8. Grievances thus built up in the public sector, over both real wages and differentials. As Ulman and Flanagan wrote, "Pressure builds up for a quantum jump in lagging public wages and salaries. . . . During the French wage explosion of 1968, the greatest wage increases tended to be concentrated among groups of public employees whose wages had been subject to the most determined government restraint."[64] And Hayward agreed: "It was the failure of the incomes policy imposed in the public sector on the basis of these [Toutée's] proposals that contributed notably to the unrest which led to the general strike of May–June 1968."[65]

In the private sector, the government used price controls and contractual agreements with individual companies and sectors to enforce wage restraint. From 1964 through 1965 prices were controlled, and this provided a direct incentive to hold back wage increases. In 1966 a new form of agreement was instituted, the *contrat de programme*. These agreements gave producers pricing freedom to build up profit margins in exchange for guarantees on exports, investments, and wages. They were confidential between the government and the company or trade association involved; trade unions neither participated in establishing the agreements nor had rights to knowledge of their contents. The agreements were policed by biannual examinations by the Ministry of Finance and the Commissariat du Plan; the penalty for increasing wages above the government norm was a reimposition of price controls. By 1969 these agreements covered 85 percent of French industry.[66] How successful they were in restraining money wage increases in the private sector is difficult to say. In each of the years 1965 to 1967, money wage increases were about 6 percent (see table 10-9, column 1), whereas they had been about 10 percent in the preceding four years. What seems clear is that in 1967, the one full year in which these agreements were in operation, businesses took the opportunity to increase prices to increase profitability and wages increased 2.78 percent less than "room" (see table 10-9, column 3).

The government sought to improve profitability and international competitiveness as well as wage restraint by structural changes in

64. Lloyd Ulman and Robert J. Flanagan, *Wage Restraint: A Study of Incomes Policies in Western Europe* (Berkeley: University of California Press, 1971), p. 239.
65. J. E. S. Hayward, "State Intervention in France: The Changing Style of Government-Industry Relations," *Political Studies,* vol. 20 (September 1972), p. 290.
66. Ibid., p. 291.

Table 10-9. *Room Calculations and Mergers, France, 1960–67*

Year	Nominal wage increases (percent change in wages and salaries per employee) (1)	"Room" for nominal wage increases (percent change in value of GDP per worker) (2)	Difference (col. 2 − col. 1) (3)	Value of mergers (millions of francs) (4)
1960	7.96	5.7	−2.26	165
1961	9.58	11.26	1.68	230
1962	11.70	9.22	−2.48	202
1963	11.32	6.66	−4.66	298
1964	8.50	2.88	−5.62	164
1965	6.20	7.14	0.94	279
1966	6.34	6.11	−0.23	817
1967	5.79	8.57	2.78	759

Sources: Column 1, OECD Economic Surveys, *France*, March 1970, table D, p. 74; column 2, ibid., table A, p. 71, and table F, p. 76; column 4, Ezra N. Suleiman, "Industrial Policy Formulation in France," in Steven J. Warnecke and Ezra N. Suleiman, eds., *Industrial Policies in Western Europe* (New York: Praeger Publishers, 1975), table 1.1, p. 27.

industry. The agreements discussed above were also used to tie companies into the government's plans for reorganizing industry.

With the 5th Plan (1966–70) the "industrial imperative" was more clearly expressed. "The irrevocable acceptance of economic competition" imposed a policy of selective growth. The accent was placed on the need for restructuring the main branches of industry by bringing into being one or two major groups within each branch. . . . The State played a decisive role, whether by setting an example in the public sector (oil, chemicals, aircraft industry) or by providing a large share of the finance required in the private sector (iron and steel, information systems), or again by taking a series of incentive measures (tax reliefs, government contracts).[67]

Column 4 of table 10-9 shows the success of the government in bringing about large-scale mergers from 1966 on. The mergers were accompanied by rationalization. According to Okun's law, a higher rate of unemployment is associated with lower growth in productivity. But the growth of productivity in 1965 and 1966 declined little from its rate during the years of great activity, 1961–64; in a similar comparison, in the 1950s productivity fell from 5.1 percent for 1955–57 to 2.3 percent for 1958–59 (see table 10-2). This suggests that businesses took advantage of loose labor markets to bring about substantial rationalization during the mid 1960s. Many observers have pointed to the relationship between these changes and the general strike of May 1968. Dubois, Durand, and

67. OECD, *The Industrial Policy of France* (Paris: OECD, 1974), p. 35.

Erbès-Seguin surveyed the structural transformations of industry in the mid 1960s and observed, "Given such an economic background, May 1968 can be seen as being less of an upheaval than may be thought."[68]

The administration was aware that these developments might cause problems in the labor market. After 1965 it put pressure on the CNPF to negotiate, particularly on issues of employment. The principal agreement arrived at, the Lorraine Iron and Steel Agreement of July 1967, placed various responsibilities on the employer to minimize the effect of structural change. Few agreements were reached, however, and employers were half-hearted in their support. In an analysis shortly after May 1968, the causes of the May strike waves, at least with respect to the private sector, were summarized by the government's *Rapport sur les problèmes posés par l'adaptation du Vème plan* as "a failure to comprehend the resistance to change, to prepare the groundwork for unprecedented dislocations resulting from mergers, combinations, business failures, layoffs, and dismissals, which accompanied modernisation. The changes on the labour market had come with greater rapidity than anticipated, too much reliance had been placed on the automatic adjustments, the mobility, of the market mechanism."[69]

Our framework for the analysis of strike waves suggested that, in a weakly organized labor market, the accumulation of grievances—"bottling-up"—was a necessary condition for a strike wave. By 1968 there was an accumulation of grievances in the labor market for all the reasons described above: wage restraint in both public and private sectors and rationalization in industry. Because of weak organization, what was also needed was some signal to which workers could respond in the knowledge that their action would be similar to that in factories elsewhere. In general, this occurs in a tight labor market, as in 1962–63 or 1955–57. The events of May 1968, however, showed that where the sense of grievance is strong enough and the external signal clear enough, a strike wave can occur in a loose labor market. The near insurrectionary success of the student revolt in Paris in early May provided the necessary signal, and by the end of May, France was engulfed in a massive general strike.

The instability of the labor market, which enabled grievances to build up, characterized France and Italy but not other countries. Why, then,

68. Pierre Dubois, Claude Durand, and Sabine Erbès-Seguin, "The Contradictions of French Trade Unionism," in Crouch and Pizzorno, eds., *The Resurgence of Class Conflict*, vol. 1; *National Studies*, p. 58.

69. OECD, *Manpower Policy in France* (Paris: OECD, 1973), p. 41.

were there strike waves elsewhere? To this there are two related answers. First, the strike waves elsewhere were not as dramatic as those in France and Italy. But second, they *did* occur largely because grievances developed and there was no safety valve. The German and British experiences illustrate this: in both countries, the unions cooperated with the government in imposing wage restraint, and in Germany they did not feel able, for legal or other reasons, to intervene effectively at the plant level to prevent rationalization. Hence workers, especially in the public sector in the United Kingdom and in iron and steel and engineering in Germany, were left without institutional recourse.

One important point remains to be made about May 1968, namely, that it produced little change compared to the Hot Autumn in Italy in 1969. The reason lies substantially in the difference between the behavior of the CGT and that of the CGIL. The CGIL, with a flexibility that reflected the internal changes in the Italian unions from the late 1950s on, channeled the upsurge of worker militancy into the establishment of shop-floor power in large factories. The CGT, on the other hand, was determined to bring the movement of May 1968 to an end as quickly as could be decently arranged. It was not interested in developing power on the shop floor that might challenge its own control; it was concerned instead lest the general strike become insurrectionary and thus be used by the government to take measures against the Communist party. The significance of May 1968 was not that it was a revolution that failed— few enough workers were interested in such a possibility; what was missed was the opportunity for the CGT to develop a real and powerful trade union movement based on the shop floor.[70]

Divergent Reactions to the May Events

The French government reacted to the events of May 1968 in two opposed ways. The first corresponded to the direct economic problem generated by the Grenelle agreement between the government, the unions, and the CNPF, which settled the general strike. The agreement provided for an increase in money wages of about 14 percent, implying

70. An excellent account of May 1968 is given in David Goldey, "A Precarious Regime: The Events of May 1968," in Philip M. Williams, with David Goldey and Martin Harrison, eds., *French Politicians and Elections, 1951–1969* (Cambridge: Cambridge University Press, 1970), pp. 226–60.

a substantial increase in real wages and consequent decline in profitability and international competitiveness. This first policy sought to rebuild profitability by reflation, exploiting the existence of short-run increasing returns; at the same time, the government gambled that real wages could be reduced by price increases without effective opposition from workers. The second policy, which followed the first, corresponded to the indirect problem that the May events had underlined: the conflict between labor-market instability and medium-term economic requirements. When rising real wages had made the first strategy redundant through 1969, a second strategy—that of institution building designed to reduce labor-market instability—was developed. In the year following May 1968 the government gambled with the labor market while rebuilding profits; in the three subsequent years, through 1972, it attempted to build an effective system of industrial relations.

Rebuilding Profits, Ignoring the Unions

In the immediate aftermath of the May events the government took the rebuilding of profitability as its objective. In figure 10-1, the government's options in achieving this objective are set out geometrically. Empirical work suggests that prices are based on average costs at normal use of capacity, as opposed to actual average costs.[71] With constant short-run returns—that is, with average productivity constant—unit profit margins are determined by the real wage alone; the margins are invariant with respect to changes in the level of activity. With the real wage held constant, however, short-run increasing returns to labor imply that unit profitability rises as output and employment increase.[72] This is shown in panel A of figure 10-1. The curves $\pi_0 \, \pi_0$ and $\pi_{pre68} \, \pi_{pre68}$ are isoprofit curves, the former tracing out the combinations of the real wage and the level of employment at which unit profits are zero, the latter the combinations at which unit profits are equal to the pre–May 1968 level. The $\pi_{pre68} \, \pi_{pre68}$ schedule must pass through the point A if E_{pre68} is the level of employment before May 1968, and $F(E, 0)$ is the pre–May 1968 negotiable real wage schedule. It is to the level of profits immediately before May that, it will be assumed, government policy aimed to return.

71. OECD Economic Surveys, *France,* February 1972, p. 16.
72. The microeconomic justification of the implied failure of businesses to equate the real wage with the marginal product of labor is that, as oligopolies, they face a kinked demand curve; the reasoning is set out in chapter 1.

Figure 10-1. *Rebuilding Profitability in France after May 1968:
The Available Options*

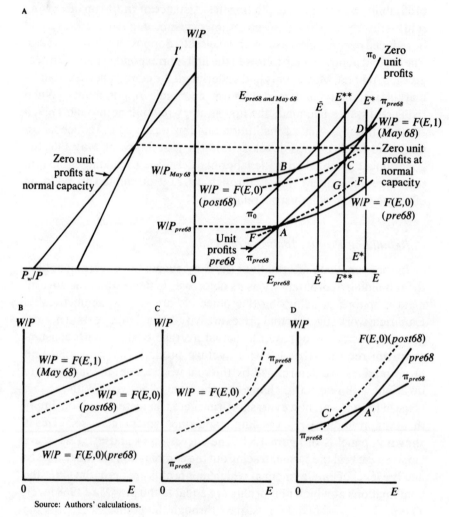

Source: Authors' calculations.

The negotiable real wage schedule of May 1968 is $F(E, 1)$; it implies
that before any changes in aggregate demand and employment had been
brought about the economy was at point B. Given the lack of effective
bargaining institutions to maintain $F(E, 1)$, the applicable real wage
schedule after May 1968, $F(E, 0)$ (*post68*), was at least no higher than
$F(E, 1)$. A possible configuration is shown in figure 10-1, panel B.

In order to move to a point on $\pi_{pre68}\,\pi_{pre68}$ while remaining on the line $F(E, 0)$ (*post68*), three policies, not mutually exclusive, were available.

1. The $\pi_{pre68}\,\pi_{pre68}$ schedule could be shifted up; in the short run this could be and was achieved by reducing employers' social security contributions (see below).

2. In principle, $F(E, 0)$ (*post68*) could have been shifted down; since this would have required an incomes policy, and since such a policy was no more politically feasible than in 1964, this was not a serious possibility.

3. Given $F(E, 0)$ (*post68*) and $\pi_{pre68}\,\pi_{pre68}$, the government could adopt an employment policy to attain a point on both schedules; in panel A of figure 10-1 the requisite point is C. The belief of the government was that such a point could be reached by reflation. This was indeed the policy followed: short-run increasing productivity would both rebuild profitability and enable the required level of real wages to be paid.

One qualification needs to be made to the above schema: the classification of policies assumed that the schedule $F(E, 0)$ (*post68*) was known, and that it intersected the line $\pi_{pre68}\,\pi_{pre68}$ at a level of employment above E_{pre68}. The assumption that it was known is incorrect, at least in the short run. Further, in the short run, even given the level of employment, the government can influence the real wage. Its ability to do so in 1968 and 1969 was based in particular on its discretion over renegotiating the Grenelle settlement of the May events to take account of subsequent increases in the cost of living. Thus one possibility was that the government might attempt to impose too low a real wage. This is illustrated by point G in figure 10-1, panel A: assume that FF is the π_{pre68} line (instead of $\pi_{pre68}\,\pi_{pre68}$); the government sets $E = E^{**}$ in the mistaken belief that $F(E, 0)$ (*post68*) passes through the point G; and by refusing to reopen the Grenelle settlement, the government causes the real wage to fall from B to G. While profitability is restored by this policy, it can work only in the very short run. And the risk is run that when a visible and common grievance is created the rise of the real wage from G to C through micro market mechanisms will be superseded by a new strike wave and end in a real wage higher than C.

The second problem associated with $F(E, 0)$ (*post68*) is that it may not intersect with $\pi_{pre68}\,\pi_{pre68}$; alternatively, the intersection may occur at a level of employment below E_{pre68}. The former case is illustrated in panel C of figure 10-1, the latter in panel D. In neither case can reflation restore profitability except in the very short run. And in both cases attempts by the government to keep the real wage down carry dangers similar to those suggested in the preceding paragraph.

The strategy actually followed by the government from May 1968 to the middle of 1969 had three strands. The element of the strategy most widely remarked corresponded to policy 3 above. This was the reflation of demand designed to secure the increase in profitability as a result of short-run economies of scale. According to figure 10-1, panel A, aggregate demand was increased so as to raise employment from E_{pre68} to E^{**}; hence the intention was to move from B to C, and thus back to the pre-Grenelle isoprofit line, $\pi_{pre68}\ \pi_{pre68}$. An OECD summary of the official French position was that "the dynamics of the new strategy would be to capitalise on the possibilities for rapid increases in productivity that seemed realistically possible with a moderately strong expansionary policy."[73]

The reflation policy was complemented by partial fiscalization of the contributions of employers to social security in particular and by changes in price controls. These were type 1 policies, since they had the effect of shifting the isoprofit line upward. Little evidence is available on the details of the changes in price controls. Controls seem to have been used in the immediate aftermath of May to allow businesses not to pass on in the form of lower prices the cost reductions attributable to fiscalization and to move their prices closer to world prices. With an ambiguity that occurs at other points in the Grenelle agreement, clause 13 states: "The CNPF asked that, as from July 1968, French businesses should not be subject to stricter price controls than those pertaining to their competitors in other EEC countries."[74]

The third strand of the strategy was to absorb the money wage increases of the Grenelle settlement by subsequent price increases. To describe the policy in these terms, however, is somewhat misleading. Suppose, for example, that the bargaining power of the unions at Grenelle, shown as $F(E, 1)$ in figure 10-1, panel A, had been effectively consolidated thereafter: thus $F(E, 0)$ (post68) would have been identical with $F(E, 1)$. In that case, if employment was maintained at E_{pre68}, price increases could not have reduced the real wage below $W/P_{May\ 68}$ because subsequent wage increases would have returned the economy to B. It is therefore clearer to state the third strand of the strategy as follows: the government gambled that $F(E, 0)$ (post68) was sufficiently far below $F(E, 1)$ that union pressure to reopen negotiations in March 1969 for

73. OECD, *Manpower Policy in France*, p. 41.
74. Reynaud, *Les Syndicats en France*, vol. 2, p. 250.

cost-of-living increases could be ignored. The Grenelle agreement, clause 12, had stated: "The government will meet with unions and CNPF, in March 1969, to examine with them in the general economic and financial context, the evolution of purchasing power during 1968." The government interpreted this clause literally: while acknowledging the substantive price increases that had occurred during 1968, they denied any commitment to compensating wage increases.

The government envisaged, in this third element in its strategy, that price increases through 1968 would absorb the increases in money wages and that subsequent pressure for cost-of-living wage increases could be ignored. Even if this pressure could be ignored, however, a problem arose over declining international competitiveness. For, if the wage increases were fully passed on in the form of high prices, French competitiveness would fall at an equal rate. Thus the strategy required, for completeness, a devaluation of the franc. This would have restored competitiveness and fully annulled the initial increase in real wages. However, de Gaulle refused devaluation in late 1968 for reasons that had essentially to do with foreign policy. The legacy of the economic strategy was a deterioration of international competitiveness and a gamble on labor-market quiescence, which by mid 1969 was beginning to look increasingly risky.

Why did the government choose to gamble in this manner? In the first place, the election of a conservative Gaullist majority in June 1968, as a backlash to the events of May, made it politically infeasible to attempt to enlist union cooperation in restraining wages. And in the second place, it would have been difficult, to say the least, to secure such cooperation.

An impediment to effective union action was the hostility between the CGT and the CFDT, which the events of May 1968 brought into the open. The CFDT strategy of supporting militant local action, often among less highly skilled workers, was greatly boosted by the radical ideology of May. This CFDT strategy conflicted both with the CGT's relative neglect of less highly skilled workers and with its tactics of building large-scale national protest strikes. The radical ideology of workers' control, which had soaked into large sections of the "porous" CFDT during the May events, conflicted with the central planning and nationalization approach of the CGT and the PCF.[75] Thus, although the CFDT moved leftward ideologically as a result of the May events, the

75. Ross, "Party and Mass Organization," p. 529.

CGT felt threatened by the competition. At least until the middle of 1969 there was little effective cooperation between the two confederations.

The unions also set store by the government commitment in the Grenelle agreement to establish trade-union rights legally in the plant. Enacted in December 1968, the Law on Trade Union Rights in the Company allows nationally representative unions to establish a local in each company of more than fifty employees; to designate up to four union officials (depending on firm size) who would be protected against unemployment, would have time off with pay, and would be given physical facilities; to collect dues on the premises, though outside working hours, and to hold a monthly meeting of members under similar conditions; to distribute pamphlets and be provided with a notice board. The CGT did not see this law as a step toward plant-level bargaining. Instead, the designated officials were seen as representatives of the union. Although in practice only officials acceptable to the work force would be appointed by the union, the appointment was legally for the union to make. The CGT opposed the "autonomous" interpretation— that the officials were primarily the representatives of the work force— with their view that they had gained a legal entrée, which they could control, into the plants. Thus the law was of great value to the CGT. The unambiguous commitment to it in the Grenelle agreement is in apparent conflict with the ambiguity of the cost-of-living reopener clause. One hypothesis is therefore that the government and the CGT implicitly agreed that the CGT would moderate wage demands in return for the legislation. If the hypothesis is correct, the strategy ranks as an incomes policy with institutional protection—that is, with an agreed shift downward of $F(E, 0)$ (*post68*)—rather than as a gamble—that is, taking the risk that $F(E, 0)$ (*post68*) may be higher than the government assumed.

Finally, the May events, unlike the Hot Autumn of 1969 in Italy, modified but did not fundamentally alter the balance of power. As will be seen, the workers gained more power both in the plants and at higher levels, but the increase in power was of uncertain extent and still left the government free, at least in the short run, to ignore the unions.

How successful, in the short run, were the three elements of the government's economic strategy? It is possible to gain a rough idea of orders of magnitude by a two-step procedure. In the first step the effects of the three elements—expansion, fiscalization, and changes in money wages—on unit costs are evaluated. In the second step these effects are compared with concurrent price increases to discover the effects on profitability. The crudeness of this exercise needs to be stressed: the quarterly data used are not strictly comparable, and several rough assumptions have been made about parameters. However, the French "experiment" attracted attention, some observers regarded it as a successful adjustment to the strike waves of the late 1960s, and it was a method followed in no other large country.

In table 10-10, columns 3, 4, and 5, the effects on unit costs of the three elements of the government's strategy are evaluated. Column 5 shows the percentage change in unit costs at normal capacity operation, $\overline{uc}$, eliminating the effects of expansion, and without account of fiscalization. Thus column 5 gives a measure of the effect of wage changes on unit costs. In the second and third quarters of 1968 the net effect was on the order of 8 percent. The increase in wages was 12 percent, and the difference is accounted for by trend productivity growth and a slow growth of unit material costs. The low growth of $\overline{uc}$ in the last quarter of 1968 and the first quarter of 1969 reflects the low rate of wage increases after the Grenelle settlement.

Column 4 shows the effect of economic expansion in reducing unit costs. The variable $\tilde{uc}$ is the percentage change in unit labor costs—difficult to convert into unit costs because of the form of the data—with no allowance for fiscalization. Thus $\tilde{uc} - \overline{uc}$ provides a rough measure of the cost-reducing effect of expansion. This was less marked than has sometimes been supposed. Much of the increase in the use of capacity (see table 10-11) in 1968 took place without an increase in employment, while in 1969 the expansion required a sizable increase in the number of jobs. Hence column 4 in table 10-10 shows reductions in 1968, balanced by increases in unit costs in 1969.

Column 3 gives a measure of the effect on unit costs of fiscalization: uc is the actual change in unit labor costs, so $uc - \tilde{uc}$ is the change caused by fiscalization. This element unambiguously reduced unit costs in both 1968 and 1969.

A measure of the development of profitability, albeit rough, is provided by a comparison of the rate of price inflation of industrial goods with the inflation of unit costs. The last quarter of 1968 and the first and second quarters of 1969 are seen as quarters in which the losses of profitability of the second and third quarters of 1968 were recouped. Except during 1968 itself, expansion of the economy appears not to have been as important an influence as is sometimes believed. The net cumulative effect of expansion between the second and third quarters of 1968 was

Table 10-10. Rebuilding Profitability, France, 1968–69

Year and quarter	Rate of inflation of industrial prices $(\dot{p})$ (1)	Percent change in unit labor cost $(\dot{uc})$ (2)	Percent change in unit labor cost because of fiscalization $(\dot{uc} - \dot{\overline{uc}})$ (3)	Percent change in unit labor cost because of expansion $(\dot{\overline{uc}} - \dot{\overline{uc}})$ (4)	Percent change in unit cost at normal capacity $(\dot{\overline{uc}})$ (5)	Hourly wage rates in manufacturing (6)	Inflation rate minus rate of change in unit labor cost $(\dot{p} - \dot{uc})$ (7)
1968:2	−1.5	3.01	...	−0.76	3.77	5.99	−4.51
3	1.7	3.26	...	−0.82	4.08	6.16	−1.56
4	2.8	−3.92	−1.50	−2.78	0.36	1.82	6.72
1969:1	3.5	0.85	−2.43	3.07	0.21	1.66	2.65
2	2.3	0.06	−0.20	−0.26	0.52	2.15	2.24
3	3.2	2.54	−0.20	1.76	0.98	2.29	0.66
4	...	...	...	...	...	1.82	6.72

Sources: Column 1, INSEE, *Fresque historique*; columns 2–6, computed from OECD Economic Surveys, *France*, successive issues.

Table 10-11. *Percentage of Firms Operating at Full Capacity, France, 1967–69, from Four Monthly Surveys*

Year and quarter	Percent	Year and quarter	Percent	Year and quarter	Percent
1967:1	. . .	1968:1	15	1969:1	35
2	20	2	23	2	42
3	17	3	28	3	43

Source: OECD Economic Surveys, *France*, 1970, diagram, p. 22; the figures represent the percentage of firms reporting their inability to expand production, from a survey of manufacturing industries made by INSEE.

to increase unit costs by 0.05 percent. Fiscalization reduced unit costs by 4.33 percent cumulatively during the same period. And the policy of allowing prices to increase while wages were held back was also of importance: a comparison of columns 1 and 5 gives an indication of this effect.

Toward a New Society

In 1968 and 1969 the consequences for profitability of the May events appeared to have been solved. To the extent that the solution involved allowing domestic prices to rise in relation to world prices, however, long-run balance-of-payments difficulties were created. And insofar as the solution relied on a lower rate of unemployment, the consequences for real wages were beginning to emerge by the middle of 1969. The "gamble on wages" was not working: to be successful, devaluation required lower real wages to reduce p/p_w (the ratio of domestic to world prices), and the rise in wages, even without devaluation, threatened to eat into profits.

Thus the methods of attacking the immediate economic difficulties of May 1968 worked only in the short run. The long-term problems had not been faced when Pompidou became president in June 1969. These were of two sorts. First, the May events had brought about changes in the system of industrial relations, in the form of increases of uncertain extent in the power of the work force from the shop floor up. Second, the May events underlined the dangers of labor-market instability, thus raising the need to come to grips with the underlying causes.

The election of Pompidou and the appointment of Jacques Chaban-Delmas as prime minister signaled a major change of policy. While the "Gaullist" strategy of industrialization was to be maintained as the centerpiece of economic policy, it was acknowledged that such a strategy in an insufficiently institutionalized labor market generated strains that were seen as a central contributory factor to the strike waves of May 1968. By the same token, the policy of holding back public-sector wages through the Toutée system had aggravated the instability of the labor market. The perceived danger in a repetition of the May events was not only economic: it was also political. The government was thus prepared to pay a substantial price to be able to attack the root causes. Institution-alization of the labor market in both the public and private sectors would eliminate the causes of the May events; in addition, it fitted into a framework for dealing with the consequence of these strikes—the increase, however uncertain, in the power of unions and workers at most levels. But this approach neglected the short-run economic problem of moderating the growth of real wages. For if the outcomes of negotiations were to be enticing enough for unions to involve themselves in a more deeply institutionalized system, the real-wage requirements of the bal-ance of payments and profitability might not be met. The government appears to have had in mind a strategy for the longer run: institutionali-zation would reduce instability by involving unions in effective bargain-ing; in turn unions would shed their political links and focus on the economic interests of their members as their goals; finally, the result would be "pragmatic" unions with which, implicitly or explicitly, the government could negotiate over incomes policy, rationalization of industry, and labor-market policy.

The government acted on two fronts. It attempted to develop effective wage bargaining in the public sector, and in the private sector it helped and pushed the Patronat into bargaining with the unions at all levels. This was the general aim of involving the unions in effective bargaining; a particular aim was to provide through such bargaining the type of redundancy, training, and work conditions seen as the necessary social framework for the strategy of industrialization.

Wage Bargaining in the Public Sector

To be drawn into public-sector wage bargaining, the unions needed to be convinced that negotiations would be with the management of the public undertaking and not with the state. Previously, as Jacques Delors, Chaban's social counselor and the architect of his policy toward indus-trial relations, argued, "even with the Toutée procedure, the negotiating parties had the impression that it was the State which unilaterally took the decision." Negotiations "without the intervention of the State" were put forward as "the advantages of the *contrat de progrès* [as the public-sector wage bargains were called] for the social partners."[76] The state, however, was not to be without influence on the general form the *contrats de progrès* were to take. The government's desire was for multiyear contracts designed to reduce the unpredictability of industrial relations: it was intended that increased prices and productivity, national or firm-specific, during the life of the contract would be contingently compensated to prevent a buildup of worker discontent, that no strikes over matters covered by the contract would be permitted while it was in effect, and that although the unions would be able to denounce, or terminate, the contract, three months' notice would be required. National as well as firm-specific factors would enter into the determination of wages, both to provide incentives and to enable workers to understand needs other than those related to their own industry.

The first important agreement in the public sector was signed in December 1969 between Electricité et Gaz de France (EGF) and the main unions, with the exception of the CGT. The agreement was to run for two years and provided for annual wage increases according to the formula

$$\dot{W} = 1 + 0.5G\dot{D}P + 0.15\,(\dot{Q}_{E,G} - 2.5\dot{E}_{E,G}),$$

where *GDP* is the value of gross domestic product, and $Q_{E,G}$ and $E_{E,G}$ are output and employment, respectively. Thus the formula echoed the main lines of the government requirements.

It was significant that the agreement was not signed by the CGT, which was suspicious of both the general Chaban initiative and the particular form it took in the EGF contract. The underlying reasons for the reticence of the CGT can be found in our earlier analysis of CGT-PCF relations and PCF strategy. The aim of the CGT was for high-level, high-visibility bargaining, as often as possible and with as little commitment as possible. This implied freedom to denounce contracts at the most opportune moment. More specifically, the CGT feared identification of the worker with the interests of the industry or the national economy. What it wanted from negotiations was wage increases without strings attached and guaranteed only against subsequent price increases.

76. Reynaud, *Les Syndicats en France*, vol. 2, p. 269.

In this light, the EGF contract seemed a trap: on the one hand, it was economically attractive, but it was also a multiyear agreement, with an effective labor peace clause, linking the interests of workers to the industry and the national economy and in the process fudging the notion of maintenance of the real purchasing power of the wage increase. The CGT held a token strike and called and won a referendum in the industry against the agreement.

The hostility of the CGT was backed up by moves toward unity on the part of the CFDT and the CGT. In late 1969 regular contacts between the two federations commenced again. In the 1970 CFDT congress, the class struggle was formally endorsed. By mid 1970 the CFDT had been won over into opposing labor peace clauses and multiyear contracts. And in December 1970 a new unity-in-action agreement was signed.

The government accepted most of the demands of the CGT in the main subsequent *contrats de progrès*—in 1970 in the railways in February, in the coal mines in March, and in the Paris Transport System in October, and in early 1971 in the railways and mines again, in Renault, and in EGF.[77] With Chaban's aim of union involvement—of the CGT and the CFDT in particular—this was an understandable compromise. The *contrats de progrès* from then on have embodied a straight money wage increase with a safeguard clause on prices. In the 1971 agreements, the safeguard clause took a threshold form; for any rise in the consumer price index of more than 4 percent, there would be one-for-one compensation for wages.[78]

If Chaban failed to incorporate all the original ideas into the *contrats de progrès,* he succeeded in part in the aim of drawing the unions in the public sector into a somewhat closer negotiating relationship with the government. This had its costs: the unions came to believe that they could get guaranteed increases in real wages; the government, as Barre was to discover, had to run greater risks than before if it was to switch again to the option of ignoring the unions. Chaban achieved a more predictable system of negotiations and union involvement in the public sector, but it fell far short of providing a framework for incomes policy bargaining after 1974 in which real wages would be moderated to restore profitability.

77. Delamotte, "Recent Collective Bargaining Trends," pp. 369–70; and OECD Economic Surveys, *France,* April 1971, annex 2, pp. 67–69.
78. Ibid.

The Development of Bargaining in the Private Sector

Chaban had two goals in promoting bargaining in the private sector. The first corresponded to the consequences of the May events and the second to their causes. The consequence, the growth of worker power within a still anarchic system of industrial relations, and the general cause, the underlying instability of the labor market, were to be met by the institutionalization of bargaining relationships. The specific cause of the May events, at least with respect to the private sector, was located in the inability of the labor-market mechanism to meet the problems caused by rapid modernization of industry. What was needed was to use bargaining in the private sector to develop institutions that would appropriately augment or replace the market. In particular, measures were required to provide greater employment security and improved training and unemployment benefits to meet necessary redundancies. This entailed interconfederal agreements between the CNPF and the union centrals that could be articulated down to the industrial level. Such high-level agreements had the added advantage of CGT support.

It was not only the government that actively canvassed such changes in the private sector. The CNPF itself had been moving, first slowly in the mid 1960s under pressure from the government, then more strongly under the influence of an analysis of the May events similar to that of the government. Within the Patronat, however, there was considerable opposition to change, particularly among the small and medium-sized firms. There were several reasons for this opposition. The profitability of smaller firms was thought unlikely to have been improved by the 1968–69 expansion, on the assumption that small firms, generally able to behave competitively in pushing output to the point of zero marginal profits, do not have significant short-run economies of scale; thus the need to restore profitability was likely to have been of greater importance than long-run stability. Second, the unions were weak in small companies, so little was to be gained and much potentially might be at risk through "giving away" institutionalization. Finally, the program of high-level negotiations entailed a more centralized structure of power in the CNPF, and this reduced the influence of small firms.

To overcome the opposition and to meet the organizational requirements, a major centralization of the CNPF,[79] the most significant change since its reinception in 1946, was brought about by the largest companies, which in effect financed the confederation. The powers of the president and the executive committee to negotiate agreements binding on CNPF members were increased, and they were charged with "determining the general policy of the organization." Particularly between 1969 and 1971 under François Ceyrac, as vice president for social affairs (he became president in 1972), the CNPF participated in the negotiation of a series of agreements at the interconfederal level. The important agreements were on employment security in February 1969, training both for employed manual workers and for those made or about to be made redundant in July 1970 (a further agreement was made in 1971 for white-collar workers), salary status (carrying with it additional security) in February 1970, and maternity leave in July 1970. The content of the agreements as they affected employment security and unemployment provisions will be discussed later.

These agreements were not realized solely at the instance of a reformed CNPF. In both content and style of negotiation they reflected the demands made by the CGT as early as the mid 1960s. Thus, unlike the *contrats de progrès,* these agreements found some consensus with the principal union confederation. Of importance too was the impetus from the government, in the form of persuasion, financial help—the costs of the measures were borne in part by the government—and legislative extension. The agreements were, in effect, tripartite negotiations in which the government was an essential partner.

The significance of these developments went beyond the content of the accords. While the CNPF had made moves before 1968 in the direction now followed, the moves had been hesitant and had been made largely at the insistence of the government. But now the CNPF, or at least the large firms, took an important part of the initiative. This not only implied a change in attitude; it also meant that business was prepared to bear at least part of the cost, given the international price constraint, of expensive reforms. The implication is that the members of the CNPF were shaken by the May events into realization of the importance of dealing with the unions.

The initiative of the government was directed toward wage bargaining in the public sector and—with the CNPF—at interconfederal agreements

79. For details of CNPF, see Reynaud, *Les Syndicats en France,* vol. 1, pp. 33–62.

in the private sector. These developments affected bargaining at other levels in the private sector in two ways. The interconfederal agreements were articulated down to sectoral agreements. Between April and December 1970, for example, eighteen industry or regional agreements on salaried status were recorded. The second effect was an "imitation" in the private sector of the *contrats de progrès*. Five million private-sector workers were estimated to have been covered in the early 1970s by agreements with cost-of-living reopeners.[80]

With these changes, induced by the government or the CNPF, went an increase in bargaining at both the industry and plant levels. This increase stemmed from the changes in workers' perceptions of their potential power brought about by the events of May 1968. While there are no adequate statistics, plant-level bargaining certainly increased after 1968. This was aided by the law of trade-union rights in the plant. In addition, an amendment in 1971 to the law of 1950 on collective bargaining established the validity of plant-level agreements, among other things. "The changes in men's minds as well as in the law are such that there can no longer be any question of refusing to bargain at this level."[81] One statistical indicator of this change is the numbers of strikes in successive years after 1968. As can be seen in column 1 of table 10-12, the average number of strikes in 1969–73 was 75 percent higher than the average number for the years 1960–67. If comparison is made with column 1 of table 10-1, moreover, the numbers of strikes in the period 1969–73 appear less sensitive to labor-market indicators than in the earlier period.

Two further sets of statistics support the view that union activity grew significantly at the plant level during the period 1968–73. The law of December 1968 allowing the establishment of union locals within the plant was reflected in the near doubling of locals between 1969 and 1973 in about 30,000 companies surveyed by the Ministry of Labor; this is set out in column 2 of table 10-12. A similar, though less regular, increase is observed in the number of establishments holding *comité d'entreprise* elections (see table 10-12, column 3).

But these developments require qualification. First, the increase in worker power at the plant level should not be exaggerated; most employers still maintained the ability to make most decisions; the growth

80. Delamotte, "Recent Collective Bargaining Trends," p. 371.
81. Ibid., p. 373.

Table 10-12. *Strikes, Plant Unions, and Comité d'Entreprise Elections, France, 1967–73*

Year or period	Number of strikes (1)	Percent of companies surveyed having union locals (2)	Number of establishments holding comité d'entreprise elections (3)
1967	1,675	. . .	3,734
1968	. . .	. . .	6,154
1969	2,207	21.92	5,736
1970	2,742	27.54	7,242
1971	4,318	31.28	6,916
1972	3,464	35.34	11,124
1973	3,731	40.00	. . .
Average, 1969–73	3,292	. . .	. . .
Average, 1960–67	1,883	. . .	. . .

Source: Jean-Daniel Reynaud, *Les Syndicats en France*, vol. 2: *Textes et documents* (Paris: Editions du Seuil, 1975), pp. 106, 117, 221.

in bargaining was not comparable to that which occurred in Italy during the same period. Second, the CGT was suspicious of and the CFDT, in the early 1970s, was ambivalent about increases in institutionalized bargaining, especially when any form of future commitment was involved. Finally, most employers, though perhaps not the largest, were deeply hostile to union implantation and were not prepared to accept it as established.

Despite the qualifications, changes had occurred. Their economic consequences can be gauged roughly by some simple econometrics. The theory of the labor market in an open oligopolistic model translates into a positive relation between changes in real wages and labor-market tightness. On the assumption that money wage increases reflected consumer price increases lagged six months, the period 1960–67 yielded

$$\dot{W} - \dot{P}_{c-1/2} = 5.496 - 4.029d \ln(U - V),$$
$$(2.938)$$

$$R^2 = 0.59$$

where the term in parentheses is the *t*-statistic. If the same equation is estimated for the five-year period 1969–73, the result is

$$\dot{W} - \dot{P}_{c-1/2} = 5.146 - 1.912d \ln(U - V).$$
$$(3.169)$$

$$R^2 = 0.77$$

What emerges directly from a comparison between these two equations is a reduced sensitivity of real wages to labor-market tightness. The coefficient of the change in the logarithm of unemployment less vacancies is about halved in absolute value. While no weight can be attached to equations with so few degrees of freedom, they confirm the predictable result of institutionalization, that it reduced the instability of the labor market. It should be noted that this structural shift did not come about because of a lower variance of labor-market tightness. In fact, the variance of $d \ln (U - V)$ is not greatly different between the two periods:

	Average of $d \ln (U - V)$	Standard deviation of $d \ln (U - V)$
1960–67	0.036	0.4024
1969–73	− 0.086	0.3079

Another route by which to examine the effect of the institutionalization in reducing instability is a direct comparison of the standard deviation of changes in real wages between the two periods. This confirms the results of the equations above, since the standard deviation of $\dot{W} - \dot{P}_{c-1/2}$ is 2.097 for the earlier period and 0.668 for the later period.

The cost of the institutionalization can be computed in two ways. The simplest way is to compare average increases in real wages during 1969–73 with increases in real wages during 1964–67. Both were periods of adjustment to sharp increases in real wages in 1962–63 and 1968. In the earlier period the adjustment was attempted by deflation, in the latter by institutionalization. The short-run net costs of the latter, though not any putative long-run benefits, may thus be examined in this comparative fashion. The average increase in real wages between 1964 and 1967 was 3.85 percent a year; between 1969 and 1973 it was 5.31 percent a year.

The second way to examine the cost of institutionalization is through "room" calculations, as set out in table 10-13. Here, paradoxically, 1968 is the only year in which wage increases were within the room allowed if constant profitability was to be maintained. As was seen earlier, this may be accounted for by the initial government strategy, employed from May 1968 to mid 1969; the room in 1969 does not include fiscalization and is therefore lower than it in fact was. From 1969 on, the room allowed for wage increases was consistently exceeded. This may be attributed to the institutionalization and the increase in bargaining power.

624   FRANCE

Table 10-13. *Wage Changes and Room, France, 1968–73*

Year	"Room" (percentage change in nominal GDP per employee) (1)	Percentage change in wages and salaries per employee (2)	Difference (col. 1 − col. 2) (3)
1968	14.47	10.89	3.58
1969	8.67	12.59	−3.92
1970	8.52	10.35	−1.83
1971	9.92	10.15	−0.23
1972	10.37	10.55	−0.18
1973	11.09	12.61	−1.52

Source: OECD Economic Surveys, *France,* successive issues.

Changing Terms of Trade and Industrial Reorganization

On top of the failure to adjust between 1969 and 1973 there was the need for additional adjustment posed by the external problems, similar to those faced by other governments of industrial countries, that the French government faced from 1974 on. In 1973 and 1974 the terms of trade deteriorated on account of the increases in the prices of commodities in 1973 and in that of oil in 1974. And the world recession in demand, which gathered pace during 1974, has persisted to the present. The deterioration of the terms of trade was partially reversed in 1975, although they again declined sharply in 1979–80. And some recovery took place in world demand during the four quarters from the middle of 1975 and again in 1978, although in neither case was it sustained.

These external developments directly created further problems of real adjustment. The change in the terms of trade implied reduced unit profitability and international competitiveness. To restore these variables to their original levels, given the development of labor productivity, required a reduction in real wages from the level they would otherwise have attained. The room for wage increases and actual wage increases are shown in table 10-14.

After 1974 the government adopted two strategies toward collective bargaining and real wages. It was suggested in the last section that the government could choose one of three broad strategies: positive institution building; maintenance of collective bargaining (without further institutionalization); or neglecting unions and imposing low wage growth by deflation or an incomes policy or both. Institution building was ruled out by its cost in productivity and competitiveness, at least in the short run. From 1974 to mid 1976 the government followed the second alternative. Jacques Chirac, the Gaullist leader and President Giscard d'Estaing's first prime minister, pursued a policy that avoided overt conflict with the unions and maintained employment of workers in the primary sectors. Real wages continued to rise rapidly, and no reorganization of the economy took place. When it became clear that this strategy had failed, the government tried the option of neglecting the unions to some extent. From 1976 to the National Assembly elections of April 1978, in which Giscard's Independent Republicans and the Gaullists retained their majority, Raymond Barre, the prime minister, imposed an incomes policy designed to hold down real wages and rebuild profitability. The Barre plan, however, did not attack fundamental problems of the reorganization of industry. After the 1978 elections a new approach was taken, which combined elements of the Barre plan with the lifting of price controls, justified by a move toward a more liberal economy. Accompanying this were more serious, but also *dirigiste,* attempts to realize changes in industries that were no longer seen as internationally competitive. At the same time, the approach of the 1981 presidential election made the government much more cautious than it had been in the mid 1960s.

The lack of adjustment between 1974 and 1976 was the result of a keen sense of the need for political compromise and caution. After 1974 the hands of the state were tied by political constraints. In the 1960s the unspoken community of interests between de Gaulle and the French Communists had given the state a free hand industrially and electorally to impose its economic policies. Industrially the CGT held back from genuine bargaining and from exploiting discontent; electorally the PCF made no serious attempts to develop an alliance with the Socialists. Four related and reinforcing changes from the late 1960s on contributed to the appearance of a fundamentally new political climate, which lasted until the Socialist-Communist split of 1977 and which was revived later in a somewhat altered form. These were a commitment by the PCF to cooperation with the Socialists; a reinvigoration of the Socialist party under François Mitterrand, together with acceptance by the party of a strategy based on the Communist-Socialist alliance; a movement by the majority toward the political center, first under Pompidou, then under Giscard; and finally, an increase in the importance among industrial

Table 10-14. *Wages, Prices, and Room, France, 1974–79*
Percent

Year	Increases in hourly wage rates (1)	Increases in consumer prices (2)	Compensation of wage and salary earnings, including contributions to social security (3)	Column 3 less employers' contributions to social security (4)	Price increases in GDP (5)	"Room" (nominal GDP per worker)[a] (6)	"Room" adjusted for terms of trade[b] (7)	Increases in real wages (col. 1 − col. 2) (8)	Excess of "room" (col. 7) over col. 3 (9)
1974	19.1	13.7	16.7	16.4	11.1	13.5	9.5	5.4	−7.2
1975	17.3	11.7	17.3	15.3	14.0	14.9	16.8	5.6	−0.4
1976	14.9	9.6	15.7	15.1	9.6	13.8	12.9	5.3	−2.8
1977	12.7	9.5	13.1	12.3	8.9	11.3	10.7	3.2	−2.4
1978	12.6	9.3	12.7	12.5	9.9	13.1	14.4	3.3	1.7
1979	13.0	10.7	14.5	. . .	10.1	13.2	12.6	2.3	−1.9

Sources: Columns 1, 2, and 5, OECD *Economic Surveys, France,* successive issues; column 3, 1975–79, OECD *Economic Surveys, France,* successive issues; 1974, *Eurostat National Accounts,* 1977, pp. 30–31; column 4, OECD *Economic Surveys, France,* May 1980, p. 55, n. 72.
a. Percentage increase in nominal GDP less percentage increase in civilian employment.
b. Column 6 less percentage inflation of GDP plus inflation of domestic expenditure.

workers of the CFDT, which at the same time moved closer to the Socialist party.

The Communist party had strong reasons for cooperating with the Socialists. The PCF strategy of the 1960s—sitting back while de Gaulle's economic policies produced discontent and presumably eventual electoral benefits to the Communists—had failed with the events of May 1968; the failure was registered by the lack of electoral advance. While such a strategy was safe as long as the Socialist party was in effect leaderless and isolated from power by the demise of the other center parties in the 1960s, it was no longer so when the Socialist party reasserted itself organizationally and electorally. The PCF also feared what might follow Gaullism. Giscard confirmed the fear of a move toward the political center. Such a move entailed the danger that reformist policies could slowly wean the Communist voter away. And indirectly the possibility opened of a rapprochement between Giscard and the Socialists that might permanently "emarginate" the Communists. On the shop floor, the advance of the CFDT, linked to the Socialist party, put in question, at least in the long run, the *cordon sanitaire* that the CGT had previously been able to raise between the government and the industrial worker.

The advance of the Socialist party was stimulated by the failure of Gaullism in the 1960s. Gaullism forced the Socialists to choose between support of the government and opposition to it, and opposition, unlike in the Fourth Republic, required cooperation with the Communists if a real challenge was ever to be mounted. The lack of success of de Gaulle by the late 1960s made the Socialist choice an increasingly clear one. And the Socialist party, in the common program (*programme commun*) with the PCF, presented the electorate from 1972 on with a real alternative to the majority. In both the National Assembly elections of 1973 and the presidential election (between Giscard and Mitterand) of 1974, the right-wing alliance of Giscardiens and Gaullists beat the Communist-Socialist alliance only by narrow margins.

The move toward the center under both Pompidou and Giscard was in part a competitive response to the relative success of the left. It also, as noted earlier, reflected a belief in the need for institutional change thrown up by the events of May 1968. Chaban's program for a "new society" expressed these beliefs. Giscard had an additional motive. He could not automatically command the loyalty of the Gaullists. His centrist approach offered, at least initially, an opportunity to gain his own electoral constituency and thus present the Gaullists with a choice between acceptance of his leadership, on the one hand, and political isolation on the right, on the other.

To these political factors was added a shift in the system of industrial relations. The events of May 1968 considerably strengthened the CFDT industrially, at the same time moving it leftward politically. Two strategies, sometimes complementary and sometimes competitive, have dominated the approach of the CFDT industrially. One has been the encouragement of worker militancy wherever it has occurred, without overmuch concern for the "winnability" of strikes. The other has been concerned with developing a strategy of negotiation at all levels, in the hope of making advances both in members' conditions and in the machinery of bargaining. The uneasy coexistence of these two approaches—of *gauchisme* and "permanent negotiation"—was reflected in a political ambivalence between a radical left position and one close to Mitterand and the leaders of the Socialist party.

These developments in the CFDT—the increase in industrial strength and the political changes—have had two consequences. The first was increased competition for the CGT; the CGT could no longer neglect local movements, nor could it afford to back out of serious negotiations. Thus, as noted, the Communist party could no longer assume that isolation with the CGT on the political left would be without cost in working-class Communist votes or CGT members. The second, however, was a reduction of the possibility of participation by the CFDT in wage restraint. In principle, there has always existed—in 1979 as in 1964—the possibility of a bargain between the government and the CFDT by which, for instance, wage moderation might be traded for bona fide bargaining requirements of employers. In 1974, however, the CFDT saw its hope for industrial change in a Socialist-Communist government. Even if wage restraint was an imaginable strategy for the CFDT leaders, moreover—as it might have been with a leftist government—the leftward movement of the union made the idea impossible while Giscard and Chirac were in power.

The difficulty of securing wage restraint was compounded by the hostility of the CGT toward it. This did not imply a strong sense of unity between the CGT and the CFDT. On the contrary, they regarded each other with suspicion. The CGT still saw its mission, albeit with greater flexibility than in the 1960s, as the staging of mass demonstrations against policies of the government and business for the electoral benefit of the Communist party. The *gauchiste* tendencies of the CFDT thus outflanked the CGT's left, while the desire for *négociation permanente* challenged its right. Such unity as there was stemmed from the common desire for a Socialist-Communist government, and this was sufficient for both confederations to reject, without consideration, any attempts at wage restraint.

Combined with these changes in the CFDT was an overall increase in union power. This increase should not be exaggerated: in the 1970s the French unions remained the weakest by far of the unions in our sample of countries. There was some improvement in shop-floor organization in the private sector, however, and in particular an increase in bargaining strength in the public sector, because of government encouragement of negotiations under Chaban.

From 1974 to late 1976 policy formation was dominated by consider-ations of political compromise. The long-run goal of the government remained the growth of the French economy within the free world. To that end, the recovery of profitability and the maintenance of competi-tiveness were of central importance. The short-run goal of the govern-ment, however—to maintain a workable parliamentary majority through the 1970s—was dominant because of the narrow gap between the majority and the left. The presidential strategy for achieving this electoral objective involved, at least initially, movement toward the center—as opposed to polarization of left and right. Its implications, as applied to economic management, were three: first, to reject a policy of confron-tation with the unions; second, to maintain the growth of real wages; and third, to maintain employment of workers in the primary sector or soften for them the consequences of unemployment, if a lower level of activity was required for external equilibrium. The government was also concerned about inflation, but it was not prepared, to the end of 1976, to put any of these three seriously at risk to lower the rate of inflation.

From the beginning of 1974 to the end of 1976, economic policy passed through three stages. In the first, which prevailed during the first half of 1971, no attempt was made to deflate the economy or to hold down wages or prices. This led to accelerating inflation and a growing balance-of-trade deficit. During the second stage, which lasted from mid 1974 to mid 1975, the government did not counter the effects on the French economy of the world recession. Instead, minor fiscal deflation was combined with price controls, and in addition a French version of a tax-based incomes policy was designed as an effort to hold down wage increases. Unemployment, especially of secondary workers, increased sharply during this stage; but the government acted to cushion the effect on primary workers by subsidizing unemployment heavily and pressuring corporations to limit the number of redundancies. The rise in unemployment corrected the balance-of-trade deficit and moderated the rate of inflation. But unemployment reached a high level, and profits bore the brunt of price controls, of make-work employment, and of low use of capacity. So, with world trade picking up somewhat from the second half of 1975, the government switched course. In the third stage, which lasted from mid 1975 to mid 1976, reflation of the economy was combined with renewed controls on prices. This led to a further massive balance-of-trade deficit without dealing with the underlying problems.

Between early 1974 and the introduction of the Barre plan at the end of 1976, price controls passed through three stages. From April 1, 1974, to October 1, 1974, separate arrangements were provided for industrial production, distribution, and services. Distributive margins were to be somewhat curtailed. In pricing industrial products and services, increases in the cost of materials, energy, and intermediate goods incorporated in production were allowed to be fully passed on; with respect to other cost components, fixed limits on increases were to be set by agreement between the price administration and the industry concerned. As sanctions, businessmen were liable to fines of from 60 to 200,000 francs and imprisonment, and legal proceedings could now be instigated on the first offense. This set of arrangements was supposedly tightened in September 1974 and designed to run until September 1975.

These measures of price control provided only limited incentives for businesses to hold down costs. In December 1974 a contingent levy on excess profits, the *prélèvement conjoncturel,* was legislated to stiffen business resistance against high wage increases. Inflation had accelerated through 1974, and the levy should be seen in the context of the package of measures put into effect in the second half of 1974. These measures were designed to counter the accelerating inflation and the deterioration of the trade balance. The latter objective was effected, if ephemerally, by the sharp reduction in economic activity. But in seeking to reduce inflation the government was constrained to pull its punches. Neither mass redundancies in industry nor incomes policy was perceived as feasible. The desire of the government to protect jobs in the primary sector blunted the effectiveness of the substantial increase in unemployment in 1975 over its level in 1974. Incomes policy within the framework of collective bargaining was ruled out by the unions. As the OECD observed in the 1975 survey:

In the field of incomes policy, it would be desirable if management and labour could agree, at enterprise, sector or national level, on reasonable norms for wage growth consistent with economic equilibrium. But given the French workers' traditional aversion to such a policy, they would first have to be convinced that the result would not be a more moderate trend in wage incomes alone.[82]

There was in any case no serious possibility that the CFDT or the CGT would have been prepared to restrain wages to help the government. The alternative of an imposed policy—such as the Barre plan—was regarded as politically infeasible.

The *prélèvement conjoncturel* was designed to avoid these problems by penalizing increases in value added—and hence wage increases—above a certain level. It operated as follows. The government set a norm for the amount by which the value added of a company could increase during the company's accounting year. If the company's value added increased by more than the norm the excess was taxed at a rate of 33⅓ percent; no tax was paid if the increase in value added was less than or equal to the norm. The norm was composed of two parts. If P_{va} is price and Q_{va} is volume of value added, the percentage increase in value added can be written as the sum of an increase in current price plus productivity and an increase in factor employment:

$$d \log (P_{va}Q_{va}) \equiv [d \log P_{va} + d \log Q_{va} - d \log F] + d \log F,$$

where F is a factor-price-weighted index of factor inputs; thus the bracketed term is the nominal productivity increase and $d \log F$ the increase in factor employment. The first part of the norm was a percentage increase, common to all companies, which represented the maximum size of the bracketed term for the individual company before the levy came into effect for that company. In 1975 this was fixed at 14.3 percent, which represented an optimistic view on the part of the government of the sum of the average rate of inflation and growth of productivity. To this figure companies had to add the percentage increase during their accounting year in their own F. The construction of $d \log F$ was to be as follows: let E_{it} be the number of i-type workers in accounting year t, w_i their wage, D_t the value of depreciation, and K_t gross book value of assets at the end of t:

$$d \log F_t \equiv [\Sigma_i(w_i E_i / \Sigma w_i E_i) \dot{E}_{it}] \frac{\Sigma w_{it} E_{it}}{\Sigma w_{it} E_{it} + D_t}$$

$$+ \frac{D_t}{\Sigma w_{it} E_{it} + D_t} \cdot \dot{K}_t.$$

Despite its complexity the *prélèvement conjoncturel* had a short life. It was abolished in September 1975, after having been in effect only eight months. It failed to provide adequate sanctions, because high wage increases in the public sector made it difficult to hold down wages in the private sector, given the continuance of tight labor markets. Further, in 1975 concern for company profitability was increasing. The same need, to counter declining profitability in 1975, led to an easing of price controls to allow pricing of a range of manufactured goods to move more closely in line with world prices. But before examining the function of price controls in the Barre plan, we must turn to a main cause of the declining profitability in 1975: job protection during a recession in output.

The government envisaged some rise in unemployment during 1975, though it appears to have been surprised by the size of the deflation that took place. Its official forecast, published in September 1974, was of a 3.7 percent growth in real GDP in 1975.[83] By autumn of 1975 GDP had fallen 1.2 percent, and the index of industrial production by 7.5 percent.[84] Unemployment rose sharply in parallel. From close to 2 percent in each of the four years 1971–74, the rate jumped to 3.4 percent in 1975 (see table 10-15).

Some reflation of the economy occurred in 1976. GDP rose 5.25 percent and industrial production 8.75 percent. Unemployment, however, increased, from 3.4 percent to 4.2 percent. The reason for this abnormal movement in unemployment lies in part in its restricted definition: it does not include partial unemployment—that is, short-time working. In October 1975, 5 percent of workers were working fewer than forty hours a week; only 0.6 percent had been working such short hours in October 1973; short-time layoffs accounted for 1,242,000 days

83. Ibid., p. 55.
84. OECD Economic Surveys, *France*, February 1977, p. 41.

Table 10-15. *Unemployment Rates, by Age and Sex, France, 1968–76*

Age group and sex	1968	1969	1970	1971	1972	1973	1974	1975	1976
Under 25	3.3	3.3	3.2	4.0	4.2	4.1	4.9	8.0	10.4
Male	3.0	3.0	3.0	3.0	3.6	3.4	3.6	6.9	7.7
Female	3.7	3.7	3.6	5.1	5.0	4.9	6.5	9.2	13.4
24–49	1.2	1.2	1.0	1.4	1.5	1.3	1.4	2.5	2.9
Male	1.1	1.0	0.8	1.0	1.1	1.0	1.0	2.1	2.3
Female	1.6	1.5	1.4	2.1	2.2	1.8	2.1	3.3	3.8
Over 50	1.5	2.0	1.6	2.0	2.2	1.7	1.7	2.2	2.9
Male	1.5	1.9	1.5	1.8	2.0	1.6	1.4	2.0	2.5
Female	1.5	2.1	1.8	2.3	2.4	1.8	2.0	2.5	3.5
Average	1.7	1.8	1.6	2.0	2.2	1.9	2.1	3.4	4.2
Male	1.5	1.5	1.3	1.5	1.7	1.5	1.5	2.8	3.2
Female	2.1	2.2	2.0	2.9	2.9	2.5	3.0	4.4	5.7

Source: OECD Economic Surveys, *France*, January 1975, p. 14; ibid., February 1977, p. 19.

a month on the average in 1975, but only 324,000 days a month in 1974,[85] and the number of workers affected increased from 88,500 in 1974 to about 350,000 in 1975.[86] Unemployment was also protected from the deflation of output by a decline in hourly labor productivity and a reduction in overtime. For industry the 7.1 percent decline in value added (1975 on 1974) was composed of a 2.9 percent decline in the number of workers, a 2.5 percent decline in the number of hours worked per worker (the joint effect of overtime reduction and short-time working), and a 1.8 percent decline in hourly productivity.[87] Finally, the unemployment figure for 1975 did not include the reduction in the supply of labor induced by the recession; this was caused primarily by postponement of school leaving and a decline in labor-force participation by women;[88] a calculation by the Institut National de la Statistique et des Etudes Economiques puts the reduction at about 200,000.[89] Thus that unemployment did not decline in 1976 can be explained to a considerable extent by these masking factors.

The government's policy appears to have been geared to the mainte-

85. Collections d'INSEE (Institut National de la Statistique et des Etudes Economiques), no. 194, Servie C, no. 42 (May 1976), p. 39. (Hereafter INSEE.)

86. OECD Economic Surveys, *France*, January 1976, p. 15.

87. INSEE, p. 40.

88. OECD Economic Surveys, *France*, January 1976, p. 15.

89. INSEE, p. 43.

nance of employment of primary workers and cushioning the consequences of unemployment on them. This was achieved through a three-
part policy: redundancies were to be prevented as far as possible through
legislation (and arm-twisting); in the event of redundancy for "economic" reasons, unemployment benefits of 90 percent of earnings were
to be paid for one year; and 50 percent compensation was to be paid for
partial unemployment.

Redundancies

In January 1975 the government enacted a law concerning dismissals
for economic reasons. It applied only to cases in which ten or more
workers were dismissed during a period of thirty days for the same
economic cause. The legislation was thus not aimed at small companies.
The requirements imposed on the employer were, with minor omissions,
as follows. The *comité d'entreprise* was to be furnished with information
on the causes of the dismissals, the numbers and specializations of
workers concerned, the calendar to be followed, and the measures taken
to attempt to minimize the number of dismissals. After a minimum of
fifteen days had elapsed from the date at which the *comité d'entreprise*
received this information, the employer was to apply to the Labor
Inspectorate (a government agency) for permission to enforce the
proposed dismissals. With the application was to be forwarded the
information given to the *comité d'entreprise* and the written comments
of the *comité*. The Labor Inspectorate was then required to reach a
decision within thirty days of receipt of the application.

A second reason for believing that the government was successful in
"persuading" companies to use partial unemployment rather than
dismissals lies in the number of companies the government had in effect
to bail out as a result; since dismissals were, from the point of view of
the individual company, cost-free, the latter would presumably have
chosen dismissals over partial compensation in the absence of government arm-twisting.

Unemployment Compensation

Until October 1974 unemployment compensation came from two
sources. The state provided a minimal *aide publique* (ten francs a day in
1974), and Unedic, an organization set up in 1958 by an agreement
between the CNPF and the unions, paid 40 percent of earnings for three

months and 35 percent for nine months for those under fifty, with more generous provision for older workers (the *allocation spéciale*). In October 1974 the government forced the CNPF to conclude a new agreement with the unions; this brought the *aide publique* and the *allocation spéciale* up to 90 percent of earnings (the *allocation supplementaire d'attente*) for those dismissed for economic reasons, and was available for a maximum period of a year. The file of each recipient was to be examined after three, six, and nine months. Recipients had to pay income tax on the 90 percent. The scheme was financed by contribution to Unedic of 1.8 percent of earnings—four fifths paid by the employer and one fifth by the worker—the remainder being paid by the government; the contribution rate was increased in July 1975 to 2.4 percent of earnings.

Partial Unemployment

The marginal cost of financing unemployment compensation to the individual company of its own dismissals was effectively zero.[90] Since workers might well prefer dismissal on what amounts to full pay for one year, after which they could legally be reemployed by the company, to partial unemployment, and since companies had excess labor in 1975, the government's strategy was to use administrative controls to prevent *big* increases in dismissals.[91] The effect of these controls on profitability was modified by allowing companies to move to short-time working.

To cushion the effects of short-time working on workers, the government and the employers, separately at first, each paid a certain amount—in early 1975, 3.0 francs and 2.10 francs, respectively—for each hour less than forty worked per week. In June the CNPF and the unions concluded an agreement whereby the employers would bring up to 50 percent of previous hourly earnings whatever hourly amount the government paid, up to 470 hours a year. The government increased its payments to offset the effect on profitability. In addition, for companies in industries in which large-scale redundancies threatened, the government subsidized short-time payments to a maximum of 80 percent; in an industry agreement with the Union des Industries Métallurgiques et Minières a 60 percent subsidy was paid to steel companies.

90. Actually negative, because contributions for dismissed workers were no longer paid.

91. Thus circumventing the argument put forward by Martin Feldstein on layoffs in "Temporary Layoffs in the Theory of Unemployment," *Journal of Political Economy*, vol. 84 (October 1976), pp. 937–57.

The End of Compromise: The Barre Plan

Sooner or later the government had to face the need for adjustment, and in the autumn of 1976 a major change was made in political and economic strategy. Chirac, the Gaullist leader, was replaced as prime minister by a political independent and former professor of economics, Raymond Barre. His policies of economic compromise gave way to the first stage of the Barre plan. This first stage was an incomes policy designed to hold real wages constant, thus enabling profitability to be rebuilt by the amount of the growth in productivity. Imposed against the will and without the cooperation of the unions, by government fiat in the public sector and government pressure in the private sector, and in a labor market in which unemployment was allowed to rise from 4.6 percent in 1976 to 5.2 percent in 1977 and 1978, the policy apparently represented the strategy choice of "ignoring the unions and gambling on the consequences." As noted earlier, two arguments had weighed against such a choice in 1974. One was the development under Chaban between 1969 and 1972 of public-sector negotiations. From then on the government was seen as committed to wage bargaining in "good faith" in the public sector. The second was the narrowness of the presidential majority, a fact of increasing relevance as the National Assembly elections of March 1978 grew closer. Since neither of these considerations was less true at the end of 1976 than in 1974, why was policy changed so radically? The primary factor was the gravity of the economic situation. Increases in real wages during the years 1974–76 prevented the restoration of competitiveness and profitability. And after the minor pickup of world trade in late 1975, the deepening world recession brought home to French policymakers the difficulty of running the economy at previous growth rates if the external balance was to be preserved.

The switch in economic policy was aided by political and industrial developments. Politically the alliance of the Socialist and Communist parties was showing signs of tension, partly because of economic factors. As the economic situation grew worse, the Communist party became more concerned with the balance of gains and losses it would incur from a Socialist-Communist coalition. In particular, the CGT would now have to bear the brunt of enforcing an unpopular incomes policy if the coalition was to be administratively successful. Also, an important reason for maintaining support for the Socialists had been to remove any temptation of a Socialist-Giscardien alliance that Giscard, as a reformist president, might have offered. It was not difficult for the government to calculate that a right-wing economic policy could set the Communists free to adopt a less conciliatory attitude toward the Socialists. Aggravated by the growing success of the Socialist party in opinion polls, the discord between the two parties of the left broke into the open in 1977 and was partly responsible for Giscard's victory in March 1978.

There was also a consideration of industrial relations that eased the switch of policy. The CGT wanted to minimize industrial unrest before the election. It feared an electoral backlash against the Communists as a consequence of serious industrial disputes, especially those likely to cause inconvenience in the public sector. Within limits, and with reference to Socialist votes, the CFDT followed a similar line of reasoning. Thus both industrially and politically, Giscard was prepared to gamble on a policy required by economic considerations.

The Barre plan had four components:

1. *Public-sector wage increases.* Wage increases in the public sector were to rise strictly in line with increases in the consumer price index; the increases, at the end of each quarter, were to equal the percentage change in the consumer price index during the quarter.

2. *Private-sector wage increases.* The private sector was asked to follow the same policy for wage increases. To enforce this the government relied on four mechanisms. First, wage increases in the public sector tended—though imperfectly—to lead wage increases in the private sector; while this mechanism had only limited efficacy in the 1960s, the effect of declining profitability in the private sector and the encouragement of bargaining in the public sector during the early 1970s increased its importance. Second, the economy was allowed to move somewhat further into recession, and the government somewhat moderated its attempts to avert redundancies; thus the labor market was loosened for larger companies in the private sector, at the same time that cyclical profitability was safeguarded. Third, the exchange rate was held constant after depreciating through the first three quarters of 1976, thus enabling the slower growth of world prices to exert a disciplining force. Finally, a committee was set up, with the cooperation of the CNPF, to provide direct surveillance of the hundred largest companies; the government envisaged the use of sanctions through government purchases, subsidies on investment and exports, and price controls.

3. *Price controls.* The first stage of the Barre plan, from September 1976 until the National Assembly elections of March 1978, embodied a price policy operated primarily through the system of price controls. Prices of goods and services were frozen for the fourth quarter of 1976. Through 1977 the annual rate of increase of rents was fixed at 6.5 percent, the same rate that was to be applied to public-utility charges from April 1977. (The *prélèvement conjoncturel* was again introduced, this time to operate from January 1977, although, as on the previous occasion, it was never invoked.) No policy was enunciated for industrial prices after the freeze. As the OECD noted, however, "the price restraint agreements concluded between the government and enterprises when the freeze was over provided for some rebuilding of profit margins."[92] At the same time the rate of the value-added tax was reduced from 20 percent to 17.6 percent; this was compensated for by increases in direct taxes and social contributions so that the total tax collected as a percentage of gross domestic product remained the same in 1977 as it had been in 1976.[93]

4. *Aggregate demand.* After a growth of 5 percent in real GDP in 1976, the government aimed for a slower growth rate—3 percent—in 1977. By late 1976 the government faced four serious problems: reduced profitability and competitiveness, balance-of-payments problems, unemployment, and the need for industrial reorganization. The rhetoric of the Barre plan was directed at the rate of inflation, but inflation was unaffected by it (see table 10-12). Had the Barre plan succeeded in holding real wages constant, the government could have chosen between rebuilding profits (by allowing price-cost margins to rise by the amount of the increase in productivity) or reducing the rate of inflation (by holding margins constant). The price agreements of early 1977 envisaged the first option. The Barre plan had some success in moderating the growth of real hourly wage rates, from around 5 percent a year from 1974 to 1976 to 3.2 percent in 1977. But productivity also grew more slowly, 2.4 percent, so overall profitability did not improve. Nor did the government make any notable headway with industrial reorganization, judging it too dangerous just before an election. The only significant economic success came on the balance-of-payments front, and that—it seems reasonable to assume—was due more to the slower growth of aggregate demand than to the Barre plan.

92. OECD Economic Surveys, *France,* December 1977, p. 37.
93. Ibid., February 1979, p. 45, n. 59.

Barre: The Second Stage

After the National Assembly election in March 1978, the government developed a more radical economic policy. As before, the government insisted that wages should not rise more rapidly than prices. But prices were to be almost completely decontrolled. And drawing a distinction between viable companies in difficulties and *canards boiteux* (lame ducks), only the former were to be recipients of state aid and concern. Redundancies for "economic reasons" were to be made easier. The government now envisaged a wholesale reorganization of industry, in particular cutting textiles and steel down to levels at which they would be able to compete in the harsher climate of world industry.

The lessons of May 1968 were, however, still remembered. And some members of the government and the Patronat saw the late 1970s as a period in which a new attempt could be made to build an effective system of collective bargaining. Three arguments favored such an attempt. First, the PCF had retreated to the ghetto of opposition, pulling the CGT with it; at the same time, the CFDT—disillusioned by the failure of the left politically—had embarked on the *recentrage* of its efforts from the political sphere to the industrial; if, therefore, the government wanted to develop collective bargaining, now was the time that an "alliance" might be formed with the CFDT and Force Ouvrière, with the possibility of significant loss of support for the CGT. Second, the government did not want grievances to build up as they had in the mid 1960s with weak unions and a loose labor market. Finally, the government wished to preserve what it could of its reformist image: the popular vote in the Assembly elections had given only a 50–49 percent majority to the Giscard-Gaullist alliance.

The government policy on wages remained virtually unchanged after September 1976. There was considerable debate about its success. At one extreme the OECD in its annual economic surveys of 1979 and 1980 neither mentions the wages policy nor makes more than passing reference to the significantly lower real wage increases in the years 1977–80 (see table 10-14, column 8). The OECD argument was (implicitly) that money wage increases remained at a high level (see table 10-14, columns 1 and 3). But while this is true, it is not relevant to an evaluation of the Barre policy. The policy was specifically couched in real-wage terms. The size of increases in money wages reflects not on the wage policy but on the price policy.

The policy of "liberating" prices from controls had three aims. First, it was believed that domestic prices would, by moving to reflect world prices and marginal costs, yield the standard gains in allocation of resources. Yet the prevalence in European industry of markup, entry-preventing pricing would minimize such benefits. Second, it was believed that world price constraints, together with a high rate of exchange, would in the long term anchor domestic inflation. And third, it was believed that in the interim, prices could rise to the world level, thereby causing an inflationary spurt but enabling the rebuilding of profits. "It seems pretty clear that [Barre] has temporarily abandoned the all-out fight against inflation to make way for the new Giscard industrial plan for improving company finances. . . . But however justified the new industrial policies may be in the longer run, they did virtually nothing to curb inflation last year, while prospects for 1979 are not dramatically better," noted *The Economist* in early 1979.[94]

An alternative critique of the effects of the Barre wage policy is that the moderation of increases in real wages was primarily the result of the loosening of the labor market during the second half of the 1970s. The rise in unemployment (see table 10-16) undoubtedly increased the bargaining power of employers in wage negotiations. The greatest increase in unemployment came in 1975, however, with no perceptible effect on increases in real wages: the decline of increases in real wages coincided with the Barre policy.

We should not be surprised that the French government could affect real-wage movements significantly. On the one hand, the unions were weak, and on the other, the links between the government and industry were close. France presented a contrast, at least before 1981, to other countries in which incomes policies usually have to be bought from unions. In France it was with industry that the contract was required to be sealed: "It is a safe bet that Mr. Ceyrac was not only involved in framing the liberal industrial policy from the start but that he struck a deal with the premier: in return for the lifting of price controls he would make sure that companies did not wreck the anti-inflation effort by releasing the brake from wages."[95] But this raises another doubt. Why

94. *The Economist,* "Survey," January 27, 1979, p. 16.
95. Ibid., p. 18. At this time Ceyrac was president of the CNPF.

Table 10-16. *Unemployment, Vacancies, and Measures*
of Competitiveness, France, 1974–79

Year	Number of unem- ployed (thousands)	Unfilled vacancies (thousands)	Relative unit labor costs (percent)	Relative average values of exports of manufactures (percent)
1974	498	205	97.6	96.1
1975	840	109	106.0	104.4
1976	933	124	102.9	102.5
1977	1,073	104	99.1	100.0
1978	1,167	87	98.9	98.9
1979	1,350	88	. . .	. . .

Sources: Columns 1 and 2, OECD Economic Surveys, *France,* successive issues; columns 3 and 4, OECD Economic Surveys, *France,* May 1980, p. 25.

was the incomes policy not more successful? Both the government and the CNPF reiterated the policy at intervals and in no uncertain terms until the middle of 1979,[96] and from late 1980 until May 1981 both government and business were again on the offensive.

There were several reasons for the slippage between the intentions of the government and the outcome. First, the government was sensitive to its political popularity: the beginning of the period from mid 1979 to mid 1980, during which the policy was publicly downplayed, coincided with the first opinion poll that showed more respondents dissatisfied than satisfied with the performance of the president.[97] Second, the wage policy was concerned, for political reasons, with reduction of inequality as well as with moderation of real wages; initially the government pursued this policy by increasing the minimum wage, the *salaire minimum interprofessionnel de croissance,* faster than the increase in prices. After that had been seen to have had an inflationary effect,[98] the government asked for industry agreements in which the less well paid grades received larger increases than higher grades, but this too probably led to compensating changes in earnings at the plant level.[99] A further factor was the effect of individual promotions.[100] Finally, especially in

96. See, for example, a report of the Paris ministerial press conference, *Le Monde,* June 29, 1979, p. 40.

97. *Le Monde,* September 15, 1979, p. 10.

98. Income Data Services, International Report, no. 87 (December 1978), p. 1; ibid., no. 82 (October 1978), p. 1.

99. *L'Express,* December 20, 1980, p. 48.

100. Ibid.

the public sector, the government was keen not to have to impose agreements. It was eager that public-private differentials should not grow in case effective opposition to its policies should emerge; it also did not wish to so stifle pay negotiations in the public sector as to prevent the development of other types of negotiations that it was trying to encourage in the private sector.

For these reasons, the incomes policy showed a certain slippage. Later, in response to the oil price increases of 1979–80, the system of indexation itself came under attack. Yvon Chotard, vice-president of the CNPF, argued in a letter to CNPF officials in November 1980, "Wages should increase neither more slowly nor faster than prices. . . . Experience shows that this can only be done if [industrywide wage increases] are about two points below the increase in the cost of living."[101] The argument in favor of breaking indexation schemes recalls the policies pursued by de Gaulle in 1958–59 and in 1969, but, as L'Express noted, "It is useless to hide the fact that the maintenance of purchasing power is a pillar of the country's political equilibrium. Thus it is necessarily part of the electoral strategy of the government and of the President."[102]

The policy of the government on nonpay questions was likewise a mixture of economic realism and electoral trimming. The growth of unemployment appears to have been dictated primarily by balance-of-payments considerations. The slow growth of the world economy imposed a slow rate of growth on France: "An expansionary policy is quite inappropriate since it would aggravate the balance-of-trade deficit," Barre explained in June 1979.[103] This did not mean opposition to expansion of the French economy in line with the rest of the world. "My feeling," the prime minister noted earlier, "is that the European countries, together with Japan and the USA, could act together to bring about a recovery."[104] The level of unemployment was thus broadly determined by the growth of French output that was permitted by world growth and by improvements in productivity that increased unemployment in the short run, although in the long run, together with wage policy, they lessened the balance-of-payments constraint. After the 1978 election the government adopted tougher policies on industrial reorganization, thereby

101. See L'Express, November 22, 1980, p. 46, for the attribution of a similar position to a senior official of the administration.
102. L'Express, December 20, 1980, p. 48 (translated by author).
103. Le Monde, June 29, 1979, p. 40 (translated by author).
104. Ibid., July 21, 1978, p. 23 (translated by author).

accepting an increase in unemployment in relation to GDP. "The period 1974-78 was one long electoral campaign, marked by various polls with which the various sides measured their forces. Only after March 1978 did the government feel safe enough to allow industrialists more leeway in the labor market."[105] In steel—despite strong union protests and some evidence of compromise by the government—textiles, and other declining industries, wholesale reorganization and redundancies took place.

On the other hand, the government encouraged the CNPF to develop negotiations with the unions over a range of issues: unemployment benefits, hours worked, and guarantees of minimum annual earnings. But despite this encouragement and the desire of the leaders of the CFDT to show its members the benefits of a strategy of negotiations, the CNPF was unprepared to make the type of concessions necessary for significant breakthroughs. The government also substantially strengthened the system of labor tribunals, the *prud'hommes* (literally, wise men), to deal with grievances in the private sector (apart from large-scale redundancies, which remain under the aegis of the Labor Inspectorate). This fitted in with the concern of the government not to allow the accumulation of avoidable grievances—large-scale redundancies during a period of industrial reorganization being unavoidable.

Some elements of the government surrounding Robert Boulin, the minister of labor, were initially prepared to move further toward the development of collective bargaining. The ministry commissioned an analysis from a group of experts, presided over by Professor Gérard Adam, who reported in late 1978. The report

paints a fairly gloomy picture of collective bargaining in France, which it describes as irregular, unstructured, and marked by intermittent bursts of feverish activity. It claims that many of the difficulties stem from the authorities' lack of trust in the ability of employers and unions to regulate labour affairs, from the traditional paternalism of French companies, from an unwillingness to reach compromise solutions, and from the persistent gap between minimum guarantees laid down in agreements and actual conditions of employment.[106]

It called for the availability of much greater information on the content of agreements. It questioned the system of "representative" unions, suggesting that a union should be able to sign an agreement only if it had acquired a certain proportion of votes in the relevant works councils

105. Suzanne Berger, "Lame Ducks and National Champions: Industrial Policy in the 5th Republic" (Massachusetts Institute of Technology, December 1978).

106. Incomes Data Services, International Report, no. 79 (August 1978), pp. 1-3.

elections. Legislation in the past had set up an elaborate framework for collective bargaining, but needed were laws to bring about fruitful negotiations between employers and unions. To this end the report proposed that a central agency should have the power to define areas and levels at which negotiations should take place and, as a last resort, should be able to require the two sides to negotiate.

This approach coincided with an important change of strategy in the second largest union, the CFDT. From the early 1970s on, the CFDT had accepted a Marxist analysis of society and had moved some distance toward the CGT-PCF view that no genuine advance could come without a change of regime. But many within the union remained hostile and in favor of collective bargaining. The rupture of the left in late 1977 convinced the leaders of the CFDT of the need to "recenter" its activities toward industrial collective bargaining. An electoral victory was now less likely. More important, the CFDT became skeptical of the possibility of reform in the event of victory. The PCF saw the path to economic recovery as leading through nationalization, subsidies, and a retreat to protectionism; the CFDT believed that reorganization of industry was necessary and wished to control its pace and shape its direction through a mixture of planning and collective bargaining.[107] The CFDT also doubted whether the PCF would allow the development of effective bargaining even if the regime were to change. *Recentrage* toward collective bargaining thus solved two problems: it could give the CFDT a power base in industry in the absence of political changes, and could therefore give it independence in bringing about the political changes. But for effective bargaining to develop, legal changes had to take place in the company's obligation to negotiate. "The company constitutes an essential center of decision-making for the work force, since it determines actual earnings, conditions and hours of work, security of employment and training. . . . It is therefore necessary to organize the right to negotiate at company level,"[108] the head of the CFDT legal service argued. The CFDT did not believe that the employer should be under obligation to make an agreement, but he should be required to "meet the unions at a specified time and place . . . discuss seriously the union's claims, formulate serious counterproposals, give the union all the information necessary for the negotiation, continue the discussion for a certain period

107. Rapport sur la politique économique de la CFDT, October 29–31, 1980.

108. J. P. Murcier, "Réflexions sur la négociation collective en France," *Droit Social,* July–August 1979.

of time, and not impose any unilateral decision during the negotiations."[109]

Between the CFDT and a part of the government there existed a
certain degree of consensus. But the government did not take the
opportunity to develop a new legal framework. Three reasons for this,
all related, can be offered. First, the strategy of "institutionalization"
carried the risk that it would increase the power of the CGT—the largest
union and therefore the potential beneficiary—without reducing its
allegiance to the PCF, and the rejection by another union federation,
Force Ouvrière, of a proposal for joint action with the CFDT reduced
the likelihood of an alliance of "reformist" unions strong enough to
challenge the CGT. Second, the growth of unemployment greatly undermined the possibility that worker militancy would be effective and
thus reduced the short-term case for more "responsible" unionism.
Finally, business recovered from its "bad" years of the mid 1970s, when
the government placed many obstacles in the way of redundancies and
rationalization; it was making good use of exceptionally weak labor
markets and was in no mood to alter the balance of power on the shop
floor, at least without a struggle—or, as things turned out, a Socialist
victory in the elections of 1981.

Conclusion

France has enjoyed considerable success in growth of productivity.
It has been less successful in holding down its rate of inflation. Of all of
the countries surveyed it has had the least success in developing an
effective system of collective bargaining. Contacts between the government and the unions were suspicious and generally unproductive. The
unions remained weak industrially, and the largest union has looked for
political rather than industrial solutions. The conservative governments
and the large employers had a close two-way relationship: the employers,
when suitably pressured, managed incomes policies and invested or
expanded in required directions; in exchange, the government gave them
access to credit and financial aid, provided state orders, and operated
price controls (including abolition of them) to enable profit margins to
be built up.

109. Ibid.

These summary statements of economic performance and institutional behavior are interrelated. The rapid growth of productivity of French industry was at least in part the result of the ability of businesses to exercise a high degree of managerial discretion. In turn this can be explained by the chronic failure of French unions to build up effective bargaining strength on the shop floor—despite the hostility of their rhetoric toward management and despite the real hostility of large sections of the work force toward their employers.

The responsibility does not lie wholly with the unions. Aware of the economic advantages of an unorganized work force and fearful of the translation of union rhetoric into bargaining demands, businesses generally acted to frustrate the development of effective negotiations. Most companies, especially those that are family-controlled, have preferred unorganized labor markets despite their attendant instability: longer periods, when productivity—and grievances—both grew, and shorter periods, with more frequent strikes and substantial wage increases, when the discontent could no longer be contained.

At certain stages, some of the larger companies and the government—with an eye to the benefits of long-run stability and the desire to preserve a center-right government in office—moved toward increased institutionalization of industrial relations. Indeed, in part as a result, the level of seriousness of bargaining in the 1970s was greater than in the two preceding decades. But in our cross-country comparison, the level in France remained the lowest. Why, in a country with a centralized and powerful administration, did successive center-right governments never push strongly enough for change?

A government, if concerned solely with fostering industrialization, must (if it can) adopt policies that enable business to increase productivity and that at the same time ensure that labor's share is, on the average, held suitably in check. The choice for the government between the maintenance of unorganized labor markets, on the one hand, and institutionalization, on the other, can be seen in that light. With unorganized labor markets, productivity has been safeguarded because businesses have had freedom, within limits, to determine work practices, employment, and type of investment. When governments have been concerned about aggregate wage developments they have been able to pressure companies into containing wage increases, again within limits. With weak unions and strong links between government and industry, incomes policies could be run through industry.

The main threat of unorganized labor markets to the government as "industrial manager" has been their instability. The government, however, has developed an economic policy response to such instability. This is based on the assumption that strike waves, with unorganized labor, cannot last; the militancy will run its course and then subside. The policy response is, let money wages rise by the amount necessary to end the strikes; then, as the militancy ebbs, let prices rise by the amount of the increases in money wages, safeguard the balance of payments by devaluation, and ensure that real wages fall rapidly (or grow minimally) as soon as the strike wave is over by cutting any de facto indexation of wages and reducing subsequent increases in money wages to the minimum. This type of response to instability goes some way toward explaining the high and variable French rate of price inflation. It also explains why—so long as it did not threaten the regime itself—such instability could be accommodated.

With a much smaller electoral gap between right and left in the 1970s, the attractions of institutionalization to the government became stronger. So long as the industrialists' private domain—the factory—was not encroached upon, effective negotiations were developed under state impulse in the public sector and, in the private sector, at the national level. But for the government as "industrial" as opposed to "electoral" manager, the claims of institutionalization were less pressing. A necessary condition for the compatibility of institutionalization with industrial growth is a measure of understanding by the unions of the limits on increases in real wages set by the economy's growth in productivity; equally, compatibility requires acceptance by unions that under some conditions world economic developments may require industrial reorganization. But the relationship of the CGT to the Communist party continued to cast doubt on the possibility of such a "rules-of-the-game" consensus. And the CGT was too well established as the most important union to permit the government to set up the game with the CFDT and Force Ouvrière.

As much as the opposition of employers, the relationship of the CGT and the PCF has also prevented the development of institutionalization under the independent pressure of the unions. Had the unions been united in their determination to convert worker militancy in one of its heightened phases—especially in May 1968—into permanent shop-floor power, there are no particular reasons to believe it would have been impossible. Just such a transformation was brought about in Italy in

1968–69 against equally hostile employers; there the CGIL was little constrained by the Italian Communist party and was much concerned to develop effective industrial power. In France, on the other hand, the PCF has always regarded the CGT as essential to its electoral ambitions. For the Communist party, the role of the CGT lies in preserving the hostility of the work force toward employers and government. The development of collective bargaining would threaten that role in several ways. It would serve to legitimate the employer as social partner and thus to hold out the possibility of social progress under a non-Communist regime. It would give the CGT an independent power base, putting at risk the party's control over its affiliated union federation. And it would increase the autonomy of the various industrial unions affiliated with the CGT. The development of stronger bargaining institutions, and hence of more effective policies of wage restraint, would appear to require either a weakening of the CGT in relation to the other labor federations— especially the more bargaining-minded CFDT—or a weakening of the control of the French Communist party over the CGT, in the dramatically altered political environment of the 1980s, or both.

XI

Conclusions

Collective bargaining is a prewar inheritance that was shaped when a high rate of unemployment was endemic. It predated the Keynesian revolution in economic thought, which was to hold out the prospect of securing and maintaining full employment primarily through the creation of aggregate demand by public authority rather than through the reduction of costs and prices by private enterprise under the pressure of cyclically intensified competition. In fact, collective bargaining institutions were frequently designed with an eye to restraint of such competition—an objective that not infrequently suited the masters as well as the men. The labor movements, of course, also looked to collective bargaining as an instrument for achieving growth and redistribution of income as well as better nonpecuniary conditions of work, affecting employees' efforts, safety, health, and social security off the job. In Europe, however, governments soon assumed primary responsibility for social security, although in some instances these public programs were administered by the trade unions, and the unions in Europe were better able to rely on their chosen political instruments for progress in this area than were American unions before the New Deal.

The European Experience

During the postwar period the market environment differed considerably from the environment in which collective bargaining had developed and which had tended to restrain its ability to increase costs. In the early years of reconstruction unemployment levels were generally high, but this reflected shortages of plant and equipment, and demand for labor increased strongly. By the end of the 1950s, unemployment rates had declined to low levels, except in Italy. The availability of foreign labor—and, in Italy, of labor in the underdeveloped south—meant that labor supplies were less inelastic than was suggested by the rates of recorded unemployment. Inflows of foreign labor, however, were limited by demand at going wage levels; the new migrants were largely unskilled, moreover, and could not fill shortages of skilled labor. Extensive tariff reductions in the late 1950s and early 1960s exposed the countries of Western Europe to increased competition, especially from the United States, where unit labor costs declined in the early 1960s while they were rising in Europe.[1] Increased international competition was reflected in declining profit shares during the first half of the 1960s, but growth in world trade contributed to increased growth rates in gross national product (GNP) and hence in the demand for labor.[2] The terms of trade, moreover, had been improving steadily since the beginning of the 1950s.

Thus for nearly two decades market developments tended to increase the potential bargaining power of unions. In the mid 1960s, however, the economic environment of collective bargaining reached a plateau, if not a climacteric, in permissiveness. The latter half of the decade was marked by relatively steep recessions and weak recoveries in most of the countries, and unemployment rates were higher, or at least no lower, than they had been in the early 1960s. Growth rates, in real per capita gross domestic product (GDP), were also generally lower, but not in Austria, the Netherlands, or Italy. Meanwhile, international competition widened and intensified as imports rose more strongly in relation to GDP, and constrained world prices increased pressure on domestic industries to minimize unit costs. Industry responded by squeezing out more labor-intensive firms and by increasing capital intensity, shaking out labor, and raising production standards in large firms. In addition, there were the two primary sources of increase in nonwage costs: the continued rapid growth of government transfer payments and other social welfare programs, both absolutely and in relation to GDP, which was reflected in increased employment taxes, and the sharp deterioration in the terms of trade after the early 1970s.

These developments since the mid 1960s have tended to increase the resistance of employers under collective bargaining, but this resistance

1. Between 1961 and 1964, the average annual rate of increase in unit labor costs in Denmark, France, West Germany, Italy, the Netherlands, and Sweden was 4.4 percent; in the United States the average rate of decline was 1.1 percent. See Arthur Neef, "Unit Labor Costs in the United States and 10 Other Nations," *Monthly Labor Review*, vol. 95 (July 1972), p. 6.

2. Paul McCracken and others, *Towards Full Employment and Price Stability* (Paris: Organisation for Economic Co-operation and Development, 1977), table A.21, p. 307; OECD, *Economic Growth, 1960–1970: A Mid-Decade Review of Prospects* (Paris: OECD, 1966), pp. 43–45.

was countered by rising expectations and heightened militancy on the part of the workers. Replacement in the work forces and in the unions of members of the prewar and wartime generations with members of the postwar generation tended to raise average levels of minimally acceptable compensation and of other conditions of work and to lower strike thresholds. Memories of prewar unemployment and, especially in Germany and Austria, of hyperinflation became less influential as determinants of current expectations and decisions; workers came increasingly to expect that real compensation would be raised by unions and employers under collective bargaining and that full employment could and would be assured by official policy. It is interesting that the wildcat strikes at the end of the 1960s had typically been preceded by declines in the rate of increase in real wages, rather than in their absolute levels. The strikers were not deterred by recession; rather, they reacted against requirements of increased effort that were associated with recession and competitive pressures. Austria and Norway, the two countries in which industrial activity was not disrupted at that time, also saw very little deflation.

The bargaining aggressiveness of the workers was also heightened by the thrust of social egalitarianism, which in the political sphere was reflected in increased tax progressivity, social transfer payments, and other public expenditures and activities. In the domain of collective bargaining it was reflected in egalitarian wage demands. Wage egalitarianism in Italy and Britain became pronounced at the end of the 1960s, when strikes in those countries were associated with an outbreak of militancy, in Britain among low-paid public-sector workers and in Italy among semiskilled production workers. In each case, the outbreak occurred within a union movement in which the interests of skilled groups had previously tended to prevail, a development that recalls the organization of American semiskilled workers in industrial unions during the 1930s. In Norway, Sweden, and the Netherlands, union confederations negotiated for compression of wage differentials within more centralized bargaining structures throughout most of the postwar period. But groups of more highly paid employees regarded as highly inequitable both egalitarian wage bargains and the combined effects of inflation on the disposable income of their members, progressive income tax structures, and higher average direct and indirect tax rates and contributions to social security. Thus bargaining aggressiveness was heightened within the ranks of both the more highly paid and those whose wages were low. Efforts to compress and to restore relative wage—and salary—incomes led to various forms of leapfrogging: negotiated wage drift in the firm or plant and negotiation of "drift compensation" within central contractual agreements; competitive wage bargaining among craft and industrial unions where the craft unions remained in separate organizations, as in Denmark and to some extent in Britain, and between unions in the private sector and those in the public sector, where the opportunities for securing drift were not great; and even the formation of aggressive federations of middle managers and professionals, notably in Sweden and the Netherlands.

The Effects of Changed Environments and Expectations

Changes in bargaining environments and in the attitudes of workers combined to weaken bargaining structures that had originally been conducive both to employer resistance and to union restraint. Industry-wide and even more highly centralized bargaining facilitated united resistance on the part of employers, which could take the form of financial support for struck or locked-out firms and even, as in Germany and Sweden, sympathy lockouts that were designed to drain union treasuries. On the union side, bargaining was largely concentrated at the level of the national unions or the central confederations, which were more restrained than groups of workers at the plant level. Furthermore, the potential for aggressiveness in bargaining among the latter, which is based on a reasonable perception of the inelasticity of demand, was not exploited.[3] Employees were typically organized into works councils, which were not incorporated into the union structures and which have been restricted to a cooperative, rather than an adversary, relationship with the employer. Demand was also perceived as almost completely inelastic in the public sector, and here too the adversary relationship was supposed to be minimized: whether by legal prohibitions or established custom, strikes were taboo and wage movements in the government sector were supposed to follow wage movements in the private sector. The Scandinavian model, according to which wage changes are determined by changes in world prices and in productivity in the open sector—a competitive sector—assigns the role of follower to the sheltered sector, which includes the government.

Employers' associations were weakened, however, when firms granted

3. See chapter 1.

CONCLUSIONS 653

wage increases in excess of contractually negotiated increases, whether in order to attract or retain skilled labor in short supply or as part of their efforts to "rationalize" in response to the challenge of international competition. The ability of employers' associations to resist union demands by secondary lockouts was limited, moreover, since nationwide stoppages, in the Scandinavian countries, or even regional shutdowns, in Germany, invited government intervention in the short-term interests of the consuming public or the balance of payments. Meanwhile, wage drift tended to undermine the authority of the unions and the confederations as it weakened the position of their social partners on the other side of the bargaining table. The union establishments were threatened by the efforts of groups of workers at the grass roots to advance or protect their real or relative wages, as well as by the efforts of such groups to resist or reverse managerial initiatives to improve the efficiency of labor. Bargaining vacuums in the work place came to be filled by the activities of militant worker representatives. In Britain, where highly autonomous shop stewards existed during World War II, the vacuum never existed in the postwar period. In some instances their bargaining militancy was augmented by radical political input. In many more, it was marked by impatience with and insubordination to the union establishment. The wildcat strikes at the end of the 1960s and later were often directed against unions and confederations as well as against employers, and union negotiators in some countries subsequently came under pressure to bargain with greater intensity in order to retain sufficient support among the members.

Bargaining intensity also increased in the public sectors, where considerable bargaining potential had traditionally been left unexploited, as it had at the plant level in private industry. The growth of the public sector meant that increased proportions of a country's work force became sheltered from competitive pressures and liberated from the fear of unemployment. Public employees also liberated themselves from the old taboos against striking in essential services and in the civil service. Unions in the public sector, especially those in which relatively large proportions of the members were in the higher tax brackets, became less content to follow wage patterns set by unions in the internationally competitive sector and this in turn tended to increase bargaining intensity in the latter groups.

Evidence of structural weakening and decentralization contributed to the belief that neither employer resistance nor union restraint could be counted on to restrict labor costs sufficiently to permit the coexistence of politically acceptable levels of employment, growth, international competitiveness, and inflation. This belief was strengthened after the early 1970s, when more restrictive demand policies were undertaken in most countries in response to intensified external pressures and after inflation rates had increased sharply during the preceding four years. Unemployment reached and remained at new highs in these groups of countries for the rest of the decade, but inflation failed to fall back to the levels of the 1960s; indeed, it rose dramatically in Italy and the United Kingdom. Rates of increase in money wages also at least remained at the high levels reached in the late 1960s, although in Germany wage inflation fell back to pre-1969 levels after 1975. Wage-change estimating equations, including our own, indicate the occurrence of "structural breaks" in the early 1970s, after which money wages demonstrated greater responsiveness to price increases. (Germany again proved to be an exception.) This behavior is consistent with "real-wage protection" in the face of inflationary pressures. And real compensation continued to increase in the face of deterioration in the terms of trade and international recession. Rates of increase were reduced below growth rates during the 1960s and early 1970s, but they rose in relation to productivity, so profitability declined sharply during the period 1974–78. The behavior of real wages in general suggested that unions in Western Europe responded to adverse movements in the terms of trade and to demand deflation in the 1970s with increased bargaining intensity.

Nor, it should be added, did negotiated wages give way before the rapidly rising increases in social welfare payments. The latter entailed increased taxes on both employees and employers. Increased payroll taxes should induce increased resistance by employers in collective bargaining; however, the coefficients of the employer-contribution variables in our wage-change estimating equations for the Netherlands and Germany—countries with extensively developed systems of social welfare—were not significantly negative. Unionists were not disposed to shoulder their share of the increased tax burden of supporting the economically inactive, while they pressed for the expansion of social welfare through political channels.

Endogenous Management of Demand

If the inertial properties of wage behavior and the inflationary process appeared to indicate the inefficiency of demand deflation, could not the remedy lie in still more—or more sustained—restrictive monetary-fiscal policy? This course was implied by the international monetarist model, the influence of which grew as the 1970s wore on. It continued to encounter resistance, however, from Keynesians who were reluctant to subordinate high-level employment as an objective of policy, from members of the business communities who feared further deterioration of profitability, and from unionists as well. The last could exert both political and economic pressure on the policymaking authorities. The most direct political channel was furnished by various left-of-center political parties, of which unions represented powerful constituencies.

Policymaking could also be constrained by the bargaining power of unions. This happened when, notably under centralized bargaining, the level of real wages was low enough to permit full employment within the unionized sectors of the work force but too high to prevent substantial unemployment among young people and women, who were newcomers to the labor force.[4] Then the unions could live more comfortably with higher levels of both aggregate unemployment and real wages than the government. Lacking the leverage on the union derived from a credible threat of deflation, the authorities would find themselves under pressure to attempt to reduce real wages and increase employment by inflationary demand management or depreciation of the currency. But the combination of higher employment and lower real wages thus achieved would be unstable, since at the higher level of employment the unions could at least restore the original level of real wages. This would force on the government a policy of accelerating monetary growth (or depreciation) as the price of maintaining the level of unemployment preferred by the government.

Of course, these pressures were not necessarily decisive. They did not always prevail over pressures exerted on behalf of deflationary alternatives, even when the unions' political allies were in office. Yet

---

4. After the mid 1970s, these groups contributed disproportionately to the prevailing higher levels of unemployment. The growth of real wages obviously did not preclude the entry and employment of foreign labor in large numbers, and the German union movement was credited with acceptance of such immigration. Many foreign workers filled low-paying jobs that native labor avoided, however, and in this respect could be regarded as complementary to native labor. The guest workers were supposed to be employed at the ruling union wage levels, moreover, so, to the extent that they were so employed, they served as a determinant of their rates of entry. But exit rates could not be similarly controlled, and when unemployment rose in the mid 1970s, official barriers to the entry of migrants from outside the European Economic Community were erected and attitudes toward the resident foreigners hardened.

even under these circumstances unionists could exert influence on economic policymaking through channels that bypassed the established political and bargaining institutions. During the early 1970s, the possibility that further labor unrest would be provoked by another recession had to be taken into account by monetary and fiscal authorities. It is interesting that strong deflationary policies were eschewed in Italy, France, and Britain. These countries had conservative governments in office, which might ordinarily have been less disposed than their leftist opponents to risk higher inflation rather than greater unemployment—especially since inflation had been on the rise in all three countries. In addition, their national unions and confederations were not in strong positions to exercise bargaining restraint, which tended to increase the risk of higher inflation. In Germany, a second outcropping of wildcat strikes in 1973 lent some weight to earlier claims that, in an unsettled climate of labor relations, usually strong and conservative unions had been induced to bargain more intensely, normally combative employers to accommodate the unions more readily, and even the autonomous and conservative Bundesbank to accommodate the employers when they posted price increases. In Sweden, a dose of deflation was administered by a Social Democratic government in 1971. But in this instance the policy was justified by reference to a balance-of-payments problem, and even so, deflation was delayed—and thus ultimately made more severe—partly because it had been feared that it would intensify the labor unrest that had existed in Sweden.

During the second half of the 1970s the pressures on stabilization policy that were generated by union bargaining and political behavior were overbalanced by the strong external pressures that ultimately weakened the postwar commitment to full employment and expectations of high rates of growth in most of the countries. Nevertheless, as minimally acceptable levels of both employment of their members and real compensation were threatened, unions in many cases responded not only with greater bargaining intensity but with extra political activity in support of a variety of public subsidy programs designed to minimize unemployment. Exerting pressure for subsidies could appeal to unions as less painful and more efficient than exercising self-restraint in bargaining in economically distressed industries in which management was unable to offer effective resistance. The former approach could be combined with the extension and invocation of legislated or negotiated requirements that employers give notification in advance of contemplated dismissals or layoffs, which gave the unions involved time in which to mobilize public opinion and to secure official intervention. In many instances subsidies were accompanied by nationalization; conversely, the prior existence of public ownership facilitated subsidization. Such lame-duck socialism, together with the enlargement of training programs and other forms of subsidy to both firms and employees in the private sector, could be effective in minimizing open unemployment, as it was particularly in Sweden and Norway. But subsidies also reduced productivity and they aggregated into increased government deficits, which worked at cross purposes with tight monetary policy. This was in contrast to the original aim of active labor market policies, which had been designed by the Swedish trade union economists Gösta Rehn and Rudolf Meidner to reduce unemployment by increasing the mobility of labor and thereby to increase productivity and facilitate the adoption and implementation of noninflationary monetary and fiscal policies.

The Tax Burden on Collective Bargaining

While collective bargaining was helping to protect and advance real wages in the face of declining growth, rising unemployment, adverse movements in the terms of trade, and increasing taxes, it was also becoming less efficient in advancing and even protecting real after-tax wage rates of union members. Tax-push inflation is a potential problem in any economy in which unions attempt to shift onto wages any increases in direct taxes or in employees' contributions to social security while employers shift onto prices any increases in indirect taxes or employers' contributions to social security. Despite its interest, econometric examination of the tax-push hypothesis has been sparse, but the Organisation for Economic Co-operation and Development reported evidence of forward shifting for Denmark, West Germany, and Sweden but not for France, the Netherlands, or the United Kingdom.[5]

Where such effects exist, as in economies with high rates of inflation and steeply progressive income taxes, it may be impossible for unions to advance real disposable earnings at any rate of money-wage increase.In order to see this, consider the proportionate rate of change of real disposable (after-tax) income, $(w/p)_d$:

(1) $$(\dot{w/p})_d = [(1 - t_m)/(1 - t_a)]\, \dot{w} - \dot{p},$$

5. OECD, *Public Expenditure Trends* (Paris: OECD, June 1978), pp. 81–87.

where t_m and t_a are respectively the marginal and average tax rates, and $(1 - t_m)/(1 - t_a)$ is the elasticity of disposable income with respect to an increase in pretax nominal income. (The progressiveness of a tax structure varies with the elasticity. If the elasticity is zero, all increases in income will be taxed away; if it equals unity, the tax system is proportional.)

If prices are a constant markup on unit labor costs, then the growth of real disposable income can be described as

$$(2) \qquad (w/p)_d = [(1 - t_m)/(1 - t_a)]\, \dot{w} - (\dot{w} - \dot{q} + \dot{\tau}),$$

where $\dot{q}$ is the rate of growth of labor productivity and $\dot{\tau}$ that of indirect tax rates and employers' contributions to social security. This formulation illustrates the dilemma of a union movement. Negotiated wage increases simultaneously increase disposable income and prices, but the effects are not symmetrical. Markup pricing produces a proportionate response of prices to wages, but with progressive taxation, nominal disposable income rises less than proportionately. The conditions under which wage gains under collective bargaining will actually reduce disposable real income can be ascertained by rearranging equation 2 to

$$(3) \qquad (w/p)_d = \dot{w}\left[\frac{(1 - t_m)}{(1 - t_a)} - 1\right] + (\dot{q} - \dot{\tau}).$$

Since the data reviewed in table 1-8 indicate that the income tax systems in the countries under study are progressive, an increase in the rate of money-wage inflation unambiguously reduces real disposable income below what it would have been otherwise. With positive money-wage increases real disposable income will be positive only if the wedge between wages and prices provided by productivity growth less indirect tax growth $(\dot{q} - \dot{\tau})$ is sufficiently large. It can be seen from equation 3 that real disposable income will decrease when

$$\dot{q} - \dot{\tau} < \dot{w}\left[1 - \frac{(1 - t_m)}{(1 - t_a)}\right].$$

Thus for closed economies with progressive income tax structures— elasticities of disposable income in the range of 0.6 to 0.7, for example— constant indirect taxation, and growth in productivity of around 3 to 4 percent a year, real disposable income will decline if nominal wage increases exceed 8–10 percent a year. If indirect taxes are increasing, the critical wage increase is lower.

The limitations on collective bargaining are even more severe in open economies in which developments in world markets determine price changes in some industries. The expression for the growth of real income in an open economy is

$$(4) \qquad (w/p)_d = \dot{w}\left[\frac{(1 - t_m)}{(1 - t_a)} - e_N\right] + e_N(\dot{q}_N - \dot{\tau}) - e_T\dot{p}_T,$$

in which the subscripts T and N denote the "tradable" and "nontradable" sectors of the economy and the e_i are the respective shares of each sector in the consumer price index.[6] Two quite different cases emerge from equation 4, the critical relation being that between $(1 - t_m)/(1 - t_a)$ and e_N. If the share of nontradables in the consumer price index (CPI) is *greater* than the tax-elasticity term, then—as in the closed economy— higher money-wage inflation reduces the increases in disposable income. The condition for a reduction in disposable real income is

$$(5) \qquad e_N(\dot{q} - \dot{\tau}) - e_T\dot{p}_T < \dot{w}[e_N - (1 - t_m)/(1 - t_a)].$$

While there are many possibilities, it is clear that with a relatively high rate of increase in world prices, a relatively low rate of productivity in the nontradables sector—services, construction, government, and so on—and increasing indirect taxation—not an unusual combination in the 1970s—the left-hand side of equation 5 can easily be negative, and thus real disposable income will decline with *any* increase in money wages. The combined effects of inflation and progressive taxation can render collective bargaining impotent as a vehicle for advancing disposable real income.

If, on the other hand, $e_N < (1 - t_m)/(1 - t_a)$, higher money-wage inflation *increases* real disposable income above what it would have been otherwise. The condition for an increase in real disposable income is that money-wage inflation is greater than

$$[e_T\dot{p}_T - e_N(\dot{q}_n - \dot{\tau})]/[(1 - t_m)/(1 - t_a)] - e_N.$$

In that case, sufficiently large rates of money-wage inflation could secure

6. For a derivation of this expression and application to Swedish data, see Lars Calmfors, "Inflation in Sweden," in Lawrence B. Krause and Walter S. Salant, eds., *Worldwide Inflation: Theory and Recent Experience* (Washington, D.C.: Brookings Institution, 1977), p. 532.

any increase in real disposable income, but this suggests equally that sole reliance on collective bargaining for that purpose would be destabilizing.

The Policies

The limited efficiency and feasibility of demand management in restraining real wages could suffice to account for the revival of incomes policies in the 1970s, and indeed some of the new policies were intended to improve the political acceptance of deflation and thus to combine restraint in wage bargaining with deflationary, rather than inflationary, monetary and fiscal policies. In the 1950s and 1960s these policies had often been ineffective in restraining domestic inflation on a sustained basis, and their failures were frequently punctuated by loud wage and price explosions. On the other hand, real wage movements had been restrained in Germany, Sweden, the Netherlands, and even Britain, and the new policies placed more explicit emphasis on the "real" objectives of improving international competitiveness and profitability. Reluctance by unionists to comply with policies of wage restraint, moreover, was potentially diminished in the countries in which high marginal rates of taxation were visibly reducing the real returns on collective bargaining, although in Sweden opposition to formal incomes policy as a matter of principle was not relaxed until the closing years of the 1970s. Finally, high and rising unemployment together with dramatically adverse international developments in the 1970s posed a more credible threat of job loss to unionized as well as nonunion sectors of the work force than had been raised before, and this too disposed unions to accept incomes policies.

But adversity could not ensure that the new policies would be more effective than the older ones had been, if only because real wage restraint could not ensure maintenance of or return to satisfactorily high levels of employment. Unionists were asked to incur known costs in exchange for possible gains. Two other types of risk arose from incomplete compliance. In the first place, if a union complies by restraining negotiated wage rates while local drift payments are not subject to restraint, the union as an organization will be seen as delivering a smaller fraction of the compensation of its members. The bargaining unions, moreover, will not receive much credit for negotiating the norm. As a result, even

strongly organized trade union movements, such as the Dutch Nederlands Verbond van Vakverenigingen, suffered erosion of membership
support. In the second place, unions found that if they complied with a
policy of restraint while other groups did not, they would be subject to a
double penalty. If by accepting a reduction in their actual or potential
real wages they contributed to an abatement of inflation, they would also
contribute to a rise in the real wages of noncompliers. The compliers
would suffer a loss in both real and relative wages as a reward for good
citizenship in creating a public good. Even if all groups were agreed that
wage restraint was desirable under the circumstances, who would be
willing to take the first step?

We have seen how, in the absence of national wage policy, such a
public-good problem arose within unionized labor markets and how
some union movements sought escape from their prisoner's dilemma by
erecting their own centralized bargaining institutions. Under an economywide incomes policy, an analogous procedure would be to provide
some form of legal enforcement which, by giving the policy the force of
law, could buttress centralized bargaining institutions—on both sides—
which had been weakened during the postwar period. But, true to theory,
legal enforcement could be effective only when it was accompanied by
a substantial consensus in favor of compliance; then it could round up
the strays—or, as the British put it, the "rogue elephants"—and make
compliance easier for the majority of unions and employers. Sometimes
government fiat could be effective after negotiations had broken down.
This happened in Denmark, Norway, and the Netherlands, where, in
the late 1970s, an implicit consensus seems to have been reached, which
took the form of a sequence that featured the promulgation of tightly
restrictive wage norms, in real terms, following the breakdown of
negotiations, which in turn sometimes followed the granting of concessions by the government on taxes or social welfare. But where consensus
was lacking, government fiat could not prove an effective substitute.
The wildcat strikes in the late 1960s and early 1970s were in defiance of
the law in many instances, and strikes of government employees revealed
the low estate to which legal doctrines of sovereignty had fallen in the
domain of industrial relations. Resort to restrictive labor legislation
backfired in Britain and the Netherlands when, in the face of union
defiance, such measures were withdrawn, repealed, or held in abeyance.

Sometimes sufficient consensus could be generated by appeal to
public-spiritedness in the face of a certifiable national emergency or in

an appeal to partisan political loyalty. In the former case, currency or balance-of-payments crises could sometimes serve as the economic equivalent of war, especially when reinforced by the intervention of the International Monetary Fund, and induce both social partners to rally round the incomes policy. But the effectiveness of exhortation tended to erode with the passage of time in the face of market pressures and adverse distributional consequences, and as early postwar predispositions to consensus yielded to heightened personal expectations while repetition and more flexible exchange rates robbed balance-of-payments difficulties of some of their shock value. Political loyalties could form a basis of compliance when Labor, Social Democratic, or even Communist parties appealed to their union allies for bargaining restraint in order to help them remain in office or to win electoral contests with conservative parties. But union support of political friends and their incomes policies often was predicated on the willingness of the latter to offer various forms of compensation, which were designed to limit or counter the risks of compliance.

Conservative as well as left-of-center governments were occasionally willing to extend compensation for wage restraint. It was typically under the latter—as in Germany, Norway, Holland, and Austria—that social-contract policies were sometimes characterized by formal multilateral institutions in which government ministries and even the central bank were included. Nevertheless, both sides could accept one premise on which a case for the social contract could be erected: that government policies had been contributing to the pressures on collective bargaining to generate inflationary wage behavior. Wage inflation can be generated when the pricing objectives of employers and the money-wage objectives of workers and their unions fail to produce consistent real-wage objectives. A real-wage offer consistent with the pricing targets of employers is likely to be influenced by excise taxes, taxes on profits, and social security taxes as well as a standard markup factor. At the same time, the real-wage target of workers is likely to depend on income and excise tax rates as well as on expected prices, relative wages, and so on.[7] As governments increased the taxes levied on each of the parties, they drove home a wedge that widened the gap between their real bargaining objectives. Since some of the principal variables that could be altered to

7. For an example, see John Pitchford and Stephen J. Turnovsky, "Some Effects of Taxes on Inflation," *Quarterly Journal of Economics,* vol. 90 (November 1976), pp. 523–39.

induce more consistent real-wage objectives were controlled by the government, a case could be made for bringing the government to the bargaining table.

Of course a case could also be made against institutionalizing the intrusion of private interest groups into the domain of public policymaking, and this, it might be noted, complemented the laissez-faire indictment of incomes policy as an intrusion into the private domain of wage and price setting. Left and centrist opinion tended to accept both forms of intervention in principle, holding that the latter was necessary and that, in consequence, the former was justified. Incomes policy could be regarded as a policy of the second best: in a world inhabited by large-scale organizations in strategic labor and product markets and by large-scale government, institutional restraint is necessary to produce results that would issue from the completely unregulated behavior of income-maximizing and rationally foresighted workers and firms under atomistically competitive conditions. In terms of figure 1-1 in chapter 1, incomes policy could increase employment from E_1 to E_0 by reducing the real wage rate from w_1 to w_0. Conservatives became increasingly uneasy with the second-best approach, warning that it could combine the worst of both possible worlds of government regulation and corporate encroachment on parliamentary sovereignty without delivering improved economic performance. Toward the end of the decade, administrations were installed in Britain and France that turned their backs on social-contract policy and offered monetarism and—in the case of Britain—certain legal restraints on unionism in its place. In other countries, however, especially where corporate traditions were strong, the ideological case against social-contract policy carried less weight.

The most telling objections were pragmatic and emerged from discussion of or experience with specific policies that could, it was hoped, serve a compensatory purpose, although not all were originally designed with that end in view. Compensation has been designed for individual wage earners and also for unions—for their political gratification and institutional protection. In some instances the purpose of compensation has been to protect real incomes, as by wage indexation, price controls, tax reduction, or increased social benefits. In others the purpose has been to further egalitarian objectives, as by some combination of collective bargaining and tax and welfare policies. Sometimes the idea has been to offer nonpecuniary compensation, mainly in the form of participation by workers in management or ownership of an enterprise or in preserving or improving the legal environment of the unions. In most instances incomes policies, formal or otherwise, employed these devices in various combinations, relying more heavily on some than on others and omitting some altogether. The whole could add up to either more or less than the sum of its parts, as the strengths or deficiencies of one element either offset or reinforced those of another in a particular mixture. Instances of such interactions are discussed in the preceding chapters, in the context of each country's experience; in the following pages we wrench each candidate for compensation out of the actual settings in which it was found and discuss each in relative isolation.

Wage Indexation

Although wage-indexation systems were important in the incomes policies of several of the countries in our sample during the 1970s, the indexation systems did not uniformly arise from the compensatory motives noted earlier. There has been in fact considerable variation among countries in the extent of wage indexation. In some, such as Denmark, Italy, and Norway, indexation systems were a well-established aspect of pay long before the 1960s and 1970s. In others, such systems have never developed—in Austria and Sweden, for example— or have been prohibited by law, as in Germany.[8] Both the timing and uneven incidence of wage-indexation arrangements across European countries reflect the complex nature of the relations between wage indexation, collective bargaining arrangements, and public policy objectives. Most commonly, wage-indexation clauses have been a quid pro quo for contracts of fixed duration when future price behavior is uncertain. The attitude of union leaders toward the desirability of indexation arrangements, however, has varied considerably across countries. While some unions have insisted on indexation as the price for long-term agreements, others have resisted it on the grounds that automatic payment mechanisms impair their ability to negotiate increases in real wages and reduce the institutional security of their labor organizations.

8. For further discussion of the timing and variation of wage-indexation policies among countries, see S. A. B. Page and Sandra Trollope, "An International Survey of Indexing and Its Effects," *National Institute Economic Review*, no. 70 (November 1974), pp. 46–60; Anne Romanis Braun, "Indexation of Wages and Salaries in Developed Economies," *IMF Staff Papers*, vol. 23 (March 1976), pp. 226–71.

Under incomes policy, wage indexation is presumably assigned the function imputed to wage-level rigidity by implicit contract theory: risk-averse workers insure themselves against cyclical reduction in real wage levels by paying their employers a premium in the form of lower average wages.[9] Despite—or because of—the real-wage-protection goals of unions, however, every European country that introduced or extended wage-indexation systems as compensatory devices during the 1970s attempted subsequently to move in the reverse direction, and in countries in which wage indexation was already well established, the indexation arrangements posed difficult problems for incomes policy. Efforts to use indexation as a compensatory tool were basically limited to France, as part of the Grenelle agreement in 1968 and of the *contrats de progrès* in the early 1970s; Italy, with the revision of the *scala mobile* during confederal negotiations in 1975; and the United Kingdom, with the introduction of threshold agreements in 1973–74. And in the Netherlands, indexation, which was first accepted in exchange for a long-term agreement by a large Dutch multinational company in 1965, was rapidly extended in the early 1970s to cover almost all collective bargaining agreements. None of these attempts was notably successful. At the same time, countries with extensive preexisting systems of indexation allocated significant incomes policy resources to reduction of the effects of the indexation system on the domestic cost structure, for wage-indexation payments accounted for an increasing proportion of growth in earnings during the 1970s. Other governments may have resisted the notion of using indexation as a compensatory device precisely because of the observed fact that wage-indexation systems tended to become a target rather than a tool of incomes policy.

The basic difficulty with the use of wage indexation as a compensatory device was that governments in the 1970s could not readily assume the position of the relatively risk-neutral insurer in which implicit contract theory placed the private employer. Wage-indexation arrangements are at best suited for inducing restraint in money wages as part of nominal incomes policies. Because indexation systems are normally inconsistent with reductions in real wages and indeed, from the perspective of compensation, have been introduced to eliminate the risk of real-

9. Martin Neil Baily, "Wages and Employment Under Uncertain Demand," *Review of Economic Studies,* vol. 49 (January 1974), pp. 37–50; Costas Azariadis, "Implicit Contracts and Underemployment Equilibria," *Journal of Political Economy,* vol. 83 (December 1975), pp. 1183–1202.

wage reductions, indexation was an inappropriate policy tool for a real incomes policy under the macroeconomic circumstances of the 1970s. During periods of increased world prices—for example, the surge in the prices of raw materials and oil in the early 1970s—indexation systems that are based on a full CPI interfere with the adjustment in real incomes that may be called for by the changing international terms of trade. International price increases then have a twofold effect on domestic prices. First, they enter the index directly to the extent that imported goods and services are consumed directly and indirectly to the extent that imported raw materials and intermediate goods are used in domestic production. Second, international price increases automatically enter the domestic labor cost structure by way of wage-indexation arrangements and contribute to a secondary pressure on prices. In this manner international price increases can trigger a wage-price spiral that retards the requisite real-wage adjustments or causes them to occur at a higher rate of inflation. Increases in indirect taxes on employer's contributions to social security can produce similar results.

In the absence of indexation unions could seek to protect the real incomes of their members by negotiating increases in contractual rates. There is a chance that real incomes policies could prevent such negotiated increases in rates, but they could not prevent indexation arrangements from generating equivalent increases in earnings if such arrangements were exempt from policy norms. Thus policy officials were generally unwilling to acquiesce in completely unfettered indexation arrangements during the inflation of the 1970s, and in practice, indexation systems often became a target rather than an instrument of incomes policy, requiring governments to become as inventive in their treatment of indexation arrangements as they were in their earlier designs of wage guidelines.

To the extent that indexation is ultimately a product of bargaining power, the latter can provide substitutes for it. In general, collective bargaining systems have proved to be quite adaptive to legal restraints on indexation. When collective bargaining provisions that index wages to prices were forbidden by law, as in France, at the time of a devaluation in late 1958, and West Germany, under interpretations of the Monetary Law of June 1948, clauses that shortened the duration of contracts in inflationary periods by providing for automatic renegotiation of collective bargaining agreements when inflation or the cost-of-living index exceeded a particular threshold appeared in collective bargaining agreements. When price indexation is forbidden, indexation to alternative correlated series, such as nominal GNP or production, is an alternative institutional response.[10]

Given the limitations on outright prohibition, three different approaches to restraint of the effects of wage-indexation arrangements have been adopted in multilateral negotiations between governments and the parties to collective bargaining during the 1970s. The first has been to create special "net," or sanitized, price indexes to be used for the purpose of wage indexation. A net price index is simply a less comprehensive version of a general consumer price index. Typically, a net price index omits the effects of indirect taxes and subsidies—as in the Netherlands, for example. On the other hand, where subsidies and indirect taxes have not been removed from the index, national government policy can regulate to some extent movements in the price index and achieve an indirect influence over wage-indexation payments. During the 1970s policy officials argued that energy prices should also be omitted, since they reflected changing terms of trade, and in Denmark, the deduction of energy prices from the wage index in the late 1970s was regarded as a signal achievement in the effort of the government to reduce the effects of the indexation arrangements on labor costs. In general, the presence of indexation during inflationary periods focuses conflict on the contents of the index. The index can become the issue.

The second approach has been to bargain over the parameters of the indexation system—particularly the degree of automatic compensation for a given increase in the index and the frequency of indexation adjustments, as in Norway, Denmark, and Italy, for example. In general, compensation has been considerably less than 100 percent, so wage-indexation arrangements have not fully removed compliance risk, even when they were based on a net price index, for workers and institutions. On the other hand, partial compensation permits the coexistence of wage indexation and a real incomes policy. Employers and policy officials have generally attempted to reduce the degree of compensation or the number of adjustments.

A third approach, adopted only in Denmark, permits indexation payments but provides that the amounts due under wage indexation be paid into special blocked pension accounts. This is not an approach in which unions have been willing to acquiesce indefinitely, and during a period of sustained inflation this method ultimately raises the subsidiary

10. Braun, "Indexation of Wages and Salaries," p. 264.

issues of when and how to dispose of the blocked indexation payments, which in the case of Denmark grew to be a significant proportion of consumption expenditures. An alternative method has been to keep indexation payments out of the cost structure by granting employers one-time subsidies equal to the amount of a periodic indexation payment.

Efforts such as these to tinker with a wage-indexation system as part of an overall incomes policy strategy rest on the untenable assumption that the various components of total compensation are determined more or less independently. But this assumption is belied theoretically by Adam Smith's durable observations concerning equalizing wage differentials and empirically by analyses of wage behavior under collective bargaining in several of the foregoing chapters. As was true of other forms of wage regulation, efforts to weaken indexation arrangements proved to be futile to the extent that other components of the compensation package were altered to compensate for the loss of indexation payments. There is some evidence that wage drift served this purpose in Denmark. More broadly, econometric analyses of earnings behavior in Italy and the Netherlands revealed full compensation for price changes before the introduction of wage-indexation arrangements, suggesting that such arrangements may simply formalize prior bargaining behavior rather than alter the underlying wage-determination process radically. When the unions strongly preferred indexation over other devices, they were able to resist pressures on the authorities from employers to weaken or renounce it, as happened in Denmark, Britain, the Netherlands, and Italy. Conversely, when employers or authorities encouraged escalation as a way of preventing real wages from rising by guaranteeing them at existing levels or, as in Italy, to strengthen the authority of the more moderate central federations, they found it impossible to prevent increases in real wages by direct negotiation.

Price Controls

Price controls were assigned a secondary, even "cosmetic," function under incomes policies that assumed markup models of pricing, as under oligopolistic competition, and were intended by the authorities at least to maintain profit margins. Price controls were supposed to facilitate wage restraint, either by increasing the bargaining resistance of employers or by inducing restraint on the union side. In France, when Communist-led unions were not disposed to cooperate with conservative governments, price controls were often the only workable part of incomes policy, at least in the private sector, and were supposed to stiffen the resistance of employers to wage increases. In Denmark a law of 1971 that was intended to prevent the passthrough of wage drift, which embarrassed and weakened the union federation, was supposed to elicit both abstinence from the employers and restraint from the unions. In fact unions frequently demanded price control as a quid pro quo, to prevent erosion of both relative and real wages—if all incomes are frozen but the productivity of labor increases, then the share of profits will increase in time under a wage-price squeeze, whereas, if union wage restraint caused a growth of compensation that matched the growth in the productivity of labor, then there would be no adverse distributional consequences. In time, however, the opposite danger could arise. With compensation increasing in *excess* of growth in productivity, a price-control policy produces a profit squeeze and reduced incentives to invest.

Price controls have the additional disadvantage that they can at most protect workers from domestic inflationary surges. Increases in world prices cannot be controlled, and in practice countries have exempted import and export prices from price-control systems. While this merely makes explicit the redistribution required by changing terms of trade, the effects of such exemptions on workers are analogous to indexing wages to a "net" price index with import prices removed, and unions and union members may perceive such partial regulation as leaving them insufficient protection against the risk of a loss of real earnings to warrant money-wage restraint. Normally, on the production side of the economy, increases in the prices of imported raw materials or intermediate goods will further squeeze profits, unless price-control legislation allows for the passthrough of international prices. If so, however, the subsequent increase in domestic prices of products with imported components will erode the power of price controls as a compensatory device from the perspective of unions. Conversely, the existence of wage indexation would help to cancel the cost-reducing effect of depreciation of the exchange rate; in Denmark it precluded adoption of the latter alternative following the oil price increases in 1973–78.

From the perspective of a basic incomes policy objective of the period—the achievement of adjustments in real wages—price controls share the same general deficiency as wage-indexation systems. Since the underlying costs are likely to be controlled as effectively as prices, real wages are unlikely to decline, and profitability is unlikely to improve. On the other hand, a price freeze could be invoked before wage negotiations, as in Norway, in order to avoid anticipatory price increases and a provocative widening of profit margins that could touch off a subsequent increase in wage inflation. There is evidence, however, that reliance on this type of policy to avoid anticipatory increases ultimately lengthens the period of anticipation in future bargaining rounds. As the parties themselves came to anticipate the use of controls preceding collective bargaining negotiations in Denmark, the period of anticipation lengthened and controls had to be imposed further and further in advance of negotiations.

Furthermore, continuing reliance on price controls would necessitate increased recourse to subsidies—in the form of reduced contributions by employers to social security, for example, if, as suggested earlier, price controls lost their effectiveness in securing wage restraint. Financing subsidies by increased domestic or foreign borrowing would cause larger government deficits or higher interest rates and would ultimately involve sacrifice of one or more of the original policy objectives. To the extent that the subsidies could be financed out of indirect tax increases, this problem would be reduced, but at the expense of another and more highly regarded area of compensation: tax reductions.

Tax and Benefit Compensation

By focusing on real disposable income, rather than real gross income, as a target of incomes policy, governments could in principle use tax policy to offset for workers the effects of real-wage restraint needed to restore competitiveness. Indeed, interest in integrating tax policies with policies of wage restraint was perhaps the principal reason that many European incomes policies in the 1970s moved in the direction of "consensus" arrangements and further away from attempts at uncompensated restraint of the outcomes of the bargaining process. But it became apparent that tax reduction could be effective both as an incentive to wage restraint and as a component of stabilization policy only to the extent, first, that it was an effective if not superior substitute for collective bargaining in securing increases in disposable wage income; second, that it yielded significant reductions in cost inflation; third, that through cost reductions it delivered anticipated reductions in the rate of price inflation; and fourth, that the distributional outcome was acceptable to the unionized wage earners.

Tax cuts could be a promising substitute for wage restraint where marginal tax rates were high and also where wages and prices had been responsive to increases in taxes. Both of these conditions were well satisfied in Sweden and Denmark, but in countries in which the income tax structure was less progressive, the government's leverage in multilateral negotiations was weaker. And in countries in which changes in tax rates did not appear to exert so strong an influence on wage movements, swapping tax cuts for wage restraint would not in itself yield generous returns as a purely anti-inflationary policy. Even the modest potential leverage afforded by tax-push was "given away" in Denmark, where prior indexation of income taxes to prices, and later to earnings, left the government with relatively little to trade for union wage restraint.[11]

In the second place, negotiated wage restraint induced by tax reductions could not yield significant reductions in cost inflation when negotiated wages constituted a relatively small portion of labor-cost increases. During the 1970s nonwage labor costs and wage drift contributed the greater portion of total cost increases in most European countries. Unions themselves often contributed to such cost increases through the exertion of political pressure for the enlargement of social security benefits and employers' contributions, and employers were generally unable to shift these increased tax burdens to the unions in the form of smaller wage increases under normal bilateral bargaining. As a result, these legislated items of welfare and cost were often made subject to multilateral negotiations under the social contract. During the 1970s employers' contributions were sometimes subsidized in the interest of price restraint or increased profitability, as they were in France after 1968 and in Italy. Sometimes, however, the contributions were increased together with benefits in attempts to secure bargaining restraint, as they were in Sweden in 1970–71, 1973, and 1977. In Denmark a countrywide stoppage occurred in 1973 after the employers' federation had attempted to insert in the collective agreement a pledge from the unions to refrain from pressuring a Social Democratic government for social legislation that would require an increase in employers' contributions.

In the third place, while social contracts based on tax compensation could offer unionists a given increase in their disposable money incomes, they could not guarantee that increase in real terms, because the offer

11. Lloyd Ulman and Robert J. Flanagan, *Wage Restraint: A Study of Incomes Policies in Western Europe* (Berkeley: University of California Press, 1971), pp. 216–17, 245–61.

was not tied to price behavior—unless it was accompanied by indexation. As a result, the approach could not provide definite insurance against the compliance risk of a loss of real earnings. Negotiated wage restraint induced by government tax concessions, for example, ended abruptly in 1976–77 in the United Kingdom following a year in which inflation substantially exceeded forecasts and real wages fell by 7 percent. In its inability to control the behavior of key variables that it hoped to influence, social-contract policy suffered from the same deficiency that characterized its predecessors when they were betrayed by overconservative forecasts of economic activity during the 1960s. Under both types of incomes policy unions were supposed to make definite concessions in exchange for uncertain rewards—whether the latter were in the form of real disposable incomes or simply increased employment.

There remains a question of fiscal feasibility, which has been raised when social-contract packages providing for tax reductions or increases in social-welfare payments or other government spending caused increased budgetary deficits or foreign borrowing. Both actions have an expansionist effect on aggregate demand and tend to increase wage drift. When levels of employment and capacity utilization were relatively low and the balance-of-payments position was favorable, policies that predicated the adoption of tax reductions or increased spending on welfare programs could indeed offer an effective inducement to the unions in the form of increased employment, even in countries in which, as in Austria and Germany, marginal tax rates were not critically high. On the other hand, the Scandinavian countries, where heavily progressive tax systems prevailed, enjoyed exceptionally low rates of unemployment, except for Denmark in the second half of the 1970s. Under such conditions deficits caused by tax-cut incentives to wage restraint could prove destabilizing, unless offset by sufficiently vigorous economic growth or a sufficiently favorable balance-of-payments position. Under conditions of high-level employment, the social contract could be more successful as a device for allocating the gains from economic growth than for sharing the burdens of a retrenchment in real wages. The period of apparent success with the Norwegian multilateral bargaining experiment, for example, was possible in part because prospective revenues from North Sea oil and gas deposits enabled the government to set higher targets for the growth of real disposable income than would have been possible otherwise. During this period the government in effect ignored the balance-of-payments constraint. With the need to adjust to greater austerity during the late 1970s, the social-contract approach fell apart and gave way to a wage and price freeze.

Equity and Equality

Compensated incomes policies also generated wage drift when they conflicted with prevailing views of distributional equity. Incomes policies were frequently designed to accommodate the distributional objectives of unions in exchange for restraint of the average real wage, and part of the appeal of incomes policies to some unions may have been that they appeared to offer an opportunity to achieve redistributional goals that had been difficult to achieve in collective bargaining. In several countries efforts to increase the relative wages of low-income workers through collective bargaining had been thwarted or diluted by the tendency of high-wage workers to obtain wage drift. To the extent that these efforts to narrow certain wage differentials eventually succeeded, it was at the cost of considerable institutional strain and an inflationary interaction between negotiated wage rates and wage drift.

In some instances efforts to narrow the wage structure through incomes policy involved constructing wage guidelines for the benefit of low-paid wage earners. This could take the form of specifying minimum and maximum absolute increases, as the British did under a Conservative government in 1972–74 and under a Labour government in 1976, or of allowing the distribution of the permissible percentage increase to be allocated within bargaining units by negotiations. In other instances, indexation arrangements sometimes called for flat rate increases, as in Norway and Denmark, for maximum increases, or for price compensation that varied inversely with income levels, as in the Netherlands. The form of the revision of the *scala mobile* in Italy in 1975 was designed to bring about the compression of wage differentials. At times, however, some unions accepted policies that had a regressive distributional effect. Both the income tax reductions that some governments offered as an inducement to wage restraint and increases in indirect taxes that were sometimes imposed to pay for income tax reductions and increased transfer payments had a regressive thrust.

In principle, there was no reason that a social-contract package could not be balanced so as to yield distributional neutrality or any desired level of progressivity or regressivity. In practice, however, the union side was frequently divided within itself over the issues of wage distribution or lacked sufficient authority to impose a settlement on itself. Neither condition could be cured by the structure of norms, indexation arrangements, or tax changes under incomes policy. British experience provides a leading case in point. Until the mid 1960s, British incomes policies tended to hold back the growth of income among low-wage groups, especially government employees, and this contributed significantly to the subsequent militancy of public-sector unions. Together with a realignment of power in favor of the semiskilled workers within the two largest unions in the Trades Union Congress (TUC), this led to incomes policies in the 1970s that favored low-wage workers until they yielded serious discontent among the highly paid workers, which caused a split in the union movement and at the end of the decade helped to undermine the policies.

Efforts to increase the incomes of low-paid workers at the expense of the salaried sector encouraged the development of separate collective bargaining organizations and more militant collective bargaining activities among salaried employees. When the Swedish unions sought in 1980 to impose a real reduction in salaries in order to make room for a rise in real wages, a militant federation of salaried employees resisted strongly, the central federation was unable to restrain the unions in the public sector, and nationwide strikes and lockouts ensued. In the Netherlands attempts by the blue-collar federation to bargain more explicitly "for" the salaried employees stimulated the latter to form their own organization, which ultimately gained entry into the Social and Economic Council over the resistance of other unions. The establishment and growth of independent unions of the middle and upper salariat reflected the combined effects on their real and relative incomes of inflation, progressive income tax structures, and relative increases in the supply of more highly educated labor, but these very developments limited the feasibility of further altering the distribution of labor income between salaries and wages through central bargaining.

Although unions might have been attracted to incomes policies because they appeared to offer them an opportunity to achieve redistributional goals that they could not achieve in collective bargaining, in fact, incomes policies ran into the same problems in achieving permanent alterations in the wage structure—a factor that ultimately contributed to the erosion of union support.

Thus efforts to raise the relative wages of low-wage workers, whether by incomes policy or by collective bargaining and whether or not they were effective, provoked feelings of inequity among those higher up in the income distribution and were sometimes conducive to wage drift. Incomes policies and unrestricted collective bargaining encountered similar problems in attempting to achieve permanent alterations in the wage structure, and incomes policies proved to have no inherent advantage over collective bargaining in achieving a more egalitarian wage structure. Indeed, the inflationary interaction between negotiated wage objectives and wage drift is often politically less acceptable when it is the outcome of an incomes policy than when it is the result of unrestricted collective bargaining.

Wage Drift and Tax-based Incomes Policy

It is clear from the preceding paragraphs and the more extensive analyses in the country chapters that wage drift continued to limit the achievements of European incomes policies during the 1970s as it had in earlier decades. In virtually every country in which a statistical analysis was possible, our wage-change estimating equations indicated that wage drift was sensitive to labor-market pressure. At the same time, in our statistical analyses we uncovered very little evidence of a significant negative relation between changes in wage drift and changes in negotiated rates, and we found no evidence at all of a compensatory equal proportionate relation, which would have implied that changes in negotiated rates have been exactly offset by opposite changes in drift and hence could not affect total money earnings and real wages. Thus more drift may be generated by increasing demand for labor, but it may or may not equal or exceed the reduction in negotiated wage increases induced by a given tax cut. If drift does equal or exceed the reduction in negotiated wage increases, real wages may be maintained or increased at excess-demand levels of employment. If, on the other hand, drift is less than the reduction in negotiated wage increases, real wages might be reduced, and the increase in demand for labor would be consistent with conditions of equilibrium in the labor market.

Drift could thus be symptomatic of policy effectiveness as well as policy failure, but even in the former case it had to be reckoned as a net cost of the policy. The greater the amount or extent of drift, the more difficult the task of restraining negotiated rates. And drift itself is an element of earnings that could not be controlled by social-contract negotiations, despite some strenuous efforts to do so. Since the domain of institutionalized collective bargaining has traditionally been restricted to the level of the industrial or multi-industrial sector in most European countries, wage drift has emerged from local ad hoc pressures or managerial policies.

Where systems of wage determination are decentralized, as in North America, however, tax-based incomes policies (TIPs) that use the tax system to reward compliance or to penalize noncompliance with pay or price objectives have been proposed to provide incentives for wage and price restraint to decentralized decisionmakers.[12] In the context of a social contract, the tax penalty or reward of a TIP may be based on adherence to the pay objectives of the negotiators but assessed on the basis of the growth of the total wage bill per worker for a firm or group of employees rather than the growth of negotiated rates. Since this measure of compliance includes wage drift, employers and workers at the plant level have an incentive to consider the consequences of pay increases that exceed contractual provisions.

When TIPs were adopted or discussed as an alternative to first-generation or social-contract policies in Europe during the 1970s, it was with the purpose of encouraging negotiated wage restraint in a limited number of situations in which collective bargaining itself was decentralized or weakly established—the *prélèvement conjoncturel* policy in France in 1975, for example. As is typical of decentralized bargaining systems, wage drift was a minor element of growth in earnings in these countries. On the other hand, in countries having centralized bargaining structures and considerable wage drift, TIPs have not been introduced, and the social-contract arrangements and earlier incomes policies that were developed to moderate the growth of negotiated wages were generally unsuccessful in mitigating wage drift, although employers in Denmark and Norway repeatedly attempted in negotiations to obtain commitments to reduce drift. While TIP arrangements address the decentralized nature of wage-drift decisions more effectively than social-contract negotiations, they also tend to shift the costs of incomes policy from workers to the government, which must pay for whatever compliance is achieved under most TIP plans. They also present certain

12. See Henry C. Wallich and Sidney Weintraub, "A Tax-Based Incomes Policy," *Journal of Economic Issues,* vol. 5 (June 1971), pp. 1–19; Arthur M. Okun and George L. Perry, eds., *Curing Chronic Inflation* (Washington, D.C.: Brookings Institution, 1978); Robert J. Flanagan, "Real Wage Insurance as a Compliance Incentive," *Eastern Economic Journal,* vol. 5 (October 1979), pp. 367–78.

administrative difficulties, and they eliminate the exercise of discretion-ary judgment in isolated cases in which it might be advisable to tolerate violations of the norm and thus allow drift to serve as a safety valve for the general policy. Nevertheless, it is by no means clear that these costs are great in relation to the benefit in reduced wage drift of integrating a TIP approach with centralized bargaining procedures. In minimizing drift, moreover, tax-based policies might help to protect centralized union and bargaining institutions from the corrosive influences to which they had been subjected in the postwar period, including incomes policies themselves. Concern about such influences was reflected in the approach of union movements to codetermination and to various proposals and measures for institutional reform.

Codetermination, Capital Sharing, and Other Nonmaterial Compensation

At least in principle the inclusion of elements of nonpecuniary compensation in a tacit or explicit social-contract package might abate the difficulties presented unions by a sacrifice of real wages or by distributional tension. Although not initially designed as compensatory incentives for wage restraint, a variety of worker-participation and capital-sharing schemes were considered as devices to encourage com-pliance with wage objectives during the 1970s. At the plant level, codetermination has included such traditional cooperative institutions as works councils, as well as ''job enrichment'' innovations intended to make factory work less monotonous and regimented—by self-managing work teams, greater flexibility and rotation in work assignments, and involvement of production employees in inspection, quality control, and planning, for example. Management hoped that by increasing job satis-faction these programs would increase productivity through encouraging the voluntary abandonment of restrictive work practices and reducing absenteeism. At the company level, the instrument of codetermination, notably in Germany and the Netherlands, has been the supervisory board of directors with legally determined proportions of directors who are either elected directly by the employees or are selected by the elected works councils. At the company, industry, or economywide level, proposals were advanced in Germany, Sweden, Denmark, and the Netherlands to create funds from contributions of shares of stock that would be equal in value to some proportion of excess profits or of the wage bill. Although these plans differed significantly in detail, all the proposals provided that the funds would be administered by unions either alone or together with public representatives.

European union leaders accepted that declining profitability had to be arrested when that seemed necessary to improve competitiveness and to avert more serious unemployment. The potential appeal of codetermination arrangements as part of a social contract was tied to the fact that incomes policies typically provided unions with no guarantees that across-the-board wage restraint would deliver intended levels of aggregate employment or that the latter, even if achieved, would not be characterized by the incidence of serious structural unemployment—notably in sectors adversely affected by international competition. European unions, which had achieved only limited protection of employment through collective bargaining, had long supported public policies and institutions that addressed unemployment at the level of the firm, including requirements of specified advance notification of dismissals and mandatory severance pay. As unemployment deepened during the 1970s, unions in various countries pressed for the strengthening of existing protective devices and added what Dutch unionists referred to as nonmaterial demands for codetermination and shorter workweeks to incomes policy discussions. Unions felt that labor representatives would have more influence over the microeconomic decisions governing employment at the plant level to the extent that investment plans and proposed plant closings or relocations had to be disclosed to works councils and at the company level to the extent that labor directors would be advised and consulted beforehand and vote on such matters as budgets, investment in labor-saving equipment, proposals to close plants at home, or investments in new facilities abroad. Such notification and consultation would permit labor directors to delay—if not to veto—policies concerning the size and distribution of the work force. It thereby could provide unions with a greater opportunity for the development of restrictive practices and the retention of excess labor.

Codetermination—insofar as it meant, led to, or helped shop-floor job control—appealed to activists within unions or confederations that exercised wage restraint at the industry or national level. Such activists were opposed to restraint and tended to be politically left-wing. They tended to be concentrated in the ranks of the younger unionists, among the shop stewards in Britain and their equivalents in Italy, and among the intellectuals in union research staffs in Germany. Only in France was the goal of autogestion (literally, "self-management") the official policy of a union, the non-Communist, left-wing Confédération Française Démocratique du Travail. Proponents of these ideas were frequently less interested in collective bargaining than in control of management, less concerned with an egalitarian distribution of wages than with the share of profits and the ownership of industrial assets, and completely out of sympathy with the centralization of authority within unions and within government. As a result, they could see in codetermination a way not merely to achieve greater growth without more profits, but to accomplish the socialization of private enterprise without bureaucratic nationalization—the old idea of the self-governing workshop or producer cooperative.

Nevertheless, there were two general difficulties with codetermination arrangements that reduced their potential value to union movements as a nonmaterial substitute for wage increases. First, codetermination at the work place could serve to strengthen ties between union members and their employers, on the one hand, and the works councils on the other. Second, codetermination arrangements elevate the profitability of the enterprise as a determinant of relative wages at the expense of solidarity or egalitarianism and thus exacerbate the conflict between the achievement of greater equality in the distribution of earnings and greater equality in the functional distribution of income. To the extent that more profitable firms and industries pay wage drift in excess of the uniform negotiated wage increase, solidaristic wage policy is disrupted; under codetermination drift would become what has been characterized as "institutionalized selfishness." On the other hand, to the extent that unions conforming to a solidaristic policy accepted less than the more profitable firms and industries were able to pay, the share of profits would be increased—but the alternative would be to raise the solidaristic wage target above the ability of the less profitable employers in the economy to pay.

It was to avoid this dilemma and to remove pressures for decentralization of bargaining that in Sweden the blue-collar labor federation, Landsorganisationen i Sverige (LO), produced its own proposal for an excess-profits tax. (The original version of the Swedish plan called for the establishment of company dividend funds, and the unions in sectors in which excess profits were low were quick to point out that transforming wages into worker-controlled dividends would do nothing to further the cause of solidarity other than pooling the industry-level funds into an aggregate fund.) In Sweden and other countries the notion of investment without profits appealed to the socialist elements of some labor federations, and capital-sharing plans were proposed in order to obtain the financial means of reallocating funds among sectors. The interest in these plans raised the possibility that they might be used as an element of compensation in wage-restraint policies.

These proposals left the bulk of the rank-and-file workers uncompensated and unmoved, however. In the first place, the planned funds suffered from a free-rider problem: the benefits of additional profits generated by the activities of workers at any one plant accrue to a general fund and thus benefit workers generally. Workers responsible for the gains receive a tiny fraction of the benefits, and the link between action and reward is likely to be too weak to provide a powerful incentive for increased profits through greater productivity in the work place. In the second place, some of these plans did not include individual ownership of the newly created shares, nor did the Dutch idea of financing the pension fund out of the proceeds of profit sharing offer much of an incentive to employed unionists to forgo wage increases. In Sweden and Denmark, moreover, the profit-and-capital-sharing plans also aroused resentment on the grounds that they represented a radical departure from the traditional Social Democratic emphasis on redistribution of income to the older Marxist emphasis on the redistribution and socialization of productive wealth. Finally, the idea of further strengthening what was already the strongest and most centralized institution in Sweden, the LO, aroused considerable popular concern among the electorate.

As it happened, none of the countries actually adopted such fund proposals, which were pushed into the political arena by the central labor movements. This does not mean that codetermination and profit sharing in one form or another can be ruled out in the future. If growth rates remain low or decline and the potential for direct pecuniary compensation remains low, and if rates of unemployment cum inflation exceed the bounds of popular tolerance, the political feasibility of these incentives to compliance could improve. In the 1970s, however, the tradeoff between anticipated economic gain from reduced wage inflation and political cost in potential social and institutional change was regarded as unacceptably steep.

Institutional Protection

Recourse to compensation and even legal compulsion could not obviate reliance on centralized bargaining institutions—notably central federations and big national unions—in developing and implementing wage policy. There appeared to be significant diseconomies of scale in the development of a consensus policy. The smaller the average size of the participating unit, the more parochial the perspectives that will be represented in the process of policy formulation; the larger the number of participating organizations, the more the process will have to contend directly with the problems of distribution. Since central institutions have typically been predisposed to more restrained settlements than their affiliates, the stronger or more influential the central organization, the easier it is to internalize the resolution of differences within its ranks before it proceeds to bargain over broader distributional issues. Central and synchronized bargaining and consistent conformity to patterns set by key settlements in open sectors of the economy have been hallmarks of generally strong bargaining institutions in Austria, Sweden, Norway, Germany, and the Netherlands. But elsewhere, craft unionism, autonomous and militantly led groups in the work place, and ideologically driven rivalry among union movements with parallel or overlapping jurisdictions have been conducive to less well coordinated and competitive wage behavior, which yields itself less readily to attempted restraint. Bargaining structures everywhere have been subject to pervasive decentralizing influences imparted by intensified international competition, rationalization, economic egalitarianism, and incomes policies.

Compensatory devices were supposed to minimize institutional strain caused by incomes policy by reducing the negotiated levels of real compensation that were minimally acceptable to the members, but sometimes they were infeasible or inefficient—as when tax reductions contributed to budgetary deficits and wage drift. And when compensatory devices were effective in reducing returns to the members from collective bargaining, by the same token they reduced the value of union membership. In part compensatory measures operated as a public good, of benefit to other sectors of the community as well as to unionists. The members could also regard the government—and especially, as in Britain, a Labour goverment—as the source of their compensatory gains, although these gains were in truth the product of political bargaining with the unions. Thus unions in Britain, Scandinavia, the Netherlands, and Germany had some reason to fear that their self-restraint in the public interest would be repaid by loss of the loyalty of their members or even loss of their affiliation. That they nevertheless persevered, to an extent that an American observer would regard as remarkable, could be ascribed to the fact that in Europe union affiliation has been a product of strong ideological or confessional traditions as well as of material utilitarianism, and courageous leaders could draw on this inheritance. But union loyalty that has an ideological base may be vulnerable to ideologically or politically motivated dissidents, or even to breakaway movements, as in Sweden and in Italy, the leaders of which have sometimes seized on bargaining restraint by the union establishment to make their causes effective with the rank and file.

For these reasons, it has sometimes been proposed that incomes policies incorporate features that might offer the unions some protection against erosion of the support of their members or that, alternatively, might preserve or strengthen their own authority. Institutional protection could assume a variety of forms. To begin with, inclusion of the union side in a formal, highly visible central bargaining or concerted-action process might confer on it status as an estate of the realm and, in the process, enable it to gain public credit for any public goods that it might negotiate in exchange for forgoing some private gains for its own members. Thus in Norway renewal of multilateral bargaining in 1975 restored the authority of the central hierarchy of the Landsorganisasjonen i Norge (LO), which had suffered from a reversion to decentralized negotiations the year before. In Germany the provision in the Law for the Promotion of Stability and Growth of 1967 for formal concerted action among the unions, employers' associations, the Bundesbank, and government ministries elevated the status of the Deutscher Gewerkschaftsbund (DGB); it helped the unions to follow through with the Düsseldorf program of the DGB, which in effect had turned the movement away from its earlier Marxist disposition. In Sweden the bilateral negotiations between the unions and the employers' federations of their "central frame agreements" so ostentatiously excluded formal intervention by the government that they highlighted the position of the LO as a senior partner in the determination of macroeconomic policy. And in Italy the decision of the large firms then in control of the employers' association to offer complete wage indexation under the *scala mobile* in 1975 enabled Confindustria to bargain directly with the union confederations in central negotiations, instead of with their affiliated industrial unions. Thus it was hoped to reduce the power of the *delegati* and the *consigli* in the plants.

Union movements were also expected to convert codetermination and profit sharing from agents of decentralization—since the individual firm is the locus of either workers' incentives or worker control—into devices that could strengthen the positions of their own central institutions. We have already referred to proposals for pooling profits and shares into central union-administered funds. Codetermination could be designed so as to give national unions, which have largely been confined to industrywide bargaining over wages, a more direct and official presence in the firm when questions of growing importance concerning employment were being decided. This was done in Germany by providing that some specified number of labor directors on the supervisory board be nominated by the majority union in the firm and that they include at least one director who was not a company employee. In the Netherlands a social-contract package that was put forward by the union federation balanced the potentially decentralizing effects of an extension of codetermination with a proposal for joint industry committees that would negotiate over job issues. In Britain, on the other hand, a proposal to restrict nominations of labor directors to a single joint committee of union representatives would have institutionalized the de facto power enjoyed by the senior shop stewards at the expense of their respective national unions, because the stewards bore the brunt of imposing a restrictive incomes policy on the members. But neither this proposal nor any system of labor directors was adopted.

In more down-to-earth moves, in some labor movements the problem of union security was addressed, the problem becoming more acute when the unions were expected to bargain with restraint. Laws requiring the "extension" of negotiated terms to nonsignatory firms lost most of their effectiveness in protecting union jobs in the high-employment climate of postwar Europe; instead they intensified a problem of free riders. In the Netherlands and Germany some unions sought the answer in restricting certain negotiated gains to their own members; in Germany members-only bargaining was also attempted but was held to be illegal. Another approach was to negotiate closed-shop agreements. In Germany these too were outlawed, but in Britain, where they had been lawful, the unions successfully resisted and ultimately, in 1971, made unworkable a law that would have forbidden them. Dutch unions called a nationwide strike in 1971 that prevented the government from putting into effect a new law that would have authorized it to invalidate specific negotiated agreements as well as to require approval of their contents in advance. Finally, the French wildcat strikes of 1968 were followed by the Law on Trade Union Rights in the Company, which tended to strengthen the authority of the Confédération Générale du Travail, which had led the strikes from behind.

But if, as suggested earlier, institutional protection can be considered to be a form of nonpecuniary compensation, it came at a nonpecuniary cost, against which the economic gains from compliance with incomes policy had to be weighed. In some cases the costs were held to be excessive at the time. De facto parity representation of labor directors in Germany fell into that category. So did the union-controlled capital-sharing funds; competitive proposals, advanced by conservatives and business groups, lacked those features that tended to strengthen the authority of central union bodies. Efforts to secure members-only bargaining in Germany were unsuccessful; in the Netherlands union success along these lines was limited by resistance from workers on the one hand and by employers' associations on the other, on the grounds that such compensation took the form of wage drift and weakened their own authority. The most successful examples of institutional protection appeared when the British and Dutch unions were able to block, repeal, or nullify legislation that would have restricted the area of legal freedom enjoyed until then by the unions in those countries. These were essentially defensive victories; they did not increase the authority of the central federations, moreover. The historical record nevertheless provides an instructive contrast between the Conservative governments in Britain in the 1950s and the Conservative government that came to power at the end of the 1970s and attempted to reduce the power of the unions. The former were willing to leave the potential bargaining power of the unions—the maximum negotiable wage—intact in exchange for an undertaking on their part to reduce their rate of bargaining intensity. The latter was unwilling to engage in policy bargaining with the unions, choosing instead to follow a course that combined reliance on deflation with an intended reduction in the maximum negotiable wage at any given level of employment.

The Predisposition to Consensus

Diseconomies of scale in the negotiation of social contracts were not confined to the union side. Even when the unions were sufficiently unified to minimize and internalize differences among wage-earning groups, a multiplicity of other interests could prevent the achievement of a working consensus. The amount of compensation and protection required to generate sufficient wage restraint could contribute to heterogeneity and fragmentation outside the union group. An attempt to resolve one set of distributional issues could exacerbate others. We have already cited the wage-salary issue as an example of the formation or invigoration of autonomous white-collar federations, which ultimately made it more difficult for blue-collar unions and management to conclude their own bilateral settlements in Sweden and, to a lesser extent, the Netherlands. In addition, when social-contract bargaining transfers more of the total distributional function of society to the legislative process, it may simultaneously channel distributional conflict into the political process. In Denmark parliamentary involvement in multilateral negotiations was associated with a proliferation of political parties, and a succession of fragile governing coalitions and instability in industrial relations contributed to such political fragmentation and instability.

Where the party system itself was centralized to begin with, as in a system characterized by two major parties or by the ability to erect strong coalitions, it could offer more effective resistance to such destabilizing influences by internalizing some of the distributional problems which arose outside the collective bargaining system. Economies of scale were greater and the prospects for effective wage restraint improved when the official as well as the private parties to social-contract bargaining possessed the capability of centralized decisionmaking. Austria, Germany, and, at least until the late 1970s, Sweden could count on such double-barreled capability. Under those conditions, a well-centralized union movement could reinforce, rather than weaken, the stability of a political system through its ability to absorb a fair amount of wage restraint; in effect it could reciprocate for any institutional protection that the government would be able to supply to the union

686   CONCLUSIONS

side. In Austria an exceptionally unified and centralized union movement, with strong ties to the shop stewards, has underwritten a higher
degree of parliamentary stability. Austria's social contracts issue from
an elaborately formalized, although extralegal, set of procedures involving the government and four large interest groups, including the Austrian
Federation of Labor. But it is hardly an exaggeration to regard the
process as unilateral. Austrian wage determination is the product of the
ultimate economy of scale: the general secretary of the labor federation,
the Oesterreichischer Gewerkschaftsbund (OeGB), has doubled in brass
as the speaker of the lower house of the parliament.

Since Austria and Germany combined outstandingly low rates of
inflation and unemployment with high rates of growth in the 1970s (see
figure 5-2), foreigners eyed their social-contract institutions—especially
the Austrian model—with great interest. But institutionalized concerted
action had been tried elsewhere, and it survived the 1970s intact only in
Austria. In Germany, where formal concerted action was abandoned in
1972, the unions and the authorities were able to continue the substance
of concerted action without the public trappings. A centralized union
movement was highly visible in Austria as it bargained with itself over
wage movements and, at critical junctures, proved to be a crucial
determinant of economic policy as well. But the Germans managed to
bargain with consistent restraint in less centralized fashion and over a
much larger economy. And the Swedes found that a trade-union movement that was only slightly less tightly centralized and politically
influential than the OeGB could not always function with sufficient
restraint to satisfy both the economy's requirements of external balance
and the labor movement's own objective of distributional equity.

The Austrians, however, did differ from the Swedes—and from
people in other countries too—in explicitly refusing to saddle their
bargaining system with redistributional tasks; the latter were left to the
legislative process, where the interests of the unions were well represented. In Germany redistribution was tacitly dropped as a bargaining
objective in the early 1960s. Whereas the strengthening of centralized
authority in the Swedish union movement and bargaining system had
been in good part motivated by a commitment to egalitarian bargaining,
centralized authority in Austria and a well-articulated bargaining system
in Germany did not depend on that type of commitment. In addition,
German and Austrian unionists joined their fellow citizens in assigning
high priority to domestic price stability as well as to international

competitiveness as policy objectives. This tended, of itself, to locate union policy targets close to the official targets and, to that extent, to minimize the bargaining restraint required for compliance with official policy. Meanwhile, the relatively strong disposition of these unions to pursue their distributional objectives through the legislative process meant that they could be more efficiently compensated for bargaining restraint by tax or welfare measures than could unions which looked more to bargaining to yield distributional change.

Taken together, these two characteristics of unionism in Austria and Germany reflected a relatively strong predisposition to consensus, which was less vulnerable to the postwar forces of erosion in those two countries than elsewhere. It was founded in part on a unique historical experience that imposed itself strongly on the national consciousness: the hyperinflation of the 1920s and the tragic political events that followed it. It was also rooted in a traditional acceptance of the function of government in providing for the economic security of the individual and the obligation of private interest groups to exercise restraint in the national public interest. Envious foreigners have emphasized the value of the centralized and unified union structures that they claim were rewards for losing the war—although some of the visitors, who helped in the process of industrial reconstruction, retained their own archaic models. But structural streamlining was only part of these success stories; other ingredients were supplied by prewar survivals. These sustaining traditions were not all unique to these two countries, but neither were they readily exportable—especially to lands where laissez-faire was the doctrinal inheritance and concerted action found itself inhibited, as if tugged by an unseen hand.

It must also be appreciated that the greater durability of consensus in Germany and Austria owed much to its effectiveness—as well as the other way around—and that its effectiveness was reflected in economic performance that was strong in both relative and absolute terms. In Germany predisposition to consensus was effective in protecting an initially undervalued currency and then a favorable balance-of-payments position. Under those circumstances wage restraint, together with monetary and fiscal restraint, could yield prompt returns, and the prospect of success could in turn serve as an added incentive to restraint on subsequent occasions. And as long as the absence of such a positive incentive was reflected in weaker wage restraint and other disinflationary policies abroad, Germanic virtue would be rewarded by foreign vice.

Incomes Policy and Unemployment—A Look Ahead

What lies ahead for incomes policy? Obviously, it could not preclude recourse to deflation in the second half of the 1970s, nor could it prevent inflation from rising with unemployment or real wages from squeezing profits. Compensatory arrangements, pecuniary and otherwise, were sometimes effective in securing union support of incomes policies and even of restrictive macroeconomic policies, but often they were either inefficient as incentives or too risky or costly in economic or political terms under prevailing conditions. By the end of the decade, incomes policies had lost much popular support and political appeal, while the political stock of monetarism had risen along with apparent tolerance of—or resignation to—unemployment. Nevertheless, incomes policy is likely to survive as an important component of overall macroeconomic policy, less formally and ostentatiously, perhaps intermittently, but possibly more cost-effectively. What are the bases of this prognosis?

To begin with, the structural characteristics of contemporary economies, for which incomes policies have been supposed to compensate, are not likely to disappear in the near future. To the extent that oligopolistic and monopolistic market structures survive international competitive erosion—further rationalization and loss of capacity in traditional, heavily unionized manufacturing industries, for example— and to the extent that proposed policies that could cause the reduction of union bargaining potential, such as restrictive labor legislation on the one hand, or possibly profit sharing under participatory arrangements on the other, remain politically infeasible, there will continue to be a second-best case for incomes policies.

In the second place, policy failures after 1973 must be attributed in part to the occurrence of some exceptionally severe surprise shocks of external origin that falsified expectations and invalidated the forecasts on which private wage setting and price setting and public policymaking were based. Since incomes policies had previously proved vulnerable to forecasting errors, their failures in the 1970s revealed a built-in weakness of this class of policies. The quadrupling of oil prices in 1973–74, however, their subsequent doubling in 1979, and the structural dislocations caused by intensified competition from outside the area did constitute a particularly nasty set of shocks to the environment in which the incomes policies were implanted. It must be remembered that incomes policies in this period were introduced in response to problems of unprecedented severity in postwar Europe.

And yet conditions of greater slack in labor and product markets in the second half of the 1970s were more conducive to the effectiveness of incomes policies than the tighter conditions that had prevailed in labor markets during the two preceding decades, when earlier policies had registered some success in restraining real wages. Real wages, although rising in relation to productivity, rose much less rapidly after 1973 than they had earlier in the decade. Unemployment rates, which rose sharply in most countries, were not conducive to demand-generated wage drift, which had frequently constituted a threat to incomes policies at higher levels of employment. Thus looser labor markets not only would have exerted some restraint on real wage movements in the absence of incomes policies; they were also conducive to greater effectiveness of such policies.

In some countries, moreover, incomes policies fulfilled a broader function after the early 1970s than they had earlier. Incomes policy had been designed originally to substitute for deflation and to be applied during upswings and at high levels of employment. While the view had indeed been expressed that policies of direct wage restraint could operate more effectively as a complement to deflation, when they would "work with the market," that was feasible only where union movements were weak, economically and politically, as they were in France and Italy during the second half of the 1960s. Elsewhere union support for wage restraint, when it was forthcoming, was offered on the condition that demand management would be expansionist. The authorities retained the option of relying on deflation without support of incomes policy, but after the wildcat strikes at the end of the 1960s, this option became less feasible and less efficient. After threats to external equilibrium had created a more urgent need for stronger stabilization measures and had won greater acceptance of deflation, however, incomes policy could be regarded less as a substitute for deflationary measures and more as a complement to them.

As analyzed in the first chapter, a combination of direct wage restraint, to reduce bargaining intensity, and deflation was applicable to a situation in which the official target level of real wages was exceeded by the wage level minimally acceptable to the union membership at the existing level of employment and hence was not attainable by exclusive reliance on incomes policy. The greater the efficiency of incomes policy in reducing real wages at higher levels of employment is, the smaller the increase in unemployment required to secure the desired level of real wages. The greater the efficiency of incomes policy, in other words, the greater the efficiency of deflation. Austria was able to implement its hard-currency option—in effect, pegging the schilling to the deutsche mark—while suffering only a modest increase in unemployment, to a rate that remained the lowest in the group. Denmark, on the other hand, was obliged to adopt the same exchange-rate policy because depreciation was ruled out by its demonstrated inability to induce wage restraint.

The acceptability of a double-barreled policy of deflation and wage restraint, however, varied considerably among countries and unions. In the north, the reception was chilly. While Denmark was forced to rely heavily on deflation, Sweden continued to rely on its central bargaining system for wage restraint as it rejected deflation and resorted to subsidization. Open unemployment was kept at low levels, but Sweden's "bridging" strategy required recourse to depreciation of the currency, which imposed a serious strain on its bargaining system. In the south, and elsewhere as well, the reception was warmer. In Italy, as in Austria and Britain, the union movements supported policies that combined wage restraint with deflation. Italy managed to reduce the growth of real wages as much as Denmark had with no greater increase in unemployment—although at higher levels—than there was in Austria. In the first two countries the unions did so despite opposition from employers' associations—in Italy in 1976–77, when the Confederazione Generale Italiana del Lavoro (CGIL) refused to join the demands of employers for reflation while urging wage restraint plus the abandonment of make-work and other restrictive practices, and in Austria in 1977–78, when the OeGB, after persuading the government to adopt the hard-currency option, negotiated with restraint while rejecting income tax reductions proposed by the employers. In all three countries union support of these double-barreled policies was essential at the time: in Italy and Britain because bargaining power on the shop floor had prevented layoffs and dismissals, in Austria and Britain because of the political influence exercised by the unions within and through governing labor parties with which they were affiliated. Indeed, union support of wage restraint with deflation, where it was forthcoming, was in good part politically motivated—with the CGIL supporting the "austerity" program adopted by the Italian Communist party in its bid for electoral respectability and political power, and with the TUC supporting the Labour government in its insistence on fiscal orthodoxy and discipline.

Thus union support of incomes policies cum deflation was not based solely on their presumptive economic merits. Wage restraint under conditions of unsatisfactorily high unemployment, moreover, was accepted by unions as a short-term expedient that should be sufficient as well as necessary for reflation to more satisfactory levels of employment. And in Germany and the Netherlands union leaders were embittered by the failure of unemployment to recede after they had accepted the need for restraint of real wages. But their moral case was stronger than their economic case. If it has been necessary to accept wage restraint with high unemployment in order to achieve target levels of real wages and profitability, reflation would have meant possibly raising the real-wage rate above target and reducing profitability correspondingly, unless there were sufficient improvement in such other determinants of profitability as trend productivity and the terms of trade.

Certainly German and other like-minded authorities placed incomes policies in more of a monetarist perspective. They regarded them as helpful in minimizing unemployment only in the sense that still higher levels of unemployment would have been necessary without them—that things would be worse than the status quo without incomes policies but not necessarily better with them. The German unions were told that the persistence of a high rate of unemployment after real wages had fallen to lower levels during the recession of 1974–75 meant simply that real wages were still too high and that more restraint was needed. This was in the spirit of what was referred to as the reprivatization of unemployment: in a regime of flexible exchange rates, the central bank could control the money supply and the price level, which would leave real wages and employment to be determined in the labor markets, primarily through collective bargaining.

This was stern doctrine, yet it could be distinguished from the monetarist approach of the British Conservatives under Prime Minister Thatcher, which ruled out incomes policy, at least in principle, because the government believed that a change in the industrial relations system was at once a precondition for more rapid growth in productivity and inconsistent with union cooperation on wage restraint. In the other approach variability of bargaining intensity and oligopolistic market structures were taken into account, and *dirigisme* was thus accorded limited influence in the determination of wages and employment. Recourse to the classic mixture of incomes policy and reflation was not necessarily precluded but cash on the barrelhead was demanded: reflation contingent on demonstrated wage restraint. In late 1974 the German government and the central bank made implementation of a set of expansionist policies contingent on lower wage settlements the following year. In 1978 a British Labour chancellor reduced tax cuts from their intended levels after the TUC withdrew active support from a social contract under which real wages had been declining at an annual rate of 7 percent.

This approach might have foreshadowed the importance of wage-restraint policies in the future—limited, but responsive to a need. It assumes that levels of employment associated with macroeconomic policies that are tied exclusively to the rate of inflation would not always be politically acceptable. During the 1970s politically acceptable levels of unemployment seemed to be raised by the need to cope with disturbances of external origin and also by previous and current increases in transfer payments and subsidies. But persistence of high levels of unemployment could reduce public tolerance; scaling back social-welfare programs almost certainly would do so. There is no reason to believe that the higher levels of acceptability reached in the 1970s will prove less mutable than the earlier lower levels of tolerance proved to be. In any event, if the rate of unemployment remains, or reemerges as, a target of economic policy in its own right—and, of course, as long as it is not the only target—policies of direct wage restraint will be included in the policymaker's kit of tools. The durability of the employment objective can account for the phoenixlike quality of incomes policies.[13]

---

13. Karl-Olof Faxén has suggested that the greater durability of incomes policies and their institutions in various small countries has reflected the desire of the parties to minimize industrial conflict rather than to achieve macroeconomic objectives and that the important attribute of such policy structures is centralized bargaining. In fact, centralized bargaining is conducive to bargaining restraint along with peaceful industrial relations. On the one hand, centralized bargaining creates the potential for a squeeze on the share of profits in income, as Faxén points out, because mediational intervention by the government constrains the resistance of employers in the interest of avoiding "national emergency disputes." On the other hand, under conditions of oligopolistic competition centralized bargaining institutions are more conducive to self-restraint than are decentralized organizational units. Hence it would be against the interests of employers to support centralized bargaining institutions unless these institutions produced outcomes consistent with macroeconomic objectives. Karl-Olof Faxén, "Incomes Policy and Centralized Wage Foundation" (Stockholm: Swedish Employers Confederation, 1982).

As the authorities find sufficient reasons to return to incomes policies, what are the incentives to compliance that are likely to be demanded by or offered to the unions when the economic environment is initially characterized by very low growth, high unemployment, and large domestic and external deficits? As long as any given country's policy options are subject to severe external constraints, the unions therein are likely to be offered thin gruel indeed. Deficit-increasing cuts in taxes and increases in benefits are all but ruled out. Instead, the unions might be called on to practice wage restraint in an effort to avert (or minimize) reductions in social welfare—to soften a tradeoff between social welfare and employment that threatens to achieve a prominence in the 1980s comparable to the prominence achieved by the Phillips tradeoff in the 1960s and 1970s. In addition, the meager store of pecuniary compensation might improve the chance of adopting one or more of the items of institutional compensation or protection that had proven politically impracticable in the 1970s. In particular, extensions of nationalization of industry or participatory management and capital-sharing schemes could be enacted, despite their lack of political appeal, by left-of-center governments in pursuit of higher levels of employment, at the insistence of their union supporters. By offering the community a swap of more employment for less capitalism, European unions could play down the method of collective bargaining as an archaic survival while nourishing their own socialist inheritances. They would seek to protect their own institutional integrity by representing their members more directly in plants and boardrooms and central forums for concerted action and less intensely at the bargaining table.

Bargaining intensity might also be reduced in exchange for more subsidies and other forms of protection of industries that have been suffering from loss of international competitiveness. This would amount to a strengthening of the unions' prior pressure for protectionism by giving them something to trade for it. It would indicate willingness by the unions to accept bargaining restraint in return for more jobs, but it would also be indicative of their insistence that governments live up to their end of the social bargain. The well-known hitch is that protectionism in one country may invite competitive emulation and ultimately prove self-defeating.

But if beggar-my-neighbor policies could be avoided by some concerted action among nations to synchronize their domestic economic policymaking, external constraints would be reduced, more expansionist policies could be adopted, and incomes policies would be made more cost-effective. Reliance on politically controversial nonpecuniary incentives could be lessened, and the latter could be considered on their own merits. Tax reductions would become more feasible and more effective as incentives to compliance with incomes policy, as part of a visible policy of increasing aggregate employment. And the pressure to prop up lame ducks would be reduced by the increased availability of jobs in other sectors, although problems connected with wage structure would remain. Finally, if authorities were in a better position to deliver higher levels of employment through expansionist policies, they would be in a better position to make such policies at least partially contingent on bargaining restraint. For hard experience has left unionists more willing to acknowledge the existence of a relation between real wages and unemployment and with increased awareness that collective bargaining is no exception to the rule that in increasingly complex and dynamic democratic societies powerful private institutions must learn to practice self-restraint.

Index